Resources for Jewish Genealogy

in the Boston Area

Warren Blatt

Jewish Genealogical Society of Greater Boston

1996

Library of Congress Catalog Card Number: 96-75919

Resources for Jewish Genealogy in the Boston Area /
        Edited by Warren Blatt.
              p.   cm.
        Includes index.
        ISBN 0-9652151-0-5
          1. Massachusetts--Genealogy--Archival resources-
-Massachusetts--Directories. 2. Jews--Genealogy--
Archival resources--Massachusetts--Directories.
I. Blatt, Warren S.   II. Jewish Genealogical Society
of Greater Boston.   III. Title
1996   96-75919

TABLE OF CONTENTS

ABBREVIATIONS

AJGS . . . . Association of Jewish Genealogical Societies

AJHS . . . . American Jewish Historical Society
(see page 33)

BPL . . . . Boston Public Library
(see page 55)

FHLC . . . . Family History Library Catalog
(see page 87)

HIAS . . . . Hebrew Immigrant Aid Society
(see page 40)

IGI . . . . International Genealogical Index
(see page 87)

JCAM . . . . Jewish Cemetery Association of Massachusetts
(see page 111)

JGFF . . . . Jewish Genealogical Family Finder
(see page 2)

JGSGB . . . . Jewish Genealogical Society of Greater Boston
(see page 4)

LDS . . . . Latter-Day Saints (Mormons)
(see page 85)

NAMP . . . . National Archives Microfilm Publication

NEHGS . . . . New England Historic Genealogical Society
(see page 161)

ACKNOWLEDGEMENTS

Many people assisted in the preparation of this book.

AMERICAN JEWISH HISTORICAL SOCIETY:

Fred Davis did a magnificent job with the overwhelming task of coordinating the AJHS efforts for the JGSGB. The JGSGB volunteers included: Eugene Hirshberg (Boston HIAS); Karen Kushner (New York City Childcare Association institutions); David Kohen (New York Court Papers); Seth Korelitz (Baron de Hirsch Fund); Elana Horowitz and Brian Ferber (American Jewish Committee Office of War Records); David Rosen (vertical files Landsmanschaftn records). A number of Brandeis students helped enter data on manuscript collections in the electronic database; Gabriel Feldberg was responsible for final input and assisted in trouble-shooting. The JGSGB would also like to thank everyone at the AJHS for their cooperation and encouragement: Holly Snyder helped initiate the project and oversee research; Michelle Feller-Kopman contributed time and resources to continue the work; Ellen Smith and Stanley Remsburg offered their expertise; and, Dr. Michael Feldberg's enthusiastic executive leadership made all of this possible.

BOSTON PUBLIC LIBRARY:

Thanks to: Henry Scannel, Alice Kane, Mary Frances O'Brien and Joseph Maciora at the BPL; and JGSGB volunteers Prof. Morton Rubin and Barbara Grant.

BRANDEIS UNIVERSITY LIBRARIES:

Thanks to: JGSGB volunteer Ed Cohler; and Dr. Charles Cutter at Brandeis.

HARVARD UNIVERSITY LIBRARIES:

Thanks to: JGSGB volunteers Mike Gerver and Fay Bussgang.

HEBREW COLLEGE LIBRARY:

Thanks to: Dr. Maurice Tuchman and Shalva Seigel at Hebrew College Library.

JEWISH CEMETERY ASSOCIATION OF MASSACHUSETTS:

Thanks to: Miriam Drukman at JCAM.

MASSACHUSETTS ARCHIVES:

Thanks to: William Milhomme at the Massachusetts Archives.

MASSACHUSETTS INSTITUTE OF TECHNOLOGY:

Thanks to: JGSGB volunteer Mike Gerver.

NATIONAL ARCHIVES, NEW ENGLAND REGION:

Thanks to: Jim Owens and Walter Hickey at the Archives; JGSGB volunteers Nancy Arbeiter and Sharla Levine.

NATIONAL ARCHIVES, PITTSFIELD:

Thanks to: Walter Hickey at the Archives.

NEW ENGLAND HISTORIC GENEALOGICAL SOCIETY:

Thanks to: David Dearborn and Jerome Anderson at NEHGS.

REGISTRY OF VITAL RECORDS AND STATISTICS:

Thanks to: JGSGB volunteers Arthur Rubin and Jim Yarin; and the staff at the Registry.

STATE LIBRARY OF MASSACHUSETTS:

Thanks to: Prof. Morton Rubin; and Brenda Howitson at the State Library.

The courthouse chapters (MIDDLESEX REGISTRIES OF DEEDS AND PROBATE, SUFFOLK REGISTRIES OF DEEDS AND PROBATE) were written by Jim Yarin and edited by Debra Bernstein.

Carol Coplin Baker undertook the laborious task of scanning the microfilms of the Boston passenger ship arrivals, to create the catalog which appears as Appendix D.

Thanks to Ellen Smith for allowing us to use the introductory section on the history of the Jews in Boston.

Lauren Davis, Jim Yarin and Debra Bernstein helped proofread the manuscript, and offered numerous useful suggestions.

I'd like to thank Debra Bernstein for her dedication and hard work in canvassing the various research facilities, editorial work, and general assistance during the final stages of the preparation of this book.

Introduction

This book is intended to serve as a guide for researchers of Jewish genealogy in the Boston area. In that regard, it focuses on resources pertaining to Jews of any time and place, as well as regional secular resources of the late nineteenth and twentieth centuries. All of the resources described here are accessible within the greater Boston area.

Previous guides to New England genealogy, of which there are many, focus on early American records: the Massachusetts Bay settlements, the Colonial period, Revolutionary War records, town records, and so on. Little or none of this information is of use to a researcher looking for Jewish ancestors. This guide attempts to avoid covering these topics; there are many other fine publications that comprehensively survey those resources, notably:

> Lindberg, Marcia Wiswall. *Genealogist's Handbook for New England Research.*
> 3rd edition. (Boston: New England Historic Genealogical Society, 1990, 1985, 1993). 178 pages.

> Schweitzer, George K. *Massachusetts Genealogical Research.* (Knoxville, TN: The Author, 1990). 279 pages.

This guide was inspired by and modelled after the (New York) Jewish Genealogical Society's outstanding book *Genealogical Resources in the New York Metropolitan Area* (1989), edited by Estelle M. Guzik, though it is not nearly as ambitious in scope. This guide concentrates only on items that would be of interest to a Jewish genealogist, i.e. local resources after 1850, since the vast majority of Jewish Americans do not have roots in this country before that date.

This book is organized in two major sections, which complement each other. The first section covers major **Record Types**: Census Records, Naturalization Records, Passenger Lists, and Vital Records (birth, marriage, and death records). The second section, the bulk of this guide, covers **Record Locations**, the institutions where genealogical materials can be found. Appendices contain bibliographies of Yizkor Books, manuscript collections, and Jewish periodicals available in libraries in the Boston area.

Record Types: Each of the major record types fundamental to American Jewish genealogy is covered in a brief section summarizing the types of information that can be found in these records, and how and where they can most easily be accessed through local institutions.

Record Locations: Each local institution and its relevant holdings are described in detail. The facility's address, hours, and directions are all included, along with other hints on using the facility's resources.

Getting Started

If you're just starting to research your Jewish family history, you should definitely begin by reading either of the following books:

Kurzweil, Arthur. *From Generation to Generation: How to Trace Your Jewish Genealogy and Personal History.* (New York: HarperCollins, 1994). 388 pages. ISBN 0-06-270097-9. [First edition was: (New York: William Morrow, 1980). 353 pages].

Rottenberg, Dan. *Finding Our Fathers: A Guidebook to Jewish Genealogy.* (New York: Random House, 1977). 401 pages. [Reprints: Baltimore: Genealogical Publishing Co., 1986, 1995. ISBN 0-8063-1151-7].

These two books were the pioneering works that helped inspire the modern Jewish genealogical movement, in the late 1970's. Both books are a great inspiration for beginners. However, many of their sources are out-of date; Jewish genealogy has advanced a great deal in the last dozen years. More recent sources are described below. Both of the books are widely available, at all libraries included in this publication, many of the vendors listed below, at most public libraries, and available from any good bookstore.

Avotaynu: The International Review of Jewish Genealogy is a quarterly publication, founded in 1985, devoted to Jewish genealogical issues: new record sources, tips on research, travel experiences, book reviews, "Ask the Experts" column, summaries of articles in other sources, stories on the human side of genealogy, and more. It is the premier publication documenting the field today. *Avotaynu* subscriptions are $29.00 per year, and back issues ($8.00 each) are available from the publisher: Avotaynu, Inc., 155 North Washington Ave., Bergenfield, NJ 07621. 1-800-AVOTAYN.

The Jewish Genealogical Family Finder (JGFF) is a computer-generated compilation of surnames and towns currently being researched by over 2,600 Jewish genealogists worldwide. It contains over 32,000 entries: 13,000 ancestral surnames and 6,000 town names, and is indexed and cross-referenced by both surname and town name. The JGFF was created by Gary Mokotoff, publisher of *Avotaynu*, is maintained by the Jewish Genealogical Society, Inc. of New York. Any member of a Jewish Genealogical Society (JGS) may submit up to 16 names/towns for inclusion in the JGFF, free of charge. Additional names are $2.50 per 16 submitted. After searching the JGFF for genealogists with similar research interests, you can contact them for exchange of information. The JGFF is a great networking tool, which is updated quarterly. A copy of the JGFF is available at HEBREW COLLEGE LIBRARY (see page 103), and the JGSGB has a recent copy, which is brought to all Society meetings. To add your ancestral names and towns to the JGFF, write to the New York JGS at P.O. Box 6398, New York, NY 10128.

Other useful resources for Jewish genealogy include:

Encyclopedia of Jewish Genealogy, Volume I: Sources in the United States and Canada. Edited by Arthur Kurzweil and Miriam Weiner. (Northvale, NJ: Jason Aronson, Inc., 1991). 226 pages. A summary of North American record repositories and their holdings, with some useful appendices.

Where Once We Walked: A Guide to the Jewish Communities Destroyed in the Holocaust, by Gary Mokotoff and Sallyann Amdur Sack. (Teaneck, NJ: Avotaynu Press, 1991). 514 pages. A gazetteer of over 21,000 Central and Eastern European localities, arranged alphabetically and phonetically, with references for each locality.

Jewish Genealogy: A Source Book of Family Histories and Genealogies. By David S. Zubatsky and Irwin M. Berent. (New York: Garland, 1984, 1991). 2 volumes: 422, 452 pages. A guide to published and manuscript genealogies in archives and libraries, arranged by surname. A third volume is in progress.

Genealogical Resources in the New York Metropolitan Area. Edited by Estelle M. Guzik. (New York: Jewish Genealogical Society, 1989). 404 pages. A detailed guide to every agency in New York City and environs that could provide data useful to Jewish genealogical research.

A Dictionary of Jewish Surnames from the Russian Empire. By Alexander Beider. (Teaneck, NJ: Avotaynu, Inc., 1993). 782 pages. A comprehensive scholarly study of Jewish surnames in the Pale of Settlement.

American-oriented genealogical guides are available at any public library. Beware that these works usually focus strictly on Anglo-American ancestry, concentrating on such topics as Revolutionary and Civil War records, land records, pioneer trails, church and town records, etc. They typically ignore sources important for Jewish researchers, such as immigration and naturalization records, but are useful for their methodology. Some recommended books are:

Greenwood, Val D. *The Researcher's Guide to American Genealogy.* 2nd edition. (Baltimore: Genealogical Publishing Co., 1990). 623 pages.

Doane, Gilbert H. and James B. Bell. *Searching for Your Ancestors: The How and Why of Genealogy.* 6th edition. (Minneapolis: University of Minnesota Press, 1992). 352 pages.

Everton, George B. *The Handy Book for Genealogists.* 8th edition. (Logan, UT: Everton Publishers, 1991). 392 pages.

Eakle, Arlene and Johni Cerny, eds. *The Source: A Guidebook of American Genealogy.* (Salt Lake City: Ancestry, Inc., 1984). 786 pages.

Ancestry's Red Book: American State, County and Town Sources. Edited by Alice Eichholz. Revised Edition. (Salt Lake City: Ancestry, Inc., 1992). 858 pages.

Guide to Genealogical Research in the National Archives. (Washington, D.C.: National Archives and Records Service, 1985). 304 pages.

The National Archives in Washington sells some publications, in addition to the above *Guide*, which can be useful. They are described in the free booklet *Aids for Genealogical Research* (29 pp), available from the National Archives Trust Fund Board, Washington DC, 20408. Among the publications offered is a series subtitled *A Select Catalog of National Archives Microfilm Publications*, which list the reel-by-reel contents of many of the National Archives microfilmed records (Census records, Passenger Lists, Naturalization Indexes Military Records, etc). These catalogs can be very useful for locating the correct reel of microfilm on which to find a record of your ancestor.

<u>Vendors</u>: The following firms sell genealogical books and supplies:

Ancestry, Inc.
P.O. Box 476
Salt Lake City, UT 84110-0476
(800) 531-1790
http://www.ancestry.com

Avotaynu, Inc.
155 North Washington Ave.
Bergenfield, NJ 07621
(800) AVOTAYN
http://www.avotaynu.com

Genealogical Publishing Co.
1001 N. Calvert St.
Baltimore, MD 21202-3897
(410) 837-8271

Genealogy Unlimited, Inc.
P.O. Box 537
Orem, UT 84059-0537
(800) 666-4363
http://www.itsnet.com/~genun

Heritage Books, Inc.
1540-E Pointer Ridge Pl.
Bowie, MD 20716
(800) 398-7709
http://www.heritagebooks.com

Hearthstone Bookshop
5735-A Telegraph Road
Alexandria, VA 22303
(703) 960-0086

All of the books mentioned in this section are available from one or more of the above vendors.

The <u>Jewish Genealogical Society of Greater Boston</u> (JGSGB) is an organization established in 1981 to develop and promote the growth, study and exchange of ideas among people interested in Jewish genealogical research. The JGSGB conducts monthly meetings and workshops on a wide range of topics; provides access to extensive research materials; and publishes a quarterly newsletter, *Mass-Pocha*. Over 300 members are an important resource unto themselves, with interests and expertise in many areas. We encourage you to join and participate. For more information contact:

Jewish Genealogical Society of Greater Boston
P.O. Box 610366
Newton Highlands, MA 02161-0366

(617) 283-8003
http://www.jewishgen.org/boston/jgsgb.html

The JGSGB is one of 60 such groups throughout the world devoted to Jewish genealogy. For the address of a Jewish Genealogical Society near you, send a self-addressed stamped envelope to: Association of Jewish Genealogical Societies (AJGS), P.O. Box 50245, Palo Alto, CA 94303. The list of all Jewish Genealogical Societies worldwide is published annually in the Spring issue of *Avotaynu*, and is also available on the Internet at the *JewishGen* World Wide Web site (see below). Many of these groups publish fine journals and newsletters, including *Dorot* (New York), *Mishpacha* (Washington) and *Roots-Key* (Los Angeles). Back issues of these journals are available at HEBREW COLLEGE LIBRARY (see page 106).

On the <u>Internet</u>, there are a growing number of resources. The *JewishGen* discussion group can be found on usenet as "soc.genealogy.jewish", as well as in mailing-list form. On the World Wide Web, the *JewishGen* home page can be found at "http://www.jewishgen.org".

The Jews of Boston
A Visitor's Guide

by Ellen Smith

For three hundred and fifty years Jews have lived in Boston, but no one had written their history. In celebration of its centenary (1895-1995), the Combined Jewish Philanthropies of Greater Boston commissioned that history as its gift to the community.

Edited by Jonathan D. Sarna and Ellen Smith, *The Jews of Boston* (Boston: Combined Jewish Philanthropies, 1995) consists of twelve essays by eleven authors, over 250 illustrations, appendices, and an extensive bibliography, tracing the history of the Boston Jewish community from its early tentative beginnings through its emergence in the 20th century as one of the most influential American Jewish communities. A brief summary of that story follows, and a guide to some of the sites that mark the tale.

Boston is rich in early American history, but its Jewish history begins surprisingly late. While there were pre-Revolutionary Jewish communities in Newport, Rhode Island; New York City; Philadelphia; Richmond, Virginia; Charleston, South Carolina; and Savannah, Georgia during the 17th and 18th centuries, Jews largely passed Boston by. Nevertheless, as Judge Samuel Sewall remarked, early Boston was "seldom wholly without them." Their names are retrievable from court, census, and tax records, and occasional references in surviving letters and diaries.

These early Jews of Boston lived in a city without an organized Jewish community and without any Jewish institutions. Among them, two individuals catch our eye. Each adopted a radically different strategy for defining the place a Jew might create for himself in the culture of early America. Their choices augur the variety of approaches generations of American Jews to come would explore, and established Boston as an intellectual and experimental center for defining the balance between being Jewish and being American.

Judah Monis arrived in Cambridge, Massachusetts in 1722, after two years in New York City. European born and trained in Hebrew and rabbinics, Monis proposed to the Overseers of Harvard College that he teach Hebrew to the undergraduates and tutors. The Overseers agreed, and in 1722 Monis was hired as the first Instructor in Hebrew at Harvard, a position he would hold until 1760. He was the first Jew awarded an A.M. degree by Harvard, and in 1735 he published the first textbook of the Hebrew language in North America: *A Grammar of the Hebrew Tongue*.

But there was a catch. Harvard required its faculty to be Christian. A month before he assumed his teaching position, Monis converted to Christianity.

Monis maintained throughout his life that he converted from conviction, not convenience. His life presents one example — if an extreme example — of how a Jewish individual made a place for himself in Boston history. Without the support of Jewish institutions, a Jewish community, or even other Jewish individuals, Monis entered the life of Cambridge as a Christian. He voluntarily left a mature Jewish community in New York City, and he seems never to have looked back. Monis charted the most radical path a Jew could follow in taking advantage of American opportunities.

Moses Michael Hays and his family chose a different path. Like Monis, Hays arrived in Boston as a mature adult. Like Monis, the Hays clan moved in the first circles of society and business. But unlike Monis, the Hays clan chose to live their lives publicly and actively as Jews.

Hays arrived in Boston immediately after the American Revolution, already an experienced trader with his eyes on the markets of the Far East. Recognizing the need for a stable currency and a secure insurance industry to underwrite such ventures, he joined with other Boston business leaders to found what is now the Bank of Boston and several key insurance companies. Hays was also active in the North American Masonic movement, even sponsoring his good friend, Paul Revere, as his Deputy in the Boston lodge that now bears Hays' name.

Hays and his wife, Rachel Myers Hays, raised four daughters, a son, and their orphaned nephews and niece (children of Reyna Hays Touro and Rabbi Isaac Touro, after whom Newport's Touro Synagogue is named). Like Moses Hays, the Hays and Touro children matured to become civic and business leaders. Judah Hays was an early proprietor of the Boston Athenaeum. Abraham and Judah Touro helped to fund the Massachusetts General Hospital. Judah Touro also donated $10,000 to help finish the Bunker Hill Monument in the Charlestown section of Boston; a plaque commemorating his contribution and that of industrialist Amos Lawrence was placed at its base.

Hays and his family conducted their very public lives as practicing Jews at a time when Jewish families in Boston probably numbered less than twenty. Hays and Rachel conducted religious worship services in their home, dispensed charity at their back door, and acquired a substantial Hebrew-language library, much of which survives in private and public hands. The family's legacy of major Boston institutions was matched by their legacy of religious persistence and pride. For the Hays, family itself became community — spiritually and culturally sustaining — a public example that in Boston, one could live successfully both as fully-integrated citizen and Jew.

With the migration of German and Central European Jews to the United States beginning in the 1840s, Boston acquired its first permanent Jewish community. Here, too, Boston's Jewish history diverges from most of American Jewish history. Throughout much of America, the mid-19th century Jewish immigration came heavily from the German-speaking regions of southwestern Germany. In Boston, the majority of the "German" immigrants were Polish, migrating from the eastern territories (especially Posen) annexed by Germany in the late 18th century. Generally more traditional and Yiddish-speaking than their German-Jewish counterparts in other American cities, Boston's Jews put a "Polish" stamp on its city's fledgling Jewish culture.

This "Polish" character of Boston's Jewish community is reflected in its early synagogues. Boston's first congregation, Ohabei Shalom (organized 1842), was predominantly Polish; its German members broke off in 1854 to form congregation Adath Israel (Temple Israel). Nonetheless, Boston's Jewish community was tightly knit and tiny. From approximately 500 individuals on the eve of the Civil War, the community numbered only 5,000 by 1880 at a time when Boston's overall population reached 800,000. In Boston's old South End, just south of the Boston Common and the current Theatre District, the small Jewish community married each other, worked for one another, and prospered more quickly than any other mid-19th century ethnic group in Boston.

Little remains of the physical presence of Boston's earliest 19th-century Jewish community. The old South End has been commercialized and transformed into the Theatre District. But Ohabei Shalom's second synagogue building survives. Built as a Universalist Church in 1839, Ohabei Shalom purchased the building at 76 Warrenton Street in 1863 and worshipped there until 1886. The building stands today as the Charles Playhouse. And Temple Israel's magnificent 1885 synagogue built at 600 Columbus at the corner of Northampton still stands. Designed by the architectural firm of Weissbein and Jones, the brick building incorporated two towers with Stars of David atop its steeples, 10 commandments above the central gable, and a Star of David rose window. The building combined these Jewish symbols with architectural features of German Romanesque-revival synagogues, and Catholic and Protestant American churches — a full statement of what American Jewish religious architecture could be. This strongly declarative Jewish building was enormously influential, and two generations of Boston synagogue architecture imitated its basic form.

In the same years that Boston's Central European Jews began moving south, Boston's next great wave of Jewish immigrants arrived. Whereas the Central European Jewish community was tiny and made little general impact on Boston as a whole, the Eastern European migrations had enormous and immediate effect. By 1895 there were 20,000 Jews in Boston, and 40,000 by 1900. In 1910 65,000 Jews lived in Boston, reaching 80,000 by the World War I; another 35,000 Jews lived in the greater Boston area. They came via New York City, but also through the East Boston Immigration Building, the direct port of entry into Boston for almost a century.

Boston Matzo Baking Company, 10 Parmenter Street, North End, Boston, ca. 1894.
American Jewish Historical Society, Waltham, Massachusetts.

The new immigrants settled in Boston's South, North and West Ends, in East Boston, and in the neighboring cities of Chelsea, Revere, Malden, and East Cambridge. In the otherwise Italian North End of Boston, the Jewish immigrants congregated west of Hanover Street, along Salem and Prince Streets, and across to Endicott and Cross. In the West End they lived more generally among a widely mixed ethnic population, tending to the northwestern streets destroyed during the urban renewal of the 1950s and 1960s, and along the back side of Beacon Hill.

Only two former West End synagogue buildings remain. The present African Meeting House on Smith Court on Beacon Hill was built in 1806 as the first American church built by free blacks. From 1899 to 1972 the building served as the *landsmanshaft shul*, Anshe Libawitz. Today it is restored as America's oldest free black church and it is open to public as part of the Black Freedom Trail. The Vilna Shul at 14-19 Phillips Street on Beacon Hill is the only surviving synagogue built by Boston's Eastern European immigrant community. Recently granted historic landmark status, the building is being restored as a cultural center and museum of Boston Jewish history by the Vilna Center for Jewish Heritage. The West End's modern Charles River Park Synagogue on Martha Road is the modern amalgam of several historic West End congregations.

The North End, too, still boasts traces of what was once equivalent to Boston's vibrant, if modest, "Lower East Side." The present Knights of Columbus Hall stands on Baldwin Place where Boston's premier immigrant orthodox Congregation Beth Israel worshiped from 1889-1920 in a former Baptist Church. As you face the site, the building to the left with a faint Jewish star carved above the doorway once housed a Talmud Torah school. Jerusalem Place off Salem Street nearby still bears the name of its former shul. Along Hanover Street, rented rooms served as synagogues, factories, and kosher provisioners. The 1896 Benoth Israel Sheltering Home on 15 Cooper Street, which once provided temporary shelter to needy immigrant women and children, still stands, as does the building across the street, originally established as a medical dispensary for men. But the most dominant Jewish structure in the North End today is Boston's new Holocaust Memorial on Blackstone Street, dedicated in October 1995.

The social service organizations built by Boston's East European immigrants suggest the complexity and the pressures that immigration brought to bear on the Boston Jewish Community. Though the Central European Jewish community had established varieties of charitable organizations throughout the 19th century, none were able to absorb or cope with the massive immigration at the turn of the century.

It was thus with the aim of centralizing community fundraising and responsibly dispersing it, that on April 25, 1895, five Jewish charitable organizations — the United Hebrew Benevolent Society, the Hebrew Ladies Society, the Leopold Morse Home for the Aged and Infirm Hebrews and Orphanage, the Free Employment Bureau, and the Charitable Burial Association — created the Federation of Jewish Charities, the first federated charitable organization in the nation. Subsequent American Jewish federations, Catholic Charities, and even the United Way, are all modeled on Boston's Federation plan. The Federation joined the self-generated Eastern European charitable institutions in providing community self-sufficiency: a trend repeated in many other American Jewish communities. The records of such early community organizations, when available, provide a wealth of information about American Jewish families and their daily lives.

Like their Central European counterparts, the Eastern European immigrants, too, quickly succeeded in America. By the First World War, the majority of Jewish residents had moved from the North and West Ends, west to Brookline, Allston-Brighton, and Newton, and primarily south, to the growing suburbs of Roxbury and Dorchester. There, between 1920 and the 1960s, almost half of Boston's Jewish population lived along a three-mile stretch of Blue Hill Avenue between Grove Hall and Mattapan Square. At its peak in the 1930s, those numbers reached nearly 80,000.

The physical legacy of the Roxbury and Dorchester community is enormous and abiding. Dozens of major synagogue buildings, schools, and community halls were constructed along with wooden triple-deckers, brick apartments, and businesses to support the community. Most of those buildings are still in use today as the churches, mosques, and community centers of Boston's African-American community.

Congregation Agudath Israel Anshei Sfard, 220 Woodrow Avenue, Dorchester (Boston), Massachusetts.
Built in 1923, the "Woodrow Avenue Shul" housed one of the more than fifty
Jewish congregations in Roxbury, Dorchester, and Mattapan between 1920 and 1970.
The building serves today as a Haitian Seventh Day Adventist Church.
American Jewish Historical Society, Waltham, Massachusetts.

Today the Jews of Boston live in three major areas. Many people leaving Roxbury and Dorchester in the 1950s and 1960s moved to Boston's southern suburbs (especially Milton, Randolph, and parts of Quincy); today, Sharon boasts a growing and vibrant Jewish population, including an important orthodox community. Other Jewish families moved to the northern suburbs, up as far as Marblehead. The majority of Jews in the 20th century moved west to Brookline, Newton, Framingham, and now beyond.

The third great wave of immigration into Boston occurred after the Second World War, and this time it came from America itself. Drawn by the universities, medical schools, and high-tech industries, young second- and third-generation American-born Jews came to the "hub of the universe" for jobs and education, and stayed. The presence of a large youthful Jewish population has left its stamp in the area's strong Hillel movement; the creation of "alternative" worship communities including the pioneering *Havurah Shalom* and the resulting *havurah* movement; and a strong tradition of student activism. These younger American Jewish immigrants have been joined by post-War Eastern European immigrants, and more recently, Soviet Jews.

Boston's contemporary Jewish community has helped to create or expand Jewish shops and restaurants along Harvard Street in Brookline; Hebrew College; three modern Jewish community centers (in Brookline, Newton, and Stoughton); new synagogues in the western and southern suburbs; and Brandeis University. The American Jewish Historical Society, located on the campus of Brandeis University, holds a wealth of material on Boston Jewish History. All are good stops for a visitor seeking present-day "Jewish Boston."

So what, in its history and present character, makes Boston unique among American Jewish communities? Historian Jonathan Sarna has argued three traits. The first is the lateness of the community's establishment, and the "Polish" character of its population and culture. The second is the depth of local antisemitism: in Boston, Louis D. Brandeis observed, "Antisemitism seems to have reached its American pinnacle." That antisemitism has been expressed in social and cultural exclusion of Jews (including from clubs, hotels, and Harvard University in the 1920s). It has also been expressed intellectually, politically, and physically. The Protestant Anti-Immigration Restriction League originated among Boston's elite "Brahmin" leaders who despaired of America's turn-of-the-century immigrants ever fitting into or benefiting the nation. Father Charles Coughlin's national anti-Jewish radio broadcasts in the 1930s and his political Union Party did better in Boston than any other American city. Locally, Father Leonard Feeney rallied his antisemitic followers. Physical violence against Jews escalated throughout the early 1940s. The 1944 appointment and leadership of Archbishop, later Cardinal, Richard Cushing improved Boston's Catholic-Jewish relations enormously.

Lastly, Boston's Jewish community is distinguished by its intellectuality and achievement. Historian Stephen Whitfield joins Jonathan Sarna in stressing this point. Whitfield argues further that in Boston, more than any other American city, the theoretical possibilities of how ethnic cultures might thrive in America were most consciously worked out. Mary Antin lived and proposed assimilation as the program American immigrants should follow. Louis Brandeis offered the alternative of Zionism, arguing that by enhancing the positive links between Americanism and Judaism, both ethnic and American aspects would be strengthened, to the advantage of both. Horace Kallen, who influenced Brandeis' early ideas on Zionism, developed the concept of "cultural pluralism," likening America's ethnic mix to a symphony orchestra where each member has different sheet music and instruments, but together all play a symphony.

And what a symphony it has been! From Judah Monis and Moses Michael Hays, through the Central and Eastern European immigrations, to Boston's American-born Jewish population, and to Boston's Jewish theorists of American-ethnic culture, Boston has provided America with some of its best examples and experiments for finding a creative balance between being American and being Jewish. The experiment is, of course, continuing. And if the Boston Jewish community has a lesson to teach from its own history, perhaps it is this: that the history of Jews in America is indeed one of choice, and remains our own to be written.

Ellen Smith is Curator of the American Jewish Historical Society, Waltham, Massachusetts, and co-editor with Jonathan D. Sarna of *The Jews of Boston* (Boston: The Combined Jewish Philanthropies of Greater Boston, Inc., 1995).

CENSUS RECORDS

Census records have been taken by the U. S. Federal Government every ten years, since 1790. Federal census records are available for 1790, 1800, 1810, 1820, 1830, 1840, 1850, 1860, 1870, 1880, 1900, 1910 and 1920. The 1890 census records were destroyed in a fire in 1921. However, an 1890 census of Civil War veterans and their widows is a partial substitute.

In the censuses of 1840 and before, only the head of the household was listed; all others in the household were merely counted, according to age group and sex. More information was added in each subsequent census. Beginning in 1850, the names of all persons were recorded, along with age, sex, occupation, marital status, and other information, including state or country of birth. Beginning with the 1880 census, the birthplaces of the father and mother of each person are also given. Beginning in 1900, the year of immigration is shown for each foreign-born person. The complete set of questions asked on each census is listed at the end of this section (page 15).

Below is a list of all available federal census records, the National Archives Microfilm Publication (NAMP) on which they were published, the total number of microfilm reels, and the reels that pertain to Massachusetts in each census.

1790	First Census	NAMP M637	(12 rolls)	Mass.: Roll #4
1800	Second Census	NAMP M32	(52 rolls)	Mass.: Rolls #13-19
1810	Third Census	NAMP M252	(71 rolls)	Mass.: Rolls #17-22
1820	Fourth Census	NAMP M33	(142 rolls)	Mass.: Rolls #47-55
1830	Fifth Census	NAMP M19	(201 rolls)	Mass.: Rolls #59-68
1840	Sixth Census	NAMP M704	(580 rolls)	Mass.: Rolls #173-202
1850	Seventh Census	NAMP M432	(1,009 rolls)	Mass.: Rolls #303-345
1860	Eighth Census	NAMP M653	(1,438 rolls)	Mass.: Rolls #486-534
1870	Ninth Census	NAMP M593	(1,748 rolls)	Mass.: Rolls #600-659
1880	Tenth Census	NAMP T9	(1,454 rolls)	Mass.: Rolls #519-568
1900	Twelfth Census	NAMP T623	(1,854 rolls)	Mass.: Rolls #631-697
1910	Thirteenth Census	NAMP T624	(1,784 rolls)	Mass.: Rolls #571-633
1920	Fourteenth Census	NAMP T625	(2,076 rolls)	Mass.: Rolls #679-752

Federal law requires that the records of each decennial census remain closed to the public for a period of 72 years after the enumeration date. For census records of 1930 and later, write to Personal Census Service Branch, Bureau of the Census, P.O. Box 1545, Jeffersonville, IN 47130. (812) 288-3300. Ask for Form BC-600. The current search fee is $40.00. Access is restricted to the persons in the record or their heirs.

A complete reel-by-reel contents listing of all census microfilms is available in National Archives Census catalogs. The catalogs are $2.00 each, and may be ordered from the National Archives Trust Fund, NEPS Dept. 630, P.O. Box 100793, Atlanta, GA 30384. The catalogs are also available at the various local institutions where census records are available, described below.

- *1790-1890 Federal Population Censuses.* (#200032). 96pp. (1979).
- *1900 Federal Population Census.* (#200031). 84pp. (1978).
- *1910 Federal Population Census.* (#200009). 44pp. (1982).
- *1920 Federal Population Census.* (#200042). 88pp. (1991).

Microfilm contents descriptions are also in the Family History Library Catalog. Look in the FHLC under the heading "UNITED STATES - CENSUS - [Year]" (see page 85).

Arrangement: All census records are organized geographically, by "Enumeration Districts" (E.D.s). An E.D. is a region assigned to a census enumerator, who went from door to door writing down information about the persons in each household.

Indexes: Privately compiled and printed indexes of census records are available for most states for 1790 through 1860 or 1870. Most of these indexes were prepared by Accelerated Indexing Systems International (AISI) of Bountiful, Utah, a private company. For Massachusetts, state-wide indexes have been prepared only through 1850:

- *Massachusetts 1800 Census Index.* (AIS, 1973) 250 p. 70,000+ entries.
- *Massachusetts 1810 Census Index.* (AIS, 1976) 192 p. 79,000+ entries.
- *Massachusetts 1820 Census Index.* (AIS, 1976) 222 p. 91,000+ entries.
- *Massachusetts 1830 Census Index.* (AIS, 1976) 274 p. 105,000+ entries.
- *Massachusetts 1840 Census Index.* (AIS, 1978) 344 p. 142,000+ entries.
- *Massachusetts 1850 Census Index.* (AIS, 1978) 934 p. 369,000+ entries.

1860: There is a published index for the city of Boston only: *Boston, MA 1860 Federal Census Index.* (AIS, 1989) 359 p.

1870: The 1870 Federal Census for Massachusetts has been indexed by a private company, Carroll Genealogical Indexing, 22 Eddie St., Quincy, MA 02169. Searches can be requested for $20.00 for up to 3 names, and $5.00 for each additional name search. There are no plans to publish this index in the near future. An index for Hampden county has been published: *Hampden Co., MA 1870 Federal Census.* (AIS, 1991) 912 p.

1880: There is a partial index for all states, prepared by the Work Projects Administration (WPA) during the 1930's. This index includes only households with children under age 10. The 1880 index for Massachusetts is available on microfilm (NAMP T754, 70 rolls). This index is arranged according to the Soundex indexing system.

1890: The 1890 Census was destroyed in a fire, thus there is no index. However, there was a special census of Civil War veterans and their widows taken in that year. This is available on NAMP M123 (118 rolls) for states Kentucky through Wyoming (alphabetically) only. Massachusetts is on reels #11-16. These schedules have been indexed: *1890 Massachusetts Census Index of Civil War Veterans or their Widows*, compiled by Bryan Lee Dilts (Index Publishing, 1985) 222 p.

1900: There is a complete Soundex index (which includes all households) for all states, prepared by the WPA. The 1900 index for Massachusetts is NAMP T1051 (314 rolls).

1910: There are Soundex indexes for only 21 states. These are mostly states with poor civil registration; no Northeast states are indexed. However, see the research strategy for Massachusetts below.

1920: There is a complete Soundex index for all states. The 1920 index for Massachusetts is NAMP M1567 (326 rolls).

Availability: The NATIONAL ARCHIVES - NEW ENGLAND REGION in Waltham is the best and most complete source for U.S. Federal census records. Each National Archives regional branch has the complete set of census schedules and indexes on microfilm, 1790 to 1920, covering the entire country (see page 143). The BOSTON PUBLIC LIBRARY microtext department has census microfilms and all available indexes for the six New England states (see page 66). The

MASSACHUSETTS ARCHIVES has copies of the census records (1790-1900) and printed indexes (1790-1850) for Massachusetts only. It also has the original Massachusetts federal census records for 1850, 1860 and 1870 (see page 126). The NEW ENGLAND HISTORIC GENEALOGICAL SOCIETY has a very incomplete set of census microfilms, but they do have nearly all of the printed indexes. All census microfilms are also available through FAMILY HISTORY CENTERS (LDS). Look in the FHLC under "UNITED STATES - CENSUS - [Year]" (see page 85). You can also borrow census microfilms for a fee through the National Archives Microfilm Rental Program (P.O. Box 30, Annapolis Junction, MD 20701-0030); and the American Genealogical Lending Library (P.O. Box 244, Bountiful, Utah, 84011).

Research strategy for the unindexed 1910 Federal Census for Massachusetts:

The smaller towns can be searched manually, but this search can be prohibitive for larger cities such as Boston, Worcester, Lowell or Fall River. For these cities, the following strategy can be pursued, using published City Directories and a valuable research aid.

1) Look in the 1909 or 1910 City Directory, alphabetically, for the person's surname, to locate their street address. (City Directories are available at the NATIONAL ARCHIVES - NEW ENGLAND REGION, BOSTON PUBLIC LIBRARY, STATE LIBRARY OF MASSACHUSETTS, MASSACHUSETTS ARCHIVES, NEHGS, and through LDS FAMILY HISTORY CENTERS).
2) Find the cross-street section of the Directory, and find the nearest intersecting street for that address.
3) Look at the city map in the Directory, and locate the intersection where the address is located. From the map location, determine the Ward number that contains the address.
4) Use the book *A Research Aid for the Massachusetts 1910 Federal Census*, compiled by Mary Lou Craver Mariner and Patricia Roughan Bellows (Sudbury, MA: Computerized Assistance, 1988; 115 pages), to translate the Ward number into an Enumeration District. (Available at the NATIONAL ARCHIVES - NEW ENGLAND REGION). The book will also guide you to the correct census microfilm reel number.
5) Get the correct census microfilm reel. Within the film, find the Enumeration District, the street, the address, and finally the entry for the person you're looking for.

A similar research strategy will work for other large U.S. cities, using the National Archives microfiche publication *Cross Index to Selected City Streets and Enumeration Districts, 1910 Census*, NAMP M1283 (50 microfiche cards), in place of steps 2, 3, and 4 above. This guide is available at the NATIONAL ARCHIVES - NEW ENGLAND REGION and through all LDS FAMILY HISTORY CENTERS (see FHLC under "UNITED STATES - CENSUS - 1910 - INDEXES). This cross index translates street addresses into Census Enumeration Districts, for 39 selected cities across the country. After locating the correct E.D., then use the *1910 Federal Population Census* catalog to determine the correct microfilm reel number. The 39 cities in NAMP M1283 are:

Akron, OH	Elizabeth, NJ	New York City:	Reading, PA
Atlanta, GA	Erie, PA	- Brooklyn	Richmond, VA
Baltimore, MD	Ft. Wayne, IN	- Manhattan & Bronx	San Antonio, TX
Canton, OH	Gary, IN	- Richmond	San Diego, CA
Charlotte, NC	Grand Rapids, MI	(no index for Queens)	San Francisco, CA
Chicago, IL	Indianapolis, IN	Oklahoma City, OK	Seattle, WA
Cleveland, OH	Kansas City, KS	Omaha, NE	South Bend, IN
Dayton, OH	Long Beach, CA	Paterson, NJ	Tampa, FL
Denver, CO	Los Angeles	Peoria, IL	Tulsa, OK
Detroit, MI	(and county), CA	Philadelphia, PA	Wichita, KS
District of Columbia	Newark, NJ	Phoenix, AZ	Youngstown, OH

Mortality Schedules:

For the censuses of 1850, 1860, 1870 and 1880, other information was gathered, "non-population census schedules", which included agricultural, industrial, mortality and social statistics. The mortality schedules are of interest to genealogists, for they list all deaths which occurred in the 12 months prior to the census date. The schedules are arranged alphabetically by county, thereunder alphabetically by town. The original non-population schedules for Massachusetts are at the MASSACHUSETTS ARCHIVES, and are also available on microfilm, NAMP T1204, "Federal Non-Population Census Schedules, Massachusetts, 1850-1880" (40 rolls). The microfilms are available at the NATIONAL ARCHIVES - NEW ENGLAND REGION, and through FAMILY HISTORY CENTERS (LDS) (see the FHLC under "MASSACHUSETTS - CENSUS - [Year]"). Mortality schedules for Massachusetts on NAMP T1204:

1850	Rolls #9-10	(2 reels).
1860	Roll #17	(1 reel).
1870	Rolls #22-23	(2 reels).
1880	Rolls #37-40	(4 reels).

Massachusetts State Censuses:

There were several **state** censuses taken by the Commonwealth of Massachusetts. The original records of the censuses of 1855 and 1865 are available at the MASSACHUSETTS ARCHIVES (see page 126), and microfilm copies are available there and through FAMILY HISTORY CENTERS (LDS) (See the FHLC under the heading "MASSACHUSETTS - CENSUS - [Year]"). The records are arranged geographically (alphabetical by county, thereunder alphabetical by town) and contain information similar to the contemporary federal census. 1855: 43 volumes (31 microfilm reels). 1865: 41 volumes (37 microfilm reels).

The 1855 and 1865 Massachusetts state census records for over seventy towns in Essex, Middlesex and Plymouth counties have now been transcribed and indexed in individual volumes published by Ann S. Lainhart, available for purchase from the author at P.O. Box 1487, Boston, MA 02117. These indexes are available at the BOSTON PUBLIC LIBRARY Microtext Department, the NEW ENGLAND HISTORIC GENEALOGICAL SOCIETY [Ref F74...] and through all FAMILY HISTORY CENTERS (LDS) (see the FHLC under "MASSACHUSETTS, [County], [Town] - CENSUS - [Year]").

For some towns in the 1855 and 1865 state census, enumerators provided the exact town of birth, instead of just state or country. There were also state censuses taken in Massachusetts every ten years between 1875 and 1945, but the original schedules were apparently destroyed, according to the State Archives. Only the statistical summaries remain.

Many other states also took state censuses, usually in years between the Federal census. Notable among the 20th-century state censuses are New York (1905, 1915, 1925), New Jersey (1905, 1915), and Rhode Island (1905 to 1935). For details see *State Census Records* by Ann S. Lainhart (Baltimore: Genealogical Publishing Co, 1992).

Federal Population Census, 1790-1920 -- Data Elements Included:

1790   Name of family head; number of free white males of 16 years and up; free white males under 16; free white females; slaves; other persons.

1800   Name of family head; if white, age and sex; race; slaves.

1810   Name of family head; if white, age and sex; race; slaves.

1820   Name of family head; age; sex; race; foreigners not naturalized; slaves; industry (agriculture, commerce, and manufactures).

1830   Name of family head; age; sex; race; slaves; deaf and dumb; blind; foreigners not naturalized.

1840   Name of family head; age; sex; race; slaves; number of deaf and dumb; number of blind; number of insane and idiotic and whether in public or private charge; number of persons in each family employed in each of six classes of industry and one of occupation; literacy; pensioners for Revolutionary or military service.

1850   Name; age; sex; race; whether deaf and dumb, blind, insane or idiotic; value of real estate; occupation; birthplace; whether married within the year; school attendance; literacy; whether a pauper or convict. Supplemental schedule for slaves, and persons who died during the year.

1860   Name; age; sex; race; value of real estate; value of personal estate; occupation; birthplace; whether married within the year; school attendance; literacy; whether deaf and dumb, blind, insane or idiotic, pauper or convict; number of slave houses. Supplemental schedule for slaves, and persons who died during the year.

1870   Name; age; race; occupation; value of real estate; value of personal estate; birthplace; whether parents were foreign born; month of birth if born within the year; month of marriage if married within the year; school attendance; literacy; whether deaf and dumb, blind, insane or idiotic; male citizens 21 and over, and number of such persons denied the right to vote for reasons other than rebellion. Supplemental schedule for persons who died during the year.

1880   Address; name; relationship to family head; sex; race; age; marital status; month of birth if born within the census year; sickness or temporary disability; whether blind, deaf and dumb, idiotic, insane, maimed, crippled, bedridden or otherwise disabled; school attendance; literacy; birthplace of person and parents. Supplemental schedule for persons who died during the year.

1890   General schedules - destroyed. Supplemental schedules for Union veterans of the Civil War and their widows.

1900   Address; name; relationship to family head; sex; race; age; marital status; number of years married; for women, number of children born and number now living; birthplace of person and parents; if foreign born, year of immigration and whether naturalized; occupation; months not employed; school attendance; literacy; ability to speak English; whether on a farm; home owned or rented and if owned, whether mortgaged.

1910   Address; name; relationship to family head; sex; race; marital status; number of years of present marriage; for women, number of children born and number now living; birthplace and mother tongue of person and parents; if foreign born, year of immigration, whether naturalized, and whether able to speak English, or if not, language spoken; occupation, industry, and class of worker; if an employee, whether out of work during the year; literacy; school attendance; home owned or rented; if owned, whether mortgaged; whether farm or house; whether a survivor of Union or Confederate Army or Navy; whether blind or deaf and dumb.

1920   Address; name; relationship to family head; sex; race; age; marital status; if foreign born, year of immigration to the U.S., whether naturalized, and year of naturalization; school attendance; literacy; birthplace of person and parents; mother tongue of foreign born; ability to speak English; occupation, industry, and class of worker; home owned or rented; if owned, whether free or mortgaged, mortgage data.

NATURALIZATIONS

Introduction:

Naturalization records, or citizenship papers, are one of the most useful items for determining your immigrant ancestor's place of origin. Not all aliens were naturalized, but when they were, the documentation process in the court records can provide a goldmine of information.

Some useful books on Naturalization records are:

Newman, John J. *American Naturalization Processes and Procedures, 1790-1985.* (Indianapolis: Indiana Historical Society, 1985). 43 pages. {The most complete study of U.S. Naturalization and Citizenship laws. With sample forms, thorough appendices, and bibliography}.

Neagles, James C. and Lila Lee Neagles. *Locating Your Immigrant Ancestor: A Guide to Naturalization Records.* Revised edition. (Logan, UT: Everton Publishers, 1986). 153 pages. {A survey of the holdings of pre-1907 Naturalization records in county courthouses throughout the U.S.}.

Naturalization laws are complicated, and were not made uniform until 1906. Usually several different documents needed to be filed with the court, in order to complete the process of Americanization:

- *Declaration of Intention* or "First Papers" was frequently completed and filed with a court soon after immigration into the country. Look for these documents in the port cities where the immigrant landed.

- *Petition for Naturalization* or "Final Papers" was filed after a stay of five years in this country (during most of our history). These papers included a Petition for Citizenship, an Oath of Allegiance, and Affidavit of witnesses.

- *Certificate of Citizenship*, which was issued to the new citizen. A stub was retained by the court. Usually, these documents provide very little information, but usually do include the location of the court, which is the key to finding the other naturalization papers.

During the period from 1790 to 1906, naturalizations could be performed in **any** court: federal, state, county or local. The Massachusetts courts which were authorized to perform naturalizations are: Supreme Judicial Court (1790-present), Court of Common Pleas (1790-1860), Superior Court (1860-present), Police Courts (1790-1855), Superior Court of Suffolk County (1856-60), Municipal Court of Boston (1858-1860), District, Police, and Municipal Courts (1855-1906). In addition, the U.S. District and Circuit Courts (Federal courts) performed naturalizations.

1790 - 1855	Supreme Judicial Court, courts of common pleas, police courts.
1855 - 1856	Massachusetts legislature suspended jurisdiction of all Massachusetts courts (Feb 1855 to Mar 1856).
1856 - 1858	Supreme Judicial Court, Court of Common Pleas, Superior Court of Suffolk County.
1858 - 1860	Supreme Judicial Court, Court of Common Pleas, Superior Court of Suffolk County, Municipal Court of Boston.
1860 - 1885	Supreme Judicial Court, Superior Court.
1885 - 1906	Supreme Judicial Court, Superior Court, district, police and municipal courts.
1906 - 1991	Supreme Judicial Court, Superior Court.

After 1906, the Bureau of Immigration and Naturalization was set up, and this agency has kept records on all naturalizations since then. If your ancestor was naturalized after 1906, you can write to the INS at the following address for a copy of Form G-641 to request records.

Immigration and Naturalization Service
Freedom of Information, Room 5304
425 Eye Street NW
Washington, DC 20536

(202) 514-1554

However, requests to the INS usually take many months to be filled. Fortunately, most of the original Massachusetts court naturalization records have been centralized in one of two locations, which can be readily accessed. In most other parts of the country, determining which court naturalized your ancestor is the most difficult part of the search. Researchers seeking New England naturalizations are spared looking through all of these various record sources by virtue of a comprehensive index (see below).

New England Naturalization Records:

Massachusetts naturalization records are generally available at one of two locations: the NATIONAL ARCHIVES - NEW ENGLAND REGION in Waltham, or the MASSACHUSETTS ARCHIVES at Columbia Point. The National Archives regional branch holds two important series of records: the WPA indexes and dexigraphs (1790-1906) and the records of the U.S. District and Circuit courts of Massachusetts. The State Archives holds abstracts of Massachusetts naturalizations, 1885-1931, as well as many county court records. Each is described below.

1) WPA Index and Dexigraphs. One of the projects undertaken by the Work Projects Administration (WPA) in the 1930s was the indexing and photocopying of all "old law" naturalization records from various courts throughout the country: city, county, state and federal courts, from 1786 through 1906, when the administration of all naturalizations came under the authority of the Immigration and Naturalization Service (INS). The project was never completed, but fortunately, indexes were completed for the New England States and New York City.

The WPA index cards for New England are in drawers at the NATIONAL ARCHIVES - NEW ENGLAND REGION in Waltham. They have also been microfilmed (NAMP M1299, 117 reels), and thus are available at the National Archives in Washington, at the BOSTON PUBLIC LIBRARY microtext room, and through all FAMILY HISTORY CENTERS (LDS). The index cards are filed in three separate groups: Connecticut (121 drawers, microfilm reels #1-38); Rhode Island (27 drawers, reels #39-46); and Maine, Massachusetts, New Hampshire and Vermont (228 drawers, reels #47-117). The cards in each group are arranged by the name of the petitioner, according to the Soundex system. Each 3x5 index card shows the following information: name, address, name and location of the court, certificate number or volume and page, date of naturalization, and country of birth. Other fields on the cards which might be filled in include: date of birth or age, date and port of arrival in U.S., names and addresses of witnesses.

When the indexes were made, the WPA also produced "dexigraph" copies of the naturalization certificates themselves — 5" x 8" photostat-like cards. The dexigraphs are also at the NATIONAL ARCHIVES - NEW ENGLAND REGION in Waltham. The original records stayed in the courts. However, the National Archives branch in Waltham has the original naturalization records from all **federal** courts in New England (U.S. District and Circuit Courts), and from some local Connecticut courts. See page 147.

2) <u>Federal Court Records</u>. The National Archives branch has the originals of all Naturalization records of **Federal** Courts (U.S. District and Circuit Courts) in the six New England states, for 1790 through the 1970's. (Note that the functions of the U.S. Circuit Courts were absorbed by the U.S. District Courts in 1911). Alphabetical indexes to the naturalizations in the U.S. District Court in Boston are available on microfilm at the Archives (NAMP M1545). 1906-1926 are on reels #1-27, 1927-1966 are on reels #28-115. The naturalization records for 1906-1929 are also on microfilm (NAMP M1368, 330 reels); original records are available at the Archives for other time periods.

The NATIONAL ARCHIVES - NEW ENGLAND REGION does accept mail requests for naturalization information. Turnover is up to 10 working days. The researcher should provide the name, place and approximate date of naturalization. The search is free. If a record is found, you will be billed a minimum of $6.00.

3) <u>State Abstracts, 1885-1931</u>. The MASSACHUSETTS ARCHIVES at Columbia Point has a few naturalization resources. It holds **abstracts** of naturalizations from Massachusetts **state and local** courts for 1885-1931, in 49 volumes. These records are arranged chronologically by year, and each annual volume is indexed separately, making them difficult to use. The resources of the NATIONAL ARCHIVES - NEW ENGLAND REGION should be consulted first. These abstracts do not provide much genealogical information themselves, but they are useful in locating the original court records.

4) <u>County Records</u>. Naturalization records in county and local courts generally remain in court jurisdictions. The MASSACHUSETTS ARCHIVES has no jurisdiction over these records, only over state records. However, some Massachusetts county courts have turned their records over to the State Archives for safe keeping. These records are kept in the vault at the State Archives, and must be accessed by the staff.

Naturalization records from Massachusetts courts accessioned by the State Archives include the Superior Courts of: Bristol County (1805-1990), Essex County (1906-1982), Franklin County (1853-1976), Hampden County (1812-1987), Hampshire County (1849-1988), Middlesex County (1842-1991), Plymouth County (1812-1977), Suffolk County (1859-1885), and Worcester County (1809-1984). Also District Court naturalization records, 1885-1906, from Fall River, Ware, Northampton, Malden, Dedham, Quincy, Plymouth, Chelsea, Worcester Central and Dudley/Webster. They also have the naturalization records of the Suffolk County Supreme Judicial Court, 1790-1859; and the Lowell Police Court, 1832-1906. See page 126 for details. See Appendix C (page 232) for a list of all Massachusetts towns and counties.

New York City:

Soundex index cards were also made by the WPA for all <u>New York City</u> courts, 1790-1906, and are available at the NATIONAL ARCHIVES - NORTHEAST REGION in New York City (201 Varick Street) (NAMP M1674). Microfilm copies of these index cards (294 reels) are available through FAMILY HISTORY CENTERS (LDS) (see FHLC under "NEW YORK, NEW YORK (CITY) - NATURALIZATION AND CITIZENSHIP - INDEXES"), and at the NEW YORK PUBLIC LIBRARY [*ZI-538].

FHL Microfilms:

Here is a list of microfilms of Massachusetts naturalization records in the LDS (Mormon) Family History Library. They may be borrowed through any of the FAMILY HISTORY CENTERS (LDS) (see page 85). These microfilm listings were extracted from the 1993 microfiche edition of the FHLC, under the headings "MASSACHUSETTS - NATURALIZATION AND CITIZENSHIP" and "MASSACHUSETTS, [County] - NATURALIZATION AND CITIZEN-SHIP". The county naturalization records, then located in Massachusetts county courthouses, were microfilmed by the Mormons in 1986-1992 (Many have since been transferred to the MASSACHUSETTS ARCHIVES). Check the FHLC for microfilm numbers.

Immigration and Naturalization Service:
* Index to New England Naturalization petitions, 1791-1906. [National Archives, 1983 (NAMP M1299)]. Soundex index to photocopies of naturalization documents filed in New England states. [CT reels #1-38; RI reels #39-46; ME, MA, NH, VT reels #47-117]. (117 reels). Originals at NATIONAL ARCHIVES - NEW ENGLAND REGION.

U.S. District Court (District of Massachusetts):
* Naturalization records, 1906-1917. [National Archives, 1988 (NAMP M1368)]. Most volumes individually indexed. (55 reels). {Note: The full series from the National Archives contains 330 rolls, and covers 1906-1929}.
* Naturalization index cards, 1790-1926. [GSU, U.S. District Court, Boston, 1985]. Index to U.S. District Court and U.S. Circuit Court in Mass. [1790-1906 A-Z, 10½ reels; 1907-1926 A-Z, 6½ reels]. (17 reels).

Barnstable County:
* Superior Court, Declarations 1907-1935. (2 reels).
* Superior Court, Naturalizations, 1907-1933. (3 reels).

Berkshire County:
* District Court (Berkshire City), Records and Index, 1885-1906. (6 reels).
* Court of Common Pleas, Records, 1843-1856. (5 reels).
* Superior Court, 1856-1885. (2 reels).
* Superior Court, 1906-1932; Index 1829-1936. (6 reels).
* Superior Court, 1866-1941. (9 reels).
* Superior Court, 1856-1887. (2 reels).
* Superior Court Clerk, Index 1815-1906. (2½ reels).
* Court of Common Pleas, Index 1815-1985. (9 reels).

Bristol County:
* 1st District Court (Taunton), Civil Docket books, 1884-1895. (1 reel).
* 1st District Court (Taunton), Card file index 1885-1906. (2 reels).
* 1st District Court (Taunton), Declarations, 1896-1906. (1 reel).
* 1st District Court (Taunton), Petitions and Index, 1885-1906. (10 reels).
* 1st District Court (Taunton), Primary declarations, 1885-1906. (1 reel).
* 1st District Court (Taunton), Final applications, 1896-1906. (1 reel).
* 1st District Court (Taunton), Declarations, papers, 1885-1906. (5 reels).
* 4th District Court (Attleboro), Dockets and records, 1904-06. (2 reels).
* Superior Court, Declarations 1856-1885, Petitions 1906-1921. (34 reels).
* Court of Common Pleas, Index 1805-1906. (1 reel).
* New Bedford City Hall, Applications for Naturalization, 1886-1900. (1 reel).

Dukes County: No records in FHLC.

Essex County: No records in FHLC.

Franklin County:
- District Court, Applications, 1899-1906. (1 reel).
- District Court, Declarations and Index, 1896-1906. (2 reels).
- Superior Court, Naturalization Indexes, 1811-1900, 1900-1991. (4 reels).

Hampden County:
- District Court of Eastern Hampden (Palmer), Dockets and Index, 1896-1906. (1 reel).
- Court of Common Pleas, Primary declarations, 1853-1877. (2 reels).
- Court of Common Pleas, Primary and Final, 1853-1874. (8 reels).
- Court of Common Pleas, Primary and Final, 1840-1852. (5 reels).
- Police Court (Springfield), Papers and Indexes, 1885-1906. (18 reels).
- Superior Court, Declarations of Intention, 1875-1893. (2 reels).
- Superior Court, Declarations of Intention, 1906-1931. (21 reels).
- Superior Court, Pending (1851-1890), Dismissed (1886-1887). (1 reel).
- Superior Court, Petitions, Declarations and Orders, 1906-1931. (48 reels).
- Superior Court, Petitions of military personnel, 1918. (1 reel).
- Superior Court, Primary and Final, 1853-1906. (4 reels).
- Superior Court, Primary and Final, 1879-1906. (9 reels).
- Superior Court, Final admission, 1875-1880. (5 reels).
- Various courts, Index 1812-1853. (1 reel).
- Superior Court, Index 1812-1906 (2 reels), Index 1906-1986 (14 reels).

Hampshire County:
- District Court (Ware), Final Dockets, 1903-1906. (1 reel).
- District Court (Northampton), Dockets, 1885-1906. (1 reel).
- Superior Court, Records, 1849-1934. (13 reels).
- Superior Court, Index, 1840-1986. (3 reels).

Middlesex County:
- Courts, Records, 1841-1884. (5 reels).
- Courts, Index, 1800-1885. (1 reel).

Nantucket County: No records in FHLC.

Norfolk County:
- Superior Court, Naturalization records and indexes, 1806-1958. (15 reels).

Plymouth County:
- 3rd District Court, Papers, Dockets and Index, 1885-1906. (2 reels).
- 4th District Court (Wareham), Applications 1885-1906. (1 reel).

Suffolk County:
- Courts, Petitions and executions, 1782-1910. (2 reels). (Court of Common Pleas 1782-1850, Superior Court 1850-1907)
- District Court, East Boston, Applications and Papers, 1885-1906. (2 reels).
- Superior Court, Primary and Final 1864-1888, Card Index 1856-1884. (5 reels).

Worcester County:
- Superior Court, Naturalization records 1916-1929. (1 reel).

PASSENGER LISTS

Lists of passengers arriving at U.S. ports have been maintained by the Federal government since 1820. U.S. Passenger Arrival Lists generally provide the name, age and country of origin for each arriving person. Relatively few U.S. lists prior to 1890 show the town or city of origin; later lists frequently provide the specific place of last foreign residence and/or birthplace. These passenger lists, which are arranged chronologically by date of arrival for each port, provide more details for 20th century arrivals than for the 19th century.

The following works provide excellent how-to and background material on passenger list research. The National Archives publication *Immigrant and Passenger Arrivals* is particularly useful for locating the correct reel of microfilm.

Tepper, Michael. *American Passenger Arrival Records: A Guide to the Records of Immigrants Arriving at American Ports by Sail and Steam.* (Baltimore: Genealogical Publishing Co., 1988, 1993). 142 pages. {A scholarly and comprehensive guide to U.S. passenger arrival records}.

Colletta, John P. *They Came in Ships.* (Salt Lake City, UT: Ancestry Publishing, 1989, 1993). 108 pages. {An easy-to-use guide for beginners, with step-by-step instructions}.

Guide to Genealogical Research in the National Archives. (Washington, D.C.: National Archives and Records Service, 1985). Pages 41-57. {Contains a summary, by port, of all passenger lists held by the National Archives in Washington}.

Immigrant and Passenger Arrivals: A Select Catalog of National Archives Microfilm Publications. 2nd edition. (Washington, DC: National Archives Trust Fund Board, 1983, 1991). 171 pages. {A reel-by-reel listing of all National Archives microfilms of passenger lists}.

The National Archives in Washington has custody of these lists, which have been microfilmed. Indexes to most ports were prepared by the WPA, but they were not completed. The following chart shows the five major U.S. ports of entry on the Atlantic coast:

Port	Passengers	Lists	Indexes
● New York	24.0 M	1820-1957	1820-1846, 1897-1948
● Boston	2.0 M	1820-1943	1848-1891, 1902-1920
● Baltimore	1.5 M	1820-1948	1820-1952
● Philadelphia	1.2 M	1800-1945	1800-1948
● New Orleans	0.7 M	1820-1945	1853-1952

The second column shows the number of passengers, in millions, that arrived at each port between 1820 and 1920. There are also lists for several minor ports, as well as the Canadian border. As you can see, the large majority of passengers arrived at New York, and there are large gaps in the indexes, especially for periods of major Jewish immigration.

Passenger Arrival Lists were kept by the U.S. Customs Service until 1891, when this function was taken over by the Immigration and Naturalization Service (INS). The forms prescribed by federal law in 1893 for an immigration passenger list included the following information for each passenger: full name; age; sex; marital status; occupation; nationality; last residence; final destination; whether in the U.S. before, and if so, when and where; and whether going to join a relative and if so, the relative's name, address and relationship. The format of the immigration passenger list was revised in 1903 to include race, in 1906 to include a personal description and birthplace, and in 1907 to include the name and address of the nearest relative in the immigrant's home country.

Because the passenger lists are organized by port, and then chronologically by date of arrival, it is most important to know the place and date your ancestor arrived, in order to locate the correct list. For some ports, name indexes have been prepared, covering certain dates (see below). For unindexed years, it is necessary to know the exact date of arrival; otherwise you will need to scan many lists in order to find your ancestor. If you do not know your ancestor's date of arrival, it is often easier to first find their naturalization papers, which usually include the date and port of arrival and the name of the ship. You can then access then correct ship list.

If you know the name of the ship upon which your ancestor arrived, you can find the dates on which that ship arrived in the *Morton Allan Directory of European Passenger Steamship Arrivals* (New York: Immigration Information Bureau, 1931; Reprint, Baltimore: Genealogical Publishing Co., 1987). It lists the names of vessels arriving by year, steamship company, and date of arrival at the ports of New York, 1890-1930, and of Baltimore, Boston and Philadelphia, 1904-1926. This can help narrow down your search.

Once you know the date of arrival and the name of the ship, you can order a copy of the ship passenger list directly from the National Archives in Washington (see "Ordering Copies" on page 28 below), or search the microfilm yourself.

Although there have been Jews in North America since 1654, most did not arrive until the late 19th or early 20th century. Here are Jewish population figures for the United States:

1790	1,500	1860	150,000
1826	6,000	1880	280,000
1840	15,000	1925	4,500,000

Boston Passenger Lists:

Boston passenger arrival lists, held at the National Archives in Washington, have been microfilmed. There are two microfilm series covering the Boston passenger lists, and three indexes. National Archives Microfilm Publication M277 (115 reels) contains the lists for the period <u>1820-1891</u>. There is an alphabetical card index of passenger names from 1848 to 1891, on microfilm series NAMP M265 (282 reels), described below. However, this index must be used with caution. Although this index is on a National Archives film, the cards were prepared from Massachusetts State passenger lists held by the MASSACHUSETTS ARCHIVES, rather than the National Archives' own collection of Federal lists, so some problems arise. Names appearing in one version of a list might not appear in the other, and entire lists found in one collection may be missing from the other. If you do not find the name you are looking for in this index, always check the approximate date of arrival in the film of the National Archives passenger lists (NAMP M277) just in case.

All original U.S. Federal Customs passenger lists for the port of Boston before 1883 were destroyed in a fire at Boston in May 1894. Most of the lists on microfilm series M277 are copies of original passenger lists, 1820-1874. Those for the period January 1883 thru July 1891 are the original passenger lists from the Boston customhouse. There are **no** Federal lists available for the period April 1874 thru December 1882. For this period, an alternate source must be used. A Massachusetts state law of 1848 required a payment of $2.00 for each passenger landed from abroad, and required that passenger lists be kept, specifying names, ages, occupations, and birthplaces. These "State Lists" extending from 1848 to 1891, not only bridge the ten-year gap from 1874 to 1883 in the Customs passenger lists, but also overlap the copies (1848-74) and the extant originals (1883-91), thereby providing an extra measure of cover. The "State Lists" are available only at the MASSACHUSETTS ARCHIVES.

An index covering Boston Passenger Arrivals, 1848-1891, was prepared from the "State Lists" by the Work Projects Administration (WPA) during the 1930s. This index is arranged alphabetically by passenger surname, and contains most of the information which is contained on the original lists: name, age, sex, occupation, nationality, last residence (usually country), if in the US before, and destination (state). It also indicates the name of the ship, the date of its arrival in Boston, and the list number. Note that wives and children arriving on the same ship are sometimes indexed separately, but are usually noted on the same card as other family members. It is important to note that these passenger lists generally do **not** provide the name of the city where the immigrant originally lived. The index is on 4x6 cards, and is kept in the vault at the MASSACHUSETTS ARCHIVES. There is no public access, but a staff member can search the index for you. However, this index has been microfilmed by the National Archives (NAMP M265, 282 reels), which is widely available.

Later Boston passenger lists, 1891-1943, have been microfilmed on NAMP T843 (454 reels). Microfilm indexes are available for 1902-1920, in two separate series. NAMP T521 (11 reels) is an alphabetical card index covering January 1902 through June 1906. NAMP T617 (11 reels) is an alphabetical index covering July 1906 through December 1920. The 1902-1906 index is on handwritten 3x5 cards, one card per family, in strict alphabetical order. Each card lists the passenger's name, age, number of family members, citizenship, ship name, date of arrival, and list number. The 1906-1920 index is more difficult to use. These typewritten 3x5 cards are arranged in **rough** alphabetical order, by the first two or three letters of the surname. There are several unrelated entries on each card, one line for each passenger. Card for arrivals before 1910 contain the passenger's name, age, citizenship, ship name, date of arrival, page and line number. Cards for arrivals after 1910 contain only the passenger name, age, sex, line, page and volume number; the date of arrival and ship name are **not** given. To correlate the volume numbers with an arrival date (and microfilm number), see the National Archives' *Immigrant and Passenger Arrivals* microfilm catalog, pages 26-30. The catalog gives a reel-by-reel breakdown of all microfilmed passenger lists, showing the volume numbers, inclusive dates and/or alphabetical portion covered by each reel. This information is also listed in the *Family History Library Catalog* (FHLC), the Mormon catalog.

There is no index for the period of mid-1891 through 1901. However, a finding aid has been prepared for this book by Carol Coplin Baker. A guide to the ships entering Boston harbor during this period, with their corresponding arrival dates and microfilm location, appears as Appendix D (see page 238).

There are no comprehensive indexes covering the period after 1920 for Boston. However, there are book indexes available for 1899 through 1940 (except 1901) on NAMP T790 (107 reels). The book indexes contain an alphabetical listing of passengers on a particular vessel, and are arranged chronologically by the date of arrival of the ship.

Availability:

The microfilms of the Boston passenger lists are available for viewing at several institutions in the Boston area.

• The NATIONAL ARCHIVES - NEW ENGLAND REGION in Waltham is most convenient location. The Archives has the most complete set locally, holding all Boston passenger list microfilms up through 1930, all three alphabetical indexes (1848-1891, 1902-1906, 1906-1920), and the book indexes through 1919. All microfilms are readily available in open cabinets. See page 143.

• The NATIONAL ARCHIVES - PITTSFIELD has a complete set: microfilms of the passenger lists through 1943, all three alphabetical indexes (1848-1891, 1902-1906, 1906-1920), and the book indexes through 1940. All microfilms are readily available in open cabinets. See page 154.

• The MASSACHUSETTS ARCHIVES at Columbia Point holds the originals and the only microfilm copies (76 reels) of the "State Lists", 1848-1891, as well as the original index cards for the same period. Also available at the State Archives is the Registry of Vessels for Boston, 1848-1892 (4 reels). See page 124.

• The BOSTON PUBLIC LIBRARY Microtext Room has microfilm copies of the lists thru 1918, the three alphabetical indexes, and the book indexes thru 1916. See page 66.

• All microfilmed lists are also available through all FAMILY HISTORY CENTERS (LDS). Look in the *Family History Library Catalog* (FHLC) Locality section under the heading "MASSA-CHUSETTS, SUFFOLK, BOSTON - EMIGRATION AND IMMIGRATION" for details on each microfilm and film numbers for ordering. See page 85.

One additional source for Jewish immigrants to Boston are the records of HIAS (Hebrew Immigrant Aid Society) of Boston, held at the AMERICAN JEWISH HISTORICAL SOCIETY (AJHS) in Waltham. The HIAS collection includes 25,000 index cards for immigrants arriving between 1882 and 1929. Each card usually includes the immigrant's name, date of arrival, steamship, from where they came and where they were headed. These cards are especially useful for locating those who arrived between mid-1891 and 1901, the period for which there are no indexes to the government lists. See page 40.

Summary of Boston Passenger Lists:

•	1820 - 1891	NAMP M277	115 reels
•	1891 - 1943	NAMP T843	454 reels

(Sep 22 1820 - Mar 31 1874,
Jan 1 1883 - Jul 29 1891)
(Aug 1 1891 - Dec 31 1943)

Summary of Boston Passenger List Indexes:

•	1820 - 1848	Alphabetical	NAMP M334, 188 reels (incomplete)
•	1848 - 1891	Alphabetical	NAMP M265, 282 reels
•	1892 - 1901	No index available	
•	1902 - 1906	Alphabetical	NAMP T521, 11 reels (Jan 1 1902 - Jun 30 1906)
•	1906 - 1920	Alphabetical	NAMP T617, 11 reels (Jul 1 1906 - Dec 31 1920)
•	1920 -	No index available	

A few additional arrival lists are in a separate 16 reel series (NAMP M575) called "Copies of Lists of Passengers Arriving at Miscellaneous Ports on the Atlantic and Gulf Coasts and Ports on the Great Lakes", covering 1820-1873. This includes assorted ports such as Galveston, Texas; Portland and Falmouth, Maine; and many small ports in New England. The 188-reel "Supplemental Index" (NAMP M334), is an (incomplete) companion to this series, but it also includes various other ports, including some Boston arrivals.

New York Passenger Lists:

The great majority of Eastern European immigrants entered the U.S. via the port of New York. The New York passenger lists are on two National Archives Microfilm Publications: NAMP M237 contains Customs passenger lists for 1820-1897 (675 reels), and NAMP T715 contains Immigration lists for 1897 to 1957, on a staggering 8,892 reels of microfilm. Unfortunately, no Boston area institution has the complete set of these later New York passenger lists, because of the immense size of the series.

There are several <u>indexes</u> to the New York passenger lists. The only index to early lists (NAMP M261, 103 reels) is a alphabetical index for 1820-1846. For later lists, there is an alphabetical index for 1897-1902 (NAMP T519, 115 reels), a Soundex index covering 1902-1943 (NAMP T621, 744 reels), and a Soundex index covering 1944-1948 (NAMP M1417, 94 reels). There are also book indexes for 1906-1942 (NAMP T612, 807 reels). Unfortunately, there is **no** comprehensive index for New York for the 1847-1897 period. (However, see "Published Indexes" below). The best way to find an ancestor in these lists is to first locate their Naturalization papers, which usually include the name of the ship and exact date of arrival. You can then access the correct ship list.

The specific date of arrival and name of the ship are provided on the alphabetical indexes for 1820-1846, 1897-1902, as well as in the Soundex index for 1902 to mid-1910. From mid-1910 forward, the index card gives **only** the line, page and volume number; the date of arrival and name of the ship are **not** stated. To correlate the volume numbers with an arrival date (and microfilm number), see the National Archives' *Immigrant and Passenger Arrivals* microfilm catalog, pages 55-126 (or see the FHLC under the heading "NEW YORK, NEW YORK (CITY) - EMIGRATION AND IMMIGRATION").

Locally, the BOSTON PUBLIC LIBRARY Microtext Department has the early series of New York lists (1820-1897, plus alphabetical index 1820-1846). See page 66. All FAMILY HISTORY CENTERS (LDS) have access to the New York Passenger list and index microfilms up until 1942. Look in the FHLC under the heading "NEW YORK, NEW YORK (CITY) - EMIGRATION AND IMMIGRATION" for film numbers. See page 85.

The complete set of New York passenger lists are available at the NATIONAL ARCHIVES, PITTSFIELD. See page 154. The NATIONAL ARCHIVES in Washington and the NATIONAL ARCHIVES NORTHEAST REGION branch in New York City (201 Varick Street) also have the complete set.

Summary of New York Passenger <u>Lists</u>:

•	1820 - 1897	NAMP M237	675 reels
•	1897 - 1957	NAMP T715	8,892 reels	(Jun 16 1897 - Jul 3 1957)

Summary of New York Passenger List <u>Indexes</u>:

•	1820 - 1846	Alphabetical	NAMP M261, 103 reels	
•	1847 - 1897	No index available		
•	1897 - 1902	Alphabetical	NAMP T519, 115 reels	(Jun 16 1897 - Jun 30 1902)
•	1902 - 1943	Soundex	NAMP T621, 744 reels	(Jul 1 1902 - Dec 31 1943)
•	1944 - 1948	Soundex	NAMP M1417, 94 reels	

Other Ports:

Passenger lists exist for other major U.S. ports, as well as smaller New England ports. Major ports include Baltimore (1820-1948), New Orleans (1820-1945), and Philadelphia (1800-1945) on the East coast, and San Francisco (1893-1953) and Seattle (1890-1957) on the West Coast. These lists are held by the National Archives in Washington, and are not available locally, other than borrowing through the FAMILY HISTORY CENTERS (LDS).

The NATIONAL ARCHIVES - NEW ENGLAND REGION in Waltham and NATIONAL ARCHIVES - PITTSFIELD both hold microfilm copies of lists and indexes for several smaller New England ports: New Bedford, MA (1902-42, 8 reels, index 2 reels); Portland, ME (1893-1943, 35 reels, index 1 reel); and Providence, RI (1911-43, 49 reels, index 2 reels). The Pittsfield branch also holds copies of the arrival lists for the port of Philadelphia, 1800-1882, and index for 1800-1906.

Canadian Border Crossings:

Many immigrants arrived in the U.S. via Canada. Fares of Canadian steamship companies were often lower, and encouraged people bound for the United States to travel through Canada. Immigration stations were set up along the Canadian border in 1895, and lists of immigrants were maintained, containing information very similar to that found in immigration passenger lists. The headquarters of the INS was in St. Albans, Vermont, and therefore the Canadian border crossing lists are often referred to as the St. Albans lists. These lists are now in the custody of the National Archives, and have been microfilmed. There are two main series of lists: one covering all ports 1895-1954 (M1464, 640 reels), and a smaller series covering entries via Pacific ports 1929-1949 (M1465, 25 reels). There are two Soundex indexes to these records: M1461 covers 1895-1924 (400 reels), and M1463 covers 1924-1952 (98 reels). The NATIONAL ARCHIVES - NEW ENGLAND REGION and NATIONAL ARCHIVES - PITTSFIELD both have the complete microfilm series. The microfilms may also be borrowed via FAMILY HISTORY CENTERS (LDS).

For ships arriving at Canadian ports, The National Archives of Canada (395 Wellington St., Ottawa K1A 0N3 Canada) has microfilm copies of passenger manifests for ships arriving at six ports, including Quebec (from 1865) and Halifax (from 1880) up to 1919. These lists are arranged chronologically; there is **no** name index. Canadian records after 1920 are subject to restrictions of the Privacy Act. Inquiries on these later records may be addressed to: Query Response Centre, Citizenship and Immigration, 300 Slater Street, Ottawa, Ontario K1A 1L1 Canada. (613) 957-7667.

Hamburg Passenger Lists:

Another source for locating immigrants' ancestral towns are the emigration records kept by the port of Hamburg, Germany. A large percentage of Eastern European Jewish immigrants left via the port of Hamburg, after traveling overland from Hungary, Poland or Russia. The Hamburg lists, covering 1850 through 1934, list each passenger's name, age, sex, occupation, and place of birth and residence. The lists are indexed by year by the first letter of each passenger's surname, so some searching is required. These lists and indexes have been microfilmed, and are available in the U.S. through all FAMILY HISTORY CENTERS (LDS). An excellent overview of these lists appears in *The Encyclopedia of Jewish Genealogy*, pages 9-12, with a reel-by-reel listing on pages 163-167.

Published Indexes:

There are some privately-compiled published indexes to passenger lists, most covering Colonial immigrants, or a particular ethnic group for a small set of years. See the bibliographies in Colletta or Tepper for a complete list. The largest of these indexes is *Passenger and Immigration Lists Index: A Guide to Published Arrival Records...*, edited by P. William Filby (Detroit: Gale Research Co., 1981 et sequa). This series indexes previously published passenger lists, and focuses on the 17th, 18th and early 19th centuries. Currently at 14 volumes and covering 2½ million passengers, one additional volume is published annually.

Within the last ten years, many compilations for various national and ethnic groups have been published, with names extracted from the passenger lists held by the National Archives. Much indexing is being done by the Temple-Balch Center for Immigration Research in Philadelphia. The largest of these projects is *Germans to America*, edited by Ira Glazier (Wilmington, Delaware: Scholarly Resources, Inc.), which covers arrivals of German passengers for Jan 1850 through Nov 1884 so far. This ongoing series (50 volumes published since 1988) is available at major libraries.

A published index for Russian immigrants is now in progress, covering Russian (and Polish and Finnish) arrivals at U.S. ports: *Migration from the Russian Empire: Lists of Passengers Arriving at the Port of New York*, edited by Ira Glazier (Baltimore: Genealogical Publishing Co.) The first two volumes were published in 1995, and contain arrivals for Jan 1875 - Apr 1886, and include 105,000 names (of the 2.3 million Russians who arrived 1871-1910). Over half of the listed passengers are Jewish. This ongoing series will continue through 1910, funding permitting, in about 50 volumes, and will take many years to complete. The next volume is expected in late summer 1996.

These published indexes are available at a number of locations, the most accessible of which is the NEW ENGLAND HISTORIC GENEALOGICAL SOCIETY (see page 164). The NATIONAL ARCHIVES, PITTSFIELD (see page 154) also has most of the major published passenger arrival indexes.

Also, the LDS Family History Library has begun a major volunteer effort to computer index the New York passenger arrival lists of 1897-1924, which is slated to be completed about the year 2000. Thus the next few years should see major progress in this area.

Ordering Copies of U.S. Passenger Lists:

If you already know an approximate date of arrival and the name of a ship, you can order a copy of a ship passenger list directly from the National Archives in Washington, without searching microfilm yourself. This is accomplished by submitting National Archives Form NATF-81, "Order for Copies of Ship Passenger Arrival Records", available from the address below.

> General Reference Branch (NNRG)
> National Archives and Records Administration
> 7th and Pennsylvania Avenue NW
> Washington, DC 20408

The search is free, and you will be charged $10.00 if the requested passenger is found and you wish to receive a copy of the passenger list. These are large actual-size copies, measuring 18" x 24", providing much information.

The National Archives will search either indexed or un-indexed lists, depending upon the following criteria:

Indexed passenger lists: The National Archives will search indexes if you can supply the following information: Full name of passenger, port of entry, and approximate date of arrival. The following indexes exist:

- Baltimore (1820-1952)
- Boston (1848-1891 and 1902-1920)
- New Orleans (1853-1952)
- New York (1820-1846 and 1897-1948)
- Philadelphia (1800-1948)
- minor ports (1820-1874 and 1890-1924)

Un-indexed passenger lists: will not be searched without more specific information. Searches of lists through 1892 require: Full name of passenger, port of entry, approximate date of arrival, and name of the vessel; OR full name of passenger, port of entry, port of embarkation, and exact date of arrival. To search un-indexed lists after 1892, they require: the full name of passenger, port of entry, name of the vessel, the exact date of arrival, and the names and ages of accompanying passengers, if any.

Always be aware that no one can do your genealogy as well as you can — no one else will be as thorough. The National Archives staff will not check alternate spellings of names, broader ranges of dates, alternate ports, etc., nor will they notice things that only you can: names of relatives traveling aboard the same ship, etc. It is always best to search the original records yourself, rather than depending upon someone else to do it for you. This is true in all areas of genealogy: do not depend upon compiled or secondary sources — always go to the original source. Searching passenger lists and indexes can be challenging and time-consuming, but it pays off in the end. You can find your immigrant ancestor on a ship manifest, if you work at it.

VITAL RECORDS
(Birth, Marriage, Death)

In the United States, the registration of Vital Statistics (Births, Marriages, Divorces, Deaths) is the jurisdiction of the individual States. The Federal Government does **not** maintain files or indexes of these records. These records are filed either in a State vital statistics office, or in a city, county or local office in some states. To obtain a copy of any of these certificates, one must write to the vital statistics office in the State or area where the event occurred.

The names and addresses of the Vital Statistics offices for all 50 states (and territories) are available in the government booklet *Where to Write for Vital Records (Births, Deaths, Marriages and Divorces)* [U.S. Department of Health and Human Services, March 1993, 30 pages]. This booklet is available for $2.25 from the U.S. Government Printing Office, Washington, DC 20402-9325, Tel. (202) 512-1800, or at any U.S. Government Printing Office Bookstore, such as the one at 10 Causeway Street in Boston. The addresses and information for states neighboring Massachusetts are provided at the end of this section.

Massachusetts:

Access to Massachusetts Vital Records can be divided into three time periods:

- Pre-1841   (At local offices; also Printed transcripts)
- 1841-1900   (At MASSACHUSETTS ARCHIVES)
- 1901-date   (At REGISTRY OF VITAL RECORDS AND STATISTICS)

From the earliest times, the towns of Massachusetts were the official keepers of vital records of their inhabitants. In 1841, in conformity with a new law, the towns began reporting their births, marriages and deaths to the state, so that after that date, the records became available at both the town and state levels. Original town records from the time of the town's origin to the present are available in the towns (town clerk, archives or library). From 1841-1900 the official duplicates which were filed with the state are at the MASSACHUSETTS ARCHIVES (see page 124), and from 1901 forward, the records are still at the REGISTRY OF VITAL RECORDS AND STATISTICS (see page 175).

Massachusetts vital records are also widely available elsewhere, other than the above government sources. Alternate sources for Massachusetts vital records include the LDS FAMILY HISTORY CENTERS (see page 85), which has microfilm copies of all Massachusetts vital records through 1899, and indexes through 1971. (See the FHLC under "MASSACHUSETTS - VITAL RECORDS" for post-1841 records; look under "MASSACHUSETTS, [COUNTY], [TOWN] - VITAL RECORDS" for pre-1841 records, or check the Massachusetts section of the IGI).

The MASSACHUSETTS ARCHIVES at Columbia Point, in addition to the 1841-1900 records, also has a microfilm copy of the **indexes** up through 1971. The only copy of the records to which these indexes refer are at the REGISTRY OF VITAL RECORDS AND STATISTICS on Tremont Street, but it's usually easier to use the indexes at the Archives, due to the Registry's limited hours. The State Archives also has most of the pre-1841 vital records available on microfilm. (See page 124).

Alternative sources for copies of Massachusetts vital records: The BOSTON PUBLIC LIBRARY microtext department (see page 63) has the Holbrook Institute's Massachusetts Vital Records Collection on microfiche (see next paragraph). The NEW ENGLAND HISTORIC GENEALOGICAL SOCIETY (NEHGS) has the 1841-1899 records on microfilm, plus all of the available pre-1841 printed indexes. They also have photocopies of the 1901-1976 death indexes. See page 161.

Microfiche copies of Massachusetts vital records and indexes can be purchased from the Archive Publishing (formerly the Holbrook Research Institute), 57 Locust Street, Oxford, MA 01540. Holbrook has filmed actual town documents, for over 210 Massachusetts towns, from their founding through the 1890's. Also available from Holbrook are microfiche copies of the state-wide indexes of births, marriages, and deaths for 1841-1895, filmed at the Massachusetts Archives. The microfiche are $6.00 each.

- Birth Index   1841-1895: 52 volumes   (417 fiche)
- Marriage Index   1841-1895: 42 volumes   (327 fiche)
- Death Index   1841-1895: 39 volumes   (310 fiche)

Neighboring States:

Connecticut:

Vital Records Section
Department of Health Services
150 Washington Street
Hartford, CT 06106

State Office has records since July 1897. For earlier records, write to Registrar of Vital Statistics in town or city where event occurred.

Copies are $5.00 each. Make check payable to Department of Health Services. To verify current fees, call (203) 566-2334.

Maine:

Office of Vital Records
Maine Department of Human Services
State House Station 11
Augusta, ME 04333-0011

State office has records since 1892. For earlier records, write to the municipality where the event occurred.

Copies are $10.00 each. Make check payable to Treasurer, State of Maine. To verify current fees, call (207) 289-3184.

New Hampshire:

Bureau of Vital Records
Health and Welfare Building
6 Hazen Drive
Concord, NH 03301

State office has records since 1640. Copies of records may be obtained from State office or from City or Town Clerk in place where event occurred.

Copies are $10.00 each. Make check payable to Treasurer, State of New Hampshire. To verify current fees, call (603) 271-4654.

Rhode Island:

Division of Vital Statistics
Rhode Island Department of Health
Room 101, Cannon Building
3 Capitol Hill
Providence, RI 02908-5097

State office has records since 1853. For earlier records, write to Town Clerk in town where event occurred.

Copies are $10.00 each. Make checks payable to General Treasurer, State of Rhode Island. To verify current fees, call (401) 277-2811.

Vermont:

Vermont Department of Health
Vital Records Section
Box 70
60 Main Street
Burlington, VT 05402

Division of Public Records
US Route 2 - Middlesex
133 State Street
Montpelier, VT 05402

Department of Health has records since 1981. For earlier records, write to the Division of Public Records.

Copies are $5.00 each. Make checks payable to Vermont Department of Health. To verify current fees, call (802) 863-7275 (Department of Health) or (802) 828-3286 (Division of Public Records).

New York:

The situation for vital records in New York State is quite complicated. Large cities in New York each kept their own vital records until 1914, and New York City continues to do so. Further complicating matters are marriage records in New York City, which are maintained separately by each borough.

For New York State (excluding New York City):

Vital Records Section
State Department of Health
Empire State Plaza
Tower Building
Albany, NY 12237-0023

(Mailing address is above; they are actually located at):
733 Broadway
Albany, NY 12207

State office has records since 1880. For records before 1914 in Albany, Buffalo or Yonkers, or before 1880 in any other city, write to the Registrar of Vital Statistics in the city where the event occurred. For the rest of the state (except New York City), write to the state office.

Copies birth and death records are $15.00 each; marriage records are $5.00. Make checks payable to New York State Department of Health. To verify current fees, call (518) 474-3075.

For New York City:

Division of Vital Records
NYC Department of Health
P.O. Box 3776
New York, NY 10007

Archives Division
Department of Records and Information Services
31 Chambers Street
New York, NY 10007

Bureau of Vital Records has birth records since 1910 and death records since 1949. For earlier records (Births 1865-1909, Marriages 1847-1865, Deaths 1865-1948), write to the Archives Division.

Copies of birth and death records are $15.00 each; Make certified checks payable to New York City Department of Health. To verify current fees, call (212) 619-4530.

Copies of marriage records are $10.00 each, and must be obtained from the City Clerk's Office in the correct borough. See *Where to Write for Vital Records* for details and addresses.

Many New York City vital records have recently been microfilmed by the Mormons, and are therefore accessible through FAMILY HISTORY CENTERS (LDS) (see page 85), as an alternate source to the government repositories listed above. The following microfilms are available:

- All Boroughs (City-wide):
    Birth certificate indexes, 1881-1965 (30 films).
    Marriage certificate indexes (grooms) 1888-1937 (12 films).
    Death certificate indexes, 1888-1965 (20 films).

- Bronx (Bronx County):
    Death certificates, 1898-1919 (91 films).
    Marriage indexes, brides, 1898-1937 (4 films).

- Brooklyn (Kings County):
        Birth certificates, 1866-1897 (94 films).
        Marriage certificates, 1866-1937 (410).
        Death certificates, 1862-1897 (339).
        Death certificates, 1898-1920 (341).
        Coroner's reports and journals, 1897-1914 (25).
        Card index to birth certificates, 1866-1897 (34).
        Card index to death ledger, 1848-1866 (7).
        Card index to death certificates, 1862-1898 (78).

- Manhattan (New York County):
        Birth registers and index, 1847-48, 1853-73 (28 films).
        Birth certificates and index, 1866-1897 (543).
        Birth certificates and record, 1898-1900 (49).
        Marriage certificates, 1866-1937 (1,361).
        Marriage index, grooms, 1866-1910 (15).
        Marriage index, brides, 1866-1937 (59).
        Death registers, 1798-1865 (19).
        Death certificates, 1866-1919 (1,038).
        Card index to deaths, 1868-1890 (104).
        Coroner's inquisitions, 1823-1898 (101).

- Queens (Queens County):
        Marriage certificates, 1898-1937 (40 films).
        Marriage certificate indexes: grooms 1881-1937; brides 1905-1937 (10).
        Death certificates, 1898-1919 (89).
        Indexes to births in towns and villages, 1847-1897 (7).

- Staten Island (Richmond County):
        Birth certificates, 1898-1909 (10 films).
        Marriage certificates, 1897-1937 (28).
        Death certificates, 1898-1920 (23).

For more information about the above records, including a reel-by-reel breakdown of film contents, consult the FHLC Locality catalog (see page 87) under the heading "NEW YORK, [County] - VITAL RECORDS". For the city-wide indexes, see under "NEW YORK, NEW YORK (CITY) - VITAL RECORDS - INDEXES". Brooklyn was an independent city before the five boroughs of New York City were incorporated in 1898; for Brooklyn records before 1898, see under "NEW YORK, KINGS, BROOKLYN - VITAL RECORDS".

Other sources of New England state vital records:

The NEW ENGLAND HISTORIC GENEALOGICAL SOCIETY (see page 167) has many state vital records on microfilm, including Maine, New Hampshire, Rhode Island and Vermont.

FAMILY HISTORY CENTERS (LDS) also have microfilms, including:

- Maine — indexes to vital records, 1892-1922 (332 films)
- New Hampshire — index to pre-1900 deaths (60 films)
- Vermont — index to vital records, 1871-1908 (120 films)

For other states, look in the FHLC Locality section under "[State] - VITAL RECORDS".

AMERICAN JEWISH HISTORICAL SOCIETY

Facility Director: Dr. Michael Feldberg, Executive Director
Holly Snyder, Archivist
Michelle Feller-Kopman, Librarian
Ellen Smith, Curator

Address: 2 Thornton Road
Waltham, MA 02154

Phone Number: (617) 891-8110   FAX: (617) 889-9208

Hours of Operation:

Monday to Friday: 9:00am - 4:30pm
Materials may not be requested from the collection after 4:15.
Please call for summer hours.

Directions:

By Car: **From Route 128 (I-95) North**: take Exit 26, Route 20 East towards Waltham. At the 3rd set of lights (1 mile, shortly after the intersection with Rt. 117) turn right onto South Street. Go 0.8 miles to the main entrance of the Brandeis University campus, just after the pedestrian overpass. Turn right off of South Street and make a hard right at the fork. Follow the road up the hill and around for about ½ mile to Lot E.

From Route 128 (I-95) South: take Exit 24 for Route 30. Go straight at the end of the exit ramp across Route 30 / Commonwealth Avenue onto River Street. Follow River Street for 1½ to 2 miles (it will change names to South Street) to the Brandeis University campus on your left.

From Brookline: 1) take Route 9 west to Route 128 North and follow directions given above, or 2) take Commonwealth Avenue west crossing over Route 128 and make a right onto River Street.

From Cambridge: go to Watertown Square and take Main Street through Watertown and Waltham to South Street. (2nd traffic light after Shaw's Super Market, just at the fork with a Shell gas station). Make left onto South Street to Brandeis University campus, which is on the right.

Once at Brandeis: Take the campus road to the right, one-half way around the campus (you will be traveling counter-clockwise). At the crest of a hill, the road will fork; you will see the side of a large white concrete building. That is the AJHS. Drive to the right of the building and park in the designated spots in front of it. Be sure to ask for a parking permit when you enter the building.

By Bus: **From Boston**: Take No. 57 bus (Watertown Limited) from Kenmore Square to the end of the line. Ask driver where to get bus to Waltham (Cedarwood). Cross over Charles River and Main Street and take No. 70 bus (Cambridge-Watertown-Waltham) to end of line (Cedarwood). Ask driver how to get to Brandeis. Cross Route 20, go up Cedarwood Avenue three short blocks to Thornton Road. Turn left on Thornton to end of street (one block). There is a door in gate on right, and Society building is on right, just inside gate.

By Commuter Rail:

The Acton/Fitchburg Line of the MBTA Commuter Rail line originates at North Station in Boston and stops at Porter Square, Belmont Center, Waverly, Waltham, **Brandeis-Roberts**, Kendal Green, Hastings, Silver Hill, Lincoln, Concord, W. Concord, and points west. Service starts early in the morning and continues until midnight. Trains leave about every 1 to 2 hours. Call (617) 222-3200 for information. The walk between the station and the AJHS is over a half mile and up hill on campus.

Description of Institution:

The AMERICAN JEWISH HISTORICAL SOCIETY collects, preserves and publishes historical materials on the Jewish experience on the American continent. It is the oldest national ethnic historical society in the United States. Headquartered on the Brandeis University campus, the AJHS has the most significant collection of American Judaica in the world.

The Society's research library-museum-archive includes a research library of 30,000 volumes; over 40 million manuscripts, letters and other material dating back to the 16th century; millions of pages of newspapers and magazines; paintings, and a Yiddish film library and theater/music collection. The archives includes records of various Jewish organizations and personal papers of diverse Jewish personalities. These artifacts document the growth and accomplishments of American Jewry. The AJHS has been referred to as "The National Archives of the Jewish People in America".

HISTORY

The AJHS was founded in 1892, on the initiative of Cyrus Adler and Oscar S. Straus, to promote the study of American Jewish history. Cyrus Adler (1863-1940) was "one of the foremost influences in establishing the pattern of American Jewish cultural, philanthropic, and communal life." He was involved as founder and/or president of numerous Jewish institutions, such as: the Jewish Publication Society of America; the Jewish Theological Seminary, New York; Dropsie College, Philadelphia; the American Jewish Committee; the National Jewish Welfare Board. Oscar Solomon Straus (1850-1926) was the first Jew to serve in a U.S. presidential cabinet, under Theodore Roosevelt, and was the first president of the AJHS.[1]

Under Isidore S. Meyer, Librarian and Editor of the *American Jewish Historical Quarterly* from 1930 to 1961, the Society's collections grew to encompass many significant institutional collections, including that of the National Jewish Welfare Board, which sponsored the Society's activities for many years.

Nathan M. Kaganoff took over as librarian of AJHS in 1962, when it was housed at the Jewish Theological Seminary in New York. "The library that Kaganoff inherited when he came to the AJHS has been charitably described as a 'mess'. Housed in a cramped suite of rooms..., it consisted of piles of books and manuscripts, most of them uncatalogued. Kaganoff soon created order."[2] In 1968, the AJHS transferred all of its holdings to a modern building constructed by the Society on the Brandeis campus in Waltham, Massachusetts, where it is today.

Kaganoff was librarian of the AJHS from 1962 until his death in 1992. Over those years, he wrote 58 installments of an article entitled "Judaica Americana," which appeared in the AJHS quarterly. These were annotated bibliographies of literature published since 1960 and received by the AJHS, and total over 10,000 citations. Recently, these were republished by Carlson Publishing as *Judaica Americana* in two volumes, and constitute by far the most comprehensive bibliography ever published on American Jewish history. Each bibliography is a different topic. For instance, "Local History" includes citations numbered 654 to 1630. The bibliography for "Genealogy" covers 211 citations numbered 5577 to 5789, listed mostly by surname.

PHILOSOPHY

The original purpose of the Society was to counter the rising anti-Semitism of the times by helping to chronicle and preserve the record of Jewish contributions to America. The founders sought to demonstrate that Jews were an integrated and accepted part of American life from the first. The collections originally focused on prominent and successful Jews, such as Cyrus Adler, Max James Kohler, Commodore Uriah Phillips Levy, Emma Lazarus, etc.

---

[1] *Standard Jewish Encyclopedia*, Cecil Roth, Editor-in-Chief (Doubleday & Company, Garden City, New York, 1962), p. 95, 31, 1763.

[2] Jonathan Sarna, in introduction to *Judaica Americana,* by Nathan Kaganoff, p. ix, (Carlson Publishing, Brooklyn, New York, 1995), published under the auspices of the American Jewish Historical Society.

Since the early years of the century, the Society's collecting philosophy has grown and matured to provide what the current Executive Director, Dr. Michael Feldberg, calls "a balanced view of the social, political, economic, and cultural life of the Jewish people that is as rich and complex and varied as that of any other ethnic group." In the last three decades, AJHS has especially focused on collecting records of national Jewish organizations, including the Council of Jewish Federations and Welfare Funds, the American Jewish Congress, and the Synagogue Council of America. "Those records serve as a repository of not just Jewish issues, but of national-policy issues," according to Dr. Feldberg.[3]

This philosophy is reflected in some of the recent acquisitions, which include the records of the American Association for Ethiopian Jews, Action for Soviet Jewry, and the National Conference on Soviet Jewry.

The term "American" as used in the AJHS name, includes all of the Americas. While most of the material in the collections does relate to the US, there are also strong collections on Canada, Central and South America, and the Caribbean.

The Society publishes the distinguished quarterly journal *American Jewish History* (formerly *American Jewish Historical Quarterly*), and a newsletter, *Heritage*. It puts on exhibitions, lectures, symposia, conferences, Jewish history tours, and other public programs. The AJHS is supported by several thousand members scattered worldwide. The collections are used by professional scholars, students, amateur researchers, and genealogists. The Society is open to the public, without charge, throughout the year. Tours are available and staff lectures can be arranged with advance notice.

AJHS COMPARED TO AJA

There is a separate institution which is sometimes confused with the AJHS. It is also devoted to the history of American Jews, but the two differ in important ways. The American Jewish Archives (AJA) is located at the Hebrew Union College-Jewish Institute of Religion in Cincinnati, Ohio, and is related to Reform Judaism. By comparison, AJHS is secular, meaning that it is not related to any one branch of Judaism. AJA was established in 1947 by Jacob Rader Marcus, who was to be its guiding spirit until his death in 1995. The AJA focuses on the United States, while the AJHS encompasses Jewish life in all of the Americas. The AJA emphasizes biographical materials, synagogue records, religious matters, and papers of scholars; whereas the AJHS' collection of such is small. The AJA collection does not have much in the way of institutional papers; whereas the AJHS is very strong in this area. Also, the AJA is solely an archive, whereas the AJHS also has sizable collections of books, photographs, paintings, ritual objects, and artifacts.

One other difference: the AJA benefits from a published finding aid to their holdings; the AJHS unfortunately, does not. However, recently, an electronic database of the AJHS' manuscript collections has been completed. As discussed below, a significant effort has been underway, on the part of the Jewish Genealogical Society of Greater Boston, to compile a consolidated database of holdings that would be useful for genealogists.

A PRESENCE IN NEW YORK (AGAIN)

In the fall of 1995, the AJHS Board of Trustees signed an agreement to participate in the Center for Jewish History, a major research center for the study of modern Jewish history, soon to be constructed at 15 West 16th Street in New York City. The Center for Jewish History is a joint venture sponsored by the American Jewish Historical Society, the YIVO Institute for Jewish Research, the Leo Baeck Institute, and the Yeshiva University Museum. Occupancy of the Center by the four institutions is expected sometime in late 1997 or early 1998.

The Society's plan is to relocate their headquarters and many of their archival, book and museum holdings to the Center. However, the Trustees are also committed to continuing the Society's presence, as funding permits, either in its current location on the Brandeis campus or elsewhere in the Boston area. The Society plans to retain collections with a Boston or New England provenance in that location.

---

[3] *Chronicle of Higher Education*, Nov. 18, 1992, p. A10.

Description of Resources:

There is much material of unique genealogical value amongst the vast holdings of the AJHS. A few examples: the records of several New York City Jewish orphanages such as the Hebrew Orphan Asylum of Manhattan are kept here; the collections of the Industrial Removal Office contain records of relocation of many Jews to the U.S. interior for industrial and agricultural work; papers of mohels and rabbis and temple records contain details of particular Jewish communities; the records of the Boston office of the Hebrew Immigrant Aid Society (HIAS) document the stories of thousands of new arrivals at the turn of the century through the Port of Boston; data assembled by the American Jewish Committee Office of War Records and the Jewish Welfare Board attest to the significance of the role that Jewish servicemen played in WWI and WWII respectively.

Most AJHS material deals with American Jewry, but there is some information on previous generations in Europe. For instance, genealogies and biographical works can be found here. In addition, landsmanschaftn records are listed by the old-country town.

Due to the diversity of items and the ways in which they came to be at the AJHS, accessing this information can be difficult. The cataloguing system had been idiosyncratic over many of the years of the society's major acquisitions. There is no published or on-line catalog and one card catalog cannot cover all items. Users must search several places to find a potential source of information, and are ultimately dependent on the excellent staff for assistance. Over the past few years, new leadership has expressed an interest in improving access to the collections, making the material available as it was always intended.

AJHS material is currently organized into several categories, or types, of collections. These categories do not particularly correspond to a genealogist's research. Most categories are catalogued in the main card catalog; some separately. The categories are:

A. INSTITUTIONAL RECORDS
B. PERSONAL PAPERS
C. PERIODICALS
D. EPHEMERA
E. VERTICAL FILES
F. READING ROOM AND LIBRARY COLLECTIONS

In addition to the main card catalog, there are six additional series of index cards. These are all shown below. The numbers in parentheses correspond to the sets of index cards found along the back wall of the main reading room, from left to right:

(1) Main card catalog. Contains index cards for Books, Institutional Records, Personal Papers, and Ephemera categories. There are also some other series of cards interfiled with these.
(2) Vertical files catalog.
(3) Names index of the Stephen Wise Papers.
(4) Names index of the Milton Steinberg Papers.
(5) Names index of the Rabbi Tobias Geffen Papers.
(6) NY Incorporation Papers locality index.
(7) 19th Century Periodicals index.

A. INSTITUTIONS

Each Institutional manuscript collection consists of papers of a particular organization, and is designated with an "I" at the beginning of the call number. There are over 200 such collections. Included are synagogues, national Jewish organizations, local Jewish organizations, landsmanschaftn, immigrant aid societies, military organizations, fraternal organizations and burial societies. A complete list of these collections is provided in Appendix E. Additional description is warranted on a few of the organizations that hold significant genealogical interest.

1. Synagogues.

The records of over two dozen synagogues are in the institutional category. However, many other synagogue collections are included in other categories at AJHS, such as ephemera (a few) and vertical files (many). For details on each of these collections, see Appendix E, under the name of the synagogue. Congregations in the institutional category include those from the following cities:

San Francisco, CA; Savannah, GA; Waukegan, IL; New Orleans, LA; Boston, MA; Cambridge, MA; Chelsea, MA; Dorchester, MA; Lexington, MA; Revere, MA; Springfield, MA; New York, NY; Brooklyn, NY; Philadelphia, PA; Charleston, SC; Nashville, TN; Montreal, Canada.

2. Baron de Hirsch Fund. This collection is of major interest for Jewish genealogists. Baron Maurice de Hirsch (1831-1896) lived in Munich, Brussels, and Paris. He was a banker and philanthropist, especially for Jewish causes. His total benefactions exceeded $100,000,000.

The Baron de Hirsch Fund was incorporated in New York State in 1891 to serve Jews fleeing Eastern Europe and migrating to the US. The Fund offered protection for immigrants through port work, relief, temporary aid, promotion of suburban industrial enterprises, removal from urban centers through the Industrial Removal Office, land settlement, agricultural training, and trade and general education. In 1894, the Baron de Hirsch Agricultural College was opened in Woodbine, New Jersey — the first school in the US to impart secondary education in agriculture. During the Nazi era, the Fund spent large sums of money for German Jewish relief. Later, its chief activity was support of the Jewish Agricultural Society, created in 1900 by the Fund and its European counterpart, the Jewish Colonization Association, to promote the Jewish farm movement.[4]

This major collection has been inventoried and re-catalogued through the work of Seth Korelitz, the 1994-95 Leo Wasserman Fellow at Brandeis; and a finding aid is available. The finding aid includes lists of names. The overall collection includes four sub-parts: the fund itself, Jewish Agricultural Society, Woodbine Colony, and the Trade School. The Industrial Removal Office is a separate, but related organization.

a. The papers of the Baron de Hirsch Fund itself take up 79 boxes, in call number I-80. These are predominantly administrative papers and include a large number of deeds and property transfer records. Boxes 5 and 6 contain files of 30 student aid recipients. Box 47 includes information about students and a list of applicants to study at Delphi Agricultural College. Box 60 includes requests by German-Jewish refugees in the 1930's, for financial assistance. Box 78 has a list of 71 Jewish farmers with significant information about each.

b. Jewish Agricultural Society. This organization was formed in 1900 by the Baron de Hirsch Fund to promote farming among Jews in the US. The Society settled about 4900 families on farms, placed nearly 22,000 farm employees in 31 states, and extended almost $15,000,000 in loans to farmers in 41 states.[5] Records are in 7 boxes and span 1901-1978 under call number I-206.

---

[4] *Standard Jewish Encyclopedia*, op. cit., p. 239, 910-911.

[5] Ibid., p. 1038.

Box 2 contains general information about 12 Jewish farmers in Sullivan and Ulster Counties, New York; Hamilton, TX; Janesville, WI, and Clayton, Millville, and Vineland, NJ. Box 7 contains loan applications, which include some biographical information.

c. Woodbine Colony. Woodbine is a town in New Jersey which was founded by the Baron de Hirsch Fund as a Jewish agricultural colony with an industrial annex. The first 60 families, mostly from southern Russia, arrived in 1892, and an agricultural school was established in 1895. In 1903, the colony became the first all-Jewish municipality in the US. Failure of the colony's original agricultural plans eventually led to a predominance of industry. During WWII, the Fund withdrew support. The Jewish population declined steadily, and by 1958, numbered 315 out of a total 2500.[6] The Woodbine Colony records themselves, from 1890-1933, are under call number I-53. The collection contains records pertaining to all aspects of the colony, including histories, reports, correspondence, and photographs. The material is arranged chronologically, not indexed.

Boxes 1-9 contains the records of individual property holders, about 250 people. These names can be found in the finding aid. Box 11 includes a listing of those employed in the town from 1895-1919. Boxes 12-14 are records of Woodbine companies.

Box 16 includes information on certain Romanian families being settled; in addition, there are lists of families farming, along with their mortgage information. Other lists include "nationality stats," class lists, and sports team lists. Information on Texas farmers includes descent information.

Box 22 contains a small amount of correspondence regarding people who were looking to be reunited with family members.

d. Woodbine Agricultural School. The collection for the Woodbine Agricultural School spans 1893-1927, under call number I-54.

Boxes 3 and 5a contain student records: correspondence regarding applications, medical exams, admissions, and inquiries. There are lists of graduates covering 1893 to 1918. Boxes 9-10 involve 63 "scholarship students" to other schools: Delphi and the NY State Institute of Applied Agriculture in Farmingdale, NY.

e. Trade School. The Baron de Hirsch Trade School in New York records span 1890-1935, under call number I-55. The school trained students in trades such as plumbing, electrical, sign painting, carpentry, and woodwork.

Boxes 1-9 are graduate records. At least in box 1, these records are bound, with an index. These include: name, class and department, address, age, nationality. Some include: how long in the US, means of support, occupation, parent or guardian's name, and name of employer.

Box 10 holds class pictures, by class and department, for the years 1925-1968. A number of these are labeled with the name underneath each person shown. Boxes 13, 16-18 are students files, with a good deal of useful information; there are files on applications, graduates by department, student lists by department, student bound record book, various statistics, etc.

Boxes 21-24 hold class ratings for the years 1899-1935. Box 32 involves questionnaires sent out to alumni of 1920's classes, asking for such information as whether the graduate was working, whether working in the field in which trained, where working, etc. Boxes 36-38 hold records of workers 1892-1935.

---

[6] Ibid., p. 1925.

3. <u>Industrial Removal Office</u>. The IRO was a US organization largely funded by the Baron de Hirsch Fund that sought to encourage new immigrants in the US to leave the large population centers on the East Coast and settle in the interior of the country. It received funds from several other sources, notably the Jewish Colonization Association.[7]

A finding aid to the IRO collection was organized by Robert Rockaway, currently of Tel Aviv University. This 100+ box collection, under call number I-91, includes almost 44,000 "records of removal" from 1899 to 1922 in box numbers 6-12, as well as correspondence from immigrants and local agents.

Anyone who has ever wondered "How is it that Jews ended up in Sheboygan, WI, or Wilkes-Barre, PA", or the like, might find the answer in the IRO records. In the records of 1904-1914, Jews were "removed" to the following locations:

ALABAMA
  Birmingham
  Demopolis
  Mobile
  Montgomery
  New Decatur
ARKANSAS
  Ft. Smith
  Little Rock
  Pine Bluff
CALIFORNIA
  Los Angeles
  San Francisco
COLORADO
  Boulder
  Colorado Springs
  Cripple Creek
  Greeley
  Pueblo
CONNECTICUT
  Uncasville
DELAWARE
  Wilmington
FLORIDA
  Jacksonville
  Pennsacola
  Ybor City
GEORGIA
  Atlanta
  Augusta
  Columbus
  Macon
  Savannah
IOWA
  Burlington
  Cedar Rapids
  Chariton
  Clinton
  Council Bluffs
  Des Moines
  Dubuque
  Keokuk
  Marshalltown
  Mason City
  Muscatine
  Oskaloosa
  Ottumwa
  Perry
  Shreveport

  Sioux City
  Waterloo
ILLINOIS
  Champaign
  Danville
  Decatur
  Rock Island
  Rockford
  Springfield
  Streator
INDIANA
  Evansville
  Ft. Wayne
  Gary
  Indianapolis
  Lafayette
  Logansfront
  Logansport
  Muncie
  Shelbyville
  South Bend
  Terre Haute
KANSAS
  Great Bend
  Hutchinson
  Lawrence
  Leavenworth
  Topeka
  Wichita
KENTUCKY
  Louisville
  Paducah
LOUISIANA
  Lake Charles
  New Orleans
MASSACHUSETTS
  Boston
  Fall River
  North Adams
MAINE
  Portland
MICHIGAN
  Bay City
  Detroit
  Grand Rapids
  Jackson
  Kalamazoo
  Traverse City

MINNESOTA
  Minneapolis
  Winona
MISSOURI
  Aurora
  Boonville
  Clinton
  Hannibal
  Joplin
  Kansas City
  Lexington
  Louisiana
  Mexico
  Moberly
  Sedalia
  St. Joseph
  St. Charles
  St. Louis
MISSISSIPPI
  Natchez
  Vicksburg
NORTH DAKOTA
  Starkweather
NEBRASKA
  Beatrice
  Grand Island
  Hastings
  Lincoln
  Nebraska City
  North Platte
  Omaha
NEW JERSEY
  Woodbine
NEW YORK
  Albany
  Buffalo
  Elmira
  Rochester
  Syracuse
OHIO
  Akron
  Alliance
  Bellaire
  Canton
  Chickasha
  Cincinnati
  Cleveland
  Columbus
  Dayton

  Kent
  Lima
  Lorain
  Marietta
  Marion
  Murray City
  Sandusky
  Springfield
  Toledo
  Youngstown
  Zanesville
OREGON
  Portland
PENNSYLVANIA
  Allentown
  Altoona
  Erie
  Harrisburg
  Lancaster
  Pittsburgh
  Reading
  Scranton
  Unionstown
  Warren
  Wilkes-Barre
SO. CAROLINA
  Charleston
  Columbia
  St. Stephens
SOUTH DAKOTA
  Sioux Falls
TENNESSEE
  Chattanooga
  Knoxville
  Memphis
  Nashville
TEXAS
  Austin
  Beaumont
  Dallas
  Ft. Worth
  Gainsville
  Houston
  Marshall
  Palestine
  San Antonio
  Sherman
  Tyler
  Waco

VIRGINIA
  Lynchburg
  Newport News
  Richmond
WASHINGTON
  Seattle
  Spokane
WISCONSIN
  Beloit
  LaCrosse
  Milwaukee
  Racine
  Sheboygan
WEST VIRGINIA
  Wheeling
WYOMING
  Cheyenne

---

[7] Ibid., p. 961.

The IRO materials contain administrative records and correspondence pertaining to all aspects of the organization. Of special importance to genealogical researchers: correspondence with local agents regarding immigrants sent to specific cities and towns listed above, records listing all persons relocated from New York (with all pertinent details), follow-up records on these individuals, and letters from the relocated immigrants to the IRO on various matters. The collection is arranged geographically, and not indexed. Where information is available, there is often very detailed data.

4. Boston HIAS (Hebrew Immigrant Aid Society). Under call number I-96, the HIAS records of most importance to genealogical researchers are the individual arrival records. These are arranged alphabetically, for immigrants arriving in Boston, Massachusetts, or Providence, Rhode Island, between 1870 and 1929. There are also incomplete chronological lists of ship arrivals and ships' passenger lists between 1904 and 1953. The records are arranged alphabetically by arrival and by case record, not indexed.

The Boston branch of the Hebrew Immigrant Aid Society started when an earlier, local group affiliated with New York's Hebrew Sheltering and Immigrant Aid Society in 1913. The name was shortened some time later. In 1977, the local Boston office was closed and all functions transferred to New York. The Boston HIAS records are now at AJHS. The records are stored in 233 numbered Hollinger boxes, with brief description labels. The records of interest to genealogists comprise most of the material and fall into three categories: arrival cards, individual case files, and passenger lists.

Individual Arrival Records are in boxes #223-233 are labeled "Boston HIAS Box #..., Individual Arrival Records 1882-1929," followed by an alphabetic designation. These boxes contain approximately 25,000 index cards. Each card is either an individual or family record of arrival, with more or less of the following information listed: ship name or other transport used, age, sex, marital status, next destination, financial arrangements, whether or not detained by U.S. Immigration, relationships, U.S. person responsible for immigrants, etc. The cards are alphabetically arranged, by surname.

Individual Case Files are contained in two groups of boxes, each box labeled "Boston HIAS Box #..., Papers, Individual Cases." Boxes #1-#179 covers the 1920's through the early 1960's; and boxes #181-#210 contain some early records, but are mostly post-WWII, into the 1970's. These boxes contain an estimated 12,000 individual files, filed alphabetically. Each box contains approximately 50 to 60 files of individual records, by name, alphabetically arranged. In most cases, the original last name given is on the file, but searchers should be aware that spelling and name changes are always a possibility. Many name changes occurred during the correspondence period, and file headings may be by original name, other spelling, Anglicized version, or by the name of the U.S. correspondent making the inquiry. Although most records are European, there are many from Latin America, India, China, Israel, and elsewhere. Each of the individual case files may or may not contain any of the following: Correspondence, Request for Immigration, Certificate of Support by U.S. Residents, Visa Application, Certificate of Good Moral Character, Certificate of Funds Transmitted, etc. Many cases, but not all, resulted in admission to the U.S.

The remaining material, in boxes #180, #211-#222, labeled "Boston HIAS Box #...," contain a variety of passenger lists, ship arrival schedules, lists of DP's (Displaced Persons), correspondence, HIAS information, and administrative files.

Recently, Eugene M. Hirshberg, a volunteer member of the Jewish Genealogy Society of Greater Boston, has recently compiled a comprehensive description of the HIAS collection, along with an inventory. The inventory lists the files in each box.

5. <u>American Jewish Committee Office Of War Records. World War I.</u> This collection offers a good amount of in-depth data regarding 4-5,000 Jewish soldiers that served in the U.S. military during World War I. It was donated many years ago, at the insistence of Max Kohler (1871-1934), a lawyer and historian who played a critical role in the project, and who was also a devoted member of the AJHS.

Following World War I, in 1921, the American Jewish Committee undertook a project to document the military service of those Jews that served in the United States Armed Forces during the war. Cyrus Adler was Chairman of the Board of the A.J.C. at the time, and had a hand in planning the community surveys. The A.J.C. was able to determine who in the military was Jewish through the records of the various American Jewish communities, and through the records of the Office of Military Chaplains, a section of the War Department.

In all, about 250,000 Jewish soldiers served in the United States military during World War I, 40,000 of whom volunteered. About 3500 Jews were killed in action or died of wounds received in battle. Jews, who made up 3 per cent of the United States population, contributed 5% to the entire death roll of the U.S. Army. The number of Jews wounded was estimated at 12,000.

According to a cover letter sent with each questionnaire, over 150,000 Jewish servicemen took part in the study. This figure is hard to prove, and is probably an exaggeration, an attempt to coax more former soldiers into taking part in the survey.   In any case, the surveyors were especially interested in documenting those whose service was exemplary, i.e., Jews who were wounded or killed, or, received a citation, or were officers. Recent inquiries to the American Jewish Committee in New York City could provide no concrete information as to the whereabouts of additional survey responses.

Each four-sided survey questionnaire is entitled, "War Record of American Jews", with the following explanatory note: "Compiled by the Office of War Records of the American Jewish Committee, in cooperation with the Jewish Welfare Board and other leading organizations, as a permanent memorial of Jewish Service in the World War and as a contribution to American and Jewish history."

Each questionnaire asks for the following information: "name in full; present service or business address; legal residence; date and place of birth; birthplace of parents; education (if college or university graduate, give name of institution, date of graduation and degree obtained); brief summary of civilian career before joining service; full name and highest rank; arm of service (Army, Navy, Marine Corps, or Uniformed Auxiliary Service); branch (such as Infantry, Field Artillery, Medical Corps, Pay Corps, etc.); method of entrance into service (enlisted, enrolled, drafted, commissioned, or volunteered); date of entrance into service; rank or rating upon entrance into service and first organization, unit, station, or ship; promotions or official recommendations for promotion received, with dates thereof; length of time spent overseas or afloat, counting toward service chevrons; duties and general location of organization, unit or ship; participated in the following actions; casualty — killed in action or by accident, died of wounds or disease, gassed, shell-socked, or taken prisoner — please give circumstantial details as to nature of casualty, time and place, name of hospital, etc., etc. Copies of official documents are particularly desired; names and addresses of other Jews in the service, particularly — Jewish commissioned officers, Jewish casualties, Jewish citations."

The AMERICAN JEWISH HISTORICAL SOCIETY collection contains about 5,000 of such questionnaires. Answers are handwritten on the forms, and photographs and related correspondence are occasionally attached.

The collection "American Jewish Committee Office of War Records" consists of twenty-one boxes. The war records begin in box two, and the war records of Jewish soldiers continue from there until box 18. Box 1 consists of inter-office correspondence of the A.J.C., and boxes 18-21 consist of letters to the A.J.C. of non-Jews mistakenly sent war records questionnaires who wished to qualify that they were not Jews. The records are divided into different headings: some records are filed according to the city they come from, and some are filed according to the branch of service and rank, and some according to both. Others are filed according to soldiers with a certain rank that were wounded. Each file in itself is in alphabetical order. Upon looking at the files, everything is self explanatory. An interesting file is folder #9 in box 1. It includes correspondence from those Jews that, while they admit to being Jewish, refused to take part in the survey for one reason or another.

The boxes of war records (#2-18) are labeled more or less along the lines of the following three parameters. It is therefore helpful, but not essential, to know into which of these categories a serviceman fit in order to search:
— Private, or Non-Commissioned Officer, or Officer
— Army, Navy, Aviation, Airforce, or Civilian War Worker
— Citation, Wounded, Casualty, or Dead.
A finding aid has been prepared by Brandeis student researchers Elana Horowitz and Brian Ferber.

6. National Jewish Welfare Board, Bureau of War Records 1940-1969. As collection #I-52, the Bureau of War Records alone constitutes a large institutional collection, totaling 672 boxes. The Bureau of War Records Collection relates to the work that the Bureau performed in describing and analyzing the role and contribution of Jews to the United armed forces during World War II. (This is just one part of the National Jewish Welfare Board records. The National Jewish Welfare Board, now better known as the Jewish Community Centers Association, has been the central organization of Jewish community centers throughout the United States since its founding in 1917. The AJHS has other records, some as yet unprocessed, including those from the USO — United Service Organization, and YMHAs — Young Men's Hebrew Associations).

The Bureau of War Records collection includes studies and listings of Jewish casualties, awards and officers, as well as studies of Jewish doctors, dentists, farmers, and refugees in service. It also includes community studies relating to Jews in and Jewish soldiers from: Fort Wayne and Hammond, Indiana; Boston and Lynn, Massachusetts; Trenton, New Jersey; Youngstown, Ohio; Allentown, Pennsylvania; and New York City. In addition, there are folders dealing with the role of Jews in the Canadian armed forces and the Korean War. There is a typed outline of the collection and a listing of the subject files. There are also population studies and studies of distinctive Jewish names. The final report of the Bureau was not published, but is contained in the collection. Isidor Kaufman's 1947 book, *American Jews in World War II* is based on BWR papers. Approximately 550,000 Jews served in the US Armed Forces during World War II.

The records are greatest genealogical importance are the many tens of thousands of data cards of individuals in the service. Each card is labeled: wounded, prisoner, award, missing, death. The cards are ordered alphabetically by name. Additionally, about half of the individuals have been indexed geographically. The card index is accessible on-site, while the remainder of the collection is stored in an off-site warehouse.

7. National Jewish Welfare Board, Army-Navy Division, Papers 1917-1955. As #I-180, this collection deals with the branch of the JWB that interceded for the needs and interests of Jewish military personnel. The Army-Navy Division name was officially introduced in 1918. This collection takes up 343 boxes. It consists mainly of surveys, reports, photographs, and correspondence of JWB personnel and U.S. Military chaplains, directed toward or concerned with the Jewish men in the Armed Forces.

This collection contains scattered information on individuals. A box list is available for the collection; the collection is stored in an off-site warehouse.

8. National Jewish Welfare Board, Papers of Aryeh Lev (Jewish chaplaincy records). Aryeh Lev was the director of the JWB's Commission on the Jewish Chaplaincy following WWII. This collection contains information on individual Jewish chaplains in the Korean and Vietnam Wars. A finding aid is available. Collection I-249, in 58 boxes.

9. New York City Court Records. A better title for the collections in this group, all of them genealogically important, would be: "Manhattan Court Records of Cases with Jewish Names." They consist of microfilm and bound photocopies of court records now in the New York City Hall of Records. The first three collections contain material primarily of interest for the pre-1860 period; the fourth, Incorporation Papers, deals with all Jewish or Jewish-related organizations incorporated in New York City between 1848 and 1920. These four collections are indexed — the index is on cards which are interfiled in the main card catalog, except for the Incorporation Papers card index, which is found in separate drawers from the main catalog. There are two more groups of materials which have never been fully processed these span approximately 1830s-1910.

All of this material has been recently described and inventoried by David Kohen, a member/volunteer of the Jewish Genealogical Society of Greater Boston.

The collections are copies of selected court records from the County of New York, New York, that is, from the Borough of Manhattan in New York City. The history of these copies is somewhat obscure, but apparently, in the early 1960s, Professor Leo Hershkowitz of Queens College and the Institute for Early New York History went through older records on file at the New York Hall of Records and extracted those records with Jewish sounding names. The records selected were then indexed and copied. AJHS has duplicate copies of the extracted records in two different formats: bound volumes of photocopies, and reels of microfilm.

At some later date, AJHS was offered boxes of original court papers relating to litigants with Jewish sounding names. The court was going to dispose of these papers, but AJHS accepted them as part of the historical record. These original documents have never been fully catalogued. However, a name index has been prepared and is interfiled in the main card catalog. Details on each collection follow.

a. *Mayor's Court Selected Briefs 1674-1860*. This collection, #I-151, holds approximately 6,000 court documents in 23 bound volumes or 13 reels of microfilm. It is arranged chronologically and indexed by last name of litigant. The index is interfiled in the main card catalog.

Collection I-151 consists of handwritten pleadings and other court papers filed in civil lawsuits in the Mayor's Court of the City of New York, also known at various times as the High Court of Chancery, the New York Inns (of Court) and the Marine Court of New York City. The handwriting is often difficult to decipher. The court papers include summons, complaints, surety bonds, affidavits, warrants, jury lists and briefs.

b. *Selected Naturalization Certificates 1816-1845*. Collection #I-152 holds approximately 500 certificates in one bound volume or one reel of microfilm. It is arranged alphabetically and indexed by the last name of declarant. The index is interfiled in the main card catalog.

Collection I-152 consists of an alphabetical set of Declarations of Intention or Affidavits of Intention filed with the Court of Common Pleas for the City and County of New York or with the New York Superior Court from 1829-1845 and of Reports of Aliens made to the Clerk of the Court from 1816-1828. The only genealogically relevant information contained in the later Declarations and Affidavits is the identification of the particular "foreign Prince, Potentate, State or Sovereignty" to which further allegiance is renounced, for example, the "Grand Duke of Hesse Cappell" or the "Authorities of the Free City of Frankfort." This reference will identify the prior citizenship and, by implication, the place of birth or prior residence of such person. The majority of the declarants came from the various Germanic states, other central European countries such as Switzerland or Romania, or from England. The very small number of earlier Reports of Aliens from the period 1816-1828 specifically list name, sex, place of birth, age, nation and allegiance, place from whence migrated, occupation and place of actual or intended settlement.

c. *Selected Insolvent Debtors Cases 1787-1861*. Collection #I-153 contains approximately 2,000 cases in nine bound volumes or five reels of microfilm. It is arranged alphabetically, and indexed by last name of debtor. The index is interfiled in the main card catalog.

Collection I-153 consists of documents filed with the Supreme Court of the State of New York for the City and County of New York in insolvency cases. The bulk of the documents consist of Insolvent Assignments each of which, like a modern bankruptcy, involves a discharge of the debtor's debts and an assignment of his assets to be sold or managed for the benefit of his creditors. The documents sometimes contain a reference to a legal notice published in a newspaper or a schedule of creditors. A small number contain an inventory of the debtor's assets.

d. *Incorporation Papers*. Collection #I-154 consists of selected incorporation papers, 1848-1920. There are approximately 10,000 organizations represented in 81 bound volumes or 27 reels of microfilm. They are arranged by year of filing and document filing number within each year. They are indexed by cross references to name of organization, general type of organization, and European town (if any) to which the organization relates. The index is located in separate card drawers to the right of the main card catalog.

Collection I-154 consists of legal filings made by Jewish-related not-for-profit organizations incorporated in New York County. The organizations include fraternal societies, political clubs, professional associations, synagogues, landsmanshaftn, benevolent organizations, social clubs, burial societies, charities and neighborhood facilities. The filings are very similar to modern corporate filings and include original certificates of incorporation, consolidation or change of corporate name. Each certificate of incorporation includes the name of the organization, the purposes or objects for which it was formed, the principal office or territory of principal operation (for example, the "Borough of Manhattan"), the names and addresses of the initial directors or trustees or officers, and the names of the incorporators. The papers are organized by year of filing and by the document number for such year assigned by the filing office.

e. *Partially Processed Original Documents*. These are selected filings in New York County Court cases, circa 1852-1909. There are approximately 500 court documents in 39 archival containers arranged by general type of case. They are not indexed.

This collection consists of pleadings and other legal papers filed with the New York Supreme Court for New York County and other courts in lawsuits which have litigants with Jewish sounding names. The original documents have been sorted into archival containers based upon the type of case. Each archival container contains a handwritten list of the cases located therein. The types of cases are identified on the outside of the archival containers as follows:

Marriage, Divorce & Guardianship	9 containers	Court Motions	6 containers
Business & Finance Cases	12 containers	Property & Real Estate Cases	1 container
Organizational Disputes	4 containers	Personal Injury Cases	1 container
Personal Finance Cases	5 containers	Assault & Battery & Slander	1 container

f. *Unprocessed Original Documents*. These are Selected Filings in New York County Court Cases, circa 1837-1910. There are approximately 1,000 court documents in 10 large cardboard shipping boxes. They are not arranged and not indexed.

These 10 cardboard boxes contain pleadings and other legal papers which were apparently packed randomly by court officials and never unpacked by AJHS. The cases appear to be similar to the types of cases which were sorted into the archival containers listed above. Each box appears to contain in excess of 100 documents without any listing whatsoever. A handwritten list of approximately 300 case names and descriptions found in an archival container labeled, "Record of Original Documents" may be a partial listing of these documents.

10. Jewish Childcare Association of New York. There are five parts to this major collection, which includes the archives of six inter-related institutions of the 19th and 20th centuries:

Hebrew Orphan Asylum of Manhattan
Hebrew Orphan Asylum of Brooklyn
Home for Hebrew Infants
Hebrew Infant Asylum of New York
Hartman Homecrest
Hebrew Sheltering Guardian Society

Approval to use some material is required from the Jewish Child Care Association of New York City. These collections were described in an in-depth article by Nancy Arbeiter in *Avotaynu*, Vol. XI, No. 1 (Spring 1995), pages 28-33.

Other Institutional Collections:

Besides the institutional collections listed above, which are of clear genealogical importance, there are over 200 others, which together document a large part of Jewish life in the United States. There are the large holdings of the national organizations such as the Council of Jewish Federations and Welfare Funds, the American Jewish Congress, and the National Conference on Soviet Jewry. Other holdings may reflect one or another era or grouping of American Jews. These collections can provide historical background, if not genealogical data. See Appendix E.

B. PERSONAL

Personal Papers collections are papers of an individual, and are organized by surname. There are over 600 of them, and they include a wide range of Jews, many of them notable. Samuel Gompers, Rebecca Gratz, Uriah Philips Levy, Arthur Waskow, Stephen S. Wise, Molly Picon, Milton Steinberg, Harry Houdini are just a few.

For genealogical purposes, some of these collections will be of interest only to someone interested in that particular individual or their family. However, many of these personal papers contain material of great historical importance. Very often, these individuals were involved in important aspects of American Jewish life, and their papers would include mentions of their colleagues.

There are three important personal paper collections which contain so much material that is of historical interest that separate indexes on cards exist for them:

- *The Milton Steinberg Papers, 1903-1908*, #P-369, has a names index. Rabbi Milton Steinberg (1903-1950) was a talented lecturer and teacher. He officiated at the Conservative Park Avenue Synagogue in New York from 1933 until his death.[8]

- *The Rabbi Tobias Geffen Papers, 1888-1968*, #P-516, has a communities and correspondents index. Tobias Geffen was an important figure in the Orthodox Community between 1910 and 1970, and played a central role among rabbis in the South.

- *The Stephen S. Wise Papers, 1884-1968*, #P-134, is the largest of the three. It also has a names index. Rabbi Stephen S. Wise was perhaps the most influential American Jew of the first half of the 20th century. He was a supporter of progressive Judaism, and an energetic promoter of political liberalism. There was not an area of significance to the American Jewish community in which he did not involve himself, as his papers bear out. His voluminous correspondence with religious, political, and social leaders of his time provide a fascinating view of recent history. Since his

---

[8] Ibid., p. 1758.

contacts were so wide-reaching, the index itself is quite a valuable genealogical resource. The Wise papers should be consulted on microfilm at the Brandeis library periodicals room. The finding aid to the collection is needed to cross-reference the index numbers with the microfilm volumes. The finding aid can be found on the short book cases in the periodicals room in the Goldfarb Library; these cases are directly in front upon entering the room, before reaching the microfilm readers.

The personal papers of certain rabbis contain vital records: his own personal records of circumcisions, marriages, and burials performed by him. Mohel books are listings by several ritual circumcisers of infants. There are mohel records for New York City, Philadelphia, Baltimore, Washington, D.C., Newport, R.I., Surinam, and other locations. Some examples:

- P-72, Polack, M. 910 circumcisions 1836-1862 in MD, VA, PA, NC, SC, DC, "47 different locations".
- P-118, Cohen, Jacob Raphael. 500 records of marriages, deaths, circumcisions, from 1776-1843 in Pennsylvania, New York, and Quebec.
- P-385, Selz, Abraham, of Niederstettin, Germany, and later of Baltimore, Maryland. Circumcisions of 450 boys in Niederstettin and surrounding towns, 1853-1881.
- I-112, Curaçao Jewish Community. 147 documentary and printed materials on 4 rolls of microfilm, including births (1723-1891), deaths (1883-1912), and other material.

Over 50 of the personal paper collections are genealogical charts, with the following surnames:

Abravanel-Mickleshavski	Ehrenreich	Kolbin	Morgenthau	Rankus
Borison	Epstein	Konheym	Moses	Rosenbaum
Capin	Ewenczyk	Leeson	Moses-Loeb	Rothnagel
Caro	Feibelman	Levitansky	Moss	Sachs
Chazin	Fidanque	Lewisohn	Moss-Harris	Samuels
Chimene	Franks	Lipschitz	Nathan	Sawyer
Cone	Geffen	Lipsey	Nones	Schwab
Dan	Goldstone	List	Oberlander	Schwarz-Lewi
Davidson	Halberstam	Lopes-Moses	Oppenheim	Stux
DeLeon-Hendricks	Halfin	Mauerberger	Phillips	Trager
Dellar	Ichenhauer	Mayerberger	Rabinowitz	Velleman
Dulken	Jacobs	Mielziner	Rabson	Wistenetzky
	Josephthal	Milontaler		

There are another approximately 50 genealogies, as yet uncatalogued.

C. PERIODICALS

The AMERICAN JEWISH HISTORICAL SOCIETY has the second largest collection of Jewish newspapers of the Americas in the world (second only to the Hebrew Union College in Cincinnati), the earliest of which date from the 1840's. Over 1000 titles exist, in English, Hebrew, Yiddish, German, Ladino, and other European languages. A large portion of these are local Jewish newspapers and are likely to contain notices of births, marriages, deaths, etc. Another useful group of periodicals includes those specific to the history of a locality: journals of a local Jewish historical society, for example. Another large group consist of journals of national organizations or specific interests and are unlikely to be fruitful for genealogists.

By way of example, the periodicals held by the AJHS range from a professional yearly publication like *Yearbook of Jewish Social Service* (formerly *Yearbook of Jewish Social Work* until 1951; New York, holdings include most years from 1930-1968) to a bi-monthly local periodical like *The Arizona Post*, Tucson, Arizona (held are most years from 1954 to 1968).

On October 31, 1994, a fire in an off-site warehouse in Stoughton, MA, threatened the Society's collection of American Jewish newspapers and magazines. Due to the quick actions of responding fire departments and the operation of the warehouse's sprinkler system, the collection was saved from destruction. Although only a few newspapers were singed by the fire and none were actually burned, about a quarter of the collection was completely soaked through by water, including several of the very rare and unique publications. In all, about 1000 titles were affected. The AJHS staff took immediate action to save these precious holdings. After consulting with the nation's leading experts on archival disasters, the wet newspapers and magazines were loaded onto a freezer trailer, and subsequently dried and cleaned. The material is now being held in storage facilities in three different locations in eastern Massachusetts.

The microfilming of the AJHS newspaper holdings will take several years. During that time, many of the newspapers — especially those in fragile condition — will be inaccessible to researchers. The AJHS staff will be happy to work with researchers to locate alternate repositories of specific titles, where possible, if the AJHS' copies are inaccessible.

Among the affected items are hundreds of rare, valuable and unique materials. Examples include the first issue of Rabbi Isaac Mayer Wise's *The Israelite* (1854), *The Asmonean* (1849-1858), the *American Jewess* (1880s), and *Sinai* (Baltimore, 1850s-1860s). Many of the Society's Latin American and Caribbean newspapers and periodicals were also soaked, including some from Buenos Aires, Argentina, where the Jewish community's archives were destroyed in the 1994 bombing there. Estimates for all of the restoration and microfilming work exceed $500,000. Insurance will pay for part of the cost, and the Society has received an emergency grant from the National Endowment for the Humanities. To help meet costs not covered by these sources, the AJHS has set up a Preservation Fund, for which contributions are currently being accepted.

The last three columns of card drawers at the AJHS contain the "19th Century Periodicals Index." This is a card index to six 19th-century American Jewish periodicals. These periodicals are on microfilm, and are part of the AJHS/Brandeis Joint Depository Project. The periodical microfilms themselves are held in the periodicals section of the Goldfarb library, a separate facility within walking distance on the Brandeis campus. Articles are indexed by: subject, city or town, and names of prominent people. The six newspapers indexed, with their index codes and range of dates held are: A: *Asmonean* (New York City, 1849-1858); I: *American Israelite* (Cincinnati, 1854-1927); M: *Jewish Messenger* (New York City, 1857-1902); O: *Occident* (Philadelphia, 1843-1869); S: *Sinai* (New York City); and Z: *Zeitgeist* (1880-82, in German).

In addition to the above, there are other periodicals owned by AJHS which are on microfilm and held in the same Brandeis periodicals area. Substantial titles represented there on microfilm: *Buffalo Jewish Review*, 1917-1968, 30 reels; *Carolina Israelite*, 1944-1962, 2 reels; *Cleveland Yiddish Velt*, 1913-1952, 33 reels; *The Hebrew*, San Francisco, 1864-1906, 7 reels; *Jewish Advocate*, Boston, 1905-continuing, 109+ reels; *Jewish Ledger*, New Orleans, 1895-1927, 19 reels; *Jewish Messenger*, New York, 1857-1902, 24 reels; *Jewish Review & Observer*, Cleveland, 1899-1958, 29 reels; *Wyoming Jewish Press*, 1930-1940, 1 reel. See Appendix B, page 230 for a complete list of AJHS titles held at Brandeis.

There are numerous indexes to Jewish periodicals. The AJHS itself has prepared two monumental indexes to the journal they themselves have published over the years. The indexes have been recently published by Carlson Publishing: *An Index to Publications of the American Jewish Historical Society* covers volumes 21-50 (1913-1961), and *An Index to American Jewish Historical Quarterly / American Jewish History*, which covers volumes 51-80 (1961-1991). These works total over 1100 pages. The index to volumes 1-20 of the Publications of the American Jewish Historical Society was published previously.

Family newsletters in the periodicals collection include these surnames: Ser, Charlap, Grad, Klein, Indianer, Pearl, Strauss, and others.

The AJHS also has several Jewish genealogy periodicals including *Avotaynu* (1985-), *Search* (1980-1992); *Toledot* (1977-1980), *Dorot* (JGS NY), and *Mass-Pocha* (JGS Boston). Publications of other Jewish genealogical societies are held in the vertical files and on microfiche.

D. EPHEMERA

These collections typically consist of ongoing publications of Jewish-related organizations. As these collections are not printed materials and are very large — usually 1 or two cartons, occasionally 5 to 20 cartons — nor highly unique, they were classified in this category instead of as institutions. The publications most often include yearbooks, proceedings, reports, catalogs, bulletins, news releases, brochures, and miscellaneous publications.

There are approximately 200 such collections. The complete list can be found in Appendix E. All have call numbers starting with "MS-" (this category was formerly, and confusingly, called "manuscript") and then another two or three capital letters, followed by the actual catalog number. The capital letters denote the type of organization as follows: ED = educational, FED = federation, INS = institution, JCC = Jewish community center, MD = medical organization, NAT = national organization, SYN = synagogue, FRA = fraternal, HOL = Holocaust, LAB = Labor, LOC = Local, SOJ = Soviet Jewry, MIS = missionary (this last category attempts to incorporate various attempts to proselytize and worse).

Under MS-ED, one finds such schools as: Baltimore Hebrew Teachers College (bulletins, catalogs, and miscellaneous publications, 1 carton); Gratz College, Philadelphia (registers, prospectuses, and miscellaneous publications, 1 carton); Jewish Theological Seminary of America, Los Angeles (constitution, annual reports and registers, scripts, addresses, periodicals, etc., 10 cartons).

Under MS-FED, there are five federations from Chicago, New York, and Philadelphia. The MS-INS institutions are: Cleveland's Bellefaire, a Jewish orphan home; and two New York homes for the aged. The MS-JCC category holds: Jewish community centers in Buffalo; Charleston, SC; New York; Fitchburg, MA; New Haven, CT; St. Louis, MO; Yonkers, NY.

Examples of MS-NAT national organizations: Alpha Epsilon Phi Fraternity, Anti-Defamation League of Bnai Brith, Canadian Jewish Congress, Hadassah, and Junior Hadassah (this collection contains yearbooks 1924-1974), Jewish Braille Institute of America, National Council of Jewish Women, Zionist Organization of America.

MS-SYN synagogues are from: Arleta, CA; Arlington, VA; Baltimore, MD; Boston, MA; Brookline, MA: Brooklyn, NY; Chicago, IL; Cleveland, OH; Detroit, MI; Flint, MI; Hampden, CT; Hartford, CT; Honolulu, HI; Monroe, NY; New York, NY; Newport, RI; Philadelphia, PA; Pittsburgh, PA; Providence, RI; Rochester, NY; San Francisco, CA; Sioux City, IA; Washington, DC; Westmount, Quebec. While this is a complete list of cities represented here, synagogues are also found in the institutional or vertical file or library categories.

E. VERTICAL FILES

Vertical files are often small collections, each being folder size, rather than a full box. The collections consist of a few types of Jewish organizations. Specifically, these types are: landsmanschaftn (137 files in 9 boxes), synagogues (20 boxes), organizations, Jewish schools (15 boxes), and foreign collections (10 boxes, mostly from England), Holocaust and Soviet Jewry.

Vertical files are indexed in their own, separate, card catalog. School and synagogue records are indexed by the name of the town. The publications of most local Jewish genealogical societies are found in vertical files.

Landsmanschaften societies material in the vertical files were documented by David Rosen, and a description follows. Landsmannschaften societies were formed by Jewish immigrants who came from the same home town in Europe and settled near each other in the new host country. Their aims were: mutual aid, European relief, access to a cemetery and burial assistance, preserving memories of the old country, and simply socializing. They were founded mainly from the 1890s through WWI, and the organizations lasted until the immigrant generation died out, their descendants moved away, and Jews disappeared from post-WWII Europe. A few still function for social or charitable purposes.

The landsmannschaften represented in the AJHS collections come almost entirely from the United States and Canada, and include both local organizations, such as the Amdur Benevolent Association of New York, and organizations with national scope, such as the United Gallician Jews of America.

The publications vary in content and thus in their value as genealogical sources. A typical item is a souvenir program from a society's anniversary dinner and contains a list of committee members and officers, group photographs, a message from the president, and a list of the full membership followed by several pages of advertisements purchased by local businesses, friends, and society members. Some of the membership lists include addresses and some include individual member photos. Sixty-four of the 137 collections have some form of this membership information. The language is sometimes English, sometimes Yiddish, and often a mixture of the two.

Following are a selection of some of the more useful and interesting documents for genealogists:

> **Akkerman Benevolent Association Golden Anniversary** (1905-1955), New York. This souvenir program contains a list of officers, brief biographies of founders, and a history of Akkerman on the Black Sea, and of the Akkerman people in New York. (64 pages, English)

> **Keidaner Association 30th Anniversary** 1900-1930, New York. A souvenir program with a list of 355 members, a memorial list with 70 names, and most interesting: four family groups showing 3 or 4 generations of the descendants of members Gabriel Litchman, Louis Solomon, Dovid Epshtein, and Moshe Zusman. (112 pages, English/Yiddish).

> **The Keidaner Association** also contributed 72 issues of their Monthly Bulletin, covering the period March, 1935 - September, 1941.

> **The United Rzeszower Relief Committees** contributed two post-WWII lists of over 800 survivors of WWII, former members of the Jewish community of Rzeszow, Poland.

> **The American Sokolover Independent Verein** is represented by their "Jubilee Book, 40 Years in Chicago, 1941", containing the story of Sokolov immigrants to Chicago, photographs and names of members, and a memorial list. (264 pages, English/Yiddish).

Towns in Europe that sent large Jewish contingents to the New World may be represented by more than one landsmanschaft group in the vertical file collection. For example, Bialystok has ten, Lodz has six.

Here is a list of the towns in the vertical file collection. An asterisk '*' indicates members' list included; modern town names are in parentheses:

Akkerman (Belgorod Dnestrovskiy)*, Amdur (Indura)*, Belchatow*, Białystok*, Brezine (Brzeziny), Chenstochov (Częstochowa), Goniondz-Trestin (Goniądz/Trzcianne)*, Grodno*, Homl (Gomel)*, Ivansk (Iwaniska)*, Kamenetz-Podolsk (Kaments-Podolskiy), Kartuz-Bereze (Bereza), Keidan (Kedainiai), Keltz (Kielce)*, Kishinev*, Kolbaschow (Kolbuszowa), Kozow (Kozova)*, Krakau (Krakow)*, Krynki*, Liady (Lyady)*, Łódź*, Lubch (Lyubcha), Lublin*, Maramaros-Sziget (Sighet), Nieshvies (Nesvizh)*, Nowo-Radomsk (Radomsko)*, Ober-Vishiv (Viseu de Sus), Odessa*, Oran (Varena), Ostrov*, Ottyn (Otynya)*, Pinsk*, Plinsk (Plonsk), Pliskov*, Rakow, Rowne (Rovno), Ruzhin*, Rzeszow*, Shat (Seta)*, Shelib (Vselyub), Shendishov (Sędziszow)*, Sierptz (Sierpc), Slutzk*, Smela*, Smill*, Smorgon*, Sokolov (Sokolow)*, Tarnigrod (Tarnogrod), Tarnow*, Tlust (Tust), Toporow* (Toporov), Turov*, Velize (Velizh)*, Vilna (Vilnius)*, Warschau (Warszawa)*, Wishkove* (Wyszkow), Wolozin (Volozhin), and Zashkov*.

A detailed inventory of the collection by David Rosen is available at AJHS. In addition, AJHS has many records of fraternal, social, and mutual aid associations. There are also records of some congregations associated with landsmanschaftn. These can be found in categories other than the vertical files. Some of the institutional manuscripts collections are: Independent Slonimer Benevolent Society (Slonim) [I-126]; Radomer Culture Society (Radom) [I-125]; Anshey Dowig Association (Daugai) [I-219]; Meretz Relief

Association (Merkine) [I-217]. The library collection contains some landsmannschaft publications; check the main card catalog under the name of the town. And the collection of New York Incorporation papers [I-154] contains incorporation papers of approximately 10,000 Jewish-related organizations incorporated in New York City between 1848 and 1920, which includes many landsmanschaftn (see page 44 above).

Reading Room, American Jewish Historical Society.
Photograph by Shawn London '98, Courtesy of the **Justice**, The Independent Student Newspaper of Brandeis University.

F. READING ROOM AND LIBRARY COLLECTIONS

The library collection consists of over 30,000 published (non-archival) materials, mostly held in closed stacks and a few on the open shelves in the main reading (reference) room, classified via the Library of Congress (LC) system. Certain categories of books may be genealogically useful, as detailed below.

General reference works include: *Who's Who in American Jewry* 1926, 1928, 1938-39, 1980 editions; and *Who's Who in World Jewry* 1955, 1965, 1972 editions. Other reference works on open access include *American Jewish Yearbook* (1899-present), *American Jewish History* (1893-date), as well as Jewish encyclopedias, and Jewish historical journals. All of these are on open shelves in the main room.

An index of persons mentioned in early volumes of the *American Jewish Yearbook* is integrated in the main card catalog.

Most of the standard genealogical reference works from the last twenty years of Jewish genealogy can be found in the reading room, including: Kurzweil, Rottenberg, Mokotoff, Sack, etc.

Approximately 200 published genealogies are found here in book form. As with genealogies in manuscript form, these are listed in the main card catalog by author and title, and probably under the family name. Some collected genealogies in the library collections include: Neil Rosenstein, *The Unbroken Chain: Biographical Sketches and Genealogy of Illustrious Jewish Families from the 15th-20th Century*, 1990, 2 volumes; George Sackheim, *Scattered Seeds*, 2 volumes; and Malcolm Stern, *First American Jewish Families*, 1991.

Published **community histories** on particular Jewish American communities are an important subset of the library collection. There is a very large collection of local histories at AJHS, which vary greatly in content. Some are the result of extensive scholarly research, others have been written by various local individuals or institutions. While there is no alphabetical central listing there are at least two very helpful finding aids:

1) The main card catalog. This file, typical of nearly all libraries, has material indexed alphabetically by title, author, and subject. However, any given subject may have been indexed in a number of ways.

   A local community may be found under the community name, but the index card for a given location (City, State, Province, Country, area, etc.) may also have a description or cross-reference of great value. Do not overlook the possibility of a card for a neighborhood or area of a city (West End, North Shore, Suburban), or a state (Worcester County, Western Mass.), or a country (Far West, South, New England).

   A given Congregation may be found under "Congregation...", "Synagogue...", or "Temple...", or by name. It may also be found under a book title or author, or under a location name, as above.

2) *Judaica Americana*, by Nathan Kaganoff. Volume 2 lists nearly 1,000 published Jewish local histories for the Western Hemisphere on pages 71-169. These are serially numbered, and listed in alphabetical order by author. To find the item referred to, check the main card catalog for the library call number.

Since the AJHS tries to limit its focus to the Americas, its collection of yizkor books is very small. Approximately 30 volumes relating to locales in Poland, Ukraine, and Belarus can be found. The books are in closed stacks, and must be requested by call slip.

Research policies:

As there is only a small staff, it is recommended that visiting researchers call in advance to make a research appointment and discuss their area of focus. The Reading Room operates on a "closed stack" basis. Individual items must therefore be requested from a staff person. There are request forms to fill out for this purpose. Some large collections are stored off-site and must be requested at least two weeks in advance, although the most frequently used material is housed on-site. Call ahead to make sure that the materials you wish to use will be there.

Researchers should note that most of the AJHS archival collections are quite fragile. Because of the uniqueness of these materials, which exist at AJHS and no place else in the world, AJHS has special regulations designed to ensure their preservation for future generations of researchers. AJHS encourages all interested researchers to use its holdings, but to help AJHS preserve them for use by all interested researchers, both now and in the future.

There is no charge for anyone doing research on-site. For someone who is remote from the site, paid research may be done by library and archival staff, at the discretion of the staff. This will depend on the time available and the likelihood of finding relevant materials. Current rates for paid research are $35 per hour, plus postage and copying. Members of the Society ($50/yr.) receive priority service and a 20% discount on all service fees and copy charges. There are separate rates for researching specific collections — for example, the records of the Hebrew Orphanage Asylum and the Beth Din of Queens. Sending a letter with all particulars is highly recommended, in order to increase the chances of successful research.

Photocopies may be made for researchers at staff discretion, based on copyright restrictions, fragility of the items, and the intended use of materials. Copying will be performed for the researcher by a member of the Staff. Please check with the AJHS Reference Librarian to obtain the current fee schedule for photocopy services.

Description of Facility:

Upon entering, researchers should sign in the register book. Personal belongings must be checked, keeping only pencils and notepads. Free lockers are available: make a U-turn around to the left, walking around the low shelves, at the end of the short hall. There are regulations to read and sign. If you came by car, be sure to request a parking permit.

Research is done in the one main reading room, at four tables which each have four chairs. Since some materials, such as ledgers and registers, can be large, four people at a table might be crowded. This happens rarely, but busy times come at random.

In the main reading room, card catalogs are along the back wall and are fully accessible. A card file for periodicals is kept separately, and can only be accessed by the staff. There are actually seven different card catalogs along this wall, and it can be confusing. They have been numbered here for clarity. The main card catalog (1) starts at the upper left side, with "A." (Note below that there are separate card indexes interfiled within the main catalog). About half-way along the wall, the main catalog ends, with "Z." After the main catalog come the smaller, but important card indexes. Working towards the right, the next three drawers make up the index for Vertical Files (2). Next are three card indexes, each to a specific personal collection: Names index of the Stephen Wise Papers (3); Names index of the Milton Steinberg Papers (4); and Communities and Correspondents index of the Rabbi Tobias Geffen Papers (5). To the right of this is a card index to localities found in the New York Court Incorporation Papers (6). The final card set, taking up the last three columns of drawers, is the 19th-century periodicals index (7).

Along the side walls are book cases. Some of these book cases are open shelves, holding mostly reference works, which researchers may browse and use. Some of the book cases are locked, with glass fronts, and contain the rare book collection. Current issues of Jewish historical journals and many Jewish genealogical periodicals can be found in the low shelves in the interior of the room.

As one faces the card catalog, rest rooms are down stairs at the left side. A museum / display area is upstairs at the right side. Food, in the way of sandwiches, salads, sodas, coffee, etc., may be obtained in the Usdan Student Center, which is a two-minute walk away. By car, there are a few other eateries just off-campus. Please ask the staff for recommendations and directions.

Microfilmed periodicals are accessible at the Goldfarb Library (see page 73), a few minutes walk away on the Brandeis campus, through a joint depository arrangement between the Society and Brandeis University. Before leaving the AJHS building, check to make sure where the microfilm is; most microfilms of manuscript materials are held at the AJHS and can be taken to Goldfarb upon deposit of a driver's license. The microform facilities are located on the second level of the Goldfarb Library, in the periodicals area. A librarian there must unlock the cabinets holding AJHS collections. Be sure to mention that you are researching materials owned or co-owned by the AJHS, as the staff person may not be familiar with the name of an individual collection. Most of the microfilm readers there can make copies, using coins. Change can be made at the Brandeis periodicals desk. Hours may vary, especially during summer, holiday, and break periods; call the Brandeis periodicals department at (617) 736-4678.

Restrictions on use:

The Society's collections do not circulate and all materials must be used on site. One can only use pencil to take notes. Use of laptop computers is encouraged and outlets are accessible.

Doing research at the AJHS:

Preparation is the key to successful research at any research institution. If a researcher wants access to particular items, conferring with AJHS staff in advance can assist in locating materials promptly and efficiently. Some material is stored off-site at two not-nearby warehouses which are not accessible to the public. Such material might only be brought to headquarters weekly. (Although the most-often-requested material is on-site). Furthermore, access to some material might require special permissions, which can take time. Again, all of the library and archival material is in closed stacks, and can only be retrieved by the staff, who may be busy with other researchers at any given time.

If a researcher wants to peruse the holdings, familiarity with the categories of holdings, as shown below, is necessary.

In searching for an individual, keep in mind that some card index series are interfiled in the main card catalog, including an name index to early years of the *American Jewish Yearbook* (these have a reference to "AJYB"), and an index to the New York City Mayor's Court Records. Depending on the individual's involvement with American Jewish organizations and activities, an individual might show up in the name or correspondent indexes to the personal collections of Stephen Wise, Milton Steinberg, and Rabbi Tobias Geffen, so these might be checked next.

Beyond these indexes, look at the collections of institutions or individuals with which the person was associated. For instance, if the person had been resident in a New York City Jewish childcare institution or had noteworthy service in World War I, this would recommend for searching these collections. Some of these collections are enormous, but some of the most important institutional collections have finding aids and/or indexes. Many of the other important collections are well enough organized to make finding an individual a reasonable project. However, it is rarely a simple task.

In searching for a location, again, check the main card catalog first. Next, check the separate card index to vertical files. In searching for an old-country location, also check the separate locality card index to the New York Incorporation Papers, as they include incorporation papers of many landsmanschaftn. Researchers should note, however, that "old country" materials are not a collection focus of the AJHS. Accordingly, the likelihood of finding information on a particular location is strictly "hit or miss."

Consolidated Database. As part of its work to catalog genealogical resources at the AJHS, the Jewish Genealogical Society of Greater Boston has designed and implemented an electronic database of manuscript collections. The database allows searching by locale of interest, surname, or keyword, in the name, description, or geographic location of the collection. The collections included are: Organizations (I=institutional), Personal papers (P=personal), and MS=Ephemera.

Some of the material in this chapter originally appeared in *Avotaynu: The International Review of Jewish Genealogy*, Volume XI, Number 3 (Fall 1995).

BOSTON PUBLIC LIBRARY

Facility Director: Arthur Curley, Director and Librarian

Address: 666 Boylston Street (at Dartmouth Street)
Copley Square
Boston, MA 02117

Phone Number: (617) 536-5400

Hours of Operation:

Monday to Thursday: 9:00 am to 9:00 pm
Friday and Saturday: 9:00 am to 5:00 pm
Sunday (October-May):   1:00 pm to 5:00 pm
Closed other Sundays and legal holidays.

Directions:

By Car: Storrow Drive to Beacon St., to Exeter St. Left on Exeter St. 4 blocks.
Copley Place parking garage on Exeter beyond Library (expensive).
By MBTA: Green Line to Copley Square Station.
Orange or Purple (Commuter) or Amtrak Lines to Back Bay Station.

Description of Institution:

The BOSTON PUBLIC LIBRARY is one of the most famous institutions of its kind. Its original orientation was Yankee-Brahmin, from the time of its founding in 1852. The McKim Building, now the Research Library, was dedicated in 1895 as a "palace for the people".

> The Library was opened in Copley Square, amidst elegant townhouses and supporting institutional services patronized by Boston's elite. The dynamics of the western move from the original peninsula neighborhoods with the filling of the Charles River's Back Bay is richly described by Walter Muir Whitehall, *Boston: A Topographical History* (Cambridge: Belknap & Harvard University Presses, 1959; 2nd ed. 1968) [F73.3.W57]. The attraction of the Boston Public Library for Americanizing immigrants is depicted by Mary Antin, *The Promised Land* (Boston: Houghton, Mifflin, 1912; 2nd ed. 1969) [E169.5.A66.1969].

In the succeeding decades the Central Library and its 27 branches expanded services. The Kirstein Business Branch, located downtown, near Old City Hall, off School Street, is named for Louis Kirstein, a leading merchant from the German-Jewish community of the late 19th century. The 1972 annex to the BPL by architect Philip Johnson became the General Library. Today the emphasis is directed to Boston's minority and ethnic population, students, the business community, and professional and technical people. With state support, library cards are issued to bona-fide residents and students throughout the Commonwealth of Massachusetts. Interlibrary loans and exchanges of a variety of audio-visual materials are available. Library services are linked to budgets, which have been hard hit by federal, state and area economic cutbacks. There is increasing urgency to tap the good will of corporate and civic interests.

Description of Resources:

A. General Library — All circulating books and current periodicals are located in this annex building (Johnson Building), on open shelves. Large green catalog books list items catalogued through 1975. More recent acquisitions are cataloged on public-accessible computer terminals located throughout the building.

For Jewish genealogy, relevant books include those that provide backgrounds to neighborhoods in which Jews have lived in Boston. These include the North, West and South Ends near the waterfront, settled before the First World War. Jews moved down Blue Hill Avenue to Roxbury, Dorchester and Mattapan, as well as westward to Allston-Brighton, then Brookline, which is outside the city limits. Jews became predominantly suburban after the second World War, though enclaves continue in Boston neighborhoods such as Brighton, Jamaica Plain, Hyde Park, West Roxbury and Back Bay student areas. The following selections are helpful:

Ehrenfried, Albert. *A Chronicle of Boston Jewry: from the Colonial Settlement to 1900.* (Boston: privately printed, 1963). 771 pp. [F73.9.J5E5]. (Typescript photocopy). [also Soc. Sci. Ref. F73.9.J5E5].

Fein, Isaac M. *Boston - Where It All Began: A Historical Perspective of the Boston Jewish Community.* (Boston: Boston Jewish Bicentennial Committee, 1976). 83 pp. [Res. Library F73.9.J5F44].

Feldman, Steven and the Staff of Genesis 2 (Jewish student publication). *Guide to Jewish Boston and New England.* (Cambridge & Boston: Donald J. Perlstein, Publisher, Charles River Printing, 1986). Combined Jewish Philanthropies of Greater Boston, Sponsor. [F73.9.J5G84 1986x]. (also in Research Library, Bates Hall section 55).

Grossman, Brigite S. *Experiencing Jewish Boston.* (Boston: Jewish Community Center of Greater Boston, 72 Franklin Street {now relocated in Newton}, 1981). 53 pp. [F73.9.J5G76].

Sarna, Jonathan and Ellen Smith. *The Jews of Boston: Essays on the occassion of the centenary (1895-1995) of the Combined Jewish Philanthropies of Greater Boston.* (Boston, Combined Jewish Philanthropies of Greater Boston, 1995). 353 pp. [F73.9.J5 J47 1995x]

Schindler, Solomon. *Israelites in Boston: A Tale Describing the Development of Judaism in Boston.* (Boston: Berwick and Smith, 1889). [*F73.9.J5S3].

The following books provide backgrounds for Jewish immigrant neighborhood settlement:

Bushee, Frederick A. *Ethnic Factors in the Population of Boston.* (New York: Hall, 1903; reprint: Arno Press, 1970). 171 pp. [F73.5.B989.1970].

Firey, Walter. *Land Use in Central Boston.* (Cambridge: Harvard University Press, 1947; reprint: New York: Greenwood Press, 1968). 367 pp. [HD268.B7F5. 1968]. {North End, South End, Beacon Hill, Back Bay}.

Fried, Marc and Ellen Fitzgerald. *The World of the Urban Working Class.* (Cambridge: Harvard University Press, 1973). 410 pp. [HN80.B7F7]. {West End urban redevelopment, 1950's-1960's}.

Handlin, Oscar. *Boston's Immigrants, A Study in Acculturation, 1790-1880.* (Cambridge, MA: Belknap Press of Harvard University Press, 1959). 382 pp. [F73.9.A1H3]. {Focus on Irish experience, but also includes Germans with some Jewish immigrants among them}. (Revised edition, 1979 is [Soc. Sci. Ref. F73.9.A1H3 1979]).

Levine, Hillel and Lawrence Harmon. *The Death of an American Jewish Community: a tragedy of good intentions.* (New York: The Free Press, Macmillan, 1992). 370 pp. [F73.9.J5 L48 1992]. {Roxbury-Dorchester-Mattapan}.

Thernstrom, Stephan. *The Other Bostonians: Poverty and Progress in the American Metropolis, 1880-1970.* (Cambridge: Harvard University Press, 1973). 345 pp. [HN80.B7T45]. {Contrasts mobility of Jews, Irish, Blacks, and others}.

Warner, Sam B. *Streetcar Suburbs: The Process of Growth in Boston 1870-1900.* (Cambridge: Harvard University and M.I.T. Presses, 1962; 2nd edition, 1982). 208 pp. [HN80.B7W3.1982x]. {Effect of electrified public transportation on the growth of Roxbury, Dorchester, and Jamaica Plain in the early 20th century, encouraging migration from downtown neighborhoods}.

Wieder, Arnold A. *The Early Jewish Community of Boston's North End*. (Waltham, MA: Brandeis University, 1962). 100 pp. [F73.9.J5W5]. {A sociological study of an East European immigrant neighborhood, between 1870 and 1900}. (also [Soc. Sci. Ref. F73.9.J5W5]).

Woods, Robert Archey. *The City Wilderness*. (Boston: Houghton, Mifflin, 1898; reprint, Arno Press, 1970). 319 pp. [HN80.B7W8.1970b]. {South End}.

Woods, Robert Archey. *Americans in Process: A Settlement Study*. (Boston: Houghton, Mifflin, 1902; reprint, Arno Press, 1970). 389 pp. [F735.W85 1970] [HV 4196.87.S8y]. {North End & West End}.

Woods, Robert Archey and Albert J. Kennedy. *The Zone of Emergence: Observations on the lower, middle and upper working class communities of Boston, 1903-1914*. (Cambridge: M.I.T. Press, 1962, 1969). 219 pp. [HN 80.B7K4.1969]. {Roxbury and Dorchester plus waterfront neighborhoods beyond North, West and South Ends}.

A limited number of books specifically useful for the genealogist includes:

Doane, Gilbert H. *Searching for your Ancestors: The How and Why of Genealogy*. 6th edition (Minneapolis: University of Minnesota Press, 1992). [CS16.D6.1992].

Pine, Leslie G. *The Genealogist's Encyclopedia*. (New York: Weybright and Talley, 1969). 360 pp. [CS9.P48.1960b] [also in REF collection].

Rubincam, Milton, and Jean Stephenson, eds. *Genealogical Research Methods and Sources*. (Washington, D.C.: American Society of Genealogists, 1980). 456 pp. [CS16.G43 1980] [also in REF collection].

Many books on Jewish history in English can be found in the General Library under call number DS135, including:

Beizer, Mikhail. *The Jews of St. Petersburg: Excursions through a noble past*. (Translated from the Russian) (Philadelphia: Jewish Publication Society, 1989). 328 pp. [DS135.R93 L463 1989].

Gutman, Israel. *The Jews of Warsaw, 1939-1943*. (A translation from the Hebrew *Yehude Varshah*). (Bloomington, Indiana: University Press, 1982). 487 pp. [DS135.P62 W27313 1982].

There are some Yiddish-language books in the foreign-language book section on the Mezzanine.

There are many tables, desks and chairs located on all levels of the General Library (Johnson Building), to accommodate several hundred readers. Peak periods are when students come during mid-afternoons.

There is a passage from the first floor of the General Library to the Research Library (McKim Building) via its open courtyard. There is also access to the Research Library from the second floor periodicals area: a passageway to the left of the Periodicals Reference Desk will lead to the Science Reference Department on the second floor of the Research Library. From there, walk through to the Card Catalog Room to Bates Hall and the rest of the McKim Building.

Boston Public Library

Central Library

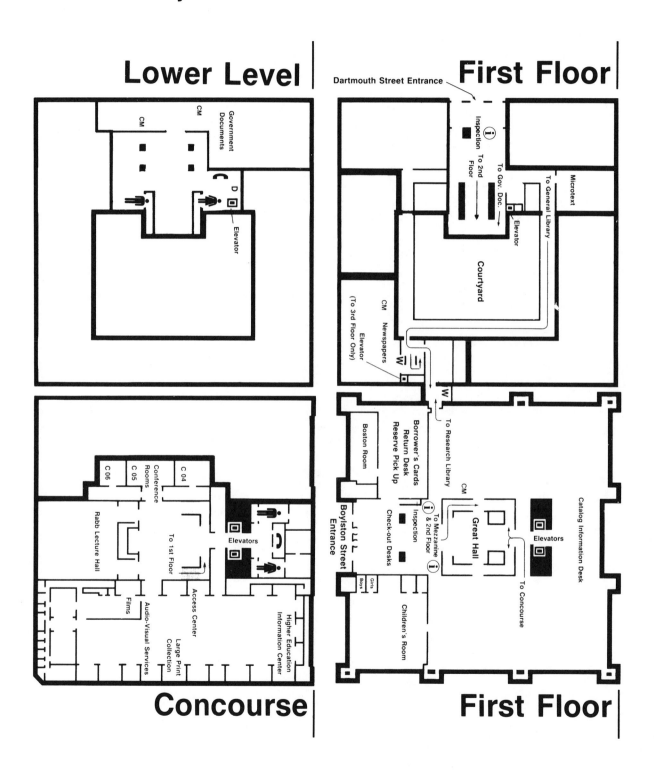

Lower Level

First Floor

Dartmouth Street Entrance

Government Documents

CM

CM

Elevator

D

Inspection

i

To 2nd Floor

To Gov. Doc.

To General Library

Microtext

Elevator

Courtyard

CM Newspapers

Elevator (To 3rd Floor Only)

W

W

To Research Library

Concourse

C 06

C 05

C 04

Conference Rooms

Rabb Lecture Hall

To 1st Floor

Elevators

Films

Audio-Visual Services

Access Center

Large Print Collection

Higher Education Information Center

First Floor

Boston Room

Borrower's Cards
Return Desk
Reserve Pick Up

Boylston Street Entrance

Inspection

Check-out Desks

i

To Mezzanine & 2nd Floor

i

CM

Great Hall

Elevators

Catalog Information Desk

To Concourse

Boys

Girls

Children's Room

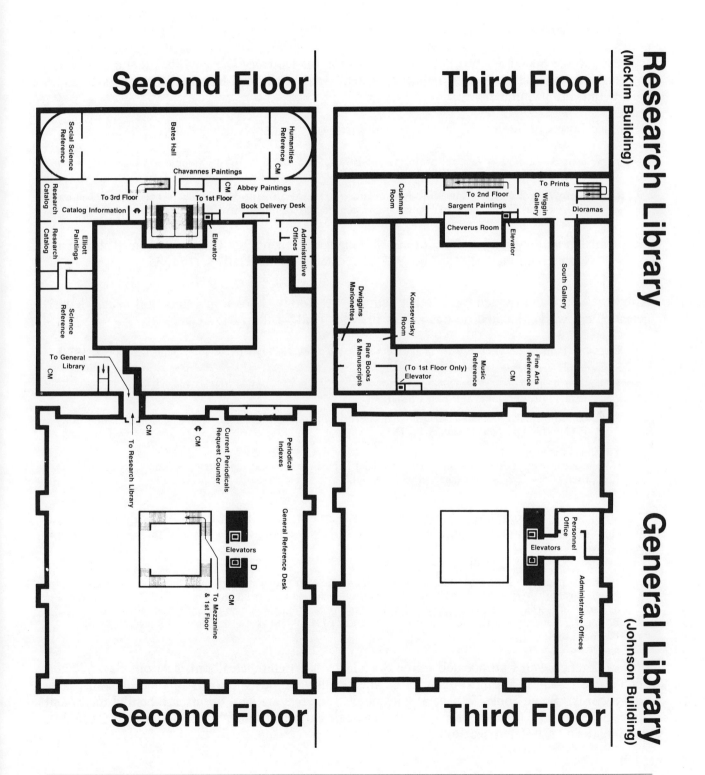

Research Library
(McKim Building)

Second Floor

Social Science Reference

Bates Hall

Humanities Reference

CM

Chavannes Paintings

CM

Abbey Paintings

To 3rd Floor

To 1st Floor

Catalog Information

Book Delivery Desk

Research Catalog

Elliott Paintings

Research Catalog

Elevator

Administrative Offices

Science Reference

To General Library

CM

Third Floor

Cushman Room

To Prints

To 2nd Floor

Wiggin Gallery

Sargent Paintings

Dioramas

Cheverus Room

Elevator

Dwiggins Marionettes

Koussevitsky Room

South Gallery

Rare Books & Manuscripts

(To 1st Floor Only) Elevator

Music Reference

CM

Fine Arts Reference

General Library
(Johnson Building)

Second Floor

CM

CM

To Research Library

Current Periodicals Request Counter

Periodical Indexes

General Reference Desk

Elevators

D

CM

To Mezzanine & 1st Floor

Third Floor

Personnel Office

Elevators

Administrative Offices

B. Research Library — This is where genealogists seeking specific data will spend most of their time. The Research Library (McKim Building), is the original 1895 library building, with its grand entrance on Dartmouth Street. All materials must be used within the area where they are located, or delivered by request. A library card is needed for items not on open shelves.

1. <u>Social Science Reference Room and Bates Hall Reading Room</u> are located on the second floor of the McKim Building. Bates Hall is the main reading room, facing Dartmouth Street. The Social Science Reference Room is located at the north end of Bates Hall. Background books, maps, and catalogs are accessible; other materials, kept in closed stacks, must be requested at the Social Science Reference Desk or at the Delivery Desk (with call slip, according to catalog number; library card required). Requested books are delivered to readers in Bates Hall within 20-30 minutes.

Reference books of interest to Jewish genealogists, on open shelves, include:

Encyclopaedia Judaica. (New York: Macmillan, 1971). [Ref BM50.E53]. 16 Volumes + Yearbooks, located in Bates Hall, section 55.

Great Soviet Encyclopedia. (New York: Macmillan, 1981). [AE5.B58]. 31 volumes + index, located in Bates Hall, section 49. This is an English translation of *Bolshoi Sovyetskaya Entsikolpediia* (Moscow, 1976). [AE55.B623]. 30 volumes, in Bates Hall, section 51.

Translation <u>dictionaries</u> for dozens of languages, including Czech, Polish, Lithuanian, Hungarian, etc., [Ref. PG . . .] are located in Bates Hall, section 35.

Amidst American-oriented and other ethnic genealogy books are the following Jewish genealogical works, located on open shelf in Bates Hall, section 01:

Kaganoff, Benzion C. *A Dictionary of Jewish Names and Their History.* (New York: Schocken Books, 1977). 250 pp. [CS3010.K28].

Rottenberg, Dan. *Finding Our Fathers: A Guidebook to Jewish Genealogy.* (New York: Random House, 1977). 401 pp. [Soc. Sci. Ref. CS21.R58].

Sack, Sallyann Amdur. *Guide to Genealogical Research in Israel.* (Baltimore: Genealogical Publishing Co., 1987). 110 pp. [Z6374.B5S23.1987].

Zubatsky, David S. and Irwin M. Berent. *Jewish Genealogy: A Sourcebook of Family Histories and Genealogies.* (New York & London: Garland Publishing Co., 1984, 1990). 2 volumes. [Ref Z6374.B5Z79.1984 (shelved with CS31)].

The <u>Social Science Reference Room</u>, at the north end of Bates Hall, contains many background histories of Boston, neighboring localities, counties, states, the United States, and foreign countries.

Of special interest to Jewish genealogists should be an article on "Judaism" by Rabbi Harry Levi of Temple Israel, Boston, covering the 1880-1930 period of institutional and leadership building, pp. 617-625, Chapter 8, part 3 of Herlihy, Elizabeth M., ed. *Fifty Years of Boston.* (Subcommittee on Memorial History of the Boston Tercentenary Committee, 1932). [Soc. Sci. Ref F73.3.B858] [see also General Library photocopy F73.3.D818 1975x].

Local reference works are located in the Social Science Reference Room, sections S22-S27, on open shelves. These are local histories of Massachusetts cities and towns, including some early vital records. Some books of general genealogical interest are kept on reserve behind the Social Science Reference Desk (including most that begin with call leter "Z"). Others are located in the Social Science Reference Room or in Bates Hall:

Andereck, Paul A. and Richard A. Pence. *Computer Genealogy: A Guide to Research Through High Technology*. (Salt Lake City: Ancestry, Inc., 1991). [Ref CS14.C645 1991]. (Bates Hall, section 01).

Cerny, Johni and Wendy Elliott, eds. *The Library: A Guide to the LDS Family History Library*. (Salt Lake City: Ancestry, Inc., 1988). 746 pp. [Z675.C5 L4 1988x]

Currer-Briggs, Noel. *Worldwide Family History*. (London: Routledge & Kegan Paul, 1982). 230 pp. [CS9.C87].

Doane, Gilbert H. and James B. Bell. *Searching for Your Ancestors: The How and Why of Genealogy*. 6th edition. (Minneapolis: University of Minnesota Press, 1992). [CS16.D6.1992]. (Bates Hall, section 1).

Eakle, Arlene and Johni Cerny, eds. *The Source: A Guidebook of American Genealogy*. (Salt Lake City: Ancestry Publishing Co., 1984). 786 pp. [Ref CS49.S65.1984].

Everton, George B., Sr., ed. *The Handy Book for Genealogists*. Revised and enlarged, 7th edition. (Logan, Utah: Everton Publishers, 1981). 370 pp. [Ref CS47.E9.1981].

Filby, P. William and others, ed. *Passenger and Immigration Lists Index*. 14 volumes, 1982 et sequa. (Detroit: Gale Research Co.) [Soc. Sci. Ref. CS68.P363]. {Focuses on 17th-19th century immigrants}. (Bates Hall, section 1).

Guide to Genealogical Research in the National Archives. (Washington, D.C.: National Archives and Records Service, 1982). [Soc. Sci. Ref. Z5313.U5U54 1982]. (Bates Hall, section 1).

Guzik, Estelle M., ed. *Genealogical Resources in the New York Metropolitan Area*. (New York: Jewish Genealogical Society, 1989). 404 pp. [Z5313.U6N523 1989] [also copy in microtext dept].

Kaminkow, Marion J. *Genealogies in the Library of Congress: A Bibliography*. (Baltimore: Magna Carta Book Co., 1972). 2 volumes. [Z5319.U53]. *First Supplement (1972-1976)*, 1977. 285 pp. *Second Supplement (1976-1986)*, 1987. 861 pp. [Soc. Sci. Ref. Z5319.U53].

Kemp, Thomas Jay. *International Vital Records Handbook*. (Baltimore: Genealogical Publishing Co., 1990). 355 pp. [Ref CS24.K46 1990x].

Accessible <u>Atlases</u> and <u>Gazetteers</u> are located near the Social Science Reference Desk, and in Bates Hall, section 13. Of interest among the current collection are:

Atlas del Mundo. Commemorating the 50th Anniversary of the Great October Social Revolution, 1917-1967. (Moscow: Chief Administration of Geodesy and Cartography under the Council of Ministers of the U.S.S.R., 1967). [Ref G1019.R957313.1967].

Penzler, Johannes, ed. *Ritter's Geographisch-Statistisches Lexikon*. 2 volumes. (Leipzig: Otto Wigand, 1906). [Ref G103.R6]. (In German). Located in Bates Hall, section 13.

The Columbia Lippincott Gazetteer of the World. (New York: Columbia University Press, 1962). [G103.L7.1962].

Where Once We Walked: A Guide to the Jewish Communities Destroyed in the Holocaust. By Gary Mokotoff and Sallyann Amdur Sack. (Teaneck, NJ: Avotaynu, Inc., 1991). 514 pp. [DS135.E8 M65 1991].

Slownik Geograficzny Królestwa Polskiego i innych krajów slowiańskich. [Geographical Dictionary of the Kingdom of Poland and other Slavic Countries]. Edited by Filip Sulimierski. 15 volumes. (Warsaw: Sulimierski i Walewski, 1880-1902). [DK403.S55], behind Social Sciences Reference Desk. {Comprehensive historical gazetteer of pre-war Poland and other Russian Empire territories. In Polish.}

Hundreds of works of local Jewish history, including Yizkor books, can be found in the old card catalog under the heading "JEWS IN [Town Name]". See Appendix A (pages 193-225) for a complete bibliography of Yizkor books with call numbers. The Research Library catalogs should be consulted for other European Jewish-oriented materials, e.g.:

Gilbert, Martin. *The Holocaust: A History of the Jews of Europe during the Second World War*. (New York: Holt, Rinehart & Winston, 1985). 959 pp. [Soc. Sci. Ref. D810.J4 G525 1985].

Gilbert, Martin. *Atlas of the Holocaust*. (New York: Wm. Morrow, 1993). 282 pp. [G1797.21.E29 G58 1993]

Gutman, Israel, editor-in-chief. *Encyclopedia of the Holocaust.* 4 volumes. (Jerusalem: Yad Vashem; Tel Aviv: Sifriat Poalim Publishing House; New York: Macmillan; London: Collier Macmillan, 1990). [D804.3.E53.1990]. (Bates Hall, section 08).

Alpert, Nachum. *The Destruction of Slonim Jewry: the story of Slonim Jewry during the Holocaust.* (Translated from the Yiddish) (New York: Holocaust Library, 1989). 370 pp. [DS135.R93 S542].

Sack, Sallyann Amdur and Suzan Fishl Wynne, eds. *The Russian Consular Records Index and Catalog.* (New York: Garland Reference Library of Social Science, 1987). 897 pp. [CS856.J4S23.1987].

2. The <u>Print Department</u> is located on the third floor of the McKim Building. Here there are files on Boston neighborhoods. Some categories show photographic "Street Views" of the North, West and South Ends and Roxbury before the first World War. Jewish life, per se, is not depicted.

3. The <u>Manuscript Department</u> is also located on the third floor of the McKim building. One collection of note is the Judaica (West End) Collection, also known as the Fannie Goldstein collection, which preserves contempory materials and ephemera assembled in the 1920s-1960s by Ms. Goldstein, a librarian with the West End Branch of the BPL, on a range of subjects of her interest. This collection of 73 boxes contains scrapbooks, newspaper clippings, and material on Jewish books and organizations. Access to this Special Collection may be requested at the Research Library Services Office (Mon-Fri 9am-5pm) located on the second floor behind the Book Delivery Desk. A brief inventory is available in this office.

4. The <u>Microtext Department</u> is probably the most useful facility for supplying raw data for individual genealogical interests. The microtext facilities are located on the first floor of the McKim Building. The Microtext Reference Desk, with professional staff, catalogs and card files are located here. Many bound index volumes are available on open shelves, and there is public access to many microfilm/fiche reading machines and tables to accommodate several dozen researchers, in the main room and an anteroom. A library card is required to access microtext materials from the reference desk.

a. <u>Newspapers</u> -- The BPL has the largest collection of newspapers on microfilm in the state, with over 3,500 titles. Microfilm copies of most local, regional, many national and some international newspapers, dating from the early 19th century to the present, may be requested from the Reference Desk librarians.

Newspaper holdings are listed in a catalog at the Reference Desk: *United States Newspapers on Microform at the Boston Public Library*. (Boston: Boston Public Library, March 1987), plus librarian updates (155 pages, Massachusetts newspapers are listed on pages 11-118). Approximately three months of the most current newspapers may be read at leisure in the <u>Newspaper Room</u>, located off the McKim Building courtyard.

Many newspaper indexes for Boston and major American cities are available in bound volumes on open shelves. Most date only from the 1970's, however, *The New York Times* Index dates from its inception in 1851, and the London *Times* Index dates from 1823. A few other newspaper indexes are available, listed in a folder at the Reference Desk.

The *Boston Jewish Advocate*, a weekly available on microfilm since May 5, 1905, is the most useful newspaper for those interested in local and global Jewish activities, personages, institutions, etc. (Also available at HEBREW COLLEGE LIBRARY, BRANDEIS UNIVERSITY LIBRARY and the AMERICAN JEWISH HISTORICAL SOCIETY).

Other Jewish newspapers on microfilm:
- *Boston Hebrew Observer* (Boston) Jan 1883 - Jan 1886 (weekly)
- *Jewish Herald* (Boston) Jun 1893 - Aug 1894 (weekly)
- *Jewish World* (Boston) Jan 1939 - Dec 1942 (weekly)
- *Jewish Civic Leader* (Worcester) Jan 1960 - Dec 1967 (weekly)
- *Jewish Weekly News* (Springfield) Mar 1952 - Jan 1974 (weekly)
- *Daily Forward* (Boston) 1919 - 1941
- *Daily Forward* (New York) Jan 1957 - Dec 1965 (daily)
- *Carolina Israelite* (Charlotte) Feb 1944 - Feb 1968 (monthly)
- *Southern Israelite* (Atlanta) Jan 1959 - Dec 1971 (weekly)
- *National Jewish Post and Opinion* (Indianapolis) Sep 1945 - Nov 1965 (weekly)
- *Jewish Post* (Winnipeg) Jan 1968 - Jun 1969 (weekly)
- *Jewish Chronicle* (London) Nov 1841 - date (weekly)
  with index 1841-1900 and 1947-48.
- *Palestine Weekly* (Jerusalem) 1919 - 1931 (weekly)
- *Jerusalem Post* (Jerusalem) 1934 - date (daily)

The Microtext Department has also acquired 115 reels of microfilm of German Jewish periodicals, 1768-1938 (45 titles from the Leo Baeck Institute, New York), via the Clearwater Publishing Co., New York. [Micro DS 136.G3 G37 1980xx].

b.   Obituary notices of interest to Jewish genealogists may be researched from microfilmed newspapers and indexes cited above. *The Boston Globe* is currently the most ubiquitous metropolitan newspaper, though *The Boston Herald* is more populist. For the first half of this century, Boston Jews were more likely to read the *Traveler* or the (Hearst) *Record*, *American*, or *Advertiser*; the *Post* appealed to Democrats and the *Herald* to Republicans; the *Boston Transcript* was quite elitist. This should guide researchers using the Obituary card file boxes, located in the rear anteroom, openly accessible. Oldest records exist for the *Boston Transcript*, 1875-1941. It also includes *The Boston Herald*, 1953-1984, and *The Boston Globe*, 1953-1982 (all with gaps).

A database of contemporary obituaries from *The Boston Globe* and *The Boston Herald* is available on an online terminal located towards the department anteroom. This database can be searched by a number of parameters and will provide the newspaper name and date of an obituary's appearance. Obituary coverage begins with 1990. Access to this database is also available on the Internet, via the Library's gopher [gopher.bpl.org] or Web site [http://www.bpl.org].

c.   Holbrook Microfiche -- Massachusetts vital records (birth, marriage and death records) from the 1600's through the 1890's, by town. These are copies of original town vital records for over 210 Massachusetts towns (including Boston), microfiched by Archive Publishing (formerly the Holbrook Research Institute). See the list of available towns and inclusive dates at the Reference Desk.

Also available are microfiche copies of the state-wide indexes to Massachusetts birth, marriage and death records, 1841-1895, filmed by Holbrook at the MASSACHUSETTS ARCHIVES. See page 30 for more information.

- Birth Index   1841-1895   52 volumes   417 fiche
- Marriage Index   1841-1895   42 volumes   327 fiche
- Death Index   1841-1895   39 volumes   310 fiche

d.   City Directories -- Bound volumes for **Boston** 1932-1981 are located on open shelves in the microtext department anteroom; microfilm reels for 1861-1931 are also located here (67 reels, [F73.2.A3]). The earliest directories, for 1789-1860, on microfilm, may be requested at the Reference Desk. (But be aware of the constricted boundaries of the city during this period, before major annexations of existing neighborhoods). No Boston City Directories have been issued since 1981, due to major residential transiency and urban renewal.

City directories for other regional localities and 72 major U.S. cities are available on microfilm, through the Reference Desk. See *City Directories of the United States, 1860-1901: Guide to the Microfilm Collection*. (Woodbridge, CT: Research Publications, Inc., 1983). Index on pp 485-487. Microfilmed directories are in four series -- I: thru 1860, II: 1861-1881, III: 1882-1901, IV: 1902-1935. The Microtext department has all of parts I, II and III, and portions of part IV. For most major cities, it has all four parts (through 1935). [Micro Z5771.2.C58.1984]. A card file drawer near the Microtext Department entrance provides an alphabetical list of City Directories on microfilm, and what years are available for each.

The Microtext Department also has City Directories for London, England, for 1677 through 1855. [DA 679.A133].

The Humanities Department catalog contains City Directories in storage at the BPL warehouse in Charlestown. [These directories were formerly at the BPL's Roslindale Branch (for New England localities, pre-1970's), and at the East Boston Branch (for over 100 localities outside New England)]. There is a list of these directories at the Humanities Department Reference Desk. The Kirstein Business Branch has the most recent City Directories. Historical directories can be requested for delivery to the BPL at the Book Delivery Desk (second floor, Abbey Room). It takes a few days for delivery; there is no charge.

[Note: The NEW ENGLAND HISTORIC GENEALOGICAL SOCIETY has a major collection of City Directories for Boston and most localities in New England, as well as other regions, in original volumes. Other collections of Massachusetts City Directories exist at the STATE LIBRARY OF MASSACHUSETTS in the State House on Beacon Hill, and at the MASSACHUSETTS ARCHIVES at Columbia Point.]

e. Annual Boston City Residents Lists (also known as "Assessed Polls" and "Voter Registration" lists, are known colloquially as "street" lists or "police" lists, since data is gathered in person at the beginning of each year). They complement the City Directories by listing all adults of voting age, rather than head-of-household only, plus age, gender, nationality, occupation, place of previous year's residence, and political party preference for primary balloting. The streets are alphabetically arranged within precincts and wards. Their jurisdictions must first be ascertained through files in the Government Documents Department, located on the lower level of the McKim Building. Only the most recent lists are located there, arranged by alphabetically by name (a fairly recent innovation) and by the traditional ward/precinct numbers. Lists from the 1860's into the 1920's must be ordered (with library card) from the New England Deposit Library via the Book Delivery Desk (second floor, Abbey Room). Microfilm lists for 1913-1931 should be requested from the Microtext Reference Desk librarian. Lists for later decades are can be requested at the Government Documents Reference Desk, by year and ward/precinct. Or you can consult alternate sources, such as the STATE LIBRARY OF MASSACHUSETTS (see page 183).

f. Sanborn Fire Insurance Maps of Boston districts and other New England localities, for the 1870's to 1950's, on microfilm. The Sanborn Map Company produced 700,000 sheets of detailed maps for 12,000 cities and towns in North America. These maps show details of every building. For the New England States, see catalog (Teaneck, NJ: Chadwyck-Healey), 1983. [Micro G12**.G475.S3 1983x]. The maps for each state are arranged alphabetically by town.

• Connecticut	(1884-1950)	19 reels	[Micro G1241.G475.S3]
• Maine	(1884-1949)	8 reels	[Micro G1216.G475.S3]
• Massachusetts	(1867-1950)	48 reels	[Micro G1231.G475.S3]
• New Hampshire	(1880-1950)	7 reels	[Micro G1221.G475.S3]
• Rhode Island	(1880-1950)	7 reels	[Micro G1236.G475.S3]
• Vermont	(1879-1959)	5 reels	[Micro G1226.G475.S3]

The original maps are at the Library of Congress (see *Fire Insurance Maps in the Library of Congress: Plans of North American Towns*. Washington, DC: Library of Congress, 1981 [Micro Z6026.I7U54]).

g. Telephone Books -- Microfilm copies exist for greater Boston for 1910-1978, and for most major American cities, since 1976, on Phone-Fiche. The most current edition is in the Humanities Department; older editions are located in the Microtext Department.

Most current telephone directories, worldwide, are located in the Humanities Department (second floor of McKim Building, south end of Bates Hall).

h. U.S. Census Schedules -- Microfilm copies for the six New England states cover 1790-1920 (except 1890, which was lost). Soundex indexes for the 1880, 1900 and 1920 censuses are also available. Printed alphabetical indexes are available for all New England states 1790-1850. For 1860, printed indexes for CT, NH, RI, VT and the city of Boston are available; For 1870, only RI. Request these indexes from the Reference Desk.

Also available is the 1890 Census of Civil War Veterans, with related indexes (see Military Records, below); and the published indexes to the 1855 and 1865 Massachusetts state censuses (see page 14). Other U.S. Census data (mostly abstracts and statistical material) are located in the Government Documents Department.

[Note that federal census records for the entire country, 1790-1920, with all indexes, are available on open shelves at the NATIONAL ARCHIVES - NEW ENGLAND REGION in Waltham, see page 144].

i. Ship Passenger Lists -- Microfilms of passenger lists for the Port of **Boston** cover 1820-1918 (with some gaps, notably Apr 1874 - Dec 1882) (NAMP M277, 115 reels, 1820-1891; NAMP T843 partial, 248 reels, 1891-1918). Alphabetical name indexes to these lists cover 1848-1891 (NAMP M265, 282 reels), Jan 1902 - June 1906 (NAMP T521, 11 reels), and 1906-1920 (NAMP T617, 11 reels). There are also book indexes for April 1899 - April 1916 (NAMP T790 partial, 62 reels). The book indexes contain an alphabetical listing of passengers on a particular vessel, and are arranged by the date of arrival of the ship. [JV6461.A6]. [Note: Later Boston passenger lists (through 1943), alphabetical indexes (through 1920) and book indexes (through 1940) are available at the NATIONAL ARCHIVES - NEW ENGLAND REGION]. See page 21 for details on these and other passenger lists.

New York Passenger Arrival Lists for 1820-1897 (NAMP M237, 675 reels) and the alphabetical index for 1820-1846 (NAMP M261, 103 reels) have been acquired on microfilm from the National Archives in Washington. [F128.25.P377.1957x].

Lists and indexes for 'Other Atlantic and Gulf Ports' cover 1820-1874 (Lists: NAMP M575, 16 reels; Indexes: NAMP M334, 188 reels) [JV6461.A62]. Passenger lists and indexes for New Bedford (1902-1954), Portland (1893-1954) and Providence (1911-1954) ports are also available.

Morton Allan Directory of European Passenger Steamship Arrivals (New York: Bernard Publishing Co., 1931), with supplement (New York: Readex, 1976) [HE945.A2D5] (in microtext room). Lists the names of vessels arriving by year, steamship company, and exact date of arrival at the ports of New York, 1890-1930, and of Baltimore, Boston and Philadelphia, 1904-1926.

There is also "Registers of Vessels Arriving at the Port of New York, New York, from Foreign Ports, 1789-1919" on microfilm (NAMP M1066, 27 reels). This collection of ledgers is a chronological listing of ship arrivals; it does not contain passenger's names.

Passenger Lists of the Holland America Line: 1900-1940. (Lisse: MMF Publications, 1994). 272 microfiche. [Micro HE945.H55P3 1994x] {See *Avotaynu* VIII:4, p57; X:4, p83}.

j. Naturalization Indexes -- Microfilm indexes for the six New England states cover 1791-1906. This index was created by the Work Projects Administration (WPA) during the 1930's. The original index cards and dexigraph copies of the naturalization documents are at the NATIONAL ARCHIVES - NEW ENGLAND REGION in Waltham. NAMP M1299 (117 reels) [F3.1646 1983x]. See page 16 for details on this index.

k. County Probate Court Records -- Microfilmed records for Suffolk County (which includes Boston), Middlesex County, and Hampshire County. The index volumes are on open shelves. The original records are being transferred to the MASSACHUSETTS ARCHIVES by the Registrars of Probate. Changing jurisdictional boundaries over time should be noted. Check with the Reference Desk librarian for possible later or additional listings.

- Suffolk County   Records: 1636-1907   72 reels [F72.S9M43]
                                Indexes: 1636-1893 (3 vols), 1894-1909 (2 vols)
- Middlesex County   Records: 1648-1910   ?? reels [F72.M7M43]
                                Indexes: 1648-1871 (1 vol), 1870-1910 (1 vol)
- Hampshire County   Records: 1660-1820   12 reels [KFM2451.9.H35]
                                Indexes: At beginning of each volume.

l. Military and Veterans' Records -- Selected microfilm indexes for New England cover 1789-1903, with emphasis on the Civil War. The Microtext Department has copies of the 1890 Census of Civil War veterans and their widows, for five New England states and New York. (Records for Connectucut are not included, since all records for states A-K were destroyed in a fire). The records are on microfilm, with printed indexes available in book form. See Dilts, Bryan Lee, ed. *1890 Massachusetts Census Index of Civil War Veterans or their Widows*. (Salt Lake City, UT: Index Publishing), 1985, [E494.D85.1985], and similar indexes for other states.

- Maine   2 reels   [HA411.1890.A303]
- Massachusetts   6 reels   [HA431.1890.A303]
- New Hampshire   1 reel   [HA511.1890.A303]
- Rhode Island   1 reel   [HA611.1890.A303]
- Vermont   1 reel   [HA671.1890.A303]

m. AJGS Microfiche -- Indexes prepared by the Association of Jewish Genealogical Societies. Also available at HEBREW COLLEGE LIBRARY (see page 106 for content details of these microfiche):
- Jewish Genealogical Consolidated Surname Index. 1989. (3 microfiche) [CS31J485]
- Gazetteer of Eastern Europe. Daitch-Mokotoff Soundex Sequence (7 microfiche); Alphabetic Sequence (8 microfiche). 1989. [DJK6.G394]
- Black Book of Localities Whose Jewish Population Was Exterminated by the Nazis. 1989. (2 microfiche) [D804.3.B533.1989x].

n. *Yad Vashem Archives of Destruction: A Photographic Record of the Holocaust*. (245 microfiche), 1981. [Micro D810.J4.Y25.1981x].

Finding Aids:

There are two main card catalogs for the Research Library:

> Pre-1981 card catalog, on paper 3x5 cards in the catalog rooms (2nd floor, McKim Building, north side), and microtext photocopies located throughout the building. Contains items catalogued before 1981.
> Post-1980 computer catalog, available on terminals located throughout the building. Contains items catalogued after 1980.

Online computer catalog terminals with public access are located throughout both buildings.

- Terminals in the General Library provide information on the circulating collections in the General Library, BPL neighborhood branches, and the six other regional MBLN public libraries.
- Terminals in the Research library cover books in the non-circulating Research Library collections at the Boston Public Library.

Both catalogs may be accessed via direct dial-up on the Internet. Terminal specifications are: VT100 emulation, 1 stop-bit, no parity, baud rates 300-9600 bps.

> For direct dial-up:
> MBLN circulating collections   (617) 859-7506   login: library
> BPL Research Library collections   (617) 536-2545   login: bpl
>
> Internet addresses:
> MBLN circulating collections   telnet://mbln.bpl.org login: library
> BPL Research Library collections   telnet://bpl.org   login: bpl

Reference assistance in general may be found by contacting (617) 536-5400, x256.

Fees/Copies:

Access to all materials is free and open to the public. BPL library cards can be issued to all residents and students in the Commonwealth of Massachusetts. Guest cards, valid for one month, are available for out-of-state visitors.

The Boston Public Library is a member of the Metro-Boston Library Network (MBLN). Other members of this network include the public libraries of Brookline, Cambridge, Chelsea, Lexington, Malden and Newton. A card obtained at any one of these libraries may be used at the Boston Public Library for borrowing books from the circulating collections in the General Library and using the reference-only materials in the Research Library.

There are about 15 coin-operated photocopy machines dispersed throughout the building. Photocopies are 10¢ each. The Microtext Department has 20 microfilm readers, 4 microfiche readers, and 3 microform printers. Microform copies cost 25¢ to 75¢, depending upon size (8½" x 11" up to 11" x 17"). Duplicate microfiche can be made at 50¢ each.

Arrangements can be made for the staff to photocopy items, only if specific citations are given (author, title, specific page numbers). Requests may be made in writing or in person (no telephone requests). Minimum charge $3.00.

Restrictions on Use:

No materials in the Research Library circulate.

Items from the BPL may be borrowed via inter-library loan (within Massachusetts only), for all items except those in the reference collection ("REF" in the call number). These items must be used within the borrowing library (no home use).

Note that while microfiche duplicates can be made from many titles found in the Microtext Department, the duplication of any Massachusetts vital records on microfiche produced by Archive Publishing (formerly the Holbrook Research Institute, see page 64) is prohibited by that micropublisher.

The library staff will not undertake any genealogical research. However, they will answer short bibliographic queries by telephone or by mail; there is no charge.

BOSTONIAN SOCIETY - LIBRARY

Facility Director: Philip Bergen, Librarian

Address: 15 State Street, Boston
(3rd floor of the National Park Service's Visitor Center)

Mailing Address: Old State House
206 Washington Street
Boston, MA 02109-1773

Phone Number: (617) 720-1713   FAX: (617) 720-3289

Hours of Operation: Monday to Friday, 9:30am - 4:30pm
Closed weekends and all legal holidays.

Directions:

By Car: (Not advised). Public parking at Government Center Garage, and scattered lots in the financial district.

By MBTA: Green Line to Government Center; Orange or Blue Line to State Street; or Red Line to Downtown Crossing.

By foot: (Most Recommended). The BOSTONIAN SOCIETY and the National Park Service's Visitor Center are readily accessible at the confluence of Washington, State and Devonshire Streets. The Old State House is a national landmark, marked by the red-striped pavement of Boston's Freedom Trail.

Description of Institution:

The BOSTONIAN SOCIETY was founded in 1881 as a civic effort to save the 1713 Old State House from being dismantled after decades of deterioration. This unique building serves both as the Society's headquarters and a museum, where Boston's cultural history is preserved and displayed.

The Society's reference library is a key research component in its educational mission. This has been expanded to include immigrant populations and changing neighborhoods.

Description of Resources:

"The Library's resources encompass more than 6,000 volumes, over 1,000 maps and architectural plans, and a selection of rare manuscripts and broadsides dating from Colonial times. The Society's extensive collection of Boston views comprises over 10,000 photographs, prints, drawings and watercolors."

Jewish genealogists are most likely to value the local historical context which the BOSTONIAN SOCIETY provides. It has collaborated with the AMERICAN JEWISH HISTORICAL SOCIETY in such exhibitions as *On Common Ground, 1649-1980*. (See AJHS catalog, 1981 [F73.9.J5.05]).

Other useful materials include Sanborn, Hopkins and Bromley atlases and maps of Boston neighborhoods, directories dating back to 1789, voter registration lists since 1930, photographs of street scenes from mid-19th and 20th century neighborhoods, and bibliographical references.

a. <u>Atlases and Maps</u>. [See STATE LIBRARY OF MASSACHUSETTS Special Collections Department (page 182) for similar references].

    1. <u>Sanborn Insurance Atlases</u> include:

        The 1867 *Sanborn Insurance Atlas* of downtown Boston is one of three copies known to exist. It antedates the Great Fire of November 1882 which destroyed much of downtown Boston. In 1989 the BOSTONIAN SOCIETY acquired Part One, corrected to 1871.

        Other catalogued *Sanborn Insurance Atlases* include:
        Boston, Massachusetts, 1919-1931, including vol. 3, Roxbury; vol. 5, East Boston and Charlestown; vol. 6, Brighton; vol 8, Jamaica Plain, Roslindale and West Roxbury; vol. 9, Dorchester (1908, 1911); vol. 10, Germantown, Roslindale and West Roxbury; vol. 11, Hyde Park, Dorchester and West Roxbury.

    2. Atlases and maps published by <u>G. M. Hopkins</u> (Philadelphia) include:

        County of Suffolk, 1873-74.

    3. Atlases and maps published by <u>G. W. Bromley</u> (Philadelphia) include:

        City of Boston and Back Bay [also Beacon Hill, North End, South End and West End], 188?, 1890, 1898, 1908, 1922, 1928.
        Charlestown, 1892; Charlestown and East Boston, 1912.
        Dorchester, 1898, 1910.
        Hyde Park, 1912.
        Roxbury, 1890, 1906, 1915.
        West Roxbury, 1889, 1896, 1905, 1924.
        [Town of] *Brookline*, 1913, 1919.

b. Selected <u>bibliographical references</u>, catalogued under "Jews--Massachusetts--Boston". [See also BOSTON PUBLIC LIBRARY (page 56) and STATE LIBRARY OF MASSACHUSETTS (page 183) references].

Ehrenfried, Albert. *A Chronicle of Boston Jewry from the Colonial Settlement to 1900.* (Boston: privately printed, 1963). [F73.9.J5E5].

Friedman, Lee M. *Three Centuries of American Jewish History in Massachusetts.* (Boston: reported by Florence M. Gillette, 1954, typescript Nov 16, 1954). [E.184.J5.F7] [Vault].

Hentoff, Nat. *Boston Boy.* (New York: Knopf, 1986). [PS 3558.E 575.Z464].

Levine, Hillel and Lawrence Harmon. *The Death of an American Jewish Community.* (New York, Free Press, 1992). [F73.9.J5L48].

Schindler, Solomon. *Israelites in Boston.* (Boston: Berwick and Smith, 1889). [F73.9J5.S3].

Stack, John Francis. *The City as a Symbol of International Conflict: Boston's Irish, Italians and Jews, 1935-1944.* (Ann Arbor, Michigan: University Microfilms, 1977; Westport, Conn: Greenwood Press, 1979). [F73.9J7.S71, ...S7].

Wieder, Arnold A. *The Early Jewish Community of Boston's North End.* (Waltham, Mass: Brandeis University, 1962). [F73.9J5.W5].

Other volumes of more tangential Jewish genealogical interest may be found under specific Boston neighborhoods, historical and biographical works for which the collection is famous.

A core Jewish neighborhood during the late 19th and well into the 20th century was the old West End. The BOSTONIAN SOCIETY mounted an exhibition during the fall of 1992 on the entire multi-ethnic history of this enclave, as part of its restoration of the Old State House. It published a collection of essays on the subject, edited by staff members Shawn Fisher and Carolyn Hughes, *The Last Tenement: Confronting Community and Urban Renewal in Boston's West End*. (Boston: The Bostonian Society, 1992). [HT 177.B6.L37].

Two recent publications with vintage photographs of Boston, including immigrant neighborhoods, are:

Bergen, Philip. *Old Boston in Early Photographs, 1850-1918.* (New York, Dover, 1990). [F73.37 B773 1990].

Campbell, Robert and Peter Vanderwarker. *Cityscapes of Boston: An American City Through Time.* (New York: Houghton Mifflin, 1992). [NA735.37C36 1992].

Finding Aids:

The Library maintains a comprehensive card file that catalogues its bibliographic holdings by subject, author, and title, using the Library of Congress system. Additional lists exist for the maps and collection of oversized photographs.

Description of Facility:

The Library is part of an office suite on the third floor of the National Park Service's Visitor Center. Access is usually via elevator, though there is also a staircase. Public entry to the Library is through a secured door, and visitors are supposed to identify themselves and advise the staff of their general purpose and needs. Reference staff is located near this entrance.

Visiting researchers may work at one of six places around a table off the entryway. At the discretion of the staff, researchers may be permitted access to the atlases and photographs, and to directories and registries in the stacks. Microfilms and microfiche are not prevalent, except for 100 volumes of scrapbooks which depict newspaper clippings of historical and biographical (obituary) interest.

Fees/Copies:

Photocopying charge is 25¢ per exposure, with a $1 minimum charge. Permission is influenced by fragility of the materials and copyright limitations.

Photographic reprints of images in the collection are available at the rate of 8"x10" glossy for $25 (where negative exists, and $45 (where negative is lacking). Color transparencies of art works may be borrowed for $50 loan fee per item. Duplicates of slides may be made for $1.50 per slide.

There is no charge for the general visitor or telephone service. Research fees for staff reference work of more than 30 minutes, at the discretion of the Librarian, at a rate of $30 per hour.

Restrictions on Use:

Materials may not leave the facility; access to stacks is by permission only.

BRANDEIS UNIVERSITY LIBRARIES

Facility Director: Dr. Charles Cutter, Head of Judaica and Special Collections

Address: 415 South Street
P.O. Box 9110
Waltham, MA 02254-9110

Phone Numbers: (617) 736-4621   (Information Recording)
(617) 736-4670   (Reference/Information)
(617) 736-4625   (Circulation)

Hours of Operation:

When the University is in Session:

	Mon-Thur	Fri	Sat	Sun
• Goldfarb/Farber	8:30-midn	8:30am-8pm	10am-8pm	noon-midn
• Reference Services	9am-10pm	9am-5pm	10am-5pm	noon-10pm
• Judaica Office	9am-5pm	9am-3pm	closed	closed

When University is not in session:
- • Goldfarb/Farber   Mon-Fri 8:30am-5:30pm
- • Reference Services   Mon-Fri 9:00am-5:00pm

Call Judaica (x4685), Creative Arts (x4681) and Information (x4621) to confirm Library hours.

Directions:

By Car: **On Route 20 going west:** From Watertown Square, go past Moody Street where signs point to Waltham center to the left. Continue on Rte. 20 (Main St.) to the intersection of Rte. 20 and Rte. 117, which is .65 miles past Moody Street and there is a Shell station in the middle of a fork. Take the left fork (still Rte. 20) and immediately thereafter turn a sharp left onto South Street. Continue on South Street to the Brandeis Main entrance (0.8 miles) on your right, described below.

On Route 20 going east: From Route 128 (I-95) take Exit 26, Route 20 East towards Waltham. At the 3rd set of lights (1 mile, shortly after the intersection with Rt. 117) turn right onto South Street. Go 0.8 miles to the main entrance of the Brandeis University campus, just after the pedestrian overpass. Turn right off of South Street and make a hard right at the fork.

From the Route 30 Exit of Route I-95 (128): If you exited Rte. I-95 going south (Exit 25), at the stop light at the top of the exit ramp, take go straight across Rte. 30 onto River Road (not well marked). If you exited Rte. I-95 going north (Exit 24), at the top of the ramp turn left, towards Newton/Wayland, crossing over Rte. 95 and turn right at the stoplight onto River Road. On River Road (which changes its name to South Street after crossing the bridge over Rte. I-95), go to the Brandeis Main entrance (1.6 miles) on your left, described below.

At the main entrance of the Brandeis campus, there is a short semi-circular drive with an information booth at the head at which you can obtain a permit for parking your car (free) and directions to the proper parking space and from thence to the Library. There are several libraries on campus, so ask for the Goldfarb Library or the Main Library. If an officer is not at the booth, turn right and go up the hill, past the Castle, past the student center, past a small parking lot on your left in which there is a small, cylindrical, brick structure. A short distance past the little parking lot is a large parking lot, E, on your right. Park there and walk back down the road into the little parking lot with the cylindrical brick structure to a stairway in its downhill corner. At the bottom of the stairs, the library will be on your right. Walk past it, up a flight of stairs and turn right for the main entrance to Goldfarb Library on your right.

By MBTA: On the "T", you may take the Green Line (Riverside "D" train) to the Riverside station. A cab from there is about $7.50. Trains run every 10-15 minutes. The train runs through Boston, Brookline and Newton, terminating at Riverside.

By Commuter Rail:
The Acton Line of the MBTA Commuter Rail line originates at North Station in Boston and stops at Porter Square, Belmont Center, Waverly, Waltham, **Brandeis-Roberts**, Kendal Green, Hastings, Silver Hill, Lincoln, Concord, W. Concord, and points west. Service starts early in the morning and continues until midnight. Trains leave about every 1 to 2 hours. Call (617) 222-3200 for information. There is also a bus that runs between Brandeis-Roberts. The walk between the station and the library is over a half mile and up hill on campus.

Description of Institution:

The University was founded in 1948. Its Library contains 120,000 volumes of Judaica. It is a library, not an archive, and therefore contains only published materials.

Description of Resources:

The strength of the Brandeis Library is in its holdings of books and periodicals, pertaining to Jews, in all languages, including a very strong holding of 19th century and earlier material.

- Rabbinic works, if you have a Rabbi in your ancestry
- Periodicals, if you want to look up lists or events in your ancestors' life
- Gravestone listings for cemeteries that may no longer be extant
- History of Jews in many places, from great countries to small towns
- Works specifically for Jewish genealogists
- Jewish encyclopedias

The collection is too varied and vast to include all items of each type, so the following are suggestive examples in each category. However, an attempt has been made to list almost all Jewish periodicals of the 19th century and earlier, in Appendix B (page 226). Similarly, the bibliography of Yizkor Books in Appendix A (pages 193-225), lists almost every Yizkor Book in the collection.

1.   Jewish Genealogy - General Reference

Kurzweil, Arthur. *From Generation to Generation: How to Trace your Jewish Genealogy and Family History.* New York, c1980, 1994. [CS21 .K87 1994] -- Judaica Ref

Rottenberg, Dan. *Finding Our Fathers: A Guidebook to Jewish Genealogy.* New York 1977, 1986. [CS21 .R58 1986] -- Judaica Ref

The Encyclopedia of Jewish Genealogy. Kurzweil & Weiner, eds. Northvale, NJ, c1991. [CS21 .E53 1991] -- Judaica

Kranzler, David. *My Jewish Roots: A Step-by-step Guide to Tracing and Recording your Genealogy.* New York, [1979]. [+CS21 .K69] -- Judaica Ref

Jewish Genealogy Society of Greater Washington. *Jewish Genealogy Beginner's Guide.* Edited by Irene Saunders Goldstein. Washington DC, c1991. [Z6374 .B5 J4 1991] -- Judaica

Sack, Sallyann Amdur. *A Guide to Jewish Genealogical Research in Israel.* Revised edition. Baltimore, Genealogical Publishing Co., 1995 [Jud ref Z6374 .B5 S23]

Guzik, Estelle M. *Genealogical Resources in the New York Metropolitan Area.* New York, Jewish Genealogical Society, 1989. [Jud ref Z5313 .U6 N523]

2. Jewish Genealogical Periodicals

Avotaynu: The International Review of Jewish Genealogy. Teaneck, NJ 1985- . Quarterly. {English}
  [+CS3010 .A96] -- Judaica

Archiv fur jüdische Familienforschung. Vienna, Austria 1912-[1914]. [CS3010 .A7]

Jüdische Familien-Forschung. Berlin, 1924-1938. 14 volumes (50 issues). [DS135.G3 A253] -- Stacks

Toledot. Flushing, N.Y. 1977-1982. Quarterly. {English} [CS3010 .T6] -- Judaica

Mass-pocha: Newsletter of the Jewish Genealogical Society of Greater Boston. Boston 1992- . Quarterly.
  [+CD59 .M3] -- Judaica

3. Individual Families

Baer, Berthold. *Stammtafeln der Familie Speyer* (Speyer Family Tree). {German} Kumpf & Reis, 1896
  [+CS3018 .S6]

Dicker, Herman. *A Jewish family trail: the Dickers and their mates.* Express Print. Co., 1977.
  [CS432 .J4 D53]

Doroshkin, Yitzchak Yankl. *Roots of the Granadier (Grand) family: from Zhitkovitch (a shtetl in White Russia)
  to America.* J. I. Doroshkin, 1977. [+CS432 .J4 D6]

Gottheil, Richard James Horation. *The Belmont-Belmonte family, a record of four hundred years, put together
  from the original documents in the archives and libraries of ...* Priv. print., 1917. [+CS409 .B4 1917]

4. Rabbinic Genealogy

There are extensive holdings for rabbinic genealogy. Try doing a subject search,
s=Rabbis, in LOUIS. Note the reference by L. Lowenstein below, a rare and little known
holding.

Halperin, Raphael. *Atlas ets-hayim.* 1978- . 20 volumes. [BM750 .H35] -- Judaica

Rosenstein, Neil. *The Unbroken Chain: biographical sketches and the genealogy of illustrious Jewish families
  from the 15th-20th century.* 2 volumes. New York, 1990. [CS432 .J4 R67 1990] -- Judaica Ref

Sackheim, George I. *Scattered seeds: the descendents of Rabbi Israel, one of the martyrs of Rozanoi, ...*
  Skokie, Illinois c1986. [+CS39 .S27 1986] -- Stacks.

Friedman, Nathan Zevi. *Otsar ha-Rabbanim Agodoth.* {Hebrew} Greenberg, Tel Aviv, 1975.
  [JudRef +BM7 50.F3.1975] {20,000 rabbis, 970 to 1970}.

Eisenstadt, Israel Tobiah. *Da'at Kedoshim - Zichronoth l'Toldoth ha Mishpochoth Eisenstadt, Bachrach,
  Ginzburg,...* {Hebrew} St. Petersburg, 1898. [DS115.E37]

Lowenstein, Leopold. *Mafteah ha-haskamoth Index Approbationum* [Index to Rabbinic Approbations].
  {Hebrew script} Frankfort am Main, 1923. [Z7070 L6]

Chaim ben Joseph Michal. *Or ha Chaim - Jewish Scholars and Their Books.* {Hebrew} Frankfort am Main,
  1891. [Z7070 M48]

Schwartz, Pinchas Zelig ha Cohen. *Shem ha Gedolim li-gedole Hungaryah.* {Hebrew} Paks, Hungary, 1913.
  438 pp. [Z7070 S4 1913a Judaica reference] {Hungarian rabbis and their works}.

Greenwald, Leopold (Jekutiel Jehudah). *Lifnei Shtei Meot Shanah, Toledot haRav Eleazar Kalir v'Zman.*
  {Hebrew} Hadar Linotyping and Publishing, NY, 1952. [BM755.K34.G7]

Perles, Moses Meir. *Megillat Yuhasin.* [Descendants of Maharshal] {Hebrew} Warsaw, 1739, 1864, 1911.
  [BM750 P37 1864.]

Abramowitz, Mayer Simcha. *Chachmei Yisroel of New England: pictorial history of the New England
  Orthodox rabbinate.* Worcester, Mass.: Nathan Stolnitz Archives, c1991. 114 pp. [BM750 .A29 1991]

5.   18th and 19th Century Jewish History

Gelber, Natan Michael. *Aus Zwei Jahrhunderten - Beitrage zur Neueren Geschichte der Juden.* {German} Vienna and Leipzig, 1924. [DS125.G4]

Graetz, Heinrich Hertz. *History of the Jews.* Philadephia, Jewish Publication Society of America, 1898. [DS118 .G73]

Hirszhorn, S. *Di geshikhter fun yidn in Polyn fun fir yorikn soym bis der Velt Milkhome, 1788-1914* [History of Jews in Poland from the Four-Year Sejm to WWI, 1788-1914]. {Yiddish} Warsaw, 1923. [DS135.P6.H5]

Stein, A. *Die Geschichte der Juden in Boehmen.* {German} Brno, 1904. [DS135 C95 S7]

Balaban, Maier. *Dzieje Zydow w Galicyi.* {Polish} Lwow, 1914. [DS 135 .P6 B245]

Brawer, Abraham Jacob. *Studies in Galician Jewry.* {Hebrew} Jerusalem, 1956. [DS135 P62 G3215]

Dubnow, Simeon. *Pinkas ha Medinah.* [Records of the Councils of Lithuania from 5383 to 5521 (1623 to 1761)]. {Hebrew} Berlin, 1925. [DS 135 L5 C62 1925a]

Weinryb, Bernard Dov. *The Jews of Poland, A Social and Economic History of the Jewish Community in Poland from 1100-1800.* Philadelphia, 1972. [Main Reserve DS135 .P6 W38]

Greenwald, Leopold (Jekutiel Jehudah). *Leflagoth Yisrael b'Ungaria.* [Jewish Community in Hungary]. {Hebrew}. Dewa, Rumania, 1929.

Rosenberg, Leo. *Die juden in litauen; Geschichte, Bevolkerung und Wirtschaft, politische Forderung.* {Yiddish} Berlin, 1918. [DS 135.L5 R6]

Moses, L. *Inschriften und Urkunden aus den Siebengemeinden.* [Inscriptions and Documents from Burgenland]. {German} [DS 101.J8]

6.   Town, City and Area Histories

A few representative books are listed here, and a more complete mention of towns with cataloged books are listed following.   These studies include references to prominent members of the communities, and sometimes family histories.   Check the card catalogs under "Jews--[Country]--[City]".

a.   Selected books with historical focus on particular towns or regions:

Dicker, Herman. *Piety and Perseverance: Jews from the Carpathian Mountains.* Sepher-Hermon Press, c1981. [DS135 .R93 Z273]

Greenwald, Leopold. *Korot ir Presburg u-gedoleha* (Bratislava) {Hebrew} 1911. [Main Microforms BM40.H28 HI0099]

Greenwald, Leopold (Jekutiel Jehudah). *Matsevet Kodesh* (Sighet, Romania and Mattersburg, Austria). {Hebrew} Hadar Linotyping and Publishing Co, New York, 1952. [DS135.R72 S5]

Pollak, Max. *Die Juden in Wiener-Neustadt.* {German} Jüdischer Verlag, Vienna. [DS135 .A92 V556]

Kaminsky, Gladys. *History of the Jewish Community of Columbus, Indiana.* Indiana, 1978. [F534 .C7 K3]

Feinstein, A.L. *Ir Tehillah* [History of Brest-Litovsk]. {Hebrew} Warsaw, 1885. [DS135 .R93 B7]

Wachstein, Bernhard. *Urkunden und Akten zur Geschichte der Juden in Eisenstadt und den Siebengemeinden.* [Documents and Records for the History of the Jews in Eisenstadt and Burgenland] {German and Hebrew} Vienna and Leipzig, 1926. [DS 135 .A9 W315]

Steinschneider, Hillel Noah Maggid. *Ir Vilna.* {Hebrew} Vilna, 1900. [DS135 R93 V56]

Avron, Dov. *Pinkas ha-Kesherim shel Kehilat Pozna (1621-1835).* {Hebrew} Jerusalem, 1966/67. [DS135 P62 P65]

Volbrinski, David ben Moses Tsevi Hirsh. *Le-Korot ir Navahrdok u-rabaneha: pelekh Minsk be-medinat Lita me-reshit zeman yediat hofeta ve-ad ata.* Tel-Aviv, 1968/69. [BM750 .V64 1968] -- Stacks

b. Towns with catalogued books providing historical material:

Belarus: Antopol, Baranavichy, Belitsa (Grodno), Bereza, Biaroza, Brest, Delyatichi, Derevna, Devenishki, Dolginovo (Minsk), Druia, Dzerzhinsk, Eremichi (Grodno), Grodno, Ilia, Indura, Ivenets, Kamin (Ivenets), Karlin, Kobrin, Kobylnik, Kozhan Gorodok, Kurenets, Lida, Lipnishki, Luninets, Lyakhovichi, Lyubcha (Grodno), Minsk, Mir, Mogilev, Molchad, Mosty, Nesvizh, Nevel (Vitebsk), Novogrudok, Oshmiana, Peski (Grodno), Pinsk, Pruzhany, Rubezhevichi, Shklou, Slonim, Slutsk, Smorgon, Sopotskin, Stolin, Svir, Svisloch (Grodno), Turets (Grodno), Vileika (Minsk), Vitebsk, Volkovysk, Zel'va.

Germany: Aachen, Ahlem, Alsenz, Altdorf (Baden), Altona, Alzey, Ansbach, Augsburg, Aurich, Ausse, Bad Mergentheim, Bad Nauheim, Bad Segeberg, Baden, Baden-Baden, Baden-Wurttemberg, Bamberg, Barmen (Wuppertal), Bavaria, Bayreuth, Beckum, Bendorf, Berlichingen, Berlin, Bielefeld, Bingen, Bodensee-Oberschwaben region, Bonn, Borken (Kreis), Bovenden, Brandenburg (Electorate), Braunschweig, Bremen, Bremerhaven Region, Brunswick, Buhl, Celle, Cologne, Cuxhaven, Dachau, Darmstadt, Delmenhorst, Detmold, Dorsten, Dortmund, Dresden, Duisburg, Dusseldorf, Leipzig, Eifel, Eitorf, Emden, Emmerich, Endingen, Erfurt, Eschwege, Essen, Esslingen am Neckar, Feldafing, Floss, Franconia, Frankfurt am Main, Freiburg im Breisgau, Friedrichstadt, Fulda, Gailingen, Gedern, Geldern, Giessen, Goppingen, Goslar, Gottingen, Grafschaft Bentheim (Landkreis), Grosskrotzenburg, Gutersloh, Guttstadt, Hagene, Hagen (Arnsberg), Halberstadt, Halle, Halle an der Saale, Haltern, Hamburg, Hamm, Hanau, Hannover, Hansa towns, Harburg, (Schwaben), Heidelberg, Heilbronn (Landkreis), Heldenbergen (Nidderau), Helmstedt, Hennef-Sieg, Hesse, Hessen, Hildesheim, Hochberg, Hochst am Main, Hof, Hohenlimburg, Hohenlohe, Hohenzollern, Illingen (Saarland), Iserlohn, Jebenhausen, Julich, Karl-Marx-Stadt, Karlsruhe, Kassel, Kitzingen, Koblenz, Konigsberg, Konigstein im Taunus, Konigswinter, Konstanz, Krefeld, Kurmainz, Ladenburg, Lahr (Ortenaukreis), Landau in der Pfalz, Langenbrucken, Leipzig, Lemgo, Linnich, Lippe, Lissa, Lower Saxony, Lubbecke, Lubeck, Magdeburg, Mainz (Rhineland-Palatinate), Malsch, Mannheim, Marburg, Marktbreit, Marktheidenfeld, Mecklenburg, Mecklenburg-Strelitz, Memmingen, Meppen, Merzig, Michelstadt, Mingolsheim, Moers, Moisling, Munden, Munich, Munster, Munster in Westfalen, Neuweid, Nidderau, Niederstetten, Niederwerrn, Nienburg, Nordhorn, North Rhine-Westphalia, Nuremberg, Oberfranken, Offenbach am Main, Oldenburg, Ostfriesland, Ottensoos, Paderborn, Palatinate, Pirmasens, Posen (Province), Potsdam, Prussia, Recklinghausen, Regensburg, Rhein-Sieg-Kreis, Rheingau-Taunus-Kreis, Rheinhessen, Rhine Province, Rhineland, Rhineland-Palatinate, Ritzebuttel (Hamburg), Rothenburg ob der Tauber, Ruppichteroth, Russelsheim, Saarland, Saarlouis (Landkreis), Saxony, Schaumburg-Lippe, Schleswig-Holstein, Schnaittach, Schoningen, Schwabisch Hall (Landkreis), Schwetzingen, Seesen (Lower Saxony), Sieg, Siegen, Siegen-Wittgenstein (Kreis), Singen, Soest, Spenge, Speyer, Stade, Steiermark, Steinheim, Stommeln, Strassburg, Stuttgart, Suhl, Sulzburg, Swabia, Telgte, Thuringia, Tiengen, Treptow (Berlin), Trier, Tubingen, Ulm, Unna, Unterfranken, Viersen, Waldeck-Frankenburg, Wandsbek, Warburg, Weinheim an der Bergstrasse, Weissensee (Berlin), Werl, Westphalia, Wiesbaden, Witten, Worms, Wuppertal, Wurttemberg, Wurzburg, Zirndorf (Furth), Zwickau.

Lithuania: Dusetos, Gargzdai, Jonova, Kaunas, Kedainiai, Kelme, Marijampole, Merkine, Siauliai, Svencionys, Telsiai, Utena, Valkininkas, Vilnius.

Moldova: Beltsy, Bendery, Bricheva, Iasi = Jassy, Kapreshty, Kishinev = Chisinau, Lipkany, Ungeny.

Poland: Amszynow, Bardo, Belchatów, Biala Podlaska, Biala Rawska, Bialobrzegi (Radom), Białystok, Biecz, Bielsk Podlaski, Bobrka, Bodzentyn, Bransk, Brzeziny, Chełm, Chmielnik, Chrzanow, Ciechanowiec, Cieszanow, Czerwony Bor (Łomża), Częstochowa, Czyzew, Dabrowa, Debica, Deblin, Dynów, Dzialoszyce, Falenica, Garwolin, Gdansk, Gniewoszow, Goniądz, Gostynin, Grajewo, Grojec (Warsaw), Hrubieszow, Jaroslaw, Jedwabne, Kaluszyn, Karczew, Kazimierz, Kielce, Kock, Kolbuszowa, Kolno, Konin, Koprzywnica, Krakow, Krasnik, Krynica-Wies, Krzemieniec, Kurow (Lublin), Lancut, Lask, Lodz, Łomża, Łosice, Lowicz, Lubartow, Lublin, Lukow (Siedlce), Miechow (Krakow), Miedzyrzec, Miedzyrzec Podlaski, Miedzyrzecz, Mikhov, Mikulince, Mława, Mogielnica, Nieswiez, Nowy Sacz, Nowy Targ (Nowy Sacz), Opoczno, Ostrołęka, Ostrów Lubelski, Ostrowiec Swietokrzy, Oswiecim, Otwock, Pabianice, Parysow, Piotrków Trybunalski, Płock, Płonsk, Przasnysz, Przedecz, Przemysl, Przytyk, Pulawy, Pultusk, Raciąz, Radom, Radomysl Wielki, Radzymin, Radzyn Podlaski, Rozan, Ryki (Warsaw), Rypin, Sandomierz, Siedlce, Sierpc, Skierniewice, Sokolow, Sokolow Podlaski, Sokoly, Sosnowiec, Stanislawow, Starachowice, Staszow (Tarnobrzeg), Stawiski, Stok, Suprasl, Suwałki, Swietokrzyski, Szczebrzeszyn, Tarnow, Tluszcz, Tomaszow Lubelski, Tyszowce, Warsaw, Węgrów, Wierzbnik, Wiskitki, Wislica, Wislowiec, Wloclawek, Wlodawa, Wolomin, Wysokie Mazowieckie, Wyszkow, Wyszogrod, Zabludow, Zaklikow, Zamość, Zarki, Zawiercie, Zelechow, Zgierz, Zloczew, Zwolen (Radom), Zychlin, Zyrardow.

Romania: Bacau, Bistrista (Bistrista-Ncascaud), Bivolari, Brichany, Bucharest, Cluj, Darabani, Dej, Dumbraveni, Edinita, Gherla, Halmeu, Hirlau, Huedin, Iclod, Maramures, Marculesti, Oradea, Piatra Neamt, Radauti, Ruscova, Salaj, Sighet, Sighetu-Marmatiei, Stefanesti, Tasnad, Tirgu-Mures, Transnistriyah, Transylvania, Turt.

Ukraine: Aleksandriya (Rovno), Babiy Yar, Berdichev, Beregovo, Berezhany, Bershad, Borislav, Borshchev, Brody, Buchach, Budanov, Chernovtsy, Dnepropetrovsk, Dobromil, Donetsk, Drogobych, Dubno, Dubovo, Gliniany, Goloskov (Ivano-Frankovsk), Gorokhov, Goshcha, Gusiatin, Ignatovka (Volynsk), Kalush, Kamenets-Podolskiy, Kamin-Kashyrskyi, Kharkiv, Khmelnitskii, Khorostkov, Khotin, Khust, Kiev, Klesov, Kolomyia, Komarno, Kosov, Kostopol, Krasnostav (Khmelnits), Krymskaia oblast, Kuty (Ivano-Frankovsk), Lanovtsy, Lopatin, Lutsk, Lviv = Lvov, Lyuboml, Matzeev, Mlyniv, Mukachevo, Muravitsa, Nadvornaya, Novoselitsa (Chernova), Novoukrainka, Odessa, Olyka, Ostrog, Podgaitsy, Podgorodtsy, Poznan, Radekhov, Radziwillow, Ratno, Respublika Krym = Crimea, Rogatin, Rovno, Rozhishche, Rudki (Lvov), Sarny, Sasov, Sekiryany, Shargorod, Shpola, Shumskoye, Skala-Podilska, Skalat, Skole, Slavuta, Slovechno, Sofyovka (Volynsk), Sokal, Sokyriany, Sosnovoye, Stawiszcze, Strusov, Stryj, Svalyava, Terebovlia, Ternopil, Torgovitsa, Tuchyn, Turiysk, Turka, Tutchin, Ugnev, Ustilug, Uzhhorod, Vakhnovka, Vinogradov, Vishnevets, Vladimir-Volynskii, Vladimirets, Volhynia Region, Vystosk, Yampol (Khmelnits), Yanov, Yavorov, Zabolotov, Zakarpatska Region, Zborov, Zholkva, Zinkov, Zolkiew, Zolochev (Lvov).

7. Jewish Onomastics (Names)

Beider, Alexander. *A Dictionary of Jewish Surnames from the Russian Empire*. Avotaynu, NJ, c1993. [Jud Ref CS3010 .B43 1993]

Kaganoff, Benzion C. *A Dictionary of Jewish Names and Their History*. Schocken, New York, 1977. [CS3010 .K28]

Singerman, Robert. *Jewish and Hebrew Onomastics: a Bibliography*. Garland, NY 1977. [Jud Ref Z6824 .S5]

Numerous publications are under "Names, Personal -- Jewish" and "Names, Personal -- Hebrew", specific to certain places: Prague, France, Germany, Greece, Hungary, Israel, Rome, Sicily, etc.

8. Jewish gravestones

There are many collections of gravestone inscriptions, especially for Germany, of which these represent just a few:

Wachstein, Dr. Bernhard. *Die Grabschriften des Alten Judenfriedhofes Eisenstadt*. {German and Hebrew} Vienna, 1922. [DS135.A9.W25]

Frankl, Ludwig August. *Inschriften des Alten Judischen Friedhofes in Wien*. {German and Hebrew} Vienna, 1855. [DS135 A92 V53]

Gelber, Nathan Michael. *Aus dem Pinax des alten Judenfriedhofes in Brody (1699-1831)*. Jahrbuch der Juedisch-Literarischen Gesellschaft v 13 pp 119-141. Frankfort am Main, 1920. {German} [DS101.J8]

Scheiber, Alexsander. *Jewish Inscriptions in Hungary, from the 3rd century to 1686*. Budapest: Akademiai Kiado; Leiden: Brill, 1983. 433 pp. [DS135 .H9 S29 1983] {Revised English version of: *Magyarorszagi zsido feliratok a III. szazadtol 1686*, 1960}.

Firkowitsch, Abraham. *Sefer Avne zikaron: ha-me'asef reshimot ha-matsevot al kivre bene Yisrael be-hatsi ha-i Krim*. Vilna, 1872. 256 pp. [PN6297.H4 F5] {Crimea, Ukraine}

9. Bibliographic Works

Zubatsky, David S. *Jewish genealogy: a sourcebook of family histories and genealogies*. Garland Pub., 1984. [CS31 .Z8 Stacks & Jud Ref] {A guide to published and manuscript genealogies, by surname}.

Hundert, Gershon David. *The Jews in Poland and Russia: bibliographical essays*. Indiana University Press, c1984. [Z6373 .P7 H86 1984 -- Stacks & Judaica]

Roest, Maijer Marcus. *Catalog der Hebraica und Judaica aus der L. Rosenthalschen Bibliotek.* {German} 1855, Republ. by N.V. Boekhandel & Antiquariaat, Amsterdam 1966.

Roest, Maijer Marcus. *Catalog der reichhaltigen Sammlungen hebraischer und jüdischer Bucher, Handschriften, Kupferstiche, Portraits etc : nachgelassen von Giuseppe Almanzi in Padua ...* Hildesheim; New York: G. Olms, 1990. [Z6375 .R63]

Kagan, Berl. *Sefer haPrenumerantn, Hebrew Subscription Lists.* {Hebrew & English} New York, 1975. [Jud Ref +BM496.8 K33]

Jewish Newspapers and Periodicals on Microfilm. Cincinnati, American Jewish Archives, 1957. [Jud. Ref. A6944 .J4 .H4].

Zafren, Herbert C., ed. *Jewish Newspapers and Periodicals on Microfilm Available at the American Jewish Periodical Center.* Cincinnati, 1984. [Z6944 .J4 H4 1984]

The Jewish Chronicle Index. London, England. Covers 1841-1881. [AP92 .J3 -- Microforms].

Fuerst, Dr. Julius. *Bibliotheca Judaica.* {German}. Leipzig, W. Engelman, 1863. [Jud ref Z7070 .F95]

Jashunskii, I. V. *Evreiskaia periodicheskaia pechat' v 1917 i 1918 gg.* (Jewish press, 1917-1918) {Russian} Aticot, 1970. [Z6367 .I37 1970]

Braham, Randolph L. *The Hungarian Jewish catastrophe: a selected and annotated bibliography.* CCNY, NY 1984. [Jud Ref DS135 .H9 B72 1984]

Roth, Cecil. *Magna Bibliotheca Anglo-Judaica: A Bibliographical Guide to Anglo-Jewish History.* London, The Jewish Historical Society of England, 1937. 464 pp. [Z6373 .G7 R4]

Lehmann, Ruth P. *Anglo-Jewish bibliography, 1937-1970.* London: Jewish Historical Society of England, 1992. 377 pp. [Z6373 .G7 L39 1992]

10. Jewish Encyclopedias

Encyclopaedia Judaica. 16 volumes+yearbooks. Jerusalem, Encyclopaedia Judaica, 1972. [DS102.8 .E495 -- Judaica Ref]

The Universal Jewish Encyclopedia: an authoritative and popular presentation of Jews and Judaism since the earliest times. 10 volumes. New York, c1948. [+DS102.8 .U5 1948 -- Judaica Ref]

Otsar Yisrael. {An encyclopedia of all matters concerning Jews and Judaism, in Hebrew} 10 volumes. Originally published in New York, 1907-1913; Reprint: Jerusalem, 1970. [JudRef DS102.8 .O9 1907a]

Evreiskaia entsiklopediia. {Pre-revolution Jewish encyclopedia, in Russian} 16 volumes. St. Petersburg, 1906-13. [Jud Ref DS102.8 .E7]

11. Databases

The library holds a number of databases on CD-ROM. The Judaica office holds: *Index to Hebrew Periodicals*, which indexes 270 Hebrew-language journals, 1977-date. The *Tel-Hai Index to Hebrew Newspapers* indexes seven Israeli newspapers, 1985-date. These indexes are concerned primarily with social, economic and political topics. *Takdin* provides full-text retrieval of decisions of Israeli courts, and indexes Israeli legal journals. Judaica also has several Talmudic databases. At Goldfarb Reference, the *Nexis* database allows full-text access to *The Jerusalem Post*, 1989-date, as well as many other current periodicals. Ask at the Reference Desk for access.

12. Periodicals

The library has hundreds of Jewish periodicals, dating from the 17th century to the present day, on both microfilm and original form. Appendix B (page 226) lists all 19th-century and earlier Jewish periodicals in the Brandeis Library collection. 20th-century periodicals at Brandeis are far too numerous to list here. See "Finding Aids" below.

13. Holocaust Resources

The library has many works listing Holocaust victims and survivors, including:

National Registry of Jewish Holocaust Survivors. Washington, D.C.: American Gathering of Jewish Holocaust Survivors, c1993. [D804.3 .N37 1993]

Other standard works such as *Gedenkbuch, Memorial to the Jews Deported from France*, etc.

Guide to Unpublished Materials of the Holocaust Period. Edited by Jacob Robinson and Yehuda Bauer. Jerusalem, Hebrew University, Institute of Contemporary Jewry, 1970- . 6 volumes. [Ref Z6372 .R58] {Inventory of archival material at Yad Vashem}.

For a complete bibliography of Yizkor books at Brandeis, see Appendix A (pages 193-225).

14. Other works of interest

Mokotoff, Gary and Sack, Sallyann Amdur. *Where Once We Walked: A Guide to the Jewish Communities Destroyed in the Holocaust.* Avotaynu, NJ c1991. [Jud ref DS135 .E83 M65]

Mokotoff, Gary and Sack, Sallyann Amdur. *WOWW Companion: A Guide to the Communities Surrounding Central and Eastern European Towns.* Avotaynu, NJ c1995. [Jud Ref DS135.E83 M652]

Sack, Sallyann Amdur. *The Russian Consular Records Index and Catalog.* Garland, NY 1987. [Jud ref CS856 .J4 S23 1987]

Piechotka, Maria and Kazimierz. *Wooden Synagogues.* Warsaw, Arkady, 1959. [NA4690 .P49 -- Stacks]

Grimsted, Patricia Kennedy. *Archives and Manuscript Repositories in the USSR: Moscow and Leningrad.* Princeton Univ. Press, 1972. [CD1711 .G7]

Grimsted, Patricia Kennedy. *Archives and Manuscript Repositories in the USSR: Moscow and Leningrad, Supplement 1: Bibliographic Addenda.* 1976, Zug, Switzerland. [CD1711 .G7 Suppl]

Grimsted, Patricia Kennedy. *Archives in Russia 1993: a brief directory.* International Research & Exchanges Board, c1993. [CD1711 .A75 1993 -- Main Reference]

Stern, Malcolm H. *First American Jewish Families: 600 Genealogies, 1654-1988.* Ottenheimer Publishers, c1991. [Special Collections +CS59 .S76 1991]

Tidhar, David. *Entsiklopedyah le-halutse ha-yishuv u-vonav.* 19 volumes. Tel-Aviv, 1947-1971. [DS102.8 .T5] {Encyclopedia of early Jewish settlers in Palestine}.

Spanish and Portuguese Jews' Congregation (London, England). *Bevis Marks records.* Published by the Board of Elders of the Congregation. Oxford University Press, 1940-1973. 4 volumes. {Volume II: Abstracts of Ketubot of the Congregation from earliest times until 1837. Volume III: ...for the period 1837-1901. Volume IV: The circumcision register of Isaac and Abraham de Paiba. Volume V: Birth register (1767-1881) of the Spanish & Potugese Jews' congregation, London}. [DS135 .E5 L6 +]

Biuletyn Zydowskiego Instytutu Historycznego. [Bulletin of the Jewish Historic Institute]. Quarterly. Warsaw, 1951-date. [DS135 .P6 Z9] {Scholarly articles on Polish-Jewish communities, in Polish}.

Swierenga, Robert P. *The Forerunners: Dutch Jewry in the North American Diaspora.* Detroit, c1994. 465 pp. [E184.J5 S9 1994]

Wininger, Salomon. *Grosse judische National-Biographie: mit mehr als 8000 Lebensbeschreibungen namhafter judischer Manner und Frauen aller Zeiten und Lander.* Cernauti, [1925-1936]. 7 volumes. [DS115 .W5] also on 83 microfiche [DS115 .W5 1925a]

Finding Aids:

Catalogs - General

Upon entrance to the Goldfarb Library walk straight ahead to the small Reference desk on the right. Whoever is on duty there will be most helpful in locating and describing the holdings of interest. There are various computer terminals across from the Reference desk which allow access to the LOUIS system, described below. LOUIS is the primary finding aid. The old main card catalog is located behind the computer terminals. The present plan is eventually to remove the main card catalog in favor of LOUIS. However, there are many Hebrew-alphabet books and periodicals which are not in LOUIS but are in the paper card catalog. There are several other card catalogs which might be useful, specifically the current periodicals catalog and some Hebrew/Yiddish catalogs. They will be described below.

LOUIS System

LOUIS, the **L**ibrary **O**nline **U**ser **I**nformation **S**ystem, is an interactive computer catalog containing the Brandeis University Libraries' holdings. It is your first and easiest line of attack on resource retrieval but in some cases your attack may fail, see "Searching in LOUIS" below. You can dial LOUIS directly with a modem and computer. See the "External Access" section below for telephone number, parameters and instructions. LOUIS terminals are available at the library. LOUIS is generally available 24 hours a day even on days the library is closed.

LOUIS provides access to the preponderance of the Libraries' monographic titles and most of the periodical holdings. However, some of the non-Roman-alphabet items are quite elusive in LOUIS while others are just not there. About 20% of the old non-Roman-alphabet periodicals of interest for genealogical research are not in LOUIS. All titles are being added to LOUIS on an ongoing basis.

Searching in LOUIS

LOUIS can search for material by Title, Author, Subject, Call Number or Keyword. Instructions for each type of search are given on-line and expanded help is also available on-line. You don't have to know the entire name since LOUIS will respond with all items partaking of the sought partial name or number. This is a very powerful search facility but it has its weaknesses.

LOUIS presently has no facility for searching in the Hebrew, Cyrillic or other non-Roman alphabets. Most non-Roman holdings are cataloged therein but in romanized form. For the layman this presents a significant barrier to their retrieval because LOUIS is still quite literal in its search facilities and is not fully cross referenced. Moreover, the transliterations are not strictly of a piece. A given word may find more than one spelling and the use of non-alphabetic symbols is not completely standardized. Search by call number is also somewhat problematic since the use of spaces and periods in call numbers is not standardized.

If you cannot find a non-Roman item in LOUIS, find a similar item, find its subject formats and search under those formats for your item. As a last resort, go to the main card catalog where almost every single item is cataloged. If you are still stymied with older items in the Hebrew alphabet there are two more catalogs described below which are worth consulting. Finally, don't hesitate to ask the staff, particularly the people in the Judaica office who are very knowledgeable in transliteration difficulties and finding techniques.

Microforms

Microforms are of three classes: Classified, Newspapers not Classified, and Joint Periodical Depository Collection of the AMERICAN JEWISH HISTORICAL SOCIETY (see page 33).

Individual works on microfilm or microfiche can generally be found in LOUIS. The Libraries also own several major microform collections, such as *Early American Newspapers*, *English Literary Periodicals*, *Early American Imprints*, *American Culture Series*, and *United Nations Documents*. Some of these sets are represented by a single entry for the collection in LOUIS; inclusion of entries for the individual works is a long term goal. For the present, access to the individual works contained in some collections is provided by printed indexes and other specialized tools.

Appendix B (page 226) lists Brandeis' periodical holdings of the 19th century and earlier. Look there first for early periodicals, since it includes many that are difficult to find. Consult the Reference Department at the Main Library for more information about specific microform holdings, if you don't find them in LOUIS or the catalogs.

LOUIS External Access Instructions

LOUIS can be accessed by either Internet telnet or direct dial-up. Via Internet, the telnet address is "louis.brandeis.edu". Via direct dial-up, call (617) 736-4840 or 4855. Modem settings are up to 14,400 baud; 8 data bits, no parity, 1 stop bit. Log on as "louis".

Card Catalogs - Periodicals

There is a card catalog of periodicals near the main catalog. This does **not** cover periodicals in microform. This catalog may have a few periodicals which are not in the main card catalog. There is a periodicals section in the Hebraica catalogs described below which have some items not in this catalog. Also, see Appendix B.

Card Catalogs - Hebraica

While Hebrew/Yiddish holdings are cataloged in LOUIS, to a large extent, transliterations of titles and authors are often not obvious to the layman. The main card catalog contains most (perhaps not all) of the older titles and may be searched for various transliterations.

Further help is in the Judaica Reference Room. To get there, proceed past the Reference Desk and telephones to a stairway on the right. Climb it to the mezzanine. The Judaica Reference Room is to the right through double doors. The Judaica Office is on your left just after you enter the double doors.

There is a Hebrew/Yiddish catalog outside of the Judaica office which may have some holdings that are only in that catalog. It has a section that covers periodicals and about 25 drawers of cards arranged alphabetically by Hebrew letters. It is not kept up-to-date but, for earlier items where you know the Hebrew spelling, it may be easier to use than trying all of the possible transliterations.

There is also a catalog of periodicals and other material in the Judaica Office which contains some otherwise uncataloged material. The Staff people in the Judaica Office (x4685) are very helpful and knowledgeable. If there are any Judaica materials which you cannot find in the catalogs, do consult the Judaica office for assistance.

External Reference Assistance

Telephone reference assistance is available during most hours that the Library is open. Check with the Information Desk at each Library for more specific hours of service. Main Library: x4670. Judaica: x4685.

Email: Reference questions and other queries can also be sent via email by sending to "cutter@binah.cc.brandeis.edu".

Locating Books by Call Number

The objective of the finding aids is to yield a call number and collection in which the item can be found. Most items will be either in the stacks or the microforms collection. A few items of interest may be in Special Collections or the Cage. If the item of interest is in Microforms, there is a stairway to the left just as you enter the library. Take it down one level to the Microforms section which is well marked.

If the item is in the Cage or Special Collections, you must consult with a Staff member in the Judaica Office. The item must be used in the Office.

If the item is in the stacks, the library is large. The list following is the current list of the floors on which specific call numbers are located. However, it is not completely descriptive for the Jewish genealogist. Many of the large general Jewish references are located in the Judaica Reference Room. Many of the items which you will find of use are in the DS section of the stacks and in the nearby Judaica section on the Mezzanine. When the call number is preceded by a +, the book is not located with its brethren but is in a separate section for tall books for that call number. Here are the Library of Congress classification subject headings. There are specific instructions posted on the floors given below.

A	General Works & Encyclopedias 3	
B	Philosophy, Psychology & Religion . . . . . Mezz	
C	Archaeology, Genealogy & Biography 3	
CS	Genealogy 3	
D	History: Eastern Hemisphere 3	
DS	Israel and Jews in the Diaspora . . . . . Mezz	
E-F	History: Western Hemisphere 3	
G	Geography & Anthropology 1	
H	Social Sciences 1	
J	Political Science 1	
K	Law 1	
L	Education 2	

M	Music . . . . 3 & 4	
N	Fine Arts 4	
P	Language & Literature 2	
PJ	Oriental & Semitic Languages & Lit. . . . Mezz	
Q	Science (also in Science Library) 2	
R	Medicine (also in Science Library) 2	
S	Agriculture 2	
T	Technology 2	
TR	Photography 4	
U-V	Military & Naval Science 2	
Z	Bibliography & Library Science . . . . Mezz	

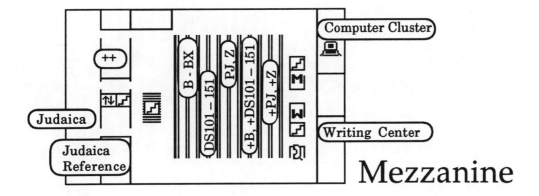

Mezzanine

Description of Facility:

The Main University Library is the Goldfarb/Farber Library for social sciences and the humanities which is the only one described here. There are also the Gerstenzang Science Library for science materials and the Intercultural Library in Intercultural Center. The maps show the main floor and mezzanine of the Main Library.

Note that there is a Copy-Card machine in back of Reserve (and some copiers too). One may buy a card for any number of copies and avoid the inconvenience of stocking up on change.

The Student Center, to the left as you leave the library, has food facilities to prevent mental deterioration during long hours of genealogical research.

Unlike many libraries, the stacks are open to the visitor. This means that you can browse in an area of interest through the stacks, often finding material you could never have found otherwise. This can make your time and effort more effective than in many of the other great Judaica libraries of the world.

There are ample tables for study everywhere but for specifically Jewish research you should choose a table on the mezzanine, either in the Judaica Reference Room or in the stacks nearby where study tables are hidden in the center of various rows in the stacks.

Fees/Copies:

Photocopy machines take either coins or plastic copycards.

Restrictions on Use:

Only Brandeis students can borrow materials.

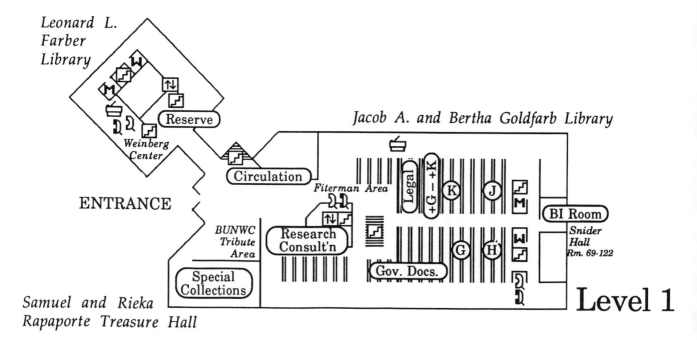

FAMILY HISTORY CENTERS (LDS)

Description of Institution:

The Church of Jesus Christ of Latter-day Saints (LDS), also known as the Mormon Church, operates the **Family History Library** in Salt Lake City, and over 2,600 **Family History Centers** worldwide. The Family History Library in Salt Lake City has the most extensive collection of materials and records of interest to genealogists in the world. Over two million rolls of microfilmed records, 523,000 microfiche, and 268,000 books are available at the library. Over 250 microfilm crews are working in 53 countries throughout the world to add to the collection daily.

The FAMILY HISTORY CENTERS (formerly known as Branch Genealogical Libraries) were established to provide access to the records in Salt Lake City, and are open to the public. Records on microfilm can be loaned to any Family History Center.

FAMILY HISTORY CENTERS are usually located in church meetinghouses, and are staffed by volunteers. There are seven FAMILY HISTORY CENTERS in the Greater Boston area: Cambridge, Weston, Lynnfield, Foxboro, Worcester, and Nashua, NH and Warwick, RI.

Weston:
Facility Director:	Maude Bentall
Address:	130 Brown Street, Weston, MA 02193
Phone Number:	(617) 235-2164, (617) 235-9892
Hours of Operation:	Tuesday 7:00pm - 9:00pm
	Friday 9:00am - 3:00pm
	Saturday 9:00am - 3:00pm
Directions:	On Route 30, 3.2 miles west of Route 128. The Church is a beige brick building on south side of Route 30.

Lynnfield:
Facility Director:	Judy Lubinski
Address:	400 Essex Street, Lynnfield, MA 01940
Phone Number:	(617) 334-5586
Hours of Operation:	Wednesday 10:00pm - 9:00pm
	Friday 10:00am - 4:00pm
	Saturday 10:00am - 4:00pm (2nd and 4th Saturdays only)
Directions:	Route 128 to Exit 41 (Main St. Lynnfield). Turn right off exit ramp onto Main St. Follow Main St. through center of town, for 1.3 miles, bearing left at center of town. Make right onto Essex Street (1st street on right, ¼ mile past center of town). The Church is on the left, past the high school (about 1 mile).

Foxboro:
Facility Director:	Marilyn Meyers
Address:	76 Main Street, Foxboro, MA 02035
Phone Number:	(508) 543-0298, (508) 543-5284
Hours of Operation:	Tues, Thurs 10:00am - 3:00pm
	Wednesday 10:00am - 3:00pm, 7:00pm - 10:00pm
	Saturday 10:00am - 3:00pm
Directions:	Take Exit 7 off Route I-95. Follow Route 140 north to Foxboro Green. Go halfway around the green and continue on Route 140. The Church is on Route 140, ½ mile north of Foxboro Green, on the left.

Nashua:

Facility Director: Susan Brussard
Address: 110 Concord Street, Nashua, NH 03060
Phone Number: (603) 594-8888
Hours of Operation: Tuesday   10:00am - 2:00pm
     Weds, Thur   10:00am - 2:00pm, 6:30pm - 9:00pm
     Saturday   10:00am - 3:00pm
Directions: Take exit 7E off of Route 3 (Everett Turnpike). Go straight through 2 sets of lights. At the 3rd light, make a right onto Concord Street. The Church is 2 blocks, on the right, next to Greeley Park. The building is locked, so go to the right rear door and ring buzzer.

Worcester:

Facility Director: July Keller
Address: 67 Chester Street, Worcester, MA 01605
Phone Number: (508) 852-7000, Church # (508) 852-4030
Hours of Operation: Tuesday   7:00pm - 9:00pm
     Wednesday   10:00am - 2:00pm
     Thursday   6:00pm - 9:00pm
     Saturday   9:00am - 1:00pm
Directions: Off Route 122A near Holden line. Take Exit 2 from I-190. Go 1 mile west on Ararat Street until it ends in a T. Turn left, go 1 mile south on Holden Street, to Chester Street. Turn right on Chester Street and go 5 blocks (winding up hill, about ½ mile) to the Church, on the left. The Family History Center is in the rear corner of the building. Ring buzzer if door is locked.
The FHC is also accessible via the Worcester City Bus line, every hour.

Cambridge:

Facilty Director: Elizabeth Nelson
Address: 2 Longfellow Park, Cambridge, MA
Phone Number: (617) 491-4749
Hours of Operation: Wednesday   6:00pm - 9:00pm
     Thursday   10:00am - 12:00pm
     Saturday   9:00am - 1:00pm   (2nd and 4th Saturdays only)
Directions: Near Harvard Square. The Church is at 2 Longfellow Park, just off Brattle Street, across from the Longfellow House.

Providence, RI:

Address: 1000 Narragansett Parkway, Warwick, RI 02888
Phone Number: (401) 463-8150
Hours of Operation: Tuesday   7:00pm - 9:00pm
     Weds, Fri   10:00am - 2:00pm, 7:00pm - 9:00pm
     Saturday   10:00am - 4:00pm

The FAMILY HISTORY CENTERS are closed for bad weather, on holidays, and some for summer months; hours occasionally change. It is best to call to verify the current schedule.

Also, the NEW ENGLAND HISTORIC GENEALOGICAL SOCIETY (NEHGS) on Newbury Street in Boston has recently entered into an agreement with the LDS Family History Library in Salt Lake City, to offer LDS microfilms to NEHGS patrons. Microfilms may be borrowed from Salt Lake City at NEHGS, just as they can at any of the FAMILY HISTORY CENTERS. See page 169.

Description of Resources:

The Family History Library in Salt Lake City has an extensive collection of Jewish records from all over the world, which can be loaned to any FAMILY HISTORY CENTER. Lists of the Library's microfilms of Jewish records (primarily 19th-century birth, marriage and death records) were compiled and published by *Avotaynu*:

- Polish-Jewish records (1700+ microfilms) - Vol. II, No. 1 (January 1986)
- German-Jewish records (2100+ microfilms) - Vol. III, No. 1 (Winter 1987)
- Hungarian-Jewish records (800+ microfilms) - Vol. IV, No. 1 (Winter 1988)

These listing have been reprinted elsewhere, including *The Encyclopedia of Jewish Genealogy*, pages 178-215. However, these listings are over 10 years out of date (they used the 1985 FHLC) — new materials are constantly being added to the collection. Check the Locality section of the FHLC for an up-to-date list of holdings and catalog numbers.

Since the fall of the Soviet Union, the LDS have begun to microfilm records previously inaccessible. Jewish records from Belarus, Estonia and Slovakia have just recently become available. Check the FHLC Locality section for recent listings.

Also available on loan are: domestic and foreign census and military records, the Hamburg Passenger Lists (1850-1934), Russian Consular Records, U.S. Passenger Arrival Lists, New York City vital records (see page 31), and much much more.

Finding Aids:

Each local FAMILY HISTORY CENTER has a complete catalogue listing the holdings of the Family History Library in Salt Lake City, and several genealogical indexes:

1. *Family History Library Catalog* (FHLC), is a microfiche copy of the catalog of the Library in Salt Lake City, which describes the books and microforms in the Library's collection. The FHLC is the key to research in the library, and is updated annually. The FHLC consists of four sections: Surname, Subject, Author/Title and Locality, containing a total of over 2,500 microfiche. (See page 92 at the end of this chapter for information on how to use the Locality section).

2. *International Genealogical Index* (IGI), an index to over 200 million names of deceased persons for whom LDS Temple ordinances have been performed. It includes birth, marriage and christening dates and places from the computerized files of the LDS. Organized geographically. The IGI is updated every four years; the most recent edition was issued in 1992/93 (11,800 fiche).

3. *Family Registry*, an alphabetical list of 300,000 names being researched, with the names and addresses of individuals or family organizations who are researching these names. 180 microfiche. The *Family Registry* is being phased out and replaced by *Ancestral File*; the last edition was issued in 1993. [Note: The *Jewish Genealogical Family Finder* (JGFF, see page 2) is a more useful networking tool for Jewish family research].

FamilySearch is the latest addition to the FHCs' resources. *FamilySearch* is a series of genealogical indexes on CD-ROM (a computer system using Compact Discs), available at all local FAMILY HISTORY CENTERS. *FamilySearch* currently consists of four databases: The FHLC, the IGI, *Ancestral File*, and the Social Security Death Index:

1. *Family History Library Catalog* (FHLC). Compact disc version of the catalog of the Salt Lake City library. Same data as the microfiche edition above, but it is updated at different times. It may be searched only by Locality or Surname, but has an additional "Locality Browse" feature, incorporating all geographic localities into one alphabetic sequence. One Compact Disc.

2. *International Genealogical Index* (IGI). Compact disc version of the index to LDS Temple ordinances. Identical data as the microfiche edition above, but arranged in one alphabetical sequence per country. 33 Compact Discs (1993 edition), plus 7 discs in 1994 addendum.

3. *Ancestral File*. A linked database of over 13 million names, available only on Compact Disc. It connects individuals into families and pedigrees. This data was contributed primarily by Mormons tracing their own families. You can make paper or diskette copies of the information you find, as well as contribute information for future updates. Four Compact Discs (1993 edition).

4. Social Security Death Index. Contains over 60 million records of deaths reported to the U.S. Social Security Administration. Most of the deaths in this file date from 1962 through 1994, but the index also includes about 1.5 million people who died between 1937 through 1962. For each person listed, you can learn the Social Security Number, date of birth, month/year of death, and last place of residence. Two Compact Discs. (See page 93 for more information about Social Security records).

    Another disc contains the *Military Index*, lists of U.S. service personnel who died in Korea (1950-1957) and Vietnam (1957-1975).

Other permanent resources at each FAMILY HISTORY CENTER include:

*   *Accelerated Indexing Systems* (AIS), a microfiche index, by name, primarily from the U.S. Census through 1850 (in some states, to 1860). Some other U.S. record sources from 1608 to 1885 are also included. The error and omission rate is about 20%. (Researchers should always check the primary source, the actual census record on microfilm, if unable to find a name).

*   *PERSI* (PERiodical Source Index), an index to articles in genealogical publications, on microfiche. Indexes 2,000 genealogical periodicals by place, subject and surname.

*   A collection of "The 200 Most Frequently Used Genealogical Reference Works", on microfiche. Mostly pre-20th-century U.S. and British Isles reference works, such as gazetteers. This series is being expanded to eventually include about 900 works.

*   Research Outlines, prepared by the Family History Library in Salt Lake City, one for each U.S. State, Canadian province, and for several other countries (8-32 pages each).

*   Language translation guides ("Genealogical Word Lists") for most Western European languages (900 words, 12-15 pages each), and other miscellaneous research aids.

Some FAMILY HISTORY CENTERS have small permanent collections of books and microfilm. Lynnfield and Nashua have collections on Ireland, Germany, New England, and Maritime and French Canada. Weston has a good collection of published pre-1850 Massachusetts vital records and some New England local histories, as well as indexes to New York City births, marriages, and deaths, 1880s-1940s (nearly 100 microfilms, a gift of the JGSGB). Foxboro has over 250 microfilms on indefinite loan.

Description of Facility:

The Centers each have the following equipment:

	Weston	Lynnfield	Foxboro	Nashua	Worcester
Microfilm:					
Readers	12	5	7	8	6
Printers	-	-	-	1	-
Microfiche:					
Readers	10	10	10	6	8
Printers	1	-	-	1	-
Film/Fiche Printer:	1	1	1	-	1
Computer:	2	1	2	1	2

Fees/Copies:

There is no charge for use of the FAMILY HISTORY CENTERS' facilities, only microfilm loan fees (though donations are accepted). Microfilms are available on loan from Salt Lake City by ordering through a local FAMILY HISTORY CENTER. The basic charges are the same at each Center: to rent a film for three weeks, $3.00; for six months, $4.50; for indefinite loan, $6.00 (see Restriction below). To extend an order from 3 weeks to 6 months, there is an added charge of $1.50. There is sometimes an additional small postage charge, which varies among Centers. The typical wait for films is 2-6 weeks from the date ordered.

Microfiche may be borrowed from Salt Lake City for 15¢ each.

Copying charges vary from Center to Center: Copies of microfilm/microfiche pages are 25¢ each in Weston, Worcester and Nashua, and 35¢ (or 3/$1.00) in Foxboro. There is a charge of 5¢-10¢ for each sheet printed from the *FamilySearch* computer.

Restrictions on Use:

Microfilm and microfiche are available for use at the FAMILY HISTORY CENTER only; no materials circulate.

Books cannot be sent from the Salt Lake City Library, only microfilm/microfiche. However, you can request that a certain pages of book be photocopied, for a small fee. Ask the librarian for a "Photoduplication Order" form. You can also request that an entire book be microfilmed. Ask for a "Request to Microfilm a Book" form. Requests can take up to a year to be filled, and are often denied due to copyright permission or other restrictions.

Policies regarding the use of the *FamilySearch* computer vary among Centers: most have advance sign-up sheets for hour or half-hour sessions; at others the computer is available on a first come, first serve basis, with a time limitations.

The approval of the director is needed to place films on indefinite loan, due to space limitations and copyright restrictions.

Summary:

The Family History Library has acquired the world's largest collection of genealogical information. It has microfilm copies of original documents, most dating between roughly 1500 and 1920. The Library makes all of its microfilmed records available through FAMILY HISTORY CENTERS, located throughout the world. They are the only local source for many records. However, there are some inconveniences in using the FAMILY HISTORY CENTERS: they have limited hours; they are staffed by church volunteers, who are often not genealogists; researchers must wait for microfilms to arrive from Salt Lake City; and the facilities are sometimes crowded, causing researchers to wait for use of microfilm readers and the *FamilySearch* computer.

The Family History Library in Salt Lake City is located at 35 North West Temple Street, Salt Lake City, Utah 84150 (Telephone 801-240-2331). They will answer limited inquiries only; they will not perform any research.

Research guides can be purchased from the Family History Library. Most useful is the "United States Research Outline", available for 75¢, a 52-page guide to United States resources at the library, and where to find them in the FHLC. Also available are State Research Outlines, one for each of the fifty states, available at 25¢ each. Each 8-32 page guide describes specific records available for each state. Other research guides (mostly for Western Europe) are also available. Write to:

Family History Library
35 North West Temple Street
Salt Lake City, Utah 84150

A comprehensive guide to the holdings of the Family History Library is *The Library: A Guide to the LDS Family History Library*, edited by Johni Cerny and Wendy Elliott. (Salt Lake City: Ancestry, Inc., 1988). 746 pages. Available at most Family History Centers, and many public libraries.

The key to finding records in the FHL collection is the *Family History Library Catalog* (FHLC), the card catalog of the holdings of the library in Salt Lake City, available on microfiche at all FAMILY HISTORY CENTERS, and updated annually. The most important part of the FHLC is the LOCALITY section, where records are organized by jurisdiction: By Country, then State, then County/Province, then City/Town. They have instructional videos on "How to use the FHLC" and "How to use a Family History Center". ($5.00 each from: Salt Lake Distribution Center, 1999 West 1700 South, Salt Lake City, UT 84104, Tel. 801-240-2504). Genealogical supplies and other research guides are also available. Ask for the "Family History Publications List" (#34083).

How to use the Family History Library Catalog (FHLC):

The most important portion of the FHLC is the <u>Locality</u> section, consisting of over 1,000 microfiche. The Locality section is organized alphabetically by country, with the exception that the 50 U.S. states and 12 Canadian provinces are treated as separate 'countries'. There is a separately numbered set of microfiche for each country.

Within each country, the localities are arranged according to geographic jurisdictions, from largest to smallest. Records about the country are listed under the name of the country. Following the national records, each county or province is listed alphabetically. Records that were kept on a county or provincial level are listed under the county heading. For example, records about the province of Galicia in Austria are listed under "AUSTRIA, GALIZIEN". Records about specific localities within each county are listed in alphabetical order after the county-level records. Thus, records of the city of Kraków, such as Jewish vital records or local history, are listed under "AUSTRIA, GALIZIEN, KRAKÓW".

For U.S. states, the localities are arranged alphabetically by counties, and thereunder alphabetically by city/town name. Therefore, one should look under "[State], [County], [City]". For example: for state-wide records look under "MASSACHUSETTS"; for records of Suffolk county look under "MASSACHUSETTS, SUFFOLK"; and for records of the city of Boston look under "MASSACHUSETTS, SUFFOLK, BOSTON".

If you do not know the county or province to which a particular city or town belongs, there is a cross-reference relating cities/towns with their respective jurisdictions on the first fiche (sometimes the first several fiche) of each country. These "see" references will direct you to the form in which the entry will appear in the catalog. These references can be used almost like a gazetteer of the country. However, "see" references are made only for those localities presently included in the catalog, and not for all possible locations. Small villages are not listed, because their records are usually included with those of a larger nearby town.

In some cases, especially in Eastern Europe, borders have changed over the years, and the town your ancestor lived in may have been in different countries during different time periods. In this case, the locality catalog usually includes materials under each country the town had belonged to. For example, records for Posen, Germany (now Poznań, Poland), can be found listed under both "GERMANY, PREUSSEN, POSEN, POSEN" and "POLAND, POZNAN, POZNAN".

Some records to look for:
- Massachusetts state-wide birth, marriage and death records, 1841-1899, and indexes for 1841-1971, can be found under the heading "MASSACHUSETTS - VITAL RECORDS".
- Boston Passenger Lists, 1820-1943, are under "MASSACHUSETTS, SUFFOLK, BOSTON - EMIGRATION AND IMMIGRATION".
- New York Passenger Lists, 1820-1943 (including Ellis Island), are under "NEW YORK, NEW YORK (CITY) - EMIGRATION AND IMMIGRATION".
- The Hamburg Passenger Lists, 1850-1934, are under "GERMANY, HAMBURG, HAMBURG - EMIGRATION AND IMMIGRATION".
- U.S. Naturalization records can be found under "[State] - NATURALIZATION AND CITIZENSHIP" and "[State], [County] - NATURALIZATION AND CITIZEN-SHIP".

- U.S. Federal Census records, 1790-1920, are under "UNITED STATES - CENSUS - [Year]".
- City Directories for most major U.S. Cities, 1789-1935, can be found under "UNITED STATES - DIRECTORIES", or "[State], [City] - DIRECTORIES".
- Extensive collections of Jewish vital records from Poland, Hungary and Germany can be found under "[Country], [County], [City] - JEWISH RECORDS".
- The Russian Consular records are under "RUSSIA (EMPIRE) - EMIGRATION AND IMMIGRATION".

Browsing through the FHLC is the most effective way of learning about the many types of records that are available.

Social Security Death Index:

The Social Security Death Index lists over 60 million deceased people who had social security numbers and whose deaths occurred between 1962 and the end of 1994. By entering a person's name and an approximate birth date, if known, the following information will be displayed: name (arranged alphabetically by surname and then by given name), year of birth (as reported to social security), state that issued the social security number, year of death, and the state of residence at time of death.

An optional feature permits you to obtain more information on a specific person: full date of birth, month and year of death, social security number, and the state where the death benefit was sent to a living relative. Zip codes can be obtained for the place of death and place where death benefits were sent. A built-in Zip code directory will list the communities served by a Zip code.

Finding an entry in the Social Security Death Index can lead you to other sources of information: Knowing the date and place of death enables you to obtain a death certificate (see page 29). Knowing a Social Security Number and date of death, you can also obtain a copy of a person's original Social Security application.

By sending a letter containing the name, Social Security Number, and date of death (or using form SSA-L997, "Social Security Number Record, Third Party Request for Extract or Photocopy" available through any Social Security office or by calling 1-800-772-1213), with $7.00, you may secure a photocopy of the person's original Social Security application. The application will show the address of the applicant, date and place of birth, father's name, and mother's maiden name. If you do not know an individual's Social Security Number, the search fee is $16.50. Address your inquiry to:

Social Security Administration
Freedom of Information Officer
4H8 Annex Building
6401 Security Boulevard
Baltimore, Maryland 21235

(410) 965-3962

HARVARD UNIVERSITY LIBRARIES

Address: Widener Library and Lamont Library
Harvard Yard
Cambridge, MA 02138

Phone Numbers:

Reference and Information: (617) 495-2411   (9-5 Mon-Fri, 12-5 Sat)
Circulation Desk: (617) 495-2413   (information on library hours)
Library Privileges: (617) 495-4166

Hours of Operation:

Mon to Fri: 9:00 am to 9:45 pm
Saturday: 9:00 am to 4:45 pm
Sunday: 12:00 noon to 4:45pm

Directions:

By MBTA:
Take the Red Line to Harvard Square. Walk east on the north side of Mass Avenue along the wall around Harvard Yard. Following the third building from the corner, turn left into a gate, and you will be at the back of Widener Library. Go around the building to the broad steps and Grecian columns in the front, and go up to the second floor to get a day pass, use the card catalogs, or request books. The microfilm collection is housed in the basement of Lamont Library. To get there from Widener, go out the front entrance of Widener into Harvard Yard, and go to the right.

By Car:
Street parking is very hard to find near Harvard Square. Plan on parking some distance away and walking, or taking a long time to find a parking space, or parking in one of the (expensive) lots in the area, for example on Holyoke or JFK Streets. Parking is cheaper at University Place, located on the other side of Harvard Square beyond the Charles Hotel (on University Rd., off of Mt. Auburn St.) It is generally more convenient to take the T. If driving in from Route 2, there is parking available at Alewife station, at the end of the Red Line, which is only a 10 minute T ride from Harvard Square.

Description of Institution:

The libraries exist primarily for the benefit of the faculty, students, and research staff at Harvard University, a private institution. The Harvard University Library, dating from 1638, is the oldest library in the United States and the largest university library in the world. It now contains more than 12 million volumes, in addition to manuscripts, microforms, maps, photographs, slides and other material. The collections are housed in over 90 libraries, most located in Cambridge and Boston.

Description of Resources:

With its millions of volumes, it is impossible to give a complete or thorough description or listing of all of the potential resources available at Harvard Libaries. A good approach is to become familiar with HOLLIS (The Harvard On-Line Library Information System) and its search capabilities. See "Finding Aids" below. Some highlights are:

A. <u>Russian Business Directories</u>. A resource of great interest to genealogists is the collection of Russian business directories from the late nineteenth and early twentieth century. Many of these are available nowhere else in the United States, or only in the Library of Congress. Except for the Leningrad city directory, these do not attempt to list most people living in the region they cover, but only certain businesses and government officials. The coverage varies greatly depending on the city and the year, and the chances are against finding any particular person. However, some of them have a large percentage of Jewish businesses listed, and sometimes Jewish communal leaders. Usually people are listed by both their given names and patronymics (father's name), which makes these directories particularly useful for tracing family relationships. For further information on Russian directories and how to use them, see the article "Russian Business Directories", by Harry D. Boonin, in the Winter 1990 issue of *Avotaynu* (Volume VI, Number 4, pages 23-32).

The Russian business directories are listed in the card catalog under titles that begin with the words "Vsia ...", "Ves ...", "Pamiatnaia knizhka ...", and "Adres'-Kalendar ...". Widener has over fifty series of these books, most of them represented by just one or two books from years between 1860 and 1914. The following directories, for regions in the Jewish Pale of Settlement, or for cities that had large Jewish populations, would be of greatest interest for Jewish genealogical research:

Vsia Rossia (All Russia). 1913, volume 3. [Slav 616.35].

Vsia Moskva: adresnaia i spravochnaia kniga (Moscow). Microfilm, 20 reels. 1896-1908, 1910-11, 1923, 1927-29, 1936. [S3518].

Vsia Vil'na: adresnaia i spravochnaia kniga (Vilna). Photocopy. 1915 (2 volumes). [DK651.V4 V74x]

Ves SSSR (All USSR). 1931 (commercial-industrial). [Slav 1684.803].

Ves Peterburg, *Ves Petrograd*, and *Ves Leningrad*. 1894 through 1934. [On microfilm, Film SC 326]

Adres'-Kalendar i spravochnaia knizhka Grodenskoi gubernii. 1914. [KSE 653]. (Depository)

Pamiatnaia knizhka Grodenskoi gubernii (Grodno guberniya). 1898, 1899, 1905. [KSE 654]. (Depository)

Pamiatnaia knizhka Kaluzhkoi gubernii (Kalisz guberniya). [Slav 3160.5].

Pamiatnaia knizhka Kovenskoi gubernii (Kovno guberniya).

Pamiatnaia knizhka Lomzhinskoi gubernii (Łomża guberniya). 1885, 1893, 1906. [DK4600.L65 P35x].

Pamiatnaia knizhka Minskoi gubernii (Minsk guberniya). 1878-1914 incomplete. [KSE 655]. (Depository)

Pamiatnaia knizhka Mogilevskoi gubernii (Mogilev guberniya). 1909. [Slav 3217.15.15].

Pamiatnaia knizhka Moskovskoi gubernii (Moscow guberniya). 1909. [Slav 3162.5.270].

Pamiatnaia knizhka Petrokovskoi gubernii (Piotrkov guberniya).

Pamiatnaia knizhka Poltavskoi gubernii (Poltava guberniya). 1914. [Slav 3240.13.55].

Pamiatnaia knizhka Radomskoi gubernii (Radom guberniya). 1874. [DK4600.R3 P35x]. (Depository)

Pamiatnaia knizhka Suvalkskoi gubernii (Suwalki guberniya). 1872. [Slav 6464.289.10].

Pamiatnaia knizhka Tavricheskoi gubernii (Taurida guberniya). 1914.

Pamiatnaia knizhka Vilenskoi gubernii (Vilna guberniya). 1914. [KSE 652]. (Depository)

An inventory of these directories is *Spravochniki po istorii dorevoliutsionnoi Rossii* [Directories of the History of pre-Revolutionary Russia], by P. A. Zaionchkovskii, revised edition (Moscow: Kniga, 1978) [DK40.Z99 S67x 1978]. This book lists all pre-1917 Russian business directories that were published, as well as many other sources for historical research, and is described in the Winter 1990 issue of *Avotaynu*. Directories that are not available at Widener are often available in the Slavic section of the library of the University of Helsinki, which has by far the largest collection, and occasionally in the Library of Congress, the New York Public Library, or other research libraries with large Slavic collections. [See "Russian Sources in Western Libraries" by Harold and James Rhode, in the Winter 1990 issue of *Avotaynu* (VI, 4, pages 20-22)].

In addition to the Russian business directories, Widener Library, as one of the largest research libraries in the world, has millions of books that are difficult to find elsewhere, including some rabbinic genealogies (e.g. the Rivlin genealogy, which includes the family of the Vilna Gaon), and other books that may be of interest to Jewish genealogists.

B.   Holocaust Victim and Survivors Lists. Published volumes that contain lists of victims and survivors of the Holocaust include:

Belgium. *Memorial de la deportation des juifs de Belgique*. By Serge Klarsfeld et Maxime Steinberg. (Bruxelles: Union des deportes juifs en Belgique; New York: Beate Klarsfeld Foundation, [1982]). 600 pp. [Harv. Dep. DS135.B4 M46 1982]

France. *Memorial to the Jews deported from France, 1942-1944 : documentation of the deportation of the victims of the Final Solution in France [Memorial de la deportation des juifs de France. English]*. By Serge Klarsfeld. (New York: B. Klarsfeld Foundation, 1983). xxxix, 663 pp. [XLK 411. 5]

Germany (West). *Gedenkbuch Opfer der Verfolgung der Jüden unter der Nationalsozialistischen Gewaltherrschaft in Deutschland 1933-1945*. (Koblenz: Bundesarchiv, 1986). 2 volumes. (1,823 pp.) {Identifies 128,000 Holocaust victims in West Germany}. [WID-LC D804.3.G43 1986 F]

Germany, Aschaffenburg. *Biographisches Handbuch der Juden in Stadt und Altkreis Aschaffenburg*. By Peter Korner. (Aschaffenburg: 1993). 287 pp. [Harv. Dep. DS135.G4 A775 1993]

Germany, Bad Kissingen. *Letzte Spuren von Deutschen judischen Glaubens im Landkreis Bad Kissingen = Last traces of German Jews in the Landkreis of Bad Kissingen*. By Cornelia Binder, Michael Mence. (Wartmannsroth, Germany: C. Binder, 1992). 148 pp. [Harv. Dep. DS135.G4 B159134 1992]

Germany, Berlin. *Gedenkbuch Berlins der jüdischen Opfer des Nationalsozialismus*. (Berlin: Ed. Hentrich, 1995). 1453 pp. {Identifies 56,000 victims}.

Germany, Cologne. *Die Jüdischen Opfer des Nationalsozialismus aus Köln: Gedenkbuch*. (Köln: Böhlau, 1995). 555 pp. [Ger 6903.1.2 Heft 77]

Germany, Frankfort am Main. *Deportationsbuch der von Frankfurt am Main aus gewaltsam verschickten Juden in den Jahren 1941 bis 1944 : (nach den Listen vom Bundesarchiv Koblenz)*. Edited by Adolf Diamant. (Frankfurt am Main: Judische Gemeinde Frankfurt am Main, 1984). 175 pp. [WID-LC DS135.G4 F625 1984 PF]

Germany, Gottingen (Kreis). *Die judischen Burger im Kreis Gottingen, 1933-1945 : ein Gedenkbuch: Gottingen, Hann. Munden, Duderstadt*. By Uta Schafer-Richter und Jorg Klein. (Gottingen: Wallstein, 1992). 310 pp. [Harv. Dep. DS135.G5 A1587 1992]

Germany, Kassel. *Namen und Schicksale der Juden Kassels 1933-1945 : ein Gedenkbuch*. Beate Kleinert und Wolfgang Prinz. (Kassel: Magistrat der Stadt Kassel, Stadtarchiv, 1986). 248 pp. [WID-LC DS135.G4 K375 1986 F]

Germany, Leipzig. *Deportationsbuch der in den Jahren 1942 bis 1945 von Leipzig aus gewaltsam verschickten Juden; nach den Listen von der Israelitischen Religionsgemeinde Leipzig und dem Archiv Yad Vashim in Jerusalem*. By Adolf Diamant. (Frankfurt am Main: Selbstverlag, 1991). 217 pp. [Harv. Dep. DS135.G4 L453 1991x]

Germany, Marburg-Biednkopf. *"Unbekannt verzogen" oder "weggemacht" : Schicksale der Juden im alten Landkreis Marburg, 1933-1945.* By Barbara Handler-Lachmann, Ulrich Schutt. (Marburg: Hitzeroth, 1992). 245 pp. [Harv. Dep. DS135.G4 M3454 1992]

Germany, Soest. *Der jüdische Friedhof in Soest : eine Dokumentation in Text und Bild.* By Michael Brocke. (Soest: Mocker & Jahn, 1993). 288 pp. [Harv. Dep. DS135.G4 S6325 1993]

Hungary. *Nevek = Shemot = Names.* (New York: Beate and Serge Klarsfeld Foundation, 1991-). 3 volumes. {Vol.1: Names of the deported Jews from Hajdu county. Vols.2-3: Names of the Jewish victims of Hungarian labour battalions}. [Harv. Dep. Heb 44300.318 F]

Hungary, Budapest. *Counted Remnant: Register of the Jewish Survivors of Budapest.* (Budapest: World Jewish Congress, Hungarian Section, 1946). [Jud 3293.644.10]

Netherlands. *Alphabetische lijst van zich in Nederland bevindende Joden.* (Eindhoven: Centraal Registratiebureau voor Joden, 1945). [Widener Microforms: Film A 344.660]

Netherlands. *Liste alphabetique des personnes, en majorite Israelites, deportees par les convois partis du camp de rassemblement de malines entre le 4 Aout 1942 et le 31 Juillet 1944.* (Bruxelles, 1954). 3 volumes, in Dutch and French. [Harv. Dep. v.1=HWMWCE, v.2=HWMW88, v.3=HWMWCS]

Poland. *Pinkas ha-nitsolim (Register of Jewish survivors).* (Jerusalem: Search Bureau for Missing Relatives, Jewish Agency for Israel, 1945). 2 volumes in 1. [Harv. Dep. Heb 11490.651.5]

Poland. *Jewish military casualties in the Polish armies in World War II.* By Benjamin Meirtchak. (Tel Aviv: World Federation of Jewish Fighters, Partisans, and Camp Inmates; Association of Jewish War Veterans of the Polish Armies in Israel, 1994-1995). 2 volumes. {An updated English edition to a Polish edition published in 1993}. [Harv. Dep. DS135.P63 A1514 1994]

Poland, Lodz (Ghetto). *Getto Litzmannstadt: Bilanz eines nationalsozialistischen Verbrechens, mit Deportations und Totenlisten der aus dem Altreich stammenden Juden.* Adolf Diamant. (Frankfurt [am Main]: A. Diamant, 1986). xiv, 411 pp. [WID-LC DS135.P62 L6433 1986]

Slovakia. *Register of all persons saved from anti-Jewish persecution in Slovakia.* (Bratislava: American Joint Distribution Committee, 1945). 3 volumes. [HW5J55, HW5J5H, HW5J3S].

Sweden. *About Jews liberated from German concentration camps arrived in Sweden in 1945.* (Stockholm: World Jewish Congress, Relief and Rehabilitation Dept.: Jewish Agency for Palestine, Rescue Committee, 1946). 2 volumes. [Consult Judaica Division]

Sweden. *List of Jews who have arrived in Sweden May 1st-June 25th 1945.* (Stockholm, 1945). [Consult Judaica Dept for item].

Auschwitz (Concentration Camp). *Death Books from Auschwitz: Remnants = Sterbebücher von Auschwitz: Fragmente = Ksiegi zgonow z Auschwitz: fragmenty.* Ed. by State Museum of Auschwitz-Birkenau. (Münich: K.G. Saur, 1995). 3 volumes. {69,000 names, with dates of birth and death}.

Terezin (Concentration Camp). *Totenbuch Theresienstadt : damit sie nicht vergessen werden.* (Wien: Junius Verlag, 1987). [Harv. Dep. D805.C9 T68 1987]

C. Yizkor Books. Widener Library has a comprehensive collection of more than 500 memorial books commemorating Jewish communities destroyed in the Holocaust. These are catalogued in a variety of different places. See Appendix A (pages 193-225) for a complete bibliography with call numbers.

D. Local History. In addition to Yizkor books, Harvard libraries have thousands of volumes of local Jewish history. To find them, do a keyword search in HOLLIS under variant spellings of the name of the town. A few examples:

Documents concerning the destruction of the Jews of Grodno, 1941-1944 / edited by Serge Klarsfeld.
New York: Beate Klarsfeld Foundation, [198-?]. 6 volumes. [WID-LC D810.J4 D63 x, 1980z]

Documents concerning the fate of Romanian Jewry during the Holocaust. Edited by Jean Ancel.
([New York]: Beate Klarsfeld Foundation, [1987]. 12 volumes. [WID-LC DS135.R7 D63 x, 1987]

Kaspi, Isaac. *Megilat peraot Shedlits bi-shenat 1906.* (Tel Aviv: 1947). 43 pp. {Siedlce, Poland: massacre of 1906}. [Heb 16708.505]

Friedman, Towiah. *Toldot kehilat Yehude Radom bi-tekufat ha-shoah 1939-1945.* (Jerusalem: Hebrew Univeristy, 1974). 3 volumes. {Masters Thesis: Holocaust in Radom, Poland}. [Widener Microforms: Film A 827.042 (4)]

Lodzer togeblat. Lodz, Poland. [Widener Microforms: Film NC 791] {Microfilmed in Jerusalem, Jewish National and University Library, [1991?]. Incomplete set: 1909, 1923-1926, 1929-1932}. 15 microfilm reels. {Harvard Libraries also have five other periodicals from Lodz}.

Feinstein, Abraham Asher. *Megilat puraniyot: zikhronot al meoraot Pinsk ve-hevel Polesiyah bi-shenot ha-milhamah ha-olamit.* (Tel Aviv: [1929]). 207 pp. {WWI in Pinsk}. [Harv. Dep. Heb 16638.737.5]

Shabad, Abraham Hayyim. *Toldot ha-yamin she-avru al Hevra-Kadisha Shivah Keruim ve-al bet ha-midrash ha-gadol asher ba-ir Minsk mi-shenat 523 ad...664.* (Vilna: 664-671, 1904-1911). 2 volumes. [Harv. Dep. Heb 16638.607].

E. Business Records. The archives of R. G. Dun & Co. (half of Dun and Bradstreet) are available at Baker Library [Harvard University Graduate School of Business Administration, Cambridge, MA 02163. Telephone (617) 495-6411]. The R. G. Dun & Co. archives contain 2,600 volumes of confidential credit reports on over 2 million people for the period 1841-1890. They are organized by state and then by county, with a name index for almost every volume extant. Access is restricted.

Anyone who operated a business was probably investigated by the Dun Company, plus other professional people. An article in *American Jewish History* (Volume 72, Number 3, March 1983, p. 333) states, "A separate file was kept on doctors and lawyers. Men who were commercially active in a community, whether they were merchants, manufacturers, brokers or bankers, were almost certain to be included."

F. Map Collection. The Harvard Map Collection is a public facility on the lower level of Pusey Library. It has thousands of maps and atlases, from the 15th century to the present, gazetteers, and reference books on cartography. The collection includes original antique maps, as well as thousands of 20th-century maps of Eastern Europe, on detailed scales from 1:200,000 down to 1:25,000. There are three card catalogs: antique maps (pre-1900), modern maps (post-1900), and atlases. File cabinets hold the grid maps needed to ascertain the grid number for the sectional modern detailed maps. All materials are held in closed stacks, and must be called for by catalog number.

There are five large tables for researchers, and a small but helpful staff. The Map Collection is open Monday-Friday 9:00am-4:45pm, (617) 495-2417.

Finding Aids:

Most of the materials in the Harvard University Libraries are catalogued in a computer system known as HOLLIS (The **H**arvard **O**n-**L**ine **L**ibrary **I**nformation **S**ystem). There are HOLLIS terminals located throughout the Harvard Libraries. You can also gain direct access to HOLLIS via the Internet, or from any home computer with a modem. Help on how to use the system is available on line.

Internet: telnet://hollis.harvard.edu
Direct dial-up: (617) 496-8500   (up to 14.4 kps, 8 data bits, no parity, VT100)

 # Widener Library

Key

Billing	198
Book Return	198
Building Services	97
Cataloging	88, 191
Circulation Desk	198
Collection Development	197
Conference Room	c
Elevator	e
Fax	f
Financial Services	82
Gifts & Exchange	86
Guard	g
Interlibrary Loan	497
HOLLIS Terminals	h
Houghton Library Access	ho
Men's Room	m
Personnel	190
Photocopiers	p
Photo Services	90
Preservation	89
Privileges	195
Serial Records	196
Stack Entrance	se
Stacks Offices	100, 500
Stairs	s
Telephone	t
Tracing	tr, 198
Women's Room	w

Ground Floor

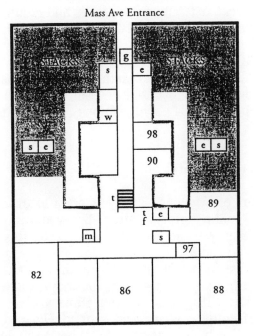

First Floor

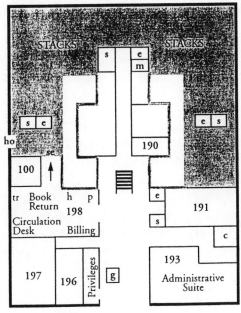

Second Floor

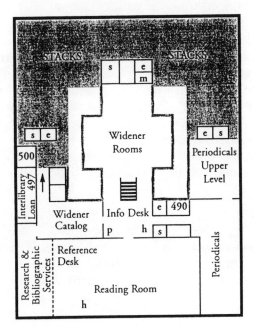

HOLLIS consists of several databases. The main database, the "Union Catalog of Harvard University" (HU) contains Widener library materials catalogued since 1978, together with retrospective catalogs of some other Harvard libraries. Another database, the "Catalog of Older Widener Materials" (OW) contains brief descriptions of some materials at Widener library catalogued before 1977. Not everything is included; some older items are still indexed only on paper cards. Other HOLLIS databases, including the "Expanded Academic Index" and "Legal Resource Index" index journal articles, and require a Harvard access code for use. The first two databases mentioned above (HU, OW) have public access.

The HOLLIS databases can be searched by Title, Author, Subject, Keyword and Catalog number. (Catalog number searches span both databases, HU & OW; other types of searches must be conducted separately on each database). There are full boolean search capabilities (AND, OR and NOT combinations), and many other sophisticated searching techniques available.

Description of Facility:

No part of Widener Library is open to the general public. However, if you have a note from your public library stating that you need material for research that is not available elsewhere, then you can get a day pass for up to six days a year, which allows you access to the card catalogue and reading rooms, and allows you to request up to five books per hour from the stacks, for use in the library. If you are associated with another university, and have a note from your university library, then you may be able to get day passes for more than six days per year. Having a day pass will not allow you to borrow books from the library; that right is limited to faculty, students and staff at Harvard, and people who have purchased a library privilege card, which costs up to $500 per year. Harvard is not a member of the Boston Library Consortium, so faculty, students, and staff at other universities in the area cannot normally borrow books from Widener through their own university libraries.

To request a book from the stacks, it is necessary to fill out a card with the call number, which is obtained from the card catalogue, and to submit it to the circulation desk. (Only users associated with Harvard, or people who have purchased a privilege card, are allowed into the stacks). Several requests (up to five) can be submitted at the same time, but it takes 15 to 30 minutes for your books to arrive. If you are planning to use the same book in the next day or two, it is recommended that you ask them to hold it for you, since it takes about a day for a book to be reshelved after it is returned, and there is no easy way for them to locate a book before it is reshelved. Books can be held for up to a week.

Government documents and the microfilm stacks are open to the public. Enter Lamont Library on the ground floor, tell the guard that you wish to use Government Documents, sign in, and descend two flights of stairs. The stacks are two floors below that.

Fees/Copies:

Photocopy machines are located throughout Widener Library. They are operated by either coins or plastic vendacards. The cards are easier to use, and may be purchased from vending machines for 70¢. Copies are 8¢ each with the cards.

HEBREW COLLEGE LIBRARY

Facility Director: Dr. Maurice Tuchman, Director of Library Services

Address: Jacob and Rose Grossman Library
43 Hawes Street
Brookline, MA 02146

Phone Number: (617) 278-4927

Hours of Operation:

	Academic Year	Summer Session	Intersessions
Monday, Thursday	9:00am-9:00pm	9:00am-5:00pm	9:00am-5:00pm
Tuesday, Wednesday	9:00am-9:00pm	9:00am-8:15pm	9:00am-5:00pm
Friday	9:00am-12:00am	9:00am-12:00am	9:00am-12:00am
Sunday	9:00am-3:00pm		

Directions:

By Car: Beacon Street to Carlton St. (¼ mile west of Audubon Circle). South on Carlton St. one block, right onto Monmouth St. Hebrew College is on the left at the next corner (Hawes St). Or Beacon Street to Kent St (½ mile east of Harvard Street). South on Kent St. two blocks, left on Beech St. to Hawes St. (one block). On-street parking usually available.

By MBTA: Green Line ("C" train; Cleveland Circle/Beacon St.) to Hawes Street stop; walk one block south on Hawes St. to Hebrew College. Or take Green Line "D" train to Longwood stop; walk one block north.

Description of Institution:

Hebrew College is an accredited non-theological institution of advanced Hebrew studies, offering undergraduate and graduate degree programs. The Library of nearly 100,000 volumes supports these programs with a comprehensive collection in all areas of Judaic study. In addition, it serves as the Jewish Public Library of the Greater Boston Area. The collection is evenly divided into Hebrew and English-language books, with a fair amount of Yiddish, German, and Russian. The library has excellent collections of: Jewish Education, including curriculum material for all levels; Responsa literature; Hasidism; Kabbalah; the mid-East and Israel; Rare books and manuscripts; and periodicals.

Description of Resources:

1. <u>Yizkor Books</u> - a collection of about 100 memorial books commemorating Jewish communities destroyed in the Holocaust. [Catalogued under call number XZD, thereunder by town name]. See Appendix A (pages 193-225) for a complete bibliography with call numbers.

   For a description of and selected excerpts from Yizkor Books, see:

   Kugelmass, Jack and Jonathan Boyarin. *From a Ruined Garden: The Memorial Books of Polish Jewry.* New York: Schocken, 1983. (275p) [XU F7]

---

2. <u>Reference Books</u> - The reference collection of non-circulating books is located directly behind the circulation desk.

Encyclopedia of Jewish Genealogy. Volume I: Sources in the United States and Canada. Edited by Arthur Kurzweil and Miriam Weiner. Northvale, New Jersey: Jason Aronson, 1991. (226p) {A summary of North American record repositories and their holdings, with some useful appendices}. [Ref WO E5]

Goldstein, Irene Saunders. *Jewish Genealogy Beginner's Guide.* 2nd edition. Washington: Jewish Genealogical Society of Greater Washington, 1991. {A 3-ring binder of useful material, with emphasis on resources in Washington, DC}. [Ref WO J48]

Greenwood, Val D. *The Researcher's Guide to American Genealogy.* 2nd edition. Baltimore: Genealogial Publishing Co., 1990. (623p). {A classic textbook on American genealogy, updated}. [Ref WO G74r]

<u>Atlases and Gazetteers:</u>

Friesel, Evyatar. *Atlas of Modern Jewish History.* New York: Oxford University Press, 1990. (159p) [Ref XKC F84a]

Gilbert, Martin. *Jewish History Atlas.* New York: Macmillan, 1977. (121p) [Ref W G5 1977]

Gilbert, Martin. *The Macmillan Atlas of the Holocaust.* New York: Macmillan, 1982. (256p) [Ref XKc G5m]

Mokotoff, Gary and Sallyann Amdur Sack. *Where Once We Walked: A Guide to the Jewish Communities Destroyed in the Holocaust.* Teaneck, NJ: Avotaynu, 1991. (514p) {A gazetteer of 21,000 Central and Eastern European localities, arranged alphabetically and phonetically, with references to other sources of information for each locality}. [Ref XKC M7w]

Mokotoff, Gary. *WOWW Companion: A Guide to the Communities Surrounding Central and Eastern European Towns.* Teaneck, NJ: Avotaynu, 1995. (197p) [Ref XKC M7wc]

Black Book of Localities Whose Jewish Population was Exterminated by the Nazis. Jerusalem: Yad Vashem, 1965. {32,000 town names are listed, by country and province. A complete alphabetical index is on AJGS microfiche, see page 106}. [Ref XKCd J45b]

Cohen, Chester G. *Shtetl Finder Gazetteer.* Los Angeles, 1980. (145p) [Ref XU C6s]

Daitch, Randy. *The Shtetl Atlas.* {Poland and Lithuania with index, Byelorussia and the Ukraine without index}. [Ref XU]

Kagan, Berl. *Hebrew Subscription Lists: With an Index to 8,767 Jewish Communities in Europe and North Africa. [Sefer HaPrenumerantn].* New York: Ktav, 1975. (384p, in Hebrew) [Ref XU ‏ כ3ם‎]

Kagan, Berl. *Jewish Cities, Towns and Villages in Lithuania Until 1918: Historical-Biographical Sketches.* New York, 1991. (796p, in Yiddish). [Ref XWh]

Schoenberg, Nancy and Stuart. *Lithuanian Jewish Communities.* New York: Garland, 1991. (502p). {A translation of portions of *Yahadut Lita*}. [Ref XWh S35]

Also see geographical reference works in Appendix A, page 195, such as *Pinkas Ha-Kehilot* and *Yahadut Lita*, as well as the gazetteers on AJGS microfiche (page 106).

<u>Biographical Works:</u>

Zubatsky, David S. and Irwin M. Berent. *Jewish Genealogy: A Source Book of Family Histories and Genealogies.* New York, 1984. (422p) {A guide to published and manuscript genealogies in archives and libraries, arranged by surname}. [Ref WO Z9j] also [WO Z9j]

Sharit Ha-Platach, Bavaria. 1945. 5 volumes in 1. {Contains names of 60,000 survivors in Bavarian Concentration Camps}. [Ref XKCz S45]

The Concise Dictionary of American Jewish Biography. By Jacob Rader Marcus. New York, Carlson Publishing, 1994. 2 volumes. (711p) {24,000 biographies, with citations}. [Ref WR C6]

Who's Who in American Jewry. 1938/39, 1955, 1965, 1972, 1980. [Ref WR48]

Who's Who in World Jewry. 1955, 1956, 1987. [Ref WR W5 1987]

Who's Who in Israel (Mi va-Mi be-Yisrael). 1985-86, 1990-91, 1994-95. [Ref WR W45]

Oversize books (kept separately, in low bookcase on the far left of the reference room):

Stern, Malcolm H. *Americans of Jewish Descent: A Compendium of Genealogy*. New York, 1991. {Data on Jewish families who settled in America before 1840}. [Ref WO S85a]

Jewish Genealogical Family Finder (JGFF). Published by the Jewish Genealogical Society (New York), updated quarterly. 1994 edition. {The master index of more than 10,000 ancestral surnames and 7,000 towns being researched by over 2,500 Jewish genealogists - a great networking tool. See page 2}. [Ref WO J4j]

Catalogs of Other Libraries:
    Harvard University - *Catalog of Hebrew Books*. (6 + 3 volumes).
    New York Public Library (NYPL) - *Catalog of Hebrew and Yiddish Titles*. (3 volumes).
    Hebrew Union College - Jewish Institute of Religion (HUC-JIR) - *Dictionary Catalog of the Klau Library, Cincinnati*. (27 volumes).

Encyclopaedias:
    Encyclopaedia Judaica. (Macmillan, New York and Keter Publishing Co., Jerusalem), 1972-1975. 16 volumes + Yearbooks. {Volume 1 contains genealogies of Hasidic rabbis, other genealogies throughout. Especially useful for local history and biography}. [Ref BZ E7j]
    Encyclopedia Judaica. (Berlin), 1928-1934. 10 volumes. {German-Jewish encyclopedia. Only volumes A-L completed}. [Ref BZ J8]
    The Jewish Encyclopedia. (Funk & Wagnalls Co., New York), 1901-1906. 12 volumes. {Contains many genealogical tables}. [Ref BZ J3]
    The Universal Jewish Encyclopedia. Isaac Landsman, ed. (New York), 1939-1941. 10 volumes. {Especially useful for American Jewish biography}. [Ref BZ U58]

3.   Genealogy Shelf - About 25 volumes of genealogical guides, reference books, and compiled family histories, including:

Frazin, Judith. *A Translation Guide to 19th-Century Polish-Language Civil-Registration Documents*. 2nd edition. Illinois, 1989. (311p) {An indispensable guide for interpreting Polish-Jewish records, including those microfilmed by the Mormons}. [WO T82]

Guide to Genealogical Research in the National Archives. Washington, 1985. (304p) {The source describing Federal records: Census, Passenger Lists, Military records, etc.}. [WO U5g]

National Archives Microfilm Guides:
These guides, published by the National Archives in Washington, describe all National Archives microfilms, with a reel-by-reel listing of film contents:
- *National Archives Microfilm Resources for Research: Catalog*. (126p) 1990. [WO M53]
- *1790-1890 Federal Population Censuses*. (96p) 1979. [WO F43]
- *1900 Federal Population Census*. (84p) 1978. [WO N5 1900]
- *1910 Federal Population Census*. (44p) 1982. [WO N5 1910]
- *1920 Federal Population Census*. (88p) 1991. [WO N5 1920]
- *Immigrant & Passenger Arrivals*. (171p) 1991. [WO U85i]
- *Genealogical & Biographical Research*. (77p). 1983. [WO U85g]
- *Military Service Records*. (330p) 1985. [WO N3m]

Guzik, Estelle. *Genealogical Resources in the New York Metropolitan Area*. New York, 1989. (404p) {A detailed guide to every agency in New York and environs that could provide data of use to Jewish genealogical research}. [WO G36] [Ref WO G9r]

Kranzler, David. *My Jewish Roots: A Practical Guide to Tracing and Recording Your Genealogy and Personal History*. New York, 1979. (88,14p) [WO K7m]

Kurzweil, Arthur. *From Generation to Generation: How to Trace Your Jewish Genealogy and Personal History*. New York, 1980. (353p) {The best book for beginners, with a very personal approach to each step}. [WO K9f]

Kurzweil, Arthur. *My Generations, A Course in Jewish Family History*. [WO K9m]

Rottenberg, Dan. *Finding Our Fathers: A Guidebook to Jewish Genealogy*. New York, 1977. (401p) {The pioneer "how-to" work of modern Jewish genealogy}. [WO R6f]

Sack, Sallyann Amdur. *A Guide to Jewish Genealogical Research in Israel*. Baltimore, 1987. (110p) {Guide to the accessibility and holdings of each agency}. [WO A58g]

Stern, Malcolm. *Tracing Your Jewish Roots*. Cincinnati, 1977. (15p) [WO S85t]

Wolfman, Ira. *Do People Grow on Family Trees? Genealogy for Kids and Other Beginners (The Official Ellis Island Sourcebook*. New York, 1991. (179p) {An excellent beginner's guide}. [WO W6d]

Zubatsky, David S. and Irwin M. Berent. *Jewish Genealogy: A Source Book of Family Histories and Genealogies*. New York, 1984. (422p) [WO Z9j] also [Ref WO Z9j]

4.   Biographies and Genealogies - Hebrew College Library contains over 350 collective biographical works. Compiled family genealogies are classified under call number WO, collective biographies under WR.

Abrams, Maynard. *The Ancestors of our Children*. Jacksonville FL, 1984. (195p) [WO A25a]

Batkin, Stanley. *The Batkin Family Genealogy*. New Jersey, 1987. (116p) [WO Batkin B25b]

Ellenbogen, Meyer. *Chevel HaKesef; Record of the Katzenelenbogen Family*. (in Hebrew) Brooklyn NY, 1937. (65,16p) [WO]

Friedmann, Nathan Zvi. *Otzar Harabanim: Rabbis' Encyclopedia: Rabbinate Era from 970 to 1970*. Bnei-Brak, Israel. (461p, in Hebrew). {Provides brief biographical information on 20,000 personalities}. [WR 8]

Gelis, Jacob. *Encyclopedia of the Sages of Eretz Israel*. Jerusalem, 1974. (2 volumes, in Hebrew) [WR]

Grad, Eli. *The Brudno Family: A Family Tree and Biographical Sketches*. Boston, 1984. (99p). With supplements, 1984-1990. [WO G7b]; *The Grad Family Newsletter*. (1986-1991). [WO G7g]; *The Lewin Family Newsletter*. (1986-1988). [WO G7l]

Gera, Gershon. *A Home in Tel Aviv: The Story of the Hoz Family*. Israel, 1987. (297p, in Hebrew) [WO]

Harkavy, Elhanan. *Dor Yesharim; a Genealogical Account of the Harkavy Family*. New York, 1903. (101p, in Hebrew) [WO]

Olswanger, Anna, ed. *Olschwanger Journal*. 1983- (63p+) [WO O58o]

Rosenstein, Neil. *The Unbroken Chain: Biographical Sketches and the Genealogy of Illustrious Jewish Families from the 15th-20th Centuries*. (1st edition) New York, 1975. (716p) [WO R58u]

Sackheim, George I. *Scattered Seeds*. Skokie, IL. (2 volumes, 2 copies) {Chronicles 13,000 descendants of Rabbi Israel of Rozanoi (d. 1659)}. [WO S25s]

Who's Who in Israel. 1952, 1956, 1966/7, 1968, 1969/70, 1973-74, 1976, 1980-81. [WR W45]

Who's Who in American Jewry. 1926, 1928, 1938/39. [WR]

Wunder, Meir. *Meorei Galacia; Encyclopedia of Galacian Rabbis and Scholars*. (in Hebrew) Jerusalem, 1978. [WR 46] also [Ref WR 46]

Other works related to genealogy include:

Beider, Alexander. *A Dictionary of Jewish Surnames from the Russian Empire*. Teaneck, NJ: Avotaynu, Inc., 1993. (782p). {The most comprehensive scholarly study of Jewish surnames in the Pale of Settlement}. [Ref CL B4d]

Kaganoff, Benzion C. *A Dictionary of Jewish Names and their History*. New York, 1977. (250p) [CL K25d]

Kolatch, Alfred J. *Complete Dictionary of English and Hebrew First Names*. New York, 1984. (488p) [CL K7n 1984]

Glazier, Ira A. *Migration From the Russian Empire: Lists of Passengers Arriving at the Port of New York*. Baltimore: Genealogical Publishing Co., 1995-present. {2 volumes to date, covering 1875-1886}. [Ref WO M5]

5. Cemetery Inscriptions - Mostly classified under WN, including:

Austria, Vienna. *Weiner hebräische Epitaphien* [Hebrew Epitaphs in Vienna]. Dr. Berhard Wachstein. Wein, 1907. (33p, in German and Hebrew) [WN]

Austria, Vienna. *Hebräische Grabsteine aus dem XIII-XV Jahrhundert in Wein und Umgebung* [Hebrew Gravestones in the 13th-15th centuries in Vienna and surroundings]. Dr. Bernhard Wachstein. Wein, 1916. (22p + illus.) [WN W3h]

Barbados, Bridgetown. *Monumental Inscriptions in the Burial Ground of the Jewish Synagogue at Bridgetown, Barbados.* [XZD Bridgetown]

Czech Republic, Prague. *Die Familien Prags. Epitaphein des Alten Jüdische Friedhofs in Prag* [Prague Families: Epitaths of the Old Jewish Cemetery in Prague]. Simon Hock, David Kaufmann. Pressburg, 1892. (402 + 36p, in German and Hebrew) {22,000 tombstone inscriptions, 9th-19th centuries} [WN]

Czech Republic, Prague. *Der Alte Prager Judenfriedhof* [The old Jewish Cemetery of Prague]. Dr. L. Jerábek. Prague, 1903. (47p + illus.) [WN Prag 1903]

Czech Republic, Prague. *Ketuvot mi-Bet ha-Almin ha-Yehudi ha-Atik bi-Prag.* [Epitaphs from the Ancient Jewish Cemetery of Prague]. Otto Muneles. Jerusalem, 1988. (508p) [XT]

Germany, Frankfort. *Die Inschriften des Alten Friedhofs der israelischen Gemeinde zu Frankfort a.M.* [The Inscriptions of the Old Cemetery of the Jewish Community in Frankfort a.M.]. Dr. M. Horovitz. Frankfort a.M., 1901. (liii + 768p, in German and Hebrew) [WN]

Germany, Hegenheim. *Der Israelitsche Friedhof in Hegenheim* [The Jewish Cemetery in Hegenheim]. Dr. Achilles Nordmann. Basel, 1910. (205p + illus., in German) [WN Basel 1910]

Germany, Mainz. *Beitrage zur Geschichte der Altesten judischen Grabsteine in Mainz.* Sali Levi.

Hungary. *Mekorot le-Korot ha-Yehudim be-Hungariyah.* Isidor Goldberger.

Israel, Tel Aviv. *Sefer Bayt HaKavarot Cheshen B'Tel-Aviv.* Tsvi Krol and Tsadik Linman. Tel Aviv, 1940. (469p) [WN]

Italy. *Hebräische Grabschriften in Italien* [Hebrew Grave Inscriptions in Italy]. Dr. A. Berliner. Frankfort a.M., 1881. (109p) {200 inscriptions, 16th-17th centuries} [WN 1881]

Poland, Warsaw. *Sefer Nichaler Olmim.* Shmuel Evninn. Warsaw, 1882. (112p, in Hebrew) 2 copies. [WN 1882]

Ukraine, Crimea. *Avne Zikaron li-Vene Yisrael be-Erets Kirim.* Abraham Firkowitz. Vilna, 1872. (256p) [XWm]

Ukraine. *Jewish Tombstones in Ukraine and Moldavia.* (Masterpieces of Jewish Art, volume 4). [Rus Art M38]

6. Microfilm - The microfilm cabinets are located on the lower level, in the first alcove on the left-hand side, after entering the main lower-level hallway.

Jerusalem Post. 1948-date. {Complete run from the founding of the State of Israel}. (140+ reels).

Boston Jewish Advocate. Weekly. 1905-date. {Complete run of the Boston-based Jewish newspaper. An important source for research on Boston Jewry}. (104+ reels).

Hebrew Newspapers, 19th-20th centuries. {*Beth Vaada La-Chachomim* (1893); *Haleumy* (1888-89); *Ha-emet* (1894); *Hameasseph* (1881); *Hapisgah* (1888-99); *Hasanegor* (1890-91); *Hatsofe* (1872); *Ho-umoh* (1915); *Yalkut Maarabi* (1904)}.

Library of Congress Judaica Section Catalogs, 1967. *Hebrew Title Catalog* (11 reels); *Yiddish Title Catalog* (5 reels).

David Kaufman Collection, Budapest. {2,840 items, including 594 manuscripts on Jewish studies: literature, Bible, Talmud, history, kabbalah, liturgy, theology, etc.} (about 84 reels).

IDC collection, Palestine, sixteenth-nineteenth centuries. {An Inter Documentation Company microfiche project containing 108 titles dealing with the Jewish population of Palestine during the Ottoman period (1516-1917)}.

Jewish Historical Institute, Warsaw. {Hebrew manuscripts, 13th-18th centuries. Folklore, biblical literature, Talmud, philosophy, history of Jews in Poland}. (56 reels).

Hebrew Union College - Hebrew Title Catalog. (1964-1971). (6 reels).

Jewish Theological Seminary (JTS) Manuscript Collection. Includes Philosophy. Belles Lettres, Kabbalah. Hebrew Incunabula, Very Rare Books, Bible Manuscripts, Liturgy Collection. (339 reels).

7. <u>AJGS microfiche</u> - Databases distributed on microfiche by the Association of Jewish Genealogical Societies (AJGS) to member societies. Hebrew College Library is the repository for the JGSGB's copy of AJGS material. Please ask a librarian for access to the microfiche.

    a. **Gazetteer of Eastern Europe - Alphabetic Sequence.** Consolidated listing of the U.S. Board on Geographic Names for 350,000 place names in Austria, Bulgaria, Czechoslovakia, East Germany, Hungary, Poland, Romania, USSR (Jewish Pale of Settlement Republics only: Byelorussia, Estonia, Latvia, Lithuania, Moldavia, Ukraine), West Germany, Yugoslavia. Shows place name, country code, latitude and longitude. (8 fiche)

    b. **Gazetteer of Eastern Europe - Soundex Sequence.** Identical database as above, indexed phonetically using the Daitch-Mokotoff Soundex System. Only shows town name and country code. (7 fiche)

    c. **Jewish Genealogical Consolidated Surname Index.** List of over 100,000 unique surnames, showing in which of ten different databases each appear. Updated 1992. Indexed using the Daitch-Mokotoff Soundex System. (4 fiche)

    d. **Black Book of Localities Whose Jewish Population Was Exterminated by the Nazis.** Alphabetical list (independent of country) of 32,000 communities in Eastern Europe where Jews lived prior to the Holocaust. Compiled by Yad Vashem. Shows pre-war town name, province, country and Jewish population. (2 fiche)

    e. **Index to "Memorial to the Jews Deported From France".** Alphabetic list of 50,000 surnames that appear in *Memorial to the Jews Deported From France*. Shows surname and convoy number. (1 fiche)

    f. **Index to Russian Consular Records.** Lists over 70,000 persons who transacted business with the Russian Czarist consulates in the United States from about 1849-1926. Shows surname, given name, place of residence and locator reference to microfilm at the U.S. National Archives which contains original documents. Indexed using the Daitch-Mokotoff Soundex System. (7 fiche)

    g. **Palestine Gazette.** List of over 28,000 persons who legally changed their name (mostly Jews) while living in Palestine during the British Mandate from 1921-1948. Shows original surname and given name, new surname and given name, nationality, city of residence, and date and page reference to the *Palestine Gazette*. Indexed by original surname, new surname. Includes index of all surnames using the Daitch-Mokotoff Soundex System. (6 fiche)

    h. **Publications of the Jewish Genealogical Societies, 1977-1990.** A complete set of all the newsletters and journals of the member societies of the Association of Jewish Genealogical Societies (AJGS), 1977-1990. Includes *Avotaynu*, *Toledot*, *Search* (Chicago), *Dorot* (NY), *Mishpacha* (Washington), and many others. See next section for contents listing. (24 fiche)

    i. **Towns and Administrative Districts in Galicia, 1877.** Alphabetical index of 6,000 towns in the province of Galicia (Austrian Poland), showing the administrative districts to which they belong, where vital records were collected. (2 fiche)

    j. **Index of Jewish Applicants for Emergency U.S. Passports, 1915-1924.** Index to U.S. Department of State Records in the National Archives. Passport applications by U.S. citizens and derivative citizens. (2 fiche)

    k. **Index of U.S. Citizens Registering at the Consular Post in Jerusalem, 1914-1918.** U.S. Department of State Consular Post Records of U.S. citizens visiting or living in Palestine. (1 fiche)

    l. **Index of Jewish Names from the U.S. Department of State Decimal File (RG 59) Series on Protection of Interests of U.S. Citizens.** U.S. State Department "Protection of Interests" files of correspondence and requests for assistance by U.S. citizens. Alphabetized in three series: Germany, Poland and Romainia, 1910-1929 (2 fiche); Austria-Hungary, 1910-1939 (1 fiche); Russia, 1910-1929 (1 fiche)

    m. **Burials in the Old Section of the Washington DC Hebrew Congregation Cemetery.** (1 fiche)

    n. **Burials in Adas Israel Congregation Cemetery in Washington, D.C., 1870-1919.** (1 fiche)

    o. *Jewish Genealogical People Finder*. Third edition, 1995. Contains over 300,000 entries submitted by over 200 Jewish genealogists. Contains name, date and place of birth and death, parents' names, spouse's name. Indexed using the Daitch-Mokotoff Soundex System. (22 fiche).

    p. **Index to Jewish Vital Statistics Records in Slovakian Archives.** Town index to birth, marriage and death records in the archives of Slovakia. For 4,000 towns, tells in which archive records are located. (1 fiche, 1993).

q. **Index to 1784 Census of Jews of Alsace**. Documents some 20,000 Jews who were enumerated in this French census. In four sequences: by surname, by given name, by town, by maiden name. (1 fiche, 1993).

r. **Jewish Residents in Canadian Censuses**. Extracts of Jewish residents gleaned from Canadian Censuses, 1861-1901, by Glen Eker. Monteal and Quebec City (1871-1901), Toronto (1861-1901), Western Canada (1861-1901), Maritime Provinces (1901), Greater Quebec Province (1871-1901) (5 fiche, 1993-95).

s. **Birth Index for Buda Jewry, 1820-1852, 1868**. Index to certain Jewish birth records of Budapest (2 fiche).

t. **Jewish Cemeteries Throughout the World**. Information on more than 7,500 cemeteries in 79 countries. (2 fiche, 1995).

u. **List of 56,000 Jewish Burials**. Initial submission to AJGS cemetery project. (3 fiche, 1995).

v. **Noms des Juifs du Maroc - Moroccan Jewish Surnames**. (1 fiche, 1995).

w. **Romanian Census Records**. Index to the census of Jews in 1824-25; 1852 census of Jews in Monesti. (1 fiche, 1995).

The *Family History Library Catalog* (FHLC) is the catalog of the Mormon Family History Library in Salt Lake City. The JGSGB has purchased portions of the FHLC Locality catalog for Hebrew College. This set of over 400 microfiche covers all of Eastern Europe, the Western republics of the former Soviet Union, most of Northern Europe, and the Northeastern United States. See page 92 for details on how to use the FHLC.

8. <u>Periodicals</u> - Hebrew College has a collection of hundreds of periodicals. Current issues of periodicals are upstairs in a large rack near the card catalog. Older issues are downstairs in the periodicals room, on the right. The *Index to Jewish Periodicals*, English and Hebrew Indexes, are located downstairs in the main hallway.

A select list of publications of Jewish historical and genealogical organizations appears below. (Not all listed holdings are complete series). Those items marked with an asterisk are also available on the AJGS microfiche (see item 7h above).

Albany Jewish Genealogical Society. *Newsletter*. [BD A46n]
American Portuguese Genealogical and Historical Society. *Bulletin Board*. [BD A615]
Ancestree. Jewish Genealogical Society of Greater Cincinnati. [BD A618]
Av va em. Jewish Henealogical Society of Tidewater (Virginia). [BD A86]
Avi Avot. Jewish Genealogical Society of Orange County (California). *[fiche #2-3] [BD A9]
Avotaynu: The International Review of Jewish Genealogy. Avotaynu, Inc., Teaneck, New Jersey. (Quarterly, 1985-) *[fiche #4-7] [BD]
Branches. Jewish Genealogical Society of Greater Miami [BD B8]
Cercle de Genealogie Juive. *Revue*. [BC C4r]
Chicago Jewish History. Chicago Jewish Historical Society. Formerly *Society News*. [BD C52s]
Chronicle. Arizona Jewish Historical Society. Southern Arizona Chapter. [BD C55]
Chronicles. Jewish Genealogical Society of Philadelphia. *[fiche #8] [BD C56]
Cleveland Kol. Cleveland Jewish Genealogy Society. [BD C59]
Discovery. San Diego Jewish Genealogical Society. [BD D55]
Dorot: Journal of the Jewish Genealogical Society. Jewish Genealogical Society, Inc. (New York). (Quarterly, 1979-). *[fiche #9-10] [BD D6]
Etz Chaim. Jewish Genealogical Society of Greater Orlando. [BD E8]
A Family Affair. Jewish Genealogical Society of Houston. [BD F3]
Family Finding. Wisconsin Jewish Genealogical Society [BD F34]
Gahelet. Igud Yotse Lita be-Yisrael (in Hebrew). [BA 4ა]
Gamsu. West Chester, PA. [BD G3]
Generations. Jewish Historical Society of Michigan. [BD G43]
Illiana Jewish Genealogical Society. *Newsletter*. [BD I4n]
Immigrant Genealogical Society. *Newsletter*. [BD I39n]
Indiana Jewish Historical Society. *Newsletter*. [BD I43n]
Indiana Jewish History. Indiana Jewish Historical Society. [BD I432]
Jewish Genealogical Society of North Jersey. *Newsletter*. *[fiche #15] Became *Yichus*. [BD J383n]
Jewish Genealogical Society of Rochester (NY). *Newsletter*. [BD J3836n]
Jewish Genealogical Society of Sacramento (California). *Newsletter*. [BD J384n]
Jewish Genealogical Society of Washington State. *Newsletter*. [BD J3842n]
Jewish Historical Society of Delaware. *Newsletter*. [BD J3843n]

Jewish Historical Society of Michigan. *Newsletter*. [BD J4n]
Landsmen: Quarterly Publication of the Suwalk-Lomza Interest Group for Jewish Genealogists. (1990-).
    [BD L33]
Latvian Jewish Courier. Jewish Survivors of Latvia. [BD L36]
Lineage. Jewish Genealogy Society of Long Island (NY). [BD L45]
Local Jewish Historical Society News. American Jewish Historical Society. [BD L62]
Maajan die Quelle. Schweizerische Vereinigung fur Judische Genealogie. [BC M3]
Mass-pocha. Jewish Genealogical Society of Greater Boston. (Quarterly, 1992-). [BD M29]
Michigan Jewish History. Jewish Historical Society of Michigan. [BD M55]
Mishpacha. Jewish Genealogy Society of Greater Washington. (1983-) *[fiche #11-12] [BD M6]
Morasha. Jewish Genealogical Society of Illinois. *[fiche #13-14] [BD M7]
Nebraska Jewish Historical Society. *Newsletter*. [BD N43n]
North Shore Jewish Historical Society (Massachusetts). *Newsletter*. [BD N7n]
Quest. Jewish Genealogical Society of Connecticut. [BD Q72]
Rhode Island Jewish Historical Notes. Rhode Island Jewish Historical Association. [BD R55]
ROM-SIG News. Jewish Genealogical Special Interest Group for Romania. [BD R6]
Roots-Key. Jewish Genealogical Society of Los Angeles. [BD R7]
The SAGA. Savannah Area Genealogical Association. [BD S3]
San Diego Jewish Genealogical Society. *Newsletter*. *[fiche #16] Became *Discovery*. [BD S33n]
San Fransisco Bay Area Jewish Genealogical Society. *Newsletter*. Became *ZichronNote*. [BD S34]
Scattered Seeds. Jewish Genealogical Society of Palm Beach County (Florida). [BD S37]
Search: International Quarterly for Researchers of Jewish Genealogy. Jewish Genealogical Society of Illinois.
    (1981-1992) *[fiche #17-20] [BD]
Shashelet (Chain). Jewish Genealogical Society of Oregon. [BD S42]
Sharsheret Hadorot. Israel Genealogical Society. [BD S43]
Shem Tov. Jewish Genealogical Society of Toronto. [BD S47]
Shemot. Jewish Genealogical Society of Great Britain. [BD S475]
Shorashim (Sources). South Orange County (California) Jewish Genealogical Society. [BD S49]
Tayerer Landsman. Jewish Genealogy Society of South Florida. *[fiche #21] [BD T37]
Texas Jewish Historical Society. *Newsletter*. [BD T42]
Toledot: The Journal of Jewish Genealogy. Toledot Press, New York. (Quarterly, 1977-1981). Edited by
    Steven W. Siegel and Arthur Kurzweil. *[fiche #22-23] [BD]
Western States Jewish History. Western States Jewish History Association.
Yichus. Jewish Genealogical Society of North Jersey. [BD Y465]
Yichus Y'all. Jewish Genealogical Society of Georgia. [BD Y466]
Z'chor. Pittsburgh Jewish Genealogical Society. *[fiche #1] [BD Z3]
ZichronNote. San Fransisco Bay Area Jewish Genealogical Society. [BD Z5]

9. Local History - About 20 books on Boston Jewry are available under call number [XZD Boston], including most of the works cited in the section on the Boston Public Library (page 56). Also of note are the Boston Jewish Community Surveys:

    1930: *Boston Jewish Communal Survey*. [XZD Boston B65]
    1967: *A Community Survey for Long Range Planing: A Study of the Jewish Population of Greater Boston*.
            [YAe C6c]
    1975: *1975 Community Survey: A Study of the Jewish Population of Greater Boston*. (125p)
            [YAe C6c 1977]
    1985: *Boston's Jewish Community: The 1985 CJP Demographic Study*. (172p) [YAe C6c 1987]

Other works on local history are available under [XZD <townname>], and some synagogue and organizational histories are classified under [YR].

10. Archival Collection - Hebrew College's archival collections include papers relating to the development of Hebrew College and Boston Jewry from 1920 onword. Manuscripts of Solomon Zucrow, 1920-1930, and Abraham Charak, 1905-1909, prominent Jewish educators in the Greater Boston area, are included in the collection.

Finding Aids:

The card catalog contains Author, Title and Subject cards integrated into one alphabetical sequence. There are a separate set of drawers for Hebrew titles. Hebrew College Library uses the Freidus classification scheme (as does the Jewish Division of the New York Public Library). Topics related to genealogy include:

X	History	
	XA - XE	History, general
	XG - XK	History, chronological
	XKC	Holocaust period
	XL - XY	History, by Country
	XL	Middle East
	XM	Balkans, Romania
	XN	Italy
	XO	Spain/Portugal
	XP	France
	XQ	Great Britain
	XS	Germany
	XT	Austria/Hungary
	XU	Eastern Europe

XV		Poland
XW		Russia
XX		Latin America
XY		United States
XZ		History, by Cities
	XZD	Local histories
W	Biography	
	WN	Cemetery Inscriptions
	WO	Genealogy
	WR	Collective Biographies
	WZ	Individual Biographies
Y	Sociology	
	YR	Synagogue Histories
Z	Zionism, Israel, Anti-Semitism	

The college publishes the quarterly *Hebrew College Today*, which describes activities at Hebrew College, updates on students and faculty, etc.

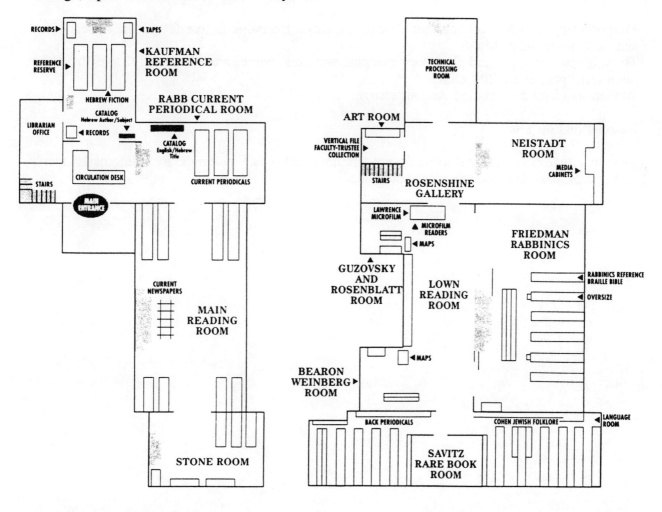

Description of Facility:

The Hebrew College Library is housed in a former mansion, built in 1907. Hebrew College moved into this Brookline building in 1951. The upper level was renovated in 1973, and the basement area was opened in 1981.

There is seating for 25 researchers upstairs, and 16 downstairs. There are two microfilm readers, one microfiche reader, and one microfilm/fiche reader/printer, located downstairs. Please ask for assistance with the microform readers.

Hebrew College is a member of the Fenway Library Consortium, a group of thirteen cooperating libraries. Materials may be borrowed from all libraries upon presentation of a valid Consortium identification card, subject to the rules of that library. In addition, Hebrew College has consortium-type relations with Boston University.

> The members of the Fenway Library Consortium are: Brookline Public Library, Emerson College, Emmanuel College, Hebrew College, Massachusetts College of Art, Massachusetts College of Pharmacy and Allied Health Sciences, Museum of Fine Arts, New England Conservatory of Music, Simmons College, Suffolk University, Wentworth Institute of Technology, Wheelock College and the University of Massachusetts (Harbor Campus).

Fees/Copies:

Membership fee is $25.00 per year (borrowing fee). Everyone is free to use the materials on site, without membership.
There is one coin-operated photocopy machine available, copies are 10¢ each. Copies from the microform printer are 20¢ each.
Written inquiries are handled without charge.

Restrictions on Use:

Reference materials and rare books do not circulate. All other materials, including newspapers, periodicals, cassettes and recordings circulate.

JEWISH CEMETERY ASSOCIATION OF MASSACHUSETTS

Facility Director:	Stanley J. Kaplan, President Miriam Drukman, Administrator
Address:	Jewish Cemetery Association of Massachusetts, Inc. 1320 Centre Street, Suite #306 Newton Centre, MA 02159
Phone Number:	(617) 244-6509

Hours of Operation:

Monday to Thursday:	9:00am - 5:00pm
Friday:	9:00am - 2:00pm
Closed Jewish Holidays.	

Directions: The JCAM office is located on Centre Street in Newton, just north of Newton Centre. Directions to member cemeteries are provided at the end of this section.

Description of Institution:

The JEWISH CEMETERY ASSOCIATION OF MASSACHUSETTS (JCAM) was founded in 1984 to meet regional needs for cemetery rehabilitation, management and preservation. To these ends it has focused on abandoned Jewish cemeteries and has encouraged affiliation by functioning cemetery associations as a necessary alternative to dissolution. JCAM has been mentored by the Combined Jewish Philanthropies (CJP) of Greater Boston and the Synagogue Council of Massachusetts. Liaisons have been established with the major Jewish service organizations, cemetery and legal services. JCAM publications include the annual *Guide to Jewish Cemeteries* and a quarterly *Newsletter*.

Description of Resources:

The JCAM office staff answers telephone and mail (preferred) inquiries, but is usually not responsive to visits. Its database can produce lists of affiliated cemeteries and names of interred individuals, often with burial dates. Maps of cemetery sites and burial plot arrangements exist for many cemeteries. Their archive has become a valuable resource for people searching for relatives' graves.

JCAM has established a computer database from the records of individual cemeteries to eventually provide a practical and historical record of all Jewish burials in the greater Boston area. The JCAM database currently contains over 65,000 individual entries from 62 cemeteries, split up into nine separate databases: Baker Street, West Roxbury (about 22,000 graves); Centre/Grove Streets, West Roxbury (5K); Woburn (14K); North Shore (7K); Everett (7K);

Brockton (4K); East Boston (2K); West (Framingham/Natick and Beth Israel Waltham, 3K); and Melrose (1K). The database contains records for each cemetery JCAM manages (but see exceptions below); it does not include those cemeteries which are privately managed.

[Exceptions: There were no written records for Sons of Benjamin (Grove Street), Beth Abraham (Grove Street), Chevra Thillim and Shary Cedeck (Centre Street). Destroyed records for Sons of Benjamin (Grove Street) and Beth Abraham (Grove Street) were reconstructed from tombstone inscriptions by the JGSGB in 1992-93, but are not in the database].

For each individual, the database contains the surname and given name, date of death (usually), and grave location (cemetery, section and lot number). For burials since 1984, the database also contains the name and address of next of kin. Some information on plot ownership is also available. The types and quality of the data vary, since the information for each cemetery comes from diverse original sources.

There is no public access to the database; all inquiries must be made through the JCAM office.

Finding Aids:

JCAM's annual *Guide to Jewish Cemeteries* lists its member cemeteries, along with a contact representative for each. The *Guide* provides maps and directions to cemetery locations. It also lists the leading funeral and cemetery service organizations in the Boston metropolitan area.

Description of Facility:

JCAM has a small one-room office, sharing a suite with the offices of the Synagogue Council of Massachusetts. There is no space for researchers.

Fees/Copies:

There is no charge for information. Inquiries may be made without fee, though donations to JCAM are suggested.

Other Resources:

Massachusetts death certificates (available at the MASSACHUSETTS ARCHIVES [for 1841-1900] and the REGISTRY OF VITAL RECORDS AND STATISTICS [for 1901-date], see page 29) list the deceased individual's burial site. Death certificates should be researched first, to ascertain the correct cemetery.

Jewish funeral directors in the Boston area include:
  • Levine Chapels   470 Harvard Street, Brookline, MA 02146
    (Established 1893)   (617) 277-8300   1-800-367-3708
  • Stanetsky Chapels   1668 Beacon Street, Brookline, MA 02146
    (Established 1892)   (617) 232-9300   1-800-842-4280
  • Schlossberg & Solomon 824 Washington Street, Canton, MA 02021-2546
                            (617) 828-6990   1-800-828-6993
  • Goldman Fisher Chapel 174 Ferry Street, Malden, MA
                            (617) 324-1122   (508) 683-2411

Resources for Jewish Genealogy in the Boston Area

Member Cemeteries:

JCAM members are divided into two categories:

- Constituent members are Jewish cemeteries which have merged assets and liabilities, including all property and archives, into JCAM.

- Sustaining members are independent cemetery associations that support the concepts of JCAM with their membership. Several sustaining members contract for one or more of the management services offered by JCAM; they are indicated in the list below with an asterisk.

Constituent:

Abramson	Baker St., West Roxbury
Ahavath Achim / Anshe Sfard of Chelsea	Lynn (Lake Shore Rd.)
Anshe Dowig Association	Centre St., West Roxbury
Bessarabian	Everett (Fuller St.)
Beth Abraham	Grove St., West Roxbury
Beth Jacob	Woburn
Beth Joseph #1 (Ohel Torah)	Woburn
Beth Joseph #2	Woburn
Beth Joseph #3	Woburn
Bresna	Centre St., West Roxbury
Butrimantzy	Baker St., West Roxbury
Chevra Chai Odom	Everett (Fuller St.)
Chevra Shaas	Baker St., West Roxbury
Chevra Thillim	Centre St., West Roxbury
Congregation Beth Israel	Centre St., West Roxbury
Congregation Chai Odom	Centre St., West Roxbury
Farband (Jewish Nat'l Workers Alliance)	Danvers (Buxton Rd.)
Guard of Moses	Everett (Fuller St.)
Hebrew Progressive	Grove St., West Roxbury
Hebrew Volin	Baker St., West Roxbury
Immigrants Mutual Aid Society (IMAS) Cemeteries:	
Roxbury Lodge / Sons of Abraham / Zviller	
	Baker St., West Roxbury
Independent Golden Crown	Woburn
Independent Pride of Boston	Baker St., West Roxbury; and Woburn
Independent Workmen's Circle	Baker St., West Roxbury
Kehillath Jacob	Baker St., West Roxbury
King Solomon Memorial Park	Centre St., West Roxbury
Knights of Zaslav	Everett
Kopiagorod	Baker St., West Roxbury
Kovner	Baker St., West Roxbury
Liberty Progressive	Everett (Fuller St.)
Lynn Hebrew Benevolent Society	Wakefield (North Ave.)
Maplewood / Lebanon Street	Malden
Meretz	Woburn
Mishna of Chelsea	Everett (Fuller St.)
Olita	Baker St., West Roxbury
Onikchty Society	Melrose (Route 99)
Ostro Hebrew Marshoe	Baker St., West Roxbury
Poali Zedeck	Everett (Fuller St.)
Polonnoe	Baker St., West Roxbury
Pultusker	Baker St., West Roxbury

Roumanian American	Danvers (Buxton Road)
Sharei Sedeck	Centre St., West Roxbury
Shari Jerusalem	Grove St., West Roxbury
Sons of Benjamin	Grove St., West Roxbury
Tifereth Israel of Winthrop	Everett (Fuller St.)
Vilkomer	Melrose (Route 99)
Vilno	Baker St., West Roxbury
Workmen's Circle	Melrose (Route 99), and Peabody (Route 114)

Sustaining:

Adath Jeshrun	Grove St., West Roxbury
Agudas Achim	Brockton
Agudas Achim	Woburn
Agudas Shalom	Everett
Agudath Israel	Baker St., West Roxbury
Ahabat Shalom	Danvers
Ahavas Achim Anshe Sfard	Everett
American Austrian	Woburn
American Friendship	Baker St., West Roxbury
Amos Lodge #27 B'nai Brith	Wakefield
Anshe Sfard of Lynn	Danvers
Atereth Israel	Baker St., West Roxbury
Beth El	Baker St., West Roxbury
Beth Israel	Everett
*Beth Israel Memorial Park	Waltham (South St.)
Beth Israel of Malden	North Reading
*Boylston Lodge Memorial Park	Baker St., West Roxbury
*Chevra Kadusha of Boston	Woburn
Chevra Mishnais / Agudas Achim	Woburn
Chevra Thillim / Boston & Chelsea	Everett
Chevra Thillim of Malden	Everett
Congregation Anshei Sfard	Baker St., West Roxbury
Crawford Street	Baker St., West Roxbury
David Vicor Cholim	Baker St., West Roxbury
Dorchester Hebrew Helping Hand	Everett
Ezrath Israel of Malden	Danvers
*Framingham-Natick Hebrew	Natick (Windsor Ave.)
Hebrew Rehabilitation Center	Baker St., West Roxbury
Hadrath Israel	Melrose
Jewish Benevolent	Grove St., West Roxbury
Jewish Civil Service	Grove St., West Roxbury
Jewish Community Center / Chelsea	Danvers
*Jewish Deedholders	Everett (Fuller St.)
Kaminker	Baker St., West Roxbury
Kenesseth Israel	Woburn
Klevaner	Everett
Knights of Liberty	Woburn
Koretz	Baker St., West Roxbury
*Lawrence Avenue	Baker St., West Roxbury
Lebanon - Tifereth Israel	Peabody (Route 128)
Linas Hatzedek #1	Everett
Lindwood Memorial Park	Randolph
Maple Hill	Peabody (Route 114)

Mishkan Tefilan Memorial Park	Centre St., West Roxbury
*Mohliver	Baker St., West Roxbury
*Montifiore Cemeteries	Everett and Woburn
Moses Mendelsohn	Grove St., West Roxbury; and Randolph
Mt. Nevo / Cong. Agudath Achim	Taunton
Netherlands	Melrose
Netzah Israel	Everett
North Russell Street Shul (Chevra Thilim)	Everett
Ohavi Sedeck	Grove St., West Roxbury
*Plymouth Rock	Brockton
*Pride of Boston	Woburn
Pride of Brockton	Brockton
*Pride of Jacob	Grove St., West Roxbury
Pride of Lynn	Lynn
Puritan	Baker St., West Roxbury
Quincy Hebrew Society	Baker St., West Roxbury
Roxbury Mutual Society	Woburn
Sharah Tfilo	Baker St., West Roxbury
Shari Jerusalem	Woburn
Sharon Memorial Park	Sharon
Shepetovka	Baker St., West Roxbury
Sons of Abraham	Baker St., West Roxbury
Staro Konstantinov	Baker St., West Roxbury
Stepiner	Baker St., West Roxbury
Temple B'nai Brith of Somerville	Peabody
Temple Beth Ed	Chelmsford
Temple Beth El of Springfield	Springfield
Temple Beth Shalom of Cambridge	Everett
Temple Beth Shalom of Peabody	Danvers
Temple Emanuel of Newton	Randolph
*Temple Emeth Memorial Park	Baker St., West Roxbury
Temple Emmanuel of Chelsea	Danvers
Temple Israel (Adath Israel)	Wakefield
Temple Israel Burial Society	Everett
*Temple Ohabei Shalom	East Boston (Wordsworth St.)
Temple Reyim (Lindwood Mem. Park)	Randolph
Temple Shalom of Medford	Peabody (Route 128)
*Tifereth Israel	Grove St., West Roxbury
Tifereth Israel of Everett	Everett
Woburn Hebrew Center	Woburn
Young Israel of Brookline	Grove St., West Roxbury
Zviller	Baker St., West Roxbury

Total of 134 cemeteries -- 52 constituent members, 82 sustaining members (including 13 cemeteries managed by JCAM, indicated with an * asterisk).

Other Cemeteries:

The following cemeteries are **not** members of JCAM, and are listed here for convenience. This is an attempt to list all other Jewish cemeteries in Massachusetts. JCAM **may** have contact information.

(Cong.) Adas Yisroeil	Grove St., West Roxbury
(Cong.) Anshe Lebovitz	Woburn
(Cong.) Anshei Sfard	Baker St., West Roxbury
(Cong.) Anshei Poland	Woburn
Agudas Achim	Fitchburg
Agudas Achim of Malden	Melrose
Agudath Achim	Fall River
Agudath Israel	Baker St., West Roxbury
Ahavas Achim Anshe Sfard	Everett
Ahavath Achim	New Bedford
B'nai Brith	Worcester
B'nai Israel	Northampton
B'nai Jacob	West Springfield
Beth David	Woburn
Beth El	Fall River
Beth Israel	West Springfield
Birsen	Everett
Chesed Shel Emeth	Danvers
Chevra Kadisha (Holy Society)	Leicester
Chevra Kadusha of Chelsea	Everett/Woburn
Chevra Mishna of Chelsea	Lynn
Chevra Mishnias / Agudas Achim	Woburn
Children of Israel	Haverhill
City of Homes	Springfield
Custom Tailors	Baker St., West Roxbury
Dodgeville	Attleboro
Hebrew Cemetery	Fall River
Jewish Community Association, Amherst	Shutesbury
Kesser Israel	Springfield
Knesset Israel	Pittsfield
Kodimoh	West Springfield
Lord Rothschild	Baker St., West Roxbury
Montifiore Synagogue	Pelham, NH
Mt. Jacob	West Gloucester
Newburyport Hebrew	Newburyport
Oak Hill / Chevra Kadusha	Peabody
Ohel Jacob	Woburn
Pride of Liberty	Baker St., West Roxbury
Prospect Hill	Millis
Rabbi Isaac Elchonon	Everett
Rodphey Sholom	Chicopee
Sons of Benjamin	Beverly
Sons of Israel	Springfield
Sons of Israel	Lawrence
Sons of Jacob	Leicester
Sons of Jacob of Salem	Danvers
Sons of Zion	Springfield
Stepiner	Baker St., West Roxbury
Sudlikov	Everett

Temple Beth El Swampscott	Peabody
Temple Emanu-El Marblehead	Danvers
Temple Emanuel	Wakefield
Temple Emanuel	Lawrence
Temple Israel Swampscott	Peabody
Temple Sinai Marblehead	Danvers
Temple Tefereth Israel Revere	Everett
Tifereth Anshe Sfard	Lawrence
Tifereth Israel	New Bedford
Worcester Hebrew Center	Auburn

Synagogues and their Corresponding Cemeteries:

The first Jewish cemetery in the Boston area was that of Temple Ohabei Shalom in East Boston, founded in 1844. The cemetery complexes on Grove and Centre Streets in West Roxbury were begun in the mid 1880s. The Woburn cemeteries were opened in the late 1890s. The cemeteries on Baker Street in West Roxbury and those in Everett were opened in the 1920s. All the other cemetery complexes were developed in the early twentieth century.

The early cemeteries were founded by diverse groups. Some were congregational cemeteries, but many others were started by other types of organizations: landsmanshaftn (associations of people from the same European ancestral town), labor unions, fraternal and charitable organizations.

Many synagogues used a particular cemetery. The following table shows some synagogues and the cemetery which the congregation used.

Shul	Shul Location	Cemetery	Cemetery Location
Ashkenaze Shul	Cambridge	Temple Beth Shalom	Everett
Baldwin Place	North End	Congregation Beth Israel	Centre St.
Blue Hill Avenue	Roxbury	Adath Jeshrun	Grove St.
Chambers Street	West End	Beth Joseph 3 (Vilna)	Woburn
Chestnut Street	Chelsea	Linas Hatzedek #2	Everett
Crawford Street	Roxbury	Beth Hamidrash Hagadol	Baker St.
Elm Street	Chelsea	Ahavas Achim / Anshe Sfard	Lynn
Emerald Street	South End	Knesseth Israel	Woburn
Fessenden Street	Mattapan	Kehillath Jacob	Baker St.
Fowler Street	Dorchester	Beth El	Baker St.
Haskins Street	Roxbury	Anshe Sfard	Baker St.
Intervale Street	Roxbury	Shepetovka	Baker St.
Kehillath Israel	Brookline	Lindwood Memorial Park	Randolph
Lawrence Avenue	Roxbury	New Palestine	Baker St.
Moreland Street	Roxbury	Atereth Israel	Baker St.
Nightingale Street	Dorchester	Congregation Chai Odom	Centre St.
North Russell Street	West End	Chevra Thillim / Anshe Sfard	Woburn
Otisfield Street	Roxbury	Shara Tfilo	Baker St.
Poplar Street	West End	Agudath Achim	Woburn
Seaver Street	Roxbury	Mishkan Tefilah	Centre St.
Shurtleff Street	Chelsea	Mishna of Chelsea	Everett
Temple Beth El	Chelmsford	Lowell Hebrew Community Center	
Temple Reyim	Newton	Lindwood Memorial Park	Randolph
Temple Emanuel	Newton	Lindwood Memorial Park	Randolph
Third Street	Chelsea	Linas Hatzedek #1	Everett
Wall Street	West End	Beth Jacob	Woburn
Walnut Street	Chelsea	Agudas Shalom	Everett
Walnut Avenue	Revere	Ahavas Achim	Everett
Wayland Street	Roxbury	Sons of Abraham	Baker St.
Woodrow Ave. (Litvash)	Dorchester	Hadrath Israel	Melrose
Woodrow Avenue	Dorchester	Agudath Israel	Baker St.

Directions to Cemeteries:

West Roxbury: **Baker Street**	From Route 128 (I-95) take Exit 15A (Dedham). Take Route 1 North for 3.2 miles to VFW Parkway. Continue 1 mile, then turn left onto Baker Street. Go ½ mile to Cemeteries on left.
Centre Street	From Route 128 (I-95) take Exit 15A (Dedham). Take Route 1 North for 1.7 miles, bear right onto Washington Street. Go ½ mile, then left onto Curve Street. Follow 1/3 mile. Cemeteries on left.
Grove Street	From Route 128 (I-95) take Exit 15A (Dedham). Take Route 1 North for 1.7 miles, bear right onto Washington Street. Go 1 mile, then right onto Grove Street. Go ¼ mile, then left at Jeshrun Road.
Lynn:	From the North, exit off Route 128 onto Route 1 South. Go to first traffic light, then left onto Route 129. From the South, take Route 128 to Route 129 East (Lynnfield Street). Follow Route 129 three miles to Wyoma Street. Take left onto Broadway. Go past St. Joseph Cemetery, turn left onto Bay State Road, then left again onto Lakeshore Road and to cemeteries at end.
Melrose:	From the South, go over the Mystic River Bridge onto Route 1 North. Go 6 miles. Exit at "Essex Street - Melrose". Go over Route 1 and back onto Route 1 South. From the North, take Route 128 to Route 1 South. Bear right off Route 1 South onto Route 99. Go 1/3 mile to cemeteries on both sides of the road.
Woburn:	From Route 93 take Exit 36 "Montvale Ave.", left at end under Route 93, then 1/3 mile to light. Take left onto Washington Street. Cemeteries are 1/3 mile on right.
Everett:	From the South, go over the Mystic River Bridge onto Route 1 North. From the North, take Route 128 to Route 1 South. Exit from Route 1 at "Sargent St." (Revere). Go right (under Route 1) to end. Then take right and next left onto Fuller Street. Cemeteries are off roadways on right.
Wakefield:	Take Route 128 to Exit 39 ("North Ave. - Wakefield"). Cemeteries are one mile on the left, before the lake.
Peabody (128):	On Route 128 North, travel past the Route 114 overpass. Go several hundred yards, then turn right off Route 128 to cemeteries.
Peabody (114):	From Route 128 North, exit at Route 114 East ("Peabody - Salem"). At the first traffic light turn left onto Esquire Road and go to end. Turn left and follow as road bears right. Cemeteries directly ahead.
Danvers:	Take Route 128 onto Route 1 North. Exit at Route 114 West ("Middleton"). Go one mile, then turn left at "Jewish Cemetery" sign. Follow road to cemeteries.
Randolph:	Take Route 128 to Exit 5A (Rte 28 South "Randolph"). Go 2 miles, past Temple Beth Am, then turn left onto Liberty Street. Follow to end. Turn left onto North Street. Cemetery entrance is ¼ mile on the right.
Framingham / **Natick:**	Take Route 9 to Route 27 South. Follow Route 27 through Natick Center (Jct Rte 135) and take first right onto Pond Street. Follow Pond Street to Lakeview Ave. Left onto Lakeview, then left onto Windsor Ave. The cemetery is a short way up on the left side of Windsor Ave.
Brockton:	Take Route 24 to Route 123 West. Make left at lights onto Pearl Street. Plymouth Rock Cemetery is ¼ mile on the right.
Sharon:	Take Route 128 to Exit 2A (Rte 138 "Stoughton"). Go ½ mile, then bear right at the first light onto Washington Street. Go three miles through Canton Center, then turn right onto High Street. Proceed over a railroad bridge, past Knollwood Memorial Park and turn right onto Dedham Street. Main Cemetery entrance is the next right.
Waltham:	From Route 128, take Exit 24 (Route 30). If exiting from north, take Route 30 West over Route 128 and turn right at traffic light onto South Street. If exiting from south, go straight at traffic light, crossing Route 30 onto South Street. Follow signs to Brandeis University. Beth Israel Memorial Park is located on right side of road beyond Brandeis University, before Waltham-Weston Hospital.
East Boston:	Exit Callahan Tunnel and take hard right turn onto Parker Street to end. Turn left onto Chelsea Street, go 0.6 miles and bear right onto Bennington Street (Route 140 North). Go .7 miles to Wordsworth Street. Turn right onto Wordsworth, go to end. Temple Ohabei Shalom Cemetery is on right. Use the last gate on right. Gate opens towards street by pulling up on white handle.

Reading Hebrew Tombstones

Hebrew Alphabet		
1	א	aleph
2	ב	bet
3	ג	gimel
4	ד	dalet
5	ה	hay
6	ו	vav
7	ז	zayin
8	ח	khet
9	ט	tet
10	י	yud
20	כ	kaf
30	ל	lamed
40	מ	mem
50	נ	nun
60	ס	samech
70	ע	ayin
80	פ	pay
90	צ	tzade
100	ק	kuf
200	ר	resh
300	ש	shin
400	ת	tav

If a tombstone is written in Hebrew (as most Jewish tombstones are - in part, if not completely), a few pointers will be helpful if you cannot read the language.

At the top of most Jewish tombstones is the abbreviation פ"נ, which stands for פֹּה נִקְבַּר , meaning "here lies".

At the end of many Jewish tombstone inscriptions you will find the abbreviation תנצב"ה, which stands for תְהִי נַפְשׁוֹ צְרוּרָה בִּצְרוֹר הַחַיִּים. This is a verse from I Samuel 25:29, "May his soul be bound up in the bond of eternal life".

If any Hebrew characters at all are written on a tombstone, they are most likely to be the person's **Hebrew name**. A Hebrew name always includes the person's father's name. This is a unique feature of Jewish tombstones, and a great boon to genealogy. The Hebrew word בן, *ben*, means "son of", as in "Yaacov ben Yitzhak". בת, *bat*, means "daughter of". On tombstones these words will often appear as ב'ר, an abbreviation for *ben reb*, meaning "son (or daughter) of the worthy", followed by the father's name.

Dates are written in Hebrew according to the **Jewish calendar**. This calendar, which starts its Year One with the Creation of the World, was probably designed by the patriarch Hillel II in the fourth century. He calculated the age of the world by computing the literal ages of biblical characters and other events in the Bible, and came up with a calendar that begins 3760 years before the Christian calendar.

The letters of the Hebrew Alphabet each have a numerical value, specified in the accompanying chart. When a Hebrew date is written, you must figure out the numerical value of each letter and then add them up. This is the date according to the Jewish calendar, not the calendar we use in every day life, known as the Gregorian calendar (also referred to as the Common Era, civil or Christian calendar). In October 1995, for example, the Jewish year was 5756. Given a Hebrew date, you need to do only a little arithmetic to change a Hebrew year into a secular year.

There is one minor complication: often a Hebrew date after the year 5000 on the Jewish calendar will leave off the number 5 in the thousands column. In other words, the Hebrew year 5680 will be written as 680 rather than 5680. To arrive at the Common Era (Gregorian) year, simply add the number 1240 to the shortened Hebrew year.

Days	
א	1
ב	2
ג	3
ד	4
ה	5
ו	6
ז	7
ח	8
ט	9
י	10
יא	11
יב	12
יג	13
יד	14
טו	15
טז	16
יז	17
יח	18
יט	19
כ	20
כא	21
כב	22
כג	23
כד	24
כה	25
כו	26
כז	27
כח	28
כט	29
ל	30

Hebrew Months:

תשרי	Tishre	Sep/Oct
חשון	Heshvan	Oct/Nov
כסלו	Kislev	Nov/Dec
טבת	Tevet	Dec/Jan
שבט	Shevat	Jan/Feb
אדר	Adar	Feb/Mar
אדר ב'	Adar II	Mar
ניסן	Nisan	Mar/Apr
אייר	Iyar	Apr/May
סיון	Sivan	May/Jun
תמוז	Tamuz	Jun/Jul
אב	Av	Jul/Aug
אלול	Elul	Aug/Sep

Here's one example: If the year is written as תרפג, the letter ת is 400, the letter ר is 200, פ is 80, and ג is 3. 400 + 200 + 80 + 3 = 683. The 5000 is usually left off, the actual year would be 5683. By using our formula, 683 plus 1240 is 1923. That is the civil year.

The Hebrew year begins on Rosh Hashanah, which appears on the Gregorian calendar in September or October. Therefore, the dates listed for the months of Tishre, Heshvan, Kislev and sometimes Tevet must be read in the civil calendar as applying to the preceding year.

The complete transposition of a Hebrew date to a Gregorian date uses a very complex formula. It is easiest to simply refer to one of the published reference works: *The Comprehensive Hebrew Calendar, 5703-5860, 1943-2100* by Arthur Spier (Jerusalem, New York: Feldheim Publishers, 1981); or *150 Year Calendar* by Rabbi Moses Greenfield (Brooklyn: Hotsaat Ateret, 1987). Most synagogues and Jewish libraries possess one of these works. Another alternative is to use one of several computer programs: CALCONV, JCAL, LUACH (PC shareware); Zmanim or HaYom (http://www.davka.com); or JOS (http://www.jewishgen.org). These programs can covert Hebrew to Gregorian dates, as well as compute Yarzheit dates for upcoming years.

For further reading:

Arthur Kurzweil, *From Generation to Generation: How to Trace Your Jewish Genealogy and Personal History.* (New York: HarperCollins, 1994). Chapter 9, pages 342-358.

Dan Rottenberg, *Finding Our Fathers: A Guidebook to Jewish Genealogy.* (New York: Random House, 1977; Reprint: Baltimore: Genealogical Publishing Co., 1986, 1995). Pages 21-22, 46-48.

Jewish Cemetery Association of Massachusetts, *Guide to Jewish Cemeteries, 1995-1996.* {Annual guide, with maps and directions to Boston area Jewish cemeteries. 64 pages. JCAM, 1320 Centre Street, Suite #306, Newton Centre, MA 02159}.

DOROT, The Journal of the Jewish Genealogical Society (New York):
 - XI, 2 (Winter 1989-90), pp 2-3: "Getting the Most Out of Your Cemetery Visit".
 - XI, 4 (Summer 1990), pg 16; and XII, 1 (Autumn 1990), pg 8: "Tools of the Trade".

Martha Marenof, *Book of Life: A Directory of Hebrew Names and Dates.* (Pittsburg: Matthews Memorial Division, 1958). {A simple list of Hebrew names, 43 pages. Available for $5.50 from the Jewish Genealogical Society of Greater Washington, P.O. Box 412, Vienna, VA 22183-0412}.

Gideon Rath, "Hebrew Tombstone Inscriptions and Dates", in *Chronicles* (Newsletter of the Jewish Genealogical Society of Philadelphia), Vol. 5, No. 1 (Spring 1986), pages 1-4.

Louis Schafer, *Tombstones of Your Ancestors.* (Heritage Books, 1991). {160 pp, paperback, $15.00. Doesn't deal specifically with Jewish tombstones}.

Lynne Strangstad, *A Graveyard Preservation Primer.* (Center for Thanatology Research, 391 Atlantic Ave., Brooklyn, NY 11217 (718) 858-3026).

Association for Gravestone Studies, 30 Elm Street, Worcester, MA 01690 (508) 831-7753. Produces a quarterly newsletter, *Markers*, and access to lending library.

Some Hebrew Phrases

Son of	"BEN"	בֶּן
Daughter of	"BAT"	בַּת
Title, i.e. "Mr."	"REB", "RAV"	רב, ר׳
Son/Daughter of the honored...		ב״ר
The Levite	"HA-LEVI"	הלוי
The Cohen (Priest)	"HA-KOHEN"	הכהן
Here Lies	"PO NIKBAR"	פ״נ
May his/her soul be bound up...		ת.נ.צ.ב.ה.
Dear, Beloved (masc.)	"HA-YAKAR"	היקר
Dear, Beloved (fem.)	"HA-Y'KARAH"	היקרה
Father	"AV"	אב
My father	"AVI"	אבי
Our father	"AVINU"	אבינו
Mother	"EEM"	אם
My mother	"EEMI"	אמי
Our mother	"EEMANU"	אמנו
My husband	"BAALI"	בעלי
My wife	"ISHTI"	אשתי
Brother	"AKH"	אח
My Brother	"AKHI"	אחי
Our Brother	"AKHINU"	אחינו
Sister	"AKHOT"	אחות
Aunt	"DODAH"	דודה
Uncle	"DOD"	דוד
Man	"ISH"	איש
Woman	"ISHAH"	אשה
Woman (unmarried)	"B'TULAH"	בתולה
Woman (married) = "Mrs."	"MARAT"	מרת
Old (masc., fem.)	"ZAKAIN", "Z'KAINA"	זקן, זקנה
Child (masc., fem.)	"YELED", "YALDAH"	ילד, ילדה
Young man/woman	"BAKHUR", "BAKHURAH"	בחור, בחורה
Died (masc., fem.)	"NIFTAR", "NIFTERAH"	נפטר, נפטרה
Born (masc., fem.)	"NOLAD", "NOLDAH"	נולד, נולדה
Year, Years	"SHANAH", "SHANIM"	שנה, שנים
Day, Days	"YOM", "YAMIM"	יום, ימים
Month	"KHODESH"	חדש
First of the Month	"ROSH KHODESH"	ראש חדש, ר.ח.

Honest, Straight	ישר(ה)	Modest	צנוע(ה)
Complete, Wholehearted	תם	Honored, Distinguished	נכבד

The First Jewish Cemetery in Greater Boston:

Between 1837 and 1843, at least ten Jewish families emigrated from Germany and Poland to Boston. These families were the nucleus for a Jewish congregation. On February 26, 1843, the original ten families, together with eight others, formally established the first Jewish congregation in Boston and in Massachusetts. At this meeting the group voted to name their congregation "Ohabei Shalom", Hebrew for "Lover of Peace".

Before 1845, the nearest Jewish cemeteries available to residents of Boston were in Newport, Rhode Island, and Albany, New York. Though there are records which show that in 1733 a one hundred square foot lot was side aside on Chambers Street in Boston as a burial ground for the "Jewish Nation", there is no evidence that it was ever used.

On July 25, 1844, the Boston City Council permitted Congregation Ohabei Shalom to purchase from the East Boston Land Company a 10,000 square foot lot for $200, for which the forty affiliated families were assessed five dollars each. That lot was located at the corner of Byron and Homer Streets in East Boston, with its present entrance on Wadsworth Street. On October 5, 1844, Ohabei Shalom was given permission to use the lot for a cemetery, which made it the first legally established Jewish cemetery in Greater Boston. The cemetery was subsequently expanded in 1868 and then again in 1874.

The cemetery is divided into six sections, containing a total of approximately two thousand grave sites, as well as a solid granite chapel with stained glass windows. The cemetery's lots and paths are bordered by flower beds and shade trees and, as was then the custom, the graves are marked by inscribed monuments and gravestones. A number of prominent founders of Boston Jewry are interred there.

MASSACHUSETTS ARCHIVES

Facility Director: Anthony DeSantis, Acting State Archivist
                         William Milhomme, Reference Supervisor

Address: The Massachusetts Archives at Columbia Point
                         220 Morrissey Boulevard
                         Boston, MA 02125

Phone Number: (617) 727-2816

Hours of Operation:

Monday to Friday: 9:00 am to 5:00 pm
Saturday: 9:00 am to 3:00 pm   (except weekends with Monday holidays)
Closed Sunday and all legal holidays
    [including three Massachusetts State and Suffolk County holidays: Evacuation Day (March 17),
    Patriots Day (third Monday in April), and Bunker Hill Day (June 17)].

Directions:

By Car: Route I-93 to either Exit 14 or Exit 15. Follow signs for UMass Boston/JFK Library. Ample free parking.

By MBTA: Take the Red Line (Ashmont Branch only) to JFK Library/Umass station. Then board free shuttle bus in the parking lot to JFK Library (buses leave MBTA station every 20 minutes from 8:45am to 5:15pm and will stop at the Archives upon request), or bus to UMass Boston (buses run every five minutes; the Massachusetts Archives are a short walk from the campus).

Description of Institution:

The MASSACHUSETTS ARCHIVES at Columbia Point, colloquially known as the "State Archives", is responsible for the custody, preservation and management of permanently valuable non-current records of the **Commonwealth of Massachusetts** and its state agencies.

Description of Resources:

1.   Vital Records: 1841-1900. The Archives holds the books of registration for births, marriages, and deaths from all Massachusetts cities and towns, 1841 through 1900. For each registration, these records usually provide name, date, place, residence, and parental information, including occupation. The Archives also holds records of added entries and corrections to vital records for the same period.

      The state-wide indexes to births, marriages and deaths are in very large typescript volumes in the back of the Research Room (also available on microfilm). The indexes are alphabetical by surname within segmented time periods; several volumes cover each five-year period (e.g. one set of volumes covers 1891-1895, one set for 1896-1900, etc).

The index volumes contain the references to the town, year, volume and page number of the actual certificates, which are available on microfilm at the Archives. The marriages are indexed by the surname of both the bride and the groom.

- Birth Index   1841-1900: 61 volumes
- Marriage Index   1841-1900: 48 volumes
- Death Index   1841-1900: 45 volumes

Massachusetts vital records for 1901 and later are available at the REGISTRY OF VITAL RECORDS AND STATISTICS (see page 175). Parallel records are transferred to the Archives at regular five-year intervals (e.g., Vital records for the years 1901-1905 will be transferred to the Archives in December 1996).

However, the Archives does have the **indexes** to the 1901-1971 vital records (as well as 1841-1900) on microfilm. The actual certificates are at the REGISTRY OF VITAL RECORDS AND STATISTICS, but it's more convenient to use the indexes at the Archives because of the Registry's limited hours. See page 29 for more information on Vital Records.

2. <u>Vital Records: Pre-1841</u>. Prior to 1841, Massachusetts vital records were kept by local governments. The city and town clerks remain the custodians of early vital records for their respective towns. The Archives has copies of the published vital records for many towns, on open shelves. Other town vital records are available at the Archives on either LDS microfilm or Holbrook microfiche.
[See inventory of the Archives' pre-1850 Vital Record holdings in *MASSOG* (Quarterly of The Massachusetts Society of Genealogists), Vol. XV, No. 1 (March 1991), pages 16-19].

3. <u>Passenger Lists</u>. The Archives holds the original Massachusetts state passenger lists, recording the names of immigrants who arrived at the port of Boston from 1848 until 1891 (when federal records-keeping programs superseded those of the state). The lists are arranged chronologically according to the date when the ship arrived in port, and are available on microfilm (76 reels).

Also available is the Registry of Vessels for Boston, 1848-1892 (4 reels). This is a chronological list giving ship name and arrival date.

Greatly facilitating the use of the Boston Passenger Lists, the Archives holds an alphabetical name **index**, covering 1848-1891, which was made by the WPA during the 1930's. The index contains most of the information which is contained on the original lists: name, age, sex, occupation, nationality, last residence (usually country), if in the US before, and destination (state). It also indicates the name of the ship, the date of its arrival in Boston, and the list number. Note that wives and children arriving on the same ship are sometimes indexed separately, but are usually noted on the same card as other family members. It is important to note that these passenger lists generally do **not** provide the name of the city where the immigrant originally lived.

The index is on 4x6 cards, and is kept in the vault. There is no public access, but a staff member can search the index for you. However, this index has been microfilmed by the National Archives (Microfilm Publication M265, 282 reels), and is available at the NATIONAL ARCHIVES - NEW ENGLAND REGION, BOSTON PUBLIC LIBRARY microtext department, and through FAMILY HISTORY CENTERS (LDS). See page 22 for more information on Boston Passenger Lists.

4.   Census Schedules. The Archives has the original Federal Census schedules for Massachusetts for 1850, 1860 and 1870. Microfilms of the Federal Census (Massachusetts only) for 1790-1900 are also available here, as are the published indexes for Massachusetts, 1790-1850. [Note that the complete Federal Census schedules (for the entire U.S., 1790-1920) are available at the NATIONAL ARCHIVES - NEW ENGLAND REGION in Waltham (see page 143)].

      The Archives also holds Massachusetts **state** census schedules, prepared in 1855 (43 volumes) and 1865 (41 volumes), originals and microfilm copies. These records are arranged geographically, and contain information similar to that of contemporary federal schedules. A number of towns have been indexed in privately published volumes. See page 11 for details on Census records.

5.   Naturalization Records. Naturalization records generally remain in court jurisdictions. However, some court records have been transferred to the MASSACHUSETTS ARCHIVES, as described below. See page 16 for more information on Naturalization records.

   a. Abstracts, 1885-1931. The Archives holds **abstracts** of naturalizations from Massachusetts **state and local** courts for 1885-1931, in 49 volumes. These records are arranged chronologically by year, and thereunder by court, making them cumbersome to use. The Archives staff highly recommends using the resources of the NATIONAL ARCHIVES - NEW ENGLAND REGION first (see page 143).

      The Naturalization abstracts are kept in the vault, and there are microfilm copies in the Research Room. They are arranged in annual volumes. Volumes for 1885 through 1921 have an alphabetical index in the front. An attempt was made to index the later records, but was never completed: a alphabetical card index exists for 1922-1923, there are unordered cards for 1924-1925, and no index exists for 1926-1931. The quantity of naturalizations in state and local courts decreased after 1906, when new federal laws went into effect. The abstracts provide the following information: name, age, occupation and residence of the naturalized person; date of naturalization; name of court; names and addresses of two witnesses. Although these records do not provide much genealogical information, the abstracts are very useful in locating the original court records.

   b. County Records. The MASSACHUSETTS ARCHIVES has no jurisdiction over **county** records, only over state records. However, some counties do turn their records over to the State Archives for safe keeping. These records, in the custody of the Judicial Archives, are held in the vault, and must be accessed by the staff. Naturalization records from Massachusetts county courts accessioned by the Archives include:

      Bristol County Superior County naturalization records for 1805-1990, with index at Archives. (Petitions starting with number 57571 are still in the Courthouse). Also Fall River District Court naturalizations, 1885-1906.

      Essex County Superior Court (Lawrence and Salem) naturalization records for 1906-1982. Pre-1906 records are still in courthouse in Salem. Indexes at Archives:

- Lawrence, card file index, 1925-1985.
- Salem, card file index, 1931-1982.
- Salem, Index to Petitions, 1906-1920 (petitions #1-9253).
- Salem, Index to Petitions, 1921-1935 (petitions #9254-18364).
- Salem, Index to Petitions, 1921-1935 (petitions #18365-24748).
- Lawrence and Salem Naturalizations, Superior Court (only), 1906-1939.
- Salem, Index to Declarations of Intention, 1929-1939.

The Archives also has naturalization records from Gloucester District Court and Newburyport District Court, with indexes.

Franklin County Superior Court naturalization records, 1853-1976. The index is still in the courthouse in Greenfield, but the individual volumes are all indexed.

Hampden County Superior Court naturalization records, 1812-1987, with index at Archives. (Petitions from number 48001 are still in the courthouse).

Hampshire County Superior Court naturalization records, 1849-1988. Also Ware and Northampton District Court records, 1885-1906. Index is at Archives.

Middlesex County Superior Court naturalization records, 1842-1991, with Index at Archives. Also have Lowell Police Court, circa 1832-1906; and Malden District Court, 1885-1906. Indexes to Lowell and Malden court records are still in their respective courthouses.

Norfolk County. Superior Court records remain in the courthouse in Dedham. The Archives has records of Dedham District Court and Quincy District Court, 1885-1906, including index.

Plymouth County Superior Court naturalization records, 1812-1977, with index at Archives. Note that this does not include Brockton Superior Court records, which remain at the courthouse. The Archives also has records from Plymouth District Court, 1885-1906.

Suffolk County. Supreme Judicial Court naturalization records and index, 1790-1859. Superior Court naturalizations, 1859-1885. (Note: After 1906 no naturalizations were performed in Suffolk County Superior Court. Researchers should check the U.S. District Court records at the NATIONAL ARCHIVES - NEW ENGLAND REGION). Also Chelsea District Court records, 1885-1906.

Worcester County Superior Court naturalization records, 1809-1984, with index at Archives. Also Worcester Central District Court, 1885-1906; and Dudley/Webster District Court, 1885-1906.

6. City Directories. City Directories for Boston, original annual volumes for 1939s-1960s (with gaps), are available on open shelves. Directories for Boston, 1861-1935 (with gaps), are available on microfilm (1861-1900, 1905, 1910, 1915, 1920, 1925, 1930, 1935). Available on microfiche are city directories for Boston 1789-1860/1; Fall River 1861-1901; Lowell 1861-1901; and Worcester 1861-1901. Each year is alphabetically arranged by surname.

7.	Probate Records. The Archives holds a very large collection of probate records for Middlesex (1648-1871), Suffolk (1636-1894), Plymouth (1686-1881), and Essex (1638-1862) counties. Probate records include wills, guardianships, trusts, administrations, adoptions, name changes, and separation support. The original records are in the vault, and printed index volumes (alphabetical by surname) are available behind the main desk. For Middlesex County, one alphabetical index volume covers 1648-1871; for Suffolk County, 3 volumes cover 1636-1894; for Essex County, index on microfilm: 1638-1840 (4 reels), 1841-1881 (5 reels).

Also available are microfilm copies of the probate records of Berkshire County (1761-1865), Worcester County (1731-1893), Plymouth County (1685-1903), and Middlesex County. These records were microfilmed by the Mormons at the respective county courthouses.

Worcester County (221 reels):
    #1:   Index, 1731-1881
    #2-21:   Docket Books
    #23-221:   Record Books, 1731-1881

Middlesex County (557 reels)

Plymouth County (164 reels):
    #1-8:   Index & Docket, 1685-1881
    #9-40:   Dockets, 1881-1967
    #41:   Probate Index, 1686-1820
    #42-43:   Docket Index, 1881-1939
    #44-164:   Probate Records, 1686-1903

Middlesex, Suffolk, Plymouth and Essex counties are the only counties for which original probate records have been accessioned by the Archives thus far. Later records in these counties, and records for other counties, are held by the Registry of Probate in the respective county.

8.	Medical Examiner's Reports. Annual returns of the records of deaths investigated by the medical examiner, 1885-1960. Records include cause of death, method of investigation, name of deceased, residence, age, and autopsy details. Deaths due to accident or suicide were investigated by the medical examiner. These records are indexed alphabetically for each year and county. Returns are now filed with the district attorney. [Use the Vital Record indexes to determine the date and county of death. These may lead you to local newspaper reports concerning the death (at BOSTON PUBLIC LIBRARY, see page 63)].

9.	State Institution Records. (Department of Mental Health, Public Health, and Corrections). The Archives has a large collection of records from various state institutions for the Blind, "Deaf and Dumb", "Lunatic", "Pauper Idiots", etc.; schools, almshouses, hospitals and prisons. Many immigrants were placed in such institutions. These records include case histories, records of admissions and dismissals, correspondence, and other details. See Restrictions and Finding Aids below.

These collections includes material (late 19th-century through the 1950's) from the Monson almshouse and primary school; Tewksbury almshouse and hospital; Pondville, Rutland Heights, North Reading and Westfield public health hospitals; the Walter E. Fernald state school; Belchertown, Danvers, Westborough and other mental institutions; the Penikese leper colony; the Lyman and Lancaster schools; and the prisons at Charlestown, Concord, Framingham, Norfolk and Walpole.

10. WPA Historical Records Survey. The project files of the Massachusetts Historical Records Survey, 1936-1942, occupy over 225 cubic feet at the Archives. The material consists of survey forms, notes, draft reports and historical sketches used in preparation for a published guide project that was never completed. Records include inventories of the records of local governments, church and synagogue records, black history, and other manuscript collections. There is a inventory of this material at the Main Desk.

Box 110 of this collection contains notes on Synagogues in Massachusetts; this work was done in 1936-1939 towards the completion of a "Directory of American Jewish Congregations", which was never finished. The bulk of this material (~2 cu. ft.) consists of one folder on each congregation, containing a brief survey: name and address of rabbi, officers, denomination, date organized, property, previous buildings, architecture, whereabouts of minute books and other records. Most congregational folders contain only 1 or 2 pages. Other folders contain Massachusetts state incorporation records and property records of synagogues, cemeteries, and other Jewish educational and religious organizations.

11. Mormon (LDS) Microfilms. A large majority of the Massachusetts records that were microfilmed by the Genealogical Society of Utah, usually available only through FAMILY HISTORY CENTERS (LDS), have been collected by the Archives (over 3,000 reels). These are early state, county, city and town records for 200 towns, and include deeds, land, court and vital records, town meeting, assessors, selectmen records, etc. A card catalog to these microfilms is available, arranged geographically (by state, county, city, town).

12. Other Records. The Archives is most noted for its vast collection of early Massachusetts records, which will not be discussed here. These include Military Records (1642-1898: Colonial, Revolutionary, 1812, Civil and Spanish-American Wars), Plymouth Colony Records, town maps and plans, legislative and executive papers, and early court records. See Finding Aids for details.

Finding Aids:

"A Guide to the Records of the Secretary of State in the Massachusetts Archives", 81 pages, (1987), is a brief inventory of the records held by the Massachusetts Archives.

Most finding aids at the Archives pertain to the "Massachusetts Archives", a vast collection of volumes containing 17th and 18th century documents (1629-1799) of the colony, province and state of Massachusetts (328 volumes).

For Boston census records 1860 and 1870, *Knights' Guide to the 1860/70 Census Records of Boston* is available at the Main Desk. The guide translates street addresses (found in the 1860/70 Boston City Directories) into census record location. (No index is currently available for the 1860 and 1870 censuses for Massachusetts).

For Probate Records (and other Court records), there is a set of loose-leaf volumes behind the Main Desk, one volume per county, prepared by the Massachusetts Judicial Archives.

For State Institution Records, see *"Guide to Social Welfare Records"* by Lizabeth Waston, May 1991 (109 pages), available at the Main Desk. The guide lists all records, their locations and restrictions, by institution.

Description of Facility:

The Massachusetts Archives is located in a large modern building, which it shares with the Commonwealth Museum, located near the UMass/Boston campus and Kennedy Presidential Library in Dorchester. When entering the building, turn to your left and sign in at the main desk. The Research Room is a glassed-in area opposite the desk. The room contains seating for 32 researchers at tables, and 16 microfilm readers.

In the back of the room are four sets of open shelves, containing printed materials, such as: the Vital Record Indexes (1841-1900), published town vital records (pre-1850), Boston City Directories (1939-1960s), printed Federal Census Indexes (Massachusetts only, 1790-1850), books on Massachusetts military records, etc.

On the left side of the Research Room are four rows of microfilm cabinets. They contain: City Directories; early court records, some Probate records; Revolutionary War Records; Census Schedules for Massachusetts: Federal (1790-1900) and State (1855, 1865); Boston Passenger Lists (State lists, 1848-1891); the Massachusetts Archives; the LDS microfilms; and the Vital Records (1841-1900) and Vital Record Indexes (1841-1971).

On the right side of the Research Room there is a large set of card catalogs, which includes finding aids to the "Massachusetts Archives" colonial records (1629-1799), and the Archives' collection of LDS microfilms of early Massachusetts town records.

Most of the archival material is kept in the vault and can be accessed only by the staff.

Fees/Copies:

There are no fees required to use the facility. No materials circulate. Photocopies are 25¢ each, and must be made by the staff. For materials up to 18"x16", photocopies are $3.00, and $3.50 for larger materials. Microfilm prints (self-service) are 50¢ each. Copies of photographs are $1.00 (existing negative) or $1.75 (negative to be made). Copies of entire microfilms can be made for $16.00.

The Archives **does** handle mail requests, and will provide certified copies of vital records and other records for $3.00 each. No fee is charged if a record can not be located. Please limit your requests to five per letter.

Rules:

a. Sign the registration book at the main desk, listing your name, address, and type of research. Photo identification should be presented to archivist at this time.
b. No personal belonging are allowed in the Research Room. This includes handbags, briefcases and coats. Lockers are available, at no charge, upon receipt of photo ID.
c. Pencils must be used to take notes! No pens or other permanent markers are allowed. Defacing records violates state law.
d. Original records must be handled with care. The existing order and arrangement of material must be maintained.

Restrictions on Use:

Access to some state institutional records (Department of Mental Health, Public Health, and Corrections) are restricted to preserve privacy, and require the permission of the State Department of Mental Health (25 Staniford Street, Boston 02114) or the Director of Records at the specified hospital. Permission to access these materials for family history research is rarely refused. The staff can assist with requests for permission.

Corrections records (prisons) after 1930 are restricted, unless you can provide a death certificate. The record becomes public sixty days after a person is deceased.

MASSACHUSETTS INSTITUTE OF TECHNOLOGY
Hayden Memorial Library

Facility Directors:
Ann J. Wolpert, 14S-216, Director of Libraries
Ruth K. Seidman, 14S-134, Head Librarian, Engineering and Science Libraries

Address: Massachusetts Institute of Technology
Hayden Memorial Library, Building 14
77 Massachusetts Avenue
Cambridge, MA 02139

Phone Numbers:

Reference and Information: (617) 253-5685 (9-8 Mon-Thu, 9-5 Fri, 1-5 Sun)
Circulation Desk: (617) 253-5671
Catalogue Information: (617) 253-5681

Hours of Operation:

Monday to Friday: 7:00 am to 12:00 midnight
Saturday: 8:00 am to 12:00 midnight
Sunday: 10:00 am to 12:00 midnight

Directions:

By MBTA: Red Line to the MIT/Cambridge Center stop (formerly Kendall Square). Cross Main Street to the entrance to the inbound side of the station if you are not already on that side, walk down Carleton Street one block until it ends at Amherst Street, go right along Amherst Street one block until it ends at Ames Street, cross Ames Street and go straight onto the MIT campus, passing the tennis courts on your left. Hayden Library will be the second building on your left.

By Car: If coming from the west along Memorial Drive, take the underpass under Massachusetts Avenue, and make a U-turn at the next opportunity. There is usually parking available on Memorial Drive, especially not too close to Mass Avenue. Hayden Library, which is on Memorial Drive, is the first building to the east of the main MIT quad, and is attached to the buildings of the quad. (The main MIT quad, on Memorial Drive, can be recognized by the domed building in the center).

Description of Institution:

The library exists primarily for the benefit of facility, students, and research staff at the Massachusetts Institute of Technology (MIT), a private institution. The MIT libraries contain more than 2.2 million volumes, more than 21,000 current subscriptions, and collections of microforms, maps, and other media.

Description of Resources:

A resource of great interest to genealogists is the <u>Map Room</u>, located on the first floor, off to the right just past the entrance to the Science Library. The Map room contains a comprehensive collection of maps published by the U.S. Army Map Service (AMS), the predecessor to the Defense Mapping Agency (DMA). The following series of maps, which are based on German maps from World War II, should be of particular interest to Jewish genealogists. They are located in drawers along the right wall of the map room.

- **Eastern Europe** at a scale of **1:250,000**, in drawer W44, call number G7010; AMS series N501. These maps cover the European part of the Soviet Union, based on its 1939 boundaries. They include even the smallest villages, down to individual city blocks. Each map covers one degree of latitude and two degrees of longitude. The maps are arranged in sets of twelve maps covering four degrees of latitude and six degrees of longitude, and are designated by two letters and a two digit number specifying the set, followed by a number from 1 to 12 specifying the map within that set. The meanings of the letter and two digit number designations are:

NJ:	36° N to 40° N	34:	18° E to 24° E
NK:	40° N to 44° N	35:	24° E to 30° E
NL:	44° N to 48° N	36:	30° E to 36° E
NM:	48° N to 52° N	37:	36° E to 42° E
NN:	52° N to 56° N	38:	42° E to 48° E
NO:	56° N to 60° N	39:	48° E to 54° E
		40:	54° E to 60° E

and within each set, the maps are numbered as follows:

1	2	3
4	5	6
7	8	9
10	11	12

For example, Kiev is on map NM36-4. The letters "NM" mean that it is in a set of maps that extends from 48° to 52° North latitude, and the number "36" means that it is in a set of maps extending from 30° to 36° East longitude. The number "4" means that it is the first of three maps in the second of four rows within the set, so this map extends from 50° to 51° N and from 30° to 32° E. For the regions north of 60° N latitude (the NP, NQ, and NR sets of maps), the numbering scheme is a little different, but those maps are of minimal interest for Jewish genealogy. There is an index map available showing the location of each map in the series (see below under Finding Aids), but you can save time by figuring out in advance which map you want to look at. The maps are arranged in alphabetical and numerical order within the drawer, although they sometimes get out of order.

- **Poland** at a scale of **1:100,000**, in drawer W36, call number G6520, AMS series M651 (GSGS series 4416). These maps extend to the 1939 boundaries of Poland. Each map covers one degree of longitude and half a degree of latitude. They are designated by a letter indicating the range of latitude, and a number indicating a range of longitude. The letters range from G in the north down to V in the south (skipping the letters I and O), and have the following meanings:

G: 55°10' N to 55°40' N
H: 54°40' N to 55°10' N
J: 54°10' N to 54°40' N
and so on, down through
V: 48°40' N to 49°10' N

The numbers range from 11 in the west to 18 in the east, and have the following meanings:

11:   16°20' E to 17°20' E
12:   17°20' E to 18°20' E
and so on, through
18:   23°20' E to 24°20' E

An exception to this numbering scheme is found in maps J-12, J-13, and J-14, which extend from 54°10' N to 54°55' N. An index map is available (see Finding Aids below).
The following maps were missing, or misfiled, as of late 1990: J-12, J-13, J-14, U-14.

- **Middle Danube** at a scale of **1:100,000**, in drawer W33, call number G6030, AMS series M671 (GSGS series 4416). These maps are a continuation to the south and southwest of the Poland series described above, and follow the same numbering scheme. They cover parts of present-day Czechoslovakia, Austria, Hungary, northern Romania, and a small part of the Ukraine, near Chernovtsy. There is an index map available (see Finding Aids below).
The following maps were missing or misfiled as of October 1990: X-13, X-15, Z-14.

- **Central Europe** at a scale of **1:100,000**, in drawer W33, call number G6030, no AMS series number given (GSGS series 4416). These are a continuation to the west of the Poland series described above, and follow the same numbering scheme. The region they cover corresponds approximately to present day Germany. There does not appear to be any index map, so it was not possible to tell which maps were missing.
The following maps were present, as of late 1990: J-4, 5, 7; K-3, 4, 7, 8; L-1, 2, 3, 6, 7, 8; M-1, 3, 4, 7, 8; N-3, 4, 5, 6, 7, 8; P-1, 2, 3, 4, 5, 6, 8; Q-1, 2, 3, 4, 5, 7, 8; R-2, 3, 4, 5, 6, 7, 8; S-1, 2, 3, 4, 5, 6, 7, 8; T-1, 2; U-2; V-2; W-2; X-2; Y-2.

- **Central Europe** at a scale of **1:250,000**, in drawer W33, call number G6030, AMS series M508 (GSGS series 4346). This series covers all of present day Germany, Poland, Austria, and Czechoslovakia, most of Hungary, and small parts of the Soviet Union and other bordering countries. Each of these maps extends over one degree of latitude and two degrees of longitude. They are designated by a letter, to indicate the range of longitude, and a number, to indicate the range of latitude. The letters range from K in the west to S in the east, and have the following meanings:

K: 6°24' E to 8°24' E
L: 8°24' E to 10°24' E
and so on, through
S: 22°24' E to 24°24' E

The numbers range from 48 in the south up to 56 in the north, and simply indicate the number of degrees latitude of the northern boundary of the map. There is an index map for this series (see Finding Aids below).
As of October 1990, the following maps were missing or misfiled: P-52, R-55, S-50, S-51.

- **Central Europe** at a scale of **1:300,000**, in drawer W33, call number G6030, AMS series M405. There appears to be no index map for this series.

- **Balkans** at a scale of **1:250,000**, in drawer W41, AMS series M506 (GSGS series 4375, 4412, and 4413). Includes call numbers G6810 (Greece and Albania), G6840 (Yugoslavia), G6880 (Romania), and G6890 (Bulgaria).

Another resource of interest to genealogists is a set of very complete gazetteers for most countries in the world, published by the **U. S. Board on Geographic Names**. Of particular interest for Jewish genealogy is the gazetteer of the U.S.S.R., published in 1970, which takes up seven volumes and has over 400,000 entries. These gazetteers are especially useful because they include former or unofficial names, with cross-references to the official name. Practically every shtetl can be located in these gazetteers. Hayden Library has most of these gazetteers, but they are not listed in the card catalogue, because they are not part of the regular library collection; they are owned by the Catalogue Department for their own use, to determine the correct subject categories for books about places whose names may have changed. As such, they are not officially available to the public. However, if you ask politely, the people in the Catalogue Department should be willing to let you use them. There is no guarantee that this access will continue to be the case, so minimize use of these gazetteers, especially if there is a reasonable alternative (see *Where Once We Walked*, page 3). The Catalogue Department is located in the Humanities Library, on the second floor of Hayden, in room 14E-210. Go all the way to the back of the library, and go through doors to the left marked "Acquisitions Catalogue Departments". The gazetteers are on shelves to the right when you enter, and are in alphabetical order by country. (Poland, unfortunately, is missing). Ask someone if it is okay to look at the gazetteers before using them.

[Note that a consolidated index to 350,00 place names in the U.S. Board on Geographic Names gazetters for Eastern European countries was prepared by the Association of Jewish Genealogical Societies, in alphabetical and Soundex sequences. The indexes are available on microfiche at the BOSTON PUBLIC LIBRARY microtext department (see page 63) and at HEBREW COLLEGE LIBRARY (see page 106)].

The following resources are also found in the Humanities Library on the second floor of Hayden. These resources are not unique to Hayden, and are available in any large research library.

Encyclopedia Britannica (1878-88). Has a good map of Russia, with old names for cities (e.g. Proskuroff instead of Chmielnitsky). [Ref AE5.E57]

Great Soviet Encyclopedia, in both Russian and English. [Ref AE55.B693, Ref AE55.B6961]

Encyclopaedia Judaica. (1971). [Ref DS102.8.E56]

Jewish Encyclopedia. (1964). [Ref DS102.8.J59]

National Union Catalogue.

Complete *New York Times*, 1851-present, on microfilm; plus indexes [Ref AI21.N53]
(Useful for steamship arrival dates earlier than those listed in the *Morton Allen Directory*, and for death notices and obituaries).

Finding Aids:

All of the books found in any of the MIT libraries are listed in an on-line catalogue, called "Barton", which may be accessed from terminals in the Science Library (first floor) and the Humanities Library (second floor).

There are some finding aids for the Map Room located along the wall to your left when you enter the room. A small card index lists the general contents of the drawers alphabetically, but with only one or two entries for each drawer. Thus, drawer W44 is listed under "USSR" but not under "Soviet Union" or "Russia", and not under any particular region or city within the USSR. A set of large gray binders labelled "DMA MAP INDEX" has index maps for most, but not all, of the series of Army Map Service maps in the drawers. These index maps are listed in alphabetical order, by the name of the series, and it is not always obvious where to look. For example, the index map for AMS series N501 is listed under "Europe, Eastern". The information included on the index maps varies, but always includes national boundaries, major cities, and major rivers, and often includes the most important town on each map in the series. These index maps are in poor condition and should be handled carefully.

Description of Facility:

The reading rooms (including the Map Room) and the stacks of the MIT libraries are open to the public, but users who are not associated with MIT are requested to sign in at the circulation desk. The Map Room is occasionally used for meetings, when it would not be open to the public. The Map Room has about ten seats around a table, but there are many more seats in the main reading room of the Science Library.

There are two photocopying machines on the first floor, which take cards, and three photocopying machines in the basement, which take cash or cards. The cards may be purchased between 9 am and 5 pm on weekdays, at the Microreproduction Lab in the basement, in quantities of 100 or 500 copies, at a slight discount from the regular cost of 10¢ per copy. There is one microfilm reader/copier, which takes cash, in the Humanities Library on the second floor.

During working hours (9am to 8am Mon-Thu, 9am to 5pm Fri, and 1pm to 5pm Sun), there is one reference librarian available for consultation in the Science Library, and one in the Humanities Library. The librarians are quite helpful, but it should be kept in mind that they have been hired to serve users from MIT.

Fees/Copies:

Photocopies and microfilm copies cost 10¢ each. Access to the reading rooms and stacks is free to the public. Students, faculty and staff associated with MIT may borrow books, and people associated with other universities in the Boston Library Consortium may borrow books not available at their own university library, if requested through their own library, with no fee. Others who want to borrow books must pay $290 per year for a library privilege card. In any case, none of the material discussed above circulates.

MIDDLESEX NORTHERN REGISTRY OF DEEDS

Address: 360 Gorham St.,
                          Lowell, MA 01853-1318

Phone Number: (508) 458-8474

Hours of Operation: Monday-Friday 8:30am-4:30pm

Directions:

By Car: Route 128 (I-95) to Route 3 North to Exit 30 North, the Lowell Connector. At the end of the Lowell Connector take a left onto Gorham Street. The registries are in the Superior Courthouse, a tenth of a mile further on the right.

Description of Resources:

The Registry holds records related to the ownership of land located in the Northern District of Middlesex County. This primarily consists of deeds (transferring ownership), mortgages and plans (detailed maps of lots and parcels). Other documents include land court records, tax liens, etc. See Appendix C on page 232 for an overview of Land Records and a list of Massachusetts cities and towns.

Finding Aids:

Older indexes are downstairs, as are the earlier record books, so you will likely do your research down there. Most of the recent indexes are on computer. Some of the recent indexes are upstairs within one of two alcove areas there. Plan indexes are upstairs in the other alcove area.

Description of Facility:

Inside the District Court building, the registry takes up two floors. The plan room is located outside the Registry in the hallway on the first floor.

Fees/Copies:

Self-service photocopies are 25¢ each. There are three copiers upstairs and two downstairs. Plans have to be ordered, and are $1-$3, depending on size. Plans may be viewed on fiche cards prior to ordering.

Restrictions on Use:

None. No books may leave the facilities under any circumstances.

MIDDLESEX SOUTHERN REGISTRY OF DEEDS

Address: 208 Cambridge St.
                           PO Box 68
                           Cambridge, MA 02141-0068

Phone Number: (617) 494-4510

Hours of Operation: Monday-Friday 8:00am-4:00pm

Note: The REGISTRY OF DEEDS tends to be very busy on the last few work days of the month. It is best to visit at other times.

Directions:

By Car: **From West of Boston**: Massachusetts Turnpike (Route I-90) to Brighton/Allston/Cambridge Exit 20 (left exit). Bear right after toll booth. Proceed straight through two traffic lights, cross over the Charles River, and take a right at the light (Memorial Drive). Follow Memorial Drive, bearing left to go under bridge (at Massachusetts Ave.), then bearing right to avoid going under bridge (at Longfellow Bridge). Pass by the Cambridgeside Galleria Mall on left. Then, two traffic lights later at the large intersection, take a left. Keep in right lane. Take first right and then enter parking lot on left. Lechmere Station is visible from parking lot — see directions for public transportation to proceed from Lechmere Station.

           From South of Boston: Take the Southeast Expressway (Route I-93) North to Storrow Drive Exit, then bear right onto Route 28 North. Proceed past the Museum of Science, bearing right. When you see Lechmere Station on your left, turn right and take an immediate left into the parking lot. See the directions for public transportation to proceed from Lechmere Station.

           From North of Boston: Take Route I-93 South to the Storrow Drive Exit, then bear right at exit onto Route 28 North. Follow directions above for South of Boston (from Route 28 North).

By MBTA: Green Line Subway "E" line to Lechmere Station. Disembark, turn left and walk to Second Street, the first street on your left. Turn left on Second Street and walk to the first intersection, Cambridge Street. The Middlesex Southern District Registry of Deeds and the Middlesex Registry of Probate are both in the Probate Courthouse on the opposite corner. Access is through the lower entrance on Cambridge Street.

Description of Resources:

The Registry holds records related to the ownership of land located in the Southern District of Middlesex County. This primarily consists of deeds (transferring ownership), mortgages and plans (detailed maps of lots and parcels). Other documents include land court records, tax liens, etc. See Appendix C on page 232 for an overview of Land Records and a list of Massachusetts cities and towns.

Finding Aids:

Grantor Index books are used to locate records of interest. In addition, Grantor Indexes after 1973 are computerized. The book indexes are divided by year or group of years, and then are sorted alphabetically by surname. The Grantor book indexes are in three different locations: the earliest books are in the basement, the books for years 1890-1973 are on the second floor, and the post-1973 indexes are in the main work room in the rear left corner.

Basic instructions for using the computers:

Press F16 key until the main menu comes up. Chose one of the grantor or grantee indexes. Start the query by entering the last name and the first initial or the full first name. Ending a first or last name with a question mark permits a wildcard match on further letters of the name. After typing in your query, press the enter key. A list of names should come up. The F4 and F5 keys can be used to move to other pages in the list. Move the cursor to the name of interest and press the enter key in order to obtain a detailed abstract for that entry. Record the following information for entries of interest: name, date, book, page (if no book and page, write down instrument number), town, transaction type, relator.

Description of Resources:

The <u>record books</u> are located as follows:

1)   Before 1930s. In the basement, around the corner to the right from the elevators. Also on microfilm in the microfilm room off the 3rd floor mezzanine.
2)   1930s - 1960. On the 3rd floor.
3)   1961 - current. Second floor. Also, the newest records are on microfilm in the microfilm room.

<u>Plans</u>: There are several ways to find a plan for a property or development:

a)   In the description in a deed or mortgage, referencing a plan.

b)   Plan Index Books. For each of three time periods (the latest ending about 1915), these index books are divided into Owner and Street indexes. In the Owner index, the books are in order by town, and within each town alphabetically by name of owner. In the Street index, the books are in order by town, and within each town alphabetically by street name (or other geographic identifier). Following the three series of book indexes for plans there is a card index for plans also divided into Owner and Street indexes.

c)   Computerized Plan Index.

There are several types of plan references:

* Book and page number. Locate that record book to find the plan. Often, instead of a page number, the term END is used. Look for the plan at the end of the referenced book. See the description for finding record books above.

* Plan book and page. Plan books are in the plan and atlas room on the fourth floor.

* Plans numbered by year. Order these plans in the Filmed Plan room on the fourth floor. These plans are taken from microfiche and printed on extra large paper, with excellent detail.

Description of Facility:

The MIDDLESEX REGISTRY OF DEEDS is one of the largest in the nation. It is located on three floors and the basement (off the first floor) in the north side of the Registry building. The second floor is where most work is done. It consists of a large work room with several long work desks with stools, and another large room off of this main room where most of the record books are located. Off of the central lobby area on the second floor, near the top of the left staircase, is the room with the Grantor Index books (1890-1973).

There are two photocopy machines in the Plan and Atlas room on the fourth floor; four on the third floor (a mezzanine overlooking the large work room); and seven on the second floor. There is one paper cutter on the fourth floor, two on the third floor and four on the first floor. The microfilm room has six reader/printers.

There are four computer terminals on the third floor, and on the second floor there are 16 in the main work room, and 30 in a separate computer room.

Fees/Copies:

There is no charge to use the facility. None of the materials circulate. Photocopies are self-service, 25¢ each (11"x17"). There is a card vending machine (taking $10.00 bills only) and a change machine (changing $1.00 and $5.00 bills into quarters). You may use either quarters or the vendor cards. Printouts from the microfilm machines are also 25¢ (8½"x11"). Plans from the Filmed Plans room are 75¢ (17"x22").

Restrictions on Use:

None. No books may leave the facilities under any circumstances.

MIDDLESEX REGISTRY OF PROBATE

Address: 208 Cambridge St.,
                       Cambridge, MA 02141-1268

Phone Number: (617) 494-4000

Hours of Operation: Monday-Friday 8:30am-4:30pm

Directions: See under MIDDLESEX SOUTHERN REGISTRY OF DEEDS

Description of Resources:

The MIDDLESEX REGISTRY OF PROBATE holds probate records starting around 1930, and divorce records starting around 1940. Older records are kept in storage, with roughly one day lead time needed to access them. The oldest records (1648-1871) are located at the MASSACHUSETTS ARCHIVES.

Finding Aids:

1. Probate Indexes:

    Book indexes for the oldest probate records are on a large, low table. They are separated into intervals of years, and then a few books divide up surnames alphabetically within each interval:

    1648-1870; 1871-1909; 1910-1924; 1925-1939; 1940-1949

    Book indexes for recent probate records are on a book table and cover the years:

    1950-1959; 1960-1969; 1970-1979; 1980-1989; 1990-date

    All books prior to 1970 are strictly alphabetical (that is, by first name also). Afterwards, the indexes are filled in manually under pre-printed surnames. A duplicate 1980-1989 probate index is kept on index cards in the large brown filing cabinet located at the edge of the probate area. These cards are in strict alphabetical sequence, unlike the 1970s book in which first names are not alphabetized.

    The most recent probate indexes are also kept in card files. A-P is in an upright card files near the large, low table; Q-Z is in the bottom drawer of the large brown file cabinet located at the edge of the probate area.

    The MIDDLESEX REGISTRY OF PROBATE also has an incomplete set of older probate index books for other Massachusetts counties, including Worcester, Essex, Norfolk and Suffolk.

2. Divorce Indexes:

    Book indexes are for yearly intervals and are located on a counter near the Family Law Clerk's help counter. They are divided into intervals covering 1935-1944; 1945-1954; 1955-1964 and 1965-1974. The remaining divorce indexes are located in nearby filing cabinets. One card file index goes from 1975-1984, and another covers from 1985 to the present.

Description of Facility:

The facility is located on the 2nd and 3rd floor in the south side of the registry building. Most of the actual files are kept on the 3rd floor. Almost everything else is on the second floor. The earliest probate index books (up until 1950) are spread out over a large table, and the later years (1951-1990) are on a counter next to the table. The most recent index is in a card file on the other side of the table.

There are probate docket books in a floor-to-ceiling book case near the back of the room, right next to the back staircase that goes up to the third floor. The docket books are on both sides of the wall/book case. Docket books are available for the earliest records (docket #1) up through current dockets. They are located at the back of the room, beginning near the back staircase. Within this shelf are books for dockets #1-221200. Around the other side of this bookshelf continue dockets #221201-551600 (through 1984). At the next shelf over are docket books for 1985-1992. The most recent docket books are located in and on top of a small table next to the shelf with the 1985-1992 books.

Active divorce files are kept downstairs, as are probate files for the past few years. Other divorce files are kept up on the third level. The divorce docket books are near the divorce card indexes.

To order a file, jot down the docket number of interest and proceed to the motions desk at the front of the room where you first entered. Order the files you need via the intercom. State the file type and the number, for example say "divorce, 1985, 6546" or "probate, 176456." (Early divorces and probate files earlier than docket #151,447 will have to be ordered from remote storage). There is a chute at the motions desk where the staff that is upstairs will send down the file. The clerk at the motions desk will take the file out of the chute and leave it for you to pick up. When you are done, place the file in the cart that is on the side of the motions desk, unless the file is of the newer kind (legal size folders), in which case you should place it in either the divorce or probate cardboard box on the table next to the cart.

For older records, currently docket numbers earlier than docket #151,447 (probates filed approximately 1915 and earlier), but which are not older than 1871 records, you will have to order the file and get it the next day. The run to storage is once a day at about noon. If you make your request prior to 10:30am, then you should be able to look at the file the same day. The list for ordering is on a clipboard at the staff desk on the third floor near the top of the front stair case. Simply help yourself to this list, and fill in the requisite information.

Fees/Copies:

Self-service photocopies. Two machines downstairs (8½"x14") and one machine upstairs (11"x17"). 25¢ per copy.

Restrictions on Use:

None. No books may leave the facilities under any circumstances.

NATIONAL ARCHIVES, NEW ENGLAND REGION

Facility Director: James Owens, Director
Stanley Tozeski, Asst. Director

Address: 380 Trapelo Road
Waltham, MA 02154

Phone Number: (617) 647-8100

Hours of Operation:

Monday to Friday   8:00 am to 4:30 pm
First Saturday of   8:00 am to 4:30 pm
   each month (unless holiday weekend)
Closed remaining Saturdays, Sundays and Federal Holidays.

Directions:

By Car: From Route 128: Exit at Trapelo Road (Exit 28A) and continue on Trapelo Road east 2.8 miles to the NATIONAL ARCHIVES - NEW ENGLAND REGION, on the right side of the road.
From Downtown Boston: Follow Storrow Drive to Mt. Auburn Street in Cambridge, to Belmont Street in Watertown. Continue on Belmont Street to Trapelo Road in Belmont and stay on Trapelo Road for 2.4 miles to the National Archives on the left.

By MBTA: From Downtown Boston: From the Park Street station take the MBTA subway train to Harvard Square. Then take the MBTA bus to Waverly Square in Belmont (runs every 15 minutes). From Waverly Square you must either walk (about a mile) or take a commercial taxi west on Trapelo Road.

Description of Institution:

The NATIONAL ARCHIVES - NEW ENGLAND REGION has custody of the permanently valuable records of field offices and divisions of **Federal** agencies in the six New England States -- Connecticut, Maine, Massachusetts, New Hampshire, Rhode Island and Vermont. It is one of thirteen such **regional archives** of the National Archives located throughout the country. Records of Federal agencies outside of Washington which are judged to have permanent administrative, legal or historical value are accessioned into the National Archives and maintained in the regional archives.

In addition, the regional archives has over 60,000 rolls of microfilm containing copies of documents located in the National Archives in Washington, DC. In order to make its holdings more accessible, the National Archives has reproduced on microfilm many of its most significant records. Microfilm publications serve the public's need for greater access to original source material. Over 200,000 rolls of microfilm have been produced by the National Archives, and select series of microfilm have been deposited in the regional archives where they can be used by researchers.

Description of Resources:

A significant amount of the records and microfilm held by the National Archives contains material of genealogical value. The most widely used records for family research are described below. [The abbreviation NAMP stands for National Archives Microfilm Publication].

1. Federal Census Records (microfilm):

   All existing Federal population census schedules, taken every ten years, for all states, from 1790 to 1920 (nearly all of the 1890 schedules were destroyed in a fire in 1921).

   Soundex indexes to the 1880, 1900 and 1920 censuses, and the partial Soundex index (21 states) to the 1910 census.

   Non-population census schedules for Massachusetts for 1850-1880, and some schedules of a special census of Union veterans and widows of veterans taken in 1890.

   Census Schedules:

a.	1790 Federal Population Census, NAMP M637	(12 rolls).
b.	1800 Federal Population Census, NAMP M32	(52 rolls).
c.	1810 Federal Population Census, NAMP M252	(71 rolls).
d.	1820 Federal Population Census, NAMP M33	(142 rolls).
e.	1830 Federal Population Census, NAMP M19	(201 rolls).
f.	1840 Federal Population Census, NAMP M704	(580 rolls).
g.	1850 Federal Population Census, NAMP M432	(1,009 rolls).
h.	1860 Federal Population Census, NAMP M653	(1,438 rolls).
i.	1870 Federal Population Census, NAMP M593	(1,748 rolls).
j.	1880 Federal Population Census, NAMP T9	(1,454 rolls).
k.	1890 Federal Population Census, NAMP M407	(3 rolls).
l.	1900 Federal Population Census, NAMP T623	(1,854 rolls).
m.	1910 Federal Population Census, NAMP T624	(1,784 rolls).
n.	1920 Federal Population Census, NAMP T625	(2,076 rolls).

   Indexes:

   1790-
   1870:   Printed indexes are available for most states and territories. Most indexes were prepared by Accelerated Indexing Systems (AIS), a private firm. Nearly all states have indexes available through 1850 (heads of household only), with some through 1860, and a few 1870.

   1880:   Soundex indexes for all states, prepared by the WPA. Index covers **only** those households with a child aged 10 or under. (Microfilm: NAMP T734-T780, 2,367 rolls). See page 12 for details.

   1890:   Alphabetical index to the fragments that survived the 1921 fire. (Microfilm: NAMP M496, 2 rolls).

   1900:   Soundex indexes for all states, all households. (Microfilm: NAMP T1030-T1083, 7,846 rolls)

1910:   Soundex indexes for only 21 states (mostly in south and west). (Microfilm: T1259-T1279, 4,642 rolls). But see research procedure, page 13.

1920:   Soundex indexes for all states and territories, all households. (Microfilm: M1548-M1605, 8,585 rolls)

Finding Aids:

1.   Description of Census Enumeration Districts, 1900. NAMP T1210. (7 rolls). Description of Census Enumeration Districts, 1910-1920. NAMP T1224. (1910: rolls 28-40; 1920: rolls 41-60).
2.   Cross Index to Selected City Streets and Enumeration Districts, 1910 Census. NAMP M1283. (50 microfiche cards). A guide relating street addresses to Enumeration Districts, for 39 cities. See page 13.
3.   Selected City Directories for use with the 1910 Census. (11 rolls). Boston, Worcester, Fall River, Lowell, MA; New York City. (Donated by JGSGB).

There is also a computer terminal available which does name-to-Soundex conversions.

Non-Population Census Schedules:

Non-population census schedules for Massachusetts from 1850-1880 (NAMP T1204, 40 rolls). Includes manufacturing, agriculture, social statistics and mortality schedules.

Special schedules of the census of Union Civil War veterans and widows of veterans taken in 1890. (NAMP M123, 118 rolls). Only for states K-W.

2.   Passenger Arrival Lists (microfilm):

Copies of most passenger arrival lists are located in the National Archives in Washington, DC. The regional archives have been given microfilm copies of many of these lists. The NATIONAL ARCHIVES - NEW ENGLAND REGION has microfilm copies of the passenger lists of vessels arriving at the ports listed below. Unless otherwise noted, the Archives has the entire series. See page 21 for details on the contents of these passenger lists.

Boston, MA:

Lists:	1820-1891	(NAMP M277, 115 rolls).
		[Note: Does **not** cover Apr 1874 - Dec 1882. See page 22].
	1891-1943	(NAMP T843, 454 rolls). Archives has only rolls #1-365 (Aug 1891 - Dec 1930).
Index:	1848-1891	(NAMP M265, 282 rolls). Alphabetical.
	1902-1906	(NAMP T521, 11 rolls). Semi-alphabetical.
	1906-1920	(NAMP T617, 11 rolls). Semi-alphabetical.
	1899-1940	(NAMP T790, 107 rolls). Archives has only rolls #1-64 (Apr 1899 - Dec 1919). These are **book** indexes, arranged chronologically.
		[Note: There are no book indexes for 1901].
Other:	Crew Lists, 1917-1943 (NAMP T938, 269 rolls).
	Archives has only rolls #1-15 (1917-1921).	

New Bedford, MA:
Lists:	1902-1942	(NAMP T944, 8 rolls).
Index:	1902-1954	(NAMP T522, 2 rolls). Alphabetical.

Portland, ME:
Lists:	1893-1943	(NAMP T1151, 35 rolls).
Index:	1893-1954	(NAMP T524, 1 roll). Alphabetical.
	1907-1930	(NAMP T793, 12 rolls). Book Indexes.

Providence, RI:
Lists:	1911-1943	(NAMP T1188, 49 rolls).
Index:	1911-1954	(NAMP T518, 2 rolls). Alphabetical.

Galveston, TX:
Lists:	1896-1951	(NAMP M1359, 36 rolls).
Index:	1896-1906	(NAMP M1357, 3 rolls). Alphabetical.
	1906-1951	(NAMP M1358, 7 rolls). Alphabetical.
Note:		Includes Galveston and various Texas subports, including Houston and Brownsville.

Miscellaneous Ports:

"Copies of Lists of Passengers Arriving at Miscellaneous Ports on the Atlantic and Gulf Coasts and at the Ports on the Great Lakes, 1820-1873". Records of the U.S. Customs Service. (NAMP 575, 16 rolls).

Canadian Border Crossings:
Lists:	1895-1954	(NAMP M1464, 639 rolls). Atlantic ports.
	1929-1949	(NAMP M1465, 25 rolls). Pacific ports.
Index:	1895-1924	(NAMP M1462, 6 rolls). Alphabetical.
		For small ports in Vermont.
	1895-1924	(NAMP M1461, 400 rolls). Soundex. For all ports.
	1924-1952	(NAMP M1463, 98 rolls). Soundex. For all ports.

3.   Naturalization Records:

Naturalization records are documents of immigrants who applied for American citizenship. These records consist of the original petition or a record of naturalization and some declarations of intention. See page 16 for details about Naturalization records. The Archives' holdings include a large number of naturalization papers of immigrants living in New England, which fall into three categories:

    i.   WPA Project Dexigraphs
    ii.   Federal Court Records
    iii.   Local Court Records

i. WPA Project Dexigraphs and Indexes (1790-1906):

During the late 1930's there was an effort by the Work Projects Administration (WPA) to copy and index Naturalization records from all courts (Federal, state, county and municipal), 1790 to 1906. Only New England, New York City, and a few other small portions were completed. The original records stayed with the courts; dexigraph copies of the originals were made, and a card index created.

The Archives has the 5" x 8" photostat negative copies ("dexigraphs") and indexes for all naturalization petitions in the six New England states, 1790-1906. See page 16 for details about this index and the dexigraphs. The Soundex card indexes to these records are located in card file drawers at the far end of the Reading Room. Once a card entry has been located, you can fill out a Reference Service Slip to see the dexigraph copy of the naturalization petition. See procedure at the end of this chapter.

ii. Federal Court Records (U.S. District and Circuit Courts):

The Archives has the originals of all Naturalization records of **Federal** Courts in the New England States, for 1790 through the 1970's. (Note that the functions of the U.S. Circuit Courts were absorbed by the U.S. District Courts in 1911).

Connecticut	1842 - 1973	New Hampshire	1873 - 1977
Maine	1790 - 1955	Rhode Island	1842 - 1950
Massachusetts	1790 - 1971	Vermont	1801 - 1972

Connecticut:

a. Connecticut - U.S. District Court at Hartford and New Haven
   • Record of Naturalization and Declarations, 13 vols., 1842-1903 (Hartford and New Haven).
   • Declarations of Intention, 1911-1955 (Hartford).
   • Petition and Record, 1911-1973 (Hartford)
   • Depositions of Witnesses, 11 boxes, 1926-1955 (Hartford).

b. Connecticut - U.S. District Court at New Haven
   • Declarations of Intention, 57 vols., 1911-1963.
   • Petition and Record, 1911-1965.
   • Petition and Record for Military Personnel, 1919.
   • Petition and Record for Military Personnel (overseas), 1942-1956.
   • Military Repatriations, 1 vol., 1920-1931.
   • Women's Repatriation, 1 vol., 1936-1972.
   • Petitions Granted/Denied, 1928-1962.
   • Depositions of Witnesses, 14 boxes, 1923-1968.
   • Name Index to Petitions, 1906-1949.

c. Connecticut - U.S. Circuit Court at Hartford
   • Declarations of Intention, for petitions numbered 1 to 200, 1893-1906.
   • Record of Naturalization, 2 vols., 1893-1906.
   • Declarations of Intention, 13 vols., 1906-1911.
   • Petition and Record, 8 vols., 1906-1911.
      (Note: Index lists these erroneously as US District Court, Hartford).

d. Connecticut - U.S. Circuit Court at New Haven
   • Declarations of Intention, 4 vols., 1906-1911.
   • Petition and Record, 3 vols., 1906-1911.

Maine:

a.   Maine - U.S. District Court:
  - Naturalization Dockets, 1856-1885.
  - Declarations of Intention (Clerk's copies), 1849-1900.
  - Petitions and Records of Naturalization, 1790-1902.
  - Naturalization Record Books, 1851-1906.
  - Declarations of Intention (submitted with petitions), 1799-1909.

b.   Maine - U.S. District Court - Southern Division (Portland):
  - Name Index to Declarations files, 1906-1955 (includes Circuit Court).
  - Declarations of Intention, 1911-1955.
  - Name Index to Petitions Filed, 1851-1944 (includes Circuit Court).
  - Petitions and Records of Naturalization, 1911-1945.
  - Petitions and Records of Naturalization of Military Personnel, 1918-1919.
  - Petitions and Records of Naturalizations Overseas, 1942-1945.

c.   Maine - U.S. District Court - Northern Division (Bangor):
  - None. (All naturalizations performed in Southern Division until about 1945).

d.   Maine - U.S. Circuit Court:
  - Declarations of Intention (Clerk's copies), 1850-1906.
  - Declarations of Intention (Originals), 1906-1911.
  - Petitions and Records of Naturalization, 1851-1906.
  - Petitions and Records of Naturalization, 1906-1911.
  - Naturalization Record Books, 1851-1906.
  - Some records included with Maine District Court, Southern Division.

Massachusetts:

a.   Alphabetic Index to Naturalizations in the U.S. District and Circuit Courts for the District of Massachusetts, 1906-1966. NAMP M1545. (115 microfilm rolls).

b.   Petitions and Records of Naturalizations in the U.S. District and Circuit Courts for the District of Massachusetts, 1906-1929. NAMP M1368. (330 microfilm rolls).
[Petitions to #119586 are on microfilm; petitions after #119586 are originals or copies of originals. See Massachusetts U.S. District Court, below].

c.   Massachusetts - U.S. District Court:
  - Declarations of Intention (Clerk's copies), 1798-1874.
  - Declarations of Intention (Originals, unbound), 1804-1874
      (includes Circuit Court declarations prior to 1845)
  - Declarations of Intention, 1874-1906.
  - Declarations of Intention, 1906-1950.
  - Petitions and Records of Naturalization (Originals, unbound), 1790-1868.
  - Name Indexes to Naturalizations, 1790-1911.
  - Naturalization Record Books, 1790-1911.
  - Petitions and Records of Naturalizations, 1868-1906.
  - Petitions and Records of Naturalizations, 1906-1970.
  - Name Index to Petitions and Records of Naturalizations, 1906-1966 (Originals).
  - Declarations of Intention (submitted with petitions), 1884-1909.
  - Petitions and Records of Naturalization for Military Personnel, 1919.
  - Depositions of Witnesses, 1911-1950.
  - 'Court Lists' of Naturalization Hearings, 1927-1951.
  - Naturalization Certificate Stub Books, 1906-1925.
  - Naturalization Case Dockets, 1908-1955.
  - Naturalization Case Files, 1912-1940.

d. Massachusetts - U.S. Circuit Court:
   - Declarations of Intention (Originals, unbound) 1845-1875
     (for earlier declarations, see Massachusetts District Court).
   - Records of Declarations Filed, 1845-1875.
   - Declarations of Intention, 1875-1906.
   - Declarations of Intention, 1906-1911.
   - Petitions and Records of Naturalization (Originals, unbound), 1845-1864.
   - Name Index to Naturalization Record Books, 1845-1871.
   - Name Index to Naturalization Records, 1845-1906.
   - Naturalization Record Books, 1845-1864.
   - Petitions and Records of Naturalizations, 1864-1906.
   - Petitions and Records of Naturalizations, 1906-1911.
   - Declarations of Intention (submitted with petitions), 1864-1909.
   - Depositions of Witnesses, 1908-1911.

New Hampshire:

a. New Hampshire - U.S. District Court:
   - Declarations of Intention, 1884-1906.
   - Declarations of Intention, 1911-1976.
   - Petitions and Records of Naturalization, 1884-1898.
   - Petitions and Records of Naturalization, 1908-1977.
   - Petitions and Records of Naturalization for Military Personnel Overseas, 1942-1955.
   - Naturalization Certificate Stub Book, 1908-1926.
   - Women's Applications for Repatriation, 1952-1967.

b. New Hampshire - U.S. Circuit Court:
   - List of Persons Naturalized or Filing Primary Declarations, 1849-1871.
   - Declarations of Intention, 1906-1911.
   - Petitions of Records of Naturalization, 1873-1906.

Rhode Island:

a. Rhode Island - U.S. District Court:
   - Declarations of Intention, 1835-1890.
   - Records of Declarations Filed, 1890-1906.
   - Declarations of Intention, 1906-1950.
   - Petitions and Records of Naturalization, 1842-1906.
   - Naturalization Records Books, 1842-1903.
   - Petitions and Records of Naturalization, 1911-1950.
   - Declarations of Intention (submitted with petitions), 1900-1925.
   - Depositions of Witnesses, 1941-1960.
   - Naturalization Certificate Stubs, 1911-1957.

b. Rhode Island - U.S. Circuit Court:
   - Record of Declarations Filed, 1888-1897.
   - Petitions and Records of Naturalization, 1843-1906.
   - Petitions and Records of Naturalization, 1906-1911.
   - Naturalization Record Books, 1842-1901.
   - Declarations of Intention (submitted with petitions), 1850-1911.
   - Naturalization Certificate Stubs, 1907-1911.

Vermont:

a.   Vermont - U.S. District Court:
- Name Indexes to Declarations and Petitions, 1801-1964.
  (includes Circuit Court to 1866).
- Records Books (copies) of Declarations Filed, 1801-1906.
- Declarations Filed, 1907-1945.
- Record Books (copies) of Petitions Filed, 1842-1906.
- Petitions and Records of Naturalization, 1908-1972.
- Petitions and Records of Naturalization, 1842-1972 (microfilm, 45 rolls).
- Petitions for Naturalization (certified unbound copies), 1904-1906.
- Declarations of Intention (submitted with petitions), 1840-1908, with gaps.

iii.   Other Naturalization Records:

Some records of **non**-Federal Connecticut courts, 1790-1974.   The records were donated to the Archives by the State of Connecticut in 1974.   Included are records of Connecticut Superior Courts, Courts of Common Pleas, County District Courts and some municipal courts.   Note that beginning in 1854, County Courts became Superior Courts.   The Courts of Common Pleas were created between 1869 and 1870.

- Ansonia City Court (New Haven County), 1893-1906.
- Bridgeport City Court (Fairfield County), 1852-1877.
- Fairfield County Court/Superior Court, 1795, 1829-1966.
- Fairfield County Court of Common Pleas, 1874-1906.
- Hartford City Court (Hartford County), 1875-1876.
- Hartford County Court of Common Pleas (at Hartford), 1876-1906.
- Hartford County Court/Superior Court (at Hartford), 1793-1908.
- Hartford County Superior Court (at New Britain), 1939-1974.
- Litchfield County District Court/Court of Common Pleas, 1874-1906.
- Litchfield County Superior Court, 1803-1973.
- Meridan City Court (New Haven County), 1903-1939.
- Middlesex County Court/Superior Court, 1795-1955.
- New Britain City Court (Hartford County), 1903-1940.
- New Haven City Court (New Haven County), 1843-1923.
- New Haven County Superior Court (at Meridan), 1936-1957.
- New Haven County Court of Common Pleas (at New Haven), 1874-1906.
- New Haven County Court/Superior Court (at New Haven), 1803-1903.
- New Haven County District Court (at Waterbury), 1881-1906.
- New Haven County District Court/Superior Court (at Waterbury), 1906-1972.
- New London City Court (New London County), 1793-1855.
- New London County Court of Common Pleas, 1874-1906.
- New London County Court/Superior Court, 1804-1974.
- Tolland County Court/Superior Court, 1825-1975.
- Waterbury City Court (New Haven County), 1854-1881.
- Windham County Superior Court, 1855-1974.

4.   Internal Revenue Service:

Internal Revenue Assessment Lists, 1862-1866:
- Connecticut   NAMP M758. (23 rolls).
- Maine   NAMP M770. (15 rolls).
- New Hampshire   NAMP M780. (10 rolls).
- Vermont   NAMP M792.   (7 rolls).
- Rhode Island   NAMP M788. (10 rolls).

5. World War II War Crimes Records:

Some of these records were captured by the Allies at the end of World War II, where they were used as evidence in the Nuernberg trails. These records were microfilmed by the U.S. government in Alexandria, VA, and were returned to the West German government.

a. Records of the U.S. Nuernberg War Crimes Trials: NI Series, 1933-1948. NAMP T301. (164 rolls, roll #127 is restricted).

b. Prosecution Exhibits Submitted to the International Military Tribunal. NAMP T988. (54 rolls).

c. War Diaries and Correspondence of General Alfred Jodl. NAMP T989. (2 rolls).

d. Mauthausen Death Books. NAMP T990. (2 rolls).
Contains name, date of birth, and date of death for about 100,000 inmates of the Mauthausen concentration camp. In German. (See *DOROT*, X, 3 (Spring 1989), pp 8-9; and *Prologue*, Fall 1983, pp 179-187, for other Holocaust resources at the National Archives).

e. U.S. Trial Brief and Document Books. NAMP T991. (1 roll).

f. Diary of Hans Frank, Governor General of German-occupied Poland, 1939-1945. NAMP T992. (12 rolls).

6. Military Records:

The Archives holds a large number of microfilm copies of U.S. military service and pension records, most relating to the Revolutionary War.

- Revolutionary War Pension and Bounty-Land Warrant Application Files. NAMP M804. (2,670 rolls).

- General Index to Compiled Military Service Records of Revolutionary War Soldiers. NAMP M860. (58 rolls).

- Compiled Service Records of Soldiers Who Served in the American Army During the Revolutionary War. NAMP M881. (1,096 rolls).

- Revolutionary War Rolls, 1775-1783. NAMP M246. (138 rolls).

- Index to Compiled Service Records of Volunteer Soldiers Who Served During the War of 1812. NAMP M602. (234 rolls).

- Indexes to Compiled Service Records of Volunteer Union Solidiers Who Served in the Civil War from:
  - Connecticut   NAMP M535. (17 rolls).   • New Hampshire   NAMP M549. (13 rolls).
  - Maine   NAMP M543. (23 rolls).   • Rhode Island   NAMP M555. (7 rolls).
  - Massachusetts NAMP M544. (44 rolls).   • Vermont   NAMP M557. (14 rolls).

- Special Census (1890) of Union Civil War Veterans and their Widows. NAMP M123. (118 rolls). Only for states K-W.

- General Index to Pension Files, 1861-1934. NAMP T288. (544 rolls).
Alphabetical index covering service between 1861 and 1916 (Civil War Union soldiers, Spanish-American War, Philippine Insurrection, Boxer Rebellion, and regular army).

- World War I Draft Registration Cards, 1917-1918. NAMP M1509.
Archives has the reels for the six New England states only, 310 reels.
Arranged by draft board. See *MassPocha* III:1 (Winter 1993/94) for details.
Finding aid at desk. Special magnifying lens available for viewing and printing.

7. Miscellaneous Records:

- Russian Consular Records (Records of Imperial Russian Consulates in the U.S., 1862-1922). NAMP M1486. (99 of 180 rolls).
  (Archives only has rolls for consulates in New York, Philadelphia, and Chicago).
- Records of Appointments of Postmasters, 1789-1971.
  (1789-1832, M1131, 4 rolls. 1832-1971, M841, 145 rolls).
- Lighthouse Keepers' Records, 1845-1912. (M1373, 4 rolls).
- U.S. Diplomatic and Consular Officer Records, 1789-1939.
  (List of U.S. Diplomatic Officers, 1789-1939, M586, 3 rolls;
  List of U.S. Consular Officers, 1789-1939, M587, 21 rolls).
- Index to U.S. Passport Applications, 1810-1906.
  (Issued to U.S. citizens traveling abroad. Passports were optional until 1928. Only the index is available, M1371, 13 rolls; the records are at the National Archives in Washington).
- Customs Records - for New England ports (228 microfilm rolls).
  (New London, New Haven, Newport, Fall River, Salem, Marblehead, Gloucester).

Description of Facility:

The Archives is housed in a modern, well-appointed facility, expanded and renovated in the summer of 1992. Its public areas include a main reading room with 40 microfilm readers and one microfiche reader, a conference/meeting room, an exhibit area, and a small research room for the use of original records. The main reading room has three tables with four chairs each. The small research room has seating for nine.

Microfilm rolls for Census records, Passenger Lists, Naturalizations and Military records are located in self-service cabinets in the reading room. Most other microfilms are in the closed stacks. Naturalization index cards for the 1790-1906 WPA dexigraphs, and most Connecticut state and local courts are located at the far end of the main reading room; other indexes are located in the stacks and must be requested from a staff member. There is a 10 minute wait for paper records (Naturalizations). See procedure below.

The Archives employs six full-time archivists and three part-time aides. Three archivist-technicians serve the public. There are also National Archives Volunteers.

Fees/Copies:

Microfilm copies: There are three microfilm copier machines — these self-service coin-fed machines cost 25¢ per page, and take quarters only.

Paper copies: There are two copiers available, 10¢ per page self-serve, or 25¢ per page if done by the staff. All original records must be copied by the staff.

Mail requests are accepted for naturalization information only. Turnover is up to 10 working days. The researcher should provide the name, place, and approximate date of naturalization. The search is free. If a record is found, you will be billed a minimum of $6.00 (overseas requests, add $2.00).

The staff sells blank forms for the various census years. The cost is 10¢ per sheet.

Restrictions on Use:

All briefcases, large bags and backpacks must be left in lockers near the entrance to the main reading room. The lockers cost 25¢ (quarters only), which is returned to you. Outerwear (coats, umbrellas, etc.) must be stored in closet at entrance to reading room.

Only pencils are allowed in the research room.

How to Access Dexigraphs and Original Records:

In order to view dexigraphs and all original records, patrons must first get a "researcher card" from a staff member. The card is good for two years. With a "researcher card", a patron who wants to view original records needs to fill out a Reference Service Slip, available from the staff in the research room. The patron should give the slip to a staff member, and the staff member will bring the records to the patron in the research room (after about a 10 minute wait, depending upon how busy they are). The material cannot be removed from the research room. If you wish to make photocopies, a staff member must make them for you, at a charge of 25¢ per page.

NATIONAL ARCHIVES, PITTSFIELD

Facility Director: Jean Nudd, Director
                             Walter Hickey, Archives Technician

Address: 100 Dan Fox Drive
                             Pittsfield, MA 01201-8230

Phone Number: (413) 445-6885   Reference Desk x26
                             (413) 445-7599   FAX

Hours of Operation:

Monday to Friday   9:00 am to 3:00 pm
Wednesday   9:00 am to 9:00 pm
Wednesday evening hours are in September thru May only.
Closed Saturdays, Sundays and Federal Holidays.

Directions:

By Car: The NATIONAL ARCHIVES—PITTSFIELD is located near the Pittsfield Municipal Airport. It is a 2½ hour drive from Boston. Take the Mass Pike (I-90) to Exit 2 (Lee). Bear right after the toll booth, onto Route 20 West. Follow Route 20 through Lee and Lenox (where it merges with Route 7 North) for 8½ miles. Just after the Pittsfield line, take a left at the traffic light with the sign to the Pittsfield Municipal Airport. Proceed ¼ mile to a sign on the right to the Federal Records Center, take the right, and follow the driveway to the top of the hill.

Description of Institution:

The NATIONAL ARCHIVES - PITTSFIELD was established in 1994 to provide greater access to microfilm copies of Federal records with high research value. It is one of thirteen such **regional archives** of the National Archives located throughout the country. The facility has over 60,000 rolls of microfilm containing copies of documents located in the National Archives in Washington, DC. In order to make its holdings more accessible, while preserving the original documents from deterioration and damage from handling, the National Archives has reproduced on microfilm many of its most significant records.

Description of Resources:

The majority of the microfilm held by the NATIONAL ARCHIVES, PITTSFIELD contains material of genealogical value. The most widely used records for family research are described below. [The abbreviation NAMP stands for National Archives Microfilm Publication].

1. Federal Census Records (microfilm):

    All existing Federal population census schedules, taken every ten years, for all states, from 1790 to 1920 (nearly all of the 1890 schedules were destroyed in a fire in 1921).

    Soundex indexes to the 1880, 1900 and 1920 censuses, and the partial Soundex index (21 states) to the 1910 census.

    Non-population census schedules for Massachusetts for 1850-1880, and some schedules of a special census of Union veterans and widows of veterans taken in 1890.

    ### Census Schedules:

a.	1790 Federal Population Census, NAMP M637	(12 rolls).
b.	1800 Federal Population Census, NAMP M32	(52 rolls).
c.	1810 Federal Population Census, NAMP M252	(71 rolls).
d.	1820 Federal Population Census, NAMP M33	(142 rolls).
e.	1830 Federal Population Census, NAMP M19	(201 rolls).
f.	1840 Federal Population Census, NAMP M704	(580 rolls).
g.	1850 Federal Population Census, NAMP M432	(1,009 rolls).
h.	1860 Federal Population Census, NAMP M653	(1,438 rolls).
i.	1870 Federal Population Census, NAMP M593	(1,748 rolls).
j.	1880 Federal Population Census, NAMP T9	(1,454 rolls).
k.	1890 Federal Population Census, NAMP M407	(3 rolls).
l.	1900 Federal Population Census, NAMP T623	(1,854 rolls).
m.	1910 Federal Population Census, NAMP T624	(1,784 rolls).
n.	1920 Federal Population Census, NAMP T625	(2,076 rolls).

    ### Indexes:

    1790-
    1870:   Printed indexes are available for most states and territories. Most indexes were prepared by Accelerated Indexing Systems (AIS), a private firm. Nearly all states have indexes available through 1850 (heads of household only), with some through 1860, and a few 1870.

    1880:   Soundex indexes for all states, prepared by the WPA. Index covers **only** those households with a child aged 10 or under. (Microfilm: NAMP T734-T780, 2,367 rolls). See page 12 for details.

    1890:   Alphabetical index to the fragments that survived the 1921 fire. (Microfilm: NAMP M496, 2 rolls).

    1900:   Soundex indexes for all states, all households. (Microfilm: NAMP T1030-T1083, 7,846 rolls)

1910:	Soundex indexes for only 21 states (none for the northeastern states). (Microfilm: T1259-T1279, 4,642 rolls). But see research procedure, page 13.
1920:	Soundex indexes for all states, all households. (Microfilm: M1548-M1605, 8,585 rolls)

Finding Aids:

1. Description of Census Enumeration Districts, 1900. NAMP T1210. (10 rolls). Description of Census Enumeration Districts, 1830-1890 and 1910-1950. NAMP T1224. (156 rolls).
2. Cross Index to Selected City Streets and Enumeration Districts, 1910 Census. NAMP M1283. (50 microfiche cards). A guide relating street addresses to Enumeration Districts, for 39 cities. See page 13.

Non-Population Census Schedules:

Non-population census schedules for Massachusetts from 1850-1880 (NAMP T1204, 40 rolls). Includes industry, agriculture, social statistics and mortality schedules.

Special schedules of the census of Union veterans and widows of veterans taken in 1890. (NAMP M123, 188 rolls). Only for states K-W.

2. Passenger Arrival Lists (microfilm):

Copies of most passenger arrival lists are located in the National Archives in Washington, DC. The regional archives have been given microfilm copies of many of these lists. The NATIONAL ARCHIVES - PITTSFIELD has microfilm copies of the passenger lists of vessels arriving at the ports listed below. Unless otherwise noted, the Archives has the entire series. See page 21 for details on the contents of these passenger lists.

New York, NY:

Lists:	1820-1897	(NAMP M237, 675 rolls).	
	1897-1957	(NAMP T715, 8,892 rolls).	
Index:	1820-1846	(NAMP M261, 103 rolls). Alphabetical.	
	1897-1902	(NAMP T519, 115 rolls). Alphabetical.	(6/16/1897-6/30/1902)
	1902-1943	(NAMP T621, 744 rolls). Soundex.	(7/1/1902-12/31/1943)
	1944-1948	(NAMP M1417, 94 rolls). Soundex.	
Other:	Registers of vessels, 1789-1919 (NAMP M1066, 27 rolls). Ship names.		
	1906-1942	(NAMP T612, 807 rolls). Book indexes.	

Philadelphia, PA:

Lists:	1800-1882	(NAMP M425, 108 rolls).
Index:	1800-1906	(NAMP M360, 151 rolls). Alphabetical.

Boston, MA:
    Lists: 1820-1891   (NAMP M277, 115 rolls).
                        [Note: Does **not** cover Apr 1874 - Dec 1882.
                        See page 22].
           1891-1943   (NAMP T843, 454 rolls). (Aug 1891 - Dec 1943).
    Index: 1848-1891   (NAMP M265, 282 rolls). Alphabetical.
           1902-1906   (NAMP T521, 11 rolls). Semi-alphabetical.
           1906-1920   (NAMP T617, 11 rolls). Semi-alphabetical.
           1899-1940   (NAMP T790, 107 rolls). These are **book** indexes,
                        arranged chronologically.
                        [Note: There **are** no book indexes for 1901].
    Other: Crew Lists, 1917-1943 (NAMP T938, 269 rolls).
           Register of Vessels, 1848-1892 (non-NARA, 4 rolls).

New Bedford, MA:
    Lists: 1902-1942   (NAMP T944, 8 rolls).
    Index: 1902-1954   (NAMP T522, 2 rolls). Alphabetical.

Portland, ME:
    Lists: 1893-1943   (NAMP T1151, 35 rolls).
    Index: 1893-1954   (NAMP T524, 1 roll). Alphabetical.

Providence, RI:
    Lists: 1911-1943   (NAMP T1188, 49 rolls).
    Index: 1911-1954   (NAMP T518, 2 rolls). Alphabetical.

Miscellaneous Ports:
"Copies of Lists of Passengers Arriving at Miscellaneous Ports on the Atlantic and Gulf Coasts and at the Ports on the Great Lakes, 1820-1873". Records of the U.S. Customs Service. (NAMP 575, 16 rolls). Also supplemental index, 1820-1874 (NAMP M334, 188 rolls).

Canadian Border Crossings:
    Lists: 1895-1954   (NAMP M1464, 639 rolls). Atlantic ports.
           1929-1949   (NAMP M1465, 25 rolls). Pacific ports.
    Index: 1895-1924   (NAMP M1462, 6 rolls). Alphabetical.
                        For small ports in Vermont.
           1895-1924   (NAMP M1461, 400 rolls). Soundex. For all ports.
           1924-1952   (NAMP M1463, 98 rolls). Soundex. For all ports.

Finding Aids:
The NATIONAL ARCHIVES, PITTSFIELD has purchased many of the privately prepared published passenger lists indexes (see page 27), which cover the unindexed 1847-1897 period for New York, including:

- *Germans to America.* (1850-1884). 50+ volumes.
- *Migration from the Russian Empire.* (1875-1886). 2+ volumes.
- *The Famine Immigrants: Lists of Irish Immigrants...* (1847-1851). 7 volumes.
- *Italians to America.* (1888-1891). 5+ volumes.

See page 164 for complete bibliographic citations for the above books.

3. Naturalization Records:

Naturalization records are documents of immigrants who applied for American citizenship. The NATIONAL ARCHIVES, PITTSFIELD holds only three microfilmed record series relating to naturalization:

a. Index to "old law" New England Naturalization Petitions, 1790-1906. NAMP M1299. (117 microfilm rolls). [Pittsfield has the index **only**. The records to which they refer are held at the NATIONAL ARCHIVES - NEW ENGLAND REGION in Waltham. See page 147].

b. Alphabetic Index to Naturalizations in the U.S. District and Circuit Courts for the District of Massachusetts, 1906-1966. NAMP M1545. (115 microfilm rolls).

c. Petitions and Records of Naturalizations in the U.S. District and Circuit Courts for the District of Massachusetts, 1906-1929. NAMP M1368. (330 microfilm rolls). [Petitions to #119586 are on microfilm; petitions after #119586 are originals or copies of originals, held at the NATIONAL ARCHIVES - NEW ENGLAND REGION in Waltham. See page 147].

4. Military Records:

The Archives holds a large number of microfilm copies of U.S. military service and pension records, most relating to the Revolutionary War.

- Revolutionary War Pension and Bounty-Land Warrant Application Files. NAMP M804. (2,670 rolls).
- General Index to Compiled Military Service Records of Revolutionary War Soldiers. NAMP M860. (58 rolls).
- Compiled Service Records of Soldiers Who Served in the American Army During the Revolutionary War. NAMP M881. (1,096 rolls).
- Revolutionary War Rolls, 1775-1783. NAMP M246. (138 rolls).

- Index to Compiled Service Records of Volunteer Soldiers Who Served During the War of 1812. NAMP M602. (234 rolls).

- Special Census (1890) of Union Civil War Veterans and their Widows. NAMP M123. (118 rolls). Only for states K-W.

- General Index to Compiled Service Records of Volunteer Soldiers who Served During the War with Spain. NAMP M871. (126 rolls).
- General Index to Compiled Service Records of Volunteer Soldiers who Served During the Philippine Insurrection. NAMP M872. (24 rolls).

- Register of Enlistments in the U.S. Army, 1789-1914. NAMP M233. (81 rolls).
- General Index to Pension Files, 1861-1934. NAMP T288. (544 rolls). Alphabetical index covering service between 1861 and 1916 (Civil War Union soldiers, Spanish-American War, Philippine Insurrection, Boxer Rebellion, and regular army).

- World War I Draft Registration Cards, 1917-1918. NAMP M1509. Pittsfield has the reels for the six New England states and New York State. Arranged by draft board. See *MassPocha* III:1 (Winter 1993/94) for details.

5. Internal Revenue Service:

Internal Revenue Assessment Lists, 1862-1866:
- Connecticut   NAMP M758. (23 rolls).
- Maine   NAMP M770. (15 rolls).
- New Hampshire   NAMP M780. (10 rolls).
- Vermont   NAMP M792.   (7 rolls).
- Rhode Island   NAMP M788. (10 rolls).

6. Miscellaneous Records:

- Russian Consular Records (Records of Imperial Russian Consulates in the U.S., 1862-1922). NAMP M1486. (180 rolls).

- Records of Appointments of Postmasters, 1789-1971.
  (1789-1832, M1131, 4 rolls. 1832-1971, M841, 145 rolls).

- U.S. Diplomatic and Consular Officer Records, 1789-1939.
  (List of U.S. Diplomatic Officers, 1789-1939, M586, 3 rolls;
  List of U.S. Consular Officers, 1789-1939, M587, 21 rolls).

- Index to U.S. Passport Applications, 1810-1906.
  (Issued to U.S. citizens traveling abroad. Passports were optional until 1928. Only the index is available, M1371, 13 rolls; the records are at the National Archives in Washington).

Description of Facility:

The NATIONAL ARCHIVES, PITTSFIELD is located in a spacious facility, opened in 1994, which it shares with the Pittsfield Federal Records Center. Most of this large modern brick building, the "Silvio O. Conte National Records Center and Regional Archives", is occupied by the Federal Records Center, which is a non-public facility used for the long-term storage of non-permanent Federal records.

The Microfilm Reading Room contains 28 brand-new microfilm readers, and two coin-operated microfilm printers. There is also one microfiche reader, and seating for 12 researchers at tables. Over 50 microfilm cabinets line the walls. It is a self-service facility. The desk attendants can help you get started, but will not do research for you.

Behind the microfilm room is a training room which seats fifty. A small cafeteria, with vending machines, a refrigerator and microwave, is located in the back of the lobby.

The staff consists of director Jean Nudd, archives technician Walter Hickey (formerly of the Waltham archives), and over fifty part-time volunteers, who are enthusiastic but inexperienced.

Differences between Pittsfield and Waltham:

The twelve other regional archives branches, including the NATIONAL ARCHIVES, NEW ENGLAND REGION in Waltham, receive the permanently valuable non-current records of Federal agencies and courts in their respective regions, and also receive copies of microfilm from the National Archives in Washington. The Pittsfield branch is different — they do **not** have custody of any original records, only duplicates of microfilm from Washington.

The microfilm holdings in Pittsfield largely duplicate those of the Waltham branch, the biggest exceptions being the New York and Philadelphia passenger lists. All of the microfilms held by Pittsfield are copies of those held in Washington. (The LDS Family History Library in Salt Lake City also has copies of nearly all of these microfilms, which can also be borrowed at any LDS FAMILY HISTORY CENTER).

Other Pittsfield holdings of interest which Waltham does not have include the World War I Draft Registration Cards for New York State, and the complete Russian Consular Records.

The greatest asset of the Pittsfield branch is the over 10,000 reels of New York passenger arrival lists, easily accessible in open microfilm cabinets. Previously, one had to travel to New York, Washington, or Salt Lake City to research these lists (although they could be borrowed via LDS FAMILY HISTORY CENTERS; and the BOSTON PUBLIC LIBRARY microtext department has the 1820-1897 lists and 1820-1846 index).

Fees/Copies:

There is no charge for the use of the facilities.

Microfilm copies: There are two coin-operated microfilm printers, which cost 25¢ per copy. Paper copies: There is one copier available, 10¢ per page self-serve.

The staff sells blank forms for the various census years. The cost is 10¢ per sheet.

Restrictions on use:

All briefcases, large bags and backpacks must be left in lockers near the entrance to the main reading room. The lockers cost 25¢ (quarters only), which is returned to you. Outerwear (coats, umbrellas, etc.) must be stored in closet at entrance to reading room.

There is a 2½ hour limit on the microfilm readers, if the facility is busy. They will reserve readers for those travelling over two hours, if they receive a written request.

NEW ENGLAND HISTORIC GENEALOGICAL SOCIETY

Facility Director: Dr. Ralph J. Crandall, Executive Director
David C. Dearborn, Head Reference Librarian
D. Brenton Simons, Director of Education

Address: 101 Newbury Street
Boston, MA 02116-3087

Phone Number: (617) 536-5740

Hours of Operation:

Office:	Monday to Friday:	9:00am - 5:00pm
Library:	Tues, Fri, Sat:	9:00am - 5:00pm
	Weds, Thurs:	9:00am - 9:00pm

[Closed Saturdays,
when they are part of a 3-day holiday weekend]

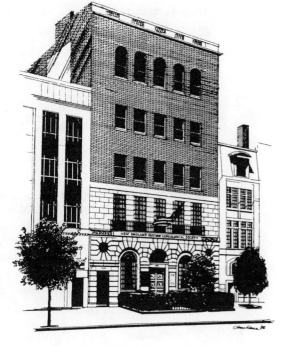

Directions:

By Car: **From the West**: Mass Pike (I-90) east, exit at Copley Square. Left on Dartmouth, three blocks north to Newbury. Limited metered street parking is available, and parking lots underground at Boylston and Clarendon (expensive).

From the South: Route I-93 (Southeast Expressway) to E. Berkeley Street. Continue past Tremont Street, over the Mass Pike, past Boylston Street, then take next left onto Newbury.

From the North: Route I-93 or Route 1 South to Expressway South (Route I-93) to Storrow Drive to Back Bay exit. A quick left and a right gets you onto Arlington Street, then take 4th right onto Newbury.

By MBTA: Green Line to Copley Station. From Boylston Street turn left onto Dartmouth, walk one block north to Newbury, turn right and walk one block to Clarendon Street. NEHGS is located on your left, two doors from the corner of Newbury and Clarendon. From Back Bay Station (Commuter Rail or Orange Line), walk four blocks north on Clarendon or Dartmouth, make right on Newbury.

Description of Institution:

The NEW ENGLAND HISTORIC GENEALOGICAL SOCIETY (NEHGS), colloqially called "HisGen", is the nation's oldest and largest genealogical society. Founded in 1845, NEHGS was the first organization specifically dedicated to the study and preservation of family history. Its library collection includes over 200,000 volumes, 10,000 reels of microfilm, and one million manuscripts, focusing on New England families, but also including nearby states and Canadian provinces. NEHGS currently has over 16,000 members.

Description of Resources:

1. ## Reading Room Reference Books

The Reading Room contains several series of books and periodicals helpful for tracing early New England ancestry.

Massachusetts Vital Records books, Systematic Series to 1850, alphabetical by town. {Published volumes of pre-1850 birth, marriage and death records,for about two-thirds of Massachusetts towns. Various publishers. A framed map on the wall shows which towns are covered}. [Ref F74 ...]

New England Marriages Prior to 1700. Clarence A. Torrey. {A manuscript index in 12 handwritten volumes of some 37,000 marriages, alphabetical by grooms' names}. [Ref F3 T6]

NEHGS Register, 1847-date. [Ref F1 N56]

The American Genealogist ("TAG"), 1922-date. [Ref F104 N6A6]. Originally *New Haven Genealogical Magazine.*

New York Genealogical and Biographical Record, 1870-date. [Ref F116 N28]

2. ## Jewish Reference Works

Standard reference works on Jewish genealogy.

Kurzweil, Arthur. *From Generation to Generation: How to Trace Your Jewish Genealogy and Personal History.* (New York, 1980). 353 pp. {The best book for beginners}. [Ref CS 21 K87]

Rottenberg, Dan. *Finding Our Fathers: A Guidebook to Jewish Genealogy.* (New York, 1977). 401 pp. {The pioneer "how-to" work of modern Jewish genealogy}. [Ref CS 21 R58]

Encyclopedia of Jewish Genealogy. Volume I: Sources in the United States and Canada. Edited by Arthur Kurzweil and Miriam Weiner. (Northvale, New Jersey: Jason Aronson, 1991). 226 pp. {A summary of North American record repository holdings, with some useful appendices}. [Ref CS21 E53 1991]

Kaganoff, Benzion C. *A Dictionary of Jewish Names and Their History.* (New York: Schocken Books, 1977). 250 pp. {Highly readable layman's view, but error prone and no references given}. [Ref CS 3010 K28]

Beider, Alexander. *A Dictionary of Jewish Surnames from the Russian Empire.* (Teaneck, NJ: Avotaynu, Inc., 1993). 782 pp. {The most comprehensive scholarly study of Jewish surnames in the Pale of Settlement}. [Ref CS 3010 B43 1993]

Singerman, Robert. *Jewish and Hebrew Onomastics: A Bibliography.* (New York and London: Garland, 1977). 132 pp. {A subject-organized list of nearly 1,200 books and articles on various aspects of Jewish names}. [Ref CS 3010 S5]

Gorr, Shmuel. *Jewish Personal Names: Their Origin, Derivation, and Diminutive Forms.* Edited by Chaim Freedman. (Teaneck, NJ: Avotaynu, Inc., 1992). 112 pp. [Ref CS 3010 G67 1992]

Guzik, Estelle M., ed. *Genealogical Resources in the New York Metropolitan Area.* (New York: Jewish Genealogical Society, Inc., 1989). 404 pp. {A detailed guide to every agency in New York City and environs that could provide data useful to Jewish (and non-Jewish) genealogical research}. [Ref F 128.25 G46]

Sack, Sallyann Amdur. *A Guide to Jewish Genealogical Research in Israel.* (Baltimore: GPC, 1987). 110 pp. [Ref CS 1504 S22]

Periodicals:
- *Avotaynu: The International Review of Jewish Genealogy.* 1985-date. [CS 31 A9]
- *Toledot.* 1977-1980. [CS 31 T64]
- *Dorot.* (New York: Jewish Genealogical Society, Inc.) 1985 (Vol. 7) to date. [E 184 J5 D6]
- *Mass-Pocha.* (Jewish Genealogical Society of Greater Boston). 1992-date. [F 75 J5 M37 1992]

Collected Genealogies:

Stern, Malcolm. *First American Jewish Families.* 3rd edition. {Genealogies of American Jewish families who arrived before 1840}. 442 pp. [Ref E184 J5 S73 1991]

Rosenstein, Neil. *The Unbroken Chain: Biographical Sketches and the Genealogy of Illustrious Jewish Families from the 15th-20th Century* (Elizabeth, New Jersey: Computer Center for Jewish Genealogy, 1990). Revised edition. 1323 pp. in 2 volumes. [CS 432 J4 R67]

Rosenstein, Neil and Charles B. Bernstein. *From King David to Baron David: The Genealogical Connections between Baron Guy de Rothschild and the Baroness Alix de Rothschild.* (Elizabeth, NJ: Computer Center for Jewish Genealogy, 1989). 68 pp. [CS 599 R684 1989]

Semigotha. Weimarer historisch-genealoges Taschenbuch des gesamten Adels jehudäischen Ursprunges. (München, 1913). 1009 pp. (1 volume, in German). [CS 28 S4] Also on microfilm.

3. Jewish Local History

Barbados. Shilstone, Eustace M. *Monumental Inscriptions in the burial ground of the synagogue at Bridgetown, Barbados.* (London, 1958). 205 pp. [F 2041 S55]

Canada. Medjuck, Sheva. *Jews of Atlantic Canada.* (St. Johns, Newfoundland, 1986). 127 pp. [F 1035 J5 M43]

Canada. Tapper, Lawrence F. *A Biographical Dictionary of Canadian Jewry 1909-1914: from the Canadian Jewish Times.* (Teaneck, NJ: Avotaynu, 1992). 245 pp. [Ref F 1035 J5 B56 1992]

Connecticut, Hartford. Silverman, Morris. *Hartford Jews, 1659-1970.* (Hartford, Conn., [1970]). 448 pp. [F104 H3 S5 1970]

Georgia, Savannah. Levy, B. H. *Savannah's Old Jewish Community Cemeteries.* (Macon, GA: Mercer Univ. Press, 1983). 118 pp. [F 294 S2 L47 1983]

Massachusetts. Kaganoff, Nathan M. *Organized Jewish Group Activities in 19th Century Massachusetts: A Checklist...* (Waltham, MA: AJHS, 1979). 2 volumes, 545 pp. + name index. [F75 J5 K3]

Minnesota. Plaut, Gunther W. *The Jews in Minnesota: The First 75 Years.* (New York: AJHS, 1959). 347 pp. [F 615 J5P53]

Missouri. Makovsky, Donald J. *The Philipsons: The First Jewish Settlers in St. Louis, 1807-1858.* (1978). 26 leaves. [F 474 S2M33]

Netherlands, Amsterdam. Verdooner, Dave. *Trouwen in Mokum.* [Jewish Marriages in Amsterdam, 1598-1811]. ('s-Grevenhage: Warray, 1991). 1,127 pp. in 2 volumes. [CS 826 J4 V47 1991]

New York City. Hershkowitz, Leo. *Wills of Early New York Jews, 1704-1799.* (New York: AJHS, 1967). 229 pp. [F 128.25 H58]

New York City. Pool, David deSola. *Portraits Etched in Stone; Early Jewish Settlers 1682-1831.* (New York: Columbia U. Press, 1952). 543 pp. [F128 J5 P2]

New York. Buffalo. Falk, Sampson. *A History of the Israelites in Buffalo* (in *Buffalo Historical Society Publication*) [F 129 B8 B88 v.1]

South Carolina. Elzas, Barnett Abraham. *The Jews of South Carolina: from the earliest times to the present day.* (1905, reprinted 1983). 352 pp. [F 280 J5 E52]

South Carolina, Charleston. Elzas, Barnett Abraham. *The Old Jewish Cemeteries at Charleston, South Carolina.* (1903). 121 pp. [F 279 C4 E5 1903]

Works on various American ethnic groups are located on Floor 5A, under the classification [E184 ...], arranged alphabetically by ethnic group. Works on American Jewry are under [E184 J5 ...]. Here are about a dozen books containing overviews of American Jewish history, plus the complete runs of two very valuable scholarly periodicals, which contain many articles on local American Jewish history:

American Jewish Archives. (Cincinnati, Ohio). 1948 to date. 46 volumes to date (1994). [E184 J5 A37]

- Index: *Index to the American Jewish Archives, Volumes I-XXIV*. By Paul F. White. (Cincinnati: AJA, 1979). 435 pp. {Covers 1948-1972}. [E 184 J5 A37 Index]

American Jewish Historical Society (AJHS) Publications, 1893 to date. 83 volumes to date (1995). Variously titled: *Publications of the American Jewish Historical Society* (1893-1961); *American Jewish Historical Quarterly* (1961-1978); *American Jewish History* (1978-date). [E184 J5 A5]

- Indexes: *Index to the Publications of the American Jewish Historical Society, Volumes 1-20*. (New York: AJHS, 1914). 600 pp. {Covers 1893-1912}. *An Index to the Publications of the American Jewish Historical Society, Volumes 21-50*. Prepared by the AJHS, introduction by Jeffrey S. Gurock. (Brooklyn: Carlson Publ. Co., 1994). 439 pp. {Covers 1913-1961}. [E 184 J5 J5 Index]

4. Atlases and Gazetteers

Mokotoff, Gary and Sallyann Amdur Sack. *Where Once We Walked: A Guide to the Jewish Communities Destroyed in the Holocaust*. (Teaneck, NJ: Avotaynu, 1991). 514 pp. {A gazetteer of 21,000 Central and Eastern European localities, arranged alphabetically and phonetically, with references to other sources of information for each locality}. [Ref DS 135 E83 M65 1990]

Cohen, Chester. *Shtetl Finder Gazetteer*. (Los Angeles, 1980). 145 pp. {Supplanted by *Where Once We Walked*, above}. [Ref DS 135 R9 C58 1989]

Gardiner, Duncan B. *German Towns in Slovakia and Upper Hungary*. (1988). 58 pp. + 18 maps. [Ref DB 2707 G37 1988]

Boston property owners maps for the late 19th and early 20th centuries can be found in large volumes in the very last aisle of Floor 5A. These highly detailed maps contain every building and owner.

An **atlas stand** in the corner of the Reading Room contains many local atlases; and world atlases and gazetteers can be found in the reference stacks under [Ref G ...].

5. Published Passenger Lists

U.S. passenger arrival lists on microfilm can be found at the NATIONAL ARCHIVES - NEW ENGLAND REGION in Waltham and elsewhere (see page 21). NEHGS has collected **published indexes** to passenger lists. Most of these compilations are of 17th and 18th century Colonial British immigrants (see under [Ref E 187.5 ...] and [Ref JV ...]). However, there are a few works listing 19th century immigrants, mostly by ethnic group or port of origin.

Filby, P. William, et al., eds. *Passenger and Immigration Lists Index: A Guide to Published Arrival Records...* (Detroit: Gale Research Co., 1981-present). 14 volumes to date. {A compilation of previously published passenger lists. One volume is published annually. Thus far listing 2½ million passengers}. [Ref CS68 P363 1981]

Dutch. Swierenga, Robert P. *Dutch Immigrants in U.S. Ship Passenger Manifests, 1820-1880: An Alphabetical Listing by Household Heads and Independent Persons*. (Wilmington, Del: Scholarly Research, Inc., 1983). 2 volumes. [E 184 D9S95 1983]

Germans. Glazier, Ira A. and P. William Filby. *Germans to America: Lists of Passengers Arriving at U.S. Ports*. (Wilmington, Del: Scholarly Resources, Inc., 1988-present). Ongoing series, 50 volumes to date, covering 1850-1884 so far. [Ref E184 G3 G38 1988]

Germans. Zimmerman, Gary J., and Marion Wolfert. *German Immigrants: Lists of Passengers Bound from Bremen to New York*. (Baltimore: Genealogical Publishing Co., 1985-93). 4 volumes. Covers 1847-1871. [E 184 G3 Z572]

Germans. Schenk, Trudy and Ruth Froelke. *The Wuerttemberg Emigration Index*. (Salt Lake City: Ancestry, Inc., 1986-93). 6 volumes {About 84,000 persons who applied to emigrate from Wüerttemberg, 1750-1900, with intended destination of each}. [Ref CS 627 W86S34 1986]

Greeks. Voultsos, Mary. *Greek Immigrant Passengers, 1885-1910*. (Worcester, Mass., 1991). 4 volumes. [E 184 G7 V68 1991]

Irish. Glazier, Ira A. *The Famine Immigrants: Lists of Irish Immigrants Arriving at the Port of New York, 1846-1851.* (Baltimore, Genealogical Publishing Co., 1983-86). 7 volumes. [Ref E 183 I6F25 1983]

Italians. Glazier, Ira A. and P. William Filby. *Italians to America: Lists of Passengers Arriving at U.S. Ports, 1880-1899.* (Wilmington, Del: Scholarly Resources, Inc., 1992-present). 5 volumes to date, covering 1880-1891 so far. [E 184 I8 I83 1992]

Russians. Glazier, Ira A. *Migration From the Russian Empire: Lists of Passengers Arriving at the Port of New York.* (Baltimore: Genealogical Publishing Co., 1995-present). 2 volumes to date, covering 1875-1886. [Ref E184 R9 M54 1995] {Also includes **Poles** and **Finns**. About half are Jewish}.

Swedes. Olsson, Nils William. *Swedish Passenger Arrivals in U.S. Ports, 1820-1850 (Except New York).* (St. Paul, North Central Publ. Co., 1979). 392 pp. [Ref E 184 S23O45]

Taylor, Maureen Alice. *Rhode Island Passenger Lists: Port of Providence, 1789-1808; 1820-1872, Port of Bristol and Warren, 1820-1871: compiled from United States Custom House Papers.* (Baltimore: Genealogical Publishing Co., 1995). 232 pp. [Ref F78 T38 1995]

Southern Historical Press. *Ships Passenger Lists, Port of Galveston, Texas, 1846-1871.* (Easley, SC, 1984). 131 pp. [F 385 S53 1984]

Smith, Clifford Neal. *Reconstructed Passenger Lists for 1850: Hamburg to...* (McNeal, Ariz.: Westland Publ., 1980-1987). 4 volumes. [CS 35 S64] [CS 35 S66] [CS 35 S645]

Aids for passenger list research include:

Filby, P. William. *Passenger and Immigration Lists Bibliography, 1593-1900: Being a Guide to Published Lists of Arrivals in the United States and Canada.* 2nd ed. (Detroit: Gale Research Co., 1988). 324 pp. {A bibliography of **published** passenger lists}. [Ref CS68 P364 1988]

Morton-Allan Directory of European Passenger Steamship Arrivals at the Port of New York, 1890-1930, and at the Ports of Baltimore, Boston, and Philadelphia, 1904-1926. (Baltimore: Gen. Publ. Co., 1987, reprint of 1931 edition). 268 pp. [CS 68 U542] [CS 68 M67 1931]

Tepper, Michael H. *American Passenger Arrival Records: A Guide to the Records of Immigrants Arriving at American Ports by Sail and Steam.* (Baltimore: GPC, 1988, 1993). 142 pp. [Ref CS 68 T49 1993]

6. Standard U.S. Reference Works

The reference section of the stacks (first six shelving units to your left upon entry into the stacks) contain an excellent collection of the standard reference books and compiled indexes to American genealogy, including published Federal census indexes for most states (1790 through 1860 or 1870), D.A.R. Lineage books, how-to works, etc.

7. Massachusetts Sources

Vital Records. Pre-1850: Published indexes, by town, in Reading Room (see #1 above).

1841-1900: NEHGS has copies of original records and indexes from the MASSACHUSETTS STATE ARCHIVES, on microfilm. (See page 124). 332 reels. [F 63 M3 Microfilm].

1901-1976: NEHGS is currently photocopying index volumes from the REGISTRY OF VITAL STATISTICS. (See page 175):

Indexes to Deaths, 1901-1976. [No catalog number; can be found in the Massachusetts section of the reference shelves]. Indexed in five-year spans (e.g. 1901-1905, 1906-1910...) Volumes 46-161.

Indexes to Marriages, 1901-1920. Volumes 49-85. {Ongoing} [Located in inquiries area at the front of Floor 5A].

Federal Census. Printed indexes to 1790-1850 Censuses; 1860 Suffolk County (Boston) [Ref F73.25 J32 1989]; 1860 Hampden County [Ref F72 H2 J32]. Original census schedules thru 1910 on microfilm (see page 168).

Massachusetts State Census of 1855, 1865. Massachusetts state census records for over seventy towns in Essex, Middlesex and Plymouth counties have been transcribed and indexed in individual volumes published since 1986 by Ann S. Lainhart. [Ref F74 ...]

Probate Indexes. Published indexes for several Massachusetts counties:
- Suffolk: 1636-1893 (3 vols.); 1894-1910 (2 vols.); 1910-1923 (2 vols.); 1923-1935 (3 vols.); 1936-1947 (3 vols.); 1948-1958 (2 vols.) [Ref F 72 S9 M45]
- Middlesex: 1648-1871, 1871-1909. [Ref F 72 M7 M55] 1910-1949. On 3 reels of microfilm [F 72 M7 Microfilm] (Cabinet #9).
- Worcester: 1731-1881 (2 vols.); 1881-1897, 1897-1910, 1910-1920. [Ref F 72 W9 M45]
- Norfolk: 1793-1900. (2 vols.) [Ref F 72 N8 M45]
- Essex: 1683-1840. (2 vols.) [Ref F 72 E7 U65 1987]
- Plymouth: 1686-1881. (1 vol.) [Ref F 72 P7 W6]. Also docket index on [F 72 P7 Microfilm]
- Bristol: 1687-1762. (2 vols.) [Ref F 72 ...] 1687-1926. On 4 reels of microfilm [F 72 B8 Microfilm] (Cabinet #8).
- Hampshire: On 4 reels of microfilm. [F 72 H2 Microfilm] (Cabinet #9).

List of Persons Whose Names Have Been Changed in Massachusetts, 1780-1892. Secretary of State, 1893. (Reprint: Baltimore: Genealogical Publ. Co., 1972). 522 pp. {Lists 16,000 Massachusetts residents who legally changed their names. Virtually no Jewish names -- mostly adoptions}. [Ref F 63 A5]

8.   City Directories

NEHGS has an extensive collection for all New England states. The Massachusetts collection is located behind the microfilm reading area of Floor 5A. Alphabetical by city. Collections for other states are shelved with that state's collection on 5A, and the end of the section for each state. The collection is slowing being converted to microfiche, in an ongoing project with the American Genealogical Lending Library (AGLL). As with all of NEHGS' collection, they are very strong for the New England states, and less comprehensive the further one gets from New England.

Massachusetts City Directories already on microfiche (Cabinet #16) include:

- Abington and Whitman [F 74 A1 H57]
- Acton and Maynard [F 74 A17 C76]
- Acushnet, Dartmouth and Westport [F 74 A22 C76]
- Athol and Orange [F 74 A87 A84]
- Attleboro [F 74 A89 A88]
- Ayer, Littleton, Groton and Harvard [F 74 A87 A94]
- Boston, 1798-1981 [F 73.2 B67 *year*]
- Cambridge [F 74 C1 C36]
- Orange [F74 O7 O73]

Many City Directories for non-New England localities were donated to the BOSTON PUBLIC LIBRARY when NEHGS moved to its present building in 1964. These books are now in storage at a BPL warehouse. (see page 64).

Directories for New York City include 1915 (2 vols.), 1916, 1917 (2 vols.), 1920, 1922/23, 1924/25 (2 vols.), and 1931. Also Queens 1912. Selected directories are available for other New York cities: Albany, Buffalo, Rochester, Syracuse, and some smaller localities.

9. <u>Vital Records</u>

Massachusetts. See under #7 "Massachusetts Sources", above.

Maine. On microfilm [F 18 M34]. Pre-1892 for about 80 towns, 141 reels. Statewide records on microfilm [F 18 M344]: for 1892-1907 (reels #1-50); 1908-1922 (reels #51-108); 1923-1936 (reels #109-165); 1937-1955 (reels #166-235). Brides Index 1895-1966 (reels #236-322), 1967-1983 (reels #323-327); Grooms Index 1956-1983 (reels #328-334). Deaths 1956-1983 (reels #335-343). Divorces 1892-1964 (reels #344-356), 1965-1983 (reels #373-375). Divorces by county (reels #357-372).

New Hampshire. On microfilm [F 33 N454]. Statewide records to 1900. Births (reels #1-98); Marriages (reels #99-200); Brides Index (reels #201-217); Divorces (reels #218-225); Deaths (reels #226-285); Miscellaneous (reels #286-288). {Records grouped by 1st and 3rd letter of surname, then alphabetical}. (Cabinet #4). Also: New Hampshire Motor Vehicles Registry, 1994. [F 33 N459 Microfiche] (Cabinet #15).

Vermont. On microfilm [F 48 V5]. Alphabetical to 1870 (reels #1-287), 1871-1908 (reels #288-407). (Cabinet #7).

Connecticut. Barbour collection: Statewide index to pre-1850 vital records, alphabetically by town [Ref F 93 C7].

Rhode Island. "Arnold" series of published vital records for 1600's-1850 (20 vols.) [Ref F 78 A75]. Printed B-M-D indexes for city of Providence, 1870s-1945 (30 vols.) [F 89 P9]. Statewide records: Births 1853-1895 (24 reels); Marriages (21 reels) and Deaths (21 reels) 1853-1900 [F 78.R55 Microfilm] (Cabinet #10).

California. Death index, 1940-1987 [F 860 C3 Microfiche] (Cabinet #16). Marriage index, 1960-1985 [F 860 C11 Microfiche] (Cabinet #16).

Oregon. Death Index, 1915-1970. [F 875 D43 Microfilm]. 14 reels. (Cabinet #11).

Washington. Death index 1907-1979. [F 890 W37 Microfilm]. 12 reels. (Cabinet #11).

Florida. Death index 1877-1992. Marriage and Divorce Index 1927-1992. [F 310 F59 1991 Microfiche] (1,797 microfiche, Cabinet #16).

Florida. Motor Vehicles Registry 1993. [F 310 F59 Microfiche] (1,314 microfiche, Cabinet #16).

Ontario, Canada. Ontario Vital Statistics Index Books: Births 1869-1896, Marriages 1873-1910, Deaths 1869-1921. (27 reels) [CS88 O6 O58 Microfilm].

Vital records for other Canadian provinces include:

   New Brunswick. Births 1810-1895, Marriages 1806-1919, Deaths 1815-1919.
   Nova Scotia. Births and Deaths 1864-1877, Marriages 1864-1918.
   Prince Edward Island. Vital records to 1900.

10. Microfilm collection

In addition to the vital records described above, NEHGS' microtext collection includes many other records, including an very complete set of New Hampshire town, county deed and probate records. They also have copies of most of the U.S. Federal Census for the New England states, through 1910 [HA 201 Microfilm]. (The complete set for the entire country is at the NATIONAL ARCHIVES - NEW ENGLAND REGION in Waltham. See page 144).

They also have a complete set of **Canadian Census** records, for 1841, 1851, 1861, 1871, 1881, 1891 and 1901 (129 reels), from the National Archives of Canada in Ottawa. [HA 741 C4 *year* Microfilm] (Cabinets #21 and #22). There are no indexes to these census records. {However, Glen Eker has compiled an index to all Jewish residents listed in the 1861-1901 Canadian censuses, available on microfiche from Avotaynu, Inc.}. They also have the 1921 Census of Newfoundland [HA 741 Microfilm].

11. Biographical Works

Biographical Dictionaries and Encyclopedias, "Who's Who"s, College classbooks...
Various "Who's Who"s and other biographical dictionaries can be found under classification [Ref CT...] and [Ref E176...]. Current editions are in the reference section on Floor 6, while older editions are downstairs on Floor 5A. Some other works:

Personal Name Index to the New York Times 1851-1974 (22 vols), 1975-1989 (5 vols). [Ref Z 5301 F28] {See the article in *Mass-Pocha* III:4 (Fall 1994), regarding use of this index}.

Directory of Deceased American Physicians, 1804-1929. (Chicago: AMA, 1993). 2 volumes. {A guide to over 149,000 medical practitioners, providing brief biographical sketches from the AMA's Deceased Physicians Masterfile}. [Ref CS 5 D56 1993]

American Jewish Biography. By Jacob Rader Marcus. (New York, Carlson Publishing, 1994). 2 volumes, 711 pp. {24,000 biographies, with citations}. [Ref E184.J5 C653 1994]

Hundreds of college classbooks, yearbooks, and alumni directories are up on Floor 6A. The collection is strongest for Harvard, Yale, Princeton and other Ivy League schools. Many series date to the turn of the century and earlier. Among others, they have books for: Amherst, Bates, Boston College, Boston University, Bowdion, Brown, University of California, Carleton, Case, University of Chicago, City College of New York, Clark, Colby, Colgate, University of Colorado, Columbia, Cornell, Dartmouth, Denison, DePauw, University of Denver, Dickenson...

12. LDS Computer

The Reading Room contains a *FamilySearch*™ computer, with all of the CD-ROMs from the LDS Family History Library in Salt Lake City: the International Genealogical Index (IGI), Social Security Death Index (SSDI), etc. This is the same material available at all LDS FAMILY HISTORY CENTERS (see page 88). They also have current nationwide telephone directories on CD-ROM, and other CD-ROM based resources. You must sign up for use of the computer, for one hour.

13. LDS Family History Center

The NEHGS has entered into an agreement with the LDS (Mormon) Family History Library in Salt Lake City, to offer LDS microfilms to NEHGS patrons. Microfilms may be borrowed from Salt Lake City, just as they could be from any of the FAMILY HISTORY CENTERS (see page 88). Use the *Family History Library Catalog* (FHLC), available at NEHGS on microfiche and CD-ROM, to locate film numbers for ordering. Current fees are $5 for a 4-week loan, $7 for a 6-month loan. Films take 2-4 weeks to arrive.

14. Other Works

Local Histories. State, Country and Town histories are on Floor 5A, arranged geographically. Within each state's section, books are arranged in two sequences: first the newer books, cataloged by the LC system (catalog numbers beginning with [F...]); then the Old system books for that state. Within each section, books pertaining to the entire state are first; followed by county-wide works, alphabetical by county; then towns, alphabetical.

Family Histories. Nearly half of NEHGS' library collection is comprised of published family histories. These are located in the stacks on Floor 6, arranged alphabetically by family surname, in two sequences. Old cataloguing system: [Gxxx], where xxx are the first three letters of the surname. New cataloguing system: [CS 71 ...].

Manuscript Collection. A collection of over one million manuscripts, mostly pertaining to early New England genealogy.

15. Some selected other books of interest:

Guide to Vital Statistics in the City of New York. (WPA: Historical Records Survey, 1942). {A survey of church records in New York City, as of 1942, including synagogues. One volume for each borough}. [Ref CD 3408 N5 H45...]

Petitions for Name Changes in New York City, 1848-1899. Abstracted by Kenneth Scott. (Washington: National Genealogical Society, 1984). 141 pp. {890 petitions for name changes}. [Ref F 128.25 S37]

United States Newspapers in the Boston Public Library. Massachusetts Newspaper Program. (Boston: The Program, 1992). 614 pp. [Ref Z 6951 B77 1992]

A Guide to Newspaper Indexes in New England. (The New England Library Association Bibliography Committee, 1978). [Ref Z 6293 N38 1978]

Szucs, Loretto Dennis. *Chicago and Cook County Sources: A Genealogical and Historical Guide*. (Salt Lake City: Ancestry, Inc., 1986). 334 pp. [Ref F548.25 S98 1986]

Thode, Ernest. *German-English Genealogical Dictionary*. (Baltimore: GPC, 1992). 286 pp. [Ref CS 6 T46]

Thode, Ernest. *Address Book for Germanic Genealogy*. (Baltimore, GPC, 1994). 174 pp. [Ref CS611 T48]

Chorzempa, Rosemary A. *Korzenie Polskie: Polish Roots*. (Baltimore: GPC, 1993). 240 pp. [Ref CS 49 C56 1993]

Register of Vital Records from the Roman Catholic parishes from the region beyond the Bug River. Reprint, with introduction by Edward W. Peckwas. (Chicago: Polish Genealogical Society, 1984). 44 pp. [CS 873 R44 1984]

Schlyter, Daniel. *Czechoslovakia: A Handbook of Czechoslovak Genealogical Research*. (GenUn, 1985). 131 pp. {Also has great info on Hungarian research}. [E 184 B67 S35

Guide to the Holdings of the American Jewish Archives. By James W. Clasper and M. Carolyn Dellenbach. (AJA: Cincinnati, 1979). 210 pp. [Ref Z 6373 U5H43]

Finding Aids:

There are two cataloguing systems in use, and two separate card catalogs: one for material catalogued since 1975, and one for pre-1975 acquisitions. The post-1975 material uses the Library of Congress (LC) cataloguing system, and pre-1975 material used a proprietary system. There is also an online computer catalog, "Sydney", which contains all material catalogued since 1987 (about 25,000 entries). Materials catalogued since September 1994 are listed **only** in the online catalog. Thus, to do a thorough search, one must search all three catalogs.

The "new" (1975-1994) card catalog begins at the left side of the reading room, and uses white labels. The cards are in one integrated alphabetical sequence: family names, authors, subjects, and places.

The "old" (pre-1975) catalog is in several sections:
- Genealogies (Yellow labels)   Alphabetical by author and family name.
                                       Family cards arranged chronologically by date of publication.
- Places (Blue labels)   Alphabetical by state, then by county and town.
- General (White labels)   Alphabetically by author and subject.

The online computer catalog overlaps the "new" catalog for 1987-1994 materials. There is currently only one access terminal, in the Reading Room. Instructions are provided there.

The <u>manuscripts</u> catalog is also in two sections, located to the right of the entrance to the stacks. The old manuscript catalog has green labels, the new catalog has orange labels. Be sure to check both catalogs. Places and names are interfiled. There is also a series of white looseleaf notebooks above the card catalog drawers, which contain inventories of the larger manuscript collections.

Description of Facility:

NEHGS is housed in a six-story building in Boston's Back Bay. The library is on the sixth floor. After signing in at the front desk, proceed by elevator to the sixth floor.

The Ruth C. Bishop Reading Room, on the sixth floor, contains the card catalogs, the reference desk, selected reference books for New England research (see section 1), and a rack containing current genealogical periodicals (about 30 titles). It also contains seven large tables, with seating for over 50 researchers.

Stacks. There are three floors of open-shelf stacks. You enter the stacks via the Reading Room on Floor 6. The main floor, 6, contains the reference section (the first six shelving units on your left); and family histories, alphabetical by surname. The lower floor, 5A, contains North American local histories, organized by state; and the microtext area. The upper floor, 6A, contains non-North American materials (mostly British Isles), church histories, college classbooks, and miscellaneous works on topics such as heraldry and gravestones.

The microtext area is located on Floor 5A of the stacks. There are 7 film readers, 3 fiche readers, and 2 microtext copiers. [Note: The microtext area will move to the newly renovated 4th floor in late 1996].

NEHGS has a staff of 35, and there are usually two or more Reference Librarians on duty, to help both beginners and more advanced researchers.

Fees/Copies:

Membership in NEHGS is $50 annually, which entitles members to unlimited use of the 200,000 volume reference library; the 20,000 volume circulating book collection; and subscriptions to the Society's two periodicals: *The New England Historical and Genealogical Register*, a scholarly quarterly; and *NEXUS*, a bi-monthly newsletter with information about Society events.

Access to the library is also available for non-members for a $10 per day fee.

Copies: Photocopies from paper or microtext are 25¢ each. Three self-service paper photocopy machines are available: one is located just to your right after entering the stacks, and two are in the reading room. You must purchase a plastic copy card from the vending machine in the hall near the elevator for $1.00, which can be refilled by putting bills into the copying machines. Microtext copies are also 25¢ each, and can be made with the copy card. Change is available at the Reference Desk.

Restrictions on Use:

To use the library, you must be a NEHGS member ($50 annually), or pay a $10 daily research fee.

The manuscript collection is available to members only. Manuscripts are kept in a locked safe area, and must be requested by members.

NORTH SHORE JEWISH HISTORICAL SOCIETY

Facility Director:	Oscar Rosen, President
	Arlene L. Kaufman, Curator
Address:	31 Exchange Street, Suite 27
	Lynn, MA 01901
Phone Number:	(617) 593-2386
Hours of Operation:	Mondays 11am-3pm, and by appointment
Directions:	Take the Lynn bus (#441, #442, #439, #455 or #426) or the MBTA commuter rail from Boston to Lynn. 31 Exchange Street is on the corner of Exchange and Union Streets, directly opposite the bus terminal. Suite 27 is on the second floor.

Description of Institution:

Founded in 1976, the NORTH SHORE JEWISH HISTORICAL SOCIETY collects and preserves memorabilia on the history of the Jewish communities of the North Shore of Massachusetts. The Society's collection includes published books and unpublished manuscripts on Jewish families in the Boston area. It has also started a funded archives project that will serve to reconstruct and preserve the history of the large and vibrant Jewish communities in Lynn, Salem, Peabody and Beverly. Special emphasis will be given to explaining the economic centrality of the shoe trades within these North Shore communities, which were the national leaders in women's shoe production.

A newsletter is published semi-annually. There is a membership fee.

Description of Resources:

The archival collection consists of thirty-one document storage cases, containing records of synagogues, Jewish organizations, etc.

Box 1   AZA Records, 1941-1962.
Box 2   Temple Beth El, Lynn. Photos and records, 1931-1963.
Box 3   Temple Beth El. 1964-1980 (moved to Swampscott).
Box 4   Temple Beth El. Photos, story Rabbi Israel Harburg and chazan Morton Shanok.
Box 5   Hadassah. Lynn. Records 1934-1981. Includes booklet "The History of Lynn Hadassah,
           1922-1993", compiled by Betty Maistleman.
Box 6   Jecomen Club. 1925-1940. Membership records, Scholarship data.
Box 7   Alpha Delta Chapter, Alpha Phi Pi, 1932.
Box 8   North Shore Jewish Historical Society (NSJHS) Art Exhibit, May 24-30, 1987.
Box 9   Brandeis University, Waltham. Bulletins and miscellaneous items.
Box 10   Congregation Ahabat Sholom, Lynn.
Box 11   Jewish Boy Scouts, Troop 4 and 19, Lynn. 1926-1945.
Box 12   Jewish Boy Scouts, Troop 4 Roster. Letters from WWII.
Box 13   Jewish Boy Scouts. Original copies of newsletter *Sachem News*, 1927-1930.

Box 14   Inside Shoe Factory: Strasnick, Weinstein and United Shoe Machinery Companies.
           {Also in NSJHS files, three drawers contain interviews, taped and transcribed, that
           formed source material for the manuscript by Stephen G. Mostov, Ph.D., for
           "Immigrant Entrepreneurs - Jews in the Shoe Trade, Lynn, 1885-1945".}
Box 15   Jewish Federation of the North Shore.
Box 16   Jewish Community Center, Marblehead. 1960-present.
Box 17   Jewish Community Center, Marblehead.
Box 18   Jewish Community Center, Marblehead. Harold Goodman Collection.
Box 19   Brickyard Exhibit, May 20, 1990. "Living and Working in the Old Neighborhood"
           Photos of businesses, The Mowhawks, groups, etc.
Box 20   Temple Israel, Swampscott.
Box 21   Peabody Hebrew School, Washington Street, Sisterhood.
Box 22   Jewish Community Center, Market Street, Lynn. YMHA-YWHA.
Box 23   Lynn YMHA-YWHA. Photos used at Reunion of 1989.
Box 24   Jewish Athletes of the North Shore. Compiled by Oscar Rosen, Ph.D., for Exhibit of
           March 5, 1990.
Box 25   Lynn Hebrew School, 1921-1961. Articles of Incorporation.
Box 26   Winer Family Genealogy.
Box 27   History of Jews of Marblehead, 1899-1950. Exhibit of Nov. 6, 1994.
Box 28   Swampscott-Marblehead Hadassah.
Box 29   British Brigade (Jewish Brigade), Palestine, 1918-1919. Photos.
Box 30   Jewish Rehabilitation Center, Swampscott.
Box 31   Peabody Boy Scouts.

In addition, other material in file drawers includes photographs, documents, booklets, etc:

- Award-winning video, also on slides, "Reason to Remember", the History of the Jews of Lynn, 1855-1940.
- Histories of Jewish communities of Haverhill, Newburyport, Gloucester, Peabody, Salem, Beverly, Lynn.
- Family Genealogies:
    - Breitman, Needleman families, in 8 volumes
    - Breitman, Velleman family, 1993
    - Lacritz family, descendants of Issac & Anna Lacritz
    - Benjamin (Bentzianov) and Revzin families
    - Hymie Joseph Adelstein, personal stories
- Photographs of Jewish veterans of the North Shore. Complete listings. An ongoing compilation, assembled by the curator, Arlene L. Kaufman.
- Complete collection of Lewis Hines photos of Ellis Island and Lower East Side, NYC.
- B'nai B'rith Women, Greater Lynn. Newsletters 1947-1961. Three souvenir journals, 1975, 1976, 1977.
- Local school class photographs (mostly Lynn):
    - Sheppard School, Class of 1919
    - Cobbet Jr. High School, Class of 1930
    - Lynn English High School, Class of 1924
    - Western Jr. High School, Class of 1929
    - Peabody High School, Class of 1918
    - Central Jr. High School, Class of 1921
- Holocaust (two file drawers)
    Holocaust survivor oral history interviews (transcribed)
    Willie Norwind correspondence searching survivors
    Twenty-three audio cassettes, Nathan Gass interviews with Holocaust survivors.

Fees/Copies:

There are no fees to use the facility, but donations are gratefully accepted.
A copying machine is available.

Restrictions on Use:

Some materials can be borrowed, on special arrangement with the Society.

REGISTRY OF VITAL RECORDS AND STATISTICS

Facility Director: Elaine Trudeau, Registrar of Vital Records and Statistics

Address: Registry of Vital Records and Statistics
Massachusetts Department of Public Health
470 Atlantic Avenue, 2nd floor
Boston, MA 02210-2224

Phone Number: (617) 753-8600   (recording)
(617) 753-8606   (for credit card requests by mail)

Hours of Operation:

Counter service for certified copies:
         Mon, Tue, Thu, Fri 8:45am - 4:45pm

Research Hours: Mon, Tue, Thu, Fri 9:00am - 12:00pm and 2:00pm - 4:30pm

Note: Research Hours sometimes change due to state budget cutbacks and other circumstances, so it's advisable to call ahead. The Registry is closed all day Wednesday.

Directions:

By Car: Atlantic Avenue runs parallel to the Central Artery (Route I-93) near Chinatown and the Financial District. Follow signs to South Station. The REGISTRY is a short distance past South Station. Street parking is difficult to find. There is paid off-street parking next to the building.

By MBTA: Take the Red Line train to South Station (also Amtrak station). Exit South Station and walk down Atlantic Avenue in the direction of the bus terminal. 470 Atlantic Avenue is a seven minute walk from South Station, just a few buildings beyond the Federal Reserve Building.

Description of Institution:

The REGISTRY OF VITAL RECORDS AND STATISTICS is a division of the Massachusetts Department of Public Health, Bureau of Health Statistics, Research and Evaluation. It is responsible for the custody of birth, marriage and death records in the Commonwealth of Massachusetts, for the years 1901 to the present.

Older Massachusetts state vital records (those from 1841-1900) have been transferred to the MASSACHUSETTS ARCHIVES at Columbia Point (see page 124).

[NOTE: The Registry's oldest records are periodically transferred to the MASSACHUSETTS ARCHIVES, typically in 5-year increments. Pending legislation in the Massachusetts State House may result in the transfer of additional records (those through 1915 or 1920) to the MASSACHUSETTS ARCHIVES].

Description of Resources:

<u>Birth Records</u>:
   Records: 1901 - 1918 (for Boston, 1901-1929, except 1919): on microfilm.
                 1919 - present (for Boston, 1919 & 1930-present):
                     certificates are bound in small volumes of about 500 records each.

   Indexes: 1901 - 1993: in bound volumes;
                 1994 - present: on computer printouts.

<u>Marriage Records</u>:
   Records: 1901 - 1918 (for Boston, 1901-1929): on microfilm.
                 1918 - present (for Boston, 1930-present):
                     certificates are bound in small volumes of about 500 records each.

   Indexes: 1901 - 1983: in bound volumes;
                 1984 - present: on computer printouts.

<u>Death Records</u>:
   Records: 1901 - 1903 (for Boston, 1901-1903 and 1914-1929): on microfilm.
                 1903 - present (for Boston, 1903-1913 and 1930-present):
                     certificates are bound in small volumes of about 500 records each.

   Indexes: 1901 - 1991: in bound volumes;
                 1991 - present: on computer printouts.

<u>Divorce Records</u>:
   Records: Copies of divorce records can be obtained only from the Registrar of the Probate
                 Court in the county where the divorce was granted.

   Indexes: 1952 - 1983 in bound volumes; 1984 - present on computer printout.
                 Includes date, name of Probate Court where divorce was granted, and court
                 docket number.

Description of Facility:

The public research room is on the second floor. Upon entering the building, proceed to the far set of elevators. Exiting on the second floor, turn left and walk to the end of the hall and enter the office on your right.

The room that you first enter is used for ordering certificates, not for research. There is a small table in this first room with forms and a window where you present your request forms for ordering certificates.

Pass through this ante-room and into the public research room. The index books and computer printouts are available in this room on open shelves. Once you find an index entry of interest, you then request from a clerk the retrieval of the certificate itself from a back room (restricted access), or you will receive a roll of microfilm.

There are seven microfilm readers, but no printers. There are no photocopiers. All information must be copied by hand from the original records. See Restrictions below.

There are three large tables and seating around those tables for 18 researchers. There is also counter space and a limited amount of space elsewhere around the room which may be used. The research room can become very crowded, due to the limited amount of space. Please be patient with the staff and other researchers, and try to limit the amount of work space you are using.

Procedures:

1. Sign in. To do research, enter the public research room and stop at the window on your immediate right to sign in and receive a stub, which you present upon leaving so that you are assessed the research fee ($3/hour).

2. Use the indexes. After signing in, proceed to the opposite end of this room where there are three large free-standing shelves with the index books you will use. Indexes are available for birth, marriage, death and divorce records. All records are indexed, and most indexes are arranged in five-year periods within the category of event (e.g. 1901-05, 1906-10, 1911-15, etc.) Within the index for each period, names are listed alphabetically.

   For some birth records, particularly older ones, if a first name is not on the original record, it may be listed as "(Female)" or "(Male)" under the last name in the index. You may also need to look under variations in spelling for the names you are researching.

   Under and inside the counter, which is next to the shelves with the index books, are the bound computer printouts for the most recent years of indexes.

   NOTE: These indexes, 1901-1971, are also available on microfilm at the MASSACHUSETTS ARCHIVES at Columbia Point (see page 124). Photocopies of the 1901-1920 marriage indexes and 1901-1976 death indexes are also available at the NEW ENGLAND HISTORIC GENEALOGICAL SOCIETY (see page 165). It's usually more convenient to use the indexes at the State Archives or NEHGS, because of the Registry's limited hours. The 1900-1971 indexes are also available on microfilm through all LDS FAMILY HISTORY CENTERS. See page 29.

3. Fill out request slip. Just in front of the shelves with the index books is a counter, and there is a box on the counter with small slips of paper that you will use to request a certificate. For any request, you will fill in the following information from the indexes on the slip of paper: name of individual; event (birth, marriage or death); year of event; volume number, and page number. After 1972, there are no volume numbers, only year and page number. For certain early years of Boston deaths (through 1930), you must identify that it is a Boston death so that you will receive the correct book of certificates; just write "Boston" prominently across the bottom of the slip.

4. Screening. Hand over the filled-in slips to the clerk who sits at a desk in the room. Staff members must screen all requests for birth and marriage records. The clerk will determine if the record you seek is in a certificate book or on microfilm. The microfilms must be retrieved by the clerk. There is a limit of only one microfilm at a time. When finished with a film, return it to the clerk's desk.

5. Access the record. The books that contain the certificates you have ordered will be brought out on a cart. Look for your slip, sticking out of the books you have ordered. You can examine as many books at a time as you wish.

6. Return the records. When finished with the books, return them to another cart where the already-examined books (without slips sticking out of them) are returned.

Fees/Copies:

In Person: There is a research fee of $3.00 per hour, charged in 15 minute intervals. A visit (no more than once per day) of less than 15 minutes is free.

Certified copies of all records are available in person, for $6.00 each. Checks should be made payable to the "Commonwealth of Massachusetts". Fill out the form in the front room and present it to the clerk at the window.

By Mail: Certified copies of all records are $11.00 each by mail. Provide the following information for each record requested:

- Birth: Name of child at birth, Date of birth, City/Town of birth, Father's name, Mother's maiden name.
- Marriage: Name of groom, Maiden name of bride, Date of marriage, City/Town of marriage.
- Death: Name of decedent, Date of death, City/Town of death, Name of spouse, and Social Security Number (if known).

Make check or money order payable to "Commonwealth of Massachusetts". Personal checks are accepted. You can request a maximum of five (5) copies per envelope. Enclose a business-sized self-addressed stamped envelope.

By Phone: Certificates can also be ordered by phone with a credit card. Call (617) 753-8606.

Restrictions on Use:

Although vital records are public records, there are a number of statutory limitations on access to these records. Only certified copies of vital records are made; no plain photocopies can be made. Use of portable photocopy machines and other means of reproducing images is prohibited by statute.

Restricted (impounded) records are accessible only to the subject, parent or guardian (for birth records), an attorney representing any of the aforementioned parties, or appropriate governmental agencies. Anyone else would require a court order for access. See specific restrictions below.

Some recent records, while being processed in the Mail, Binding and Clerk Liaison Unit, are not accessible to researchers, but certified copies of these records will be furnished to appropriate persons.

Restricted records are:

Births:
   a)   Records of children born to unmarried parents (out-of-wedlock).
   b)   Records of birth corrected for purposes of adoption or legitimation.
   c)   Records corrected for purposes of adding father's information.
   d)   Records corrected for any other purpose.
   e)   Records created after amendment.

Marriages:
   a)   Marriages of parents of persons born out of wedlock.
   b)   Bride pregnant at time of marriage (pre-1982).
   c)   Marriage records corrected for any purpose.

Deaths:
   a)   Fetal deaths (stillbirths, miscarriages).
   b)   Death records corrected for any purpose.

STATE LIBRARY OF MASSACHUSETTS

Facility Director: Gasper Caso, State Librarian, Director
Brenda Howitson, Special Collections Librarian

Address: State Library of Massachusetts
Room 341
The State House
Boston, MA 02133

Phone Number:

(617) 727-2590	(Main Library Reference)
(617) 727-2595	(Special Collections)
(617) 727-2594	(Periodicals/Newspapers)
(617) 727-5819	(FAX)

Hours of Operation:

Monday to Friday: 9:00am - 5:00pm
Closed Saturday, Sunday and all legal holidays
[including three Massachusetts State and Suffolk County holidays: Evacuation Day (March 17),
Patriots Day (third Monday in April), and Bunker Hill Day (June 17)].

Directions:

By Car: (Not advised). Closest public parking to Beacon Hill, where the State House is located, is the Boston Common Garage. Government Center Garage is further.

By MBTA: Park Street Station (Red and Green Lines) at the corner of Tremont and Park Streets is closest. All other transportation lines connect here.

By foot: Most recommended from any downtown Boston location. The golden dome of the Bulfinch-designed Massachusetts State House is a landmark at the northeast corner of Boston Common. Enter the west wing past the John F. Kennedy statue off Beacon Street.

Description of Institution:

The STATE LIBRARY OF MASSACHUSETTS was founded in 1826 to meet the information and research needs of the executive and legislative branches of state government. It is strongest in public law, public affairs, political science, Massachusetts state government publications, and state and local history. Its collection includes 825,000 volumes, 288,000 microforms, 1800 periodical and newspaper titles, and materials in a variety of other formats.

The Main Library, with its catalogs and reference desk, is located on the third floor of the Massachusetts State House, in Room 341. The Periodical and Newspaper Collection is entered through Room 442, directly above. The Special Collections Department is located in Room 55, in the basement of the West Wing.

Description of Resources:

The STATE LIBRARY OF MASSACHUSETTS is the official depository for publications of Massachusetts state agencies. Its collection forms a comprehensive record of printed materials issued by the legislative, executive and judicial branches of the state government from the 17th century to the present. The Library has collections of state agency documents and publications; public law, covering the U.S. and the 50 states; federal congressional and executive documents; a general collection of books, research reports and pamphlets on public affairs, health care, the environment, education, etc.; and a legislative biographical file. The Library has since its inception collected extensively in the area of Massachusetts history and its collection of printed local histories is the most comprehensive in the state.

Its Special Collections include rare books, maps, atlases, city directories, broadsides, almanacs, manuscript collections, prints, photographs, and scrapbooks. The focus of the Special Collections Department is on the history of Massachusetts in all of its aspects.

Most useful for Jewish genealogical research are the Periodical and Newspaper collections, Maps and Atlases, City Directories, Voting Lists, and works about Jewish communities. These materials are listed in the Library catalogs under community headings.

a. <u>Periodical and Newspaper collection</u>. Over one hundred current daily and weekly Massachusetts newspapers are received, as well as national papers such as the *New York Times* and *Washington Post*. Most older newspaper materials are given to the BOSTON PUBLIC LIBRARY for their microfilm collection (see page 63). The State Library retains microfilms of the *Boston Globe* since its founding in 1872 and the *Boston Herald* since 1881; the *Springfield Daily News* and *Republican* since 1968 and the *Worcester Telegram* since 1960. The Library also maintains a collection of late 18th and early 19th century Massachusetts newspapers.

An index to Massachusetts newspapers from 1878 to 1937 (the "Zimmer" index), compiled over the years by staff members, is available at the Library. Items indexed include political news stories of the day, some obituaries, and some general news.

An in-house card file maintained by the Library staff indexes several Boston newspapers between 1962 and 1978. It is located near the fourth floor reference desk. The commercially published *Boston Globe Index* since 1982 and *New York Times Index* since 1913 are also located here. Other commercial newspapers indexes, both in book and CD-ROM formats, are also available.

The Periodical collection of over 1,800 titles reflects the Library's specialized purpose; it is useful to government employees but probably not to most genealogists. The collection is especially strong in law reviews and journals. It also contains periodicals on history and government from the 19th and 20th centuries, especially those published in Massachusetts.

b. Atlases and Maps. The map collection, located in the Special Collections Department, is particularly strong in 19th and early 20th century maps and atlases covering Massachusetts and its communities. All of the items in the Library's map collection are accessible through its on-line catalog. Maps are cataloged under the names of the communities they depict, as well as under applicable subject headings, i.e. Boston harbor, geology, canals, etc.

The Special Collections Department has extensive archival hard copy and microfilm Atlases and Maps for Massachusetts cities and towns. Original copies date from the 17th century to the current publication *Historical Atlas of Massachusetts*, edited by Richard W. Wilkie and Jack Tager (Amherst: University of Massachusetts Press, 1991).

Of particular interest is the Library's collection of atlases by the commercial firms of G. M. Hopkins and G. W. Bromley, published between 1873 and 1931 in Philadelphia. These atlases provide highly detailed information on street patterns and addresses, shape and size of buildings, building use and occupancy, and date of construction.

Sanborn Fire Insurance maps are typified by a "paste-up" feature. This takes a "skeleton" basic neighborhood map and brings it up-to-date, thus marking changes over several decades. A convenient loose-leaf binder in the Special Collections reading room, *Municipal Holdings, 1986, of Sanborn Fire Insurance Maps*, lists available Library of Congress microfilm reels of Sanborn maps for Massachusetts cities and towns. Boston neighborhood maps begin with 1867 and continue into the 1990s. Communities with extensive coverage for the past 100 years include Cambridge, Everett, Lowell, Lynn, Malden, Newton, and Worcester, among others.

c. City Directories. The Library's extensive City Directory holdings, dating from the first Boston directory of 1789, are listed in the card catalog under the name of the community, followed by the subheading "Directories". Directories are available for almost all Massachusetts communities.

A detailed list of holdings, a loose-leaf binder entitled *City Directories and Related Lists: A Guide to Materials in the Special Collections Department* lists holdings and locations of both City Directories and Voting Lists, and their accessibility on open shelves, the stacks, or the vault.

Researchers should consult City Directories for alphabetical listing of residents and businesses within the community. Before 1930 these consisted mostly of male and widowed female household heads, males and employed females over age 21, all with occupations cited. The listing of female spouses as well as information by street address occurred after 1930. However, families are not distinguished as such within multi-family houses.

Directories also provide information about community government agencies and personnel, and religious and social organizations, cemeteries, etc. Business advertisements can sometimes reveal otherwise elusive data. The user may also want to consult a guide prepared by the Special Collections Department staff entitled "A List of buildings in Boston and vicinity depicted in the Boston city directories, 1850-1930".

City Directories have sometimes been replaced by Cole's cross-reference telephone listings after the 1970s (by street, but without name of resident). Most standard Polk City

Directories ceased publication during the 1980s because of urban renewal, suburban migrations and transiency.

City Directories are located in the Special Collections Department Reading Room on open shelves for major Massachusetts communities for the period since the 1860's. Holdings which predate that era and are in a vault, which can be accessed by the Special Collections staff on request. Directories of major cities and towns that may be found on open shelves include:

• Boston	1847-1978		• Medford	1869-1938
• Brockton	1874-1969		• Newton	1868-1980
• Cambridge	1849-1968		• Quincy	1868-1967
• Chelsea	1847-1946		• Revere	1876-1911
• Everett	1870-1940		• Salem	1866-1983
• Fall River	1866-1967		• Somerville	1869-1940
• Lowell	1868-1982		• Springfield	1859-1968
• Lynn	1867-1969		• Worcester	1866-1982
• Malden	1869-1980			

Directories for other communities, such as Massachusetts shore and river valley mill towns and suburban Brookline (1868-1968), are located in the Special Collection Department stacks, and must be requested from the staff.

d. Voting Lists. Voting Lists are sometimes called Assessors' Poll or Registrars of Voters Street Lists. They are all located in the Special Collections Department stacks, and can be accessed by a member of the staff. Availability of Voting Lists is most easily obtained via the loose-leaf binder *City Directories and Related Lists*, mentioned above.

Voting Lists are most useful for giving the names, gender, ages, occupations and addresses of potential voters. Resident mobility since the previous year is recorded with an entry that may list an earlier street address, community, state or foreign country. Within multi-family residences, specific family units are usually not identified.

Volumes for large cities are organized by wards. Residential streets may be arranged alphabetically within precincts. Correct wards and precincts must first be determined to locate the desired streets and addresses. These political boundaries change periodically, and must be ascertained through indexes, City Directories or maps, which the Special Collections staff can provide.

The Voting Lists in the Special Collections Department are original hard copies, and tend to cover the period from before the First World War until the present, with gaps. For example, Boston begins in 1910; Cambridge, 1915; Chelsea, 1917; Haverhill, 1902; Lawrence, Malden and New Bedford, 1884; Quincy, 1901; Revere, 1911; Somerville, 1853; and Worcester, 1873. Street Lists for earlier periods are available on microfilm at the BOSTON PUBLIC LIBRARY (see page 65).

e. Jewish Communities. The Library catalogs include the following works, which may be of interest for local Jewish genealogical research. See the Subject catalogs under headings such as "Jews in Boston, Massachusetts" or "Jewish ..." The old catalog (drawer 480) covers material to 1975; the new catalog (drawer 1333) covers later materials. A sampling of titles includes:

Brussel, Sylvia Ginsberg. *Community and Change: A Story of the Hasidic Community of Boston.* Ph. D. dissertation, Boston University Graduate School, 1974. 281 pp. [BM 198. B78 1974].

Ehrenfried, Albert. *A Chronicle of Boston Jewry: From the Colonial Settlement to 1900.* (Boston: privately printed, 1963). 771 pp. [974 M31:2.B 741.9j E33c].

Fein, Isaac M. *Boston - Where it all Began: A Historical Perspective of the Boston Jewish Community.* (Boston: Boston Jewish Bicentennial Committee, 1976). 83 pp. [F73.9.J5 F44].

Friedman, Lee Max. "Boston in American Jewish History". American Jewish Historical Society Publications, 1953, vol. 42, pp. 333-340. [933.A 515p].

Ginsberg, Yona. *Jews in a Changing Neighborhood: The Study of Mattapan.* (New York: Free Press, 1975). 214 pp. [F73.9 J5. G56. 1975].

Hebrew Immigrant Aid Society (HIAS). *Golden Jubilee Celebration, 1904-1954.* 21 pp. [Pam. 361.H44h].

Hebrew Ladies Home for the Aged, Dorchester, Massachusetts. *Memorial Yearbook, 1956.* 40 pp. [362.6M31:2 B741:H44y].

Jewish Advocate. *Silver Jubilee Edition. A Record of the Progress of Our Community.* March 17, 1927. 216 pp. [FN 974.5:J59].

Jewish Advocate. *Tercentenary Edition, 1630-1930. The Story of the Jew in the Progress of Massachusetts and the United States.* Vol 57, No. 19. Supplement to the issue of Oct 10, 1930, 232. [J 1970. 368].

Jewish Charities, 1895-96, 1896-97. *Federation of Jewish Charities of Boston, Annual Reports.* [362M31.2] [362H31.12] [B741: F29r].

Lebowich, Joseph. "The Jews in Boston till 1875". American Jewish Historical Society Publications, 1904, no. 12, pp. 101-112. [933.A 515p].

Levine, Hillel and Lawrence Harmon. *The Death of an American Jewish Community: A Tragedy of Good Intentions.* [Roxbury-Dorchester-Mattapan]. (New York: Free Press, 1992). 370 pp. [F73.9.J5.L48. 1992].

Massachusetts Department of Public Safety. *Report on inquiry into the circumstances with reference to a series of assaults, injuries and cases of property damage, allegedly resulting from anti-semitic feeling.* 1943. [Pam. 933. M41r].

Mirsky, Mark. *Thou Worm, Jacob: A Novel of Blue Hill Avenue, Boston.* (New York: Macmillan, 1967). 177 pp. [Pz4. M647 Th].

Neusner, Jacob. "The impact of immigration and philanthropy upon the Boston Jewish community, 1880-1914". American Jewish Historical Society Publications, 1956-57. vol. 46, pp. 71-85. [933.A 515p].

On Common Ground: The Boston Jewish Experience, 1649-1980. [Exhibition catalog]. (Waltham, Mass.: The American Jewish Historical Society, 1981). 50 pp. [F73.9.J5.05].

Wieder, Arnold A. *The Early Jewish Community of Boston's North End.* (Waltham, Mass.: Brandeis University, 1962). 100 pp. [974 M 31.2] [B 741: 9j W 64e].

Works on other Massachusetts Jewish communities, catalogued under the headings "Jews - [community] - Massachusetts", include:

Brookline. Philips, Bruce A. *Acculturation, group survival, and the ethnic community: A social history of the Jewish Community of Brookline, Massachusetts, 1915-1940.* Ph. D. dissertation. (Los Angeles: University of California at Los Angeles, 1975). 428 pp. [974M31:2 B881:9j P588a].

Malden. Klayman, Richard. *The First Jew: Prejudice and Politics in an American Community, 1900-1932.* (Malden, Mass.: Old Suffolk Square Press, 1985). 175 pp. [F74.M24 K57 1975].

Springfield. Gelin, James A. *Starting Over: The Formation of the Jewish Community of Springfield, Massachusetts, 1840-1905.* (Lanham, Maryland: University Press of America, 1984). 161 pp. [F74.S76 J54 1984].

f.   Other resources.   Other potential genealogical resources at the State Library include Massachusetts town and county histories, pre-1850 published vital records, tax valuations, legislative biographical files, government documents, and specialized directories.

Finding Aids:

The Library's holdings can be accessed in a variety of ways. For materials cataloged by the Library prior to 1975, the old card catalog, located in the Main Reading Room, must be consulted. This catalog lists materials under author and subject; for most entries, title access is not given. Most materials in the old card catalog are classified using the Dewey Decimal System.

The new card catalog, which contains material cataloged from 1975 to 1995, is a divided catalog, with one section listing material by author and title, the other section by subject. Materials in the new card catalog are classified primarily using the Library of Congress classification system. In 1995, the Library made available a computerized on-line public access catalog, containing all materials cataloged since 1978. Public access terminals for this catalog can be found in all of the public service areas of the Library. The on-line catalog is also available for remote access through the Massachusetts Library and Information Network (URL is http://www.mlin.lib.ma.us).

Consult both catalogs under community headings for such sub-topics as annual reports, assessors' valuations and taxes, atlases and maps, directories, histories, voting and poll lists.

A Guide to Massachusetts Genealogical Material in the State Library of Massachusetts is an in-house publication issued in 1985. Copies are located behind the Reference Desk of the Main Library as well as in the Special Collections Department. This loose-leaf binder comprises about 60 typed pages, organized around some 94 topical items. These include general genealogical books, community catalog sub-headings, and recommended resources outside the State Library.

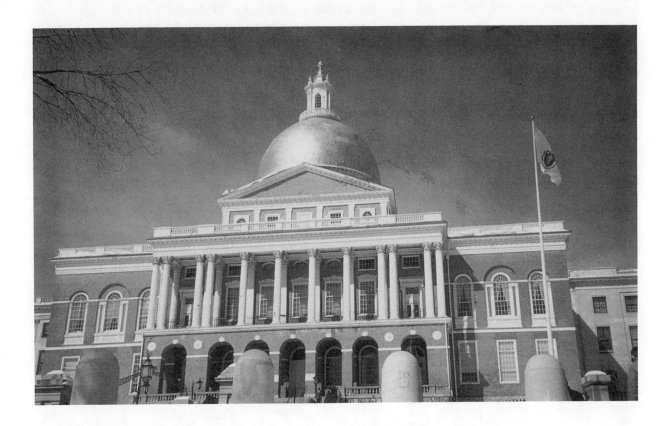

Description of Facility:

The <u>Main Library</u> reference desk and catalogs are located on the third floor in Room 341 of the Massachusetts State House. Reference books on open shelves are most useful for government research. Other holdings are in the stacks and must be accessed by a reference librarian. The <u>Special Collections Department</u> is located in Room 55, in the basement of the West Wing. Its open shelves contain directories for major Massachusetts communities. Other materials are in the stacks or in a vault, available through a reference librarian. <u>Periodicals and Newspapers</u> are on the fourth floor in Room 442. Current issues are accessible; microfilm and certain indexes must be requested from a librarian at the periodical desk.

There is space for 30 researchers around tables in the Main Library; for about 12 in the Special Collections Department; and for 15 in the Periodicals and Newspapers Department.

The State Library is an affiliate member of the Boston Library Consortium, a network of area research libraries. Through its membership in the Consortium, the collections of member libraries are available to State Library card holders via inter-library loan.

The STATE LIBRARY OF MASSACHUSETTS can be a most convenient resource for hands-on genealogical research, particularly in locating family members in community contexts. Library reference services will also direct researchers to alternative sources of information.

Fees/Copies:

The Main Library has two self-service photocopy machines at 20¢ per page. In the Special Collections Department the librarian has discretion, considering the fragility of the material, of making photocopies, also at 20¢ per page. Two microfilm readers and two microfilm reader/printers (at 25¢ per page) are available in the Periodical and Newspaper Department. A microfilm reader/printer is also available in the Special Collections Department. There are no other fees for services.

Restrictions on Use:

All visitors may have access to all facilities on site. Main Library circulation is restricted to persons who are employed by agencies of the state government, other than colleges and hospitals. Circulating materials in the Library's collection may be borrowed for a one month period and may be renewed. No materials published before 1930 and no Special Collections materials circulate.

Due to the small number of library staff, no telephone requests or correspondence requiring extensive research is possible. Researchers are most welcome to visit and use the collections on site.

SUFFOLK REGISTRY OF DEEDS

Address: Old Courthouse
                      One Pemberton Square
                      Boston, MA 02108-1772

Phone Number: (617) 725-8575

Hours of Operation: Monday-Friday 8:30am-4:30pm

Directions:

By Car: Take the Southeast Expressway (Route 3) from the South, or Routes 1 or I-93 from the North to the Storrow Drive Exit in Boston. Exit left when you see the sign for Government Center. Go 3/4 around the rotary to Cambridge Street. Follow Cambridge Street about a mile until you pass by the first high-rise office buildings on your right. Take the next right and an immediate left into the parking garage entrance. The old courthouse is above the garage.

By MBTA: Green or Blue Line MBTA to Government Center stop. Exit the station and immediately begin walking in the opposite direction from that direction you were facing. You will see Cambridge Street and a long, curved building: Center Plaza. Proceed through the opening at Two Center Plaza, up the stairs or escalator, and straight ahead into the Old Court House.

Description of Resources:

Land records for properties in Suffolk County from pre-Revolutionary days. Detailed Assessor's maps (circa 1910) are also available. Suffolk County includes the cities of Boston, Chelsea, Withthrop and Revere.

Finding Aids:

Grantor Indexes and record books are divided between the fourth and fifth floors. Older records, pre-1950s, will be found on the fourth floor. Older record books and Grantor Indexes are on microfilm on the fourth floor. For recorded land, there are card indexes also on the fourth floor.

Description of Facility:

The older registry materials and all recorded land records are on the fourth floor. The newer materials are on the fifth floor.

The 4th floor holds a large main research room which contains:

- A) Record books: from about 1910-1950
- B) Grantor and Grantee indexes: from about 1920 - 1950
- C) Indexes for recorded titles
- D) Compiled plans from the oldest record books

An adjoining room (to the far right as you enter the main 4th floor room) holds:

A) Grantor indexes: up to about 1920
B) Record books: up to about 1880

<u>Plans</u>:

Many plans have been compiled from the oldest record books and can be found in books atop of the row of filing cabinets in the fourth floor room near the entrance to the adjoining room.

For most newer plans, you will need to check in the plan indexes at the far right side of the room on the fifth floor. To order a plan that is not otherwise available to be copied, consult with the clerk in the small office at the far right side of the fifth floor room.

Fees/Copies:

Photocopies are 25¢ for 11"x17" copies. There are two photocopiers on the fourth floor and four on the fifth floor. There are paper cutters on both floors. The three microfilm reader/printers on the fourth floor are also 25¢, and yield 8½"x11" copies.

Plans from the plan room on the fifth floor cost $1.00, occasionally more. The fee must be paid to the main desk and your receipt will be your proof of payment that will allow you to receive a copy.

Restrictions on Use:

None. No books may leave the facilities under any circumstances.

SUFFOLK REGISTRY OF PROBATE

Address: Room 124, Old Courthouse
                          One Pemberton Square
                          Boston, MA 02108-1706

Phone Number: 617-725-8300

Hours of Operation: Monday-Friday 8:30am-4:30pm

Directions: See SUFFOLK REGISTRY OF DEEDS.

Description of Resources:

Probate, divorce and related records such as name changes, guardianships and Conservatorships for Suffolk County. Suffolk County includes the cities of Boston, Chelsea, Revere and Winthrop. See Appendix C on page 232 for an overview of Probate Records.

Finding Aids:

Probate indexes are available near the center of the Probate Room, near a doorway to the hallway and across from the photocopier. They are divided into eight sets, each comprised of two or three volumes for different portions of the alphabet:

> 1636-1894; 1894-1910; 1910-1923; 1923-1936;
> 1936-1947; 1948-1958; 1959-1968; 1969-1979

Card indexes continue along the wall, in these intervals:

> 1980-1983; 1984-1986; 1987-1994; 1995

Docket books are available along the walls of the room. They cover docket entries for all of the 1900s and some of the late 1800s.

Divorce indexes are available in the room that handles divorce matters. The earliest indexes are in book form, located under the counter to your right as you enter the room. Nearby are various card indexes covering later years. Certain matters of domestic law for early years, such as "separate support", "leave to marry without delay", and adoptions are kept with the probate records, and are likewise indexed together with the probate records.

Description of Facility:

If you are going to do probate research, take an immediate left after going through security, and enter into the first open door on your left. If you are going to check divorce records, continue down the hallway, pass through the double doors, and enter the office on your right.

Records are ordered in the same manner in both the probate and the domestic law rooms. Fill out a card with the docket number of the file and the information identifying you (name and address). Present the card or cards to a clerk.

Fees/Copies:

Copies are 25¢ per photocopy. There is one photocopy machine in each of the probate and the domestic law offices. Bring your own change, as there is no change makers nearby (closest are on the 5th floor).

Restrictions on Use:

None. No books may leave the facilities under any circumstances.

WORCESTER HISTORICAL MUSEUM

Address: 30 Elm Street
                            Worcester, MA 01609

Phone Number: (508) 753-8278

Hours of Operation: Tuesday - Saturday   10:00am - 4:00pm
                            Sunday   1:00pm - 4:00 pm
                            (Library is closed on Sunday, only Museum open)

Directions: Take the Massachusetts Turnpike (I-90) to Exit 11A, then take Route I-495 North, approximately 7 miles, to Route I-290 West towards Worcester. Take Exit 16 (Central Street). Make a right on East Central Street to Main Street. Take a left on Main, and a right onto Elm Street (one block on the right). Drive past the Museum after the first traffic light on Elm (because parking is around the block). Make a left on Linden (first left after passing Museum) to Pleasant (one block). Left on Pleasant to Chestnut (one block). Left on Chestnut. The Museum is on the left at the end of the block. Museum parking is directly behind the Museum. Additional parking available at the Pearl-Elm garage (on Pearl Street, one block from Museum) or Worcester Center garage (four blocks form Museum).

Description of Institution:

The WORCESTER HISTORICAL MUSEUM, founded in 1875, documents the history and heritage of this central Massachusetts city. The Museum's holdings include artifacts, manuscripts, photographs, maps, and other Worcester-related items that bear witness to the traditions and accomplishments of the city's residents.

Description of Resources:

The Museum's Research Library contains 50,000 items. Items of interest to Jewish genealogists are documents and photographs relating to Jewish families, synagogues, cemeteries, businesses, unions, schools, clubs and organizations.

- Extensive documentation of Shaarai Torah Sons of Abraham Synagogue (1904), 32 Providence Street, last remaining Jewish house of worship on Worcester's east side (first area of settlement for Worcester's Jewish population). Includes Secretary's Records, 1904-1953, and photographs and documents relating to religious and social events. See the Exhibition catalog, published in conjunction with *Shaarai Torah: Life Cycle of a Synagogue* (March-June 1991).

- Exhibition catalog, published in conjunction with *Water Street: World Within A World* (November 1983-March 1984). Focuses on the Eastern European Jewish immigrant in Worcester between 1880 and 1945.

- *Jewish Civic Leader*. Weekly newspaper, published in Worcester from 15 Mar 1926 to 15 May 1980. On microfilm.

- Worcester City Directories: 1829, 1844-1991.

- Worcester House Directories, 1888-1992.

- Atlases of the City of Worcester: 1870, 1886, 1896, 1911, and 1922.

- Sanborn Fire Insurance Maps for Worcester: 1892, 1910, 1936, 1937, 1969 and 1978.

- Hebrew Immigrant Aid Society (HIAS). Arrival cards for immigrants coming to Worcester through the port of Boston, 1907-1930. 375 cards, photocopied courtesy of the AMERICAN JEWISH HISTORICAL SOCIETY in Waltham.

- List of Jewish births, Dec. 1884 - Apr. 1894. Compiled from City Hall records by Alfred G. Isenberg, former publisher of the *Jewish Civic Leader*. 319 names with date of birth.

- Records of Hebrew Cemetery, 1896 - 1992. Worcester's first Jewish cemetery. Gives name, death date, and burial site.

- Records of Chevra Kadisha (Holy Society) Cemetery, 1926-1992. Includes name, death date, and burial site as of 2 June 1992. Includes records of Workmen's Circle Cemetery and Agudas Sons of Jacob Cemetery, now part of Chevra Kadisha Cemetery Corp.

- Marriage Records, 26 June 1907 - 7 Feb 1932, kept by Rabbi Zorach Hurowitz, of Sons of Jacob Synagogue. Gives city of residence, age, occupation, birthplace, and parents' names for bride and groom.

Appendix A

YIZKOR BOOK BIBLIOGRAPHY

Bibliography of Eastern European Memorial (Yizkor) Books
Compiled by Zachary M. Baker

With Call Numbers at Libraries in the Boston Area

Introduction:

Memorial (or yizkor) books are among the most frequently consulted published sources on individual Eastern European Jewish communities. The narrative sections that comprise the bulk of a memorial book treat the history, culture and institutions of the town's Jewish community with particular emphasis on the period between the two world wars and the Holocaust. Many memorial books also include articles on prominent local rabbinical families and lists of Holocaust martyrs, which can be of particular value to the genealogist.

Most memorial books are in Hebrew and/or Yiddish, though some also have sections in English or other languages. While some memorial books are written by individual authors, most represent the collective efforts of organizations of former townspeople (also known as *landsmannschaft* societies), which serve as the publishers of the overwhelming majority of these works.

Purchase:

Most yizkor books are published in very limited quantities, and are therefore usually difficult to find and expensive to purchase. Most books currently sell for between $40 and $100. The following establishments sell yizkor books:

J. Robinson & Co.
31 Nachlat Benjamin St.
P.O. Box 4308
Tel Aviv 65162, ISRAEL

Pinat Ha-Sefer
P.O. Box 46646
Haifa 31464, ISRAEL

Chaim Dzialowski
P.O. Box 6413
Jerusalem 91063, ISRAEL

Moshe Schreiber
Mea Shearim Street 16
Jerusalem, ISRAEL

Bibliography:

The following bibliography is adapted from Zachary M. Baker's compilation in "Appendix A" of *Genealogical Resources in the New York Metropolitan Area* (1989), and its update published by the Jewish Genealogical Society, Inc. (New York) in July 1992 (51 pp).

Copies of most memorial books can be located in the Boston area. Call numbers at Boston area libraries are listed after each book's citation:

AJHS:	American Jewish Historical Society (Waltham)
BPL:	Boston Public Library (Copley Square, Boston)
BRAN:	Brandeis University Library (Waltham)
HAR:	Harvard University Library (Harvard Square, Cambridge)
HEBC:	Hebrew College (Brookline)

This bibliography is arranged in three sections: General Reference Works, Countries and Regions, and Localities. The last two sections are arranged alphabetically by place name. Official place names are used.

Book titles are given in transliteration from Hebrew or Yiddish originals. Place names that appear within book titles are, however, not systematically translated but are instead given their official forms. English titles are supplied in brackets after the Hebrew or Yiddish titles. An asterisk (*) after an English title indicates that the translated title was supplied in the work itself. Otherwise titles have been translated by Zachary M. Baker.

The languages in which the book is written are noted at the end of each citation as follows: (H) Hebrew, (Y) Yiddish, (E) English, (F) French, (G) German, (Hu) Hungarian, (J) Judezmo, (P) Polish, (R) Russian, (Ro) Romanian, (S) Spanish, (SC) Serbo-Croatian.

The following cross-references are used:

a) A "see" reference sends the reader from an alternate spelling of a place name to the official form.
b) A "see under" reference sends the reader from the name of a locality discussed in a special chapter of a book on another locality to the full citation of the latter book.
c) A "see also" reference sends the reader to other books that include chapters on a locality.

GENERAL REFERENCE WORKS

Pinkas ha-kehilot; entsiklopediya shel ha-yishuvim lemin hivasdam ve-ad le-aher shoat milhemet ha-olam ha-sheniya [Pinkas hakehillot: encyclopedia of Jewish communities*]. Jerusalem, Yad Vashem Martyrs' and Heroes' Remembrance Authority, 1969-. [An index to the communities included in the first 9 of these volumes appeared in *Search: International Quarterly for Researchers of Jewish Genealogy*, Fall 1988, pages 17-23. The next 4 volumes were indexed in the Summer 1991 issue, pages 22-25].
Romania. vol. 1: Eds.: Theodore Lavi, Aviva Broshni. 1969. 224, 552 p., illus. (H); vol. 2: Eds.: Jan Ancel, Theodore Lavi. 1980. 5, 568 p., illus., maps (H)
Germany. vol. 1: *Bavaria.* Ed.: Baruch Zvi Ophir. 1972. 12, 683, 40 p., illus. (H,E); vol. 2: *Wuerttemberg, Hohenzollern and Baden.* Ed.: Joseph Walk. 1986. 13, 549 p., illus., maps (H); vol. 3: *Hesse, Hesse-Nassau, Frankfort.* 1992. (H).
Hungary. Ed.: Theodore Lavi. 1975. 8, 557 p., illus. (H)
Poland. vol. 1: *The communities of Lodz and its region.* Eds.: Danuta Dabrowska, Abraham Wein. 1976. 15, 285, 15 p., illus. (H,E); vol. 2: *Eastern Galicia.* Eds.: Danuta Dabrowska, Abraham Wein, Aharon Weiss. 1980. 31, 563 p., illus., maps (H,E); vol. 3: *Western Galicia and Silesia.* Eds.: Abraham Wein, Aharon Weiss. 1984. 23, 392 p., illus., maps (H); vol. 4: *Warsaw and its region.* Ed.: Abraham Wein. 1989. 24, 482 p., illus., maps (H); vol. 5: *Volhynia and Polesie.* Ed.: Shmuel Spector. 1990. 9, 341 p., illus., maps (H)
The Netherlands. Authors: Joseph Michman, Hartog Beem, Dan Michman. 1985. 10, 434 p., illus., maps, ports. (H)
Yugoslavia. Ed.: Zvi Loker. 1988. 382 p., illus., maps, ports. (H)
Latvia and Estonia. Ed.: Dov Levin. 1988. 11, 396 p., illus., maps, ports. (H)
Lithuania. Ed.: Dov Levin. 1996. 770 pp. (H)
HEBC: Ref XE 62פ (except Latvia & Estonia, Yugoslavia)
HAR: Heb 16018.749   BRAN: Ref DS135.E8 P5

Arim ve-imahot be-Yisrael; matsevet kodesh le-kehilot yisrael she-nehrevu bi-yedei aritsim u-tmeim be-milhemet ha-olam ha-aharona [Towns and mother-cities in Israel; memorial of the Jewish communities which perished...]. Ed.: Y. L. Fishman (Maimon). Jerusalem, The Rav Kuk Institute (H)
vol. 1, 1947. 371 p., ports.
vol. 2, 1948. 354 p., ports.
vol. 3, *Warsaw.* [By] D. Flinker. 1948. 308 p., ports.
vol. 4, 1950. 313 p., ports.
vol. 5, *Stanislowow.* Eds.: D. Sadan, M. Gelerter. 1952. ports., music.
vol. 6, *Brody.* [By] N. Gelber. 1956. 347 p., ports., map.
vol. 7, *Bratislava (Pressburg).* [By] Sh. Weingarten-Ha-kohen. 1960. 184 p., ports.
HEBC: XZD (except vol. 5)   HAR: Heb 16009.736
BRAN: BM290.M35

COUNTRIES AND REGIONS

Bessarabia. *Al admat Bessarabia; divrei mehkar, zikhronot, reshimot, teudot ve-divrei safrut le-kviat hadmut shel yaha-duta* [Upon the land of Bessarabia; studies, memoirs, articles, documents and essays depicting its image]. Ed. K.A. Bertini. Tel Aviv, United Assoc. of Former Residents of Bessarabia, 1959. 2 vols.: 266, 213 p., ports. (H)
BRAN: DS135.R93 B4 (vol. 1 only)   HAR: PHeb 70.95

Bessarabia. *Bessarabia ha-yehudit be-ma'aroteha; ben shtei milhamot ha-olam 1914-1940* [The Jews in Bessarabia; between the world wars 1914-1940*]. [By] David Vinitzky. Jerusalem - Tel Aviv, The Zionist Library, Gvilei Bessa-rabia, 1973. 2 vols.: 719 p., illus. (H)
BPL: DS135.R93 B48   HAR: Heb 16638.196.5
BRAN: DS135.R93 B48

Bessarabia. *Yahadut Bessarabia* [The Jewry of Bessarabia]. Eds.: K.A. Bertini et al. Jerusalem, The Encyclopaedia of the Jewish Diaspora (vol. 11), 1971. 986 columns, ports., maps (H)
HEBC: XWh Bessarabia בס'   BRAN: +DS135.E8 E55
HAR: Heb 16638.196

Bulgaria. *Yahadut Bulgaria* [Bulgaria*]. Eds.: A. Romano et al. Jerusalem, The Encyclopedia of the Jewish Diaspora (vol. 10), 1967. 1018 columns, ports., maps, facsims. (H)
BRAN: +DS135.E8 E55   HAR: Heb 16849.907 F
HEBC: XM ר47

Carpatho-Ruthenia see Karpatalja

Crimea. *Yahadut Krim me-kadmuta ve-ad ha-shoa* [The Jews of Crimea from their beginnings until the Holocaust]. Ed.: Yehezkel Keren. Jerusalem, Reuben Mass, 1981. 337 p., illus. (H)
HAR: WID-LC Hebrew DS135.R93 C752 x   BRAN: DS135.R93 K768

Galicia. *Pinkes Galicia* [Memorial Book of Galicia]. Ed.: Nechemias Zucker. Buenos Aires, Former Residents of Galicia in Argentina, 1945. 638 p., ports. (Y)
HAR: Y 967.838   BRAN: DS135.G22 P65 1945 (Cage)

Karpatalja (region). *Karpatorus* [Karpatorus*]. Ed.: Y. Erez. Jerusalem, The Encyclopedia of the Jewish Diaspora (vol.7), 1959. 590 columns, ports., facsims. (H)
HAR: Heb 16638.795 F   HEBC: XW

Karpatalja (region). *Sefer zikhron kedoshim le-yehudei Karpatorus-Marmarosh* [Memorial book of the martyrs of Karpatorus-Marmarosh]. [By] Sh. Rosman. Rehovot, 1969. 643 p., ports. (Y)
BRAN: DS135.R93 Z28   HAR: Y 975.889
HABC: XR   BPL: DS135.R93 Z28

Latvia. *The Jews in Latvia.* Ed.: M. Bobe et al. Tel Aviv, Association of Latvian and Estonian Jews in Israel, 1971. 384 p., illus. (E)
BRAN: DS135.R93 L27   HEBC: XWh L27
BPL: DS135.R93 L27

Latvia. *Yahadut Latvia; sefer zikaron* [The Jews od Latvia; a memorial book]. Eds.: B. Eliyav, M. Bobe, A. Kramer. Tel Aviv, Former Residents of Latvia and Estonia in Israel, 1953. 458 p., ports., map (H)
BRAN: DS135.R93 L37   HAR: Heb 16564.513
HEBC: XWn

Latvia. *Yidn in Letland* [Latvian Jewry]. Ed.: Mendel Bobe. Tel Aviv, Reshafim, 1972. 368 p., illus. (Y)
HEBC: XWh בל'   BRAN: DS135.R93 L253

Lithuania. *Bleter fun Yidish Lite* [Lithuanian Jews: a memorial book*]. Ed.: Jacob Rabinovitch. Tel Aviv, Hamenora, 1974. 289 p., illus. (Y,H,E)
HAR: Y 945.189   BPL: DS135.L5 B55

Lithuania. *Lite* [Lithuania], vol. 1. Eds.: Mendl Sudarsky, Uriah Katzenelenbogen, J. Kissin. New York, Jewish-Lithuanian Cultural Society, 1951. 2070 columns, viii p., ports., maps, facsims. (Y); [Lithuania], vol. 2. Ed.: Ch. Leikowicz. Tel Aviv, I. L. Peretz, 1965. 894 columns, ports., facsims. (Y)
BRAN: +DS135.L5 L5   HEBC: XWh 5ל (Oversize)
HAR: Y 954.450   BPL: BM376 L5 L5

Lithuania. *Yahadut Lita* [Lithuanian Jewry*], vol. 1. Eds.: N. Goren, L. Garfinkel et al. Tel Aviv, Am-Hasefer, 1959. 648 p., ports, maps, facsims., music (H); vol. 2. 1972 (H); vol. 3. Eds.: R. Hasman, D. Lipec et al. Tel Aviv, Association for Mutual Help of Former Residents of Lithuania in Israel, 1967. 396 p., ports., maps (H); vol. 4: The Holocaust, 1941-1945. Ed.: Leib Garfunkel. Tel Aviv, 1984. (H)
HEBC: XWh 4ל (Oversize)   BRAN: +DS135.L5 Y25
HAR: Heb 16584.481 F   BPL: DS135.L5 Y3 Folio

[Note: Volume III has been translated into English as *Lithuanian Jewish Communities*, edited by Nancy and Stuart Schoenberg (New York: Garland Publishing, 1991). 502 p.].
HAR: WID-LC DS135.R93 L556 1991
BPL: DS135.R93 L556 1991   BRAN: Ref DS135.R93 L5565 1991

Lithuania. *Yidishe shtet, shtetlekh un dorfishe yishuvim in Lite: biz 1918: historish-biograpfishe skitses* [Jewish cities, towns and villages in Lithuania*]. [By] Berl Kagan. New York, B. Kohen, 1991. ix, 791, v p. (Y)
HEBC: HAR: Y 10200.220
BRAN: Jud Ref +DS135.R93 L55493

Maramures (region). *Sefer Marmarosh; mea ve-shishim kehilot kedoshot be-yishuvan u-ve-hurbanan* [The Marmaros book; in memory of a hundred and sixty Jewish communities*]. Eds.: Sholom Yehuda Gross, Y. Yosef Cohen. Tel Aviv, Beit Marmaros, 1983. 58, 436, 151 p., illus., map, ports. (H,Y,E)
HAR: Heb 44300.117 F   BRAN: +DS135.R72 M377 1983

Poland. *Megilat Poland* [The scroll of Poland]. Part 5: Holocaust, Vol. 1. Jerusalem, Society of Religious Jews from Poland, 1961. 351 p., ports., facsims. (H,Y)
BRAN: +DS135.P6 M37

Transylvania. *Toldot ha-kehilot be-Transylvania; perakim me-sevalot ha-yehudim ve-nitsane ha-gevura bi-tekufat ha-shoa be-Hungaria* [History of the communities of Transylvania]. [By] Yehuda Shvartz. Hadera, Ha-Aguda Yad le-Kehilot Transylvania, [1976]. 293 p., illus. (H)
HAR: WID-LC HEBREW DS135.H92 T77 x   BPL: DS135.R72 T77
BRAN: DS135.R72 T77

Ukraine. *Shtet un Shtetlekh in Ukraine un in andere teyln fun Rusland; Furshungen in yidisher geshikhte un yidishn lebnsshteyger* [Cities and towns in the history of the Jews in Russia and the Ukarine*]. By Mendel Oserowitch. New York, The M. Osherowitch Jubillee [sic] Committee. 1948. 2 vols. (305, 306 p.) (Y)
HEBC: XW ש9א   HAR: Y 951.580.10
BRAN: DS135.R9 O8 (volume 2)

Ukraine. *Yidn in Ukraine* [Jews in the Ukraine*]. Eds.: M. Osherowitch, J. Lestschinsky et al. New York, Association for the Commemoration of the Ukrainian Jews, 1961-1967. 2 vols. (342 p.), ports., maps, facsims. (Y)
BRAN: +DS135.R93 U52 v1-2   HAR: Y 951.580.5
BPL: DS135.R93 U5

Zaglebie. *Pinkes Zaglembye; memorial book*. Ed.: J. Rapoport. Melbourne, Zaglembie Society and Zaglembie Community in Melbourne; Tel Aviv, Hamenorah, 1972. 82, 613 p., illus. (Y,E)
BRAN: +DS135.P62 Z256   HAR: Y 967.503
BPL: DS135.P62 Z256

LOCALITIES

Aleksandria. *Pinkas ha-kehila Aleksandria (Wolyn); sefer yizkor* [Memorial book of the community of Aleksandria (Wolyn)]. Comp.: Shmuel Yizreeli; ed.: Natan Livneh. Tel Aviv, Aleksandria Society, 1972. 314 p., illus. (H)
BRAN: DS135.R93 A576   HAR: Heb 16678.159

Aleksandrow. *Aleksander* [Aleksander - near Lodz]. Ed.: N. Blumenthal. Tel Aviv, Association of Former Residents of Aleksandrow in Israel, 1968. 391 p., ports., facsims. (H,Y)
BRAN: DS135.P62 A53   HAR: Heb 16718.161
BPL: DS135.P62 A53

Altona see under *Arim ve-imahot be-Yisrael*, volume 2.

Amdur see Indura

Amshinov (Mszczonow) see under Zyrardow

Annopol. *Rachov-Annopol; pirkei edut ve-zikaron* [Rachov-Annopol; testimony and remembrance*]. Ed.: Shmuel Nitzan. Israel, Rachov/Annapol and Surrounding Region Society, 1978. 80, 544 p., illus. (H,Y,E)
HAR: WID-LC HEB DS135.P62 R327 x
BPL: DS135.P62 R327 x

Antopol. *Antopol (Antepolie); sefer yizkor* [Antopol (Antopolie) yizkor book*]. Ed.: Benzion H. Ayalon. Tel Aviv, Antopol Societies in Israel and America, 1972. 11, 754, 170 p., illus. (H,Y,E)
BRAN: DS135.R93 A598   HAR: 16638.173.5
AJHS: DS135.P62 A5

Antopol. *Antopol (5400-5702); mi-toldoteha shel kehila ahat be-Polesie* [Antopol, 1648-1942; from the history of one Jewish community in Polesie]. Ed.: Yosef Levin. Tel Aviv, 5727 [1966/67]. 164 p., illus. (H)
HAR: 16638.173   BPL: DS135.R93 A6
BRAN: DS135.R93 A6

Apt see Opatów

Augustów. *Sefer yizkor le-kehilat Augustow ve-ha-seviva.* [Memorial book of the community of Augustow and vicinity]. Ed.: J. Alexandroni. Tel Aviv, Association of Former Residents of Augustow and Vicinity, 1966. 549p., ports. (H,Y)
BRAN: DS135.P62 A8   HAR: 16718.125
BPL: DS135.P62 A8

Baranów. *Sefer yizkor Baranow* [A memorial to the Jewish community of Baranow*]. Ed.: Nachman Blumenthal. Jerusalem, Yad Vashem, 1964. xvi, 236 p., ports., tabs., facsims. (H,Y,E)
BRAN: DS135.P62 B3   HAR: 16718.180
BPL: DS135.P62 B3

Baranowicze. *Baranovits; sefer zikaron* [Baranovits; memorial book]. Tel Aviv, Association of Former Residents of Baranovits in Israel, 1953. vi, 668 p., ports., map, facsims. (H,Y)
BRAN: DS135.P62 B37   HAR: Heb 16638.233
HEBC: XZD Baranovichi

Barylow see under Radziechow

Będzin. *Pinkas Bendin* [Pinkas Bendin; a memorial to the Jewish community of Bendin*]. Ed.: A. Sh. Stein. Tel Aviv, Association of Former Residents of Bedzin in Israel, 1959. 431 p., ports. (H,Y)
BRAN: +DS135.P62 B385   HAR: Heb 16718.217 F
AJHS: DS135.P62 B385

Będzin see also under Piotrków Trybunalski

Beligrod see under Lesko

Belitzah see Bielica

Belz. *Belz; sefer zikaron* [Belz memorial book]. Ed.: Yosef Rubin. Tel Aviv, Belz Societies in Israel and America, 1974. 559 p., illus. (H,Y)
HAR: Heb 16718.211   BPL: DS135.P62 B415

Bendery. *Kehilat Bendery; sefer zikaron* [Yizkor book of our birthplace Bendery*]. Ed.: M. Tamari. Tel Aviv, Bendery Societies in Israel and the United States, 1975. 446, 42 p., illus. (H,Y,E)
BRAN: +DS135.R93 B364   HAR: Heb 16838.238

Bendin see Będzin

Beresteczko. *Hayeta ayara...sefer zikaron le-kehilat Beresteczko ve-ha-seviva* [There was a town...memorial book of Beresteczko...and vicinity]. Ed.: Mendel Singer. Haifa, Assication of Former Residents of Beresteczko in Israel, 1961. 555 p., ports., map, facsims. (H,Y)
HAR: Heb 16678.233   BRAN: DS135.R93 B383 1960

Bereze see under Pruzana

Berlin see under *Arim ve-imahot be-Yisrael*, volume 1.

Bershad. *Be-tsel ayara.* [Bershad*]. [By] Nahman Huberman. Jerusalem, Encyclopaedia of the Jewish Diaspora, 1956. 247 p., port. (H)
HAR: Heb 16638.238   HEBC: XZD Bershad
BRAN: DS135.R93 B387

Biała Podlaska. *Podlyashe in natsi-klem; notitsn fun khurbn* [Podlasie en las garras del nazismo*]. [By] Moses Joseph Faignboim [Feigenbaum]. Buenos Aires, Committee of Friends, 1953. 241 p., illus. (Y)
HAR: YA 5074.88   BRAN: DS135.P6 F32 1953

Biała Podlaska. *Sefer Biala Podlaska* [Book of Biala Podlaska]. Ed.: M. J. Feigenbaum. Tel Aviv, Kaput Gmilut Hesed of the Community of Biala Podlaska, 1961. 501 p., ports., facsims. (H,Y)
HEBC: XZD Biala   BRAN: +DS135.P62 F3
HAR: Heb 16718.200   BPL: DS135.P62 B45

Biała Rawska. *Sefer yizkor le-kedoshei Biala Rawska* [Memorial book to the martyrs of Biala Rawska]. Eds.: Eliyahu Freudenreich, Arye Yaakobovits. Tel Aviv, Biala Rawska Societies in Israel and the Diaspora, 1972. 255 p., illus. (H,Y)
BRAN: DS135.P62 B53   HAR: Y961.710
BPL: DS135.P62 B53

Białobrzegi. *Sefer zikaron le-kehilat Bialobrzeg* [Memorial book of the Byalovzig community*]. Ed.: David Avraham Mandelboim. Tel Aviv, Yotse le-or al yede Vaad ha-ayarah Byalobzig, 1991. 396 p., illus., maps, ports. (H)
HEBC: XDZ Bialobrzegi   HAR: Heb 42956.392
BRAN: DS135.P62 R322 1991

Białystok. *Bialystok; bilder album...* [Bialystok; photo album...*]. Ed.: David Sohn. New York, Bialystoker Album Committee, 1951. 386 p. (Y,E)
HEBC: XZD Bialystok   BRAN: +DS135.P62 B5352 1951

Białystok. *Der Bialystoker yisker-bukh* [The Bialystoker memorial book*]. Ed.: I. Shmulewitz. New York, Bialystoker Center, 1982. xi, 396, 205, x p., ports., illus. (Y,E)
BRAN: +DS135.P62 B5353 1982
HAR: WID-LC YIDDISH DS135.P62 B522 x

Białystok. *Pinkes Bialystok; grunt-materyaln tsu der geshihkte fun di yidn in Bialystok biz nokh der ershter velt-milkhome* [Pinkos Bilaystok (the chronicle of Bialystok); basic material for the history of the Jews in Bialystok until the period after the First World War*]. Ed.: Yudl Mark. New York, Bialystok Jewish Historical Association, 1949-1950. 2 vols. (Y)
HEBC: XZD Bialystok   BRAN: DS135.P62 B54
HAR: Y 963.473   AJHS: DS135.P62 B54

Biecz. *Sefer zikaron le-kedoshei ayaratenu Biecz* [Memorial book of the martyrs of Biecz]. Ed.: P. Wagshal. Ramat Gan, Association of Former Residents of Biecz and Vicinity in Israel, 1960. 243 p., ports. (H,Y)
BRAN: DS135.P62 B567

Bielica. *Pinkas Bielica* [Book of Belitzah-Bielica*]. Ed.: L. Losh. Tel Aviv, Former Residents of Bielica in Israel and the USA, 1968. 511 p., ports., map, facsims. (H,Y,E)
BRAN: DS135.R93 B346   HAR: Heb 16658.211
BPL: DS135.P62 B346

Bielsk-Podlaski. *Bielsk-Podlaski; sefer yizkor...* [Bielsk-Podliask; book in the holy memory of the Bielsk-Podliask Jews*]. Ed.: H. Rabin. Tel Aviv, Bielsk Societies in Israel and the United States, 1975. 554, 44 p., illus. (H,Y,E)
BRAN: DS135.P62 B94
HAR: WID-LC HEB DS135.P62 B572

Bielsko-Biala. *Bielitz-Biala (Bielsko-Biala); pirkei avar* [chapters from the past]. [By] Elijahu Miron. Israel, 1973. 182 p., illus. (H,G)
HAR: Heb 16718.210

Biezun. *Sefer ha-zikaron le-kedoshei Biezun* [Memorial book of the martytrs of Biezun]. Tel Aviv, Former Residents of Biezun, 1956. 186 p., ports. (H,Y)
HAR: Y 966.890

Bikovsk (Bukowsko) see under Sanok

Bilgoraj. *Bilgoraj yisker-bukh* [Bilgoraj memorial book]. [By] Moshe Teitlboym. Jerusalem, 1955. 243 p., illus. (Y)
HEBC: XZD Bilgoraj

Bisk see Busk

Bitshutsh see Buczacz

Bivolari. *Avaratenu Bivolari* [Our town Bivolari]. Eds.: Moscu Abramovici et al. Haifa, Bivolari Immigrants Organization in Israel, 1981. 160, 37 p., illus. (H,Ro,E)
BRAN: +DS135.R72 B5 1981
HAR: WID-LC HEBREW DS135.R77 B529 x

Bobrka. *Le-zekher kehilat Bobrka u-benotehu* [Boiberke memorial book*]. Ed.: Sh. Kallay. Jerusalem, Association of Former Residents of Bobrka and Vicinity, 1964. 218, 38 p., ports, facsims. (H,Y,E)
BRAN: +DS135.R92 B64   HAR: Heb 16718.190 F

Bobruisk. *Bobruisk; sefer zikaron le-kehilat Bobruisk u-benoteha* [Memorial book of the community of Bobruisk and its surroundings]. Ed.: Yehuda Slutski. Tel Aviv, Former Residents of Bobruisk in Israel and the USA, 1967. 2 vols.: 871 p., ports., map, facsims. (H,Y)
HEBC: XZD Bobruisk   HAR: Heb 16638.185
BRAN: +DS135.R93 B59   BPL: DS135.R93 B59

Bolechow. *Sefer ha-zikaron le-kedoshei Bolechow* [Memorial book of the martyrs of Bolechow]. Ed.: Y. Eshel. Association of Former Residents of Bolechow in Israel, 1957. 352 p., ports. (H,Y)
BRAN: DS135.P62 B65   HAR: Heb 42800.405

Borsa. *Sefer zikaron Borsha, o: ayarat-ahavim be-yarketei ha-karpatim* [Memorial book of Borsha, or: The beloved village by the foot of the Carpathians*]. Written and edited by Gedaliahu Stein. Kiryat Motzkin, 1985. 655 p., illus., maps, ports. (H)
HAR: Heb 44300.133F

Borszczow. *Sefer Borszczow* [The book of Borstchoff*]. Ed.: N. Blumenthal. Tel Aviv, Association of Former Residents of Borszczow in Israel, 1960. 341 p., ports, facsims. (H,Y)
BRAN: DS135.R93 B6   HAR: Y 951.850

Bransk. *Braynsk; sefer ha-zikaron* [Brainsk; book of memories*]. [By] A. Trus and J. Cohen. New York, Brainsker Relief Committee of New York, 1948. 440 p., ports, facsims. (Y)
BRAN: DS135.P62 B7 1944   HAR: Y 962.250
AJHS: DS135.P62 B7

Bratislava (Pressburg) see under *Arim ve-imahot be-Yisrael*, volume 7.

Braynsk see Bransk

Brest Litovsk see Brzesc nad Bugiem

Brichany. *Britshan; Britsheni ha-yehudit be-mahatsit ha-mea ha-aharona* [Brichany; its Jewry in the first half of our century]. Eds.: Y. Amizur et al. Tel Aviv, Former Residents of Brichany, 1964. 296 p., ports, map (H)
BRAN: DS135.R93 B77   HAR: Heb 16698.225
BPL: DS135.R93 B77

Brichevo. *Pinkas Brichevo* [Memorial book of Brichevo]. Ed.: K.A. Bertini. Tel Aviv, Former Residents of Brichevo (Bessarabia) in Israel, 1970. 531 p., ports., map, facsims. (H,Y)
BRAN: DS135.R93 B785   HAR: Heb 16698.230
BPL: DS135.R93 B785

Brisk see Brzesc nad Bugiem

Brody see under *Arim ve-imahot be-Yisrael*, volume 6.

Brzesc nad Bugium. *Brisk de-Lita* [Brest Lit.(owsk) Volume*]. Ed.: E. Steinman. Jerusalem, The Encyclopaedia of the Jewish Diaspora (vol. 2), 1954-55. 2 vols. (647 p), ports., map (H,Y)
BRAN: +DS135.E8 E55   HEBC:
HAR: Heb 16718.227 F

Brzezany. *Brzezany, Narajow va-he-seviva; toldot kehilot she-nehrevu* [Brzezany memorial book*]. Ed.: Menachem Katz. Haifa, Brzezany-Narajow Societies in Israel and the United States, 1978. 28, 473 p. (H,Y,E)
BRAN: +DS135.R93 B3843   HAR: Heb 44300.120

Brzeziny. *Bzhezhin yisker-bukh* [Brzeziny memorial book*]. Eds.: A. Alperin, N. Summer. New York, Brzeziner Book Committee, 1961. 288 p., ports. (Y)
HEBC: XZD Brzezin   BRAN: +DS135.P62 B722
HAR: Y 961.340

Buczacz. *Sefer Buczacz; matsevet zikaron le-kehila kedosha* [Book of Buczacz; in memory of a martyred community]. Ed.: Israel Kahan. Tel Aviv, Am Oved, 1956. 302 p., ports., facsims. (H)
HEBC: XZD Buczacz   BRAN: DS135.R93 B8

Budapest see under *Arim ve-imahot be-Yisrael*, volume 1.

Budzanow. *Sefer Budzanow* [Book of Budzanow*]. Ed.: J. Siegelman. Haifa, Former Residents of Budzanow in Israel, 1968. 319 p., ports., maps, facsims. (H,Y,E)
BRAN: DS135.R93 B815   HAR: Heb 16678.193
BPL: DS135.R93 B815

Bukaczowce see under Rohatyn

Bukowsko see under Sanok

Bursztyn. *Sefer Bursztyn* [Book of Bursztyn]. Ed.: S. Kanc. Jerusalem, The Encyclopedia of the Jewish Diaspora, 1960. 426 columns, ports., facsims. (H,Y)
BRAN: +DS135.R93 B83   HAR: Heb 16638.195

Busk. *Sefer Busk; le-zekher ha-kehila she-harva* [Busk; in memory of our community*]. Ed.: Avrum Shayari. Haifa, Busker Organization in Israel, 1965. 293 p., ports., facsims. (H,Y,E,P)
BRAN: DS135.P62 B87   HAR: Heb 16718.194.5
BPL: DS135.P62 B87

Bychawa. *Bychawa; sefer zikaron* [Bychawa; a memorial to the Jewish community of Bychawa Lubelska*]. Ed.: J. Adini. Bychawa Organization in Israel, 1968. 636 p., ports., map, facsims (H,Y)
BRAN: DS135.P62 B93   HAR: Heb 16718.208
BPL: DS135.P62 B93

Byten. *Pinkas Byten* [Memorial book of Byten]. Eds.: D. Abramowich, M.W. Bernstein. Buenos Aires, Former Residents of Byten in Argentina, 1954. 605 p., map, facsims. (Y)
HAR: Y 10200.134; Y 951.40   BRAN: DS135.R93 B89 1954

Cakovec. *Megilat ha-shoa shel kehilat kodesh Cakovec* [Holocaust scroll of the holy community of Cakovec]. [By] Moshe Etz-Hayyim (Tibor Grunwald). Tel Aviv, 1977, 182, 12 p., illus. (H,SC)
BRAN: DS135.Y82 C343   BPL: DS135.Y82 C343
HAR: WID-LC HEBREW DS135.Y82 E87 x

Calarasi see Kalarash

Capresti see Kapreshty

Cernauti (Czernowitz) see under *Arim ve-imahot be-Yisrael*, volume 4.

Cetatea-Alba see Akkerman

Charsznica see under Miechow

Chelm. *Sefer ha-zikaron le-kehilat Chelm; 40 shana le-hurbana* [Yizkor Book in memory of Chelm*]. Ed.: Shimon Kanc. Tel Aviv, Chelm Society in Israel and the U.S., [1980/81]. 828 columns, illus. (H,Y)
BRAN: +DS135.P62 C514 1980   HEBC: XZD Chelm
HAR: WD-LC HEBREW DS135.P62 C437 x

Chelm. *Yisker-bukh Chelm* [Commemoration book Chelm*]. Ed.: M. Bakalczuk-Felin. Johannesburg, Former Residents of Chelm, 1954. 731 p., ports., facsims. (Y)
BRAN: +DS135.P62 C5   HAR: Y 961.591

Chernowitz see under *Arim ve-imahot be-Yisrael*, vol. 4.

Chervonoarmeisk see Radziwillow

Chmielnik. *Pinkas Chmielnik* [Memorial Book of Chmielnik]. Tel Aviv, Former Residents of Chmielnik in Israel, 1960. 1299 columns, ports., facsims. (H,Y)
BRAN: +DS135.P62 C52   HAR: Y 964.950F

Chodecz see under Wloclawek

Cholojow see under Radziechow

Chorostkow. *Sefer Chorostkow* [Chorostkow book*]. Ed.: David Shtokfish. Tel Aviv, Committee of Former Residents of Chorostkow in Israel, 1968. 418 p., ports., facsims. (H,Y)
HAR: Heb 16678.381   BPL: DS135.R93 K42

Chortkov see Czortkow

Chorzele. *Sefer zikaron le-kehilat Chorzel* [Memorial book of the community of Chorzel]. Ed.: L. Losh. Tel Aviv, Association of Former Residents of Chorzele in Israel, 1967. 272 p., ports., facsims. (H,Y)
BRAN: DS135.P62 C537   HAR: Heb 16718.430
BPL: DS135.P62 C537

Chrzanow. *Sefer Chrzanow* [The book of Chrzanow]. [By] Mordecai Bokhner. Regensburg, 1948. xiii, 377 p. (Y)
BRAN: DS135.P62 C538   HAR: Y 961.595

Ciechanow. *Yisker-bukh fun der Tshekhanover yidisher kehile; sefer yizkor le-kehilat Ciechanow* [Memorial book of the community of Ciechanow]. Ed.: A.W. Yassni. Tel Aviv, Former Residents of Ciechanow in Israel and in the Diaspora, 1962. 535 p., ports. (H,Y)
BRAN: DS135.P62 C539

Ciechanowiec. *Ciechanowiec; mehoz Bialystok, sefer edut ve-zikaron* [Ciechanoviec-Bialystok district; memorial and records*]. Ed.: E. Leoni. Tel Aviv, The Ciechanovitzer Immigrant Assoc. in Israel and the USA, 1964. 936, 78 p., ports., facsims. (H,Y,E)
BRAN: DS135.P62 C54   HAR: Heb 16718.775

Ciechocinek see under Wloclawek

Cieszanow. *Sefer zikaron le-kehila kedosha Cieszanow* [Memorial book of the martyred community Cieszanow]. Ed.: D. Ravid. Tel Aviv, Former Residents of Cieszanow in Israel, 1970. 331 p., ports. (H,Y)
BRAN: +DS135.P62 C56   HAR: Heb 16718.776
BPL: DS135.P62 C56

Cluj see Kolozsvar

Cmielow see under Ostrowiec

Cracow see Krakow

Csaktornya see Cakovec

Czarny Dunajec see under Nowy Targ

Czerbin see under Ostrolenka

Czernowitz see under *Arim ve-imahot be-Yisrael*, volume 4.

Czestochowa. *Churban Czenstochow - The destruction of Czenstokov - Khurbn Tshenstokhov.* [By] Benjamin Orenstein. [Western Germany], Central Farwaltung fun der Czenstochower Landsmanszaft in der Amerikaner Zone in Dajczland, 1948. 463 p., illus., ports. (Y in Latin characters).
HAR: Y 965.770.12

Czestochowa. *Sefer Tshenstokhov* [Memorial book of Czestochow]. Ed.: M. Schutzman. Jerusalem, The Encyclopedia of the Jewish Diaspora, 1967-1968. 2 vols., ports. (H,Y)
BRAN: +DS135.P62 C89   HAR: Heb 16718.778 F

Czestochowa. *Tshenstokhov; nayer tsugob-material tsum bukh "Tshenstokhover yodn"* [Czenstochov; an new supplement to the book "Czenstochover Yidn"*]. Ed.: S.D. Singer. New York, United Relief Committee in New York, 1958. 336, iv p., ports. (Y)
BRAN: +DS135.P62 C894   HAR: Y 966.525

Czestochowa. *Tshenstokhoker yidn* [The Jews of Czestochowa]. Ed.: R. Mahler. New York, United Czestochower Relief Committee and Ladies Auxiliary, 1947. cxliv, 404 p., ports., facsims. (Y)
HEBC: XZD Czestochowa   BRAN: +DS135.P62 C893
HAR: Y 10200.124

Czortkow. *Sefer yizkor le-hantsahat kedoshei kehilat Czortkow* [Memorial book of Czortkow*]. Ed.: Y. Austri-Dunn. Tel Aviv, Haifa, Former Residents of Czortkow in Israel, 1967. 435, 36 p., ports., map, facsims. (H,Y,E)
BRAN: +DS135.R93 C53   HAR: Heb 16718.773
BPL: DS135.R93 C5

Czyzewo. *Sefer zikaron Czyzewo* [Memorial book of Tshijewo*]. Ed.: Sh. Kanc. Tel Aviv, Former Residents of Czyzewo in Israel and the Usa, 1961. 1206 columns, ports., facsims. (H,Y)
BRAN: DS135.P62 C948

Dabrowa Gornicza. *Sefer kehilat yehudei Dabrowa Gornicza ve-hurbana* [Memorial book of Dombrawa Gornitza]. Eds.: N. Gelbart et al. Tel Aviv, Former Residents of Dombrowa Gornitza, 1971. 696 p., ports., facsims. (H,Y)
BRAN: +DS135.P62 D267   HAR: Heb 16718.279
BPL: DS135.P62 D267

Daugavpils. *Le-zekher kehilat Dvinsk* [In memory of the community of Dvinsk]. Haifa, [1975]. 63 p., illus. (H)
BPL: DS135.R93 D3184

Dawidgrodek. *Sefer zikaron Dawidgrodek* [Memorial book of Dawidgrodek]. Eds.: Y. Idan et al. Tel Aviv, Former Residents of Dawidgroek in Israel, [195-]. 487 p., ports. (H,Y)
BRAN: DS135.R93 D32

Debica. *Sefer Dembits* [Book of Debica]. Ed.: D. Leibl. Tel Aviv, Association of Former Residents of Debica, 1960. 204 p., ports. (H,Y)
BRAN: DS135.P62 D37

Deblin. *Sefer Deblin-Modrzyc* [Demblin-Modrzyc book*]. Ed.: D. Shtokfish. Tel Aviv, Association of Former Residents of Demblin-Modrzyc, 1969. 694 p., ports., facsims. (H,Y)
BRAN: DS135.P62 D38   BPL: DS135.P62 D38
HAR: Heb 16718.281

Debrecen. *Mea shana le-yehudei Debrecen; le-zekher kedoshei ha-kehila ve-yishevei ha-seviva* [Hundred years of Devrecen Jewry; in memory of the martyrs of Debrecen and vicinity]. [By] Moshe Eliyahu Gonda. Tel Aviv, Committee for Commemoration of the Debrecen Jewry, 1970. 264, 409 p., ports., facsims. (H,Hu)
BRAN: DS135.H92 D434   BPL DS135.H92 D434
HAR: Heb 16758.275

Dembits see Debica

Demblin see Deblin

Derecske. *Sefer zikaron le-yehudei Derecske ve-geliloteha* [Emlékkönyv Derecske és vidéke zsidósága* - Memorial to the Jews of Derecske and its environs]. [By] Arje Moskovits. Tel Aviv, Society of Derecske Emigrants in Israel, 1984. 186, [93], 185 p., illus., facsims, ports. (H,Hu)
HAR: Heb 44300.118   BPL: DS135.H92 D475 1984

Derecske see also under Debrecen

Dereczyn. *Sefer Dereczyn* [Deretchin memorial book*]. Tel Aviv, Deretchiners Societies in Israel and USA, [196-]. 494 p., ports., facsims. (H,Y)
BRAN: +DS135.R93 D437   HAR: Heb 16638.300
BPL: DS135.R93 D437

Des. *Des..., Bethlen, Magyarlapos, Retteg, Nagyilonda és kornyeke* [Des... and vicinity]. Ed.: Z. Singer. Tel Aviv, Former Residents of Des, [197-]. 2 vols. (683 p.), ports., facsims. (Hu)
BPL: DS135.R72 D47

Devenishki see Dziewieniszki

Dieveniskes see Dziewieniszki

Dinov see Dynow

Disna see Dzisna

Divenishok see Dziewieniszki

Dmytrow see under Radziechow

Dnepropetrovsk see Yekaterinoslav

Dobromil. *Sefer zikaron le-zekher Dobromil* [Memorial book Dobromil]. Ed.: M. Gelbart. Tel Aviv, The Dobromiler Society in New York and the Dobromiler Organization in Israel, 1964. 389, 138 p., ports., facsims. (H,Y,E)
BRAN: DS135.R93 D6   HAR: Heb 16718.277
BPL: DS135.R93 D6

Dobrzyn. *Ayarati; sefer zikaron le-ayarot Dobrzyn-Golub* [My town; in memory of the communities Dobrzyn-Gollob]. Ed.: M. Harpaz. [Tel Aviv], Association of Former Residents of Dobrzyn-Golub, 1969. 459, 29 p., ports., facsims. (H,Y,E)
BRAN: DS135.P62 G58   BPL: DS135.P62 G58
HAR: Heb 16718.288

Dokszyce. *Sefer yizkor Dokszyce-Parafianow* [Dokszyc-Parafianow book*]. Ed.: D. Shtokfish. Tel Aviv, Assoc. of Former Residents of Dokszyce-Parafianow in Israel, 1970. 350 p., ports., facsims. (H,Y)
BRAN: DS135.R93 D648   BPL: DS135.R93 D648
HAR: Heb 16658.277

Dolhinow. *Esh tamid - yizkor le-Dolhinow; sefer zikaron le-kehilat Dolhinow ve-ha-seviva* [Eternal flame; in memory of Dolhinow]. Eds.: Josef Chrust, Matityahu Bar-Razon. Tel Aviv, Society of Dolhinow Emigrants in Israel, [198-]. 781 p., illus., maps, ports. (H,Y,E)
BRAN: DS135.R93 D654 1984   HAR: Heb 44300.125

Drohiczyn nad Bugiem. *Sefer Drohiczyn* [Drohiczyn book]. Ed.: D. Shtokfish. Tel Aviv, 1969. 576, 67 p., illus. (H,Y,E)
BRAN: DS135.P62 D76   HAR: Heb 16718.285

Drohiczyn Poleski. *Drohiczyn; finf hundert yor yidish lebn* [Memorial book Drohichyn*]. Ed.: Dov Ber Warshawsky. Chicago, Book-Committee Drohichyn, 1958. viii, 424 p., ports., map, facsims. (Y)
HAR: Y 953.550

Drohobycz. *Sefer zikaron le-Drohobycz, Boryslaw ve-ha-seviva* [Memorial to the Jews of Drohobycz, boryslaw and surroundings*]. Ed.: N.M. Gelber. Tel Aviv, Assoc. of Former Residents of Drohobycz, Boryslaw and surroundings, 1959. 224 p., ports. (H,Y)
BRAN: +DS135.R93 D77   HAR: Heb 16638.285 F

Druja. *Sefer Druja ve-kehilot Miory, Drujsk, ve-Leonpol* [The book of Druya and the communities of Miory, Drusk and Leonpol*]. Ed.: Mordekhai Neishtat. Tel Aviv, Druja and Surrounding Region Society, 1973. 255 p., illus. (H,Y)
BRAN: DS135.R93 D78   HAR: Heb 16718.286
BPL: DS135.R93 D786

Druysk see under Druja

Dubno. *Dubno; sefer zikaron* [Dubno; a memorial to the Jewish community of Dubno, Wolyn*]. Ed.: Yakov Adini. Tel Aviv, Dubno Organization in Israel, 1956. 752 columns, ports., maps, facsims. (H,Y)
BRAN: +DS135.R93 D8   HAR: Heb 16638.273.5
BPL: DS135.R93 D8

Dubossary. *Dubossary; sefer zikaron* [Dubossary memorial book]. Ed.: Y. Rubin. Tel Aviv, Association of Former Residents of Dubossary in America, Argentina and Israel, 1965. 377 p., ports., maps, music (H,Y)
BRAN: DS135.R93 D82   HAR: Heb 16638.272
BPL: DS135.R93 D82

Dumbraveny. *Sefer Dombroven; ner-zikaron le-moshava ha-haklait ha-yehudit ha-rishonah be-Bessarabia* [Dombroven book; memorial to the first Jewish agricultural colony in Bessarabia]. Ed.: Haim Toren. Jerusalem, Dombroven Societies in Israel and The Diaspora, 1974. 8, 252 p., illus. (H,Y)
BRAN: DS135.R72 D86   HAR: Heb 4300.146
BPL: DS135.R72 D86

Dunajska Streda see Dunaszerdahely

Dunaszerdahely. *Sefer zikaron le-kehilat Dunaszerdahely* [A memorial to the Jewish community of Dunaszerdahely (Dunajska Streda)*]. [By] Abraham (Alfred) Engel. Israel, Committee of Dunaszerdahely Emigrants, 1975. 429, 157 p., illus. (H,Hu)
HEBC: XZD Dunaszerdahely   BRAN: DS135.C96 D863
HAR: Heb 16738.277   BPL: DS135.C96 D863

Dvinsk see Daugavpils

Dynow. *Sefer Dynow; sefer zikaron le-kedoshei kehilat Dynow she-nispu ba-shoa ha-hatsit* [The memorial book of Jewish Dinov*]. Eds.: Yitzhak Kose, Moshe Rinat. Tel Aviv, Dynow Society, 1979. 324 p., illus., map (H,Y)
BRAN: DS135.P62 D927
HAR: WID-LC HEBREW DS135.P62 D567 x

Dzialozszyce. *Sefer yizkor shel kehilat Dzialoszyce ve-ha-seviva* [Yizkor book of the Jewish community in Dzialoszyce and surroundings*]. Tel Aviv, Hamenora, 1973. 44, 423 p., illus. (H,Y,E)
BRAN: DS135.P62 D936   HAR: Heb 16718.276
BPL: DS135.P62 D936

Dziewieniszki. *Sefer Divenishok; yad vashem le-ayara yehudit* [Devenishki book; memorial book*]. Ed.: David Shtokfish. Israel, Divenishok Societies in Israel and the United States, 1977. 536 p., illus. (H,Y)
BRAN: DS135.R93 L557   BPL: DS135.R93 L557
HAR: WID-LC HEBREW DS135.P62 D487 x

Dzikow see Tarnobrzeg

Dzisna. *Disna; sefer zikaron le-kehila* [Disna; memorial book of the community]. Eds.: A. Beilin et al. Tel Aviv, Former Residents of Disna in Israel and the USA, 1969. 277 p., ports., facsims. (H,Y)
BRAN: +DS135.R93 D533   HAR: Heb 16718.280
BPL: DS135.R93 D533

Edineti see Yedintsy

Eger. *Yehudei Erlau* [The Jews of Eger]. Eds.: Arthur Abraham Ehrenfeld-Elkay, Tibor Meir Klein-Z'ira. Jerusalem, Eger Commemorative Committee, 1975. 64, 36, 100 p., illus. (H,Hu)
HAR: WID-LC HEBREW DS135.H92 E3439 x

Eisenstadt see under *Arim ve-imahot be-Yisrael*, volume 1.

Ejszyszki. *Eishishok, koroteha ve-hurbana* [Ejszyszki, its history and destruction]. Ed.: Sh. Barkeli. Jerusalem, Committee of the Survivors of Ejszyszki in Israel, 1960. 136 p., ports. (H,Y)
HAR: Heb 16718.154

Ekaterinoslav see Yekaterinoslav

Erlau see Eger

Falenica. *Sefer Falenica* [Falenica book*]. Ed.: D. Shtokfish. Tel Aviv, Former Residents of Falenica in Israel, 1967. 478 p., ports., facsims. (H,Y)
BRAN: DS135.P62 F3

Falenica see also under Otwock

Fehergyarmat. *Ayaratenu le-she-avar Fehergyarmat* [Our former city Fehergyarmat]. [By] Josef Blasz. Bnei Brak, 1965. 44, 52 p., ports., music, facsims. (H,Hu)
BRAN: DS135.H92 F4   HAR: Heb 16758.749
BPL: DS135.H92 F4

Felshtin. *Felshtin; zamlbukh lekoved tsum ondenk fun di Felshtiner kdoyshim* [Felshtin; collection in memory of the martyrs of Felshtin]. New York, First Felshtiner Progressive Benevolent Association, 1937. 670 p., illus. (Y,E)
BRAN: DS135.R93 F4   HAR: Y 957.490

Filipow see under Suwałki

Frampol. *Sefer Frampol* [Frampol book*]. Ed.: David Shtokfish. Tel Aviv, [Book Committee], 1966. 414 p., ports. (H,Y)
BRAN: DS135.P62 F7   HAR: Heb 16718.751
BPL: DS135.P62 F7

Frampol (Polodia) see under Kamenets-Podolskiy

Gąbin. *Gombin; dos lebn un umkum fun a yidish shtetl in Poyln* [Gombin; the life and destruction of a Jewish town in Poland*]. Eds.: Jack Zicklin et al. New York, Gombin Society in America, 1969. 228, 162 p., illus. (Y,E)
HAR: Y 962.390   AJHS: DS135.P62 G4

Gargzdai. *Sefer Gorzd (Lita); ayara be-hayehu u-be-hilayona* [Gorzd book; a memorial to the Jewish community of Gorzd*]. Ed.: Yitzhak Alperovitz. Tel Aviv, The Gorzd Society, 1980. 79, 417 p., illus. (H,Y,E)
BRAN: DS135.R93 G357   BPL: DS135.R93 L5537x
HAR: WID-LC HEBREW DS135.R93 L5537 x

Garwolin. *Garwolin yisker-bukh* [Garwolin memorial book]. Eds.: Moshe Zaltsman, Baruch Shein. Tel Aviv, Garwolin Societies, 1972. 304 p., illus. (H,Y)
BRAN: +DS135.P62 G394   HAR: Y 964.80F
BPL: DS135.P62 G394

Ger see Gora Kalwaria

Gherla see Szamosujvar

Glebokie. *Khurban Glubok... Koziany* [The destruction of Glebokie... Koziany]. [By] M. and Z. Rajak. Buenos Aires, Former Residents' Association in Argentina, 1956. 426 p., ports. (Y)
BRAN: DS135.R93 G587 1956

Glina see Gliniany

Gliniany. *Khurbn Glinyane* [The tragic end of our Gliniany*]. New York, Emergency Relief Committee for Gliniany and Vicinity, 1946. [52] p. (Y,E)
HAR: WID-LC YIDDISH D804.G4 H87

Gliniany. *Megiles Gline* [The book of Gline*]. Ed.: H. Halpern. New York, Former Residents of Gline, 1950. 307 p., (Y)
BRAN: +DS135.P62 G5   HAR: Y 963.149
AJHS: DS135.P62 G55

Glinojeck. *Mayn shtetle Glinovyetsk; un di vayterdike vandlingen Plotsk-Wierzbnik, zikhroynes* [My town Glinojeck...]. [By] Shlomo Moshkovitch. Paris, 1976. 335 p., illus. (Y)
HAR: WID-LC YIDDISH DS135.P62 G5545 x

Glubok see Glebokie

Glusk see under Bobruisk; Slutsk

Gniewaszow. *Sefer Gniewaszow* [Memorial book Gniewaszow*]. Ed.: David Shtokfish. Tel Aviv, Association of Gniewaszow in Israel and the Diaspora, 1971. 533, 19 p., ports. (H,Y,E)
BRAN: DS135.P62 G567   BRAN: DS135.P62 G567
HAR: Heb 16718.253

Golub see under Dobrzyn (*Ayarati*)

Gombin see Gabin

Gomel see under *Arim ve-imahot be-Yisrael*, volume 2.

Goniadz. *Sefer yizkor Goniadz* [Our hometown Goniadz*]. Eds.: J. Ben-Meir (Treshansky), A.L. Fayans. Tel Aviv, The Committee of Goniadz Association in the USA and in Israel, 1960. 808, xix p., ports., maps (H,Y,E)
BRAN: DS135.P62 G59   HAR: Heb 16718.239

Gora Kalwaria. *Megiles Ger*. Ed.: Gregorio Sapoznikow. Buenos Aires, Ger Societies in Argentina, Israel and the United States, 1975. 512 p., illus. (Y)
BRAN: DS135.P62 G59
HAR: WID-LC YIDDISH DS135.P62 6677 x

Gorlice. *Sefer Gorlice; ha-kehila be-vinyana u-be-hurbana* [Gorlice book; the community at rise and fall*]. Ed.: M. Y. Bar-On. [Association of Former Residents of Gorlice and Vicinity in Israel], 1962. 338 p., ports, map, facsims. (H,Y)
HAR: Heb 16718.260F

Gorodek see Grodek Jagiellonski

Gorodenka see Horodenka

Gorodnitsa see under Novograd-Volynskiy

Gorokhov see Horochow

Gorzd see Gargzdai

Gostynin. *Pinkes Gostynin; yisker-bukh* [Pinkas Gostynin; book of Gostynin*]. Ed.: J.M. Biderman. New York, Gostynin Memorial Book Committees, 1960. 358 p., ports. (Y)
BRAN: DS135.P62 G66

Goworowo. *Goworowo; sefer zikaron* [Govorowo memorial book*]. Eds.: A. Burstin, D. Kossovsky. Tel Aviv, The Govorover Societies in Israel, the USA and Canada, 1966. 496, xvi p., ports., facsims. (H,Y,E)
BRAN: DS135.P62 G67   BPL: DS135.P62 G67

Grabowiec. *Sefer zikaron le-kehilat Grabowiec* [Memorial book Grabowitz*]. Ed.: Shimon Kanc. Tel Aviv, Grabowiec Society, 1975. 432, 5, 26 p., illus. (H,Y,E)
BRAN: DS135.P62 G687   HAR: Heb 16718.255
BPL: DS135.P62 G687

Grajewo. *Grayeve ysiker-bukh* [Grayewo memorial book]. Ed.: Dr. G. Gorin. New York, Unitd Grayever Relief Committee, 1950. 51, [38], 311 p., illus. (Y,E)
BRAN: DS135.P62 G7   HAR: Y 10200.121
BPL: DS135.P62 G7

Greiding see Grodek Jagiellonski

Gritsa see Grojec

Grodek Jagiellonski. *Sefer Greiding* [Greiding book]. Ed.: Yehuda Margel. Tel Aviv, 1981. (H)
BRAN: /HTemp/2111

Grodno. *Grodno* [Grodno*]. Ed.: Dov Rabin, Grodno Society; The Encyclopaedia of the Jewish Diaspora, 1973. 744 columns, illus. (H,Y)
HEBC: XZD Grodno   BRAN: DS135.E8 E55
HAR: Heb 16718.265F

Gross Magendorf (Nagymagyar) see under Dunaszerdahely

Grosswardein see Oradea

Grozovo see under Slutsk

Gusiatyn see Husiatyn

Hajdunanas see under Debrecen

Hajdusamson see under Debrecen

Halmi. *Zikhron netsah le-kehilot ha-kedoshot Halmin-Turcz ve-ha-seviva asher nehrevu ba-shoa* [In memory of the communities of Halmin-Turcz and vicinity]. Ed.: Yehuda Shvartz. Tel Aviv, Halmin-Turcz and Vicinity Society, [1968]. 138 p., illus. (H)
HAR: Heb 16838.301

Haydutsishok (Hoduciszki) see under Swieciany

Hivniv see Uhnow

Hlusk (Glusk) see under Slutsk

Hoduciszki see under Swieciany

Holojow (Cholojow) see under Radziechow

Holszany. *Lebn um umkum fun Olshan* [The life and destruction of Olshan]. Tel Aviv, Former Residents of Olshan in Israel, 1965. 431, 136 p., ports., facsims. (H,Y)
BRAN: DS135.R93 Q5

Holynka see under Dereczyn

Homel (Gomel) see under *Arim ve-imahot be-Yisrael*, volume 2.

Horochow. *Sefer Horochow* [Horchiv memorial book*]. Ed.: Yosef Kariv. Tel Aviv, Horchiv Committee in Israel, 1966. 357, 79 p., ports., map, facsims. (H,Y,E)
BRAN: +DS135.R93 G69   HAR: Heb 16718.324
BPL: DS135.R93 G69

Horodec. *Horodets; a geshikhte fun a shtetl, 1142-1942* [Horodec; a history of a town 1142-1942]. Ed.: A. Ben-Ezra. "Horodetz" Book Committee, 1949. 238 p., ports., map, facsims. (Y)
BRAN: +DS135.R93 G67 1949   HAR: Y 952.37

Horodenka. *Sefer Horodenka* [The book of Horodenka]. Ed.: Shimshon Meltzer. Tel Aviv, Former Residents of Horodenka and Vicinity in Israel and the USA, 1963. 425, vii p., ports., map, facsims. (H,Y)
HEBC: XZD Gorodenka   BRAN: +DS135.R93 G65
HAR: Heb 16718.301   BPL: DS135.R93 G65

Horodlo. *Di kehile fun Horodlo; yisker-bukh...* [The community of Horodlo; memorial book...]. Ed.: Y. Ch. Zawidowitch. Tel Aviv, Former Residents of Horodlo in Israel, 1962. 324 p., ports., facsims. (Y)
BRAN: DS135.P62 H659   HAR: Y 963.261

Horodlo. *Kehilat Horodlo; sefer zikaron le-kedoshei Horodlo (Polin) ve-li-kedoshei ha-kefarim ha-semukhim* [The community of Horodlo; memorial book...]. Ed.: Y. Ch. Zawidowitch. Tel Aviv, Former Residents of Horodlo in Israel, 1959. 260 p., ports., fascims. (H)
HAR: Heb 16718.321

Horodno see under Stolin

Horodek see Grodek (near Bialystok)

Hoszcza. *Hoshtsh; sefer zikaron* [Hoshtch-Wolyn; in memory of the Jewish community*]. Eds.: B.H. Ayalon-Baranicka, A. Yaron-Kritzmar. Tel Aviv, Former Residents of Hoshtch in Israel, 1957. 269 p., ports., facsims. (H)
BRAN: DS135.P62 G615   HAR: Heb 16678.301

Hotin see Khotin

Hrubieszow. *Pinkas Hrubieszow* [Memorial book of Hrubieshov*]. Ed.: B. Kaplinsky. Tel Aviv, Hrubieshov Associations in Israel and the USA, 1962. 811, xviii colunms, ports. (H,Y,E,P)
HAR: Heb 16718.333 F

Husiatyn. *Husiatyn; Podoler Gubernye* [Husiatyn; Podolia-Ukraine*]. Ed.: B. Diamond. New York, Former Residents of Husiatyn in America, 1968. 146, [40], 123 p., ports. (Y,E)

Husiatyn. *Kehilatiyim: Husiatyn ve-Kopyczynce* [Two communities: Husiatyn and Kopyczynce*]. [By] Abraham Backer. Tel Aviv, Husiatyn Society, 1977. 286 p., illus. (H,Y)
HAR: WID-LC HEBREW DS135.P62 H872 x

Husiatyn. *Mibet aba; pirkei zikhronot mi-yemei yaldut be-ayarat moladeti Husiatyn* [From my parents' home; memorial chapter...]. [By] A. Y. Avitov (Birnbojm). Tel Aviv, The author, 1965. 155 p., ports. (H)
BRAN: DS135.R93 G88   HAR: Heb 16678.321

Iklad see under Szamosujvar

Ileanda (Nagyilonda) see under Des

Ilja. *Kehilat Ilja; pirkei hayim ve-hashmada* [The community of Ilja; chapters of life and destruction]. Ed.: A. Kopilevitz. [Tel Aviv], Association of Former Residents of Ilja in Israel, 1962. 466 p., ports., facsims. (H,Y)
BRAN: DS135.R93 I387 1962

Indura. *Amdur, mayn geboyrn-shtetl* [Amdur, my hometown]. [By] Iedidio Efrom. Buenos Aires, 1973. 252, 33 p., illus. (Y,S)
HAR: WID-LC YIDDISH DS135.R93 I 54

Istrik (Ustrzyki Dolne) see under Lesko

Ivano-Frankovsk (Stanislawow) see under *Arim ve-imahot*, volume 5

Ivanovo see Janow (near Pinsk)

Ivye see Iwie

Iwacewicze see under Byten

Iwie. *Sefer zikaron le-kehilat Iwie* [Ivie; in memory of the Jewish community*]. Ed.: Moshe Kaganovich. Tel Aviv, Association of Former Residents of Ivie in Israel and "United Ivier Relief" in America, 1968. 738 p., ports., map. (H,Y)
BRAN: DS135.R93 I9   HAR: Heb 16658.140
BPL: DS135.R93 I9

Iwieniec. *Sefer Iwieiec; Kamien va-ha-seviva; sefer zikaron* [The memorial book of Iwieniec, Kamien, and the surrounding region]. Tel Aviv, Iwieniec Societies in Israel and the Diaspora, 1973. 484 p., illus. (H,Y)
BRAN: DS135.R93 I8857   HAR: Heb 16658.149

Jablonka see under Nowy Targ

Jadow. *Sefer Jadow* [The book of Jadow*]. Ed.: A. Wolf Jassni. Jerusalem, The Encyclopedia of the Jewish Diaspora, 1966. 472, xxiii p., ports. (H,Y,E)
BRAN: DS135.P62 J275   HAR: Y 964.700.30
BPL: DS135.P62 J275

Jaisi (Jejsa) see under Braslaw

Janova see Jonava

Janow (near Pinsk) *Janow al yad Pinsk; sefer zikaron* [Janow near Pinsk; memorial book*]. Ed.: M. Nadav (Katzikowski). Jerusalem, Association of Former Residents of Janow near Pinsk in Israel, 1969. 420 p., ports. (H,Y)
HEBC: XZD Yanov ...   BRAN: DS125.R93 I88
HAR: Heb 16658.467   BPL: DS135.R93 I88

Janow (near Trembowla) see under Budzanow; Trembowla

Jaroslaw. *Sefer Jaroslaw* [Jaroslav book*]. Ed.: Yitzhak Alperowitz. Tel Aviv, Jaroslaw Society, 1978. 371, 28 p., illus. (H,Y,E)
BRAN: DS135.P62 J297   BPL: DS135.P62 J297
HAR: WID-LC HEBREW DS135.P62 J377 x

Jaryczow Nowy. *Khurbn Jaryczow bay Lemberg; sefer zikaron le-kedoshei Jaryczow u-sevivoteha* [Destruction of Jaryczow; memorial book to the martyrs of Jaryczow and surroundings]. [By] Mordekhai Gerstl. New York, A. Boym, 1948. 78 p., ports. (Y)
HAR: Y 964.355

Jaslo. *Toledot yehudei Jaslo; me-reshit hityashvutam be-tokh ha-ir ad yemei ha-hurban al yedei ha-natsim...* [History of the Jews of Jaslo...]. [By] Moshe Natan Even-Hayim. Tel Aviv, Jaslo Society, 1953. 360 p., maps, ports., illus. (H)
HEBC: XZD Jaslow

Jaworow. *Matsevet zikaron le-kehilat Jaworow ve-ha-seviva* [Monument to the community of Jaworow and the surrounding region]. Ed.: Michael Bar-Lev. Haifa, Jaworow Societies in Israel and the United States, 1979. 252 p., illus. (H,Y)
BRAN: +DS135.R93 Y385
HAR: WID-LC HEBREW DS135.P62 Y385 x

Jędrzejów. *Sefer ha-zikaron le-yehudei Jedrzejow* [Memorial book of the Jews of Jedrzejow]. Ed.: Sh. D. Yerushalmi. Tel Aviv, Former Residents of Jedrzejow in Israel, 1965. 490 p., ports., facsims. (H,Y)
BRAN: DS135.P62 J43   HAR: Heb 16718.441

Jedwabne. *Sefer Jedwabne; historiya ve-zikaron* [Yedwabne; history and memorial book*]. Eds.: Julius L. Baker, Jacob L. Baker; assisted by Moshe Tzinovitz. Jerusalem-New York, The Yedabner Societies in Israel and in the United States of America, 1980. 121, 110 p., illus. (H,Y,E)
HAR: WID-LC HEBREW DS135.P62 Y427 x

Jeremicze see under Turzec

Jezierna. *Sefer Jezierna* [Memorial book of Jezierna*]. Ed.: J. Sigelman. Haifa, Committee of Former Residents of Jezierna in Israel, 1971. 354 p., ports. (H,Y)
BRAN: DS135.R93 O958   HAR: Y 954.130

Jezierzany. *Sefer Ozieran ve-ha-seviva* [Memorial book; Jezierzany and surroundings*]. Ed.: M.A. Tenenblatt. Jerusalem, The Encyclopaedia of the Jewish Diaspora, 1959. 498 columns, ports. (H,Y)
BRAN: DS135.R93 O958   HAR: Heb 16638.129
BPL: DS135.R93 O958

Jod (Jody) see under Braslaw

Jonava. *Yanove oyf di breges fun Vilye; tsum ondenk fun di khorev-gevorne yidishe kehile in Yanove* [Yizkor book in memory of the Jewish community of Yanova*]. Ed.: Shimeon Noy. Tel Aviv, Jonava Society, 1972. 35, 429 p., illus. (Y,E)
BRAN: +DS135.L52 J667   HAR: Heb 16598.675
BPL: DS135.L52 J667

Jordanow see under Nowy Targ

Jozefow. *Sefer zikaron le-kehilat Jozefow ve-le-kedosheha* [Memorial book to the community of Jozefow and its martyrs]. Ed.: Azriel Omer-Lemer. Tel Aviv, Jozefow Societies in Israel and the U.S.A., 1975. 462 p., illus. (H,Y)
BRAN: DS135.P62 J697   BPL: DS135.P62 J697x
HAR: WID-LC HEBREW DS135.P62 J697 x

Kadzidlo see under Ostrołęka

Kalarash. *Sefer Kalarash; le-hantsahat zikhram shel yehudei ha-ayara she-nehreva bi-yemei ha-shoa* [The book of Kalarash in memory of the town's Jews, which was destroyed in the Holocaust]. Eds.: Noah Tamir et al. Tel Aviv, 1966. 533 p., ports., facsims. (H,Y)
BRAN: DS135.R93 K23   HAR: Heb 16698.813
BPL: DS135.R93 K23

Kalisz. *Toledot yehudei Kalish* [History of the Jews of Kalisz]. [By] Yisrael David Bet-Halevi. Tel Aviv, 1961. 448 p., illus., ports., map. (H)
HEBC: XZD Kalisz   HAR: Heb 16718.783

Kalisz. *The Kalish Book.* Ed.: I.M. Lask. Tel Aviv, The Societies of Former Residents of Kalish and the vicinity in Israel and the USA, 1968. 327 p. (E)
BRAN: +DS135.P62 K293   BPL: DS135.P62 K293

Kalisz. *Sefer Kalish* [The Kalish book*]. Tel Aviv, The Israel-American Book Committee, 1964-1968. 2 vols. (624, 598 p.), ports., facsims. (H,Y)
BRAN: +DS135.P62 K29   BPL: DS135.P62 K29
HAR: Heb 16718.783.5   AJHS: DS135.P62 K9

Kalov see Nagykallo

Kalusz. *Kalusz; heyeha ve-hurbana shel ha-kehila* [Kalusz; the life and destruction of the community]. Eds.: Shabtai Unger, Moshe Ettinger. Tel Aviv, Kalusz Society, 1980. 325, 330, 15 p., illus. (H,Y,E)
BRAN: DS135.R244 1980

Kaluszyn. *Sefer Kaluszyn; geheylikt der khorev gevorener kehile* [Memorial book of Kaluszyn]. Eds.: A. Shamir, Sh. Soroka. Tel Aviv, Former Residents of Kaluszyn in Israel, 1961. 545, [15] p., ports., facsims. (Y)
BRAN: +DS135.P62 K52   HAR: Y 966.750F

Kalwaria see under Wadowice

Kamenets-Litovsk see Kamieniec Litewski

Kamenets-Podolskiy. *Kamenets-Podolsk u-sevivata* [Kamenets-Podolsk and its surroundings]. Eds.: Abraham Rosen, Ch. Sharig, Y. Bernstein. Tel Aviv, Association of Former Residents of Kamenets-Podolsk and Its Surroundings in Israel, 1965. 263 p., ports., facsims. (H)
BRAN: +DS135.R93 K25   HAR: Heb 16678.813
BPL: DS135.R93 K25

Kamien see under Iwieniec

Kamien Koszyrski. *Sefer ha-zikaron le-kehilat Kamien Koszyrski ve-ha-seviva...* [Kamin Koshirsky book; in memory of the Jewish community*]. Eds.: A.A. Stein et al. Tel Aviv, Former Residents of Kamin Koshirsky and Surroundings in Israel, 1965. 974 columns, ports. (H,Y)
BRAN: +DS135.P62 K325

Kamiensk see under Radomsko

Kammeny Brod see under Novograd-Volynskiy

Kapsukas see Mariampole

Kapulye (Kopyl) see under Slutsk

Karczew see under Otwock

Kartuz-Bereze (Bereza Kartuska) see under Pruzana

Kaszony see Kosyno

Kazimierz. *Pinkas Kuzmir* [Kazimierz -- memorial book*]. Ed.: D. Shtokfish. Tel Aviv, Former Residents of Kazimierz in Israel and the Diaspora, 1970. 655 p., ports., facsims. (H,Y)
BRAN: DS135.P62 K377   HAR: Heb 16718.789
BPL: DS135.P62 K377

Kedainiai. *Keydan; sefer zikaron* [Keidan memorial book*]. Ed.: Josef Chrust. Tel Aviv, Keidan Societies in Israel, South America, and the United States, 1977. 39, 313 p., illus. (H,Y,E)
HAR: WID-LC HEBREW DS135.L52 K442x   BRAN: DS135.R93 L555

Kelts see Kielce

Keydan see Kedainiai

Khmelnitskii see Proskurov

Kholm see Chelm

Khorostkov see Chorostkow

Khotin. *Sefer kehilat Khotin (Bessarabia)* [The book of the community of Khotin (Bessarabia)]. Ed.: Shlomo Shitnovitzer. Tel Aviv, Khotin (Bessarabia) Society, 1974. 333 p., illus. (Y)
BRAN: +DS135.R72 H667   HAR: Heb 16678.379

Khozhel see Chorzele

Kibart see Kybartai

Kielce. *Sefer Kielce; toldot kehilat Kielce* [The history of the community of Kielce]. [By] P. Zitron. Tel Aviv, Former Residents of Kielce in Israel, 1957. 328 p., ports. (H,Y)
BRAN: DS135.P62 K5   HAR: Heb 16718.809

Kiemieliszki see under Swieciany

Kiernozia see under Lowicz

Kislowszczyzna see under Braslaw

Kisvarda. *Sefer yizkor le-kehilat Kleinwardein ve-ha-seviva* [Memorial book of Kleinwardein and vicinity]. Tel Aviv, Kleinwardein Society, 1980. 79, 190 p., illus. (H,Hu,E)
HAR: WIC-LC HEBREW DS135.H92 K577 x

Kitai-Gorod see under Kamenets-Podolskiy

Kitev see Kuty

Klausenburg see Kolozsvar

Kleck. *Pinkas Kletsk* [Pinkas Klezk; a memorial to the Jewish community of Klezk-Poland*]. Ed.: Abraham Samuel Stein. Tel Aviv, Former Residents of Klezk in Israel, 1959. 385 p., ports., map, facsims. (H,Y)
BRAN: +DS135.R93 K65

Kleinwardein see Kisvarda

Klesov see Klosowa

Klosowa. *Sefer Klosowa; kibuts hotsvei avanim a(l) sh(em)*
Yosef Trumpeldor be-Klosowa u-flugatav, measef [The story
of Kibbutz Klosova*]. Ed.: Haim Dan. Beit Lohamei
Hagetaot, Ghetto Fighters House, 1978. 405 p., illus. (H)
HAR: WID-LC HEBREW DS135.P62 K5562x
BPL: DS150.L5 R885

Knenitsh (Knihynicze) see under Rohatyn

Knihynicze see under Rohatyn

Kobryn. *Sefer Kobryn; megilat hayim ve-hurban* [Book of
Kobryn; the scroll of life and destruction]. Eds.: Betsalel
Schwartz, Y. H. Biletzky. Tel Aviv, 1951. 347 p., ports.
(H)
HEBC: XZD Kobrin   BRAN: DS135.P62 K66 1951
HAR: Heb 16620.799

Kobryn. *Kobrin (Belarus) Yizkor Book*. Eds.: Ronald and
Anita Wornick. English translation of *Sefer Kobryn* (1951).
San Fransisco, Holocaust Center of Northern California,
1992.

Kobylnik. *Sefer Kobylnik* [Memorial Book of Kobilnik*].
Ed.: I. Siegelman. Haifa, Committee of Former Residents of
Kobilnik in Israel, 1967. 292 p., ports., map (H,Y)
HEBC: XZD Kobilnik   BRAN: DS135.P62 K6614
HAR: Heb 16658.789   BPL: DS135.P62 K6614

Kock. *Sefer Kotsk* [Memorial book of Kotsk]. Ed.: E.
Porat. Tel Aviv, Former Residents of Kotsk in Israel...,
1961. 424 p., ports., map, facsims. (H,Y)
BRAN: DS135.P62 K662   HAR: Heb 16718.806

Koidanovo. *Koydenov; zamlbukh tsum ondenk fun di*
Koyenover kdoyshim [Koidanov; memorial volume of the
martyrs of Koidanov]. Ed.: A. Reisin. New York, United
Koidanover Assn., 1955. 216, [41], 207 p., ports., facsims.
(Y)
BRAN: DS135.R93 D97   HAR: Y 5750.74

Kolarovgrad (Bulgaria) see Shmula

Kolbuszowa. *Pinkas Kolbishov (Kolbasov)* [Kolbuszowa
memorial book*]. Ed.: I.M. Biderman. New York, United
Kolbushover, 1971. 793, 88 p., ports. (H,Y,E)
BRAN: DS135.P62 K6636   AJHS: DS135.P62 K652
BPL: DS135.P62 K6636

Kolki. *Fun ash aroysgerufn* [Summoned from the ashes].
[By] Daniel Kac. Warszaw, Czytelnik, Zydowski Instytut
Historyczny w Polsce, 1983. 399 p., illus., map, ports. (Y)
HAR: Y 10500.764

Kolno. *Sefer zikaron le-kehilat Kolno* [Kolno memorial
book*]. Eds.: Isaac Remba, Benjamin Halevy. Tel Aviv,
The Kolner Organization and Sifriat Po'alim, 1971. 680, 70
p., ports., facsims. (H,Y,E)
HEBC: XZD Kolno   BRAN: DS135.P62 K6645
HAR: Heb 16718.799   BPL: DS135.P62 K6645

Kolo. *Sefer Kolo* [Memorial Book of Kolo]. Ed.: M.
Halter. Tel Aviv, Former Residents of Kolo in Israel and
the USA, 1958. 408 p., ports. (H,Y)
HAR: Heb 16718.798

Kolomyja. *Pinkes Kolomey* [Memorial book of Kolomey].
Ed.: Shlomo Bickel. New York, 1957. 448 p., ports. (Y)
BRAN: DS135.R93 K6565   HAR: Y 951.790.68
AJHS: DS135.P62 K652   HABC: XZD Kolomea

Kolomyja. *Sefer zikaron le-kehilat Kolomey ve-ha-seviva*
[Kolomeyer memorial book*]. Eds.: D. Noy, M. Schutzman.
[Tel Aviv], Former Residents of Kolomey and Surroundings
in Israel, [1972]. 395 p., ports., facsims. (H)
BRAN: DS135.R93 K6567   HAR: Heb 16778.802.10

Kolonia Synajska see under Dereczyn

Kolozsborsa see Borsa

Kolozsvar. *Sefer zikaron le-yahadut Kluzh-Kolozsvar*
[Memorial volume of the Jews of Cluj-Kolozsvar*]. Ed.:
Moshe Carmilly-Weinberger. New York, 1970. 2nd edition,
1988. 156, 313 p., ports., facsims. (H,E,Hu)
HEBC: XDZ Cluj C3m   BRAN: DS135.R72 C54
HAR: Heb 16758.817 (1st ed.)   HAR: Heb 44300.158 (2nd ed.)
BPL: DS135.R72 C59

Kolozsvar. *Zikaron netsah le-kehila ha-kedosha Kolozhvar-*
Klauzenberg asher nehreva ba-shoa [Everlasting memorial of
the martyred community of Kolozsvar-Klausenberg which
perished in the Holocaust]. [Eds.]: Sh. Zimroni, Y.
Schwartz. Tel Aviv, Former Residents of Kolozsvar in
Israel, 1968. 118 p., (H,Hu), mimeo.
BRAN: DS135.R72 C59   HAR: Heb 16825.801
BPL: DS135.R72 C59

Koltyniany see under Swieciany

Konin. *Kehilat Konin be-ferihata u-ve-hurbana* [Memorial
book Konin*]. Ed.: M. Gelbart. Tel Aviv, Assoc. of Konin
Jews in Israel, 1968. 772, 24 p., map, facsims. (H,Y,E)
BRAN: DS135.P62 K673   HAR: Heb 16718.804
BPL: DS135.P62 K673

Konyar see under Debrecen

Kopin see under Kamenets-Podolskiy

Koprzywnica. *Sefer Pokshivnitsa* [Memorial book of
Koprzywnica]. Ed.: Elchanan Erlich. Tel Aviv, Former
Residents of Koprzywnica in Israel, 1971. 351 p., ports.,
facsims. (H,Y)
BRAN: DS135.P62 K6733   HAR: Heb 16718.735
BPL: DS135.P62 K6733

Kopyczynce see under Husiatyn (*Kehilatiyim*)

Kopyl see under Slutsk

Korczyna. *Korczyna; sefer zikaron* [Korczyna memorial
book*]. New York, Committee of the Korczyna Memorial
Book, 1967. 495 p., ports. (H,Y)
BRAN: DS135.P62 K6735

Korelicze. *Korelits; hayeha ve-hurbana shel kehila yehudit*
[Korelitz; the life and destruction of a Jewish community*].
Ed.: Michael Walzer-Fass. Tel Aviv, Korelicze Societies in
Israel amd the U.S.A., 1973. 61, 357 p., illus. (H,Y,E)
BRAN: DS135.R93 K666   HAR: Heb 16658.805
BPL: DS135.R93 K666

Korelicze see also under Nowogrodek

Koretz see Korzec

Koriv see Kurow

Korzec. *Korets (Wolyn); sefer zikaron le-kehilatenu she-ala aleha ha-koret* [The Korets book; in memory of our community that is no more*]. Ed.: E. Leoni. Tel Aviv, Former Residents of Korets in Israel, 1959. 791 p., ports., facsims. (H,Y)
HAR: Heb 16638.806

Kosow (East Galicia). *Sefer Kosow-Galicia ha-mizrahit* [Memorial book of Kosow - Kosow Huculski*]. Eds.: G. Kressel, L. Oliczky. Tel Aviv, Former Residents of Kosow and Vicinity in Israel, 1964. 430 p., ports., facsims. (H,Y)
BRAN: DS135.R93 K68   HAR: Heb 16638.801

Kosow Lacki. *Kosow Lacki.* Eds.: Rivka and Moshe Barlev. San Fransisco, Holocaust Center of Northern California, 1992.

Kostopol. *Sefer Kostopol; ha-yeha u-mota shel kehila* [Kostopol; the life and death of a community*]. Ed.: A. Lerner. Tel Aviv, Former Residents of Kostopol in Israel, 1967. 386 p., ports. (H)
BRAN: DS135.P62 K675   HAR: Heb 16678.805
BPL: DS135.P62 K675

Kosyno. *The Jews of Kaszony, Subcarpathia.* By Joseph Eden (Einczig). New York, 1988. v, 131 p., illus., map, ports. (E,H,Hu)
HEBC: XZD Kaszony   BPL: DS135.R93 K275 1988x
HAR: WIC-LC DS135.R93 R794 x, 1988

Kotsk see Kock

Kowal see under Wloclawek

Kowel. *Pinkes Kowel* [Memorial book of Kowel]. Ed.: B. Baler. Buenos Aires, Former Residents of Kowel and Surroundings in Argentina, 1951. 511 p., ports., facsims. (Y)
HAR: Y 10200.208

Kozamyer see Kazimierz

Kozangrodek see under Glebokie; Swieciany

Kozieniec. *Sefer zikaron le-kehilat Kozieniec* [Memorial book of the community of Kozieniec]. Ed.: B. Kaplinsky. Tel Aviv, Former Residents in Kozieniec in Israel..., 1969. 516 p., ports., map, music, facsims. (H,Y)
BRAN: +DS135.P62 K678   HAR: Y 967.955F
AJHS: DS135.P62 K678   BPL: DS135.P62 K678

Krakow. *Sefer Kroke, ir va-em be-yisrael* [Memorial book of Krakow, mother and town in Israel]. Eds.: Aryeh Bauminger et al. Jerusalem, The Rav Kuk Institute and Former Residents of Krakow in Israel, 1959. 429 p., ports., facsims. (H)
HEBC: XZD Cracow   BRAN: +DS135.P62 K678
HAR: Heb 16718.159

Krakow see also under *Arim ve-imahot be-Yisrael*, vol. 2.

Krakowiec see under Jaworow (*Matsevet zikaron...*)

Krasnik. *Sefer Krasnik.* Ed.: David Shtokfish. Tel Aviv, Krasnik Societies in Israel and the Diaspora, 1973. 673 p., illus. (H,Y)
BRAN: +DS135.P62 K9175   HAR: Heb 16718.820
BPL: DS135.P62 K69175

Krasnystaw. *Yisker tsum ondenk fun kdoyshey Krasnystaw* [Memorial book of the martyrs of Krasnystaw]. Ed.: A. Stunzeiger. Munich, Publ. "Bafrayung"--Poalei Zion, 1948. 150 p., ports. (Y)
BRAN: DS135.P62 K72 (cage)   HAR: XPA 4659

Kremenits see Krzemieniec

Kripa (Horyngrod) see under Tuczyn

Krivitsh see Krzywicze

Krosienko see under Nowy Targ

Kroshnik see Krasnik

Krosniewiec see under Kutno

Krynki. *Krinik in khurbn: memuarn* [Krinki en ruines*]. [By] Alex Sofer. Montevideo, Los Comites de Ayuda a los Residentes de Krinki de Montevideo y Buenos Aires, 1948. 269, [27] p., illus., map, ports. (Y)
HAR: Y 10020.138

Krynki. *Pinkas Krynki* [Memorial book of Krynki]. Ed.: D. Rabin. Tel Aviv, Former Residents of Krynki in Israel and the Diaspora, 1970. 373 p., ports., map, facsims. (H,Y)
BRAN: DS135.P62 K786   HAR: Heb 16718.825
BPL: DS135.P62 K786

Krzemienica see under Wolkowysk (*Volkovisker ...*)

Krzemieniec. *Pinkas Kremenits; sefer zikaron* [Memorial book of Krzemieniec]. Ed.: A. S. Stein. Tel Aviv, Former Residents of Krzemieniec in Israel, 1954. 450 p., ports., facsims. (H,Y)
HEBC: XZD Kremeniec   BRAN: DS135.R93 K7
HAR: Heb 16638.858

Krzywicze. *Ner tamid; yizkor le-Krivitsh* [Kryvitsh yizkor book*]. Ed.: Matityahu Bar-Ratzon. Tel Aviv, Krivitsh Societies in Israel and the Diaspora, 1977. 724 p., illus. (H,Y)
BRAN: DS135.R93 K746   BPL: DS135.R93 K746
HAR: WID-LC HEBREW DS135.R93 K746

Kshoynzh (Ksiaz Wielki) see under Miechow

Ksiaz Wielki see under Miechow

Kunow see under Ostrowiec

Kurow. *Yisker-bukh Koriv; sefer yizkor, matsevet zikaron le-ayaratenu Koriv* [Yizkor book in memoriam of our hometown Kurow*]. Ed.: Moshe Grossman. Tel Aviv, Former Residents of Kurow in Israel, 1955. 1148 columns, ports., facsims. (Y)
BRAN: +DS135.P62 K83   HAR: Y 962.736

Kurzeniec. *Megilat Kurenits; ayara be-hayehu u-ve-mota* [The scroll of Kurzeniec; the town living and dead]. Ed.: A. Meyerowitz. Tel Aviv, Former Residents of Kurzeniec in Israel and in the USA, 1956. 335 p., ports. (H)
BRAN: DS135.R93 K83   HAR: Heb 16638.807

Kutno. *Kutno ve-ha-seviva* [Kutno and surroundings book*]. Ed.: D. Shtokfish. Tel Aviv, Former Residents of Kutno and Surroundings in Israel and the Diaspora, 1968. 591 p., ports., facsims. (H,Y)
BRAN: +DS135.P62 K88   HAR: Heb 16718.794F
BPL: DS135.P62 K86 Folio

Kuty. *Kitever yisker-bukh* [Kitever memorial book]. Ed.: E. Husen. New York, Kitever Sick and Benevolent Society in New York, 1958. 240 p., ports. (Y)
HAR: Y 953.150

Kuzmir see Kazimierz

Kuznitz see Kozieniec

Lachwa. *Rishonim la-mered; Lachwa* [First ghetto revolt, Lachwa*]. Eds.: H.A. Malachi et al. Jerusalem, The Encyclopaedia of the Jewish Diaspora, 1957. 500 columns, ports., facsims. (H,Y)
BRAN: +DS135.R93 L24   HAR: Heb 16638.548

Lakatsh see Lokachi

Lancut. *Lancut; hayeha ve-hurbana shel kehila yehudit* [Lancut; the life and destruction of a Jewish community*]. Eds.: M. Waltzer, N. Kudish. Tel Aviv, Associations of Former Residents of Lancut in Israel and USA, 1963. 465, lix p., ports., facsims.
BRAN: +DS135.P62 L34

Lanovits see Lanowce

Lanowce. *Lanovits; sefer zikaron le-kedoshei Lanovits she-nispu be-shoat ha-natsim* [Lanowce; memorial book of the martyrs of Lanowce who perished during the Holocaust]. Ed.: H. Rabin. Tel Aviv, Association of Former Residents of Lanowce, 1970. 440 p., ports. (H,Y)
BRAN: DS135.R93 L245   HAR Heb 16678.493
BPL: DS135.R93 L24

Lapichi see under Bobruisk

Lask. *Lask; sefer zikaron* [Memorial book of Lask]. Ed.: Z. Tzurnamal. Tel Aviv, Assoc. of Former Residents of Lask in Israel, 1968. 737, 164 p., ports., facsims. (H,Y,E)
BRAN: DS135.P62 L37   HAR: Heb 16718.477
BPL: DS135.P62 L3

Lask see also under Pabianice

Leczyca. *Sefer Linshits* [Memorial book of Leczyca]. Ed.: Yitzhak Frankel. Tel Aviv, Former Residents of Leczyca in Israel, 1953. 223 p., ports. (H)
HEBC: XZD Leczyc   BRAN: DS135.P62 L43
HAR: Heb 16718.515

Lemberg see Lwow

Lenczyc see Leczyca

Leonpol see under Druja (*Sefer Druja*)

Lesko. *Sefer yizkor; mukdash le-yehudei ha-ayarot she-nispu ba-shoa be-shanim 1939-44, Linsk, Istrik... ve-ha-seviva* [Memorial book; dedicated to the Jews of Linsk, Istrik... and vicinity who perished in the Holocaust in the eyars 1939-44]. Eds.: N. Mark, Sh. Friedlander. [Tel Aviv], Book Committee of the "Libai" Organization, [1965]. 516 p., ports. (H,Y)
BRAN: DS135.P62 L47   HAR: Heb 16709.579

Levertev see Lubartow

Lezajsk. *Lizhensk; sefer zikaron le-kedoshei Lizhensk she-nispu be-shoat na-natsim* [Memorial book of the martyrs of Lezajsk who perished in the Holocaust]. Ed.: H. Rabin. Tel Aviv, Former Residents of Lezajsk in Israel, [1970]. 495 p., ports., facsims. (H,Y)
BRAN: DS135.P62 L49   HAR: Heb 16718.514
BPL: DS135.P62 L49

Libovne see Luboml

Lida. *Sefer Lida* [The book of Lida*]. Eds.: A. Manor et al. Tel Aviv, Former Residents of Lida in Israel and the Relief Committee of the Lida Jews in USA, 1970. 438, xvii p., ports., maps, facsims. (H,Y,E)
BRAN: +DS135.R93 L48   HAR: Heb 16718.490
BPL: DS135.R93 L48

Likeva see Lukow

Lineve see under Pruzana

Linshits see Leczyca

Linsk see Lesko

Lipkany. *Kehilat Lipkany; sefer zikaron* [The community of Lipkany; memorial book]. Tel Aviv, Former Residents of Lipkany in Israel, 1963. 407 p., ports. (H,Y)
BRAN: +DS135.R93 L47   HAR Heb 16838.493

Lipkany. *Lipkan fun amol* [Lipcan of old*]. By Aaron Shuster. Montreal, Author, 1957. 217 p., illus., ports. (Y)
HAR: Y 959.430

Lipniszki. *Sefer zikaron shel kehilat Lipnishok* [Memorial book of the community of Lipniszki]. Ed.: A. Levin. Tel Aviv, Former Residents of Lipniszki in Israel, 1968. 206 p., ports., map (H,Y)
BRAN: DS135.R93 L494   HAR: Heb 16658.565
BPL: DS135.R93 L494

Litevisk (Lutowiska) see under Lesko

Lizhensk see Lezajsk

Lodz. *Kehilat Lodz; ir ve-em be-yisrael* [The community of Lodz; a Jewish mother-city]. [By] Aaron Ze'ev Aescoly. Jerusalem, Ha-Mahlakah le-inyanei ha-no'ar shel ha-Histadrut ha-Tsiyonit [Youth Section of the Zionist Organization], [1947/48]. 238 p. (H)
HAR: Heb 16718.513.6

Lodz. *Lodzer Yisker-bukh* [Lodzer yiskor book*]. New York, United Emergency Relief Committee for the City of Lodz, 1943. Various pagings, ports. (Y)
HEBC: XZD Lodz   BRAN: DS135.P62 L84415

Lodz. *Yiddish Lodz; a yiskor book*. Melbourne, Lodzer Center, 1974. 13, 243 p., illus. (Y,E)
BRAN: +DS135.P62 L64

Lokachi. *Sefer yizkor le-kehilat Lokats' (Polin)* [Lokatch (Poland) Memorial book*]. By Eliezer Verbah. Jerusalem, Shimon Matlovski, 1993. 98, 32 p., illus., ports. (H,Y,E)
HAR: Heb 42956.407   HEBC: XZD Lokatch

Łomża. *Lomzhe; ir oyfkum un untergang* [The rise and fall of Lomza]. Ed.: H. Sabotko. New York, American Committee for the Book of Lomza, 1957. 371 p., ports., facsims. (Y)
HEBC: XZD Lomza 25   HAR: Y 966.470 F

Łomża. *Sefer zikaron le-kehilat Lomza* [Lomza - In memory of the Jewish community*]. Ed.: Yom-Tov Lewinski. Tel Aviv, Former Residents of Lomza in Israel, 1952. 337 p., ports., facsims. (H)
HEBC: XZD Lomza   BRAN: +DS135.P62 L65
HAR: Heb 16718.487 F

Łomża. *Lomza, moments and memories.* New York, United Lomzer Relief Committee, 1946. 27, 63 p. (E, Y)
HEBC: XZD Lomza ...

Lopatyn see under Radziechow

Łosice. *Loshits; lezeykher an umgebrakhte kehile* [Losice; in memory of a Jewish community, exterminated by Nazi murderers*]. Ed.: M. Shener. Tel Aviv, Former Residents of Losice in Israel, 1963. 469 p., ports, facsims. (H,Y)
BRAN: DS135.P62 L68 1963   HAR: Y 965.50

Lowicz. *Lowicz; ir be-Mazovia u-seviva, sefer zikaron* [Lowicz; a town in Mazovia, memorial book*]. Ed.: G. Shaiak. [Tel Aviv], Former Residents of Lowicz in Melbourne and Sydney, Australia, 1966. 395, xxii p., ports., facsims. (H,Y,E)
BRAN: +DS135.P62 L69

Lubartow. *Khurbn Levartov* [The destruction of Lubartow]. Ed.: B. Tshubinski. Paris, Association of Lubartow, 1947. 117 p., ports., facsims. (Y)
BRAN: +DS135.P62 L73   HAR: Y 964.640

Lubcza. *Lubtsh ve-Delatitsh; sefer zikaron* [Lubtch ve-Delatich; in memory of the Jewish community*]. Ed.: K. Hilel. Haifa, Former Residents of Lubtsh-Delatitsh in Israel, 1971. 480 p., ports., map, facsims. (H,Y)
BRAN: DS135.R93 L94   HAR: Heb 16718.483
BPL: DS135.R93 L94

Lubenichi see under Bobruisk

Lublin. *Dos bukh fun Lublin* [The memorial book of Lublin]. Paris, Former Residents of Lublin in Paris, 1952. 685 p., ports., facsims. (Y)
BRAN: +DS135.P62 L74   HAR: Y 10020.123

Lublin. *Lublin* [Lublin volume*]. Eds.: Nachman Blumenthal, M. Korzen. Jerusalem, the Encyclopaedia of the Jewish Diaspora (vol. 5), 1957. 816 columns, ports., map, facsims. (H,Y)
BRAN: +DS135.E8 E55   HEBC: XZD Lublin 6
HAR: Heb 16718.481.10 F

Luboml. *Sefer yizkor le-kehilat Luboml* [Yizkor book of Luboml*]. Ed.: Berl Kagan. Tel Aviv, 1974. 390, 18 p., illus. (H,Y,E)
BRAN: +DS135.R93 L957   HAR: Heb 16638.692
BPL: DS135.R93 L957

Lubraniec see under Wloclawek

Luck. *Sefer Lutsk* [Memorial book of Lutsk]. Ed.: N. Sharon. Tel Aviv, Former Residents of Lutsk in Israel, 1961. 608 p., ports., facsims. (H,Y)
BRAN: +DS135.R93 L85   HAR: Heb 16638.545

Ludmir see under Wlodzimierz

Ludwipol. *Sefer zikaron le-kehilat Ludwipol* [Ludvipol-Wolyn; in memory of the Jewish community*]. Ed.: N. Ayalon. Tel Aviv, Ludvipol Relief Society in Israel, 1965. 335 p., ports., map, facsims. (H,Y)
BRAN: DS135.R93 A97   HAR: Heb 16638.481 F
BPL: DS135.R93 A97

Lukow. *Sefer Lukow; geheylikt der khorev gevorener kehile* [The book of Lukow; dedicated to a destroyed community]. Ed.: Binem Heller. Tel Aviv, Former Residents of Lukow in Israel and the USA, 1968. 652 p., ports., facsims. (H,Y)
BRAN: DS135.P62 L96   HAR: Y 963.420
BPL: DS135.P62 L96

Luniniec. *Yizkor kehilot Luniniec/Kozhanhorodok* [Memorial book of the communities of Luniniec/Kozhanhorodok]. Eds.: Y. Zeevi (Wilk) et al. Tel Aviv, Assoc. of Former Residents of Luniniec/Kozhanhorodok in Israel, 1952. 268 p., ports. (H,Y)
BRAN: DS135.R93 L8 1952a

Lutowiska see under Lesko

Lutsk see Luck

Lvov see Lwow

Lwow. *Lwow* [Lwow volume*], part I. Ed.: N. M. Gelber. Jerusalem, Encyclopaedia of the Jewish Diaspora (vol. 4), 1956. 772 columns, ports., facsims. (H)
HEBC: XZD Lemberg   HAR: Heb 16718.479 F
BRAN: +DS135.E8 E55

Lwow see also under *Arim ve-imahot be-Yisrael*, volume 1.

Lyngmiany see under Stolin

Lynki see under Stolin

Lyntupy see under Swieciany

Lyskow see under Wolkowysk (*Volkovisker ...*)

Lyszkowice see under Lowicz

Lyuban see under Slutsk

Lyubcha see Lubcza

Mad. *Ha-kehilah ha-yehudit shel Mad, Hungaria.* [The Jewish community of Maad, Hungary*]. Ed.: Arieh Levy. Jerusalem, Mad Commemorative Committee, 1974. 154, 31 p., illus. (H,E,Hu)
BRAN: DS135.H92 M424   HAR: Heb 16751.500
BPL: DS135.H92 M424

Magyarlapos see under Des

Makow-Mazowiecki. *Sefer zikaron le-kehilat Makow-Mazowiecki* [Memorial book of the community of Makow-Mazowiecki]. Ed.: J. Brat. Tel Aviv, Former Residents of Makow-Mazowiecki in Israel, 1969. 505 p., ports., facsims. (H,Y)
BRAN: DS135.P62 M33   HAR: Heb 16718.520
BPL: DS135.P62 M33

Makow Podhalanski see under Nowy Targ

Malecz see under Pruzana

Marculeshti see Markuleshty

Margita. *Sefer yizkor le-kehilat Margareten ve-ha-seviva* [Memorial book of the community of Margareten and the surrounding region]. Ed.: Aharon Kleinmann. Jerusalem, Hayim Frank, 1979. 200, 275 p., (H,Hu)
HAR: WID-LC HEBREW DS 135.H92 M374 x

Marijampole. *Marijampole al gedot ha-nahar Sheshupe (Lita)* [Mariajampole on the river Sheshupe (Lithuania)*]. Ed.: Avraham Tory-Golub. Tel Aviv, Committee of Survivors from Marijampole in Israel, 1983. 2nd edition, 1986. 74, 245 p., illus., map, ports. (H,Y,E)
BRAN: +DS135.L5 M2 1983   HAR: Heb 44300.138

Markuleshty. *Markuleshty; yad le-moshava yehudit be-Bessarabia* [Markuleshty; memorial to a Jewish colony in Bessarabia]. Eds.: Leib Kuperstein, Meir Kotik. Tel Aviv, Markuleshty Society, 1977. 272 p., illus. (H,Y)
BRAN: DS135.R93 M335   HAR: Heb 44300.143
HAR: WID-LC HEBREW HD1516.R8 M37 x

Marosvasarhely. *Korot yehudei Marosvasarhely ve-ha-seviva* [History of the Jews in Marosvasarhely]. [By] Yitzhak Perri (Friedmann). Tel Aviv, Ghetto Fighters House, Ha-Kibbutz ha-Meuhad, 1977. (H)
BPL: DS135.R72 T576

Marvits (Murawica) see under Mlynow

Medenice see under Drohobycz

Melits see Mielec

Meretsh see Merkine

Merkine. *Meretsh; ayara yehudit be-Lita* [Meretch, a Jewish City in Lithuania]. Ed.: Uri Shefer. Tel Aviv, [Society of Meretsh Immigrants in Israel], 1988. 195 p., illus., map, ports. (H)
HEBC: XWh   HAR: Heb 44300.180
(Also see landsmanshaft archival material at AJHS, [I-217]).

Meytshet see Molczadz

Mezhirechye see Miedzyrzec-Wolyn

Mezrtish see Miedzyrzec

Miava see under Postyen

Michalovce see Nagymihaly

Michow. *Muchow (Lubelski); sefer zikaron le-kedoshei Michow she-nispu be-shoat ha-natsim ba-shanim 1939-1942* [Memorial book to the amrtyrs of Michow who perished in the Holocaust...]. Ed.: Hayim Rabin. [Israel], Former Residents of Michow, 1987. 343 p., illus., map, ports. (H,Y)
HAR: Heb 44300.205

Miechow. *Sefer yizkor Miechow, Charsznica, Ksiaz* [Miechow memorial book, Charshnitza and Kshoynge*]. Eds.: N. Blumenthal, A. Ben-Azar (Broshy). Tel Aviv, Former Residents of Miechov, Charshnitza and Kshoynzh, 1971. 314, [4] p., ports., facsims. (H,Y)
BRAN: DS135.P62 M53

Miedzyrzec. *Mezritsh; zamlbukh* [The Mezritsh volume]. Ed.: Y. Horn. Buenos Aires, Assoc. of Former Residents of Mezritsh in Argentina, 1952. 635 p., ports., facsims. (Y)
BRAN: DS135.P62 M47   HAR: YA 3274.58

Miedzyrzec. *Sefer Mezritsh; lezeykher di kdoyshim fun undzer shtot* [Mezritsh book, in memory of the martyrs of our town]. Eds.: Binem Heller, Yitzhak Ronkin. Israel, Mezritsh Societies in Israel and the Diaspora, 1978. 821 p., illus. (H,Y)
HAR: Heb 44300.164

Miedzyrzec. *Di yidn-shtot Mezritsh; fun ir breyshis biz erev der velt-milkhome* [Historia de Mezritch (Mezritch Podlasie); su población judía*]. [By] Meir Edelboim. Buenos Aires, Sociedad de Residentes de Mezritch en la Argentina, 1957. 424 p., facsims. (Y)
HAR: YA 4860.47

Miedzyrzec-Wolyn. *Mezeritsh gadol be-vinyana u-be-hurbana* [Mezhiritch-Wolyn: in memory of the Jewish community*]. Ed.: Benzion H. Ayalon-Baranick. Tel Aviv, Former Residents of Mezhiritch, 1955. 442 columns, ports., facsims. (H,Y)
HEBC: XZD Mezhiritch 4

Miedzyrzec-Wolyn. *Pinkas ha-kehila Mezhirits* [Memorial book of Mezhirits]. Ed.: Natan Livneh. Tel Aviv, Committee of Former Residents of Mezhirits in Israel, 1973. 71 p., illus. (H,Y)
HAR: Heb 16718.541   BPL: DS135.R93 M425

Mielec. *Melitser yidn* [Mielec Jews]. [By] Shlomo Klagsbrun. Tel Aviv, Nay-Lebn, 1979. 288 p., illus. (Y)
HAR: WID-LC YIDDISh DS135.P62 M434 x

Mielnica see under Kowel (*Pinkes Kowel*)

Mikepercs see under Debrecen

Mikolajow see under Radziechow

Mikulince. *Mikulince; sefer yizkor* [Mikulince yizkor book*]. Ed.: Haim Preshel. [Israel], The Organisation of Mikulincean Survivors in Israel and in the United States of America, 1985. 356, 266 p., illus., ports. (H,E)
BRAN: DS135.P62 M535 1985   HAR: Heb 44300.199

Mikulov (Nikolsburg) see under *Arim ve-imahot be-Yisrael*, volume 4.

Milosna see under Rembertow

Minkovtsy see under Kamenets-Podolskiy

Minsk. *Minsk ir va-em* [Minsk; Jewish mother city: a memorial anthology*]. Ed.: Shlomo Even-Shushan. Jerusalem, Association of Olim from Minsk and its Surroundings in Israel; Ghetto Fighters' House; Kiryat Sefer, 1975-1985. 2 vols., illus., ports. (H)
HEBC: XZD Minsk   BRAN: DS135.R93 M555
HAR: Heb 16648.607   BPL: DS135.R93 M555

Minsk-Mazowiecki. *Sefer Minsk-Mazowiecki* [Minsk-Mazowiecki memorial book*]. Ed.: Ephraim Shedletzky. Jerusalem, Minsk-Mazowiecki Societies inIsrael and Abroad, 1977. 6, 633 p., illus. (H,Y,E)
BRAN: DS135.P62 M537   BPL: DS135.P62 M567 x
HAR: WID-LC HEBREW DS135.P62 M567 x

Miory see under Druja (*Sefer Druja*)

Mir. *Sefer Mir* [Memorial book of Mir]. Ed.: Nachman Blumenthal. Jerusalem, The Encyclopaedia of the Jewish Diaspora, 1962. 768, 62 columns, ports. (H,Y,E)
HAR: Heb 16658.559   BRAN: +DS135.R93 M6
HEBC: XZD Mir   BPL: DS135.R93 M6

Mizocz. *Mizocz; sefer zikaron* [Memorial book of Mizocz]. Ed.: A. Ben-Oni. Tel Aviv, Former Residents of Mizocz in Israel, 1961. 293, [24] p., ports., facsims. (H)
HAR: Heb 16678.555   BRAN: DS135.R93 M62

Mlawa. *Mlawa ha-yehudit; koroteha, hitpathuta, kilayona - Di yidishe Mlave; geshikhte, oyfshtand, umkum* [Jewish Mlawa; its history development, destruction*]. Ed.: David Shtokfish. [Israel], Mlawa Societies in Israel and in the Diaspora, 1984. 2 vols. (536, 584 p.), illus., maps, ports. (H,Y,E)
HEBC: XZD Mlawa   HAR: Heb 44300.123

Mlawa. *Pinkes Mlave* [Memorial book of Mlawa]. New York, World Assoc. of Former Residents of Mlawa, 1950. 483, 63 p., ports. (Y)
BRAN: DS135.P62 M6

Mlynow. *Sefer Mlynow-Marvits* [Mlynov-Muravica memorial book*]. Ed.: J. Sigelman. Haifa, Former Residents of Mlynov-Muravica in Israel, 1970. 511 p., ports. (Y,H)
BRAN: DS135.R93 M637   HAR: Heb 16678.569
BPL: DS135.R93 M637

Modrzyc see Deblin

Mogielnica. *Sefer yizkor Mogielnica-Bledow* [Memorial book of Mogielnica-Bledow]. Ed.: Yisrael Zonder. Tel Aviv, Mogielnica and Bledow Society, 1972. 808 p., illus., map, ports. (H,Y)
BRAN: +DS135.P62 M63 1972   HAR: Heb 16718.581 F

Molczadz. *Sefer-zikaron le-kehilat Meytshet* [Memorial book of the community of Meytshet]. Ed.: Benzion H. Ayalon. Tel Aviv, Meytshet Societies in Israel and Abroad, 1973. 460, 12 p., illus. (H,Y)
BRAN: DS135.R93 M647   HAR: Heb 16658.555
BPL: DS135.R93 M647

Mosty see under Piaski

Mosty-Wielkie. *Mosty-Wielkie--Most Rabati, sefer zikaron* [Mosty-Wielkie memorial book*]. Eds.: Moshe Shtarkman, Abraham Ackner, A.L. Binot. Tel Aviv, Mosty Wielkie Societies in Israel and the United States, 1975-1977. 2 vols., illus. (H,Y,E)
BRAN: DS135.R93 V375
HAR: WID-LC HEBREW DS135.R93 U375

Motele see Motol

Mszczonow see under Zyrardow

Mukacevo see Munkacs

Munkacs see under *Arim ve-imahot be-Yisrael*, volume 1.

Murawica see under Mlynow

Myjava (Miava) see under Postyen

Mysleniec see under Wadowicz

Myszyniec see under Ostrołęka

Nadarzyn see under Pruszkow

Nadworna. *Nadworna; sefer edut ve-zikaron* [Nadworna, Stanislav district; memorial and records*]. Ed.: Israel Carmi (Otto Kramer). Tel Aviv, Nadworna Societies in Israel and the United States, 1975. 281, 67 p., illus. (H,Y,E)
BRAN: +DS135.R93 N326

Nadzin (Nadarzyn) see under Pruszkow

Nagylonda see under Des

Nagykallo. *Ha-tsadik me-Kalov ve-kehilato; tsiyun le-nefesh hayeha zts"l ve-le-kehila nihahedet...* [The tsadik of Kalov and his community...]. [By] Tuvia (Laszlo) Szilágyi-Windt; translated from Hungarian and edited: Yehuda Edelshtein. Haifa, [1970?]0. 208 p., facsims., illus., ports. (H)
HAR: Heb 16758.782   BPL: BM755 T23 S916

Nagymagyar see under Dunaszerdahely

Nagymihaly. *Sefer Michalovce ve-ha-seviva* [The book of Michalovce*]. Ed.: Mordechai Ben-Zeev (Mori Farkas). Tel Aviv, Committee of Former Residents of Michalovce in Israel, 1969. 240, 64, 103 p., ports., facsims. (H,E,Hu)
BRAN: DS135.C96 M537   HAR: Heb 16738.557
BPL: DS135.C96 M537

Nagyszollos. *Sefer zikaron le-kehilat Selish ve-ha-seviva* [A memorial to the Jewish community of Sevlus (Nagyszollos) District*]. Ed.: Shmuel haKohen Weingarten. Israel, Selish Society, 1976. 326 p., illus. (H)
HAR: WID-LC HEBREW DS135.H92 S 489 x

Nagyszollos. *Sefer zikaron...* [Memorial book*] - Musaf [Addenda]. Eds.: J.H. Klein, J.M. Hollander. Israel, The Committee of Olei Nagyszollos and Vicinity in Israel, 1981. 94 p., ports. (H,E)
BRAN: DS135.R93 V587 1976 Supl.

Nagytapolcsany see Topolcany

Nagyvarad see Oradea

Naliboki see also under Stolpce

Narajow see under Brzezany

Navaredok see Nowogrodek

Naymark see Nowy Targ

Nemirov see under *Arim ve-imahot be-Yisrael*, volume 2.

Nestilye see Uscilug

Neumarkt see Nowy Targ

Nevel see under Vitebsk (*Sefer Vitebsk*)

Nieswiez. *Sefer Nieswiez*. Ed.: David Shtokfish. Tel Aviv, Nieswiez Societies in Israel and the Diaspora, 1976. 531 p., illus. (H,Y)
BRAN: +DS135.R93 N58   HAR: Heb 44300.198F
HAR: WID-LC HEBREW DS135.R93 N477 xF

Nikolsburg see under *Arim ve-imahot be-Yisrael*, volume 4.

Novograd-Volynskiy. *Zvhil-Novogradvolinsk*. Eds.: Azriel Ori, Mordechai Boneh. Tel Aviv, Association of Former Residents of Zvhil and the Environment, 1962. 354, 232, 16 p., ports. (H,Y,E)
BRAN: DS135.R93 N66   HAR: Heb 16638.403

Novo Minsk see Minsk Mazowiecki

Novyi Vitkov (Wiktow Nowy) see under Radziechow

Novyi Yarichev see Jaryczow Nowy

Nowe Miasto see under Plonsk

Nowogród see under Łomża (*Lomzhe; ir oyfkum ...*)

Nowo-Swieciany see under Swieciany

Nowy Dwor (near Warszawa). *Pinkas Nowy Dwor* [Memorial book of Nowy-Dwor]. Eds.: Aryeh Shamri, Dov First. Tel Aviv, Former Residents of Nowy-Dwor in Israel, USA, Argentina..., 1965. 556, xix p., ports., map, facsims. (H,Y,E)
BRAN: DS135.P62 N6   HAR: Y 969.730

Nowy Dwor. *Ondenk bukh fun Nowy Dwor* [Memorial book of Nowy Dwor]. Los Angeles, Nowy Dwor Relief Committee, [1947]. 60 p., illus., ports. (Y)
HAR: Y 966.330

Nowy Dwor see also under Szczuczyn (*Sefer zikaron...*)

Nowy Sacz. *Sefer Sants* [The book of the Jewish community of Nowy Sanz*]. Ed.: Raphael Mahler. New York, Former Residents of Sants in New York, 1970. 886 p., ports., facsims. (H, Y)
HEBC: XZD Nowy Sacz   HAR: Y 965.760.5
BRAN: DS135.P62 N647   BPL: DS135.P62 N647

Nowy Targ. *Sefer Nowy Targ ve-ha-seviva* [Remembrance book of Nowy Targ and vicinity*]. Ed.: Michael Walzer-Fass. Tel Aviv, Townspeople Association of Nowy Targ and Vicinity, 1979. 301 p., illus. (H,Y,E)
BRAN: DS135.P62 N657 1979

Nowy Zagorz see under Sanok

Odessa see under *Arim ve-imahot be-Yisrael*, volume 2.

Okmieniec see under Braslaw

Okuniew see under Rembertow

Olkeniki. *Ha-ayara be-lehavot; sefer zikaron le-kehilat Olkenik pelekh Vilna* [Olkeniki in flames; a memorial book*]. Ed.: Shlomo Farber. Tel Aviv, Association of Former Residents of Olkeniki and Surroundings, 1962. 287, [4] p., ports. (H,Y)
HAR: Heb 16718.126

Olyka. *Pinkas ha-kehila Olyka; sefer yizkor* [Memorial book of the community of Olyka]. Ed.: Natan Livneh. Tel Aviv, Olyka Society, 1972. 397 p., illus. (H,Y)
BRAN: DS135.R93 O576   HAR: Heb 16678.109
BPL: DS135.R93 O536

Opatow. *Apt (Opatow); sefer zikaron le-ir va-em be-yisrael* [Apt; a town which does not exist any more*]. Ed.: Z. Yasheev. Tel Aviv, The Apt Organization in Israel, USA, Canada and Brzail, 1966. 441, [3], 20 p., ports. (H,Y,E)
BRAN: +DS135.P62 Q63   HAR: Heb 16718.143F
BPL: DS135.P62 O63

Opatow see also under Ostrowiec (*Ostrovtse; geheylikt...*)

Opocznow. *Sefer Opotshnah; yad vashem le-kehilah she-harvah* [The book of Opoczno]. Ed.: Yitshak Alfasi. Tel Aviv, Association of Emigrants from Opoczno and Vicinity, 1989. 394, 21 p., illus., ports., diagrams (H,Y,E)
BRAN: DS135.P62 Q65 1989   HAR: Heb 44300.171

Opsa see under Braslaw

Oradea. *A tegnap városa; a nagyváradi zsidóság emlékkönyve* [Ir ve-etmol; sefer ziakron le-yehudei Grosswardein* = A city and yesterday; memorial book to the Jews of Grosswardein]. Eds: Schön Dezsö et al. Tel Aviv, 1981. 446 p., illus., maps, ports. (Hu)

Oradea. *Sefer zikaron le-yahadut Grosswardein-Oradea-Nagyvarad ve-ha-seviva, mishnat yisoda ve-ad-hurbana* [Memorial book to the Jews of Grosswardein-Oradea-Nagyvarad and vecinity...]. Ed.: Zvi Grossman. Tel Aviv, Grosswardein Society in Israel, 1984. 451, 67 p., illus., maps, ports. (H)
HAR: Heb 44300.130

Orgeyev. *Orheyev be-vinyana u-be-hurbana* [Orheyev alive and destroyed]. Eds.: Yitzhak Spivak et al. Tel Aviv, Committee of Former Residents of Orheyev, 1959. 216 p., ports. (H,Y)
BRAN: +DS135.R72 O7   HAR: Heb 16698.113

Orhei see Orgeyev

Orlowa see under Zoludek

Oshmena see Oszmiana

Oshpitsin see Oswiecim

Osiek see under Staszow

Osipovici see under Bobruisk

Ostra see Ostrog

Ostrog. [By] Judah Loeb Levin. Jerusalem-Tel Aviv, Yad Yahadut Polin, 1966. 111 p., map, ports., illus. (H)
BPL: DS135.R93 O74

Ostrog. *Pinkas Ostrog; sefer zikaron...* [Ostrog-Wolyn; in memory of the Jewish community*]. Ed.: H. Ayalon-Baranick. Tel Aviv, Association of Former Residents of Ostrog, 1960. 640 columns, ports., maps, facsims. (H,Y)
HAR: Heb 16678.129

Ostrog. *Sefer Ostrag (Vohlin); matsevet zikaron le-kehila kedosha* [Ostrog book; a memorial to the Ostrog holy community*]. Ed.: Yitzhak Alperowitz; Chief Coordinator: Chaim Finkel. Tel Aviv, The Ostrog Society in Israel, 1987. 402, 34 p., illus., ports., map (H,Y,E,P)
HEBC: XZD Ostrog   HAR: Heb 44300.157

Ostrog. *Ven dos lebn hot geblit* [When life was blooming]. [By] M. Grines. Buenos Aires, 1954. 471 p., ports. (Y)
HAR: Y 10200.218

Ostrog see also under *Arim ve-imahot be-Yisrael*, volume 1.

Ostrołęka. *Sefer kehilat Ostrolenka* [Book of kehilat Ostrolenka*]. Ed.: Y. Ivri. Tel Aviv, Association of Former Residents of Ostrolenka, 1963. 579 p., ports. (H,Y)
BRAN: +DS135.P62 Q75   HAR: Heb 16718.129

Ostrowiec. *Ostrovtse; geheylikt dem ondenk... fun Ostovtse, Apt...* [Ostrovtse; dedicated to the memoriy of Ostrovtse, Apt...]. Buenos Aires, Former Residents of Ostrovtse... in Argentina, 1949. 217, [3] p., ports. (Y)
BRAN: DS135.P62 O8 1949   HAR: Y 961.430

Ostrowiec. *Ostrovtse; a denkmol oyf di khurves fun a farnikhtete yidishe kehile* [Ostrowiec; a monument on the ruins of an annihilated Jewish community*]. Eds.: Gershon Silberberg, M.S. Geshuri. Tel Aviv, Society of Ostrovster Jews in Israel, with the cooperation of the Ostrovtser Societies in New York and Toronto, [197-/8-]. 560, [106], 134 p., illus. maps, ports. (Y,H,E)
HAR: Heb 16718.127   AJHS: DS135.P62 O827
BPL: DS135.P62 O827

Ostrow-Lubelski. *Sefer-yizkor Ostrow-Lubelski - Yisker-bukh Ostrow-Lubelski* [Memorial-book Ostrow-Lubelski*]. Ed.: David Shtokfish. Israel, Association of Former Residents of Ostrow-Lubelski in Israel, 1987. 422 p., illus., ports. (H,Y,E)
HAR: Heb 44300.178

Ostrów-Mazowiecka. *Ostrow Mazowiecka*. [By] Judah Loeb Levin. Jerusalem-Tel Aviv, Yad Yahadut Polin, 1966. 164 p., ports., illus. (H)
HAR: Heb 16718.173.5   BPL: DS135.P62 O92

Ostrów-Mazowiecka. *Sefer ha-zikaron le-kehilat Ostrov-Mazovyetsk* [Memorial book of the community of Ostrow-Mazowiecka]. Ed.: Aryeh Margalit. Tel Aviv, Association of Former Residents of Ostrow-Mazwieck, 1960. 653 p., ports. (H,Y)
HAR: Heb 16718.173

Ostryna see under Szczuczyn (*Sefer zikaron...*)

Oszmiana. *Sefer zikaron le-kehilat Oshmana* [Oshmana memorial book*]. Ed.: M. Gelbart. Tel Aviv, Oshmaner Organization in Israel and the Oshmaner Osciety in the USA, 1969. 659, 109 p., ports. (H,Y,E)
BRAN: +DS135.R93 Q67   HAR: Heb 16718.147
BPL: DS135.R93 O67

Otwock. *Khurbn Otvotsk, Falenits, Kartshev* [The destruction of Otvosk, Falenits, Kartshev]. [By] B. Orenstein. [Bamberg], Former Residents of Otvotsk, Falenits and Kartshev in the American Zone in Germany, 1948. 87 p., ports. (Y)
HAR: Y 961.550.0

Otwock. *Yisker-bukh; Otvotsk-Kartshev* [Memorial book of Otvotsk and Kartshev*]. Ed.: Shimon Kanc. Tel Aviv, Former Residents of Otvosk-Kartshev, 1968. 1086 columns, ports. (H,Y)
BRAN: +DS135.P62 O86   HAR: Heb 16718.107
BPL: DS135.P62 O86

Ozarow see under Ostrowiec

Ozieran see Jezierzany

Ozorkow. *Ozorkow*. [By] Judah Loeb Levin. Jerusalem, Yad Yahadut Polin, 1966. 128 p., illus. (H)
BRAN: DS135.P62 Q9   HAR: Heb 16718.125.50
BPL: DS135.P62 O9

Pabianice. *Sefer Pabianice* [Memorial book of Pabianice]. Ed.: A. Wolf Yassni. Tel Aviv, Former Residents of Pabianice in Israel, 1956. 419 p., ports., facsims. (H,Y)
BRAN: DS135.P62 P32   HAR: Y 10020.137

Paks. *Mazkeret Paks* [Paks memorial book]. Ed.: D. Sofer. Jerusalem, 1962-[1972/73]. 3 vols., ports., facsims. (H)
BRAN: DS135.H92 P3   HAR: Heb 16758.731 (Vols 1&2)
BPL: DS135.H93 P3

Pápa. *Sefer zikaron Papa; le-zekher kedoshei ha-kehila ve-yishuvei ha-seviva* [Memorial book of Papa...]. [By] Jehuda-Gyula Lang. Israel, Papa Memorial Committee, [1970-]. 28 p., illus., ports. (H,Hu)
HAR: Heb 16758.730   BPL: DS135.H92 P356

Parafianowo see under Dokszyce

Parysów. *Sefer Parisov* [Parysow; a memorial to the Jewish community of Parysow, Poland*]. Ed.: Yechiel Granatstein. Tel Aviv, Former Residents of Parysow in Israel, 1971. 625 p., ports. (H,Y)
BRAN: DS135.P62 P376   HAR: Heb 16718.710
BPL: DS135.P62 P376

Perehinsko see under Rozniatow

Peroshkov see Pruszkow

Peski see Piaski

Petrikov see Piotrkow Trybunalski

Piaski. *Pyesk ve-Most; sefer yizkor* [Piesk and Most, a memorial book*]. Tel Aviv, Piesk and Most Societies in Israel and the Diaspora, 1975. 657, 17, 52 p., illus. (H,Y,E)
BRAN: +DS135.R93 P398   HAR: Heb 16638.745
BPL: DS135.R93 P398

Piatnica see under Lomza (*Lomzhe, ir oyfkum...*)

Piesk see Piaski

Piestany see Postyen

Pilev see Pulawy

Pinczow. *Sefer zikaron le-kehilat Pintshev; in Pintshev togt shoyn nisht* [A book of memory of the Jewish community of Pinczow, Poland*]. Ed.: Mordechai Shener. Tel Aviv, Former Residents of Pinczow in Israel and in the Diaspora, 1970. 480 p., ports. (H,Y)
BRAN: DS135.P62 P547   HAR: Heb 16718.737
AJHS: DS135.P62 P547   BPL: DS135.P62 P547

Pinsk. *Pinsk sefer edut ve-zikaron le-kehilat Pinsk-Karlin* [Pinsk*]. Ed.: Nachman Tamir (Mirski). Tel Aviv, Former Residents of Pinsk-Karlin in Israel, 1966-1977. 3 vols., ports., facsims. (H,Y)
BRAN: +DS135.R93 P54   HAR: Heb 16638.737
HEBC: XZD Pinsk   BPL: DS135.R93 P54

Pinsk. *Toyznt yor Pinsk; geshikhte fun der shtot, der yidisher yishev, institutsyes, sotsyale bavegungen, perzenlekh-keytn, gezelshaftlekhe tuer, Pinsk iber der velt* [A thousand years of Pinsk; history of the city, its Jewish community, institutions, social movements, personalitites, community leaders, Pinsk around the world]. Ed.: Ben-Zion Hoffman. New York, Pinsker Branch 210, Workmen's Circle, 1941. 15, 500 p., illus (Y)
BRAN: +DS135.R93 P5   HEBC: XZD Pinsk

Piotrków Trybunalski. *Piotrkow Trybunalski ve-ha-seviva* [Piotrkow Trybunalski and vicinity*]. Eds.: Yaakov Melz, N. (Lavy) Lau. Tel Aviv, Former Residents of Piotrkow Tryb. in Israel, [1965]. 1192 columns, lxiv p., ports., facsims. (H,Y,E)
BRAN: +DS135.P62 P5   HEBC: XZD Piotrkow
BPL: DS135.P62 P5

Pitshayev see Poczajow

Plantsh (Polaniec) see under Staszow

Plawno see under Radomsko

Plintsk see Płońsk

Płock. *Plotsk; bletekh geshikhte fun idishn lebn in der alter heym* [Plock; páginas de historia de la via judía de Allende el Mar*]. Ed.: Yosef Horn. Buenos Aires, Sociedad de Residentes de Plock en la Argentina, 1945. 255 p., illus., ports. (Y)
HAR: Y 10020.207

Płock. *Plotsk; toldot kehila atikat yomin be-Polin* [Plotzk; a history of an ancient Jewish community in Poland*]. Ed.: Eliyahu Eisenberg. Tel Aviv, World Committee for the Plotzk Memorial Book, 1967. 684, 96 p., ports., map, facsims. (H,Y,E)
BRAN: +DS135.P62 P566   HAR: Heb 16718.745 F
BPL: DS135.P62 P566

Płock. *Yidn in Plotsk* [Jews in Plotzk*]. [By] S. Greenspan. New York, 1960. 325 p., ports. (Y)
HAR: Y 962.810   BPL: DS135.P62 P56

Płońsk. *Sefer Plonsk ve-ha-seviva* [Memorial book of Plonsk and vicinity]. Ed.: Shlomo Zemah. Tel Aviv, Former Residents of Plonsk in Israel, 1963. 775 p., ports., map, facsims. (H,Y)
BRAN: +DS135.P62 P616   HAR: Heb 44300.261
AJHS: DS135.P62 P617

Plotsk see Płock

Plusy see under Braslaw

Poczajow. *Pishayever yisker-bukh* [Memorial book dedicated to the Jews of Pitchayev-Wohlyn executed by the Germans*]. Ed.: H. Gelernt. Philadelphia, The Pitchayever Wohliner Aid Society, 1960. 311 p., ports. (Y)
HAR: Y 962.731

Poczajow see also under Krzemieniec

Podbrodzie see under Swieciany

Podgaitsy see Podhajce

Podhajce. *Sefer Podhajce.* Ed.: Meir Simon Geshuri. Tel Aviv, Podhajce Society, 1972. 295, 17 p., illus. (H,Y,E)
HAR: Heb 16678.699   BPL: DS135.R93 P59

Pogost see under Slutsk

Pohost (Pogost) see under Slutsk

Pokshivnitsa see Koprzywnica

Polaniec see under Staszow

Polav see Pulawy

Poligon see under Swieciany

Polonnoye see under Novograd-Volynskiy

Porcsalma see under Csenger

Porisov see Parysow

Porozow see under Wolkowysk (*Volkovisker...*)

Postawy see under Glebokie

Postyen. *Gedenkbuch der Gemeinden Piestany und Umgebung.* [By] Sh. Grunwald. Jerusalem, 1969. 111, [10] p., ports. (G)
BRAN: DS135.C95 G78   BPL: DS135.C95 G78

Pozsony (Pressburg) see under *Arim ve-imahot be-Yisrael*, volume 7.

Praga. *Sefer Praga; mukdash le-zekher kedoshei irenu* [Praga book; dedicated to the memory of the martyrs of our town]. Ed.: Gabriel Weisman. Tel Aviv, Praga Society, 1974. 563 p., illus. (H,Y)
BRAN: DS135.P62 W339   HEBC: XZD Praga 89
HAR: Y 966.675   BPL: DS135.P62 W338

Premisle see Przemysl

Pressburg (Pozsony) see under *Arim ve-imahot be-Yisrael*, volume 7.

Proshnits see Przasnysz

Proskorov. *Khurbn Proskurov; tsum ondenken fun di heylige neshomes vos zaynen umgekumen in der shreklikher shkhite, vos iz ongefirt gevoren durkh de haydamakes* [The destruction of Proskurov; in memory of the sacred souls who perished during the terrible slaughter of the Haidamaks]. New York, 1924. 111 p., illus. (Y,H)
HAR: Y 954.375

Pruszków. *Sefer Pruszkow, Nadzin ve-ha-seviva* [Memorial book of Pruszkow, Nadzin and vicinity]. Ed.: D. Brodsky. Tel Aviv, Former Residents of Pruszkow in Israel, 1967. 334 p., ports., facsims. (H,Y)
BRAN: DS135.P62 P7   HAR: Heb 16718.753
BPL: DS135.P62 P7

Pruzana. *Pinkas me-hamesh kehilot harevot...* [Memorial book of five destroyed communities...]. Ed.: Mordechai Wolf Bernstein. Buenos Aires, Former Residents of Pruzana..., 1958. 972 p., ports., facsims. (Y)
BRAN: +DS135.R93 W46   HAR: Y 962.92.100

Pruzana. *Pinkas Pruzhany ve-ha-seviva; edut ve-zikaron le-kehilat she-hushmedu ba-shoa* [Pinkas Pruz'any and its vicinity (Bereze, Malch, Shershev, Seltz and Lineve); chronicle of six communities perished in the Holocaust*]. Ed.: Joseph Friedlander. Tel Aviv, United Pruziner and Vicinity Relief Committee in New York and in Philadelphia and the Pruz'ana Landshaft Association in Israel, 1983. 542, 169 p., illus., maps, ports. (H,E)
HEBC: XZC ...   BRAN: DS135.R93 P786 1983
HAR: Heb 44300.113

Przasnysz. *Sefer zikaron kehilat Proshnits* [Memorial book to the community of Proshnitz*]. Ed.: Shlomo Bachrach. Tel Aviv, Proshnitz Society, 1974. 273 p., illus. (H,Y,E)
BRAN:DS135.P62 P73   HAR: Heb 16718.752
BPL: DS135.P62 P73

Przeclaw see under Radomysl Wielki

Przedborz. *Przedborz--33 shanim le-hurbana* [Przedborz memorial book*]. Ed.: Shlomo Kanc. Tel Aviv, Przedborz Societies in Israel and America, 1977. 84, 548 p., illus. (H,Y,E)
BRAN: DS135.P62 P7358
HAR: WID-LC HEBREW DS135.P62 P796 x

Przedborz see also under Radomsko

Przedecz. *Sefer yizkor le-kedoshei ir Pshaytsh korbanot ha-shoa* [Memorial book to the Holocaust victims of the city of Pshaytsh]. Eds.: Moshe Bilavsky et al. Tel Aviv, Przedecz Societies in Israel and the Diaspora, 1974. 400 p., illus. (H,Y)
BRAN: DS135.P62 P7377   HAR: Heb 16718.762
BPL: DS135.P62 P7377

Przemysl. *Sefer Przemysl* [Przemysl memorial book*]. Ed.: Arie Menczer. Tel Aviv, Former Residents of Przemysl in Israel, 1964. 522 p., ports., facsims. (H,Y)
BRAN: DS135.P6 M45   HAR: Heb 16718.761
HEBC: XZD Przemysl

Przytyk. *Sefer Przytyk.* Ed.: David Shtokfish. Tel Aviv, Przytyk Societies in Israel, France, and the USA, 1973. 7, 461 p., illus. (H,Y)
BRAN: DS135.P62 P787   HARL Heb 16718.760
BPL: DS135.P62 P787

Pshaytsh see Przedecz

Pshedbozh see Przedborz

Pshemishl see Przemysl

Pshetslav (Przeclaw) see under Radomysl Wielki

Pshitik see Przytyk

Pulawy. *Yisker-bukh Pulawy* [In memoriam--the city of Pulawy*]. Ed.: M.W. Bernstein. New York, Pulawer Yiskor Book Committee, 1964. 494 p., ports., map., facsims. (Y)
BRAN: DS135.P62 P8   HAR: Y 964.730

Pultusk. *Pultusk; sefer zikaron* [Pultusk memorial book]. Ed.: Yitzhak Ivri. Tel Aviv, Pultusk Society, 1971. 683 p., illus. (H,Y)
BRAN: +DS135.P62 P88   HAR: Y 966.785
BPL: DS135.P62 P86

Punsk see under Suwałki

Raab see Gyor

Rabka see under Nowy Targ

Rachev see under Novograd-Volynskiy

Raciąż. *Galed le-kehilat Raciaz* [Memorial book of the community of Racionz*]. Ed.: E. Tsoref. Tel Aviv, Former Residents of Raciaz, 1965. 446, 47 p., ports., facsims. (H,Y,E)
BRAN: DS135.P62 R27   HAR: Heb 16718.839
BPL: DS135.P62 R27

Raczki see under Suwałki

Radikhov see Radziechow

Radom. *Dos yidishe Radom in khurves; ondenkbukh* [The havoc of Jewish Radom*]. Stuttgart, The Committee of Radom Jews in Stuttgart, 1948. 1 vol., illus. (Y)
BRAN: DS135.P62 R31 1948

Radom. *Radom* [Radom, a memorial to the Jewish community of Radom, Poland*]. Ed.: Abram Shmuel Stein. Tel Aviv, Former Residents of Radom in Israel and in the Diaspora, 1961. 346, [20] p., ports., facsims. (H)
BRAN: +DS135.P62 R321   HAR: Heb 16718.870F

Radom. *Sefer Radom* [The book of Radom; the story of a Jewish community in Poland destroyed by the Nazis*]. Ed.: Yitzhak Perlow; [English section]: Alfred Lipson. Tel Aviv, Former Residents of Radom in Israel and the USA, 1961. 451, [23], lxxviii, 120 p., illus., ports. (Y,E)
BRAN: +DS135.P62 R32   HEBC:
HAR: Y 967.510F

Radomsko. *Sefer yizkor le-kehilat Radomsk ve-ha-seviva* [Memorial book of the community of Radomsk and vicinity]. Ed.: L. Losh. Tel Aviv, Former Residents of Radomsk..., 1967. 603 p., ports., music, facsims. (H,Y)
BRAN: +DS135.P62 R323   HAR: Heb 16718.872 F
BPL: DS135.P62 R323

Radomyśl Wielki. *Radomysl Rabati ve-ha-seviva; sefer yizkor* [Radomysl Wielki and neighbourhood; memorial book*]. Eds.: H. Harshoshanim et al. Tel Aviv, Former Residents of Radomysl and Surroundings in Israel, 1965. 1065, liii p., ports., map, facsims. (H,Y,E)
BRAN: +DS135.P62 R3267 XX (1971)   HAR: Heb 16678.831
BPL: DS135.P62 R3267 (1971 ed.)

Radoszkowice. *Radoshkovits; sefer zikaron* [Rodashkowitz; a memorial to the Jewish community*]. Eds.: Mordechai Robinson et al. Tel Aviv, Former Residents of Radoshkowitz in Israel, 1953. 222 p., ports. (H)
HEBC: XZD Radoshkowitz   BRAN: DS135.R93 R3
HAR: Heb 16638.870

Radzanow see under Szransk

Radziechow. *Sefer zikaron le-kehilot Radikhov, Lopatyn, Witkow Nowy, Cholojow, Toporow, Stanislawcyzk, Stremiltsh, Shtruvits, ve-ha-kefarim Ubin, Barylow, Wolica-Wygoda, Skrilow, Zawidcze, Mikolajow, Dmytrow, Sienkow, ve-od* [Memorial book of Radikhov, Lopatyn, Witkow Nowy, Cholojow, Toporow, Stanislawcyzk, Stremiltsh, Shtruvits, and the villages Ubin, Barylow, Wolica-Wygoda, Skrilow, Zawidcze, Mikolajow, Dmytrow, Sienkow, etc.]. Ed.: Getsel Kressel. Tel Aviv, Society of Radikhov, Lopatyn and Vicinity, 1976. 656 p., illus. (H,Y)
HEBC: XZC ...   BRAN: DS135.R93 R287
HAR: WID-LC HEBREW DS135.R93 U4225 x
BPL: DS135.R93 U4225 x

Radzin. *Sefer Radzin* [The book of Radzin]. Ed.: I. Siegelman. Tel Aviv, Council of Former Residents of Radzin (Podolsky) in Israel, 1957. 358 p. (H,Y)
BRAN: DS135.R93 R33

Radziwiłłów. *Radziwillow; sefer zikaron* [A memorial to the Jewish community of Radziwillow, Wolyn*]. Ed.: Y. Adini. Tel Aviv, The Radziwillow Organization in Israel, 1966. 438, [15] p., ports., map, facsims. (H,Y)
BRAN: DS135.R93 R32   HAR: Heb 16638.865
BPL: DS135.R93 R32

Radzymin. *Sefer zikaron le-kehilat Radzymin* [Le livre du souvenir de la communité juive de Radzymin*]. Ed.: Gerson Hel. Tel Aviv, The Encyclopaedia of the Jewish Diaspora, 1975. 389 p., illus. (H,Y,F)
BRAN: +DS135.P62 R3287   HAR: Heb 16718.830
BPL: DS135.P62 R3287

Rakhov see Annopol

Rakishok see Rokiskis

Rakospalota. *Toldot kehilat Rakospalota* [History of the Rakospalota community]. [By] Rachel Aharoni. Tel Aviv, 1978. 52, 204 p., illus. (H,Hu)
HAR: WID-LC HEBREW DS135.H92 R342 x

Ratno. *Ratne; sipura shel kehila yehudit she-hushmeda* [Ratne; the story of a Jewish community that was destroyed]. Ed.: Nachman Tamir. Tel Aviv, Ratno Society in Israel, 1983. 331 p., illus., map, ports. (H)
HAR: Heb 44300.122

Ratno. *Yisker-bukh Ratne; dos lebn un umkum fun a yidish shtetl in Volin* [Memorial book of Ratno; the life and destruction of a Jewish town in Wolyn]. Eds.: Y. Botoshansky, Y. Yanasovitsh. Buenos Aires, Former Residents of Ratno in Argentina and the USA, 1954. 806 p., ports., map (Y)
BRAN: DS135.P62 R33   HAR: Y 10200.125

Ratsiyonzh see Raciaz

Rawa Ruska. *Sefer zikaron le-kehilat Rawa Ruska ve-ha-seviva* [Rawa Ruska memorial book*]. Eds.: A.M. Ringel, I.Z. Rubin. Tel Aviv, Rawa Ruska Society, 1973. 468 p., illus. (H,Y,E)
BRAN: +DS135.R93 R377   HAR: Heb 16664.675F
BPL: DS135.R93 R377

Raysha see Rzeszów

Rayvits see Rejowiec

Rembertów. *Sefer zikaron le-kehilat Rembertow, Okuniew, Milosna* [Yizkor book in memory of Rembertov, Okuniev, Milosna*]. Ed.: Shimon Kanc. Tel Aviv, Rembertow, Okuniew and Milosna Societies in Israel, the USA, France, Mexico City, Canada, Chile and Brazil, 1974. 16, 465 p., illus. (H,Y)
BRAN: DS135.P62 R456   HAR: Y 964.723
BPL: DS135.P62 R456

Retteg see under Des

Rimszan (Rymszany) see under Braslaw

Riskeva see Ruscova

Rogatin see Rohatyn

Rohatyn. *Kehilat Rohatyn ve-ha-seviva* [Rohatyn; the history of a Jewish community*]. Ed.: Mordechai Amihai. Tel Aviv, Former Residents of Rohatyn in Israel, 1962. 362, [15], 62 p., ports., facsims. (H,Y,E)
BRAN: DS135.R93 R63   HAR: Heb 16638.875

Rokiskis. *Yisker-bukh fun Rakishok un umgegnt* [Yizkor book of Rakishok and environs*]. Ed.: M. Bakalczuk-Felin. Johannesburg, The Rakishker Landsmanshaft of Johannesburg, 1952. 626 p., ports., facsims. (Y)
BRAN: DS135.L52 R3   HARL Y 945.159

Romanova see under Slutsk

Rotin see Rohatyn

Rovno see Rowne

Rowne. *Rowne; sefer zikaron* [Rowno; a memorial to the Jewish community of Rowno, Wolyn*]. Ed.: A. Avitachi. Tel Aviv, "Yalkut Wolyn"--Former Residents of Rowno in Israel, 1956. 591 p., ports., map, facsims. (H)
BRAN: DS135.P62 R6   HAR: Heb 16678.881

Rozan. *Sefer zikaron le-kehilat Rozan (al ha-Narew)* [Rozhan memorial book*]. Ed.: Benjamin Halevy. Tel Aviv, Rozhan Societies in Israel and the USA, 1977. 518, 96 p., illus. (H,Y,E)
BRAN: +DS135.P62 R62
HAR: WIC-LC HEBREW DS135.P62 R697 x

Rozana. *Rozhinoy; sefer zikaron le-kehilat Rozhinoy ve-ha-seviva* [Rozana; a memorial to the Jewish community*]. Ed.: M. Sokolowsky. Tel Aviv, Former Residents of Rozhinoy in Israel, 1957. 232 p., ports. (H,Y)
BRAN: DS135.P62 R73

Rozanka see under Szczuczyn (*Sefer zikaron...*)

Rozhan see Rozan

Rozhinoy see Rozana

Rozprza see under Piotrkow Trybunalski

Rozwadów. *Sefer yizkor Rozwadow ve-ha-seviva* [Rozwadow memorial book*]. Ed.: Nachman Blumental. Jerusalem, Former Residents of Rozwadow in Israel..., 1968. 349 p., ports. (H,Y,E)
BRAN: +DS135.P62 R65   HAR: Heb 16718.831
BPL: DS135.P62 R65

Rozyszcze. *Rozyszcze ayarati* [Rozyszcze my old home*]. Ed.: Gershon Zik. Tel Aviv, Rozyszcze Societis in Israel, the United States, Canada, Brazil, and Argentina, 1976. 482, 76 p., illus. (H,Y,E)
BRAN: +DS135.R93 R687

Rubeshov see Hrubieszow

Rubiezewicze. *Sefer Rubizhevitsh, Derevne ve-ha-seviva* [Rubiezewicze and surroundings book*]. Ed.: D. Shtokfish. Tel Aviv, 1968. 422 p., illus. (Y,H)
BRAN: DS135.R93 R77   HAR: Heb 16658.831

Rubiezewicze see also under Stolpce

Rudki. *Rudki; sefer yizkor-le-yehudei Rudki ve-ha-seviva* [Rudki memorial book; of the Jews of Rudki and vicinity*]. Ed.: Joseph Chrust. Israel, Rudki Society, 1978. 374 p., illus. (H,Y,E)
BRAN: DS135.R93 R737 1977

Ruscova. *Sefer le-zikaron kedoshei Ruskova ve-Soblas, mehoz Marmarosh* [Memorial book of the matryrs of Ruskova and Soblas, Marmarosh District]. Ed.: Y. Z. Moskowitz. Tel Aviv, Former Residents of Ruskova and Soblas in Israel and in the Disapora, 1969. 126 p., ports., facsims. (H,Y)
BRAN: DS135.R72 R877   HAR: Heb 16838.833
BPL: DS135.R72 R877

Ryki. *Yisker-bukh tsum fareybikn dem ondenk fun der khorev-gevorner yidisher kehile Ryki* [Ryki; a memorial to the community of Ryki, Poland*]. Ed.: Shimon Kanc. Tel Aviv, Ryki Societies in Israel, Canada, Los Angeles, France, and Brazil, 1973. 611 p., illus. (H,Y)
BRAN: DS135.P62 R778   HAR: Y 964.735

Rypin. *Sefer Rypin* [Rypin; a memorial to the Jewish community of Ripin--Poland*]. Ed.: Shimon Kanc. Tel Aviv, Former Residents of Ripin in Israel and in the Diaspora, 1962. 942, 15 p., ports., facsims. (H,Y,E)
BRAN: +DS135.P62 R83   HAR: Heb 16718.923

Rytwiany see under Staszow

Rzeszów. *Kehilat Raysha; sefer zikaron* [Rzeszow Jews; memorial book*]. Ed.: Moshe Yari-Wold. Tel Aviv, Former Residents of Rzeszow in Israel and the USA, 1967. 620, 142 p., ports., maps, facsims. (H,Y,E)
BRAN: DS135.P62 R95   HAR: Heb 16718.835
BPL: DS135.P62 R95

Saloniki. *Saloniki; ir va-em be-yisrael* [Salonique, ville-mère en Israël*]. Jerusalem and Tel Aviv, Centre de recherches sur le Judaisme de Salonique, Union des Juifs de Grèce, 1967. 358, xviii p., ports., maps, facsims. (H,F)
HEBC: XZD Saloniki ...   HAR: Heb 16918.895.5
BPL: DS135.G72 T55

Saloniki. *Zikhron Saloniki; gedulata ve-hurbana shel Yerushalayim de-Balkan* [Zikhron Saloniki; grandeza i destruyicion de Yeruchalayim del Balkan*]. Ed.: David Recanati. Tel Aviv, Committee for the Publication of the Saloniki Book, [1971/72, 1985-86]. 2 vols., illus., facsims., ports. (H,J)
HEBC: XZD Saloniki ...   HAR: Heb 16918.895.15
BRAN: +DS135.G72 T59   BPL: DS135.G72 T59

Sambor. *Sefer Sambor-Stary Sambor; pirkei edut ve-zikaron le-kehilot Sambor-Stary Sambor mireshitan ve-ad hurbanan* [The book of Sambor and Stari Sambor, the story of the two Jewish communities from their beginnings to their end*]. Ed.: Alexander Manor. Tel Aviv, Sambor/Stary Sambor Society, 1980. xlvi, 323 p., illus. (H,Y,E)
BRAN: +DS135 P62 S147 1980
HAR: WID-LC HEBREW DS135.P62 S357 x

Sammerein (Somorja) see under Dunaszerdahely

Samorin (Somorja) see under Dunaszerdahely

Sanok. *Sefer zikaron le-kehilat Sanok ve-ha-seviva* [Memorial book of Sanok and vicinity]. Ed.: Elazar Sharvit. Jerusalem, Former Residents of Sanok and Vicinity in Israel, 1970. 686 p., ports., facsims. (H,Y)
BRAN: DS135.P62 S16   HAR: Heb 16718.669
BPL: DS135.P62 S16

Sanok see also under Dynow (*Khurbn Dynow*)

Sants see Nowy Sacz

Sarkeystsene (Szarkowszczyna) see under Glebokie

Sarnaki. *Sefer yizkor le-kehilat Sarnaki* [Memorial book of the community of Sarnaki]. Ed.: Dov Shuval. Haifa, Former Residents of Sarnaki in Israel, 1968. 415 p., ports. (H,Y)
BRAN: DS135.P62 S2   HAR: Heb 16718.671
BPL: DS135.P62 S2

Sarny. *Sefer yizkor le-kehilat Sarny* [Memorial book of the community of Sarny]. Ed.: Y. Kariv. Tel Aviv, Former Residents of Sarny and Vicinity in Israel, 1961. 508, 32 p., ports., facsims. (H,Y)
BRAN: DS135.R93 S3   HAR: Heb 16638.691

Satmar see Satu Mare

Satorujhely see under Zemplenmegye

Satu Mare. *Zekhor et Satmar; sefer ha-zikaron shel yehudei Satmar* [Remember Satmar; the memorial book of the Jews of Satmar]. Ed.: Naftali Stern. Bnei Brak, 1984. 160, 240 p., illus., maps, ports. (H,Hu)
HAR: Heb 44300.131F

Schodnica see under Drohobycz

Schutt Szerdahely see Dunaszerdahely

Secureni see Sekiryany

Sedziszow see under Wodzislaw

Sekiryani. *Sekurian (Bessarabia) be-vinyana u-be-hurbana* [Sekiryani, Bessarabia -- alive and destroyed]. Ed.: Z. Igrat. Tel Aviv, [Committee of Former Residents of Sekiryani], 1954. 260 p., ports. (H)
BRAN: DS135.R93 S456

Selib (Wsielub) see under Nowogrodek

Selish see Nagyszollos

Seltz (Sielec) see under Pruzana

Semyatichi see Siemiatycze

Sendishev (Sedziszow) see under Wodzislaw

Serock. *Sefer Serotsk* [The book of Serock]. Ed.: M. Gelbart. Former Residents of Serock in Israel, 1971. 736 p., ports. (H,Y)
BRAN: DS135.P62 S477   BPL: DS135.P62 S477

Sevlus see Nagyszollos

Shchedrin see under Bobruisk

Shebreshin see Szczebrzeszyn

Shedlets see Siedlce

Shelib (Wsielub) see under Nowogrodek

Sherpts see Sierpc

Shershev see under Pruzana

Shidlovtse see Szydlowiec

Shimsk see Szumsk

Shkud see Skuodas

Shpola. *Shpola; masekhet hayei yehudim ba-ayara* [Shpola; a picture of Jewish life in the town]. [By] David Cohen. [Haifa], Association of Former Residents of Shpola (Ukraine) in Israel, 1965. 307 p., ports. (H)
BRAN: DS135.R93 S47   HAR: Heb 16678.921

Shransk see Szransk

Shtruvits (Szczurowice) see under Radziechow

Shumen (Bulgaria) see Shumla

Shumla (Bulgaria). *Yehudei Bulgaria--Kehilat Shumla* [The Jews in Bulgaria--The community of Shumla*]. [By] Benjamin Joseph Arditti. Tel Aviv, Community Council, 1968. 179 p., ports. (H)
HAR: Heb 16849.941

Shumskoye see Szumsk

Siedlce. *Sefer yizkor le-kehilat Shedlets* [Memorial book of the community of Siedlce]. Ed.: A. Wolf Yassni. Buenos Aires, Former Residents of Siedlce in Israel and Argentina, 1956. xvi, 813 p., ports., facsims. (H,Y)
BRAN: DS135.P62 S54   HAR: Y 10200.119

Sielec (Seltz) see under Pruzana

Siemiatycze. *Kehilat Semiatycze* [The community of Semiatich*]. Ed.: Eliezer Tash (Tur-Shalom). Tel Aviv, Assoc. of Former Residents of Semiatich in Israel and the Diaspora, 1965. 449 p., ports., map, facsims. (H,Y,E)
BRAN: DS135.P62 S555   HAR: Heb 16638.688

Sienkow see under Radziechow

Sierpc. *Kehilat Sierpc; sefer zikaron* [The community of Sierpc; memorial book]. Ed.: Efraim Talmi (Wloka). Tel Aviv, Former Residents of Sierpc in Israel and Abroad, 1959. 603 p., ports., map, facsims. (H,Y)
BRAN: DS135.P62 S56   HAR: Heb 16718.927

Siniawka see under Kleck

Sislevitsh see Swislocz

Skala. *Sefer Skala.* Ed.: Max Mermelstein (Weidenfeld). New York-Tel Aviv, Skala Benevolent Society, 1978. 98, 261 p., (H,Y,E)
BRAN: DS135.R93 S5294
HAR: WIC-LC HEBREW DS135.R93 S5527 x

Skalat. *Es shtarbt a shtetl; megiles Skalat* [Skalat destroyed*]. [By] Abraham Weissbrod. Ed.: I. Kaplan. Munich, Central Historical Commission of the Central Committee of Liberated Jews in the U.S. Zone of Germany, 1948. 184 p., maps, ports. (Y)
HEBC: XKCd Skalat   HAR: Y 693.576

Skalat. *Skalat; kovets zikaron le-kehila she-harva ba-shoa* [Skalat; memorial volume of the community which perished in the Holocaust]. Ed.: Haim Bronstein. Tel Aviv, The Yaacov Krol School in Petah-Tikva and Former Residents of Skalat in Israel, 1971. 160 p., ports., facsims. (H)
BRAN: DS135.R93 S537   HAR: Heb 16678.691
BPL: DS135.R93 S537

Skarzysko-Kamienna. *Skarzysko-Kamienna sefer zikaron* [The "yischor" book in memoriam of the Jewish community of Skarzysko and its surroundings*]. Tel Aviv, Skarzysko Society, 1973. 260 p., illus. (H,Y)
HAR: Heb 16718.691F   BPL: DS135.P62 S5677

Skierniewice. *Sefer Skierniewice* [The book of Skierniewice]. Ed.: Isaac Perlow. Tel Aviv, Former Residents of Skierniewice in Israel, 1955. 722 p., ports., facsims. (Y)
BRAN: DS135.P62 S57   HAR: Y 967.510.5

Sknilow   see under Radziechow

Skole   see under Galicia (*Gedenkbukh Galicia*)

Slobodka   see under Braslaw

Slonim. *Pinkas Slonim* [Memorial book of Slonim]. Ed.: Kalman Lichtenstein. Tel Aviv, Former Residents of Slonim in Israel, [1962-1979]. 4 vols., illus., ports. (H,Y,E)
BRAN: +DS135.R93 S54   HAR: Heb 16638.685 F
BPL: DS135.R93 S54

Slupia   see under Ostrowiec

Slutsk. *Pinkas Slutsk u-benoteha* [Slutsk and vicinity memorial book*]. Eds.: Nachum Chinitz, Shimson Nachmani. Tel Aviv, Yizkor-Book Committee, 1962. 450 p., ports, maps, facsims. (H,Y,E)
HEBC: XZD Slutsk   BRAN: +DS135.R93 S57
HAR: Heb 16638.686   BPL: DS135.R93 S57

Sluzewo   see under Wloclawek

Smorgonie. *Smorgon mehoz Vilna; sefer edut ve-zikaron* [Smorgonie, District Vilna; memorial book and testimony]. Ed.: E. Tash (Tur-Shalom). [Tel Aviv], Assoc. of Former Residents of Smorgonie in Israel and USA, 1965. 584 p., ports., facsims. (H,Y)
BRAN: DS135.R93 S58   HAR: Heb 16658.689
BPL: DS135.R93 S58

Smotrich   see under Kamenets-Podolskiy

Soblas   see under Ruscova

Sobolew   see under Laskarzew

Sobota   see under Lowicz

Sochaczew. *Pinkas Sochaczew* [Memorial book of Sochaczew]. Eds.: A. Sh. Stein, G. Weissman. Jerusalem, Former Residents of Sochaczew in Israel, 1962. 843 p., ports. (H,Y)
BRAN: DS135.P62 S6

Sokal. *Sefer Sokal, Tartakow... ve-ha-seviva* [Memorial book of Sokal, Tartakow... and surroundings]. Ed.: Avraham Chomel. Tel Aviv, Former Residents of Sokal and Surroundings, 1968. 576 p., ports., facsims. (H,Y)
BRAN: DS135.R93 S59   HAR: Heb 16678.680
BPL: DS135.R93 S59

Sokółka. *Sefer Sokolka* [Memorial book of Sokolka]. Jerusalem, The Encyclopaedia of the Jewish Diaspora, 1968. 768 columns, ports., facsims. (H,Y)
BRAN: +DS135.P62 S63   HAR: Heb 16718.685
HEBC: XZD Sokolka   BPL: DS135.P62 S63

Sokolovka (Yustingrad)   see Yustingrad

Sokolow. *In shotn fun Treblinka (khurbn Sokolow-Podlaski)* [In the shadow of Treblinka*]. [By] Symcha Polakiewicz. Tel Aviv, Sokolow-Podlaski Socity, 1957. 167 p. (Y)
HAR: Y 966.930

Sokolow. *Mayn khorev shtetl Sokolow; shilderungen, bilder un portetn fun a shtot umgekumene yidn* [My destroyed town of Sokolow]. [By] Peretz Granatstein. Buenos Aires, Union Central Israelita Polaca en la Argentina, 1946. 188 p., illus. (Y)
HAR: Y 962.734   BPL: DS135.P62 S64

Sokolow. *Sefer ha-zikaron; Sokolow-Podlask* [Memorial Book of Sokow-Podlask]. Ed.: Mendl Gelbart. Tel Aviv, Former Residents of Sokolow-Podlask in Israel and...in the USA, 1962. 758, [55] p., ports. (Y,H)
HAR: Y 962.732

Sokoly. *Sefer zikaron le-kedoshei Sokoly* [Memorial book of the martyrs of Sokoly]. Ed.: M. Grossman. Tel Aviv, Former Residents of Sokoly, 1962. 625 p., ports. (Y)
HAR: Y 962.737

Sokoly. *Sokoly -- be-ma'avak le-hayim* [Sokoly -- in a struggle for survival]. Trans. and ed.: Shmuel Klisher. Tel Aviv, Sokoly Society, 1975. 438 p., illus. (H)
BRAN: DS135.P62 S636 1962

Sombor   see Zombor

Somorja   see under Dunaszerdahely

Sompolno. *Dapei ed shel sarid ha-ayara Sompolno* [Pages of witness of the remnants of the town Sompolno]. [By] Yitzhak Kominkovski. Tel Aviv, Alef, 1981. 103 p., illus., ports. (H)
HAR: WID-LC HEBREW D811.5.K654 x

Sopochinie. *Korot ayara ahat; megilat ha-shigshug ve-ha-hurban shel kehilat Sopotkin* [Sopotkin; in memory of a Jewish community*]. [By] Alexander Manor (Menchinsky). [Tel Aviv], Sopotkin Society, 1960. 124 p., illus. (H)
HAR: Heb 16638.683

Sopotkin   see Sopockinie

Sosnovoye   see Ludwipol

Sosnowiec. *Sefer Sosnowiec ve-ha-seviva be-Zaglembie* [Book of Sosnowiec and the surrounding region in Zaglebie]. Ed.: Meir Shimon Geshuri (Bruckner). Tel Aviv, Sosnowiec Societies in Israel, the United States, France, and other countries, 1973-1974. 2 vols., illus. (H,Y)
BRAN: +DS135.P62 S657   HAR: Heb 16718.684
BPL: DS135.P62 S657

Stanislawcyzk see under Radziechow

Stanislawow. *Al horvotayikh Stanislawow; divrei edut le-kilayon kehilat Stanislawow ve-sevivata mipi adei-riah ve-al-pi teudot* [On the ruins of Stanislawow; concerning the annihilation of the community of Stanislawow and vicinity]. [By] Ami Weitz. Tel Aviv, 1947. 133 p. (H)
HAR: Heb 16638.684

Stanislawow also see under *Arim ve-imahot*, volume 5

Starachowice see under Wierzbnik

Starobin see under Slutsk

Starye Dorogi see under Slutsk

Stawiski. *Stawiski; sefer yizkor* [Stawiski memorial book]. Ed.: I. Rubin. Tel Aviv, Stavisk Society, 1973. 379, 5 p., illus. (H,Y,E)
BRAN: DS135.P62 S737   HAR: Heb 16718.686
BPL: DS135.P62 S737

Stepan. *Ayaratenu Stepan* [The Stepan Story; excerpts*]. Ed.: Yitzhak Ganuz. Tel Aviv, Stepan Society, 1977. 4, 364 p., illus. (H,E)
HAR: WID-LC HEBR DS135.P62 S 7432 x

Stoczek-Wegrowski. *Pinkes Stok (bay Vengrov); matsevet netsah* [Memorial book of Stok, near Wegrow]. Ed.: I. Zudicker. Buenos Aires, Stok Societies in Israel, North American and Argentina, 1974. 654 p., illus. (H,Y)
BRAN: DS135.P62 S7456

Stolbtsy see Stolpce

Stolin. *Albom Stolin* [Stolin Album]. Eds.: Phinehas Doron, Z. Blizovski. Jerusalem, 1960. 88 p., illus., ports. (H,Y)
HAR: Heb 16658.685

Stolin. *Stolin; sefer zikaron le-kehilat Stolin ve-ha-seviva* [Stolin; a memorial to the Jewish communities of Stolin and vicinity*]. Eds.: Aryeh Avatichi, Y. Ben-Zakkai. Tel Aviv, Former Residents of Stolin and Vicinity in Israel, 1952. 263 p., ports. (H)
HEBC: XZD Stolin   BRAN: DS135.R93 S72
HAR: Geb 16638.682

Stolpce. *Sefer zikaron; Steibts-Sverhnye ve-ha-seviva ha-semukhot... Rubezevits,Derevno, Nalibuk* [Memorial volume of Steibtz-Swerznie and the neighboring villages...*]. Ed.: Nahum Hinitz. Tel Aviv, Former Residents of Steibtz in Israel, 1964. 537, xxiii p., ports., map, facsims. (H,Y,E)
BRAN: +DS135.R93 S68   HAR: Heb 16658.680
BPL: DS135.R93 S68

Stramtura. *Agadot Strimtera; sipura shel kehilat yehudit me-reshita ve-ad ahrita* [Tales of Strimtra; the story of a Jewish community from beginning to end]. [By] Sh. Avni. Tel Aviv, Reshafim, [1985/86]. 270 p. (H)
HAR: Heb 44800.425

Stremiltsh (Strzemilcze) see under Radziechow

Strimtera see Stramtura

Stryj. *Sefer Stryj* [Memorial book of Stryj]. Eds.: Natan Kudish et al. Tel Aviv, Former Residents of Stryj in Israel, 1962. 260, 68 p., ports, facsims. (H,Y,E)
HEBC: XZD Stryj   BRAN: +DS135.R93 S83
HAR: Heb 16678.685

Strzegowo. *Strzegowo yisker-bukh* [Memorial book of Strzegowo]. New York, United Strzegower Relief Committee, 1951. 135, [18] p., ports., facsims. (H,Y,E)
HAR: Y 966.933

Strzemilcze see under Radziechow

Strzyzow. *Sefer Strizhuv ve-ha-seviva* [Memorial book of Strzyzow and vicinity]. Eds.: Itzhok Berglass, Shlomo Yahalomi (Diamant). Tel Aviv, Former Residents of Strzyzow in Israel and Diaspora, 1969. 480 p., ports., facsims. (H,Y)
BRAN: +DS135.P62 S75   HAR: Heb 16718.690 F
BPL: DS135.P62 S75
[English translation by Harry Langsam: *The Book of Stryzow and Vicinity*. Los Angeles, 1990, viii, 560 p., illus., ports., facsims. (E)]
HEBC: XZD Strzyzow M4

Stutshin see Szczuczyn

Suchowola. *Khurbn Sukhovolye; lexikorn fun a yidish shtetl tsvishn Bialystok un Grodne* [The Holocaust in Suchowola; in memory of a Jewish shtetl between Bialystok and Grodno]. Description by Lazar Simhah; ed. by Sh. Zabludovski. Mexico, published by a group of Suchowola landsleit in Mexico, 1947. 72 p., illus., ports. (Y)
BRAN: +DS135.P62 S58

Suchowola. *Sefer Suchowola* [Memorial book of Suchowola]. Eds.: H. Steinberg et al. Jerusalem, The Encyclopaedia of the Jewish Diaspora, 1957. 616 columns, [2] p., ports., map, facsims. (H,Y)
HAR: Heb 16718.683

Suwałki. *Yisker-bukh Suvalk* [Memorial book of Suvalk]. Ed.: Beryl Kahan [Kagan]. New York, The Suvalk and Vicinity Relief Committee of New York, 1961. 825 columns, ports., facsims. (Y)
BRAN: +DS135.P62 S85   HEBC: XVm
HAR: Y 964.910

Swieciany. *Sefer zikaron le-esrim ve-shalosh kehilot she-nehrevu be-ezor Svintsian* [Svintzian Region; memorial book of twenty-three Jewish communities*]. Ed.: Shimon Kanc. Tel Aviv, Former Residents of the Svintzian District in Israel, 1965. 1954 columns, ports., map, music, facsims. (H,Y)
BRAN: +DS135.R93 S514   HAR: Heb 16598.861 F
BPL: DS135.R93 S514

Swierzen see under Stolpce

Swir. *Ayaratenu Swir* [Our townlet Swir*]. Ed.: Chanuch Swironi (Drutz). Tel Aviv, Former Residents of Swir in Israel and... in the United States, 1959. 240 p., ports., map (H,Y)
HAR: Heb 16638.680   BRAN: DS135.R93 S922

Swir. *Haya hayeta ayarat Swir; ben shtei milhamot ha-olam* [There once was a town Swir; between the two world wars]. [By] Herzl Vayner. [Israel], Swir Society, 1975. 227 p., illus. (H,Y)
HAR: Heb 16718.680

Swizlocz. *Kehilat Swisiocz pelekh Grodno* [The community of Swisocz, Grodno District]. Ed.: H. Rabin. Tel Aviv, Former Residents of Swislocz in Israel, 1961. 159 p., ports. (H,Y)
BRAN: DS135.R93 S93

Szamosujvar. *Sefer zikaron shel kedoshei ayaratenu Számosujvar-Iklad ve-ha-seviva...* [Memorial book of the martyrs of our town Szamosujvar-Iklad and surroundings]. Eds.: Michael Bar-On, Benjamin Herskovits. Tel Aviv, Former Residents of Szamosujvar-Iklad and Surroundings in Israel, 1971. 190, 90 p., ports., facsims. (H,Hu)
BRAN: DS135.R72 G457   HAR: Heb 16838.671
BPL: DS135.R72 G457

Szczawnica see under Nowy Targ

Szczebrzeszyn. *Sefer zikaron le-kehilat Shebreshin* [Book of memory to the Jewish community of Shebreshin*]. Ed.: Dov Shuval. Haifa, Association of Former Inhabitants of Shebreshin in Israel and the Diaspora, 1984. xiv, 518 p., illus., maps, ports. (Y,H,E)
BRAN: DS135.P62 S877 1984   HAR: Heb 44300.137

Szczuczyn (Bialystok area). *Hurban kehilat Szczuczyn* [The destruction of the community of Szczuczyn]. Tel Aviv, Former Residents of Szczuczyn in Israel and..., 1954. 151 p., ports. (Y)
HAR: Heb 16718.924

Szczuczyn (Belarus). *Sefer zikaron le-kehilot Szczuczyn, Wasiliszki, Ostrin, Novidvor, Rozankan* [Memorial book of the communities Szczuczyn, Wasiliszki...]. Ed.: L. Losh. Tel Aviv, Former Residents of Szczuczyn, Wasiliszki..., 1966. 456 p., ports., map, facsims. (H,Y)
BRAN: DS135.R93 S43   HAR: Heb 16658.925

Szczurowice (Shtruvits) see under Radziechow

Szransk. *Kehilat Szransk ve-ha-seviva; sefer zikaron* [The Jewish community of Szrensk and the vicinity; a memorial volume*]. Ed.: Y. Rimon (Granat). Jerusalem, [Former Residents of Szrensk in Israel], 1960. 518, 70 p., ports., maps, facsims. (H,Y,E)
BRAN: DS135.P62 S9

Szumsk. *Szumsk... sefer zikaron le-kedoshei Szumsk...* [Szumsk... memorial book of the martyrs of Szumsk...]. Ed.: Hayim Rabin. [Tel Aviv, Former Residents of Szumsk in Israel, 1968]. 477 p., ports., map, facsims. (H,Y)
HAR: Heb 16678.900   BPL: DS135.R93 S495

Targowica. *Sefer Trovits* [Memorial book of Targovica*]. Ed.: Yitzhak Siegelman. Haifa, Former Residents of Targovica in Israel, 1967. 452 p., ports., map, facsims. (H,Y)
HAR: Heb 16678.419   BPL: DS135.R93 T64

Targu-Lapus (Magyarlapos) see under Des

Targu-Mures see Marosvasarhely

Tarnobrzeg. *Kehilat Tarnobrzeg-Dzikow (Galicia ha-ma'aravit)* [The community of Tarnobrzeg-Dzikow (Western Galicia)]. Ed.: Yaakov Yehoshua Fleisher. Tel Aviv, Tarnobrzeg-Dzikow Society, 1973. 379 p., illus. (H,Y)
HAR: Heb 16718.439F   BPL: DS135.P62 T3354

Tarnopol. *Tarnopol* [Tarnopol volume*]. Ed.: Philip Korngruen. Jerusalem, The Encyclopaedia of the Jewish Diaspora (vol. 3), 1955. 474 columns, ports., facsims. (H,Y,E)
BRAN: +DS135.E8 E55   HEBC: XZD Tarnopol 8 (2 copies)
HAR: Heb 16718.463F

Tarnów. *Tarnow; kiyuma ve-hurbana shel ir yehudit* [The life and decline of a Jewish city]. Ed.: A. Chomet. Tel Aviv, Association of Former Residents of Tarnow, 1854-1968. 2 vols. (xx, 928; 433 p.), ports., facsims., map (H,Y)
BRAN: DS135.P62 T34   HAR: CRL (Chicago)
BPL: DS135.P62 T34

Tartakow see under Sokal

Tasnad. *Tasnadl tei'ur le-zekher kehilat Tasnad (Transylvania) ve-ha-seviva ve-yeshivat Maharam Brisk, me-reshitan ve-ad le-aher y'mei ha-shoah* [Tasnad; description, in memory of the community of Tasnad (Transylvania) and the surrounding region, and the Brisk Yeshiva, from their beginnings until after the Holocaust]. [By] Avraham Fuks. Jerusalem, 1973. 276 p., illus. (H)
BRAN: DS135.R72 T373   HAR: Heb 16838.409
HEBC: XZD Tasnad   BPL: DS135.R72 T373

Teglas see under Debrecen

Telechany. *Telekhan* [Telekhan memorial book*]. Ed.: Sh. Sokoler. Los Angeles, Telekhan Memorial Book Committee, 1963. 189, 15 p., ports., map (H,Y,E)
BRAN: DS135.R93 T45   HAR: Y 965.710

Telsiai. *Sefer Telz (Lita); matsevet zikaron le-kehila kedosha* [Telsiai book*]. Ed.: Yitzhak Alperovitz. Tel Aviv, Tel Society in Israel, 1984. 505 p., illus., map, ports. (H,Y)
HAR: Heb 44300.121   BRAN: +DS135.R93 T4377 1984

Telz see Telsiai

Teplik. *Teplik, mayn shtetle; kapitlen fun fufsik yor lebn* [My town Teplik; chapters from fifty years of life]. [By] Valentin Chernovetzky. Bienos Aires, El Magazine Argentino, 1946-1950. 2 vols., illus. (Y)
HAR: Y 3991.85

Terebovlya see Trembowla

Ternopol see Tarnopol

Ternovka. *Ayaratenu Ternovka; pirkei zikaron ve-matseva* [Our town Ternovka; chapters of remembrance and a monument]. [By] G. Bar-Zvi. Tel Aviv, Ternovka Society, 1972. 103 p., illus. (H)
HAR: Heb 16678.425   BPL: DS135.R93 T47 1972

Thessaloniki see Saloniki

Tughina see Bendery

Tiktin see Tykocin

Timkovichi see under Slutsk

Tirgi-Mures see Marosvasarhely

Tishevits see Tyszowce

Tlumacz. *Tlumacz-Tolmitsh; sefer edut ve-zikaron* [Memorial book of Tlumacz*]. Eds.: Shlomo Blond et al. Tel Aviv, Tlumacz Society, 1976. 187, 533 p., illus. (H,Y,E)
HEBC: XW ...   BRAN: DS135.R93 T577
HAR: WID-LC HEBREW DS135.R93 T5687 x
AJHS: DS135.P62 T58

Tluste. *Sefer Tluste* [Memorial book of Tluste]. Ed.: G. Lindenberg. Tel Aviv, Association of Former Residents of Tluste and Vicinity in Israel and USA, 1965. 289 p., ports., map, facsims. (H,Y)
BRAN: +DS135.R93 T6   BPL: DS135.R93 T6
HAR: Heb 16638.417

Tłuszcz. *Sefer zikaron le-kehilat Tłuszcz* [Memorial book of the community of Tluszcz]. Ed.: M. Gelbart. Tel Aviv, Association of Former Residents of Tluszcz in Israel, 1971. 340 p., (H,Y)
BRAN: DS135.P62 T55   BPL: DS135.P62 T55
HAR: Heb 16718.460

Tolmitsh see Tlumacz

Tolstoye see Tluste

Tomaszów-Lubelski. *Sefer zikaron shel Tomaszow-Lub.* [Memorial book of Tomaszow-Lubelski]. Ed.: Moshe Gordon. Jerusalem, 1972. 28, 549 p., illus. (H)
BRAN: DS135.P62 T64   HAR: Heb 16718.434.5

Tomaszów Lubelski. *Tomashover (Lubelski) yisker-bukh* [Memorial book of Tomaszow Lubelski]. New York, Tomashover Relief Committee, 1965. 912 p., ports., facsims. (Y)
BRAN: DS135.P62 T65   HAR: Y 964.460

Tomaszów Mazowiecki. *Sefer zikaron le-kehilat Tomaszow Mazowiecki* [Tomashow-Mazowieck; a memorial to the Jewish community of Tomashow-Mazovieck*]. Ed.: M. Wajsberg. Tel Aviv, Tomashow Organization in Israel, 1969. 648 p., ports., map, facsims. (H,Y,E,F)
BRAN: +DS135.P62 T67   BPL: DS135.P62 T67
HAR: Heb 16718.435

Tooretz-Yeremitz see Turzec

Topolcany. *Korot mekorot le-kehila yehudit-Topolcany* [The story and source of the Jewish community of Topoltchany*]. [By] Yehoshua Robert Buchler. Lahavot Haviva, Topolcany Book Committee, 1976. 74, 64, 174 p., illus. (H,E,G)
BRAN: DS135.C96 T6
HAR: WID-LC HEBREW DS135.C96 T662 x

Toporow see under Radziechow

Torgovitsa see Targowica

Torhovytsia see Targowica

Torna (Galicia) see Tarnow

Torna (Turna nad Bodvou) see Turna

Toshnad see Tasnad

Trembowla. *Sefer yizkor le-kehilot Trembowla, Strusow ve-Janow ve-ha-seviva* [Memorial book for the Jewish communities of Trembowla, Strusow, Janow and vicinity*]. Bnai Brak, Trembowla Society, [1981?], li, 379 p., illus., maps (H,E)
BRAN: DS135.R93 T467
HAR: WID-LC HEBREW DS135.R93 T747 x

Trisk see Turzysk

Trovits see Targowica

Tuczyn. *Sefer zikaron le-kehilat Tuczyn-Kripe* [Tutchin-Kripe, Wolyn; in memory of the Jewish community*]. Ed.: B.H. Ayalon. Tel Aviv, Tutchin and Krippe Relief Society of Israel..., 1967. 383 p., ports., map, facsims. (H,Y)
BRAN: +DS135.R93 T75   BPL: DS135.R93 775
HAR: Heb 16678.415

Turbin see Turobin

Turets see Turzec

Turiysk see Turzysk

Turka. *Sefer zikaron le-kehilat Turka al nehar Stryj ve-ha-seviva* [Memorial book of the community of Turka on the Stryj River and vicinity]. Ed.: Yitzhak Siegelman. Haifa, Former Residents of Turka (Stryj) in Israel, 1966. 472 p., ports., map, facsims. (H,Y)
BRAN: DS135.R93 T8   BPL: DS135.R93 T8
HAR: Heb 16718.453

Turobin. *Sefer Turobin; pinkas zikaron* [The Turobin book; in memory of the Jewish community*]. Ed.: Meir Shimon Geshuri. Tel Aviv, Former Residents of Turobin in Israel, 1967. 397 p., ports, map, facsims. (H,Y)
BRAN: DS135.P62 T86   HAR: Heb 16718.438

Turzec. *Kehilot Turzec ve-Jeremicze; sefer zikaron* [Book of remembrance -- Tooretz-Yeremitz*]. Eds.: Michael Walzer-Fass, Moshe Kaplan. Israel, Turzec and Jeremicze Societies in Israel and America, 1978. 114, 421 p., illus. (H,Y,E)
HEBC: XZD Turetz   BRAN: DS135.R93 T784
HAR: WID-LC HEBREW DS135.R93 T664 x

Turzysk. *Pinkas ha-kehila Trisk; sefer yizkor* [Memorial book of Trisk]. Ed.: Natan Livneh. Tel Aviv, Trisk Society, 1975. 376 p., illus. (H,Y)
BRAN: DS135.R93 T796   BPL: DS135.R93 T796
HAR: 16718.437

Tykocin. *Sefer Tiktin* [Memorial book of Tiktin]. Eds.: M. Bar-Yuda, Z. Ben-Nahum. Tel Aviv, Former Residents of Tiktin in Israel, 1959. 606 p., ports., facsims. (H)
BRAN: DS135.P62 T92   HAR: Heb 16718.457

Tysmienica. *Tismenits; a matseye oyf di khurves fun a farnikhteter yidisher kehile* [Tysmienica; a memorial book*]. Ed.: Shlomo Blond. Tel Aviv, Hamenora, 1974. 262 p., illus. (H,Y)
BRAN: DS135.R93 T933   BPL: DS135.R93 T933
HAR: Y 954.550

Tyszowce. *Pinkas Tishovits* [Tiszowic book*]. Ed.: Y. Zipper. Tel Aviv, Assoc. of Former Residents of Tiszowic in Israel, 1970. 324 p., ports., facsims. (H,Y)
BRAN: DS135.P62 T98   BPL: DS135.P62 T98
HAR: Y 967.505

Ubinie (Ubin) see under Radziechow

Uhnow. *Hivniv (Uhnow); sefer zikaron le-kehila* [Hivniv (Uhnow); memorial book to a community]. Tel Aviv, Uhnow Society, 1981. 293, 83 p., illus. (H)
BRAN: HTemp 2180
HAR: WID-LC HEBREW DS135.R93 U356 x

Ujhely (Satorujhely) see under Zemplenmegye

Ujpest. *Sefer zikhronot shel k(ehila) k(edosha) Ujpest* [Memorial book of the coommunity of Ujpest]. [By] Laszlo Szilagy-Windt; Hebrew translation: Menahem Miron. Tel Aviv, 1975. 27, 325 p., illus. (H,Hu)
BRAN: DS135.H92 O9

Ungvar. *Shoat yehudei rusiah ha-karpatit--Uzhorod* [The Holocaust in Carpatho-Ruthenia--Uzhorod]. [By] Dov Dinur. Jerusalem, Section for Holocaust Research, Institute of ContemporaryJewry, Hebrew University of Jerusalem; World Union of Carpatho-Ruthenian Jews; and Hebrew School, [1983]. 6, 123, 15 p., facsims. (H)
HAR: Heb 42800.268

Ungvar see under *Arim ve-imahot be-Yisrael*, volume 4.

Urechye see under Slutsk

Uscilug. *Kehilat Ustila be-vinyana u-be-hurbana* [The growth and destruction of the community of Uscilug]. Ed.: A. Avinadav. Tel Aviv, Association of Former Residents of Uscilug, [1961]. 334 p., ports. (H,Y)
BRAN: DS135.R93 U8 1961

Ustila see Uscilug

Ustrzyki Dolne see under Lesko

Uzhorod (Ungvar) see under *Arim ve-imahot be-Yisrael*, volume 4.

Uzlovoye (Cholojow) see under Radziechow

Valkininkas see Olkeniki

Vamospercs see under Dedrecen

Vas. *Sefer zikaron mehoz Vas* [Memorial book of the region of Vas]. Ed.: Avraham Levinger. Israel, Vas Commemorative Committee, 1974. 214 p., illus. (H)
BRAN: DS135.H92 V378   BPL: DS135.H92 V378
HAR: Heb 16749.570

Vashniev (Wasniow) see under Ostrowiec

Vasilishok see Wasiliszki

Vayslits see Wislica

Velky Magar (Nagymagyar) see under Dunaszerdahely

Vengrov see Węgrow

Venice see under *Arim ve-imahot be-Yisrael*, volume 4.

Verbo see under Postyen

Verzhbnik see Wierzbnik

Vienna see under *Arim ve-imahot be-Yisrael*, volume 1.

Vilna. *Bleter vegn Vilne; zamlbukh* [Pages about Vilna; a compilation]. Eds.: Leyzer Ran, Leybl Koriski. Lodz, Association of Jews from Vilna in Poland, 1947. xvii, 77 p., ports., music, facsims. (Y)
BRAN: +DS135.R93 Y4   HAR: Y 945.673

Vilna. *Vilner zamlbukh - measef Vilna* [Vilna collection*]. Ed.: Yisrael Rudnicki. Tel Aviv, World Federation of Jews from Vilna and Vicinity in Israel, 1974. 140 p., illus., facsims. (Y,H)
HAR: Y 965.357

Vilna. *Yerusholayim de-Lita* [Jerusalem of Lithuania, illustrated and documented*]. Collected and arranged by Leyzer Ran. New York, Vilna Album Committee, 1974. 3 vols., illus. (H,Y,E,R)
BRAN: +DS135.R93 V584 v.1-2 HAR: Y 945.867.5

Vilna see also under Lithuania and under *Arim ve-imahot be-Yisrael*, volume 1.

Vilnius see Vilna

Vinogradov see Nagyszollos

Vishneva see Wiszniew

Vishnevets see Wisniowiec Nowy

Vishogrod see Wyszogrod

Viskit (Wiskitki) see under Zyrardow

Visooroszi see Ruscova

Visotsk see Wysock

Vitebsk. *Sefer Vitebsk* [Memorial book of Vitebsk]. Ed.: Baruch Karu. Tel Aviv, Former Residents of Vitebsk and Surroundings on Israel, 1957. 508 columns, ports., facsims. (H)
HEBC: XZD Vitebsk   BRAN: +DS135.R93 V67
HAR: Heb 16638.338

Vitebsk. *Vitebsk amol; geshikhte, zikhroynes, khurbn* [Vitebsk in the past; history, memoirs, destruction]. Eds.: Gregor Aronson, Jacob Lestschinsky, Avraham Kihn. New York, 1956. 644 p., ports. (Y)
BRAN: DS135.R93 V6   HAR: Y 951.506

Vitkov Novyy (Witkow Nowy) see under Radziechow

Vizna see under Slutsk

Vladimir Volynskiy see Wlodzimierz

Vladimirets see Woldzimierzec

Vloyn see Wielun

Voislavitsa see Wojslawiec

Volhyn. *Yalkut Vohlin*. Ed.: A. Avatichi. Tel Aviv, 1945-47. 2 vols.
HEBC: XZD Volhyn

Volkovisk see Wolkowysk

Volomin see Wolomin

Volozhin see Wolozyn

Voronovo see Werenow

Voydislav see Wodzislaw

Vrbové see under Postyen

Vurka see Warka

Vysotsk see Wysock

Wadowice. *Sefer zikaron le-kehilat Wadowice, Andrychow, Kalwarja, Myslenice, Sucha* [Memorial book of the communities Wadowice...]. Ed.: D. Jakubowicz. Ramat Gan, Former Residents of Wadowice... and Masada, 1967. 454 p., ports., facsims. (H,Y)
BRAN: DS135.P62 W223   HAR: Heb 16718.337

Warsaw. *Dos amolike yidishe Varshe, biz der shvel fun drim khurbn; yisker-bletekh nokh tayere noente umgekumene* [Jewish Warsaw thatwas: a Yiddish literary anthology]. Montreal, Farband of Warsaw Jews in Montreal, 1967. 848, 56 p., facsims., illus., ports. (Y)
BPL: DS135.P62 W228

Warsaw. *Pinkes Varshe* [Book of Warsaw]. Eds.: P. Katz et al. Buenos Aires, Former Residents of Warsaw and Suroundings in Argentina, 1955. 1351 columns, lvi p., ports., music, maps (Y)
BRAN: +DS135.P62 W325   HAR: Y 967.500 F

Warsaw. *Warsaw* [Warsaw volume*]. Ed.: Yitzhak Gruenbaum. Jerusalem, The Encyclopaedia of the Jewish Diaspora, 1953-1973. 3 vols. (v. 1, 6, 12), ports, maps, facsims. (H,Y)
HEBC: XZD Warsaw (vols. 1 & 12)   BRAN: +DS135.E8 E55

Warsaw see also under *Arim ve-imahot be-Yisrael*, vol. 3.

Waszawa see Warsaw

Warta. *Sefer D'Vart.* Ed.: Eliezer Estrin. Tel Aviv, D'Vart Society, 1974. 567 p., illus. (H,Y)
BRAN: DS135.P62 B375

Węgrów. *Kehilat Wegrow; sefer zikaron* [Community of Wegrow; memorial book]. Ed.: M. Tamari. Tel Aviv, Former Residents of Wegrow in Israel, 1961. 418 p., ports., facsims. (H,Y)
HEBC: XZD Wengrow   BRAN: DS135.P62 W6
HAR: Heb 16718.345

Wengrow see Wegrow

Werenow. *Voronova; sefer zikaron le-kedoshei Voronova she-nispu ba-shoat ha-natsim* [Voronova; memorial book to the martyrs of Voronova who died during the Nazi Holocaust]. Ed.: Chaim Rabin. Israel, Voronova Societies in Israel and the United States, 1971. 440 p., illus. (H,Y)
BRAN: DS135.R93 V69   BPL: DS135.R93 V69
HAR: Heb 16658.345

Wieliczka. *Kehilat Wieliczka; sefer zikaron* [The Jewish community of Wieliczka; a memorial book*]. Ed.: Shmuel Meiri. Tel Aviv, The Wieliczka Association in Israel, 1980. [9], 93 p., illus. (H,Y,E,P)
HAR: Heb 44300.144

Wieluń. *Sefer zikaron le-kehilat Wielun* [Wielun memorial book*]. Tel Aviv, Wielun Organization in Israel and the Memorial Book Committee in USA, 1971. 534, 24 p., ports. (H,Y,E)
BRAN: +DS135.P62 W638   HAR: Heb 16718.340
BPL: DS135.P62 W638

Wieruszów. *Wieruszow; sefer yizkor* [Wieruszow; memorial book]. Tel Aviv, Former Residents of Wieruszow Book Committee, 1970. 907 p., ports., maps, facsims. (H,Y)
BRAN: DS135.P62 W64   HAR: Heb 16718.341
BPL: DS135.P62 W64

Wierzbnik. *Sefer Wierzbnik-Starachowice* [Wierzbnik-Starachowitz; a memorial book*]. Ed.: Mark Schutzman. Tel Aviv, Wierzbnik-Starachowitz Societies in Israel and the Diaspora, 1973. 29, 399, 100, 83 p., illus. (H,Y,E)
BRAN: +DS135.P62 W6537   HAR: Heb 16718.338
BPL: DS135.P62 W6537

Wilno see Vilna

Wislica. *Sefer Vayslits; dos Vaysliter yisker-bukh...* [Book of Wislica]. Tel Aviv, Association of Former Residents of Wislica, 1971. 299 p., ports., map (H,Y,P)
BRAN: DS135.P62 W667   HAR: Heb 16718.339
BPL: DS135.P62 W667

Wisłowiec see Wojslawice

Wisniowiec Nowy. *Wisniowiec; sefer zikaron le-kedoshei Wisniowiec she-nispu be-shoat ha-natsim* [Wisniowiec; memorial book of the martyrs of Wisniowiec who perished in the Nazi Holocaust]. Ed.: Chaim Rabin. [Tel Aviv], Former Residents of Wisniowiec. 540 p., ports. (H,Y)
BRAN: DS135.R93 V59   BPL: DS135.R93 V59
HAR: Heb 16678.345

Wiszniew. *Vishneva, ke-fi she-hayeta ve-enena od; sefer zikaron* [Wiszniew, as it was and is no more; memorial book]. Ed.: Hayyim Abramson. Tel Aviv, Wiszniew Society in Israel, 1972. 216 p., illus. (H,Y)
BRAN: DS135.R93 V598   BPL: DS135.R93 V598
HAR: 16718.346

Witkow Nowy see under Radziechow

Włocławek. *Wloclawek ve-ha-seviva; sefer zikaron* [Wloclawek and vicinity; memorial book*]. Eds.: Katriel Fishel Thursh, Meir Korzen. [Israel], Assoc. of Former Residents of Wloclawek in Israel and the USA, 1967. 1032 columns, ports., facsims. (H,Y)
BRAN: +DS135.P62 V4   HAR: Heb 16718.344 F
BPL: DS135.P62 V4

Włodawa. *Yisker-bukh tsu Vlodave* [Yizkor book in memory of Vlodava and region Sobibor*]. Ed.: Shimon Kanc. Tel Aviv, Wlodawa Societies in Israel and North and South America, 1974. 1290, 128 columns, illus. (H,Y,E)
BRAN: +DS135.P62 W715   HAR: Heb 16718.347
BPL: DS135.P62 W715

Włodzimierz. *Pinkas Ludmir; sefer zikaron le-kehilat Ludmir* [Wladimir Wolynsk; in memory of the Jewish community*]. Tel Aviv, Former Residents of Wladimir in Israel, 1962. 624 columns, ports., facsims. (H,Y)
BRAN: +DS135.R93 V619   HAR: Heb 16718.928

Włodzimierzec. *Sefer Vladimerets* [The nook of Vladimerets]. Ed.: A. Meyerowitz. Tel Aviv, Former Residents of Vladimerets in Israel, [196-]. 515 p., ports., map (H,Y,E)
BRAN: DS135.R93 N62

Wodzislaw. *Sefer Wodzislaw-Sedziszow.* Ed.: M. Schutzman. Israel, Community Council of Wodzislaw-Sedziszow Emigrants in Israel, 1979. 437 p., illus. (H,Y)
BRAN: DS135.P62 W68

Wojslawice. *Sefer zikaron Voislavitse* [Yizkor book in memory of Voislavize*]. Ed.: Shimon Kanc. Tel Aviv, Former Residents of Voislavize, 1970. 515 p., ports., facsims. (H,Y)
HAR: Y 963.560   BPL: DS135.P62 W68

Wolborz see under Piotrków Trubunaski

Wolica-Wygoda see under Radziechow

Wolkowysk. *Hurban Wolkowysk be-milhemet ha-olam ha-sheniya 1939-1945* [The destruction of Wolkowysk during the Second World War 1939-1945]. Tel Aviv, Committee of Former Residents of Wolkowysk in Eretz-Israel, 1946. 96 p., ports. (H)
BRAN: DS135.R93 V642 1946   HAR: Heb 16638.359

Wolkowysk. *Volkovisker yisker-bukh* [Wolkovisker yizkor book*]. Ed.: Moses Einhorn. New York, 1949. 2 vols. (990 p.), ports (Y,E)
HEBC: XZD Wolkovisk   BRAN: DS135.R93 V64
BPL: DS135.R93 V64   HAR: Y 951.230

Wolma see under Rubiezewicze

Wolomin. *Sefer zikaron kehilat Wolomin* [Volomin; a memorial to the Jewish community of Volomin (Poland)*]. Ed.: Shimon Kanc. Tel Aviv, Wolomin Society, 1971. 600 p., illus. (H,Y)
BRAN: DS135.P62 W757   HAR: Y 967.960
BPL: DS135.P62 W757

Wolozyn. *Wolozyn; sefer shel ha-ir ve-shel yeshivat "Ets Hayim"* [Wolozin; the book of the city and of the Etz Hayyim Yeshiva*]. Ed.: Eliezer Leoni. Tel Aviv, Former Residents of Wolozin in Israel and the USA, 1970. 679, 35 p., ports., map, facsims. (H,Y,E)
BRAN: DS135.R93 V67   BPL: DS135.R93 V67
HAR: Heb 16718.352   HEBC: XZD Volozhyn

Wolpa see under Wolkowysk

Wsielub see under Nowogrodek

Wysock (near Rowne). *Ayaratenu Vistosk; sefer zikaron* [Our town Visotsk; memorial book]. Haifa, Association of Former Residents of Visotsk in Israel, 1963. 231 p., ports., maps (H,Y)
BRAN: DS135.R93 V9   BPL: DS135.R93 V9
HAR: Heb 16678.343

Wysokie-Mazowieckie. *Wysokie-Mazowieckie; sefer zikaron* [Visoka-Mazovietsk*]. Ed.: Iosef Rubin. Tel Aviv, Wysokie-Mazowieckie Society, 1975. 280 p., illus. (H,Y,E)
BRAN: DS135.P62 W888   HAR: Heb 16718.402
BPL: DS135.P62 W888

Wyszków. *Sefer Wyszkow* [Wishkow book*]. Ed.: David Shtokfish. Tel Aviv, Association of Former Residents of Wishkow in Israel and Abroad, 1964. 351 p., ports., facsims. (H,Y)
BRAN: +DS135.P62 W9   HAR: Heb 16718.343F

Wyszogrod. *Wyszogrod; sefer zikaron* [Vishogrod; dedcated to the memory...*]. Ed.: Hayim Rabin. [Tel Aviv], Former Residents of Vishogrod and ..., [1971]. 316, 48 p., ports., facsims. (H,Y,E)
BRAN: +DS135.P62 W958   HAR: Heb 16718.342

Wyzgrodek see under Krzemieniec

Yagistov see under Augustow

Yampol. *Ayara be-lehavot; pinkas Yampola, pelekh Volyn* [Town in flames; book of Yampola, district Wolyn]. Ed.: L. Gelman. Jerusalem, Commemoration Committee for the Town with the Assistance of Yad Vashem and the World Jewish Congress, 1963. [154] p. (H,Y)
BRAN: DS135.R93 Y3

Yanov (near Pinsk) see Janow

Yanova see Jonava

Yedintsy. *Yad le-Yedinits; sefer zikaron le-yehudei Yedinits-Bessarabia* [Yad l'Yedinitz; memorial book for the Jewish community of Yedintzi, Bessarabia*]. Eds.: Mordekhai Reicher, Yosef Magen-Shitz. Tel Aviv, Yedinitz Society, 1973. 1022 p., illus. (H,Y)
BRAN: +DS135.R72 E348   HAR: Heb 16684.467
BPL: DS135.R72 E348

Yedwabne see Jedwabne

Yekaterinoslav. *Sefer Yekaterinoslav-Dnepropetrovsk*. Eds.: Zvi Harkavi, Yaacov Goldburt. Jerusalem-Tel Aviv Yekaterinoslav-Dnepropetrovsk Society, 1973. 167 p., illus. (H)
BRAN: DS135.R93 D597   HAR: Heb 16678.447
HEBC: XZD Yekaterinoslav

Yendrikhov (Andrzchow) see under Wadowice

Yendzheva see under Jedrzejow

Yeremitz (Jeremicze) see under Turzec

Yustingrad. *Sokolievka / Justingrad; a centry of struggle and suffering in a Ukrainian shtetl, as recounted by survivors to its scattered descendants*. Eds.: Leo Miller, Diana F. Miller. New York, A Logvin Book, Loewenthal Press, 1983. 202 p., facsims., illus., maps, ports. (E,H,Y). Incl. facsim. and tr. of 1972 Mashabei Sadeh booklet.
HAR: WID-LC HEBREW DS135.R93 S5947 1983

Yustingrad. *Yustingrad-Sokolivka; ayara shenihreva* [Yustingrad-Sokolivka; a town that was destroyed]. Kibbutz Masabei Sadeh, 1972. 63, [17] p., ports., map, illus. (H)
BPL: DS135.R93 Y87

Zablotow. *Ir u-metim; Zablotow ha-melea ve-ha-hareva* [A city and the dead; Zablotow alive and destroyed]. Tel Aviv, Former Residents of Zablotow in Israel and the USA, 1949. 218 p., ports. (H,Y)
BRAN: DS135.R93 Z22

Zabludow. *Zabludow; dapim mi-tokh "yisker-bukh"* [Pages from the memorial book]. Eds.: Nehama Shavli-Shimush et al. Tel Aviv, Former Residents of Zabludow in Israel, [1986/87]. 170, 23 p., illus., map (H)
HAR: Heb 44300.201

Zabludow. *Zabludow yiskeer-bukh* [Zabludowo; im memoriam*]. Eds.: Sh. Tsesler et al. Buenos Aires, Zabludowo Book Committee, 1961. 507 p., ports., map, facsims. (Y)
HAR: Y 963.970

Zagaipol see Yustingrad

Zakopane see under Nowy Targ

Zaloshits see Dzialoszyce

Zambrow. *Sefer Zambrow; Zambrove* [The book of Zambrov*]. Ed.: Yom Tov Lewinsky. Tel Aviv, The Zambrover Societies in USA, Argentina and Israel, 1963. 627, 69 p., ports., facsims. (H,Y,E)
BRAN: +DS135.P62 Z27   HAR: Heb 16718.422

Zamekhov see under Kamenets-Podolskiy

Zamość. *Pinkes Zamosc; yizker-bikh* [Pinkas Zamosc; in memoriam*]. Ed.: Mordechai Wolf Bernstein. Buenos Aires, Committee of the Zamosc Memorial Book, 1957. 1265 p., ports., facsims. (Y)
BRAN: +DS135.P6 Z298 1957   HAR: Y 10200.146

Zamość. *Zamosc be-genona u-be-sivra* [The rise and fall of Zamosc]. Ed.: M. Tamari. Tel Aviv, Former Residents of Zamosc in Israel, 1953. 327 p., ports., facsims. (H,P)
BRAN: DS135.P62 Z3

Zaręby Kowcielne. *Le-zikhron olam; di Zaromber yidn vos zaynen umgekumen al kidesh-hashem* [For eternal remembrance; the Jews of Zaromb...]. [New York], United Zaromber Relief, 1947. 68 p., ports., map, facsims. (Y)
HAR: Microfilm A 375.79

Zarki. *Kehilat Zarki; ayara be-hayeha u-ve-khilyona* [The community of Zarki; life and destruction of a town]. Ed.: Y. Lador. Tel Aviv, Former Residents of Zarki in Israel, 1959. 324 p., ports. (H,Y)
BRAN: DS135.P62 Z35

Zaromb see Zareby Koscielne

Zarszyn see under Sanok

Zassow see under Radomysl

Zawidcze see under Radziechow

Zawiercie. *Sefer zikaron; kedoshei Zawiercie ve-ha-seviva* [Memorial book of the martyrs of Zawiercie and vicinity]. Ed.: Sh. Spivak. Tel Aviv, Former Residents of Zawiercie and Vicinity, 1948. 570 p., ports. (H,Y)
BRAN: DS135.P62 Z37   HAR: Heb 16718.435

Zbaraz. *Sefer Zbaraz* [Zbaraz: the Zbaraz memorial book*]. Ed.: Moshe Sommerstein. Tel Aviv, The Organization of Former Zbaraz Residents, 1983. 45, 128 p., illus., ports. (H,Y,E)

Zborow. *The Jewish commonwealth of Zborow.* [By] Solomon Berger. New York, 1967.
HEBC: XZD Zborov ...

Zborow. *Sefer zikaron le-kehilat Zborow* [Memorial book of the community of Zborow]. Ed.: Eliyahu (Adik) Zilberman. Haifa, Zborow Society, 1975. 477 p., illus. (H,Y)
BRAN: DS135.R93 Z37

Zdunska Wola. *Zdunska Wola* [The Zdunska-Wola book*]. Ed.: E. Erlich. Tel Aviv, Zdunska-Wola Associations in Israel and in the Diaspora, 1968. 718, 8, 55 p., ports., facsims. (H,Y,E)
BRAN: +DS135.P62 Z38   HAR: Heb 16718.423

Zdzieciol. *Pinkas Zhetl* [Pinkas Zetel; a memorial to the Jewish community of Zetel*]. Ed.: B. Kaplinski. Tel Aviv, Zetel Association in Israel, 1957. 482 p., ports., facsims. (H,Y)
BRAN: +DS135.R93 D95

Zelechow. *Yisker-bikh fun der Zhelekhover yidisher kehile* [Memorial book of the community of Zelechow]. Ed.: W. Yassni. Chicago, Former Residents of Zelechow in Chicago, 1953. 398, xxiv p., facsims. (Y)
BRAN: +DS135.P62 Z55 1953

Zelow. *Sefer zikaron le-kehilat Zelow* [Memorial book of the community of Zelow]. Ed.: Avraham Kalushiner. Tel Aviv, Zelow Society, 1976. 447 p., illus. (H,Y)
BRAN: DS135.P62 Z447
HAR: WID-LC HEBR DS135.P62 Z447 x

Zemplenmegye. *Mah tovu uhalekha Yaacov; korot yehudei mehoz Zemplen* [Vanished communities in Hungary; the history and tragic fate of the Jews in Ujhely and Zemplen County*]. By Meir Sas [Szasz]; translated from Hebrew by Carl Alpert. Toronto, Memorial Book Committee, 1986. 141, [56], 170, 214 p., illus., ports, maps, facsims. (H, Hu,E)
HEBC: XT S28v   HAR: WID-LC DS135.H92 Z467 1986

Zetel see Zdzieciol

Zgierz. *Sefer Zgierz, mazkeret netsah le-kehila yehudit be-Polin* [Memorial book Zgierz*]. vol. 1: Ed.: David Shtokfish; vol. 2: Eds.: Sh. Kanc, Z. Fisher. Tel Aviv, Zgierz Society, 1975-1986. 2 vols., illus. (H,Y)
BRAN: DS135.P62 Z487   HAR: Heb 16718.270
BPL: DS135.P62 Z487

Zhelekhov see Zelechow

Zheludok see Zoludek

Zhetl see Zdzieciol

Zholkva see Zolkiew

Zinkov. *Pinkas Zinkov* [Zinkover memorial book*]. Tel Aviv-New York, Joint Committee of Zinkover Landsleit in the United States and Israel, 1966. 239, 16 p., ports. (H,Y,E)
BRAN: DS135.R93 Z5   HAR: Heb 16678.351
BPL: DS135.R93 Z5

Złoczew (Lodz). *Sefer Zloczew* [Book of Zloczew]. Tel Aviv, Committee of the Association of Former Residents of Zloczew, [1971]. 432, [21] p., ports., facsims. (H,Y)
BRAN: +DS135.P62 Z557   HAR: Y 963.610 F
BPL: DS135.P62 Z557

Złoczow. *Sefer kehilat Zloczow* [The city of Zloczow*]. Ed.: Baruch Karu (Krupnik). Tel Aviv, Zloczow Society, 1967. 540, 208 columns, illus. (H,E)
BRAN: +DS135.R93 Z6   HAR: Heb 16718.425
BPL: DS135.R93 Z6

Zólkiew. *Sefer Zolkiew (kirya nisegava)* [Memorial book of Zolkiew]. Eds.: Natan Michael Gelber, Y. Ben-Shem. Jerusalem, The Encyclopaedia of the Jewish Diaspora, 1969. 844 columns, ports., map, facsims. (H)
BRAN: +DS135.P62 Z67   HAR: Heb 16718.420.10
HEBC: XZD Zolkiew

Zolochev see Zloczow

Zoludek. *Sefer Zoludek ve-Orlowa; galed le-zikaron* [The book of Zoludek and Orlowa; a living memorial*]. Ed.: Aharon Meyerowitz. Tel Aviv, Former Residents of Zoludek in Israel and the USA, [1967]. 329, [5] p., ports., map (H,Y,E)
BRAN: DS135.R93 Z47   HAR: Heb 16658.361
BPL: DS135.R93 Z47

Zvihil see Novograd-Volynskiy

Zwiahel see Novograd-Volynskiy

Zwoleń. *Zvolinsker yisker-bukh* [Zwolen memorial book]. New York, Zwolen Society, 1982. 564, 112 p., illus. (Y,E)
BRAN: DS135.P62 Z88 1982

Żychlin. *Sefer Zychlin* [The memorial book of Zychlin*]. Ed.: Ammi Shamir. Tel Aviv, Zychliner Organization of Israel and America, 1974. 4, 350 p., illus. (H,Y,E)
BRAN: DS135.P62 Z878   HAR: Heb 16718.424
BPL: DS135.P62 Z878

Zyrardow. *Pinkas Zyrardow, Amshinov un Viskit* [Memorial book of Zyrardow, Amishov and Viskit]. Ed.: Mordechai Wolf Bernstein. Buenos Aires, Association of Former Residents in the USA, Israel, France and Argentina, 1961. 699 p., ports., facsims. (Y)
BRAN: +DS135.P62 Z9   HAR: Y 962.963

MISCELLANEOUS

Teachers - Poland. *Lerer yizkor bukh* [Teachers memorial book]. Ed.: Hayim Solomon Kasdan. New York, Zydowski Centralna Organizacja Szkolna, 1952-54. 566 p., ports. (Y)
HEBC: XVm ...   BRAN: LC746.P7 K34

Physicians - Poland. *The Martyrdom of Jewish Physicians in Poland*. Ed.: Louis Falstein. New York, Exposition Press, 1963. 500 p. {Includes alphabetic necrology of 2500 murdered physicians}. (E)
HEBC: VK F25n   BRAN: R536.F3

Military Personnel - Poland. *Jewish Military Casualities in the Polish Armies in World War II*. By Benjamin Meirtchak. Tel Aviv: World Federation of Jewish Fighters, Partisans, and Camp Inmates, 1994-95. 2 volumes. (E)
HAR: DS135.P63 A1514 1994   HEBC:

Appendix B

BRANDEIS PERIODICALS

This appendix lists Jewish periodicals in the Brandeis Library collection (see page 73). This list is in four parts. The first two lists contain all 19th-century and earlier periodicals. The 20th-century periodicals at Brandeis are far too numerous to list here.

a) Periodicals catalogued in the LOUIS (computer catalog) system.
b) Hebrew and other items not in LOUIS.
c) Some microform periodicals recently acquired from YIVO, but not yet catalogued as of early 1996.
d) American Jewish Historical Society / Brandeis Joint Depository Collection

a. Periodicals in the LOUIS System

Abendland, Das (Prague, Czechoslovakia), 1864-1869. [DS135 .C95 A28] -- Microfilm
Allgemeine illustrirte Judenzeitung, Pest, Hungary 1860-1861. [DS101 .A178] -- Microfilm
Allgemeine israelitische Wochenschrift, Berlin 1895-1899. [DS133 .J54 -- v.4-8,189?] -- Microfiche
Allgemeine Zeitung des Judenthums, Berlin 1837-1922. [+DS133 .A44] -- Stacks & Microform.
{Note: Cohen, A.D. Verzeichnis der,..., Todesanzeigen und Nekrologe. 1837-1861. Supplement to number 48. 1864. Index to all of the obituaries published to that date.}
Alliance israelite universelle, Bulletin de. Paris, France 1861-1913. [DS101 .A3] -- Stacks & Microform
American Hebrew, The. New York, USA 1879-1902. [E184.J5 A25] -- Microfilm
American Israelite, The. Cincinnati, USA 1874. [AP92 .A53] -- Microfilm
The American Jewess. New York [etc.], USA 1895-1899. [AP92 .A54] -- Microforms.
American Jewish Year Book. Philadelphia, US 1899-present. [E184 .J5 A55] -- Stacks & Judaica
Archives israelites de France. Paris 1840-1935. [DS135.F8 A2] -- Stacks & Microfilm
Asmonean, The. New York 1849-1858. [AP92 .A8] -- Microfilm
Ben-Chananja. Szegedin, Hungary 1858-1867. [BM1 .B38] -- Stacks & Microfilm
Bikurim. Vienna, Austria 5625 [1864/65]-5626 [1865/66]. [BM1 .B52] -- Stacks
Carmel; allg[emeine] illustrirte Judenzeitung. Pest, Hungary 1861-1862. [DS101 .A178] -- Microform
Ceskozidovske listy. 1894- . Prague, Czechoslovakia. [DS135 .C95 C4] -- Special Collections.
Dr. Adolph Brull's Popular-wissenschaftliche Monatsblatter zur Belehrung uber das Judentum fur Gebildete aller Konfessionen. Frankfurt a/M, Germany 1881-1908. -- [DS101 .P6] -- Stacks.
Dr. Bloch's oesterreichische Wochenschrift. Vienna 1898-1918. [+AP93 .D6] -- Special Collections
The Everlasting nation. London 1889-1892. [DS135 .E8 A23] -- Special Collections
Evreiskiia zapiski. Riga, Latvia 1881. [DS135 .L3 E9] -- Microforms
Evrejskaja biblioteka. St. Petersburg 1871-1903. [DS135 .R9 E8]
Das Fullhorn. Bamberg, Germany 1835-1836. [DS101 .F8] -- Microforms
Gazeta de Amsterdam. Amsterdam 1675-1690. [AP93 .G3] -- Microforms
ha-Goren. St.Petersburg 1898. [DS101 .G63] -- Stacks
Havatselet = Habazeleth. Jerusalem, Israel 1863-1911. [DS101 .H25] -- Microforms
Hebraica. Chicago 1884-95. [PJ3001 .A6]
Illustrierte Gemeinde-Zeitung. Vienna, Austria 1885-1886. [DS135 .A9 I4] -- Microfilm
Illustrirte Monatshefte fur die gesammten Interessen des Judenthums. Vienna 1865-1866. [AP93 .I61] -- Microforms.
Der Israelit. Mainz, Frankfurt a/M, Germany 1860-1938. [DS133 .I75] -- Microforms & Special Collections.
Israelit und Jeschurun. Mainz, Germany 1889-1891. [Cage +DS133 .I75] -- Specials collections.
The Israelite a weekly periodical devoted to the religion, history, and literature of the Israelite. Cincinnati, USA 1854-1874. [AP92 .A53] -- Microforms
Israelitische Annalen. Frankfurt a/M, Germany 1839-1841. [DS101 .I7] -- Stacks
Der Israelitische Lehrer. Mainz, Germany 1861. [DS135 .G33 I78] -- Microforms
Israelitische Monatsschrift. Berlin 1898. [+DS133 .J783] -- Special Collections
Der Israelitische Volkslehrer. Frankfurt a/M 1851-1859. [BM1 .I8] -- Stacks
Israelitische Wochenschrift. Berlin 1899-1906. [DS133 .J56] -- Microforms
Israelitischer Jugendfreund. Berlin 1895-1904. [AP93 .I8] -- Stacks

Israelitisches Predigt-Magazin. Leipzig 1893-1894. [BM730 .A1 I8] -- Stacks

Israel's Advocate. New York 1823-1827. [Z6951 .A493] -- Microforms

Der Israelt des neunzehnten Jahrhunderts. Meiningen, Germany 1839- [DS133 .I752] -- Microforms.

Izraelita. Warsaw 1865-99. [AP93 .I95] -- Special collections

Jahrbuch fur die Geschichte der Juden und des Judenthums. Leipzig, Germany 1860-1869. [DS102 .I6] -- Stacks

Jahrbuch fur die israelitischen Cultus-Gemeinden in Ungarn und seinen ehemaligen Nebenlandern. Arad, Hungary 1860/1861- . [DS135 .H9 J32] -- Microforms

Jahrbücher für jüdische Geschichte und Literatur. W. Erras, Frankfurt a/M 1874-1885. [DS101 .J3] -- Stacks

Jahresbericht der Verwaltung der Kuranstalt für arme Israeliten in Bad Soden am Taunus. 1892-1913. [HV3193.G4 K8] -- Stacks.

Jeschurun. v. 1-9. 1856-1878 Bamberg, etc., Germany. [DS101 .J382] -- Special Collections.

Jeschurun. Berlin, Germany 1892-1895. [DS133 .J52] -- Jahrg.1-4? -- Microforms.

Jeschurun ein Monatsblatt zur Forderung judischen Geistes und judischen Lebens, in Haus, Gemeinde und Schule. Frankfurt a/M 1855-70. [DS133 .J4] -- Stacks & Microforms

Jeschurun : Wochenschrift zur Forderung judischen Geistes und judischen Lebens in Haus, Gemeinde und Schule. Hannover, Germany 1883-1887. [DS133 .J4] -- Stacks & Microforms

The Jewish Chronicle. London, England Nov. 12, 1841- . [AP92 .J3] -- Microforms & Judaica

The Jewish quarterly review. London, England 1888-1908. [DS101 .J48] -- Stacks

The Jewish year book. London, England 1896/97- . [DS135 .E5 A3] -- Stacks

Joseph. Poland 1879. [DS135 .P6 J65] -- v. 1,1879 -- Microforms

Der Jude: ein Journal fur Gewissens-Freiheit. Altona, Germany 1835. [DS135.G3 A229] -- Stacks

Der Jude; eine Wochenschrift. Leipzig 1768-72. [DS135 .G3 A213] -- Microforms

Das judische Centralblatt : zugleich Archiv fur die Geschichte der Juden in Bohmen. Prague 1882-1892. [DS101 .J83] -- Stacks

Die Judische Press. 1870-1923. Berlin, Germany [DS133 .J78] -- Microforms

Judische zeitschrift fur wissenschaft und leben. Breslau 1862-1875. [DS101 .J85] -- Stacks

Kalendar und Jahrbuch fur Israeliten. Vienna, Austria 1842/43-1867/68. [DS135 .A9 K29] -- Stacks

Kevuzat Hakhamim. Vienna 1861. [BM4057 1861a]

ha-Kokhavim. Vilna, Lithuania 1865. [AP91 .K65] -- Stacks.

ha-Levanon. Jerusalem, Israel 1863-1886. [DS101 .L42] -- Microforms

ha-Levanon. Jerusalem, Israel 1863-1886. [+ DS101 .L4] -- Stacks & Special Collections

Magazin fur die Wissenschaft des Judenthums. Berlin 1874-1893. [DS101 .M3] -- Stacks

Ha-Melits. Odessa, St.Petersburg 1860-1904. [+DS101 .M447]

The Menorah : a monthly magazine for the Jewish home... New York, USA 1886-1907. [AP92 .M5] -- Stacks

Mitteilungen zur judischen Volkskunde. Hamburg, etc. 1898-1910. [GR98 .A1 M5] -- Stacks

Mi-mizrah umi-ma'arav. Vienna/Berlin 1894-1899. [DS101 .M472] -- Microforms

Monatsblatter fur Vergangenheit und Gegenwart des Judentums. Berlin, Germany 1890-1891. [DS135 .G33 M46] -- Microforms

Monatsschrift fur Geschichte und Wissenschaft des Judentums. Germany 1851-1939. Breslau, Germany [DS101 .M6] -- Stacks

Proceedings of the ... convention of the National Council of Jewish Women. Philadelphia, USA 1897- . [E184.J5 N256] -- Stacks

Neue israelitische Zeitung. 1878-1880. [DS101 .N3] -- Microforms

Die Neuzeit. Vienna, Austria 1861-1903. [AP93 .N4] -- Microforms

The Occident and American Jewish advocate. Philadelphia, USA 1843-1869. [DS133 .O25] -- Microforms

Oesterreichisches Central-Organ fur Glaubensfreiheit, Cultur, Geschichte und Literatur der Juden. Vienna, Austria 1848- . [DS135 .A9 O3] -- Microforms

Ohel mo'ed. Cracow 1898-1901. [BM496 A1 O53]

ha-Or. Lvov 1882-83. [AP91 .O65] -- Special Collections

Or Torah. Frankfurt a/M 1874. [AP91 .O7] -- Special Collections

Or Torah. Jerusalem 1897-1901. [BM500 .O7] -- Stacks

Der Orient. Leipzig, Germany 1840-1851. [+ DS101 .O76] -- Stacks

Otsar ha-sifrut. Cracow, Poland 1887-96. [DS101 .O84]

Le Paix: revue religieuse, morale et litteraire. Paris, France 1846-1847? [DS133 .P3] -- Special Collections.

Pardes: osef sifruti. Odessa 1892-1896. [DS101 .P38]

Personalist und Emancipator. Berlin, Germany 1899-1921. [DS141 .P43] -- Microforms

Razsviet. Odessa 1860-61. [+DS135 .R9 R38]

Reichsbote Zeitschrift fur soziale wissenschaftliche und Cultus-Interesse des Judenthums. Vienna, Austria 1894. [DS135 .A9 R3] -- Microforms

Revue des études juives. Paris, France 1880- . [DS101 .R45] -- Judaica

Russkii evrei. St. Petersburg 1879-1884. [DS133 .R8] -- Microforms

Serubabel. Berlin, 1886-1889. [DS135 .G3 A2799] -- Microforms

Sinai; ein organ fur erkenntniss und veredlung des judenthums... Baltimore, USA 1856-1863. [BM197 .S5] -- Stacks
Sion'. Odessa, Russia 1861-1862. [DS135 .R9 S4] -- Microforms
Spenden-Verzeichnisse für alle Zweige jüdischer Wohlthätigkeit. Bad Durkheim, Germany 1889-1906.
  [+ DS133 .J784] -- Special Collections
Sulamith. Dessau, Germany 1806-1848. [DS133 .S8] -- Stacks
Tijdschrift. Rotterdam: 1869. [AS244 .V4 A1] -- Microforms
L'Univers israelite. Paris, France 1844- . [BM1 .U5] -- Microforms
La Verite israelite : recueil d'instruction religieuse. Paris, France 1860-1862. [BM100 .V4] -- Stacks
Voskhod zhurnal uchebno-literaturnyi politicheskii. St. Petersburg, Russia 1899- . [DS133 .V6] -- Stacks
Die Wahrheit. Prague, Czechoslovakia 1871-1872. [DS135 .C95 W3] -- Microforms
Die Wahrheit. Vienna, Austria 1885-1938. [+ DS133 .J8] -- Stacks & Microforms
Die Welt. Vienna 1897-1914. [+DS149 .A346]
Wiener Vierteljahrs-Schrift. Vienna, Austria 1853. [DS101 .W4] -- Microforms
Wissenshaftliche Zeitschrift fur judische Theologie. Frankfurt a/M, Germany 1835-1847. [DS101 .W5] -- Stacks &
  Microforms.
ha-Yehudi. London, England 1897-1913. [DS101 .Y39] -- Microforms
Yeshurun. Lvov/Breslau/Bamberg 1856-1878. [BM496 .A1 Y4] and [BM496 .A1 Y42] -- Microforms.
  [DS101 .J382] -- Special Collections
Zeitschrift fur die geschichte der Juden in Deutschland. Hsg. Prof. Dr. Ludwig Geiger. Braunschweig, Germany
  1887-1892. [DS135 .G3 A282] -- Microforms [DS135 .G3 A28] -- Stacks
Zeitschrift fur die religiosen Interessen des Judenthums. Berlin, Germany 1844-1846. [DS101 .Z35] -- Microforms
Zeitschrift fur die Wissenschaft des Judenthums. Berlin, Germany 1822-1823. [DS101 .Z42] -- Microforms &
  [DS101 .Z4] -- Stacks
Zion. Berlin 1895. [DS149 .A1 Z54] -- Microforms

b. Hebrew and Other Periodicals not in LOUIS

Ahiasaf. Warsaw 1896- . [PJ5002 .A5] -- Stacks
Der Idisher Arbayter. New York 1896-1904. [HX .I32] -- Special Collections
Der arbayter Fraynd. London 1885-1908. [HX8 .A7] -- Microforms
Die Arbayter Shtime. St. Petersburg 18?-1917. [HX8 .A743 and .A74] -- Microforms
Die Arbayter Tsaytung. New York 1890-1902. [AP91 .A7] -- Microforms
Asefat hakhamim. Koenigsberg 1877-1878. [HX8 .A8] -- Stacks
Ha-Asif. Warsaw 1884-93. [DS101 .A78] -- Stacks
Bet 'eked. Berdichov 1892. [PJ5038 .B4] -- Stacks
Bet 'eked ha-agadot. Franfurt a/M 1881. [BM510 .B48] -- Microforms
Bet ha-midrash. Cracow 1888. [BM1 .B44 ST] -- Stacks
Bet ha-midrash. Vienna 1865. [BM1 .B4] -- Stacks
Bet Talmud. Vienna 1881-89. [BM1 .B46] -- Stacks
Bikure ha'Itim. Vienna 1821-30. [DS101.B5] -- Special Collections.
Bikure ha'itim ha-hadashim, neue Folge I. Vienna 1845. [DS101 .B52] -- Stacks
Bikurim. Vienna 1865-66. [BM1 .B5] -- Special Collections
Blätter fur jüdische geschichte und Literatur. 1899-1904. [DS101.B55] -- Stacks
ha-Boker Or. Warsaw 1876-1886. [AP91 .B6] -- Microforms
Dinstagishe kurantyn-fraytagishe kurantyn. Amsterdam 1686-1687. [DS135 .N5 A534] -- Microforms
Diskuhrs fun di naye kehile. Amsterdam 1797-1809. [BM327 .A6 D58] -- Microforms
Ha-Eshkol. Cracow 1898-1913. [PJ5001 .E8] -- Stacks
Di fraye gezelshaft. New York 1895-1900. [HX8 .F72] -- Stacks
Gilyonenu. New York 1890- . [LC701 .G5] -- Stacks
Ginze Nistarot. Bamberg, Germany 1868-1878. [BM1 .G4] -- Stacks
Ha-Goren. St. Petersburg 1898. [PJ5038 .R29] (additional) -- Stacks
He-haluts. Lemberg, Breslau, Frankfurt a/M, Prague, Vienna 1852-1889. [PJ5001 .H34] -- Microforms
Hevrat kol Yisrael haverim. Zichronot. Paris 1873. [DS101 .A315] -- Stacks
'Ivri Anokhi. Brody 1865-1890. [AP91 .I8] -- Microforms
Jescherun: Zeitschrift fur die Wissenschaft des Judenthums. Lemberg 1856-1878. -- Special Collections
Das Judische Literaturblatt. Magdeburg, Germany 1872-1913. [+AP93 .J82] -- Stacks & Microforms
Judisches Volksblatt. Leipzig 1860-1863. [+DS135 .G3 A26]
Kadimah. New York 1899. [DS101 .K32] -- Microforms
Ha-Karmel. Vilna 1860-1880. [DS101 .K37] -- Stacks & Microforms
Keneset Ha-Gedolah. Warsaw 1890-91. [AP91.K4] -- Stacks

Keneset hakhme Yisrael. Odessa 1897- . [BM522 .A1 K4] -- Stacks
Keneset Ysra'el. Warsaw 1886-1889. [DS101 .K42] -- Stacks
Ha-Kerem. Warsaw 1887. [PJ5002 .K4] -- Stacks
Kerem Hemed. Vienna, Berlin 1833-56. [DS101 .K4] -- Stacks
Kochbe Jizchak, eine Sammlung ebraeisher ausaetze. Vienna 1845-1873. [DS101 .K6] -- Stacks
Kovets or ha-Torah. Jerusalem 1896/7. ?? -- Stacks
Kovets al-Yad. Berlin 1885-1903. [BM40 .K63 1885a] -- Stacks
Ha-Mabit and Ha-Mabit Le Yisrael. Vienna 1878. [DS133 .M3] -- Special Collections
Ha-Magid. Lyck, Berlin, Cracow 1856-1903. [+DS101.M32] -- Stacks, Microforms & Special Collections
Magid Mishnah. Lyck 1879-1881. [+DS101 .M322] -- Stacks
Ha-Me'assef. Koenigsberg, Berlin, Breslau, Altona, Dessau 1784-1810. [+DS101 .M44, .M439, .M441] -- Special Collections & Microforms
Ha-Me'asef. Jerusalem 1896-1914. [BM1 .M39] -- Stacks
Ha-Mevaser. Lemberg 1860- . [DS101 .M46] -- Special Collections
Mitspah. St.Petersburg 1885. [AP91 .M55] -- Microforms
Mi-mizrah umi Ma'arav. Vienna 1894-1899. [DS101 .M47] -- Microforms
Der Morgenstern. New York 1890. [AP91 .M6] -- Microforms
Di Naye Tsayt. New York 1898-99. [HX9 .N39] -- Special Collections
Ner ha-ma'aravi. New York 1894-97. [DS101 .N382] -- Stacks
Ha-Nesher. Lemberg 1863-64. [+DS101 .M46] -- Special Collections
Ha-osem. St. Petersburg 1897. [PJ5005 .A1 Y4] -- Stacks
Ha-Pisgah. NY, Baltimore, Boston, St.Louis, Chicago 1888-1900. [+DS101 .P52] -- Stacks
Ha-Pisgah. Vilna 1895-1904. [DS101 .P5] -- Stacks
Ha-Shahar. Vienna 1868-1884. [DS101 .S429] -- Special Collections & Microforms.
Ha-Shav'ua. Vienna 1898- . [+DS101 .M3224] -- Special Collections
Shem va-yafet. Lemberg 1887-88. [BM1 .S36] -- Stacks
Ha-Shilo'ah. Berlin, Cracow, etc. 1896-1926. [PJ5001 .S55] -- Microforms & Stacks
Shomer Tsion ha-Ne'eman. Altona 1854-63. [BM496 .A1 S5] -- Stacks
Shulamis. New York 1889-90. [DS149 .A1 S5] -- Microforms
Talpiyot me'asef sifruti. Berdichev 1895. [DS101 .T283] -- Special Collections
Tel Talpiyot. Vac, Hungary 1892-1938. [BM520 .T45] -- Special Collections
Torah mi-Tsiyon. Jerusalem 1887-1905. [BM496 .A1 T6] -- Microforms
Tsiyon; ve-hu otsar chadash li-hokhmi bnai Yisrael. Frankfurt a/M 1840-42. [BM1 .T83] -- Stacks
Ha-Yekev. St. Petersburg 1894. [PJ5005 .A1 Y4]
Va-yelaket. Paks, Hungary 1898-1918. [BM504 .V3]. -- Microforms
Yerushalayim. Me'asef sifruti le-hakirat erets ha-kodesh. Vienna, Jerusalem 1882-1919 . DS101 .Y42 -- Stacks
Yerushalayim; mahberet shehubrah la yahdav divre hokhmah ve-da'at. Zolkiew, Lemberg, Prague 1844-45. [DS101 .Y4] -- Stacks
Ha-Yonah o Keneset Yisrael. Berlin 1848-1851. [DS101 .Y6] -- Stacks
Yud: tsaytshrift fur ale yudishe interesn. Vienna, Cracow 1899-1902. [AP91 .Y82 1899] -- Microforms
Di Yudishe bibliotek. Cracow 1891-1904. [PJ5111 .Y74] -- Special Collections
Ha-Zefirah. Warsaw (Berlin), 1862-1931. [PJ5001 .T77] also T8 Lodz 1919-20.
Zionist Congress. Jerusalem 1897-1978. [DS149 .A45] -- Stacks

c. Uncatalogued Microforms of Yiddish and Russian Periodicals

These are Yiddish and Russian periodicals recently acquired in the Brandeis Microforms Collection from YIVO, but not yet cataloged. Inquire at the Judaica Office on the Mezzanine.

Af di Yegn tsu der Nayer Shul - education in 1920's
Albatros - 1920's literary magazine
Arbeter Tsaytung - Poale Tsiyon
Bikher Velt - Warsaw literary journal
Den - in Russian
Edinenye Odessa - in Russian
Folk un Land - Journal of Hitachdut--Labor Zionism in Poland
Folks-blat - pre-WWI Vilna weekly
Folks-gezunt - Vilna journal, important for social history

Fraye Yugnt - 20's leftist journal
Gazeta Zydowska - Paper issued in occupied Krakow
Glos Akademika - Postwar Lodz
Glos Zydowski - Warsaw 1906, 1917
Grinike Beymelekh - Vilna literary journal
Di Idishe Vokh - Warsaw
Idishes Togblat - Warsaw
Khronik fun der Yidisher Kehile in Lodzsh 1921-31 - important source for interwar Lodz
Der Komtar - Jewish politics in Kharkov
Komunistishe Fon - Kiev Communist paper

Dos Leben - St.Petersburg, 1905
Lebens-Fragen - Warsaw pre and post-WWI
Lodzer Arbeter - important source for interwar Lodz
Lodzer Folksblat - important source for interwar Lodz
Lodzer Ovendpost - important source for interwar
Lodzer Togblat - important source for interwar Lodz
Mosty - Post WWII Poland
Nasze Slowo - Post WWII Poland
Dos Naye Lebn - Bialystok, 1919-1925
Di Naye Shul - Bundist school politics
Nayer Haynt - supplement to Haynt 1924, 1925, 1931
Der Odeser Arbeter - Odessa
Dos Odeser Leben - Odessa
Polyeser nayes - Brest, late 1930's
Proletarisher fon - Kiev Communist paper 1928-29
Proletarisher gedank - Warsaw leftist paper
Prolit - Kharkov Communist paper, 1928-1932
Przyszlosc - Lwow paper, 1892-99
Przetom - Post WWII Warsaw
Rasvet - in Russian
Rotnbildung - Jewish politics in Kharkov
Di Royte Velt - Jewish politics in Kharkov
Sambatyon - Warsaw cultural paper
Shtern - Minsk Communist paper
Di Shtime Fun Bund - very early Bundist paper (1908)
Shul un Lebn - 20's Bundist educational paper
Sotsiale Meditsin - Warsaw 1928, 1930, 1936 - many important articles for social history
Dos Sotsialistishe dorf - Soviet Jewish politics, 1920s

Sovetish - Soviet literary periodical, 1934-41
Sovetishe literatur - Soviet literary periodical
Togblat - Warsaw, 1904-1911
Tshernovitser Bleter - Czernowitz, Romania (major Yiddish cultural center) post WWI
Tsentral-Komitet Fun Yidn in Poylin - Post WWII Communist politics
Tsiyonistishe Bleter - 20's Zionism in Poland
Undzer Hamer - socialist
Undzer Kind - orphans in interwar Poland
Undzer Tsayt - Warsaw
Undzer Vort - socialist
Undzer Vort - postwar Paris
Unzer bavegung - Poale Tsiyon
Unzer Byalistoker Ekspres - Bialystok
Unzer Leben - Breslau
Varshever Yudishe Tsaytung - very early (1867-81)
Varshover Radyo - popular paper
Der Veg - Petersburg pre-WWI
Der Veker - Kombund (Minsk)
Yankel Rubenshtik: Zamelbukh ... - Minsk, Byelorus -- main Yiddish cultural center in USSR
Der Yud - Warsaw, Orthodox paper
Yudishe Velt - Berlin Eastern-Jewish paper
Yudishe Folks-blat - St. Petersburg 1887-1890
Yidisher Artisten-Fareyn in Poyln - cultural life in interwar Poland
ha-Yisreeli - Minsk, 1881
Zycie Zydowskie - interesting periodical, 1906-1907

d. AJHS/Brandeis Judaica Depository Collection

Algemeyner Zshurnal. 1972-. [A991.A38] 16+ reels. {Continuing: Feb 25, 1972 - present}
American Hebrew. 1879-1950, with gaps. [E184.J5 A25] 31 reels. {New York City, Nov. 21 1879 - Nov. 6, 1884, Nov. 10, 1916 - Apr. 21, 1950}
American Israelite. Vol. 1-73. 1854-1927. 36 reels. {Cincinnati, July 15, 1854 - June 23, 1927}
American Israelite. 1854-1927. [AP92.A53] 9 reels.
Arbayter Tsaytung. 1890-1902. [AP91.A7] 7 reels.
Asmonean. 1849-1858. [AP92.A8] 3 reels. {New York City, indexed. Oct. 26, 1849 - June 28, 1858}
Aufbau. 1934-1972. [AP93.A9] 39 reels. {Oct. 1940 - Dec. 1972}
Boston Hebrew Observer. Vol 1-14. 1883-1886. Half reel. {Boston, on same reel as *Jewish Herald*}
Boston Jewish Chronicle. 1891-1893. 1 reel. {Boston, July 17, 1891 - March 10, 1893}
Di Bostoner Idishe Shtime. Vol. 1-5. 1913-1916. 1 reel. {Boston, Oct. 1, 1913 - Dec. 29, 1916}
Buffalo Jewish Review. 1917-1968. 30 reels. {Nov 9, 1917 - Dec. 27 1968}
California Jewish Bulletin. Vol 1:4 Vol 2:3 1933-1934. Half reel. {Los Angeles, May-Jun 1933, May 1934; on same reel as *California Jewish Review*}
California Jewish Press. Vol. 1, No. 1 - Vol. 3, No. 52 1956-1969. 4 reels. {Los Angeles}
California Jewish Record. Vol. 16-28. 1960-1971. 2 reels. {Oakland 1960-1966, San Francisco 1966-1971}
California Jewish Review. 1924-1929. Half reel. {Los Angeles, on same reel as *California Jewish Bulletin*. Feb. 29, 1924 - June 14, 1929}
Carolina Israelite. Vol. 1-20. 1944-1962. 2 reels. {Charlotte, NC}
Cleveland Yiddish Velt. 1913-1916, 1917, 1919, 1921-1952. 33 reels {Cleveland, July 18, 1913 - Nov. 26, 1917, Jan 7, 1919 - Nov 22, 1919, Jan. 10, 1921 - Feb. 22, 1952}
Ha-Doar. Vol. 1-3. 1921-1923. [PJ5001.D63] 1 reel.
Forverts - see *Jewish Daily Forward*
Freiheit. 1922-1929. [AP91.F75] 17 reels. {Continued by *Morgen Freiheit*. Apr. 2, 1922 - July 30, 1929}
Hapisgoh (The Summit). Vol. 1-6. 1888-1899. 1 reel. {Sept. 14, 1888 - Oct 13, 1899}
The Hebrew. Vol. 1-53. 1864-1906. 7 reels. {San Francisco, Jan. 1864 - Mar. 23, 1906}
Hebrew Observer. 1889-1890, 1897-1898. 2 reels. {Cleveland, July 9, 1889 - July 4, 1890, 1897-1898}

Humor Un Ernst. 1926 [PJ 5125.H8] 1 reel. {Buenos Aires, March 5, 1926}

Idisher Fihrer. Vol. 4. 1925-1926. 1 reel. {Boston, Aug. 11, 1925 - Oct. 15, 1926}

Idisher Immigrant. 1908-1909. [JV 6895 J6 I36] 1 reel.

Jerusalem Times. 1960. One-third reel. {Jerusalem, Jordan. On same reels as *Southern Israelite, Southern Guide.*
    Mar 4, 1960}

Jewish Advocate. 1905-present. 109+ reels. {Boston, continuing. May 26, 1905 - present}.

Jewish Daily Forward (Forverts). 1897-1946, 1980- . [AP91.F68] 213+ reels. {Continuing}

Jewish Day (Tog). 1914-1951. [AP91.T6] 131 reels. {Nov. 5, 1914 - Dec. 31, 1951}

Jewish Frontier. 1933-1968. [DS149.A324] 6 reels.

Jewish Herald. 1893-1894. Half reel. {Boston, on same reels as *Boston Hebrew Observer*}

Jewish Ledger. 1895-1927 with gaps. 19 reels. {New Orleans, 1895-1905, 1913-1914, 1895-1927 with gaps}

Jewish Messenger. 1857-1902. 24 reels. {New York City, Jan. 2, 1857 - Dec. 26, 1902}

Jewish Post. 1934-1941. 4 reels. {Patterson, NJ, Nov. 1934 - July 1941}

Jewish Progress. Vol. 21-23. 1897-1898. 1 reel. {San Francisco, Jan. 15, 1897 - Nov 18, 1898}

Jewish Review. 1895-1899 with gaps. 2 reels. {Cleveland, Nov. 8, 1895 - Oct. 30, 1896, Oct. 1, 1897 - Nov. 17,
    1899}

Jewish Review & Observer. 1899-1958. 29 reels. {Cleveland, Nov. 24, 1899 - Dec. 26, 1958}

Jewish Times. Vol. 1-11. 1869-1879. 7 reels. {New York City, English/German. Mar. 5, 1869 - Oct. 10, 1879}

Jewish Times & Observer. Vol. 36-55. 1892-1922 (incomplete). 1 reel. {San Franciso}

Jewish Tribune. 1903-1906. 1 reel. {Portland, Oregon, Apr. 24, 1903 - Feb. 9, 1906}

Maccabean. Vol. 10-13. 1906-1907. 1 reel. {New York City, Jan. 1906 - Dec. 1907}

Me-et Le-Et. 1901. [AP91.M43] 1 reel. {New York}

Memorias Curiel. 1 reel. {Curacao}

Memorias Senior. 1 reel. {Curacao}

Morgen Freiheit. 1929-1988. [AP91.F752] 103 reels. {Continues *Freiheit.* Aug. 1, 1929 - Sept. 11, 1988}

Nayeleben. Vol. 9-23. 1935-1950. [DS135.R93 B53] 4 reels.

Occident. Vol. 1-26. 1843-1869. 11 reels. {Philadelphia. Apr. 1843 - Mar. 1869}

Occident and American Jewish Advocate. 1843-1869. [DS133.025] 11 reels. {Apr. 1843 - Mar. 1869}

Occident Index. 1843-1869. [DS133.025] 21 reels.

Orthodox Union. Vol. 1-13. 1933-1946. 2 reels. {New York City, Aug. 1933 - June 1946}

Pacific Jewish Press. 1963. 1 reel. {Jan. 4, 1963}

Reflex. Vol. 6, No. 1-4; Vol. 7, No. 2, 4. 1935-1936. 1 reel. {Los Angeles. Jun. - Sept. 1935, Jan. - Mar.
    1936}

Shabes Zshurnal (Shabbath Journal). 1908. [BM 685.S423] 1 reel.

Southern Guide (Der Wegweiser). Vol. 1, No. 2. 1908. One third reel. {On same reel as *Jerusalem Times,*
    Southern Israelite, Mar. 1908}

Southern Israelite. Vol. 44, Nov 29, 1969. One third reel. {Atlanta, July 18, 1969. On same reel as *Jerusalem*
    Times, Southern Guide}

The Summit - see *Hapisgoh*

Tog - see *Jewish Day*

Torah Velt. 1978-1986. [AP91-T644] 3 reels. {Sept. 1978 - Dec. 1986}

Toren. 12 vol. 1913-1924. [DS101.Y6] 8 reels.

Wyoming Jewish Press. 1930-1940. 1 reel. {Sept. 22, 1930 - Oct. 2, 1940}

Yidisner Recorder. Vol. 1-4. 1893-1895. 1 reel. {Apr. 3, 1893 - Mar. 1, 1895}

Yidisher Shprakh. Vol. 1-15. 1941-1955. [PJ5111.Y52] 2 reels.

Miscellaneous Jewish Periodicals -
  Reel 1:
    Israelietische Almanak Voor Ned. West Indies (Surinam), 1911
    Israelietische Almanak Voor Suriname. (Surinam), 1943 - 1944
    Israelietische Almanak - Yearbook for the Jewish communities on Curacao and Aruba (Curacao) 1946 - 1951
    Home Journal. (Curacao) Vol. 1: 1-24; Vol. 2: 1-6. Nov. 1, 1889 - Jan. 15, 1891
    Shemah Israel. (Curacao) Series 1: 1-2. Jan 29, 1864 - May 30, 1865
  Reel 2:
    The Jewish Immigrant. 1908 - 1909 {New York City. English/Yiddish. Aug. 1908, 1909}
    Dr. Birnbaum's Vochenblatt. 1908 {Czernowitz}
    Der Chodesh. 1921 {Warsaw}
    Folkstimme. 1901 - 1902 {Vilna}
    Di Shtime. {Vilna}
    Shabbos Zhurnal. April 1905 {New York City}
    Shulamith. 1889 {New York City, Yiddish}

Appendix C

MASSACHUSETTS CITIES AND TOWNS

This appendix includes an overview of Probate and Land records, which are kept on the county level in Massachusetts. An alphabetical list of all Massachusetts cities and towns with their corresponding counties and districts, and addresses of the Registries of Deeds and Probate follows.

Probate Records and Land Records

If a person that you are researching owned property or other substantial assets, it might be worthwhile to conduct a search at the Registry of Deeds and Registry of Probate. In Massachusetts, probate is registered by county and land records are registered by district within each county. This appendix lists the county and district for each Massachusetts city and town. U.S. Census records (1900, 1910 and 1920) have a column listing home ownership.

Registry of Deeds

A Registry of Deeds holds land records. By researching these, you will be able to determine what property a relative owned, including who sold him the property, who held mortgages for the property, and who purchased the property from him. In addition, if ownership of the property was transferred by inheritance, the Registry of Deeds would hold a record of that transfer. Often, you will be able to determine who owned the neighboring property and be able to get a copy of a detailed map of the property's layout.

There are two types of indexes for locating the owners of recorded land: the Grantor Index and the Grantee Index. A Grantor is someone who sells or transfers property, or who grants a mortgage. The Grantee is the person who receives the property or a partial interest in the property. The indexes are organized by year or group of years, and then alphabetically by surname. It is usually easiest to begin searching the Grantor Index for an entry referencing the sale of the property. The documentation of the sale almost always provides a reference to the document recording the prior purchase of the property. The indexes reference a record book and page number, which can be used to find the original document.

Registry of Probate

A Registry of Probate holds wills, and also holds records of guardianship, adoption, divorce and name change. There will be no Probate records if the deceased had very little or no property. If spouses are joint owners of real estate, then the property automatically goes to the survivor upon the death of the first spouse, thus no record would be filed at that time. A will might contain information such as: heirs, other relatives and friends, lawyer, administrator, executor, business, real property, personal property, debtors and creditors. Probate records are filed in the county of the primary domicile at the time of death. A Registry of Probate holds indexes, which are usually arranged by year or group of years, and then alphabetically. These indexes point to a docket number, file number or book/page number.

The following is an alphabetical list of Massachusetts cities and towns with their corresponding counties. For counties with more than one Registry of Deeds, the Registry location is also listed.

TOWN/CITY	COUNTY
Abington	Plymouth
Acton	Middlesex - South
Acushnet	Bristol - South
Adams	Berkshire - North
Agawam	Hamden
Alford	Berkshire - South
Amesbury	Essex - South
Amherst	Hampshire
Andover	Essex - North
Arlington	Middlesex - South
Ashburnham	Worcester - North
Ashby	Middlesex - South
Ashfield	Franklin
Ashland	Middlesex - South
Athol	Worcester - Worcester
Attleboro	Bristol - North
Auburn	Worcester - Worcester
Avon	Norfolk
Ayer	Middlesex - South
Barnstable	Barnstable
Barre	Worcester - Worcester
Becket	Berkshire - Middle
Bedford	Middlesex - South
Belchertown	Hampshire
Bellingham	Norfolk
Belmont	Middlesex - South
Berkeley	Bristol - North
Berlin	Worcester - Worcester
Bernardston	Franklin
Beverly	Essex - South
Billerica	Middlesex - North
Blackstone	Worcester - Worcester
Blandford	Hamden
Bolton	Worcester - Worcester
Boston	Suffolk
Bourne	Barnstable
Boxborough	Middlesex - South
Boxford	Essex - South
Boylston	Worcester - Worcester
Braintree	Norfolk
Brewster	Barnstable
Bridgewater	Plymouth
Brimfield	Hamden
Brockton	Plymouth
Brookfield	Worcester - Worcester
Brookline	Norfolk
Buckland	Franklin
Burlington	Middlesex - South
Cambridge	Middlesex - South
Canton	Norfolk
Carlisle	Middlesex - North
Carver	Plymouth
Charlemont	Franklin
Chesterfield	Hampshire
Chicopee	Hamden
Chilmark	Dukes
Clarksburg	Berkshire - North
Clinton	Worcester - Worcester
Cochituate	Middlesex - South
Cohasset	Norfolk
Colrain	Franklin
Concord	Middlesex - South
Conway	Franklin
Cummington	Hampshire
Dalton	Berkshire - Middle
Danvers	Essex - South
Dartmouth	Bristol - South
Dedham	Norfolk
Deerfield	Franklin
Dennis	Barnstable
Dighton	Bristol - North
Douglas	Worcester - Worcester
Dover	Norfolk
Dracut	Middlesex - North
Dudley	Worcester - Worcester
Dunstable	Middlesex - North
Duxbury	Plymouth
East Bridgewater	Plymouth
East Brookfield	Worcester - Worcester
East Longmeadow	Hamden
Eastham	Barnstable
Easthampton	Hampshire
Easton	Bristol - North
Edgartown	Dukes
Egremont	Berkshire - South
Erving	Franklin
Essex	Essex - South
Everett	Middlesex - South
Fairhaven	Bristol - South
Fall River	Bristol - Fall River
Falmouth	Barnstable
Fitchburg	Worcester - North
Florida	Berkshire - North
Foxborough	Norfolk
Framingham	Middlesex - South
Franklin	Norfolk
Freetown	Bristol - Fall River
Gardner	Worcester - Worcester
Gay Head	Dukes
Georgetown	Essex - South
Gill	Franklin
Gloucester	Essex - South
Goshen	Hampshire
Gosnold	Dukes
Grafton	Worcester - Worcester
Granby	Hampshire
Granville	Hamden
Great Barrington	Berkshire - South
Greenfield	Franklin
Groton	Middlesex - South
Groveland	Essex - South
Hadley	Hampshire
Halifax	Plymouth
Hamilton	Essex - South
Hampton	Hamden
Hancock	Berkshire - North
Hanover	Plymouth
Hanson	Plymouth
Hardwick	Worcester - Worcester
Harvard	Worcester - Worcester
Harwich	Barnstable

Hatfield	Hampshire	Montgomery	Hamden
Haverhill	Essex - South	Mount Washington	Berkshire - South
Hawley	Franklin	Nahant	Essex - South
Heath	Franklin	Nantucket	Nantucket
Hingham	Plymouth	Natick	Middlesex - South
Hinsdale	Berkshire - Middle	Needham	Norfolk
Holbrook	Norfolk	New Ashford	Berkshire - North
Holden	Worcester - Worcester	New Bedford	Bristol - South
Holland	Hamden	New Braintree	Worcester - Worcester
Holliston	Middlesex - South	New Marlborough	Berkshire - South
Holyoke	Hamden	New Salem	Franklin
Hopedale	Worcester - Worcester	Newbury	Essex - South
Hopkinton	Middlesex - South	Newburyport	Essex - South
Hubbardston	Worcester - Worcester	Newton	Middlesex - South
Hudson	Middlesex - South	Norfolk	Norfolk
Hull	Plymouth	North Adams	Berkshire - North
Huntington	Hampshire	North Andover	Essex - North
Ipswich	Essex - South	North Attleborough	Bristol - North
Kingston	Plymouth	North Brookfield	Worcester - Worcester
Lakeville	Plymouth	North Reading	Middlesex - South
Lancaster	Worcester - Worcester	Northborough	Worcester - Worcester
Lanesborough	Berkshire - North	Northbridge	Worcester - Worcester
Lawrence	Essex - North	Northfield	Franklin
Lee	Berkshire - Middle	Norton	Bristol - North
Leicester	Worcester - Worcester	Norwell	Plymouth
Lenox	Berkshire - Middle	Norwood	Norfolk
Leominster	Worcester - North	Northampton	Hampshire
Leverett	Franklin	Oak Bluffs	Dukes
Lexington	Middlesex - South	Oakham	Worcester - Worcester
Leyden	Franklin	Orange	Franklin
Lincoln	Middlesex - South	Orleans	Barnstable
Littleton	Middlesex - South	Otis	Berkshire - Middle
Longmeadow	Hamden	Oxford	Worcester - Worcester
Lowell	Middlesex - North	Palmer	Hamden
Ludlow	Hamden	Peabody	Essex - South
Lunenburg	Worcester - North	Pelham	Hampshire
Lynn	Essex - South	Pembroke	Plymouth
Lynnfield	Essex - South	Pepperell	Middlesex - South
Malden	Middlesex - South	Peru	Berkshire - Middle
Manchester	Essex - South	Petersham	Worcester - Worcester
Mansfield	Bristol - North	Phillipston	Worcester - Worcester
Marblehead	Essex - South	Pinehurst	Middlesex - North
Marion	Plymouth	Pittsfield	Berkshire - Middle
Marlborough	Middlesex - South	Plainfield	Hampshire
Marshfield	Plymouth	Plainville	Norfolk
Mashpee	Barnstable	Plymouth	Plymouth
Mattapoisett	Plymouth	Plympton	Plymouth
Maynard	Middlesex - South	Princeton	Worcester - Worcester
Medfield	Norfolk	Provincetown	Barnstable
Medford	Middlesex - South	Paxton	Worcester - Worcester
Medway	Norfolk	Quincy	Norfolk
Melrose	Middlesex - South	Randolph	Norfolk
Mendon	Worcester - Worcester	Raynham	Bristol - North
Merrimac	Essex - South	Reading	Middlesex - South
Methuen	Essex - North	Rehoboth	Bristol - North
Middleborough	Plymouth	Revere	Suffolk
Middlefield	Hampshire	Richmond	Berkshire - Middle
Middleton	Essex - South	Rochester	Plymouth
Milford	Worcester - Worcester	Rockland	Plymouth
Millbury	Worcester - Worcester	Rockport	Essex - South
Millis	Norfolk	Rowe	Franklin
Millville	Worcester - Worcester	Rowley	Essex - South
Milton	Norfolk	Royalston	Worcester - Worcester
Monroe	Franklin	Russell	Hamden
Monson	Hamden	Rutland	Worcester - Worcester
Montague	Franklin	Salem	Essex - South
Monterey	Berkshire - South	Salisbury	Essex - South

Sandisfield	Berkshire - South	Wales	Hamden
Sandwich	Barnstable	Walpole	Norfolk
Saugus	Essex - South	Waltham	Middlesex - South
Savoy	Berkshire - North	Ware	Hampshire
Scituate	Plymouth	Wareham	Plymouth
Seekonk	Bristol - North	Warren	Worcester - Worcester
Sharon	Norfolk	Warwick	Franklin
Sheffield	Berkshire - South	Washington	Berkshire - Middle
Shelburne	Franklin	Watertown	Middlesex - South
Sherborn	Middlesex - South	Wayland	Middlesex - South
Shirley	Middlesex - South	Webster	Worcester - Worcester
Shrewsbury	Worcester - Worcester	Wellesley	Norfolk
Shutesbury	Franklin	Wellfleet	Barnstable
Somerset	Bristol - Fall River	Wendell	Franklin
Somerville	Middlesex - South	Wenham	Essex - South
Southbridge	Worcester - Worcester	West Boylston	Worcester - Worcester
South Hadley	Hampshire	West Bridgewater	Plymouth
Southampton	Hampshire	West Brookfeld	Worcester - Worcester
Southborough	Worcester - Worcester	West Newbury	Essex - South
Southwick	Hamden	West Springfield	Hamden
Spencer	Worcester - Worcester	West Stockbridge	Berkshire - South
Springfield	Hamden	West Tisbury	Dukes
Sterling	Worcester - Worcester	Westborough	Worcester - Worcester
Stockbridge	Berkshire - Middle	Westfield	Hamden
Stoneham	Middlesex - South	Westford	Middlesex - North
Stoughton	Norfolk	Westhampton	Hampshire
Stow	Middlesex - South	Westminster	Worcester - North
Sturbridge	Worcester - Worcester	Weston	Middlesex - South
Sudbury	Middlesex - South	Westport	Bristol - South
Sunderland	Franklin	Westwood	Norfolk
Sutton	Worcester - Worcester	Weymouth	Norfolk
Swampscott	Essex - South	Whately	Franklin
Swansea	Bristol - Fall River	Whitman	Plymouth
Taunton	Bristol - North	Wilbraham	Hamden
Templeton	Worcester - Worcester	Williamsburg	Hampshire
Tewksbury	Middlesex - North	Williamstown	Berkshire - North
Tisbury	Dukes	Wilmington	Middlesex - North
Tolland	Hamden	Winchendon	Worcester - Worcester
Topsfield	Essex - South	Winchester	Middlesex - South
Townsend	Middlesex - South	Windsor	Berkshire - North
Truro	Barnstable	Winthrop	Suffolk
Tyngsborough	Middlesex - North	Woburn	Middlesex - South
Tyringham	Berkshire - Middle	Woodville	Middlesex - South
Upton	Worcester - Worcester	Worcester	Worcester - Worcester
Uxbridge	Worcester - Worcester	Worthington	Hampshire
Waban	Middlesex - South	Wrentham	Norfolk
Wakefield	Middlesex - South	Yarmouth	Barnstable

Massachusetts Registries of Deeds and Probate

See the more detailed write-ups for Middlesex and Suffolk counties.

Barnstable Registry of Deeds
508-362-2511 x225
PO Box 427
Barnstable, MA 02630

Barnstable Registry of Probate
508-362-2511
Main St., PO Box 346
Barnstable, MA 02630-0346

Berkshire Northern Registry of Deeds
413-743-1003
65 Park St.
Adams, MA 01220

Berkshire Southern Registry of Deeds
413-528-0146
334 Main St.
Great Barrington, MA 01230

Berkshire Middle Registry of Deeds
413-443-7438
44 Bank Row
Pittsfield, MA 01201

Berkshire Registry of Probate
413-442-6941
44 Bank Row
Pittsfield, MA 01201

Bristol Northern Registry of Deeds
508-822-3081
11 Court St.
Taunton, MA 02780

Bristol Southern Registry of Deeds
508-993-2603
25 North 6th St.
New Bedford, MA 02740

Bristol Fall River Registry of Deeds
508-671-1651
441 No. Main St.
Fall River, MA 02720

Bristol Registry of Probate
508-824-4004
11 Court St., PO Box 567
Taunton, MA 02780

Dukes Registry of Deeds
508-627-4025
81 Main St., PO Box 5231
Edgartown, MA 02539

Dukes Registry of Probate
508-627-4703
81 Main St., PO Box 5031
Edgartown, MA 02539-5031

Essex Northern Registry of Deeds
508-683-2745
381 Common St.
Lawrence, MA 01840

Essex Registry of Probate
508-741-0201 x381
36 Federal St.
Salem, MA 01970

Essex Southern Registry of Deeds
508-741-0200 x250
36 Federal St.
Salem, MA 01970

Franklin Registry of Deeds
413-772-0239
425 Main St., PO Box 1495
Greenfield, MA 01302

Franklin Registry of Probate
413-774-7011, 12, 13
425 Main St., PO Box 290
Greenfield, MA 01301-0290

Hamden Registry of Deeds
413-748-8600
50 State St., PO Box 559
Springfield, MA 01102-0559

Hamden Registry of Probate
413-748-8600
50 State St.
Springfield, MA 01103

Hampshire Registry of Deeds
413-584-3637
99 Main St.
Northampton, MA 01060-3298

Hampshire Registry of Probate
413-586-8500
33 King St.
Northampton, MA 01060

Nantucket Registry of Deeds
508-228-7250
Town & Country Building
16 Broad St.
Nantucket, MA 02554

Nantucket Registry of Probate
508-228-2669
Broad St., PO Box 1116
Nantucket, MA 02554

Norfolk Registry of Deeds
617-461-6122, 6123
649 High St.
Dedham, MA 02026-0897

Norfolk Registry of Probate
617-326-7200
649 High St., PO Box 269
Dedham, MA 02027-0269

Plymouth Registry of Deeds
No. Russell St., PO Box 3535
Plymouth, MA 02361-3535

Plymouth Registry of Probate
508-747-6204
Russell St., PO Box 3640
Plymouth, MA 02361

Worcester Northern District Registry of Deeds
508-342-2637
84 Elm St.
Fitchburg, MA 01420

Worcester Registry of Probate
508-756-2441
2 Main St.
Worcester, MA 01608-1176

Worcester Worcester District Registry of Deeds
508-798-7717
2 Main St.
Worcester, MA 01608

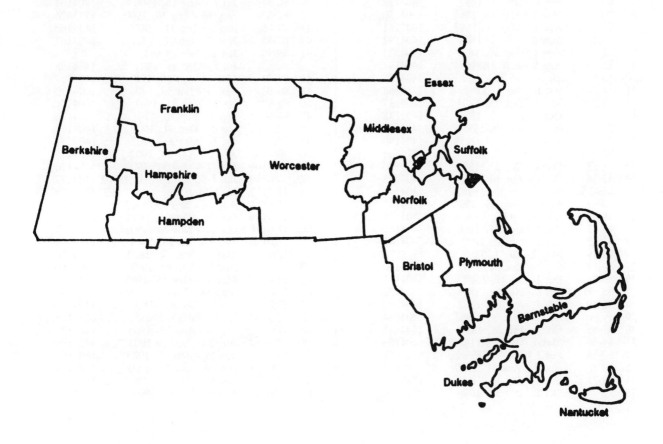

Appendix D

BOSTON SHIPS, 1891-1903

Compiled by Carol Coplin Baker

This appendix lists passenger ships entering the port of Boston, for the period of 1891-1903. This information was extracted from the first 69 reels of National Archives Microfilm Publication T843, *Passenger Lists of Vessels Arriving at Boston, MA, 1891-1943*. This work extends the *Morton Allan Directory of European Passenger Steamship Arrivals*, which lists Boston ship arrivals for 1904-1926. The entries are arranged chronologically by date of arrival, and contain: the ship name, port(s) of origin, National Archives microfilm reel number, volume and page number. At the end of this appendix is a cross-reference list, arranged alphabetically by name of ship.

For many ships, especially during the 1893-1901 period, there are **two** passenger lists for each voyage, each containing information for the same passengers. These are noted in the last "See also" column. Researchers are advised to check both lists for each ship.

Here is a table of the first 69 microfilm reels of NAMP T843, which volume number they contain, their inclusive dates, and the corresponding LDS Family History Library (FHL) microfilm number.

#	Volumes	Dates	FHL film #	#	Volumes	Dates	FHL film #
1	1-2	Aug 1 - Dec 1, 1891	1404126	36	74-75	Jan 1 - Mar 31, 1900	1404161
2	3-4	Jan 1 - Jun 30, 1892	1404127	37	76-78	Apr 1 - Jun 30, 1900	1715575
3	5	Jul 1 - Aug 31, 1892	1404128	38	79	Jan 1 - Dec 31, 1900	1404163
4	6	Sep 1 - Oct 31, 1892	1404129	39	80-81	Jul 1 - Aug 15, 1900	1404164
5	7-8	Nov 1 - Mar 31, 1893	1404130	40	82-83	Aug 16 - Sep 30, 1900	1715576
6	9	Apr 1 - May 31, 1893	1404131	41	84-86	Sep 1 - Oct 31, 1900	1404166
7	10-11	May 1 - Jul 31, 1893	1404132	42	87-88	Nov 1 - Jun 30, 1901	1404167
8	12	Aug 1 - Sep 30, 1893	1404133	43	89-90	Jan 1 - Feb 28 and	
9	13-15	Aug 9 - Mar 31, 1894	1404134			Jul 1 - Dec 31, 1901	1404168
10	16-17	Jan 1 - Jun 30, 1894	1404135	44	91-92	Mar 1 - Apr 30, 1901	1404169
11	18-20	Jun 1 - Aug 1, 1894	1715568	45	93-94	May 1 - Jun 30, 1901	1404170
12	21-23	Sep 1 - Dec 31, 1894	1404137	46	95-97	Jul 1 - Aug 31, 1901	1404171
13	24-25	Oct 1 - Apr 30, 1895	1404138	47	98-99	Sep 1 - Sep 30, 1901	1404172
14	26-27	Jan 1 - Jun 30, 1895	1404139	48	100-102	Oct 1 - Dec 31, 1901	1404173
15	28-29	May 1 - Aug 31, 1895	1404140	49	103-104	Jan 1 - Mar 31, 1902	1404174
16	30-30a	Jul 1 - Sep 30, 1895	1715569	50	105-106	Apr 1 - Apr 30, 1902	1404175
17	31-32	Sep 1 - Dec 31, 1895	1715570	51	107-108	May 1 - May 31, 1902	1404176
18	33-34	Oct 1 - Apr 30, 1896	1404143	52	109-110	Jun 1-30 & Jul 15-31, 1902	1404177
19	34a-35	Jan 1 - Jun 30, 1896	1404144	53	111-112	Jul 1-14 & Aug 1-15, 1902	1404178
20	36-37	May 1 - Aug 31, 1896	1404145	54	113-114	Aug 16 - Sep 15, 1902	1404179
21	38-39	Jul 1 - Sep 30, 1896	1404146	55	115-116	Sep 16 - Oct 11, 1902	1715577
22	40-42	Sep 1 - Dec 31, 1896	1404147	56	117-118	Oct 12 - Nov 30, 1902	1404181
23	43-45	Jan 1 - Jun 30, 1897	1404148	57	119-120	Dec 1 - Feb 28, 1903	1715578
24	46-49	May 1 - Jun 1, 1897	1715571	58	121	Mar 1 - Mar 31, 1903	1715579
25	50-52	Sep 1 - Dec 31, 1897	1404150	59	122	Apr 1 - Apr 30, 1903	1404184
26	53-54	Oct 1 - Jul 31, 1898	1404151	60	123	May 1 - May 15, 1903	1404185
27	55, 57	Jan 1 - May 31, 1898	1404152	61	124	May 16 - May 31, 1903	1404186
28	58-59	Jun 1 - Aug 31, 1898	1404153	62	125	Jun 1 - Jun 30, 1903	1404187
29	59a-60	Aug 1 - Dec 31, 1898	1404154	63	126-127	Jul 1 - Jul 31, 1903	1404188
30	61-63	Oct 1 - Feb 28, 1899	1404155	64	128	Aug 1 - Aug 19, 1903	1404189
31	64-66	Mar 1 - May 31, 1899	1404156	65	129-130	Aug 20 - Sep 10, 1903	1404190
32	67-68	Jun 1 - Jul 31, 1899	1404157	66	131	Sep 11 - Sep 19, 1903	1404191
33	69	Aug 1 - Aug 31, 1899	1715572	67	132-133	Sep 20 - Oct 14, 1903	1404192
34	70-71	Sep 1 - Sep 30, 1899	1715573	68	134-135	Oct 15 - Nov 30, 1903	1404193
35	72-73	Oct 1 - Dec 31, 1899	1715574	69	136-137	Dec 1 - Jan 31, 1904	1404194

Year	Date	Ship	From	T843 Reel#	Vol	Page	See also
1891	2-Aug	Catalonia	Liverpool/Queenstown	1	1	4	
1891	4-Aug	Ottoman	Liverpool	1	1	19	
1891	9-Aug	Cephalonia	Liverpool/Queenstown	1	1	32	
1891	11-Aug	Prussian	Glasgow	1	1	42	
1891	13-Aug	Roman	Liverpool	1	1	52	
1891	17-Aug	Samaria	Liverpool/Queenstown	1	1	70	
1891	19-Aug	Michigan	Liverpool	1	1	87	
1891	23-Aug	Pavonia	Liverpool/Queenstown	1	1	114	
1891	24-Aug	Scandinavian	Glasgow	1	1	121	
1891	27-Aug	Kansas	Liverpool	1	1	131	
1891	30-Aug	Scythia	Glasgow	1	1	154	
1891	2-Sep	Norseman	Liverpool	1	1	170	
1891	7-Sep	Catalonia	Liverpool/Queenstown	1	1	207	
1891	9-Sep	Nestorian	Glasgow	1	1	227	
1891	10-Sep	Ottoman	Liverpool	1	1	232	
1891	13-Sep	Cephalonia	Liverpool/Queenstown	1	1	252	
1891	16-Sep	Roman	Liverpool	1	1	268	
1891	22-Sep	Prussian	Glasgow	1	1	302	
1891	23-Sep	Michigan	Liverpool	1	1	312	
1891	23-Sep	Samaria	Liverpool/Queenstown	1	1	296	
1891	28-Sep	Pavonia	Liverpool/Queenstown	1	1	337	
1891	2-Oct	Kansas	Liverpool	1	2	13	
1891	5-Oct	Scythia	Glasgow	1	2	26	
1891	8-Oct	Norseman	Liverpool	1	2	45	
1891	9-Oct	Scandinavian	Glasgow	1	2	47	
1891	14-Oct	Catalonia	Liverpool/Queenstown	1	2	67	
1891	16-Oct	Ottoman	Liverpool	1	2	80	
1891	19-Oct	Cephalonia	Liverpool/Queenstown	1	2	90	
1891	22-Oct	Nestorian	Glasgow	1	2	99	
1891	22-Oct	Roman	Liverpool	1	2	102	
1891	28-Oct	Michigan	Liverpool	1	2	115	
1891	29-Oct	Samaria	Liverpool/Queenstown	1	2	122	
1891	1-Nov	Pavonia	Liverpool/Queenstown	1	2	137	
1891	3-Nov	Bavarian	Liverpool	1	2	144	
1891	5-Nov	Kansas	Liverpool	1	2	147	
1891	5-Nov	Scythia	Glasgow	1	2	158	
1891	10-Nov	Norseman	Liverpool	1	2	165	
1891	16-Nov	Catalonia	Liverpool/Queenstown	1	2	178	
1891	19-Nov	Ottoman	Liverpool	1	2	186	
1891	23-Nov	Cephalonia	Liverpool/Queenstown	1	2	195	
1891	24-Nov	Lake Superior	Liverpool	1	2	200	
1891	25-Nov	Roman	Liverpool	1	2	202	
1891	1-Dec	Michigan	Liverpool	1	2	220	
1891	4-Dec	Pavonia	Liverpool/Queenstown	1	2	235	
1891	4-Dec	Peruvian	Glasgow	1	2	230	
1891	7-Dec	Lake Huron	Liverpool	1	2	238	
1891	14-Dec	Scythia	Liverpool/Queenstown	1	2	247	
1891	17-Dec	Lake Ontario	Liverpool	1	2	251	
1891	19-Dec	Norseman	Liverpool	1	2	256	
1891	19-Dec	Samaritan	Glasgow	1	2	260	
1891	23-Dec	Catalonia	Liverpool/Queenstown	1	2	271	
1891	24-Dec	Ottoman	Liverpool	1	2	275	
1891	28-Dec	Cephalonia	Liverpool/Queenstown	1	2	283	
1892	2-Jan	Rowan	Liverpool	2	3	5	
1892	2-Jan	Scandinavian	Glasgow	2	3	7	
1892	6-Jan	Lake Superior	Liverpool	2	3	15	
1892	6-Jan	Michigan	Liverpool	2	3	17	
1892	12-Jan	Lake Huron	Liverpool	2	3	27	
1892	19-Jan	Pavonia	Liverpool/Queenstown	2	3	32	
1892	20-Jan	Norseman	Liverpool	2	3	35	
1892	28-Jan	Kansas	Liverpool	2	3	49	
1892	28-Jan	Lake Ontario	Liverpool	2	3	46	
1892	31-Jan	Ottoman	Liverpool	2	3	55	
1892	2-Feb	Cephalonia	Liverpool/Queenstown	2	3	58	
1892	4-Feb	Rowan	Liverpool	2	3	68	
1892	12-Feb	Michigan	Liverpool	2	3	82	
1892	14-Feb	Lake Superior	Liverpool	2	3	83	
1892	15-Feb	Scandinavian	Glasgow	2	3	84	
1892	16-Feb	Catalonia	Liverpool/Queenstown	2	3	87	
1892	20-Feb	Norseman	Liverpool	2	3	101	
1892	22-Feb	Lake Huron	Liverpool	2	3	103	
1892	24-Feb	Peruvian	Glasgow	2	3	107	
1892	28-Feb	Kansas	Liverpool	2	3	118	
1892	4-Mar	Ottoman	Liverpool	2	3	123	
1892	9-Mar	Samaritan	Liverpool	2	3	134	
1892	13-Mar	Roman	Liverpool	2	3	143	
1892	17-Mar	Lake Neprzon	Liverpool	2	3	161	
1892	20-Mar	Michigan	Liverpool	2	3	164	
1892	22-Mar	Catalonia	Liverpool/Queenstown	2	3	177	
1892	22-Mar	Lake Superior	Liverpool	2	3	172	
1892	24-Mar	Assyrian	Glasgow	2	3	185	
1892	24-Mar	Norseman	Liverpool	2	3	194	

Year	Date	Ship	From	Reel#	Vol	Page	See also
1892	27-Mar	Pavonia	Liverpool/Queenstown	2	3	201	
1892	30-Mar	Kansas	Liverpool	2	3	214	
1892	6-Apr	Navarro	London	2	3	234	
1892	6-Apr	Ottoman	Liverpool	2	3	238	
1892	7-Apr	Buenos Ayrian	Glasgow	2	3	240	
1892	10-Apr	Cephalonia	Liverpool/Queenstown	2	3	255	
1892	16-Apr	Roman	Liverpool	2	3	284	
1892	17-Apr	Scythia	Liverpool/Queenstown	2	3	289	
1892	19-Apr	Scandinavian	Glasgow	2	3	307	
1892	20-Apr	Michigan	Liverpool	2	3	319	
1892	25-Apr	Catalonia	Liverpool/Queenstown	2	3	353	
1892	27-Apr	Norseman	Liverpool	2	3	369	
1892	1-May	Pavonia	Liverpool/Queenstown	2	4	4	
1892	4-May	Prussian	Glasgow	2	4	29	
1892	5-May	Kansas	Liverpool	2	4	42	
1892	10-May	Ottoman	Liverpool	2	4	86	
1892	10-May	Samaria	Liverpool/Queenstown	2	4	68	
1892	15-May	Cephalonia	Liverpool/Queenstown	2	4	103	
1892	18-May	Austrian	Glasgow	2	4	123	
1892	19-May	Roman	Liverpool	2	4	150	
1892	22-May	Scythia	Liverpool/Queenstown	2	4	158	
1892	25-May	Michigan	Liverpool	2	4	178	
1892	31-May	Catalonia	Liverpool/Queenstown	2	4	201	
1892	1-Jun	Scandinavian	Glasgow	2	4	215	
1892	2-Jun	Norseman	Liverpool	2	4	224	
1892	5-Jun	Pavonia	Liverpool/Queenstown	2	4	238	
1892	8-Jun	Kansas	Liverpool	2	4	256	
1892	14-Jun	Samaria	Liverpool/Queenstown	2	4	276	
1892	15-Jun	Prussian	Glasgow	2	4	283	
1892	16-Jun	Gothia	Hamburg	2	4	295	
1892	16-Jun	Ottoman	Liverpool	2	4	297	
1892	19-Jun	Cephalonia	Liverpool/Queenstown	2	4	306	
1892	21-Jun	Roman	Liverpool	2	4	332	
1892	23-Jun	Halifax	Halifax	2	4	326	
1892	25-Jun	Slavonnia	Hamburg	2	4	351	
1892	26-Jun	Scythia	Liverpool/Queenstown	2	4	344	
1892	28-Jun	Austrian	Glasgow	2	4	356	
1892	28-Jun	Michigan	Liverpool	2	4	362	
1892	4-Jul	Catalonia	Liverpool/Queenstown	3	5	16	
1892	7-Jul	Norseman	Liverpool	3	5	30	
1892	10-Jul	Pavonia	Liverpool/Queenstown	3	5	42	
1892	13-Jul	Scandinavian	Glasgow	3	5	58	
1892	14-Jul	Kansas	Liverpool	3	5	76	
1892	18-Jul	Worcester	Charlottetown & Halifax	3	5	91	
1892	19-Jul	Ottoman	Liverpool	3	5	102	
1892	19-Jul	Samaria	Liverpool/Queenstown	3	5	97	
1892	23-Jul	Cephalonia	Liverpool/Queenstown	3	5	129	
1892	25-Jul	Prussian	Glasgow	3	5	145	
1892	27-Jul	Roman	Liverpool	3	5	153	
1892	27-Jul	Sch Willina D.	St. John, N.B.	3	5	152	
1892	30-Jul	Scythia	Liverpool/Queenstown	3	5	183	
1892	1-Aug	Michigan	Liverpool	3	5	194	
1892	7-Aug	Catalonia	Liverpool/Queenstown	3	5	229	
1892	10-Aug	Elberfeld	Hamburg	3	5	242	
1892	10-Aug	Norseman	Liverpool	3	5	253	
1892	14-Aug	Pavonia	Liverpool/Queenstown	3	5	271	
1892	15-Aug	Austrian	Glasgow	3	5	285	
1892	17-Aug	Kansas	Liverpool	3	5	308	
1892	22-Aug	Samaria	Liverpool/Queenstown	3	5	343	
1892	24-Aug	Ottoman	Liverpool	3	5	359	
1892	27-Aug	Cephalonia	Liverpool/Queenstown	3	5	385	
1892	30-Aug	Scandinavian	Glasgow	3	5	400	
1892	31-Aug	Roman	Liverpool	4	6	9	
1892	5-Sep	Scythia	Liverpool/Queenstown	4	6	38	
1892	7-Sep	Michigan	Liverpool	4	6	58	
1892	14-Sep	Catalonia	Liverpool/Queenstown	4	6	111	
1892	14-Sep	Prussian	Glasgow	4	6	139	
1892	17-Sep	Yarmouth	Yarmouth	4	6	145	
1892	18-Sep	Pavonia	Liverpool/Queenstown	4	6	169	
1892	20-Sep	Marathon	Liverpool/Queenstown	4	6	254	
1892	21-Sep	Boston	Yarmouth	4	6	165	
1892	3-Oct	Cephalonia	Liverpool/Queenstown	4	6	264	
1892	9-Oct	Scythia	Liverpool/Queenstown	4	6	276	
1892	10-Oct	Scandinavian	Glasgow	4	6	280	
1892	17-Oct	Catalonia	Liverpool/Queenstown	4	6	311	
1892	24-Oct	Pavonia	Liverpool/Queenstown	4	6	344	
1892	8-Nov	Cephalonia	Liverpool/Queenstown	5	7	19	
1892	21-Nov	Catalonia	Liverpool/Queenstown	5	7	58	
1892	22-Nov	Sternhoft	Anxhafen (Germany)	5	7	52	
1892	28-Nov	Pavonia	Liverpool/Queenstown	5	7	81	
1892	12-Dec	Cephalonia	Liverpool/Queenstown	5	7	130	
1892	13-Dec	Pickhuben	Antwerp	5	7	126	
1892	23-Dec	Carroll	Halifax	5	7	100	
1892	28-Dec	Catalonia	Liverpool/Queenstown	5	7	93	

Year	Date	Ship	From	Reel#	Vol	Page	See also
1893	6-Jan	Rhenania	Hamburg	5	8	10	
1893	9-Jan	Pavonia	Liverpool/Queenstown	5	8	19	
1893	19-Jan	Markomannia	Hamburg	5	8	34	
1893	21-Jan	Cephalonia	Liverpool/Queenstown	5	8	41	
1893	9-Feb	Catalonia	Liverpool/Queenstown	5	8	75	
1893	16-Feb	Boston	Yarmouth	5	8	84	
1893	21-Feb	Pavonia	Liverpool/Queenstown	5	8	95	
1893	25-Feb	Boston City	London	5	8	109	
1893	1-Mar	Peruvian	Glasgow	5	8	121	
1893	5-Mar	Cephalonia	Liverpool/Queenstown	5	8	138	
1893	17-Mar	Prussian	Glasgow	5	8	179	
1893	20-Mar	Catalonia	Liverpool/Queenstown	5	8	186	
1893	23-Mar	Boston	Yarmouth	5	8	198	
1893	31-Mar	Buenos Ayrian	Glasgow & Liverpool	5	8	224	
1893	2-Apr	Boston	Yarmouth	6	9	1	
1893	3-Apr	Pavonia	Liverpool/Queenstown	6	9	12	
1893	11-Apr	Scythia	Liverpool/Queenstown	6	9	45	
1893	14-Apr	Peruvian	Glasgow	6	9	69	
1893	15-Apr	Cephalonia	Liverpool/Queenstown	6	9	90	
1893	24-Apr	Catalonia	Liverpool/Queenstown	6	9	130	
1893	26-Apr	Prussian	Glasgow	6	9	153	
1893	30-Apr	Bothina	Liverpool/Queenstown	6	9	175	
1893	2-May	Colonia	Hamburg	6	9	193	
1893	7-May	Pavonia	Liverpool/Queenstown	6	9	220	
1893	11-May	Scandinavian	Glasgow	6	9	244	
1893	14-May	Scythia	Liverpool/Queenstown	6	9	264	
1893	21-May	Cephalonia	Liverpool/Queenstown	6	9	299	
1893	23-May	British Queen	London	6	9	316	
1893	25-May	Nestorian	Glasgow	6	9	325	vol 10 p. 69
1893	29-May	Catalonia	Liverpool/Queenstown	6	9	351	vol 10 p. 80
1893	3-Jun	Bothnia	Liverpool/Queenstown	7	10	118	vol 11 p. 18
1893	6-Jun	Prussian	Glasgow	7	10	134	vol 11 p. 37
1893	11-Jun	Pavonia	Liverpool/Queenstown	7	10	145	vol 11 p. 62
1893	12-Jun	Kehrovieder	Hamburg	7	10	166	vol 11 p. 73
1893	18-Jun	Scythia	Liverpool/Queenstown	7	10	169	vol 11 p. 90
1893	19-Jun	Scandinavian	Glasgow	7	10	197	vol 11 p. 103
1893	25-Jun	Cephalonia	Liverpool/Queenstown	7	10	206	vol 11 p. 128
1893	5-Jul	Catalonia	Liverpool/Queenstown	7	10	226	vol 11 p. 169
1893	5-Jul	Nestorian	Glasgow	7	10	242	vol 11 p. 183
1893	9-Jul	Bothnia	Liverpool/Queenstown	7	10	255	vol 11 p. 202
1893	16-Jul	Pavonia	Liverpool/Queenstown	7	10	265	vol 11 p. 236
1893	21-Jul	Prussian	Glasgow	7	10	278	vol 11 p. 264
1893	23-Jul	Scythia	Liverpool/Queenstown	7	10	289	vol 11 p. 280
1893	30-Jul	Cephalonia	Liverpool/Queenstown	7	10	300	vol 11 p. 317
1893	7-Aug	Catalonia	Liverpool/Queenstown	8	12	37	vol 14 p. 4
1893	8-Aug	Steinhoft	Hamburg	8	12	35	vol 14 p. 1
1893	9-Aug	Scandinavian	Glasgow	8	12	53	vol 14 p. 15
1893	13-Aug	Bothnia	Liverpool/Queenstown	8	12	83	vol 14 p. 22
1893	20-Aug	Pavonia	Liverpool/Queenstown	8	12	130	vol 14 p. 33
1893	22-Aug	Nestorian	Glasgow	8	12	145	vol 14 p. 48
1893	26-Aug	Scythia	Liverpool/Queenstown	8	12	185	vol 14 p. 52
1893	2-Sep	Cephalonia	Liverpool/Queenstown	8	12	230	vol 14 p. 66
1893	6-Sep	Prussian	Glasgow	8	12	257	vol 14 p. 83
1893	10-Sep	Catalonia	Liverpool/Queenstown	8	12	284	vol 14 p. 91
1893	17-Sep	Bothnia	Liverpool/Queenstown	8	12	319	vol 14 p. 103
1893	18-Sep	Scandinavian	Glasgow	8	12	336	vol 14 p. 118
1893	23-Sep	Pavonia	Liverpool/Queenstown	8	12	369	vol 14 p. 122
1893	1-Oct	Scythia	Liverpool/Queenstown	9	13	6	vol 14 p. 141
1893	5-Oct	Nestorian	Glasgow	9	13	23	vol 14 p. 153
1893	8-Oct	Cephalonia	Liverpool/Queenstown	9	13	46	vol 14 p. 159
1893	15-Oct	Catalonia	Liverpool/Queenstown	9	13	77	vol 14 p. 170
1893	19-Oct	Prussian	Glasgow	9	13	98	vol 14 p. 177
1893	29-Oct	Pavonia	Liverpool/Queenstown	9	13	138	vol 14 p. 182
1893	12-Nov	Cephalonia	Liverpool/Queenstown	9	13	172	vol 14 p. 194
1893	18-Nov	Catalonia	Liverpool/Queenstown	9	13	217	vol 14 p. 206
1893	5-Dec	Pavonia	Liverpool/Queenstown	9	13	233	vol 14 p. 212
1893	19-Dec	Cephalonia	Liverpool/Queenstown	9	13	267	vol 14 p. 214
1893	29-Dec	Catalonia	Liverpool/Queenstown	9	13	285	vol 14 p. 217
1894	1-Jan	Baumwall	Hamburg	9	15	10	vol 17 p. 1
1894	17-Jan	Bohemia	Hamburg	9	15	45	vol 17 p. 12
1894	22-Jan	Cephalonia	Liverpool/Queenstown	9	15	51	vol 17 p. 18
1894	8-Feb	Catalonia	Liverpool/Queenstown	9	15	86	vol 17 p. 19
1894	19-Feb	Grimm	Hamburg	9	15	108	vol 17 p. 21
1894	22-Feb	Pavonia	Liverpool/Queenstown	9	15	116	vol 17 p. 25
1894	7-Mar	Cephalonia	Liverpool/Queenstown	9	15	142	vol 17 p. 30
1894	11-Mar	Polynesia	Hamburg	9	15	157	vol 17 p. 34
1894	18-Mar	Pomeranian	Glasgow & Liverpool	9	15	173	vol 17 p. 40
1894	23-Mar	Catalonia	Liverpool/Queenstown	9	15	176	vol 17 p. 42
1894	28-Mar	Italia	Hamburg	9	15	200	vol 17 p. 47
1894	2-Apr	Pavonia	Liverpool/Queenstown	10	16	5	vol 17 p. 55
1894	3-Apr	Carthagenia	Glasgow & Liverpool	9	15	213	vol 17 p. 52
1894	5-Apr	Wandrahm	Hamburg	10	16	21	vol 17 p. 61
1894	7-Apr	Gallia	Liverpool/Queenstown	10	16	35	vol 17 p. 69

Year	Date	Ship	From	Reel#	Vol	Page	See also
1894	7-Apr	Stockholm City	London	10	16	41	
1894	17-Apr	Bothnia	Liverpool/Queenstown	10	16	61	vol 17 p. 79
1894	17-Apr	Hungaria	Hamburg	10	16	69	vol 17 p. 97
1894	18-Apr	Buenos Ayrian	Glasgow	10	16	76	vol 17 p. 108
1894	20-Apr	Prussian	Glasgow	10	16	87	vol 17 p. 110
1894	21-Apr	Catalonia	Liverpool/Queenstown	10	16	98	vol 17 p. 111
1894	27-Apr	Scythia	Liverpool/Queenstown	10	16	122	vol 17 p. 128
1894	2-May	Scandinavian	Glasgow	10	16	132	vol 17 p. 153
1894	6-May	Pavonia	Liverpool/Queenstown	10	16	154	vol 17 p. 167
1894	8-May	Polynesia	Hamburg	10	16	164	vol 17 p. 184
1894	12-May	Gallia	Liverpool/Queenstown	10	16	178	vol 17 p. 199
1894	18-May	Cephalonia	Liverpool/Queenstown	10	16	191	vol 17 p. 222
1894	19-May	Nestorian	Glasgow	10	16	197	vol 17 p. 234
1894	24-May	Catalonia	Liverpool/Queenstown	10	16	210	vol 17 p. 251
1894	28-May	Prussian	Glasgow	10	16	215	vol 17 p. 264
1894	3-Jun	Scythia	Liverpool/Queenstown	10	16	232	vol 18 p. 2
1894	10-Jun	Pavonia	Liverpool/Queenstown	10	16	250	vol 18 p. 23
1894	12-Jun	Scandinavian	Glasgow	10	16	255	vol 18 p. 40
1894	16-Jun	Gallia	Liverpool/Queenstown	10	16	265	vol 18 p. 52
1894	17-Jun	Hungaria	Hamburg	10	16	273	vol 18 p. 60
1894	24-Jun	Cephalonia	Liverpool/Queenstown	10	16	286	vol 18 p. 75
1894	27-Jun	Nestorian	Glasgow	10	16	293	vol 18 p. 89
1894	2-Jul	Catalonia	Liverpool/Queenstown	11	18	108	vol 19 p. 5
1894	2-Jul	Polynesia	Hamburg	11	18	105	vol 19 p. 3
1894	15-Jul	Pavonia	Liverpool/Queenstown	11	18	144	vol 19 p. 32
1894	18-Jul	Prussian	Glasgow	11	18	155	vol 19 p. 39
1894	22-Jul	Grimm	Hamburg	11	18	175	vol 19 p. 60
1894	28-Jul	Cephalonia	Liverpool/Queenstown	11	18	196	vol 19 p. 82
1894	4-Aug	Catalonia	Liverpool/Queenstown	11	19	103	vol 20 p. 16
1894	12-Aug	Scythia	Liverpool/Queenstown	11	19	134	vol 20 p. 51
1894	20-Aug	Pavonia	Liverpool/Queenstown	11	19	168	vol 20 p. 82
1894	26-Aug	Bothnia	Liverpool/Queenstown	11	19	210	vol 20 p. 119
1894	28-Aug	Polynesia	Hamburg	11	19	219	vol 20 p. 141
1894	1-Sep	Cephalonia	Liverpool/Queenstown	12	21	11	vol 22 p. 2
1894	10-Sep	Catalonia	Liverpool/Queenstown	12	21	73	vol 22 p. 13
1894	17-Sep	Scythia	Liverpool/Queenstown	12	21	107	vol 22 p. 113
1894	23-Sep	Pavonia	Liverpool/Queenstown	12	21	138	vol 22 p. 151
1894	28-Sep	Polaria	Hamburg	12	21	178	vol 22 p. 193
1894	30-Sep	Bothnia	Liverpool/Queenstown	12	21	200	vol 22 p. 196
1894	7-Oct	Cephalonia	Liverpool/Queenstown	12	23	24	vol 24 p. 24
1894	12-Oct	Hungaria	Hamburg	12	23	46	vol 24 p. 59
1894	15-Oct	Catalonia	Liverpool/Queenstown	12	23	58	vol 24 p. 62
1894	22-Oct	Pavonia	Liverpool/Queenstown	12	23	85	vol 24 p. 99
1894	6-Nov	Cephalonia	Liverpool/Queenstown	12	23	151	vol 24 p. 149
1894	24-Nov	Catalonia	Liverpool/Queenstown	12	23	123	vol 24 p. 187
1894	3-Dec	Pavonia	Liverpool/Queenstown	12	23	178	vol 24 p. 216
1894	9-Dec	Cephalonia	Liverpool/Queenstown	12	23	188	vol 24 p. 228
1894	19-Dec	Bolivia	Hamburg	12	23	203	vol 24 p. 247
1894	22-Dec	Catalonia	Liverpool/Queenstown	12	23	212	vol 24 p. 256
1895	6-Jan	Sicilia	Hamburg	13	25	8	vol 26 p. 10
1895	7-Jan	Pavonia	Liverpool/Queenstown	13	25	12	vol 26 p. 13
1895	14-Jan	Canadia	Hamburg	13	25	26	vol 26 p. 29
1895	21-Jan	Cephalonia	Liverpool/Queenstown	13	25	29	vol 26 p. 35
1895	1-Feb	Polaria	Hamburg	13	25	47	vol 26 p. 54
1895	4-Feb	Catalonia	Liverpool/Queenstown	13	25	51	vol 26 p. 60
1895	12-Feb	Bolivia	Hamburg	13	25	65	vol 26 p. 71
1895	18-Feb	Samaria	Liverpool/Queenstown	13	25	99	vol 26 p. 79
1895	3-Mar	Cephalonia	Liverpool/Queenstown	13	25	88	vol 26 p. 97
1895	20-Mar	Catalonia	Liverpool/Queenstown	13	25	129	vol 26 p. 119
1895	2-Apr	Pavonia	Liverpool/Queenstown	13	25	176	vol 26 p. 146
1895	6-Apr	California	Hamburg	13	25	218	vol 26
1895	14-Apr	Cephalonia	Liverpool/Queenstown	13	25	250	vol 26 p. 179
1895	21-Apr	Catalonia	Liverpool/Queenstown	13	25	310	vol 26 p. 211
1895	27-Apr	Gallia	Liverpool/Queenstown	13	25	353	vol 26 p. 231
1895	2-May	Peruvian	Glasgow	14	27	5	vol 28 p. 9
1895	6-May	Pavonia	Liverpool/Queenstown	14	27	21	vol 28 p. 30
1895	13-May	Scythia	Liverpool/Queenstown	14	27	47	vol 28 p. 88
1895	15-May	Scandinavian	Glasgow	14	27	60	vol 28 p. 123
1895	17-May	Italia	Hamburg	14	27	71	vol 28 p. 143
1895	20-May	Cephalonia	Liverpool/Queenstown	14	27	80	vol 28 p. 150
1895	27-May	Catalonia	Liverpool/Queenstown	14	27	102	vol 28 p. 207
1895	29-May	Hibernian	Glasgow	14	27	113	vol 28 p. 238
1895	31-May	Russia	Hamburg	14	27	123	vol 28 p. 252
1895	2-Jun	Gallia	Liverpool/Queenstown	14	27	128	vol 28 p. 263
1895	10-Jun	Pavonia	Liverpool/Queenstown	14	27	154	vol 28 p. 303
1895	12-Jun	Peruvian	Glasgow	14	27	163	vol 28 p. 330
1895	13-Jun	Bohemia	Hamburg	14	27	172	vol 28 p. 346
1895	16-Jun	Scythia	Liverpool/Queenstown	14	27	180	vol 28 p. 355
1895	23-Jun	Cephalonia	Liverpool/Queenstown	14	27	204	vol 28 p. 388
1895	24-Jun	Scandinavian	Glasgow	14	27	213	vol 28 p. 407
1895	1-Jul	Catalonia	Liverpool/Queenstown	15	29	6	vol 30 p. 1
1895	6-Jul	Gallia	Liverpool/Queenstown	15	29	30	vol 30 p. 14

Year	Date	Ship	From	Reel#	Vol	Page	See also
1895	9-Jul	Hibernian	Glasgow	15	29	56	vol 30 p. 28
1895	14-Jul	Pavonia	Liverpool/Queenstown	15	29	72	vol 30 p. 48
1895	21-Jul	Scythia	Liverpool/Queenstown	15	29	106	vol 30 p. 72
1895	23-Jul	Heroynia	Hamburg	15	29	127	vol 30 p. 77
1895	23-Jul	Peruvian	Glasgow	15	29	129	vol 30 p. 79
1895	27-Jul	Cephalonia	Liverpool/Queenstown	15	29	146	vol 30 p. 96
1895	5-Aug	California	Hamburg	15	29	216	vol 30 p. 139
1895	5-Aug	Catalonia	Liverpool/Queenstown	15	29	199	vol 30 p. 133
1895	6-Aug	Scandinavian	Glasgow	15	29	220	vol 30 p. 141
1895	10-Aug	Gallia	Liverpool/Queenstown	15	29	233	vol 30 p. 160
1895	18-Aug	Hibernian	Glasgow	15	29	283	vol 30 p. 214
1895	18-Aug	Pavonia	Liverpool/Queenstown	15	29	269	vol 30 p. 197
1895	23-Aug	Scotia	Hamburg	15	29	316	vol 30 p. 231
1895	24-Aug	Scythia	Liverpool/Queenstown	15	29	320	vol 30 p. 249
1895	1-Sep	Cephalonia	Liverpool/Queenstown	16	30A	15	vol 31 p. 2
1895	5-Sep	Peruvian	Glasgow	16	30A	39	vol 31 p. 43
1895	9-Sep	Catalonia	Liverpool/Queenstown	16	30A	73	vol 31 p. 82
1895	14-Sep	Gallia	Liverpool/Queenstown	16	30A	119	vol 31 p. 131
1895	18-Sep	Scandinavian	Glasgow	16	30A	145	vol 31 p. 173
1895	22-Sep	Bothnia	Liverpool/Queenstown	16	30A	180	vol 31 p. 190
1895	30-Sep	Scythia	Liverpool/Queenstown	16	30A	226	vol 31 p. 251
1895	1-Oct	Hibernian	Glasgow	17	32	2	vol 33 p. 2
1895	4-Oct	California	Hamburg	17	32	19	vol 33 p. 18
1895	6-Oct	Cephalonia	Liverpool/Queenstown	17	32	25	vol 33 p. 26
1895	15-Oct	Catalonia	Liverpool/Queenstown	17	32	78	vol 33 p. 81
1895	16-Oct	Peruvian	Glasgow	17	32	96	vol 33 p. 90
1895	27-Oct	Bothnia	Liverpool/Queenstown	17	32	119	vol 33 p. 122
1895	29-Oct	Scandinavian	Glasgow	17	32	136	vol 33 p. 131
1895	10-Nov	Cephalonia	Liverpool/Queenstown	17	32	157	vol 33 p. 156
1895	19-Nov	Catalonia	Liverpool/Queenstown	17	32	182	vol 33 p. 176
1895	25-Nov	Peruvian	Glasgow	17	32	195	vol 33 p. 189
1895	28-Nov	Italia	Hamburg	17	32	204	vol 33 p. 195
1895	1-Dec	Scythia	Liverpool/Queenstown	17	32	211	vol 33 p. 204
1895	16-Dec	Cephalonia	Liverpool/Queenstown	17	32	236	vol 33 p. 233
1895	24-Dec	Catalonia	Liverpool/Queenstown	17	32	257	vol 34-A p. 249
1896	28-Jan	Virginian	London	18	34	23	vol 34-A p. 249
1896	25-Feb	Bothnia	Liverpool/Queenstown	18	34	49	vol 34-A p. 59
1896	7-Mar	Virginian	London	18	34	64	vol 34-A p. 249
1896	26-Mar	Bothnia	Liverpool/Queenstown	18	34	94	vol 34-A p. 103
1896	31-Mar	Scythia	Liverpool/Queenstown	18	34	117	vol 34-A p. 116
1896	7-Apr	Catalonia	Liverpool/Queenstown	18	34	146	vol 34-A p. 137
1896	8-Apr	Sarmatian	Galway & Glasgow	18	34	172	vol 34-A p. 149
1896	13-Apr	Cephalonia	Liverpool/Queenstown	18	34	198	vol 34-A p. 161
1896	18-Apr	Gallia	Liverpool/Queenstown	18	34	237	vol 34-A p. 187
1896	23-Apr	Scandinavian	Glasgow	18	34	273	vol 34-A p. 211
1896	28-Apr	Bothnia	Liverpool/Queenstown	18	34	289	
1896	3-May	Pavonia	Liverpool/Queenstown	19	35	9	vol 36 p. 6
1896	8-May	Peruvian	Glasgow	19	35	65	vol 36 p. 28
1896	10-May	Catalonia	Liverpool/Queenstown	19	35	125	vol 36 p. 46
1896	17-May	Cephalonia	Liverpool/Queenstown	19	35	96	
1896	19-May	Prussian	Glasgow	19	35	173	vol 36 p. 92
1896	24-May	Scythia	Liverpool/Queenstown	19	35	190	vol 36 p. 106
1896	30-May	Gallia	Liverpool/Queenstown	19	35	218	vol 36 p. 123
1896	3-Jun	Hibernian	Glasgow	19	35	249	vol 36 p. 136
1896	7-Jun	Pavonia	Liverpool/Queenstown	19	35	264	vol 36 p. 150
1896	14-Jun	Catalonia	Liverpool/Queenstown	19	35	292	vol 36 p. 169
1896	16-Jun	Peruvian	Glasgow	19	35	314	vol 36 p. 176
1896	21-Jun	Cephalonia	Liverpool/Queenstown	19	35	328	vol 36 p. 186
1896	24-Jun	Servia	Liverpool	19	35	344	vol 36 p. 194
1896	27-Jun	Asturia	Hamburg	19	35	356	
1896	28-Jun	Scythia	Liverpool/Queenstown	19	35	359	vol 36 p. 217
1896	1-Jul	Prussian	Glasgow	20	37	1	vol 38 p. 103
1896	4-Jul	Gallia	Liverpool/Queenstown	20	37	16	vol 38 p. 113
1896	12-Jul	Pavonia	Liverpool/Queenstown	20	37	39	vol 38 p. 85
1896	16-Jul	Norwegian	Glasgow	20	37	48	vol 38 p. 27
1896	20-Jul	Catalonia	Liverpool/Queenstown	20	37	61	vol 38 p. 61
1896	26-Jul	Cephalonia	Liverpool/Queenstown	20	37	81	vol 38 p. 1
1896	29-Jul	Peruvian	Glasgow	20	37	99	vol 38 p. 28
1896	31-Jul	Servia	Liverpool	20	37	107	vol 38 p. 156-A
1896	8-Aug	Gallia	Liverpool/Queenstown	20	37	145	vol 38 p. 163
1896	10-Aug	Prussian	Glasgow	20	37	158	vol 38 p. 188
1896	15-Aug	Pavonia	Liverpool/Queenstown	20	37	174	vol 38 p. 207
1896	18-Aug	Asturia	Hamburg	20	37	191	vol 38 p. 231
1896	23-Aug	Catalonia	Liverpool/Queenstown	20	37	212	vol 38 p. 247
1896	23-Aug	Norwegian	Glasgow	20	37	213	vol 38 p. 255
1896	30-Aug	Cephalonia	Liverpool/Queenstown	20	37	250	vol 38 p. 291
1896	6-Sep	Scythia	Liverpool/Queenstown	21	39	45	vol 40 p. 14
1896	9-Sep	Peruvian	Glasgow	21	39	54	vol 40 p. 47
1896	12-Sep	Bothnia	Liverpool/Queenstown	21	39	87	vol 40 p. 60
1896	21-Sep	Pavonia	Liverpool/Queenstown	21	39	122	vol 40 p. 110
1896	29-Sep	Catalonia	Liverpool/Queenstown	21	39	168	vol 40 p. 151
1896	4-Oct	Servia	Liverpool/Queenstown	22	41	16	vol 42 p. 12

Year	Date	Ship	From	Reel#	Vol	Page	See also
1896	11-Oct	Armenian	Hamburg	22	41	61	vol 42 p. 44
1896	11-Oct	Scythia	Liverpool/Queenstown	22	41	63	vol 42 p. 47
1896	13-Oct	Peruvian	Glasgow	22	41	71	vol 42 p. 62
1896	18-Oct	Bothnia	Liverpool/Queenstown	22	41	89	vol 42 p. 75
1896	25-Oct	Pavonia	Liverpool/Queenstown	22	41	105	vol 42 p. 92
1896	8-Nov	Catalonia	Liverpool/Queenstown	22	41	138	vol 42 p. 120
1896	25-Nov	Pavonia	Liverpool/Queenstown	22	41	165	vol 42 p. 144
1896	4-Dec	Christiania	Hamburg	22	41	183	vol 42 p. 166
1896	4-Dec	Servia	Liverpool/Queenstown	22	41	185	vol 42 p. 168
1896	28-Dec	Pavonia	Liverpool/Queenstown	22	41	222	vol 42 p. 198
1897	2-Jan	Canada	Liverpool	23	43	1	vol 44 p. 1
1897	6-Jan	Cheruskia	Hamburg	23	43	6	vol 44 p. 13
1897	28-Jan	Catalonia	Liverpool/Queenstown	23	43	30	vol 44 p. 25
1897	5-Feb	Canada	Liverpool	23	43	45	vol 44 p. 38
1897	15-Feb	Cephalonia	Liverpool/Queenstown	23	43	50	vol 44 p. 41
1897	21-Feb	Bohemia	Hamburg	23	43	61	vol 44 p. 55
1897	23-Feb	Pavonia	Liverpool/Queenstown	23	43	67	vol 44 p. 63
1897	4-Mar	Catalonia	Liverpool/Queenstown	23	43	86	vol 44 p. 73
1897	13-Mar	Canada	Liverpool	23	43	90	vol 44 p. 88
1897	17-Mar	Cephalonia	Liverpool/Queenstown	23	43	97	vol 44 p. 93
1897	19-Mar	Armenian	Hamburg	23	43	113	vol 44 p. 108
1897	19-Mar	Pavonia	Liverpool/Queenstown	23	43	129	vol 44 p. 118
1897	30-Mar	Hibernian	Glasgow	23	43	136	vol 44 p. 129
1897	31-Mar	Siberian	Glasgow	23	43	168	vol 44 p. 149
1897	14-Apr	Catalonia	Liverpool/Queenstown	23	43	171	vol 44 p. 152
1897	16-Apr	Canada	Liverpool	23	43	184	vol 44 p. 175
1897	19-Apr	Cephalonia	Liverpool/Queenstown	23	43	195	vol 44 p. 1185
1897	25-Apr	Gallia	Liverpool	23	43	214	vol 44 p. 207
1897	2-May	Pavonia	Liverpool/Queenstown	23	45	7	vol 46 p. 207
1897	5-May	Scandinavian	Glasgow	23	45	22	vol 46 p. 41
1897	8-May	Cephalonia	Liverpool/Queenstown	23	45	57	vol 46 p. 86
1897	10-May	Scythia	Liverpool/Queenstown	23	45	34	vol 46 p. 54
1897	19-May	Hibernian	Glasgow	23	45	72	vol 46 p. 109
1897	23-May	Catalonia	Liverpool/Queenstown	23	45	85	vol 46 p. 143
1897	29-May	Gallia	Liverpool	23	45	101	vol 46 p. 174
1897	14-Jun	Pavonia	Liverpool/Queenstown	23	45	123	vol 46 p. 204
1897	14-Jun	Scythia	Liverpool/Queenstown	23	45	142	vol 46 p. 228
1897	16-Jun	Scandinavian	Glasgow	23	45	152	vol 46 p. 241
1897	20-Jun	Cephalonia	Liverpool/Queenstown	23	45	162	vol 46 p. 257
1897	24-Jun	Canada	Liverpool	23	45	174	vol 46 p. 277
1897	27-Jun	Hibernian	Glasgow	23	45	185	vol 46 p. 282
1897	28-Jun	Catalonia	Liverpool/Queenstown	23	45	189	vol 46 p. 292
1897	3-Jul	Gallia	Liverpool	24	48	10	vol 49 p. 2
1897	11-Jul	Pavonia	Liverpool/Queenstown	24	48	34	vol 49 p. 24
1897	18-Jul	Scythia	Liverpool/Queenstown	24	48	55	vol 49 p. 44
1897	28-Jul	Adria	Hamburg	24	48	85	vol 49 p. 87
1897	28-Jul	Scandinavian	Glasgow	24	48	81	vol 49 p. 81
1897	29-Jul	Canada	Liverpool	24	48	89	vol 49 p. 89
1897	7-Aug	Catalonia	Liverpool/Queenstown	24	48	103	vol 49 p. 107
1897	7-Aug	Gallia	Liverpool	24	48	117	vol 49 p. 125
1897	8-Aug	Peruvian	Glasgow	24	48	130	vol 49 p. 144
1897	15-Aug	Pavonia	Liverpool/Queenstown	24	48	151	vol 49 p. 157
1897	17-Aug	Constantia	Hamburg	24	48	158	vol 49 p. 175
1897	23-Aug	Scythia	Liverpool/Queenstown	24	48	182	vol 49 p. 200
1897	30-Aug	Cephalonia	Liverpool/Queenstown	24	48	224	vol 49 p. 234
1897	3-Sep	Canada	Liverpool	25	50	19	vol 51 p. 8
1897	6-Sep	Bohemia	Hamburg	25	50	64	vol 51 p. 54
1897	6-Sep	Catalonia	Liverpool/Queenstown	25	50	66	vol 51 p. 58
1897	8-Sep	Scandinavian	Glasgow	25	50	80	vol 51 p. 77
1897	11-Sep	Gallia	Liverpool	25	50	98	vol 51 p. 89
1897	19-Sep	Pavonia	Liverpool/Queenstown	25	50	151	vol 51 p. 120
1897	27-Sep	Scythia	Liverpool/Queenstown	25	50	192	vol 51 p. 168
1897	5-Oct	Cephalonia	Liverpool/Queenstown	25	52	21	vol 53 p. 16
1897	7-Oct	Canada	Liverpool	25	52	45	vol 53 p. 35
1897	11-Oct	Catalonia	Liverpool/Queenstown	25	52	77	vol 53 p. 66
1897	16-Oct	Gallia	Liverpool	25	52	101	vol 53 p. 82
1897	26-Oct	Pavonia	Liverpool/Queenstown	25	52	132	vol 53 p. 104
1897	1-Nov	Scythia	Liverpool/Queenstown	25	52	154	vol 53 p. 118
1897	3-Nov	Canada	Liverpool	25	52	165	vol 53 p. 125
1897	15-Nov	Cephalonia	Liverpool/Queenstown	25	52	191	vol 53 p. 145
1897	23-Nov	Catalonia	Liverpool/Queenstown	25	52	208	vol 53 p. 159
1897	5-Dec	Canada	Liverpool	25	52	230	vol 53 p. 168
1897	5-Dec	Pavonia	Liverpool/Queenstown	25	52	238	vol 53 p. 174
1897	17-Dec	Cephalonia	Liverpool/Queenstown	25	52	270	vol 53 p. 196
1897	28-Dec	Catalonia	Liverpool/Queenstown	26	52	281	vol 53 p. 203
1898	7-Jan	Canada	Liverpool	26	54	1	vol 55 p. 17
1898	11-Jan	Pavonia	Liverpool/Queenstown	26	54	4	vol 55 p. 27
1898	1-Feb	Catalonia	Liverpool/Queenstown	26	54	6	vol 55 p. 79
1898	11-Feb	Canada	Liverpool	26	54	8	vol 55 p. 107
1898	12-Feb	Pavonia	Liverpool/Queenstown	26	54	11	vol 55 p. 111
1898	19-Feb	Cephalonia	Liverpool/Queenstown	26	54	12	vol 55 p. 127
1898	12-Mar	Catalonia	Liverpool/Queenstown	26	54	18	vol 55 p. 181

Year	Date	Ship	From	Reel#	Vol	Page	See also
1898	17-Mar	Canada	Liverpool	26	54	20	vol 55 p. 205
1898	19-Mar	Pavonia	Liverpool/Queenstown	26	54	30	vol 55 p. 217
1898	21-Mar	Alessia	Hamburg	26	54	33	vol 55 p. 231
1898	30-Mar	Norwegian	Glasgow	26	54	35	vol 55 p. 270
1898	3-Apr	Cephalonia	Liverpool/Queenstown	26	54	33	vol 57 p. 5
1898	15-Apr	Bohemia	Hamburg	26	54	43	vol 57 p. 41
1898	18-Apr	Peruvian	Glasgow	26	54	45	vol 57 p. 66
1898	18-Apr	Scythia	Liverpool/Queenstown	26	54	50	vol 57 p. 82
1898	21-Apr	Canada	Liverpool	26	54	57	vol 57 p. 115
1898	28-Apr	Samaritan	Glasgow	26	54	69	vol 57 p. 152
1898	30-Apr	Pavonia	Liverpool/Queenstown	26	54	73	vol 57 p. 162
1898	3-May	Heroynia	Hamburg	26	54	87	vol 57 p. 208
1898	11-May	Scandinavian	Glasgow	26	54	88	vol 57 p. 235
1898	14-May	Cephalonia	Liverpool/Queenstown	26	54	92	vol 57 p. 251
1898	19-May	Christiania	Hamburg	26	54	104	vol 57 p. 272
1898	21-May	Catalonia	Liverpool/Queenstown	26	54	106	vol 57 p. 293
1898	26-May	Canada	Liverpool	26	54	111	vol 57 p. 311
1898	26-May	Peruvian	Glasgow	26	54	121	vol 57 p. 322
1898	3-Jun	Pavonia	Liverpool/Queenstown	26	54	124	vol 58 reel 28 p. 9
1898	5-Jun	Moravia	Hamburg	26	54	129	vol 58 reel 28 p. 20
1898	20-Jun	Cephalonia	Liverpool/Queenstown	26	54	132	vol 58 reel 28 p. 65
1898	21-Jun	Markomannia	Hamburg	26	54	139	vol 58 reel 28 p. 74
1898	22-Jun	Scandinavian	Glasgow	26	54	142	vol 58 reel 28 p. 86
1898	24-Jun	Canada	Liverpool	26	54	147	vol 58 reel 28 p. 109
1898	25-Jun	Catalonia	Liverpool/Queenstown	26	54	153	vol 58 reel 28 p. 116
1898	5-Jul	Peruvian	Glasgow	26	54	159	vol 58 reel 28 p. 165
1898	8-Jul	Pavonia	Liverpool/Queenstown	26	54	163	vol 58 reel 28 p. 206
1898	10-Jul	New England	Liverpool/Queenstown	26	54	167	vol 58 reel 28 p. 221
1898	22-Jul	Canada	Liverpool	26	54	177	vol 58 reel 28 p. 320
1898	22-Jul	Cephalonia	Liverpool/Queenstown	26	54	183	vol 58 reel 28 p. 327
1898	22-Jul	Moravia	Hamburg	26	54	176	vol 58 reel 28 p. 311
1898	30-Jul	Catalonia	Liverpool/Queenstown	26	54	191	vol 58 reel 28 p. 388
1898	2-Aug	Sardinia	Hamburg	28	59	4	vol 59A reel 29 p. 2
1898	4-Aug	Scandinavian	Glasgow	28	59	14	vol 59A reel 29 p. 3
1898	5-Aug	New England	Liverpool/Queenstown	28	59	26	vol 59A reel 29 p. 7
1898	12-Aug	Pavonia	Liverpool/Queenstown	28	59	82	vol 59A reel 29 p. 16
1898	16-Aug	Peruvian	Glasgow	28	59	110	vol 59A reel 29 p. 22
1898	19-Aug	Canada	Liverpool	28	59	141	vol 59A reel 29 p. 25
1898	22-Aug	Christiania	Hamburg	28	59	164	
1898	26-Aug	Cephalonia	Liverpool/Queenstown	28	59	212	vol 59A reel 29 p. 36
1898	1-Sep	Moravia	Hamburg	29	59A	46	vol 60 reel 29 p. 185
1898	2-Sep	New England	Liverpool/Queenstown	29	59A	47	vol 60 reel 29 p. 214
1898	3-Sep	Catalonia	Liverpool/Queenstown	29	59A	68	vol 60 reel 29 p. 244
1898	13-Sep	Scandinavian	Glasgow	29	59A	79	vol 60 reel 29 p. 370
1898	16-Sep	Bohemia	Hamburg	29	59A	112	vol 60 reel 29 p. 430
1898	16-Sep	Canada	Liverpool	29	59A	84	vol 60 reel 29 p. 402
1898	16-Sep	Pavonia	Liverpool/Queenstown	29	59A	105	vol 60 reel 29 p. 419
1898	21-Sep	Peruvian	Glasgow	29	59A	115	
1898	30-Sep	New England	Liverpool/Queenstown	29	59A	118	
1898	1-Oct	Cephalonia	Liverpool/Queenstown	29	59A	137	vol 61 reel 30 p. 12
1898	8-Oct	Catalonia	Liverpool/Queenstown	29	59A	152	vol 61 reel 30 p. 94
1898	15-Oct	Canada	Liverpool	29	59A	159	vol 61 reel 30 p. 150
1898	20-Oct	Moravia	Hamburg	29	59A	178	vol 61 reel 30 p. 188
1898	21-Oct	Pavonia	Liverpool/Queenstown	29	59A	179	vol 61 reel 30 p. 203
1898	29-Oct	New England	Liverpool/Queenstown	29	59A	185	vol 61 reel 30 p. 237
1898	1-Nov	Hispania	Hamburg	29	59A	199	vol 62 reel 30 p. 1
1898	4-Nov	Peruvian	Glasgow	29	59A	201	vol 62 reel 30 p. 20
1898	5-Nov	Cephalonia	Liverpool/Queenstown	29	59A	203	vol 62 reel 30 p. 25
1898	13-Nov	Catalonia	Liverpool/Queenstown	29	59A	208	vol 62 reel 30 p. 60
1898	18-Nov	Canada	Liverpool	29	59A	211	vol 62 reel 30 p. 82
1898	25-Nov	Pavonia	Liverpool/Queenstown	29	59A	220	vol 62 reel 30 p. 113
1898	26-Nov	Christiania	Hamburg	29	59A	226	vol 62 reel 30 p. 124
1898	26-Nov	Dominion	Liverpool	29	59A	223	vol 62 reel 30 p. 118
1898	2-Dec	New England	Liverpool/Queenstown	29	59A	227	vol 62 reel 30 p. 139
1898	12-Dec	Cephalonia	Liverpool/Queenstown	29	59A	234	vol 62 reel 30 p. 177
1898	17-Dec	Canada	Liverpool	29	59A	238	vol 62 reel 30 p. 193
1898	19-Dec	Catalonia	Liverpool/Queenstown	29	59A	242	vol 62 reel 30 p. 202
1898	25-Dec	Dominion	Liverpool	29	59A	244	vol 62 reel 30 p. 225
1898	31-Dec	New England	Liverpool/Queenstown	29	59A	246	vol 62 reel 30 p. 245
1899	1-Jan	Pavonia	Liverpool/Queenstown	30	63	4	vol 74 reel 36 p. 1
1899	3-Jan	Assyrian	Hamburg	30	63	11	vol 74 reel 36 p. 4
1899	12-Jan	Halifax	Halifax	30	63	29	
1899	15-Jan	Canada	Liverpool	30	63	49	vol 74 reel 36 p. 6
1899	17-Jan	Cephalonia	Liverpool/Queenstown	30	63	56	vol 74 reel 36 p. 9
1899	28-Jan	New England	Liverpool/Queenstown	30	63	88	vol 74 reel 36 p. 13
1899	3-Feb	Prince George	Yarmouth	30	63	105	
1899	12-Feb	Canada	Liverpool	30	63	119	vol 74 reel 36 p. 17
1899	21-Feb	Alessia	Hamburg	30	63	146	vol 74 reel 36 p. 22
1899	21-Feb	Cephalonia	Liverpool/Queenstown	30	63	149	vol 74 reel 36 p. 25
1899	21-Feb	Dominion	Liverpool	30	63	155	vol 74 reel 36 p. 26
1899	23-Feb	Halifax	Halifax	30	63	162	
1899	24-Feb	New England	Liverpool/Queenstown	30	63	172	vol 74 reel 36 p. 28
1899	5-Mar	Catalonia	Liverpool/Queenstown	31	64	13	vol 74 reel 36 p. 33

Year	Date	Ship	From	Reel#	Vol	Page	See also
1899	10-Mar	Canada	Liverpool	31	64	42	vol 74 reel 36 p. 36
1899	11-Mar	Ultonia	Liverpool/Queenstown	31	64	56	vol 74 reel 36 p. 44
1899	25-Mar	Cephalonia	Liverpool/Queenstown	31	64	112	vol 74 reel 36 p. 47
1899	1-Apr	New England	Liverpool/Queenstown	31	65	1	vol 74 reel 36 p. 53
1899	9-Apr	Catalonia	Liverpool/Queenstown	31	65	61	vol 74 reel 36 p. 69
1899	15-Apr	Canada	Liverpool	31	65	103	vol 74 reel 36 p. 72
1899	17-Apr	Ultonia	Liverpool/Queenstown	31	65	134	vol 74 reel 36 p. 84
1899	20-Apr	Pavonia	Liverpool/Queenstown	31	65	183	vol 74 reel 36 p. 96
1899	22-Apr	Assyrian	Glasgow	31	65	175	vol 74 reel 36 p. 91
1899	28-Apr	New England	Liverpool/Queenstown	31	65	233	vol 74 reel 36 p. 103
1899	5-May	Peruvian	Glasgow	31	66	22	vol 74 reel 36 p. 130
1899	7-May	Cephalonia	Liverpool/Queenstown	31	66	40	vol 74 reel 36 p. 135
1899	12-May	Canada	Liverpool	31	66	98	vol 74 reel 36 p. 156
1899	14-May	Catalonia	Liverpool/Queenstown	31	66	126	vol 74 reel 36 p. 172
1899	18-May	Ultonia	Liverpool/Queenstown	31	66	168	vol 74 reel 36 p. 177
1899	20-May	Hibernian	Glasgow	31	66	187	vol 74 reel 36 p. 184
1899	24-May	Pavonia	Liverpool/Queenstown	31	66	222	vol 74 reel 36 p. 189
1899	27-May	New England	Liverpool/Queenstown	31	66	236	vol 74 reel 36 p. 194
1899	28-May	Norwegian	Glasgow	31	66	275	vol 74 reel 36 p. 215
1899	9-Jun	Canada	Liverpool	32	67	45	vol 74 reel 36 p. 216
1899	10-Jun	Cephalonia	Liverpool/Queenstown	32	67	71	vol 74 reel 36 p. 230
1899	14-Jun	Peruvian	Glasgow	32	67	102	vol 74 reel 36 p. 240
1899	17-Jun	Derbyshire	Liverpool/Queenstown	32	67	120	vol 74 reel 36 p. 243
1899	18-Jun	Catalonia	Liverpool/Queenstown	32	67	137	vol 74 reel 36 p. 248
1899	24-Jun	Ultonia	Liverpool/Queenstown	32	67	169	vol 74 reel 36 p. 251
1899	28-Jun	Hibernian	Glasgow	32	67	198	vol 74 reel 36 p. 256
1899	30-Jun	New England	Liverpool/Queenstown	32	67	215	vol 74 reel 36 p. 260
1899	30-Jun	Pavonia	Liverpool/Queenstown	32	67	243	vol 74 reel 36 p. 274
1899	7-Jul	Canada	Liverpool	32	68	37	vol 74 reel 36 p. 278
1899	12-Jul	Norwegian	Glasgow	32	68	72	vol 74 reel 36 p. 285
1899	15-Jul	Cephalonia	Liverpool/Queenstown	32	68	88	vol 74 reel 36 p. 287
1899	15-Jul	Derbyshire	Liverpool/Queenstown	32	68	100	vol 74 reel 36 p. 293
1899	23-Jul	Catalonia	Liverpool/Queenstown	32	68	158	vol 74 reel 36 p. 297
1899	27-Jul	Peruvian	Glasgow	32	68	192	vol 74 reel 36 p. 300
1899	28-Jul	New England	Liverpool/Queenstown	32	68	213	vol 74 reel 36 p. 303
1899	29-Jul	Ultonia	Liverpool/Queenstown	32	68	237	vol 74 reel 36 p. 315
1899	5-Aug	Pavonia	Liverpool/Queenstown	33	69	33	vol 74 reel 36 p. 319
1899	8-Aug	Hibernian	Glasgow	33	69	70	vol 74 reel 36 p. 321
1899	12-Aug	Derbyshire	Liverpool/Queenstown	33	69	109	vol 74 reel 36 p. 326
1899	18-Aug	Cephalonia	Liverpool/Queenstown	33	69	178	vol 74 reel 36 p. 332
1899	22-Aug	Norwegian	Glasgow	33	69	234	vol 74 reel 36 p. 341
1899	25-Aug	New England	Liverpool/Queenstown	33	69	293	vol 74 reel 36 p. 344
1899	26-Aug	Catalonia	Liverpool/Queenstown	33	69	349	vol 74 reel 36 p. 370
1899	1-Sep	Canada	Liverpool	34	70	239	vol 74 reel 36 p. 375
1899	5-Sep	Peruvian	Glasgow	34	70	326	vol 74 reel 36 p. 393
1899	5-Sep	Winifredian	Liverpool	34	70	340	
1899	9-Sep	Derbyshire	Liverpool/Queenstown	34	70	68	vol 74 reel 36 p. 395
1899	9-Sep	Pavonia	Liverpool/Queenstown	34	70	81	vol 74 reel 36 p. 400
1899	12-Sep	Armenian	Liverpool	34	70	153	
1899	14-Sep	Hibernian	Glasgow	34	70	173	
1899	22-Sep	New England	Liverpool/Queenstown	34	71	115	vol 74 reel 36 p. 409
1899	24-Sep	Cephalonia	Liverpool/Queenstown	34	71	198	vol 74 reel 36 p. 436
1899	26-Sep	Norwegian	Glasgow	34	71	244	vol 74 reel 36 p. 451
1899	1-Oct	Catalonia	Liverpool/Queenstown	35	72	24	vol 74 reel 36 p. 454
1899	7-Oct	Canada	Liverpool	35	72	108	vol 74 reel 36 p. 461
1899	7-Oct	Ultonia	Liverpool/Queenstown	35	72	144	vol 74 reel 36 p. 483
1899	10-Oct	Winifredian	Liverpool	35	72	189	
1899	22-Oct	New England	Liverpool/Queenstown	35	72	265	vol 74 reel 36 p. 491
1899	4-Nov	Canada	Liverpool	35	73	19	vol 74 reel 36 p. 514
1899	15-Nov	Ultonia	Liverpool/Queenstown	35	73	62	vol 74 reel 36 p. 523
1899	17-Nov	New England	Liverpool/Queenstown	35	73	87	vol 74 reel 36 p. 529
1899	15-Dec	New England	Liverpool/Queenstown	35	73	186	vol 74 reel 36 p. 541
1899	21-Dec	Ultonia	Liverpool/Queenstown	35	73	214	vol 74 reel 36 p. 549
1900	29-Jan	Ultonia	Liverpool/Queenstown	36	75	68	vol 79 reel 38 p. 7
1900	31-Jan	New England	Liverpool/Queenstown	36	75	53	vol 79 reel 38 p. 1
1900	1-Mar	Ultonia	Liverpool/Queenstown	36	75	165	vol 79 reel 38 p. 10
1900	15-Apr	Ultonia	Liverpool/Queenstown	37	76	68	vol 79 reel 38 p. 18
1900	20-Apr	New England	Liverpool/Queenstown	37	76	117	vol 79 reel 38 p. 28
1900	30-Apr	Sardinian	Glasgow & Galway	37	76	175	vol 79 reel 38 p. 55
1900	10-May	Prince Arthur	Yarmouth	37	77	26	
1900	13-May	Hibernian	Glasgow	37	77	43	vol 79 reel 38 p. 53
1900	13-May	Prince Arthur	Yarmouth	37	77	39	
1900	18-May	New England	Liverpool/Queenstown	37	77	72	vol 79 reel 38 p. 71
1900	19-May	Ultonia	Liverpool/Queenstown	37	77	114	vol 79 reel 38 p. 96
1900	25-May	Peruvian	Glasgow	37	77	164	vol 79 reel 38 p. 105
1900	31-May	Saxonia	Liverpool/Queenstown	37	77	194	vol 79 reel 38 p. 110
1900	1-Jun	Halifax	Halifax	37	78	2	
1900	3-Jun	Kansas	Liverpool	37	78	12	
1900	7-Jun	Prince Arthur	Yarmouth	37	78	25	
1900	10-Jun	Prince Arthur	Yarmouth	37	78	41	
1900	14-Jun	New England	Liverpool/Queenstown	37	78	66	vol 79 reel 38 p. 123
1900	14-Jun	Prince George	Yarmouth	37	78	52	
1900	15-Jun	Halifax	Halifax	37	78	62	

Year	Date	Ship	From	Reel#	Vol	Page	See also
1900	17-Jun	Norwegian	Glasgow	37	78	124	vol 79 reel 38 p. 146
1900	21-Jun	Ivernia	Liverpool/Queenstown	37	78	144	vol 79 reel 38 p. 150
1900	29-Jun	Ultonia	Liverpool/Queenstown	37	78	210	vol 79 reel 38 p. 163
1900	5-Jul	Saxonia	Liverpool/Queenstown	39	80	20	vol 79 reel 38 p. 196
1900	11-Jul	Boston	Yarmouth	39	80	73	
1900	12-Jul	Peruvian	Glasgow	39	80	85	vol 79 reel 38 p. 202
1900	15-Jul	New England	Liverpool/Queenstown	39	80	107	vol 79 reel 38 p. 205
1900	15-Jul	Prince Arthur	Yarmouth	39	80	145	
1900	24-Jul	Norwegian	Glasgow	39	80	229	vol 79 reel 38 p. 227
1900	27-Jul	Ivernia	Liverpool/Queenstown	39	80	251	vol 79 reel 38 p. 229
1900	4-Aug	Ultonia	Liverpool/Queenstown	39	81	53	vol 79 reel 38 p. 240
1900	9-Aug	Saxonia	Liverpool/Queenstown	39	81	120	vol 79 reel 38 p. 245
1900	10-Aug	New England	Liverpool/Queenstown	39	81	153	vol 79 reel 38 p. 254
1900	15-Aug	Peruvian	Glasgow	39	81	263	
1900	28-Aug	Norwegian	Glasgow	40	82	246	vol 79 reel 38 p. 279
1900	30-Aug	Ivernia	Liverpool/Queenstown	40	82	302	vol 79 reel 38 p. 282
1900	7-Sep	New England	Liverpool/Queenstown	41	84	199	vol 79 reel 38 p. 297
1900	7-Sep	Ultonia	Liverpool/Queenstown	41	84	243	vol 79 reel 38 p. 322
1900	12-Sep	Saxonia	Liverpool/Queenstown	40	83	18	vol 79 reel 38 p. 331
1900	19-Sep	Bohemian	Liverpool	40	83	180	
1900	20-Sep	Peruvian	Glasgow	40	83	202	vol 79 reel 38 p. 347
1900	20-Sep	Yarmouth	Yarmouth	40	83	194	
1900	2-Oct	Norwegian	Glasgow	41	86	19	vol 79 reel 38 p. 350
1900	4-Oct	Ivernia	Liverpool/Queenstown	41	86	49	vol 79 reel 38 p. 354
1900	5-Oct	New England	Liverpool/Queenstown	41	86	111	vol 79 reel 38 p. 371
1900	7-Oct	Florida	Sydney	41	86	182	
1900	11-Oct	Commonwealth	Liverpool	41	86	228	vol 79 reel 38 p. 395
1900	14-Oct	Prince Arthur	Yarmouth	41	85	18	
1900	14-Oct	Ultonia	Liverpool/Queenstown	41	85	6	vol 79 reel 38 p. 410
1900	17-Oct	Prince George	Yarmouth	41	85	43	
1900	18-Oct	Saxonia	Liverpool/Queenstown	41	85	48	vol 79 reel 38 p. 416
1900	22-Oct	Cambrian	London	41	85	123	
1900	2-Nov	New England	Liverpool/Queenstown	42	87	13	vol 79 reel 38 p. 429
1900	5-Nov	Ivernia	Liverpool/Queenstown	42	87	65	vol 79 reel 38 p. 444
1900	8-Nov	Commonwealth	Liverpool	42	87	87	vol 79 reel 38 p. 458
1900	13-Nov	Anglican	London	42	87	113	
1900	16-Nov	Halifax	Halifax	42	87	127	
1900	18-Nov	Ultonia	Liverpool/Queenstown	42	87	138	vol 79 reel 38 p. 466
1900	25-Nov	Prince Arthur	Yarmouth	42	87	159	
1900	27-Nov	Saxonia	Liverpool/Queenstown	42	87	175	vol 79 reel 38 p. 472
1900	29-Nov	New England	Liverpool/Queenstown	42	87	190	vol 79 reel 38 p. 477
1900	7-Dec	Commonwealth	Liverpool	42	87	219	vol 79 reel 38 p. 484
1900	13-Dec	Turcoman	Liverpool	42	87	241	
1900	15-Dec	Ivernia	Liverpool/Queenstown	42	87	247	vol 79 reel 38 p. 490
1900	16-Dec	Prince Arthur	Yarmouth	42	87	261	
1900	20-Dec	Ultonia	Liverpool/Queenstown	42	87	293	vol 79 reel 38 p. 496
1900	27-Dec	Prince Arthur	Yarmouth	42	87	305	
1900	28-Dec	New England	Liverpool/Queenstown	42	87	310	vol 79 reel 38 p. 500
1901	11-Jan	Saxonia	Liverpool/Queenstown	43	90	31	vol 90 reel 43 p. 31
1901	17-Jan	Prince Arthur	Yarmouth	43	90	51	vol 90 reel 43 p. 51
1901	25-Jan	Ivernia	Liverpool/Queenstown	43	90	76	vol 90 reel 43 p. 76
1901	26-Jan	New England	Liverpool/Queenstown	43	90	87	vol 90 reel 43 p. 87
1901	30-Jan	Ontario	Hull	43	90	103	vol 90 reel 43 p. 103
1901	4-Feb	Ultonia	Liverpool/Queenstown	43	90	115	vol 90 reel 43 p. 115
1901	9-Feb	Commonwealth	Liverpool	43	90	128	vol 90 reel 43 p. 128
1901	14-Feb	Saxonia	Liverpool/Queenstown	43	90	155	vol 90 reel 43 p. 155
1901	21-Feb	Halifax	Halifax	43	90	183	vol 90 reel 43 p. 183
1901	22-Feb	New England	Liverpool/Queenstown	43	90	184	vol 90 reel 43 p. 184
1901	28-Feb	Ivernia	Liverpool/Queenstown	43	90	207	vol 90 reel 43 p. 207
1901	9-Mar	Commonwealth	Liverpool	44	91	23	
1901	12-Mar	Ultonia	Liverpool/Queenstown	44	91	48	
1901	21-Mar	Saxonia	Liverpool/Queenstown	44	91	97	
1901	23-Mar	New England	Liverpool/Queenstown	44	91	126	
1901	5-Apr	Commonwealth	Liverpool	44	92	20	
1901	14-Apr	Ultonia	Liverpool/Queenstown	44	92	90	
1901	18-Apr	Ivernia	Liverpool/Queenstown	44	92	128	
1901	19-Apr	New England	Liverpool/Queenstown	44	92	175	
1901	21-Apr	Prince George	Yarmouth	44	92	212	
1901	27-Apr	Norwegian	Glasgow	44	92	244	
1901	2-May	Saxonia	Liverpool/Queenstown	45	93	12	
1901	3-May	Commonwealth	Liverpool	45	93	92	
1901	7-May	Columbian	London	45	93	148	
1901	8-May	Peruvian	Glasgow	45	93	155	
1901	17-May	New England	Liverpool/Queenstown	45	93	203	
1901	17-May	Ultonia	Liverpool/Queenstown	45	93	242	
1901	22-May	Assyrian	Glasgow	45	93	280	
1901	22-May	Ivernia	Liverpool/Queenstown	45	93	289	
1901	31-May	Commonwealth	Liverpool	45	93	379	
1901	6-Jun	Saxonia	Liverpool/Queenstown	45	94	17	
1901	13-Jun	Peruvian	Glasgow	45	94	79	
1901	15-Jun	New England	Liverpool/Queenstown	45	94	104	
1901	18-Jun	Sagamore	Liverpool	45	94	145	
1901	22-Jun	Ultonia	Liverpool/Queenstown	45	94	165	

Year	Date	Ship	From	Reel#	Vol	Page	See also
1901	23-Jun	Anglican	London	45	94	188	
1901	25-Jun	Assyrian	Glasgow	45	94	193	
1901	26-Jun	Ivernia	Liverpool/Queenstown	45	94	198	
1901	29-Jun	Commonwealth	Liverpool	45	94	235	
1901	29-Jun	Sachem	Liverpool	45	94	272	
1901	2-Jul	Bostonian	London	46	95	8	
1901	7-Jul	Cambrian	London	46	95	39	
1901	10-Jul	Norwegian	Glasgow	46	95	52	vol 89 reel 43 p. 1
1901	11-Jul	Saxonia	Liverpool/Queenstown	46	95	65	vol 89 reel 43 p. 4
1901	12-Jul	New England	Liverpool/Queenstown	46	95	93	vol 89 reel 43 p. 18
1901	27-Jul	Commonwealth	Liverpool	46	95	208	vol 89 reel 43 p. 31
1901	27-Jul	Ultonia	Liverpool/Queenstown	46	95	233	vol 89 reel 43 p. 46
1901	1-Aug	Ivernia	Liverpool/Queenstown	46	96	1	vol 89 reel 43 p. 52
1901	9-Aug	New England	Liverpool/Queenstown	46	96	104	vol 89 reel 43 p. 69
1901	11-Aug	Cambrian	London	46	96	144	
1901	14-Aug	Caledonian	London	46	96	167	
1901	14-Aug	Saxonia	Liverpool/Queenstown	46	96	180	vol 89 reel 43 p. 82
1901	19-Aug	Columbian	London	46	97	32	
1901	23-Aug	Commonwealth	Liverpool	46	97	73	vol 89 reel 43 p. 102
1901	30-Aug	Ultonia	Liverpool/Queenstown	46	97	211	vol 89 reel 43 p. 125
1901	2-Sep	Olivetti	Halifax	47	98	29	vol 89 reel 43 p. 1
1901	2-Sep	Peruvian	Glasgow	47	98	45	vol 89 reel 43 p. 132
1901	3-Sep	Lancastrian	Liverpool	47	98	77	
1901	4-Sep	Ivernia	Liverpool/Queenstown	47	98	91	vol 89 reel 43 p. 134
1901	6-Sep	New England	Liverpool/Queenstown	47	98	175	vol 89 reel 43 p. 162
1901	6-Sep	Prince Arthur	Yarmouth	47	98	165	
1901	12-Sep	Prince Arthur	Yarmouth	47	98	302	
1901	16-Sep	Norwegian	Glasgow	47	99	22	vol 89 reel 43 p. 183
1901	16-Sep	Prince George	Yarmouth	47	99	39	
1901	19-Sep	Saxonia	Liverpool/Queenstown	47	99	63	vol 89 reel 43 p. 185
1901	21-Sep	Commonwealth	Liverpool	47	99	159	vol 89 reel 43 p. 226
1901	4-Oct	New England	Liverpool/Queenstown	48	100	38	vol 89 reel 43 p. 255
1901	5-Oct	Ultonia	Liverpool/Queenstown	48	100	89	vol 89 reel 43 p. 280
1901	10-Oct	Ivernia	Liverpool/Queenstown	48	100	162	vol 89 reel 43 p. 295
1901	18-Oct	Commonwealth	Liverpool	48	101	53	vol 89 reel 43 p. 327
1901	24-Oct	Saxonia	Liverpool/Queenstown	48	101	117	vol 89 reel 43 p. 344
1901	26-Oct	Boston	Yarmouth	48	101	163	
1901	1-Nov	New England	Liverpool/Queenstown	48	102	1	vol 89 reel 43 p. 368
1901	5-Nov	Bonavista	Halifax	48	102	39	
1901	8-Nov	Ultonia	Liverpool/Queenstown	48	102	57	vol 89 reel 43 p. 382
1901	14-Nov	Ivernia	Liverpool/Queenstown	48	102	85	vol 89 reel 43 p. 387
1901	25-Nov	Commonwealth	Liverpool	48	102	145	vol 89 reel 43 p. 401
1901	29-Nov	Saxonia	Liverpool/Queenstown	48	102	175	vol 89 reel 43 p. 412
1901	30-Nov	New England	Liverpool/Queenstown	48	102	195	vol 89 reel 43 p. 422
1901	12-Dec	Kingstonian	London	48	102	240	
1901	14-Dec	Ultonia	Liverpool/Queenstown	48	102	243	vol 89 reel 43 p. 427
1901	19-Dec	Ivernia	Liverpool/Queenstown	48	102	265	vol 89 reel 43 p. 431
1901	26-Dec	Bonavista	Halifax	48	102	300	
1901	26-Dec	Bostonian	London	48	102	299	
1902	6-Jan	Cambian	London	49	103	15	
1902	17-Jan	Ultonia	Liverpool/Queenstown	49	103	41	
1902	18-Jan	New England	Liverpool/Queenstown	49	103	47	
1902	9-Feb	Boston	Yarmouth	49	103	127	
1902	12-Feb	Bucentaur	Calcutta	49	103	131	
1902	13-Feb	Boston	Yarmouth	49	103	135	
1902	23-Feb	Boston	Yarmouth	49	103	154	
1902	24-Feb	Ultonia	Liverpool/Queenstown	49	103	157	
1902	28-Feb	Ivernia	Liverpool/Queenstown	49	103	169	
1902	6-Mar	Bonavista	Halifax	49	104	75	
1902	9-Mar	Boston	Yarmouth	49	104	82	
1902	13-Mar	Boston	Yarmouth	49	104	122	
1902	13-Mar	Saxonia	Liverpool/Queenstown	49	104	89	
1902	18-Mar	Commonwealth	Naples	49	104	208	
1902	21-Mar	Merion	Liverpool	49	104	222	
1902	24-Mar	Ultonia	Liverpool/Queenstown	49	104	250	
1902	27-Mar	Ivernia	Liverpool/Queenstown	49	104	267	
1902	3-Apr	Boston	Yarmouth	50	105	5	
1902	3-Apr	Sardinian	Glasgow & Galway	50	105	20	
1902	6-Apr	Boston	Yarmouth	50	105	79	
1902	6-Apr	New England	Liverpool/Queenstown	50	105	86	
1902	10-Apr	Boston	Yarmouth	50	105	124	
1902	13-Apr	Boston	Yarmouth	50	105	142	
1902	16-Apr	Pomeranian	Glasgow & Galway	50	105	158	
1902	18-Apr	Commonwealth	Liverpool	50	105	175	
1902	24-Apr	Ivernia	Liverpool/Queenstown	50	106	12	
1902	24-Apr	Virginian	London	50	106	149	
1902	27-Apr	Merion	Liverpool	50	106	160	
1902	30-Apr	Norwegian	Glasgow	50	106	193	
1902	1-May	Boston	Yarmouth	51	108	1	
1902	2-May	New England	Liverpool/Queenstown	51	108	14	
1902	2-May	Ultonia	Liverpool/Queenstown	51	108	62	
1902	9-May	Halifax	Halifax	51	108	110	
1902	11-May	Boston	Yarmouth	51	108	114	

Year	Date	Ship	From	Reel#	Vol	Page	See also
1902	13-May	Caledonian	London	51	108	123	
1902	16-May	Commonwealth	Liverpool	51	108	142	
1902	16-May	Devonian	Liverpool	51	108	135	
1902	22-May	Ivernia	Liverpool/Queenstown	51	107	62	
1902	25-May	Merion	Liverpool	51	107	148	
1902	30-May	New England	Liverpool/Queenstown	51	107	178	
1902	1-Jun	Prince George	Yarmouth	52	109	49	
1902	3-Jun	Ultonia	Liverpool/Queenstown	52	109	60	
1902	4-Jun	Prince George	Yarmouth	52	109	85	
1902	6-Jun	Halifax	Halifax	52	109	91	
1902	6-Jun	Saxonia	Liverpool/Queenstown	52	109	94	
1902	13-Jun	Commonwealth	Liverpool	52	109	164	
1902	19-Jun	Ivernia	Liverpool/Queenstown	52	109	222	
1902	19-Jun	Olivetti	Halifax	52	109	211	
1902	22-Jun	Merion	Liverpool	52	109	271	
1902	23-Jun	Columbian	London	52	109	287	
1902	27-Jun	New England	Liverpool/Queenstown	52	109	299	
1902	30-Jun	Anglian	London	52	109	331	
1902	3-Jul	Saxonia	Liverpool/Queenstown	53	111	60	
1902	6-Jul	Prince Arthur	Yarmouth	53	111	118	
1902	11-Jul	Commonwealth	Liverpool	53	111	155	
1902	11-Jul	Ultonia	Liverpool/Queenstown	53	111	183	
1902	16-Jul	Ivernia	Liverpool/Queenstown	52	110	41	
1902	20-Jul	Merion	Liverpool	52	110	64	
1902	25-Jul	New England	Liverpool/Queenstown	52	110	112	
1902	28-Jul	Halifax	Halifax	52	110	166	
1902	29-Jul	Boston	Yarmouth	52	110	176	
1902	31-Jul	Boston	Yarmouth	52	110	189	
1902	31-Jul	Saxonia	Liverpool/Queenstown	52	110	196	
1902	8-Aug	Commonwealth	Liverpool	53	112	51	
1902	10-Aug	Ultonia	Liverpool/Queenstown	53	112	91	
1902	12-Aug	Cambroman	Naples & Genoa	53	112	125	
1902	13-Aug	Ivernia	Liverpool/Queenstown	53	112	166	
1902	17-Aug	Merion	Liverpool	54	113	23	
1902	21-Aug	New England	Liverpool/Queenstown	54	113	85	
1902	25-Aug	Halifax	Halifax	54	113	159	
1902	26-Aug	Prince George	Yarmouth	54	113	175	
1902	28-Aug	Saxonia	Liverpool/Queenstown	54	113	198	
1902	31-Aug	Sachem	Liverpool	54	113	313	
1902	5-Sep	Commonwealth	Liverpool	54	114	93	
1902	6-Sep	Ultonia	Liverpool/Queenstown	54	114	150	
1902	10-Sep	Ivernia	Liverpool/Queenstown	54	114	235	
1902	14-Sep	Merion	Liverpool	54	114	371	
1902	15-Sep	Victorian	Liverpool	54	114	408	
1902	18-Sep	New England	Liverpool/Queenstown	55	115	39	
1902	24-Sep	Saxonia	Liverpool/Queenstown	55	115	191	
1902	3-Oct	Commonwealth	Liverpool	55	116	25	
1902	3-Oct	Ultonia	Liverpool/Queenstown	55	116	71	
1902	8-Oct	Ivernia	Liverpool/Queenstown	55	116	143	
1902	10-Oct	Halifax	Halifax	55	116	243	
1902	12-Oct	Merion	Liverpool	56	117	63	
1902	17-Oct	Halifax	Halifax	56	117	108	
1902	18-Oct	New England	Liverpool/Queenstown	56	117	118	
1902	19-Oct	Columbia	London	56	117	155	
1902	31-Oct	Halifax	Halifax	56	117	225	
1902	1-Nov	Commonwealth	Liverpool	56	118	1	
1902	3-Nov	Ultonia	Liverpool/Queenstown	56	118	44	
1902	9-Nov	Merion	Liverpool	56	118	120	
1902	13-Nov	Ivernia	Liverpool/Queenstown	56	118	144	
1902	23-Nov	Boston	Yarmouth	56	118	226	
1902	24-Nov	Columbian	London	56	118	230	
1902	27-Nov	Saxonia	Liverpool/Queenstown	56	118	286	
1902	1-Dec	New England	Liverpool/Queenstown	57	119	1	
1902	7-Dec	Ultonia	Liverpool/Queenstown	57	119	37	
1902	8-Dec	Merion	Liverpool	57	119	55	
1902	11-Dec	Halifax	Halifax	57	119	69	
1902	19-Dec	Ivernia	Liverpool/Queenstown	57	119	87	
1902	25-Dec	Boston	Yarmouth	57	119	127	
1902	25-Dec	Halifax	Halifax	57	119	130	
1902	29-Dec	Commonwealth	Liverpool	57	119	143	
1903	12-Jan	Boston	Yarmouth	57	120	108	
1903	12-Jan	Ultonia	Liverpool/Queenstown	57	120	61	
1903	13-Jan	Merion	Liverpool	57	120	114	
1903	25-Jan	Admiral Dewey	Kingston, Jamaica	57	120	148	
1903	25-Jan	Boston	Yarmouth	57	120	146	
1903	5-Feb	Boston	Yarmouth	57	120	183	
1903	12-Feb	Boston	Yarmouth	57	120	223	
1903	17-Feb	Hurworth	Newcastle	57	120	260	
1903	17-Feb	Ultonia	Liverpool/Queenstown	57	120	235	
1903	18-Feb	Merion	Liverpool	57	120	247	
1903	2-Mar	Canada	Liverpool	58	121	9	
1903	5-Mar	Boston	Yarmouth	58	121	25	
1903	6-Mar	Saxonia	Liverpool/Queenstown	58	121	33	

Year	Date	Ship	From	Reel#	Vol	Page	See also
1903	28-Mar	Canada	Liverpool	58	121	265	
1903	29-Mar	Ultonia	Liverpool/Queenstown	58	121	286	
1903	2-Apr	Boston	Yarmouth	59	122	4	
1903	2-Apr	Winfredian	Liverpool	59	122	14	
1903	3-Apr	Saxonia	Liverpool/Queenstown	59	122	16	
1903	9-Apr	Halifax	Halifax	59	122	200	
1903	19-Apr	Mayflower	Liverpool	59	122	277	
1903	24-Apr	Ultonia	Liverpool/Queenstown	59	122	356	
1903	1-May	Saxonia	Liverpool/Queenstown	60	123	1	
1903	4-May	Buenos Ayrean	Glasgow & Galway	60	123	103	
1903	4-May	Devonian	Liverpool	60	123	101	
1903	8-May	Halifax	Halifax	60	123	129	
1903	9-May	New England	Liverpool/Queenstown	60	123	130	
1903	14-May	Carpathia	Liverpool	60	123	202	
1903	16-May	Mayflower	Liverpool	61	124	7	
1903	23-May	Ultonia	Liverpool/Queenstown	61	124	74	
1903	26-May	Corean	Glasgow & Galway	61	124	116	
1903	29-May	Saxonia	Liverpool/Queenstown	61	124	135	
1903	30-May	Commonwealth	Liverpool	61	124	212	
1903	5-Jun	New England	Liverpool/Queenstown	62	125	15	
1903	10-Jun	Ivernia	Liverpool/Queenstown	62	125	58	
1903	13-Jun	Mayflower	Liverpool	62	125	123	
1903	14-Jun	Sarmatian	Glasgow	62	125	152	
1903	19-Jun	Ultonia	Liverpool/Queenstown	62	125	232	
1903	25-Jun	Saxonia	Liverpool/Queenstown	62	125	274	
1903	26-Jun	Commonwealth	Liverpool	62	125	324	
1903	4-Jul	New England	Liverpool/Queenstown	63	126	12	
1903	8-Jul	Ivernia	Liverpool/Queenstown	63	126	55	
1903	11-Jul	Mayflower	Liverpool	63	126	99	
1903	18-Jul	Ultonia	Liverpool/Queenstown	63	127	15	
1903	24-Jul	Commonwealth	Liverpool	63	127	118	
1903	24-Jul	Saxonia	Liverpool/Queenstown	63	127	74-	
1903	27-Jul	Sarmatian	Galway & Glasgow	63	127	156	
1903	31-Jul	New England	Liverpool/Queenstown	63	127	185	
1903	6-Aug	Ivernia	Liverpool/Queenstown	64	128	86	
1903	10-Aug	Mayflower	Liverpool	64	128	157	
1903	15-Aug	Ultonia	Liverpool/Queenstown	64	128	224	
1903	20-Aug	Saxonia	Liverpool/Queenstown	65	129	1	
1903	21-Aug	Commonwealth	Liverpool	65	129	80	
1903	28-Aug	New England	Liverpool/Queenstown	65	129	222	
1903	2-Sep	Ivernia	Liverpool/Queenstown	65	130	24	
1903	5-Sep	Mayflower	Liverpool	65	130	125	
1903	7-Sep	Sarmatian	Galway & Glasgow	65	130	218	
1903	11-Sep	Canada	Liverpool	66	131	12	
1903	12-Sep	Ultonia	Liverpool/Queenstown	66	131	50	
1903	17-Sep	Saxonia	Liverpool/Queenstown	66	131	161	
1903	18-Sep	Commonwealth	Liverpool	66	131	271	
1903	21-Sep	Devonian	Liverpool	67	132	32	
1903	22-Sep	Admiral Dewey	Port Arthur, Jamaica	67	132	46	
1903	25-Sep	New England	Liverpool/Queenstown	67	132	76	
1903	28-Sep	Prince George	Yarmouth	67	132	175	
1903	29-Sep	Buenos Ayrian	Glasgow	67	132	177	
1903	30-Sep	Ivernia	Liverpool/Queenstown	67	132	183	
1903	2-Oct	Mayflower	Liverpool	67	133	30	
1903	10-Oct	Columbus	Liverpool	67	133	176	
1903	12-Oct	Ultonia	Liverpool/Queenstown	67	133	223	
1903	15-Oct	Saxonia	Liverpool/Queenstown	68	134	10	
1903	16-Oct	Commonwealth	Liverpool	68	134	69	
1903	22-Oct	Prince Arthur	Yarmouth	68	134	116	
1903	29-Oct	Ivernia	Liverpool/Queenstown	68	134	160	
1903	1-Nov	Mayflower	Liverpool	68	135	12	
1903	4-Nov	Columbus	Liverpool	68	135	42	
1903	14-Nov	Ultonia	Liverpool/Queenstown	68	135	80	
1903	15-Nov	Commonwealth	Liverpool	68	135	105	
1903	19-Nov	Saxonia	Liverpool/Queenstown	68	135	171	
1903	27-Nov	Romanic	Liverpool	68	135	228	
1903	2-Dec	Devonian	Liverpool	69	136	1	
1903	3-Dec	Ivernia	Liverpool/Queenstown	69	136	5	
1903	6-Dec	Boston	Yarmouth	69	136	55	
1903	6-Dec	Cretic	Liverpool	69	136	41	
1903	20-Dec	Cymric	Liverpool	69	136	90	
1903	21-Dec	Ultonia	Liverpool/Queenstown	69	136	99	
1903	24-Dec	Saxonia	Liverpool/Queenstown	69	136	129	
1903	27-Dec	Republic	Liverpool	69	136	145	

Ship	Year	Date
Admiral Dewey	1903	25-Jan
Admiral Dewey	1903	22-Sep
Adria	1897	28-Jul
Alessia	1898	21-Mar
Alessia	1899	21-Feb
Anglian	1902	30-Jun
Anglican	1900	13-Nov
Anglican	1901	23-Jun
Armenian	1896	11-Oct
Armenian	1897	19-Mar
Armenian	1899	12-Sep
Assyrian	1892	24-Mar
Assyrian	1899	03-Jan
Assyrian	1899	22-Apr
Assyrian	1901	22-May
Assyrian	1901	25-Jun
Asturia	1896	27-Jun
Asturia	1896	18-Aug
Austrian	1892	18-May
Austrian	1892	28-Jun
Austrian	1892	15-Aug
Baumwall	1894	01-Jan
Bavarian	1891	03-Nov
Bohemia	1894	17-Jan
Bohemia	1895	13-Jun
Bohemia	1897	21-Feb
Bohemia	1897	06-Sep
Bohemia	1898	15-Apr
Bohemia	1898	16-Sep
Bohemian	1900	19-Sep
Bolivia	1894	19-Dec
Bolivia	1895	12-Feb
Bonavista	1901	05-Nov
Bonavista	1901	26-Dec
Bonavista	1902	06-Mar
Boston	1893	16-Feb
Boston	1893	23-Mar
Boston	1893	02-Apr
Boston	1900	11-Jul
Boston	1901	26-Oct
Boston	1902	09-Feb
Boston	1902	13-Feb
Boston	1902	23-Feb
Boston	1902	09-Mar
Boston	1902	13-Mar
Boston	1902	03-Apr
Boston	1902	06-Apr
Boston	1902	10-Apr
Boston	1902	13-Apr
Boston	1902	01-May
Boston	1902	11-May
Boston	1902	29-Jul
Boston	1902	31-Jul
Boston	1902	23-Nov
Boston	1902	25-Dec
Boston	1903	12-Jan
Boston	1903	25-Jan
Boston	1903	05-Feb
Boston	1903	12-Feb
Boston	1903	05-Mar
Boston	1903	02-Apr
Boston	1903	06-Dec
Boston City	1893	25-Feb
Bostonian	1901	02-Jul
Bostonian	1901	26-Dec
Bothina	1893	30-Apr
Bothnia	1893	03-Jun
Bothnia	1893	09-Jul
Bothnia	1893	13-Aug
Bothnia	1893	17-Sep
Bothnia	1894	17-Apr
Bothnia	1894	26-Aug
Bothnia	1894	30-Sep
Bothnia	1895	22-May
Bothnia	1895	27-Oct
Bothnia	1896	25-Feb
Bothnia	1896	26-Mar
Bothnia	1896	28-Apr
Bothnia	1896	12-Sep
Bothnia	1896	18-Oct
British Queen	1893	23-May
Bucentaur	1902	12-Feb
Buenos Ayrean	1903	04-May
Buenos Ayrian	1892	07-Apr
Buenos Ayrian	1893	31-Mar
Buenos Ayrian	1894	18-Apr
Buenos Ayrian	1903	29-Sep
Caledonian	1901	14-Aug
Caledonian	1902	13-May
California	1895	06-Apr
California	1895	05-Aug
California	1895	04-Oct
Cambian	1902	06-Jan
Cambrian	1900	22-Oct
Cambrian	1901	07-Jul
Cambrian	1901	11-Aug
Cambroman	1902	12-Aug
Canada	1897	02-Jan
Canada	1897	05-Feb
Canada	1897	13-Mar
Canada	1897	16-Apr
Canada	1897	24-Jun
Canada	1897	29-Jul
Canada	1897	03-Sep
Canada	1897	07-Oct
Canada	1897	03-Nov
Canada	1897	05-Dec
Canada	1898	07-Jan
Canada	1898	11-Feb
Canada	1898	17-Mar
Canada	1898	21-Apr
Canada	1898	26-May
Canada	1898	24-Jun
Canada	1898	22-Jul
Canada	1898	19-Aug
Canada	1898	16-Sep
Canada	1898	15-Oct
Canada	1898	18-Nov
Canada	1898	17-Dec
Canada	1899	15-Jan
Canada	1899	12-Feb
Canada	1899	10-Mar
Canada	1899	15-Apr
Canada	1899	12-May
Canada	1899	09-Jun
Canada	1899	07-Jul
Canada	1899	01-Sep
Canada	1899	07-Oct
Canada	1899	04-Nov
Canada	1903	02-Mar
Canada	1903	28-Mar
Canada	1903	11-Sep
Canadia	1895	14-Jan
Carpathia	1903	14-May
Carroll	1892	23-Dec
Carthagenia	1894	03-Apr
Catalonia	1891	02-Aug
Catalonia	1891	07-Sep
Catalonia	1891	14-Oct
Catalonia	1891	16-Nov
Catalonia	1891	23-Dec
Catalonia	1892	16-Feb
Catalonia	1892	22-Mar
Catalonia	1892	25-Apr
Catalonia	1892	31-May
Catalonia	1892	04-Jul
Catalonia	1892	07-Aug
Catalonia	1892	14-Sep
Catalonia	1892	17-Oct
Catalonia	1892	21-Nov
Catalonia	1892	28-Dec
Catalonia	1893	09-Feb
Catalonia	1893	20-Mar
Catalonia	1893	24-Apr
Catalonia	1893	29-May
Catalonia	1893	05-Jul
Catalonia	1893	07-Aug
Catalonia	1893	10-Sep
Catalonia	1893	15-Oct
Catalonia	1893	18-Nov
Catalonia	1893	29-Dec
Catalonia	1894	08-Feb
Catalonia	1894	23-Mar
Catalonia	1894	21-Apr
Catalonia	1894	24-May
Catalonia	1894	02-Jul
Catalonia	1894	04-Aug
Catalonia	1894	10-Sep
Catalonia	1894	15-Oct
Catalonia	1894	24-Nov
Catalonia	1894	22-Dec
Catalonia	1895	04-Feb
Catalonia	1895	20-Mar
Catalonia	1895	21-Apr
Catalonia	1895	27-May
Catalonia	1895	01-Jul
Catalonia	1895	05-Aug
Catalonia	1895	09-Sep
Catalonia	1895	15-Oct
Catalonia	1895	19-Nov
Catalonia	1895	24-Dec
Catalonia	1896	07-Apr
Catalonia	1896	10-May
Catalonia	1896	14-Jun
Catalonia	1896	20-Jul
Catalonia	1896	23-Aug
Catalonia	1896	29-Sep
Catalonia	1896	08-Nov
Catalonia	1897	28-Jan
Catalonia	1897	04-Mar
Catalonia	1897	14-Apr
Catalonia	1897	23-May
Catalonia	1897	28-Jun
Catalonia	1897	07-Aug
Catalonia	1897	06-Sep
Catalonia	1897	11-Oct
Catalonia	1897	23-Nov
Catalonia	1897	28-Dec
Catalonia	1898	01-Feb
Catalonia	1898	12-Mar
Catalonia	1898	21-May
Catalonia	1898	25-Jun
Catalonia	1898	30-Jul
Catalonia	1898	03-Sep
Catalonia	1898	08-Oct
Catalonia	1898	13-Nov
Catalonia	1898	19-Dec
Catalonia	1899	05-Mar
Catalonia	1899	09-Apr
Catalonia	1899	14-May
Catalonia	1899	18-Jun
Catalonia	1899	23-Jul
Catalonia	1899	26-Aug
Catalonia	1899	01-Oct
Cephalonia	1891	09-Aug
Cephalonia	1891	13-Sep
Cephalonia	1891	19-Oct
Cephalonia	1891	23-Nov
Cephalonia	1891	28-Dec
Cephalonia	1892	02-Feb
Cephalonia	1892	10-Apr
Cephalonia	1892	15-May
Cephalonia	1892	19-Jun
Cephalonia	1892	23-Jul
Cephalonia	1892	27-Aug
Cephalonia	1892	03-Oct
Cephalonia	1892	08-Nov
Cephalonia	1892	12-Dec
Cephalonia	1893	21-Jan
Cephalonia	1893	05-Mar
Cephalonia	1893	15-Apr
Cephalonia	1893	21-May
Cephalonia	1893	25-Jun
Cephalonia	1893	30-Jul
Cephalonia	1893	02-Sep
Cephalonia	1893	08-Oct
Cephalonia	1893	12-Nov
Cephalonia	1893	19-Dec
Cephalonia	1894	22-Jan
Cephalonia	1894	07-Mar
Cephalonia	1894	18-May
Cephalonia	1894	24-Jun
Cephalonia	1894	28-Jul
Cephalonia	1894	01-Sep
Cephalonia	1894	07-Oct
Cephalonia	1894	06-Nov
Cephalonia	1894	09-Dec
Cephalonia	1895	21-Jan
Cephalonia	1895	03-Mar
Cephalonia	1895	14-Apr
Cephalonia	1895	20-May
Cephalonia	1895	23-Jun
Cephalonia	1895	27-Jul
Cephalonia	1895	01-Sep
Cephalonia	1895	06-Oct
Cephalonia	1895	10-Nov
Cephalonia	1895	16-Dec
Cephalonia	1896	13-Apr
Cephalonia	1896	17-May
Cephalonia	1896	21-Jun
Cephalonia	1896	26-Jul
Cephalonia	1896	30-Aug
Cephalonia	1897	15-Feb
Cephalonia	1897	17-Mar
Cephalonia	1897	19-Apr
Cephalonia	1897	08-May
Cephalonia	1897	20-Jun
Cephalonia	1897	30-Aug
Cephalonia	1897	05-Oct
Cephalonia	1897	15-Nov
Cephalonia	1897	17-Dec
Cephalonia	1898	19-Feb
Cephalonia	1898	03-Apr
Cephalonia	1898	14-May
Cephalonia	1898	20-Jun
Cephalonia	1898	22-Jul
Cephalonia	1898	26-Aug
Cephalonia	1898	01-Oct
Cephalonia	1898	05-Nov
Cephalonia	1898	12-Dec
Cephalonia	1899	17-Jan
Cephalonia	1899	21-Feb
Cephalonia	1899	25-Mar
Cephalonia	1899	07-May
Cephalonia	1899	10-Jun
Cephalonia	1899	15-Jul
Cephalonia	1899	18-Aug
Cephalonia	1899	24-Sep
Cheruskia	1897	06-Jan
Christiania	1896	04-Dec
Christiania	1898	19-May
Christiania	1898	22-Aug
Christiania	1898	26-Nov
Colonia	1893	02-May
Columbia	1902	19-Oct
Columbian	1901	07-May
Columbian	1901	19-Aug
Columbian	1902	23-Jun
Columbian	1902	24-Nov
Columbus	1903	10-Oct
Columbus	1903	04-Nov
Commonwealth	1900	11-Oct
Commonwealth	1900	08-Nov
Commonwealth	1900	07-Dec
Commonwealth	1901	09-Feb
Commonwealth	1901	09-Mar
Commonwealth	1901	05-Apr
Commonwealth	1901	03-May
Commonwealth	1901	31-May
Commonwealth	1901	29-Jun
Commonwealth	1901	27-Jul
Commonwealth	1901	23-Aug
Commonwealth	1901	21-Sep
Commonwealth	1901	18-Oct
Commonwealth	1901	25-Nov
Commonwealth	1902	18-Mar
Commonwealth	1902	18-Apr
Commonwealth	1902	16-May
Commonwealth	1902	13-Jun
Commonwealth	1902	11-Jul
Commonwealth	1902	08-Aug
Commonwealth	1902	05-Sep
Commonwealth	1902	03-Oct
Commonwealth	1902	01-Nov
Commonwealth	1902	29-Dec
Commonwealth	1903	30-May
Commonwealth	1903	26-Jun
Commonwealth	1903	24-Jul
Commonwealth	1903	21-Aug
Commonwealth	1903	18-Sep
Commonwealth	1903	16-Oct
Commonwealth	1903	15-Nov
Constantia	1897	17-Aug
Corean	1903	26-May

Ship	Year	Date
Cretic	1903	06-Dec
Cymric	1903	20-Dec
Derbyshire	1899	17-Jun
Derbyshire	1899	15-Jul
Derbyshire	1899	12-Aug
Derbyshire	1899	09-Sep
Devonian	1902	16-May
Devonian	1903	04-May
Devonian	1903	21-Sep
Devonian	1903	02-Dec
Dominion	1898	26-Nov
Dominion	1898	25-Dec
Dominion	1899	21-Feb
Elberfeld	1892	10-Aug
Florida	1900	07-Oct
Gallia	1894	07-Apr
Gallia	1894	12-May
Gallia	1894	16-Jun
Gallia	1895	27-Apr
Gallia	1895	02-Jun
Gallia	1895	06-Jul
Gallia	1895	10-Aug
Gallia	1895	14-Sep
Gallia	1896	18-Apr
Gallia	1896	30-May
Gallia	1896	04-Jul
Gallia	1896	08-Aug
Gallia	1897	25-Apr
Gallia	1897	29-May
Gallia	1897	03-Jul
Gallia	1897	07-Aug
Gallia	1897	11-Sep
Gallia	1897	16-Oct
Gothia	1892	16-Jun
Grimm	1894	19-Feb
Grimm	1894	22-Jul
Halifax	1892	23-Jun
Halifax	1899	12-Jan
Halifax	1899	23-Feb
Halifax	1900	01-Jun
Halifax	1900	15-Jun
Halifax	1900	16-Nov
Halifax	1901	21-Feb
Halifax	1902	09-May
Halifax	1902	06-Jun
Halifax	1902	28-Jul
Halifax	1902	25-Aug
Halifax	1902	10-Oct
Halifax	1902	17-Oct
Halifax	1902	31-Oct
Halifax	1902	11-Dec
Halifax	1902	25-Dec
Halifax	1903	09-Apr
Halifax	1903	08-May
Heroynia	1895	23-Jul
Heroynia	1898	03-May
Hibernian	1895	29-May
Hibernian	1895	09-Jul
Hibernian	1895	18-Aug
Hibernian	1895	01-Oct
Hibernian	1896	03-Jun
Hibernian	1897	30-Mar
Hibernian	1897	19-May
Hibernian	1897	27-Jun
Hibernian	1899	20-May
Hibernian	1899	28-Jun
Hibernian	1899	08-Aug
Hibernian	1899	14-Sep
Hibernian	1900	13-May
Hispania	1898	01-Nov
Hungaria	1894	17-Apr
Hungaria	1894	17-Jun
Hungaria	1894	12-Oct
Hurworth	1903	17-Feb
Italia	1894	28-Mar
Italia	1895	17-May
Italia	1895	28-Nov
Ivernia	1900	21-Jun
Ivernia	1900	27-Jul
Ivernia	1900	30-Aug
Ivernia	1900	04-Oct
Ivernia	1900	05-Nov
Ivernia	1900	15-Dec
Ivernia	1901	25-Jan
Ivernia	1901	28-Feb
Ivernia	1901	18-Apr
Ivernia	1901	22-May
Ivernia	1901	26-Jun
Ivernia	1901	01-Aug
Ivernia	1901	04-Sep
Ivernia	1901	10-Oct
Ivernia	1901	14-Nov
Ivernia	1901	19-Dec
Ivernia	1902	28-Feb
Ivernia	1902	27-Mar
Ivernia	1902	24-Apr
Ivernia	1902	22-May
Ivernia	1902	19-Jun
Ivernia	1902	16-Jul
Ivernia	1902	13-Aug
Ivernia	1902	10-Sep
Ivernia	1902	08-Oct
Ivernia	1902	13-Nov
Ivernia	1902	19-Dec
Ivernia	1903	10-Jun
Ivernia	1903	08-Jul
Ivernia	1903	06-Aug
Ivernia	1903	02-Sep
Ivernia	1903	30-Sep
Ivernia	1903	29-Oct
Ivernia	1903	03-Dec
Kansas	1891	27-Aug
Kansas	1891	02-Oct
Kansas	1891	05-Nov
Kansas	1892	28-Jan
Kansas	1892	28-Feb
Kansas	1892	30-Mar
Kansas	1892	05-May
Kansas	1892	08-Jun
Kansas	1892	14-Jul
Kansas	1892	17-Aug
Kansas	1900	03-Jun
Kehrovieder	1893	12-Jun
Kingstonian	1901	12-Dec
Lake Huron	1891	07-Dec
Lake Huron	1892	12-Jan
Lake Huron	1892	22-Feb
Lake Neprzon	1892	17-Mar
Lake Ontario	1891	17-Dec
Lake Ontario	1892	28-Jan
Lake Superior	1891	24-Nov
Lake Superior	1892	06-Jan
Lake Superior	1892	14-Feb
Lake Superior	1892	22-Mar
Lancastrian	1901	03-Sep
Marathon	1892	20-Sep
Markomannia	1893	19-Jan
Markomannia	1898	21-Jun
Mayflower	1903	19-Apr
Mayflower	1903	16-May
Mayflower	1903	13-Jun
Mayflower	1903	11-Jul
Mayflower	1903	10-Aug
Mayflower	1903	05-Sep
Mayflower	1903	02-Oct
Mayflower	1903	01-Nov
Merion	1902	21-Mar
Merion	1902	27-Apr
Merion	1902	25-May
Merion	1902	22-Jun
Merion	1902	20-Jul
Merion	1902	17-Aug
Merion	1902	14-Sep
Merion	1902	12-Oct
Merion	1902	09-Nov
Merion	1902	08-Dec
Merion	1903	13-Jan
Merion	1903	18-Feb
Michigan	1891	19-Aug
Michigan	1891	23-Sep
Michigan	1891	28-Oct
Michigan	1891	01-Dec
Michigan	1892	06-Jan
Michigan	1892	12-Feb
Michigan	1892	20-Mar
Michigan	1892	20-Apr
Michigan	1892	25-May
Michigan	1892	28-Jun
Michigan	1892	01-Aug
Michigan	1892	07-Sep
Moravia	1898	05-Jun
Moravia	1898	22-Jul
Moravia	1898	01-Sep
Moravia	1898	20-Oct
Navarro	1892	06-Apr
Nestorian	1891	09-Sep
Nestorian	1891	22-Oct
Nestorian	1893	25-May
Nestorian	1893	05-Jul
Nestorian	1893	22-Aug
Nestorian	1893	05-Oct
Nestorian	1894	19-May
Nestorian	1894	27-Jun
New England	1898	10-Jul
New England	1898	05-Aug
New England	1898	02-Sep
New England	1898	30-Sep
New England	1898	29-Oct
New England	1898	02-Dec
New England	1898	31-Dec
New England	1899	28-Jan
New England	1899	24-Feb
New England	1899	01-Apr
New England	1899	28-Apr
New England	1899	27-May
New England	1899	30-Jun
New England	1899	28-Jul
New England	1899	25-Aug
New England	1899	22-Sep
New England	1899	22-Oct
New England	1899	17-Nov
New England	1899	15-Dec
New England	1900	31-Jan
New England	1900	20-Apr
New England	1900	18-May
New England	1900	14-Jun
New England	1900	15-Jul
New England	1900	10-Aug
New England	1900	07-Sep
New England	1900	05-Oct
New England	1900	02-Nov
New England	1900	29-Nov
New England	1900	28-Dec
New England	1901	26-Jan
New England	1901	22-Feb
New England	1901	23-Mar
New England	1901	19-Apr
New England	1901	17-May
New England	1901	15-Jun
New England	1901	12-Jul
New England	1901	09-Aug
New England	1901	06-Sep
New England	1901	04-Oct
New England	1901	01-Nov
New England	1901	30-Nov
New England	1902	18-Jan
New England	1902	06-Apr
New England	1902	02-May
New England	1902	30-May
New England	1902	27-Jun
New England	1902	25-Jul
New England	1902	21-Aug
New England	1902	18-Sep
New England	1902	18-Oct
New England	1902	01-Dec
New England	1903	09-May
New England	1903	05-Jun
New England	1903	04-Jul
New England	1903	31-Jul
New England	1903	28-Aug
New England	1903	25-Sep
Norseman	1891	02-Sep
Norseman	1891	08-Oct
Norseman	1891	10-Nov
Norseman	1891	19-Dec
Norseman	1892	20-Jan
Norseman	1892	20-Feb
Norseman	1892	24-Mar
Norseman	1892	27-Apr
Norseman	1892	02-Jun
Norseman	1892	07-Jul
Norseman	1892	10-Aug
Norwegian	1896	16-Jul
Norwegian	1896	23-Aug
Norwegian	1898	05-Jun
Norwegian	1898	28-May
Norwegian	1899	12-Jul
Norwegian	1899	22-Aug
Norwegian	1899	26-Sep
Norwegian	1900	17-Jun
Norwegian	1900	24-Jul
Norwegian	1900	28-Aug
Norwegian	1900	02-Oct
Norwegian	1901	27-Apr
Norwegian	1901	10-Jul
Norwegian	1901	16-Sep
Norwegian	1902	30-Apr
Olivetti	1901	02-Sep
Olivetti	1902	19-Jun
Ontario	1901	30-Jan
Ottoman	1891	04-Aug
Ottoman	1891	10-Sep
Ottoman	1891	16-Oct
Ottoman	1891	19-Nov
Ottoman	1891	24-Dec
Ottoman	1892	31-Jan
Ottoman	1892	04-Mar
Ottoman	1892	06-Apr
Ottoman	1892	10-May
Ottoman	1892	16-Jun
Ottoman	1892	19-Jul
Ottoman	1892	24-Aug
Pavonia	1891	23-Aug
Pavonia	1891	28-Sep
Pavonia	1891	01-Nov
Pavonia	1891	04-Dec
Pavonia	1892	19-Jan
Pavonia	1892	27-Mar
Pavonia	1892	01-May
Pavonia	1892	05-Jun
Pavonia	1892	10-Jul
Pavonia	1892	14-Aug
Pavonia	1892	18-Sep
Pavonia	1892	24-Oct
Pavonia	1892	28-Nov
Pavonia	1893	09-Jan
Pavonia	1893	21-Feb
Pavonia	1893	03-Apr
Pavonia	1893	07-May
Pavonia	1893	11-Jun
Pavonia	1893	16-Jul
Pavonia	1893	20-Aug
Pavonia	1893	23-Sep
Pavonia	1893	29-Oct
Pavonia	1893	05-Dec
Pavonia	1894	22-Feb
Pavonia	1894	02-Apr
Pavonia	1894	06-May
Pavonia	1894	10-Jun
Pavonia	1894	15-Jul
Pavonia	1894	20-Aug
Pavonia	1894	23-Sep
Pavonia	1894	22-Oct
Pavonia	1894	03-Dec
Pavonia	1895	07-Jan
Pavonia	1895	02-Apr
Pavonia	1895	06-May
Pavonia	1895	10-Jun
Pavonia	1895	14-Jul
Pavonia	1895	18-Aug
Pavonia	1896	03-May
Pavonia	1896	07-Jun
Pavonia	1896	12-Jul
Pavonia	1896	15-Aug
Pavonia	1896	21-Sep
Pavonia	1896	25-Oct
Pavonia	1896	25-Nov
Pavonia	1896	28-Dec
Pavonia	1897	23-Feb
Pavonia	1897	19-Mar
Pavonia	1897	02-May
Pavonia	1897	14-Jun
Pavonia	1897	11-Jul
Pavonia	1897	15-Aug
Pavonia	1897	19-Sep
Pavonia	1897	26-Oct

Pavonia	1897	05-Dec
Pavonia	1898	11-Jan
Pavonia	1898	12-Feb
Pavonia	1898	19-Mar
Pavonia	1898	30-Apr
Pavonia	1898	03-Jun
Pavonia	1898	08-Jul
Pavonia	1898	12-Aug
Pavonia	1898	16-Sep
Pavonia	1898	21-Oct
Pavonia	1898	25-Nov
Pavonia	1899	01-Jan
Pavonia	1899	20-Apr
Pavonia	1899	24-May
Pavonia	1899	30-Jun
Pavonia	1899	05-Aug
Pavonia	1899	09-Sep
Peruvian	1891	04-Dec
Peruvian	1892	24-Feb
Peruvian	1893	01-Mar
Peruvian	1893	14-Apr
Peruvian	1895	02-May
Peruvian	1895	12-Jun
Peruvian	1895	23-Jul
Peruvian	1895	05-Sep
Peruvian	1895	16-Oct
Peruvian	1895	25-Nov
Peruvian	1896	08-May
Peruvian	1896	16-Jun
Peruvian	1896	29-Jul
Peruvian	1896	09-Sep
Peruvian	1896	13-Oct
Peruvian	1897	08-Aug
Peruvian	1898	18-Apr
Peruvian	1898	26-May
Peruvian	1898	05-Jul
Peruvian	1898	16-Aug
Peruvian	1898	21-Sep
Peruvian	1898	04-Nov
Peruvian	1899	05-May
Peruvian	1899	14-Jun
Peruvian	1899	27-Jul
Peruvian	1899	05-Sep
Peruvian	1900	25-May
Peruvian	1900	12-Jul
Peruvian	1900	15-Aug
Peruvian	1900	20-Sep
Peruvian	1901	08-May
Peruvian	1901	13-Jun
Peruvian	1901	02-Sep
Pickhuben	1892	13-Dec
Polaria	1894	28-Sep
Polaria	1895	01-Feb
Polynesia	1894	11-Mar
Polynesia	1894	08-May
Polynesia	1894	02-Jul
Polynesia	1894	28-Aug
Pomeranian	1894	18-Mar
Pomeranian	1902	16-Apr
Prince Arthur	1900	10-May
Prince Arthur	1900	13-May
Prince Arthur	1900	07-Jun
Prince Arthur	1900	10-Jun
Prince Arthur	1900	15-Jul
Prince Arthur	1900	14-Oct
Prince Arthur	1900	25-Nov
Prince Arthur	1900	16-Dec
Prince Arthur	1900	27-Dec
Prince Arthur	1901	17-Jan
Prince Arthur	1901	06-Sep
Prince Arthur	1901	12-Sep
Prince Arthur	1902	06-Jul
Prince Arthur	1903	22-Jul
Prince George	1899	03-Feb
Prince George	1900	14-Jun
Prince George	1900	17-Oct
Prince George	1901	21-Apr
Prince George	1901	16-Sep
Prince George	1902	01-Jun
Prince George	1902	04-Jun
Prince George	1902	26-Aug
Prince George	1903	28-Sep
Prussian	1891	11-Aug
Prussian	1891	22-Sep
Prussian	1892	04-May
Prussian	1892	15-Jun
Prussian	1892	25-Jul
Prussian	1892	14-Sep
Prussian	1893	17-Mar
Prussian	1893	26-Apr
Prussian	1893	06-Jun
Prussian	1893	21-Jul
Prussian	1893	06-Sep
Prussian	1893	19-Oct
Prussian	1894	20-Apr
Prussian	1894	28-May
Prussian	1894	18-Jul
Prussian	1896	19-May
Prussian	1896	01-Jul
Prussian	1896	10-Aug
Republic	1903	27-Dec
Rhenania	1893	06-Jan
Roman	1891	13-Aug
Roman	1891	16-Sep
Roman	1891	22-Oct
Roman	1891	25-Nov
Roman	1892	13-Mar
Roman	1892	16-Apr
Roman	1892	19-May
Roman	1892	21-Jun
Roman	1892	27-Jul
Roman	1892	31-Aug
Romanic	1903	27-Nov
Rowan	1892	02-Jan
Rowan	1892	04-Feb
Russia	1895	31-May
Sachem	1901	29-Jun
Sachem	1902	31-Aug
Sagamore	1901	18-Jun
Samaria	1891	17-Aug
Samaria	1891	23-Sep
Samaria	1891	29-Oct
Samaria	1892	10-May
Samaria	1892	14-Jun
Samaria	1892	19-Jul
Samaria	1892	22-Aug
Samaria	1895	18-Feb
Samaritan	1891	19-Dec
Samaritan	1892	09-Mar
Samaritan	1898	28-Apr
Sardinia	1898	02-Aug
Sardinian	1900	30-Apr
Sardinian	1902	03-Apr
Sarmatian	1896	08-Apr
Sarmatian	1903	14-Jun
Sarmatian	1903	27-Jul
Sarmatian	1903	07-Sep
Saxonia	1900	31-May
Saxonia	1900	05-Jul
Saxonia	1900	09-Aug
Saxonia	1900	12-Sep
Saxonia	1900	18-Oct
Saxonia	1900	27-Nov
Saxonia	1901	11-Jan
Saxonia	1901	14-Feb
Saxonia	1901	21-Mar
Saxonia	1901	02-May
Saxonia	1901	06-Jun
Saxonia	1901	11-Jul
Saxonia	1901	14-Aug
Saxonia	1901	19-Sep
Saxonia	1901	24-Oct
Saxonia	1901	29-Nov
Saxonia	1902	13-Mar
Saxonia	1902	06-Jun
Saxonia	1902	03-Jul
Saxonia	1902	31-Jul
Saxonia	1902	28-Aug
Saxonia	1902	24-Sep
Saxonia	1902	27-Nov
Saxonia	1903	06-Mar
Saxonia	1903	03-Apr
Saxonia	1903	01-May
Saxonia	1903	29-May
Saxonia	1903	25-Jun
Saxonia	1903	24-Jul
Saxonia	1903	20-Aug
Saxonia	1903	17-Sep
Saxonia	1903	15-Oct
Saxonia	1903	19-Nov
Saxonia	1903	24-Dec
Scandinavian	1891	24-Aug
Scandinavian	1892	02-Jan
Scandanavian	1892	15-Feb
Scandanavian	1897	05-May
Scandanavian	1897	16-Jun
Scandanavian	1897	28-Jul
Scandinavian	1897	08-Sep
Scandinavian	1891	09-Oct
Scandinavian	1892	19-Apr
Scandinavian	1892	01-Jun
Scandinavian	1892	13-Jul
Scandinavian	1892	30-Aug
Scandinavian	1892	10-Oct
Scandinavian	1893	11-May
Scandinavian	1893	19-Jun
Scandinavian	1893	09-Aug
Scandinavian	1893	18-Sep
Scandinavian	1894	02-May
Scandinavian	1894	12-Jun
Scandinavian	1895	15-May
Scandinavian	1895	24-Jun
Scandinavian	1895	06-Aug
Scandinavian	1895	18-Sep
Scandinavian	1895	29-Oct
Scandinavian	1896	23-Apr
Scandinavian	1898	11-May
Scandinavian	1898	22-Jun
Scandinavian	1898	04-Aug
Scandinavian	1898	13-Sep
Sch Willina D.	1892	27-Jul
Scotia	1895	23-Aug
Scythia	1891	30-Aug
Scythia	1891	05-Oct
Scythia	1891	05-Nov
Scythia	1891	14-Dec
Scythia	1892	17-Apr
Scythia	1892	22-May
Scythia	1892	26-Jun
Scythia	1892	30-Jul
Scythia	1892	05-Sep
Scythia	1892	09-Oct
Scythia	1893	11-Apr
Scythia	1893	14-May
Scythia	1893	18-Jun
Scythia	1893	23-Jul
Scythia	1893	26-Aug
Scythia	1893	01-Oct
Scythia	1894	27-Apr
Scythia	1894	03-Jun
Scythia	1894	12-Aug
Scythia	1894	17-Sep
Scythia	1895	13-May
Scythia	1895	16-Jun
Scythia	1895	21-Jul
Scythia	1895	24-Aug
Scythia	1895	30-Sep
Scythia	1895	01-Dec
Scythia	1896	31-Mar
Scythia	1896	24-May
Scythia	1896	28-Jun
Scythia	1896	06-Sep
Scythia	1896	11-Oct
Scythia	1897	10-May
Scythia	1897	14-Jun
Scythia	1897	18-Jul
Scythia	1897	23-Aug
Scythia	1897	27-Sep
Scythia	1897	01-Nov
Scythia	1898	18-Apr
Servia	1896	24-Jun
Servia	1896	31-Jul
Servia	1896	04-Oct
Servia	1896	04-Dec
Siberian	1897	31-Mar
Sicilia	1895	06-Jan
Slavonnia	1892	25-Jun
Steinhoft	1893	08-Aug
Sternhoft	1892	22-Nov
Stockholm City	1894	07-Apr
Turcoman	1900	13-Dec
Ultonia	1899	11-Mar
Ultonia	1899	17-Apr
Ultonia	1899	18-May
Ultonia	1899	24-Jun
Ultonia	1899	29-Jul
Ultonia	1899	07-Oct
Ultonia	1899	15-Nov
Ultonia	1899	21-Dec
Ultonia	1900	29-Jan
Ultonia	1900	01-Mar
Ultonia	1900	15-Apr
Ultonia	1900	19-May
Ultonia	1900	29-Jun
Ultonia	1900	04-Aug
Ultonia	1900	07-Sep
Ultonia	1900	14-Oct
Ultonia	1900	18-Nov
Ultonia	1900	20-Dec
Ultonia	1901	04-Feb
Ultonia	1901	12-Mar
Ultonia	1901	14-Apr
Ultonia	1901	17-May
Ultonia	1901	22-Jun
Ultonia	1901	27-Jul
Ultonia	1901	30-Aug
Ultonia	1901	05-Oct
Ultonia	1901	08-Nov
Ultonia	1901	14-Dec
Ultonia	1902	17-Jan
Ultonia	1902	24-Feb
Ultonia	1902	24-Mar
Ultonia	1902	02-May
Ultonia	1902	03-Jun
Ultonia	1902	11-Jul
Ultonia	1902	10-Aug
Ultonia	1902	06-Sep
Ultonia	1902	03-Oct
Ultonia	1902	03-Nov
Ultonia	1902	07-Dec
Ultonia	1903	12-Jan
Ultonia	1903	17-Feb
Ultonia	1903	29-Mar
Ultonia	1903	24-Apr
Ultonia	1903	23-May
Ultonia	1903	19-Jun
Ultonia	1903	18-Jul
Ultonia	1903	15-Aug
Ultonia	1903	12-Sep
Ultonia	1903	12-Oct
Ultonia	1903	14-Nov
Ultonia	1903	21-Dec
Victorian	1902	15-Sep
Virginian	1896	28-Jan
Virginian	1896	07-Mar
Virginian	1902	24-Apr
Wandrahm	1894	05-Apr
Winfredian	1903	02-Apr
Winifredian	1899	05-Sep
Winifredian	1899	10-Oct
Worcester	1892	18-Jul
Yarmouth	1892	17-Sep
Yarmouth	1892	21-Sep
Yarmouth	1900	20-Sep

AJHS MANUSCRIPT COLLECTIONS

The appendix lists manuscript collections at the AMERICAN JEWISH HISTORICAL SOCIETY (see page 33). It is in three parts: Institutional collections, Personal Papers, and Ephemera.

A. INSTITUTIONAL MANUSCRIPT COLLECTIONS

NAME	TYPE	CALL #	CITY, STATE	SIZE
Adler, Selig (1909-), Collector, material pertaining to the Jewish Community of Buffalo, N.Y.	Institutional	I-108	Buffalo, NY	1 box (117 items)
Aleph Beth Club	Fraternal	I-276	St. Paul, MN	1 box
America-Israel Society	National	I-272		1 box
American Association For Jewish Education (founded 1939)	Institutional	I-75		29 boxes
American Economic Committee For Palestine	National	I-288		
American Jewish Committee - Office Of War Records	Institutional	I-9		21 boxes - 9.5 linear feet
American Jewish Committee. San Francisco Collection Committee (1906-1907)	Institutional	I-86		1 box
American Jewish Conference (established in 1943 as the American Jewish Assembly; Terminated its activities in 1949)	Institutional	I-67		10 boxes
American Jewish Congress	Institutional	I-77		246 boxes
American Jewish Historical Exhibition, 1901-1902 (proposed)	Institutional	I-21		186 items
American Jewish Press Association (established 1943? as The American Assoc. of English-Jewish Newspapers, Reorganized 1960)	Institutional	I-62		2 boxes
American Jewish Relief Committee For Sufferers From The War (founded 1914, Dissolved 1919)	Institutional	I-83		1 box
American Jewish Tercentenary Celebration Papers 1951-1956	Institutional	I-11		7 boxes
American League For A Free Palestine	Political	I-278		1 box
American League To Combat Anti-Semitism	Political	I-263		1 box
American Society For Jewish Farm Settlements in Russia, Inc.	Agricultural	I-129		10 items
American Zionist Council	Political	I-284		2 boxes
Anshey Dowig Association	Landsmanshaft	I-219	Boston, MA	42 items
Arab Blacklist Papers	Political	I-187		1 vol., 5 supplements
Aryeh Lev Papers	Military	I-249		58 boxes
Association for the Free Distribution of Matsot to The Poor	Institutional	I-106	New York, NY	1 box (12 items)
Association For The Sociological Study Of Jewry	Academic	I-207		2 boxes
Audits & Surveys, Inc.		I-209		3 folders
B'nai Brith Arnon Centennial Lodge #39	Fraternal	I-30	New York, NY	131 pages
B'nai Brith. Manhattan-Washington Lodge #19	Institutional	I-31		30 items, 6000 pages
B'nai Brith. Missouri Lodge	Fraternal	I-194		1 item
B'nai Brith. Mt. Sinai Lodge #270	Institutional	I-29		2 items, 786 pages
B'nai Brith. Washington Irving Lodge #312	Institutional	I-29		1 item, 180 pages
B'nai Moses Congregation	Synagogue	I-264	Muscatine, IA	9 items
B. Manischewitz Co.		I-283		1 box
Barbados Jewish Community	Communal	I-139	Barbados	26 pages
Baron De Hirsch Fund (established 1890)	Institutional	I-80		63 boxes
Baron De Hirsch Trade School	Institutional	I-55	New York, NY	58 boxes + misc.
Beth Hamidrosh Hagadol	Synagogue	I-247	St. Louis, MO	1 reel
Beth Joseph Center (est. 1924 as Beth Yehudah, Center, became Beth Joseph 1932, dissolved 1989)	Community	I-262	Rochester, NY	2 boxes
Bickur Cholem Ukadishu	Fraternal	I-60	Chicago, IL	3 cartons-3 ledger books
Blue Card, Inc.	National	I-253		12 items
Board Of Delegates Of American Israelites	Institutional	I-2		4 cartons (1500 items)
Breira		I-160		2 boxes
Breira, Inc.	Political	I-250		16 boxes
Brownsville, N.Y.	Memoranda	I-138	Brooklyn, NY	2 pages
Cambridge Hebrew Women's Aid Society (founded 1897 as the Cambridge Hebrew Ladies' Charitable Society; name changed in 1919)	Institutional	I-113	Cambridge, MA	1 box
Camp Council		I-214	Philadelphia, PA	25 items

Camp Equinunk		I-246	Equinunk. PA	9 items
Canadian Jewish Herald - Magen David Adom Papers		I-165		175 items
Carvalho & Hirsch		I-195		1 page
Central Committee Of America In Aid Of Starving Jews In Russia	Institutional	I-15		
Central Conference Of American Rabbis	National	I-215		220 items
Central Jewish Organization	National	I-212	Boston, MA	1 item
Chaltham County Georgia, Sheriff's Office.		I-196	Savannah, GA	1 page
Chebra Gemilath Chesed	Burial Society	I-130	Boston, MA	215 pages
Chevra Kadisha Gemilath Chesed Shel Emeth (a.k.a. Chevra Kadisha Agudath Achim)	Burial Society	I-132	Fall River, MA	1 item
Chevra Kadusha	Religious	I-185	Boston, MA	3 boxes
Citizens	Other	I-198	Chicago, IL	1 page
Citizens	Correspondnce	I-149	St. Paul, MN	1 item
City College, Dept. Of Romance Languages Investigating Committee	Institutional	I-98	New York, NY	1 box
City Court Of The City Of New York	Legal	I-151	New York, NY	23 folios, 13 film reels
City Court Of The City Of New York	Institutional	I-49	New York, NY	297 boxes
Civil War Centennial Jewish Historical Commission	Institutional	I-40		114 items
Clara De Hirsch Literary Society	Educational	I-275	Minneapolis, MN	
Columbia Religious And Industrial School For Jewish Girls (founded 1888, incorporated 1907)	Institutional	I-24	New York, NY	91 items
Combined Jewish Philanthropies	Charity	I-220	Boston, MA	3 boxes
Committee On Cooperation	National	I-174		1 box
Community Relations Conference	National	I-171		
Concerned Jewish Students Of Greater Boston (est. 1970)		I-157	Boston, MA	200 pages
Congregation Mikveh Israel	Institutional	I-26	Philadelphia, PA	105 items
Congregation Adath Jeshurun	Synagogue	I-244	Philadelphia, PA	5 items
Congregation Ahaveth Achim	Synagogue	I-222	Chelsea, MA	9 items
Congregation Am Echod, Minute Book	Institutional	I-79	Waukegan, IL	1 box
Congregation Anshai Russia. A History, by Abraham Noah Ravitz		I-225	Newark, NJ	2 items
Congregation Anshei Libovitz	Institutional	I-103	Boston, MA	5 boxes
Congregation Beth Elohim	Institutional	I-107	Charleston, SC	25 items
Congregation Beth Hamidrash Hagadol	Synagogue	I-239	Boston, MA	3 items
Congregation Beth Israel	Synagogue	I-131	Boston, MA	2 items
Congregation Beth Israel	Institutional	I-51	Cambridge, MA	3 boxes
Congregation Bnai Israel	Synagogue	I-221	Revere, MA	8 items
Congregation Bnai Jacob	Synagogue	I-148	Montreal, Canada	1 item
Congregation Gates Of Prayer (established 1850)	Synagogue	I-133	New Orleans, LA	2 items
Congregation Glory Of Israel (Tiphereth Israel)	Synagogue	I-229	Brooklyn, NY	2 boxes
Congregation Kahal Adath Yeshurun Em Anshe Lubtz	Institutional	I-10	New York, NY	6 linear feet
Congregation Kenesseth Israel	Synagogue	I-266	Boston, MA	34 items
Congregation Kesser Israel	Synagogue	I-150	Springfield, MA	18 pages
Congregation Linas Zedeck Beth Israel	Institutional	I-101	Chelsea, MA	2 ledgers and 6 items
Congregation Mesilath Yeshurim And Talmud Torah	Synagogue	I-128	New York, NY	minutebooks and ledgers
Congregation Mikve Israel	Synagogue	I-277	Savannah, GA	1 box
Congregation Mishkan Israel	Institutional	I-114	Dorchester, MA	1 box
Congregation Ohava Emes	Synagogue	I-252	Nashville, TN	2 items, 56 pages
Congregation Rodeph Shalom	Synagogue	I-242	Philadelphia, PA	18 items
Congregation Shearith Israel	Institutional	I-4	New York, NY	6 cartons
Congregation Sherith Israel	Institutional	I-97	San Francisco, CA	
Congregation Anshe Sefard	Synagogue	I-269	Boston, MA	2 items
Coordinating Committee Of Jewish Organizations Dealing With Employment Discrimination in War Industries	Political	I-169		
Coordinating Committee Of National Jewish Organizations for the United National Clothing Collection for War Relief	National	I-175		75 pages
Council Of Jewish Federation And Welfare Funds	Institutional	I-69		395 boxes
Council Of Jewish Federations. Oral History Interviews	Institutional	I-59		4 boxes
Curaco Jewish Community	Institutional	I-112	Curacao	1 box (207 items)
Damascus Affair	Political	I-238		32 items
Delaware Valley College Of Science And Agriculture (founded 1896 by Rev. Joseph Krauskopf)	Institutional	I-36		420 items
Description Of Wedding, Nineteenth Century		I-144	Lexington, MO	3 pages
East Lexington Hebrew Congregation, Temple Bnai Jacob	Institutional	I-102	Lexington, MA	1 ledger book
East Side Emergency Loan Fund	Loan Assoc.	I-140	New York, NY	2 pages
Executive Committee On The Celebration of the 250th Anniversary of the Settlement of the Jews in the United States	Institutional	I-16		1 box
Federation Of Jewish Women's Organizations	Fraternal	I-208	New York, NY	8 boxes
First Baltimore Hebrew Guards (Formed in 1846)	Military	I-134	Baltimore, MD	1 item
First Radomer Congregation	Synagogue	I-124	New York, NY	2 ledgers
Freedom Seder Collection	Institutional	I-64		600 items
Freemasons. King Solomon's Lodge #279	Institutional	I-39		8 items, 139 pages
Friends Of Ida Kaminska Theatre Foundation Inc. (incorporated 1970, dissolved 1975)		I-122		3 boxes (2500 items)

Galveston Immigration Plan (1907-1914)	Institutional	I-90		6 boxes
Gan Chaim Corporation Limited		I-251		
General Jewish Council	National	I-170		18 boxes
German Hebrew Benevolent Society of the City of NY	Institutional	I-46	New York, NY	1 item
Graduate School For Jewish Social Work	Institutional	I-7	New York, NY	6 boxes
Hamilton House	Immigrant Aid	I-281	New York, NY	1 box
Hartman-Homecrest	Orphan	I-233	New York, NY	1 box
Harvard University	Other	I-199	Cambridge, MA	1 page
Hebra Tarumot Hakodesh (founded London 1824; American branch in existence, 1832-185?)	Institutional	I-33		18 items
Hebra Shel Bikur Holim Ugemilut	Burial Society	I-147	Philadelphia, PA	7 pages
Hebrew Benevolent Society Of The City Of New York		I-258	New York, NY	3 items
Hebrew Congregation - Madison, Wisconsin	Institutional	I-19	Madison, WI	1 volume
Hebrew Custom Tailors Cemetery Association		I-260	Boston, MA	3 items
Hebrew Educational Alliance, Congregation Toras Moshe	Synagogue	I-231	Boston, MA	21 items
Hebrew Emigrant Aid Society Of The United States	National	I-184		1 item
Hebrew Female Orphans Dowry Society of the U.S.	Institutional	I-22		1 item
Hebrew Free Loan Society	Loan Society	I-205	Pittsfield, MA	2 ledgers
Hebrew Free Loan Society Of Boston (established 1912 as Hebrew Free Loan Society, reorganized under present name 1937)	Institutional	I-115	Boston, MA	2 boxes
Hebrew Immigrant Aid Society	Institutional	I-96	Boston, MA	248 boxes
Hebrew Infant Asylum Of The City Of New York	Orphanage	I-166	New York, NY	2 boxes (11 items)
Hebrew Orphan Asylum		I-230	Brooklyn, NY	5 boxes, 5 ledgers
Hebrew Orphan Asylum	Institutional	I-42	New York, NY	14 boxes, 9 ledgers
Hebrew Orphan Asylum (founded 1822 as Hebrew Benevolent Soc., various name changes until 1906, merged 1940 into Jewish Child Care Association)	Institutional	I-42	New York, NY	62 boxes, 35,000 items
Hebrew Relief Society	Charity	I-155	New York, NY	
Hebrew Sheltering Guardian Society Of New York (founded 1879, merged into Jewish Child Care Assoc. of New York in 1940)	Institutional	I-43	New York, NY	9 boxes
Hebrew Teachers Association of Greater Boston, 1934-56	Institutional	I-119	Boston, MA	3 boxes
Hecht Neighborhood House (founded 1889 as Hebrew Industrial School; changed name 1922; merged with YMHA of Boston in 1958/59 to YMHA-Hecht House)	Institutional	I-74	Boston, MA	27 boxes
Home For Hebrew Infants	Orphan Society	I-232	New York, NY	2 boxes, 1 ledger
Immigrants Mutual Aid Society, Inc., Boston	Institutional	I-109	Boston, MA	2 boxes
Independent Order of Brith Abraham, Dr. Gaster Lodge No. 689	Institutional	I-104	Boston, MA	1 box
Independent Order of Brith Abraham, Sag Harbor Lodge No. 297	Institutional	I-99	Sag Harbor, NY	1 ledger
Independent Order of Ahawas Israel, United Brethren Lodge No. 139	Institutional	I-100	Sag Harbor, NY	3 ledgers + 20 items
Independent Slonimer Benevolent Society, New York		I-126	New York, NY	2 boxes
Industrial Removal Office	Institutional	I-91		123 boxes
Informal Committee On Commemoration Of The Jewish Military Chaplaincy	Institutional	I-44		815 items
Inquisition Records	Institutional	I-3	Mexico	20 boxes
Institute For Jewish Life	Cultural	I-168		11 boxes
Intercollegiate Zionist Federation Of America	Institutional	I-57		1 box
Jamaica, West Indies	Institutional	I-82	Jamaica	1 box
Jewish Academy Of Arts And Sciences (founded 1927)	National	I-121		2 boxes
Jewish Agricultural Society	Agricultural	I-206		7 boxes
Jewish Book Council Of America		I-259		5 boxes
Jewish Child Care Association		I-235	New York, NY	13 boxes, 17 scrapbooks
Jewish Children's Clearing Bureau	Institutional	I-81		1 box
Jewish Chronic Disease Hospital	Hospital	I-245	Brooklyn, NY	2 boxes
Jewish Community Council Of Metropolitan Boston (established 1944)	Community	I-123	Boston, MA	211 boxes, 4 albums
Jewish Community Council Of Metropolitan Boston - Maciver Report Papers	Institutional	I-78		3 boxes
Jewish Community Of Zvehil, Poland	Appreciation	I-141	Zvehil, Poland	1 page
Jewish Culture Club	Fraternal	I-179	Boston, MA	Recordbook
Jewish Family And Children's Service		I-218	Boston, MA	50 items
Jewish Family And Children's Service Of Denver	Institutional	I-65	Denver, CO	57 boxes
Jewish Frontier - Anniversary Speeches	Speeches	I-142		12 pages
Jewish Historical Committee	Historical	I-137	Boston, MA	12 pages
Jewish Historical Society Of Illinois	Institutional	I-34	Chicago, IL	12 items
Jewish Hospital Association Of Philadelphia		I-243	Philadelphia, PA	5 items
Jewish Immigration Committee (1908-1917)	Institutional	I-84	New York, NY	1 box
Jewish Ministers Cantors Association Of America	Music	I-287		1 box
Jewish Music Forum		I-255	New York, NY	1 box
Jewish Peace Fellowship	Political	I-189		19 boxes
Jewish Public Relations Council	National	I-176	Pittsburgh, PA	7 pages
Jewish Reconstructionist Foundation, Inc.	Institutional	I-71		47 boxes
Jewish Sabbath Alliance Of America	Religious	I-282		1 box

Jewish Sisters Mutual Aid Society	Institutional	I-72	New York, NY	5 boxes
Jewish Social Service Organization Of Schenectady		I-261	Schenectady, NY	7 items
Jewish Student Press Service	National	I-248		7 boxes
Jewish Vocational Aid Society		I-216	Boston, MA	100 items
Jewish War Veterans Of The United States	Institutional	I-32		277 items
Jews For Urban Justice	Political	I-159	Washington, DC	300 pages
Joint Advisory Committee	National	I-191		11 boxes
Kadimah Zionist Club	Institutional	I-116	Boston, MA	5 items
Kehilla Of New York City		I-274	New York, NY	1 box
Kesher Shel Barzel (Founded 1860, Dissolved 1903)	Institutional	I-28		9 guidebooks, 2 pamphlets
Khebrat Sha'arey Beenah	Synagogue	I-226	New York, NY	1 item
Kishinev Protest Meeting, Committee Of Arrangements	Institutional	I-25		22 items
Labor League	Labor	I-267	Brockton, MA	4 items
Labor Lyceum Workmen's Circle	Labor	I-268	Brockton, MA	1 item
Louisa May Alcott Club		I-210	Boston, MA	1 item
Lynn Hebrew Young Men's Aid Association (1903-1971)	Institutional	I-73	Lynn, MA	3 boxes
M. & E. Meyer & Co.		I-183	Selma, AL	1 page
Maimonides Octocentennial Papers	Institutional	I-12		3 boxes - 1500 items
Madison House	Immigrant Aid	I-279	New York, NY	1 book
Marks Bros.	Advertising	I-193	Philadelphia, PA	1 item
Massachusetts Board Of Rabbis	Institutional	I-56	MA	1 box
Massachusetts Observance of the American Jewish Tercentenary	Institutional	I-63		4 boxes
Meretz Relief Association	Landsmanshaft	I-217	Boston, MA	2 boxes
Moegenthau Commission		I-143		1 item
Mosaic (a publication of Harvard/Radcliffe Hillel)	Fraternal	I-178	Cambridge, MA	30 items
Moss Rehabilitation Hospital	Institutional	I-38	Philadelphia, PA	1 box
Mt. Sinai Hospital (founded 1852 as Jews Hospital, name changed 1866)	Institutional	I-37	New York, NY	12 items
National Association Of Hillel Directors	Institutional	I-41		1000 items
National Association Of Jewish Social Workers	Institutional	I-88		2 boxes
National Citizens Committee	Institutional	I-23		2 boxes, 777 items
National Citizens Committee For Fairness To The President	National	I-177		3 boxes
National Committee For The Relief Of Sufferers By Russian Massacres	Institutional	I-5		2 cartons (900 items)
National Committee On Post-War Immigration Policy	National	I-173		1 box
National Community Relations Advisory Council	National	I-172		29 boxes
National Conference On Soviet Jewry	National	I-181		72 boxes
National Honey Board		I-271		1 box
National Jewish Immigration Council	Institutional	I-85		1 box
National Jewish Population Study	National	I-254		137 boxes
National Jewish Welfare Board, Army-Navy Division	National	I-180		343 boxes
National Jewish Welfare Board, Bureau Of War Records	Institutional	I-52		672 boxes
National Refugee Service	Institutional	I-92		7 boxes
Near East Crisis Collection	Institutional	I-18		20 boxes
Netherlands. States-General	Correspondnce	I-136	Jamaica	1 item
New Century Club	Institutional	I-95	Boston, MA	2 boxes
New England Jewish Free Press		I-158	Boston, MA	75 pages
New England Jewish Music Forum		I-270	Boston, MA	9 boxes
New England Student Struggle For Soviet Jewry	Student	I-237		200 pages
New York (county) Hall Of Records	Legal	I-153	New York, NY	9 folios, 5 microfilm reels
New York (county) Hall Of Records	Legal	I-154	New York, NY	81 folios, 27 microfilm reels
New York (county) Surrogate's Office. Inventories Of Estates		I-203	New York, NY	18 items
New York Association For Jewish Children	Orphanage	I-236	New York, NY	2 boxes, 1 ledger
New York City Committee On Jewish Affairs	Religious	I-190	New York, NY	500 pages
New York City Comptroller		I-257	New York, NY	6 items
New York State Assembly	Political	I-213	New York, NY	5 items
New York State Court Of Common Pleas	Legal	I-152	New York, NY	1 folio, 1 microfilm reel
Noah Benevolent Society	Orphan Assoc.	I-186	New York, NY	27 boxes
North American Relief Society For The Indigent Jews In Jerusalem, Palestine	Institutional	I-14		1 box
Oheb Shalom Congregation, Congregation Beth Torah	Synagogue	I-228	Newark, NJ	14 items
Organization Of Jewish Colonies In America	Institutional	I-47		3 boxes
Palestine Emergency Fund	National	I-289	New York, NY	1 box
Palestinian Educational Association	Institutional	I-117		2 pages
Paris Hebrew Benevolent Association	Burial Society	I-135	Paris, TX	11 pages.
People's Relief Committee	Institutional	I-13		49 boxes & 13 scrapbooks
Phi Epsilon Pi (founded 1904, absorbed in 1970 by Zeta Beta Tau)	Institutional	I-76		53 boxes
Philadelphia City Treasurer		I-192	Philadelphia, PA	76 items
Philadelphia Y.M.H.A. and Y.W.H.A.	Community	I-241	Philadelphia, PA	5 boxes
Protest Committee Of Non-Jewish Women Against The Persecution Of Jews In Germany (est. 1933)	Political	I-156		4 pages

Purim Association, 1862-1902	Institutional	I-20		3 items
Radomer Culture Center	Cultural	I-125	New York, NY	1 box
Rassco Israel Corporation	National	I-280		1 box
Rehabilitation Services		I-256	Boston, MA	75 items
Round Table Club, Philadelphia (est. 1912)		I-145	Philadelphia, PA	
Sabbath Observance Association	Religious	I-273	New York, NY	1 box
School For Jewish Communal Work (1916-1919)	Institutional	I-89	New York, NY	1 box
Seder Ritual Committee founded by Rufus Learsi Israel Goldberg in 1952, has functioned under American Jewish Congress)	Institutional	I-50		200 items
Seligman Solomon Society	Institutional	I-6		5 Cartons
Slonimer Ladies' Bikur Cholim Unter-Stutzungs Verein, New York. (est. 1913)	Fraternal	I-127	New York, NY	ledger book
Society For The Advancement Of Judaism	Institutional	I-70		7 boxes
Society Of Jewish Social Workers (1908-1914?)	Institutional	I-87	New York, NY	2 boxes
Spinoza Tri-Centennial Celebration Collection	Institutional	I-17		1 box - 320 items
Standard Club		I-252	Nashville, TN	1 item
Student Collection	Institutional	I-61		
Surinam Jewish Community	Institutional	I-94	Surinam	45 items
Swiss Treaty	Institutional	I-35		14 items
Synagogue Council Of America	Institutional	I-68		55 boxes
Temple Beth El	Institutional	I-111	Bimingham, MI	8 boxes
Temple Beth-El	Synagogue	I-265	Corsicana, TX	3 items
Training Bureau For Jewish Communal Service	Institutional	I-8	New York, NY	5 boxes
Union Of Orthodox Jewish Congregations Of America	Institutional	I-66		15 boxes
United Hebrew Benevolent Association	Orphan Assoc.	I-211	Boston, MA	2 items
United Hebrew Benevolent Association	Charity	I-223	Boston, MA	6 items
United Hebrew Congregation	Institutional	I-45	St. Louis, MO	1 volume (178 pages)
United Jewish Organizations	National	I-167	Philadelphia, PA	32 items
United Kosher Butchers Association, Inc.	Institutional	I-118		
United Order True Sisters, Inc., Noemi No. 11 (established 1883, dissolved In 1989)	Institutional	I-58		21 boxes
United Service For New Americans	Institutional	I-93		7 boxes
United States Sanitary Commission (founded in 1861 to improve medical conditions in the Union Army)	Institutional	I-48		2 items
University Settlement Society Of New York (1892-),	Institutional	I-27		
West End House	Immigrant Aid	I-285	Boston, MA	1 box
Wilkes-Barre, Pa. Flood.	Institutional	I-110	Wilkesbarre, PA	2 boxes
Woodbine Agricultural School	Institutional	I-54		12 boxes, 1 portfolio
Woodbine Colony	Institutional	I-53		5 ledgers, 27 boxes + misc.
Young Israel	National	I-240		1 box
Zionist House		I-286	Boston, MA	1 box

B. PERSONAL PAPERS COLLECTIONS

Abelson, Abel Eliyahu (1902-)	P-569	8 pages	
Abendanone Family (1829-)	P- 91	3 items	
Abrahams Family (NY) (1848-1867)	P-183	1 box (¼ lft)	
Abrahams, Isaac (1804-1811)	P-396	1 box	
Adams, Charles Follen (1882)	P-176	1 item, 1 photograph	
Adams, Hannah (1755-1831)	P-205	4 items	
Adler, Cyrus (1863-1940)	P- 16	6 cartons	
Adler, Felix (1882-1888)	P-401	3 pages	
Adler, Rachel Garfunkel (1899-1908)	P-645	1 box	
Aeron, Henry (1799-1799)	P-174	1 item	
Agriss, Leon (1935-1953)	P-179	150 pages	
Allen, Henry Watkins (1864-)	P-420	1 p.	
Alpert, Abraham (1903-1939)	P-544	2 boxes	
Alpert, David B. (1924-1979)	P- 82		
Amaram, David Werner	P-229	111 pages	
Andrade, Isaac (1853-1866)	P-256	2 items	
Asch, Morris Joseph (1862-1884)	P-201	2 items	
Auerhaim, Solomon (1854-1888)	P-166	24 items	
Azevedo, Moses Cohen D' (1813-1814)	P-364	ca. 200 pp.	
Barrett, Solomon I. (1844-)	P-421	1 page	
Baruch, Bernard (1923-1957)	P-200	26 items	
Baruch, Simon (1862-1870)	P-200	2 items	
Beck, James M. (1923-)	P-422	3 pages	
Bee, Barnard E. (1852-)	P-423	1 page	
Beecher, Henry Ward (1877-1887)	P-159	1 box, 7 itm	
Beer-Hoffmann, Richard (1911-1916)	P-212	2 items	
Beerman, Jacob	P-612		
Beilis, Mendel (1926-1930)	P-144	1 box	
Belmont, August (1841-1904)	P-207	7 items	
Benjamin, Judah Philip (1838-1942)	P- 45	60 items & photostats	
Benjamin, Solomon (1864-)	P-428	12 pages	
Berman, Abraham H. (1900-1966)	P-345		
Bernal, Abraham I.H. (1850-)	P-581	1 item	
Bernard, Edward (1968-1972)	P-102	2 boxes	
Bernheim, Isaac W. (1899-1938)	P-177	3 items (15 pages)	
Bernstein, Israel (1940-1968)	P- 51		
Bernstein, Samuel (1916-1918)	P-390	50 items	
Bisno, Julius (1801-1968)	P- 85	3 boxes (320 items)	
Blau, Joel (1909-1926)	P- 44	826 items	
Block, Herman W. (1913-1967)	P- 99	2 boxes	
Bloom, Sol (1927-1945)	P-253	17 items	
Bluestone, E. Michael (1920-1980)	P-362	18 boxes	
Bluestone, Joseph Isaac (1875-1975)	P-323	8 boxes	
Blumenthal, Charles (1922-1943)	P-114	33 items	
Blumenthal, Walter Hart (1900-1969)	P- 83	6 boxes (2½ lft)	
Bondi, August (1883-1906)	P-178	295 pages	
Bondi, Jonas Letters (1868-1869)	P-173	2 items	
Boruchoff, Ber (1906-1939)	P-157	1 box, ca. 236 items	
Boudinot Elias (1820-1820)	P-247	1 item	
Brandeis Louis Dembitz (1886-1940)	P-248	14 items	
Broido, Louis (1923-1976)	P-161	34 boxes	
Bromberg, Pauline (1886-1981)	P-519	3 items	
Brown Family (1885-1940)	P-628	1 box	
Brown, Joseph (1917-1919)	P-528	43 items	
Browne, Edward B.M. (1881-)	P-349	1 item	
Brownejohn, William (1786-1789)	P-299	2 items	
Calmenson, Jesse B. (1903-1952)	P-359	9 boxes	
Cardozo, Benjamin Nathan (1845-1970)	P-128	1 box	
Caro Family (1922-1962)	P-245	4 items	
Carpenter, Asa (1795-1795)	P-285	2 pages	
Castro, Henry (1843-)	P-548	1 item	
Charney, Aaron Reuben (1918-1956)	P-617	2 items	
Chazin Family	P-550	43 pages	
Chimene Family	P-389	22 pages	
Clapp John M. (1834-1834)	P-264	1 page	
Cogan, Saul (1903-1922)	P-530	47 pages	
Cohen, Augustus E. (1863-)	P-424	4 pages	

Cohen, David (1839-1839)	P-250	1 item	
Cohen, Eleazer (1800-1800)	P-249	1 item	
Cohen Family (1841-1913)	P-101	1 box	
Cohen Family of London (1775-1856)	P-373	2 items	
Cohen Family Papers (1787-1897)	P- 3	119 items	
Cohen Family Papers (1807-1888)	P-375	ca. 25 pages	
Cohen, Henry (1885-)	P-373	1 item	
Cohen, J. Barrett (1868-)	P-403	1 pages	
Cohen, Jack (of Rochester NY) (1944-1960)	P-317	ca. 900 pp.	
Cohen, Jacob Raphael (1776-1843)	P-118	3 items + 51 leaves	
Cohen, Jacob Xenab (1924-1978)	P-661	2 boxes	
Cohen, Joseph Solomon (1775-)	P-374	1 page	
Cohen, Levi (1786-1805)	P-657	1 box	
Cohen, Mordecai (1817-1829)	P-425	2 items	
Cohen, Rose (1911-1969)	P-611	3 boxes	
Cohen, S. (1864-)	P-402	1 item	
Cohen, William (1928-)	P-659	1 item	
Cohn, Aaron B. (1862-)	P-105	1 item	
Cole, Thankful Pinto	P-194	1 item	
Cone, Sydney M. (1755-)	P-158	1 box ca. 203 pages	
Constine - Coons Family (1851-1962)	P-601	11 items	
Corcos, Joseph Moses	P-119		
Costa, Da, Family (of London, Charleston, SC, and NY) (1776 1873)	P-145	1 box	
Cowen, Phillip (1876-1934)	P- 19	3 boxes (1500 items)	
Craft, Sheila (1976-1976)	P-332		
Crestohl, Leon David (1904-1963)	P- 63	6 boxes + 4 scrapbooks	
Dan Family Genealogy	P-392	10 items	
Dana Family	P-397	2 items	
Davega Family (1819-1856)	P-404	2 items	
Davidson - Borison Family	P-631		
De Lo Motta, Emanuel (1821-)	P- 68	2 items	
De Lyon, Isaac, B. (1786-)	P-406	2 pages	
Debrest, Harold (1906-1979)	P-163	1 box, ca. 30 items	
Deleon Family (1813-1861)	P-405		
Dellar, Dorothy D.	P-355	2 pages	
Diamond, David, (1928-1968)	P- 59	6 boxes	
Dias, Joseph Lopez (1819-1819)	P-199	1 item	
Drucker, Eliezer (1890-1916)	P- 42	1 box	
Duhl Family (1910-)	P-570	2 items	
Dutilh & Wachsmuth (1794-1802)	P-325	1 box	
Ehramnn, Sara Rosenfeld (1939-1939)	P-243	24 pages	
Ehrenreich Family (geneal.) (1841-1971)	P- 96	3 boxes	
Ehrenreich, Bernard C. (1876-1955)	P- 26	4 boxes	
Ehrlich Family (of Germany and Brazil) (1852-1943)	P-326	21 items	
Ehrmann, Herbert B. (1913-1970)	P- 94	5 boxes	
Einstein, Albert (1921-1945)	P-287	2 items	
Ellstein, Abraham (1925-1965)	P- 32	2 boxes	
Enedict, Herman (1860-)	P-341		
Epstein Family	P-512	7 pages	
Etting Family (of Baltimore, Frankfort aM, Philadelphia and York, PA) (1765-1862)	P-143	14 items	
Eudovich, Solomon (1902-1940)	P- 88	1 box	
Ewanczyk Family (1830-)	P-514	14 pages	
Ezekiel, Moses (1872-1908)	P-186	17 items	
Feibelman Family (1727-)	P-546	5 charts	
Fein, Isaac (1962-1964)	P-150	3 boxes	
Feingold, Beatrice	P-621		
Feldman, Joachim (1940-1942)	P-634	1 box	
Feller, Jack	P-604	2 items	
Felsenthal, Bernhard (1856-1920)	P- 21	2 boxes (800 items)	
Fidanque Family (1951-1951)	P-260	1 item	
Filemann, Jacob (1771-)	P-426	2 pages	
Filene, Edward Albert (1918-1937)	P-164	1 box	
Fine, Jacob, M.D.	P-638	1 box	
Finesilver, Moses Z. (1880-1881)	P-184	2 items	

Finzi, Camilla (1810-1816)	P-300	1 item
Fisher Family (1928-1930)	P-596	4 items
Fishman, Jacob	P- 37	2 boxes
Flexner, Simon	P-540	1 item
Fortas, Abe (1968)	P-279	4 items
Frank, Jacob (1769)	P-324	1 item
Frank, Leo Max (1915-)	P-408	1 page
Frankel Brothers (1906-1934)	P-665	1 box
Frankel, Lee Kaufer (1889-1931)	P-146	22 boxes
Franks Family (1832-1937)	P-585	6 items
		(84 pages)
Franks Family (of Halifax, London, New York, and Philadelphia)		
(1711-1821)	P-142	35 items
Franks, Bilah Abigail Levy (1733-1748)	P-142	1 box (½ lft)
Freedman, Louis A. (1762-1903)	P-276	1 item
Freund Family (1854-1885)	P-265	3 items
Friedenwald, Herbert (1908-1938)	P-261	19 pages
Friedman, M (1864-)	P-348	1 item
Gal Allon (1914-1917)	P-251	41 pages
Geffen Family	P-626	1 sheet
Geffen, Tobias (1903-1970)	P-516	31 boxes
Geller, Myron (1977-1979)	P-398	6 looseleafs,
		1 notebook
Gershwin, George (1933)	P-182	1 item
Gerzow Family	P-675	1 box
Glaser, Louis (1904-1934)	P-593	138 items
Goldberg, Arthur J.	P-409	2 items
Goldberg, Israel (1911-1964)	P- 71	4 boxes
Goldberg, Jacob	P-551	146 pages
Goldstein Family (NY) (1853-1874)	P-259	5 items
Goldstein, Harriet B.L. (1918-1919)	P- 31	3 albums,
		1 scrapbook
Goldstein, Jonah J. (1913-1967)	P- 61	25 boxes
Goldstone Family (1934-1934)	P-230	1 chart
Gomez Family (1716-1882)	P- 62	2 boxes
Gompers, Samuel (1904-1923)	P-416	5 items
Goodman, Samuel (M.D.) (1891-1971)	P-629	1 box
Gordon, Albert I. (1926-1968)	P- 86	19 boxes
Gorfinkle, Bernard Louis (1916-1956)	P-664	3 boxes
Gorovitz, Aaron (1895-1956)	P- 87	3 boxes
Gottheil Family (1897-1899)	P- 49	3 items
Gouled, Peter (1917-1968)	P-100	2 boxes
Gradwohl Family (1857-1870)	P-236	1 page
Gratz Family Papers (1753-1869)	P- 8	719 items
Greenbaum, Henry (1855-1903)	P-315	4 items
Greenbaum, Samuel	P-314	3 items
Greenberg, Meyer (1936-1978)	P-358	24 boxes
Greene Family (1910-)	P-587	4 boxes
Greenwald Family (1854-1920)	P-509	2 items
Grossbard, Sol (1919-)	P-151	123 pages
Guggenheimer, Simon (1863-)	P-504	1 page
Gurvitz, Samuel H. (1934-1939)	P-352	73 pages
Hackenburg, William B. (1880)	P-235	4 items
Hahn, Michael (1865-)	P-413	3 pages
Halfin Family (1842-)	P-584	47 items
Hamilton, Alexander	P-104	1 item
Hapgood Norman (1922-1922)	P-263	39 pages
Harkavy, Alexander (1853-1937)	P- 50	18 items +
		diary
Hart Family (1792-1897)	P- 18	10 boxes
		(4.15 lft)
Hart, Abraham (1810-1853)	P-414	3 items
Hart, Nathan (1857-1857)	P-226	8 pages
Hays Family Papers (1759-1766)	P-130	180 pages
Heiligman Family (1907-)	P-594	2 items
Hendricks Family (legal) (1798-1855)	P-376	6 items
Henry, Aaron (1804-)	P-396	2 items
Hershfield, Aaron (1894-1894)	P-322	1 item
Heyman, Louis (1843-1843)	P-244	6 pages
Heyman, Moses (1765-1765)	P-242	1 item
Hirsch, Moses (1859-1859)	P-233	5 pages
Hirschel, Solomon	P-541	2 pages
Hochheimer, Henry (1850-1900)	P- 74	one volume
Hubbard, Adolph (1918-1976)	P-647	1 box
Hurst, Fannie (1919-1933)	P-411	4 items

Hutler, Albert A. (1938-1945)	P-156	1 box
		ca. 50 items
Ichenhauser Family	P-393	9 items
Irwin, Norma (Nones) (1977-1981)	P-334	3 sheets
Isaacks, Abraham (1731-1797)	P-280	3 items
Isaacs, Emanuel (1797)	P-266	1 page
Isaacs Family of Easthampton (1741-1781)	P-272	2 items
Isaacs, Joshua (1799)	P-271	2 items
Isaacs, Michael (1819)	P-273	1 item
Isaacs, Abraham (1808-)	P-417	2 pages
Isaacs, Alexander (1869-)	P-418	
Isaacs, Jacob	P-435	1 page
Isaacs, Lazarus (1859)	P-239	14 pages
Isaacs, Myer Samuel (1878-1898)	P- 22	2 boxes
Israel, Israel (1800-1825)	P-419	7 items
Jacobs Family	P-590	
Jacobs Family of New York, Charleston & Savannah (1833)		
	P-339	5 pages
Jacobs, Phillip Collection (1760-1832)	P- 10	2 cartons
Jaffe, Solomon Elhanan (1858-1922)	P-433	33 items,
		550 pages
Johnson, Augusta Ellis (1869-)	P- 98	1 box
Jolson, Al	P-232	1 item
Jonas, Abraham (1747-1866)	P-377	23 pages
Joseph, Jacob	P-350	
Josephson, Manuel (1729-1796)	P-438	1 page
Josephthal Family	P-517	1 sheet
Judah Family (1794-1831)	P- 77	2 boxes
Judah Family (New York, Montreal, Indiana) (1784-1830)		
	P- 78	4 items
Judah Monis Papers (1723)	P-343	2 items
Judah, Moses (1831-)	P- 77	77 pages
Kagan, Solomon Robert- (1933-1955)	P- 40	328 items
Kamberg, Abraham (1917-1975)	P-148	2 boxes
Katz, Hyman (1937-1938)	P-160	1 box,
		7 items
Katz, Label A (1931-1968)	P- 92	19 boxes
Katz, Mark Jacob (1898-1919)	P- 39	200 items
Kaufman, David S. (1846-)	P-441	1 page
Kaufman, Reuben	P-663	1 box
Kayserling, Meyer (1859-1865)	P-302	9 items
Keith, George	P-191	35 pages
Keller, Jacob (1826-1834)	P-278	30 pages
Keyser, Samuel Bar Issac (1774)	P-304	1 item
Klein, Rose (1775-1832)	P-386	209 pages
Kline Joseph (1862-1862)	P-254	3 pages
Kohler, Max James (1871-1934)	P- 7	20 cartons &
		4 scrapbooks
Kohn, David (1858-)	P-443	4 pages
Kohs, Samuel Calmin (1916-1960)	P- 90	9 boxes
Kolbin Family	P-524	6 pages
Kosminsky, Nettie Friede (1880-)	P-269	ca. 250 pp.
Kraft, Louis (1914-1975)	P-673	23 boxes
Kraus, Adolf (1911-)	P-520	1 item
Krauskopf, Joseph (1919)	P-289	9 pages
Kursheedt, Israel Baer (1815-1831)	P-196	2 items
Kussy, Sarah (1898-1951)	P- 4	6 items
Lazarus, Emma (1869-1877)	P- 2	1 carton
		(170 items)
Lazarus, Jacob, Jr. (1830-)	P-415	4 pages
Lazarus, Michael (1816-1836)	P- 76	2 boxes
Le Witt, George (1921-1921)	P-311	2 pages
Leeser, Isaac (1829-1866)	P- 20	187 items
Leeson, Daniel Nathan	P-356	2 boxes
Lemkin, Raphael (1941-1951)	P-154	13 boxes,
		1 scrapbook
Leoni Family (1928-1962)	P-623	20 items
Levin, Etta L. (1794-)	P-361	ca. 200 pp.
Levine, Israel (1914-1970)	P-625	2 boxes
Levine, Leo (1933-1950)	P-646	1 box
Levy Family (of NYC) (1710-1835)	P-120	49 items
Levy Family (of Newport & New Orleans) (1746-1747)		
	P-268	3 items
Levy, Aaron (1781-1815)	P-124	10 items
Levy, Asher (1807-)	P-125	1 item

Levy, Esther (1843)	P- 79	1 folder
Levy, Haym (1795-)	P-268	1 item
Levy, Israel (1824-)	P-656	1 box
Levy, Jacob, Jr. (1837-)	P-674	1 box
Levy, Jefferson Monroe (1901-1939)	P- 48	16 items, 7 scrapbooks
Levy, Jonas Phillips (1851-1882)	P-412	
Levy, Judah Solomon (1852-)	P-660	
Levy, Juliet Lopez (1852-)	P-122	1 item
Levy, Lyon, Esq. (1848)	P-106	1 folder
Levy, Mark (1855)	P- 93	1 folder
Levy, Mark, D. (1855-)	P- 93	1 box
Levy, Samuel A. (1842-)	P-658	1 item
Levy, Uriah Philipps (1787-1944)	P- 43	131 items
Levy, William Mallory (1877-)	P-126	1 item
Lewisohn Family (1750-)	P-513	25 pages
Lichtenberg, Philip (1853)	P-168	1 item
Liebman, Joshua Loth (1940-1947)	P-636	1 box
Lifschitz, Aaron (1906-)	P-655	1 portfolio
Lilienthal, Max (1847-)	P-363	9 pages
Linfield, Harry Sebee (1907-1970)	P-346	
Lipman, Hymen L. (1842-)	P-457	2 items
Lipsky, Louis (1898-1976)	P-672	22 boxes
Lisan, Manuel (1897-1968)	P-138	1 box
Lisitzky, Ephraim E. (1934-1962)	P-627	1 box
List, Albert A. (1966)	P-277	2 pages
Litman, Ray Frank (1878-1957)	P- 46	2 boxes
Lloyd George, David (1863-1945)	P- 73	one volume
London, Hannah Ruth (1943-1978)	P-347	5 boxes
Lopez, Aaron (1752-1794)	P- 11	ca. 6800 itms 14 cartons
Lopez, Abraham (1766-)	P-381	1 page
Lopez, David (1862-)	P-458	2 items
Louzada, Aaron (1746-1756)	P-188	3 items
Lowenthal, Marvin (1890-1956)	P-140	17 boxes
Lown, Philip W. (1944-1975)	P-162	2 boxes
Lyons, Jacques Judah (1728-1776)	P- 15	12 cartons
Lyons, Judah Eleazer (1800-1837)	P-121	5 items
Lyons, Solomon (Phila.) (1788-1804)	P- 6	1 carton (18 items)
Mamon, William (1808-)	P-459	1 page
Mannheimer Family (1915-1931)	P-172	6 items
Markens, Isaac (1778-1916)	P- 47	2 boxes
Marks Family (of Phila.) (1799)	P-169	1 item
Marks, Sarah Ann (1794-)	P-399	1 item
Marks, Solomon (1814-)	P-169	2 pages
Marshall, Louis (1906-1929)	P- 24	4 boxes (608 items)
Marx, Asher (1815-1815)	P-190	2 items
Mayer, Alexander (1850-1852)	P-117	27 items
Medina, Shmuel Robles De (1763-)	P-113	1 bound item (96 leaves)
Memminger, Christopher G. (1864-)	P-460	3 pages
Menken Family (1878-1923)	P-635	1 box
Menken, Adah Isaacs (1862-1868)	P-559	8 items
Menken, Alice Davis (1882-1935)	P- 23	4 scrapbs, 3 boxes
Menuhin, Yehudi (1969)	P-275	1 item
Mesquita, Moses Gomez De (1744-1746)	P-111	60 leaves
Mielziner Family genealogy (1928-)	P-342	
Mielziner, Leo	P-610	48 pages
Milontaler Family (1875-1987)	P-553	25 items, 90 pages
Mincer Family Material (1896-1981)	P-387	7 items
Montefiore, Sir Moses Haim (1858)	P-189	1 item
Morais, Sabato (1851-1893)	P- 55	29 items + 22 clippings
Mordecai Family (1771-1907)	P-116	43 items
Mordecai, Sarah Ann (Hays) (1823-1833)	P- 70	2 bound vols & 19 items
Morgenthau Family (1808-1946)	P-613	160 pages
Morris, Robert (1798)	P-316	1 item
Morrison Family Papers (1887-1947)	P-394	ca. 30 items, scrapbook
Moses Family Papers (1767-1941)	P- 1	ca. 260 items

Moses-Loeb Family	P-357	1 sheet
Moss Family (of Phila.) (1840-1895)	P- 14	12 scrapbks
Moss, Joseph Lyons (1828-)	P-365	2 items
Moss, Sanford A. (1942)	P-192	1 page
Mossler Family (1858-1871)	P-522	2 items
Multer, Abraham J. (1954-1966)	P- 89	137 boxes
Myers-Cohen Family (1815-1819)	P-238	2 items
Naar, David (1846-1846)	P-337	4 pages
Nathan Family (1791-1918)	P- 54	22 items + notebook
Nathan, Moses (1782-1798)	P- 65	100 pages
Nathan, Moses Henry (1865-)	P-466	2 pages
Nathans Family (of Phila.) (1816-1823)	P-336	10 items
Nathans, Isaac (1819)	P-335	1 page
Navarro, Israel (1808-)	P-396	1 page
Nigrosh, Max (1919-1946)	P-542	
Noah, Mordecai Manuel (1816-1851)	P- 75	75 items
Nones Family Papers (1812-1822)	P- 5	200 pages
Nones, David B. (1810-1829)	P-366	
Noot, Simon C. (1847)	P-208	1 item
Nunez (Nunes), Samuel (1784-)	P-468	3 pages
Obermayer, Leon J. (1919-1973)	P-141	24 boxes
Oppenheim, Jeffrey (Genealogy)	P-370	1 sheet
Oppenheim, Samuel (Collection, 1650-1850)	P-255	43 boxes
Ottolengui Family (1866-)	P-499	3 pages
Pearlman, Nathan D. (1915-1952)	P- 66	9 boxes
Peerce, Jan (1972)	P-331	1 item
Peixotto, Benjamin (1870)	P-195	1 item
Peixotto, Moses Levy Maduro (1829-)	P-351	7 items
Perlman, Max (1943-1944)	P-391	15 items
Perlman, Robert (1870-1914)	P-654	1 box
Pettit, Charles (1789-)	P-470	1 page
Phillips Family (of NYC and Philadelphia) (1733-1954)	P- 17	8 boxes
Phillips, Emily (1893-1893)	P-202	13 items
Phillips, Jonas Altamont (1837-1902)	P-471	1 volume
Picon, Molly (1876-1967)	P- 38	44 boxes, 22 scrapbks
Pincus, Simon (1920-1934)	P-650	1 box
Pinto, Isaac (1765)	P-206	1 item
Polack, M. (1836-1862)	P- 72	1 bound item (150 pages)
Polier, Shad (1938-1987)	P-572	17 boxes
Polock Family (of Philadelphia) (1856)	P-197	1 item
Preuss Family	P-526	2 items
Price, Samuel (1913-1962)	P- 95	7 boxes
Pulitzer, Joseph (1883-)	P-473	3 items
Rabalsky, Benjamin (1913-1932)	P-153	1 box (ca. 200 items.
Rabinoff, George W. (1912-1971)	P- 58	11 boxes
Rabinovitz, Meyer Azriel (1906-1929)	P-367	10 items
Rabinowits, David Meir (1909)	P-257	1 item
Rabinowitz Family	P-516	
Rabson, S.M.	P-523	43 pages
Raphael, Ralph B.	P-360	2 boxes, ca. 1185 pp.
Raphael, Solomon (1787)	P-203	1 item
Raphall, Morris Jacob (1863)	P-329	2 pages
Razovsky, Cecelia (1912-1968)	P-290	6 cartons
Reis Family (1831-1880)	P-338	6 items
Rieur, Jacques (1930-1937)	P-669	1 box
Rose (Roos) Family (1772-1962)	P-129	2 items
Rosenbaum Zell Collection (1868-1973)	P-353	4 items
Rosenbaum, Michael (1865-)	P-475	1 item
Rosenberg, Louis (1843)	P-330	1 page
Rosenberg, Michael Samuel (1831)	P-291	1 item
Rosenblum, William Franklin (1910-1968)	P-327	17 boxes
Rosenfeld, Morris (1898-)	P-139	1 box
Rosenthal, Louis N. (1859-)	P-476	1 item
Rosenthal, Moses (1912-1971)	P-535	40 items
Rosenwald, Julius (1917-1927)	P-477	2 items
Roth, Benjamin (1854-1969)	P-603	5 items
Rothchild, Nathan Meyer (1834)	P-198	1 item
Rothnagel-Rankus Family	P-368	2 boxes
Rukeyser, Merryle Stanley (1924-1966)	P-293	98 pages

Sachs Family (1842-1990)	P-622	14 items	Starr, Myer	P-525	63 pages
Salit, Norman (1917-1959)	P- 35	8 boxs	Steinberg, Milton (1920-1981)	P-369	28 boxes
Salomon, Haym (1777-1967)	P- 41	6 boxes	Steinbrink, Meier (1921-1952)	P-103	1 box
Sampter, Lawrence	P- 67	60 items	Stern, Louis (1905-1915)	P-281	11 items
Samuel Family (1853-1967)	P-478	2 volumes	Stern, Morris (1867-)	P-484	1 page
Samuel, Hyman (1791)	P-305	1 item	Strakosch, Maurice	P-215	1 item
Sawyer Family (1837-)	P-538	24 pages	Strasburger Family of NY (1854-1887)	P-217	27 items
Schachter, Samuel (1885-)	P-108	1 box	Straus, Nathan (1899-1929)	P-220	8 items
Schary, Dore (1952-)	P-344		Straus, Oscar Solomon (1892-1921)	P-485	17 letters
Schatz, Boris (1905-1932)	P-571	3 items	Strauss, Abraham (1979-1919)	P-648	1 box
Schiff, Jacob Henry (1912-1918)	P-295	4 items	Strauss, Lewis Lichtenstein (1908-1973)	P-632	76 boxes
Schorz, Carl (1888)	P-283	25 pages	Sulzberger Family (1825-1923)	P-147	16 items
Schwab Family Genealogy	P-388	3 items	Sutro, Adolph Heinrich Joseph (1896-1897)	P-318	4 pages
Schwager, Charles (1909-1948)	P-301	133 pages	Szold, Henrietta (1904-1936)	P-216	6 items
Schwartz, William S. (1932-)	P-354	6 items	Taylor Family (1908-1976)	P-213	ca. 100 items
Schwarz - Lewi Family (1828-1934)	P-662	1 box	Tenzer, Herbert (1965)	P-308	1 item
Schweid, Mark (1935-1936)	P-340	ca. 150 pp.	Touro Family (1812-1854)	P-214	8 items
Scwartz, Maurice	P-494	1 item	Trounstine Family (1856-)	P-488	2 pages
Seelav, Samuel (1900-1905)	P-292	4 items	Troy, NY Merchants Union Expr Co (1870)	P-307	1 item
Seixas Family (1748-1911)	P- 60	29 items	Ungar, Louis Arthur (1893-1974)	P-137	2 boxes
Seixas, Rachel Levy Phillips (1821-1828)	P-383	3 items	Untermeyer, Samuel (1917-1932)	P-384	15 pages
Seligman Family (1870-1903)	P-107	5 items	Van Buren, Martin, Pres. (1840-)	P-131	3 items
Selz, Abraham (1853-1881)	P-385	55 leaves	Velleman, Natalie J. (1812-)	P-543	7 items
Shahn, Ben (1964-1966)	P-284	4 pages	Waksman, Selman Abraham (1886-1975)	P- 97	4 boxes
Shapiro, Harry (1953-1963)	P- 56	4 boxes	Waskow, Arthur I. (1963-1977)	P-152	15 boxes
Shecter, Louis E. (1928-1975)	P-165	2 boxes	Watts, John S. (1862-)	P-490	1 pages
Sheftall, Mordecai (1761-1873)	P- 12	3175 items	Weill, Milton (1918-1950)	P- 34	4 boxes
Shubow, Leo (1933-1958)	P-395	ca. 150 items	Weinberg, Bernard (1933-1934)	P-668	1 box
Siegal, Isaac, (1897-1944)	P- 33	1 box	Weiss, Samuel Arthur (1941-)	P-670	1 box
Silver, Harold (1925-1927)	P-149	1 box	Wheeler, Everett P. (1907-1921)	P-288	8 items
Simon, Bilah (Belle) (1774-1779)	P-238	2 items	Wilson, Woodrow (1904-1916)	P-223	2 items
Simpson, Lassack H. (1879-)	P-110		Winogradoff, Jospeh (1920-1924)	P-666	1 box
Simson Family (1713-1892)	P-109	20 items	Wise, Mrs. M. (1861-)	P-132	2 items
Sloan, Sara Wernon (1898-)	P-640	1 box	Wise, Stephen S. (1841-1978)	P-134	191 boxes
Slomovitz, Philip (1933-1967)	P- 84	500 items	Wolf, Gertrude (1910-1942)	P- 27	2 boxes
Slomovitz, Philip (1969-1973)	P-135	2 boxes			(470 items)
Slomovitz, Philip (1971-1974)	P-136	150 items	Wolf, Simon (1861-1923)	P- 25	2 boxes
Snitzer, Joeph Lazarus (1909-1944)	P- 36	2 boxes,			(342 items)
		5 scrapbooks	Wolfe, David (1809-)	P-133	1 item
Solender Family (1890-1989)	P-554	18 boxes	Wolff, Abraham (1817-)	P-491	2 items
Solis and Solis-Cohen Family (1806-1990)	P-642	6 items	Wolff, Joseph (1823-1859)	P-602	7 items
Solomon Family (of NY) (1877-1881)	P-296	3 items	Wolk Family (1902-1906)	P-643	1 box
Solomon, H. (1821)	P-294	2 items	Yulee, David Levy (1842-1866)	P-115	15 items
Solomon, Henry E. (1825-)	P-400	1 item	Zangwill, Israel (1897-1964)	P-225	ca. 125 pp.
Solomons, Adolphus Simeon (1841-1910)	P- 28	200 pages &	Zeman, Isador Louis (1911-1982)	P-549	11 items,
		4 scrapbooks			two boxes
Spiegel, Marcus M. (1860-)	P-483	1 page	Zigmond, Rabbi Maurice L. (1943-1964)	P-112	20 boxes
Spiegelberg, Willi (1883-1919)	P-303	35 pages	Zunitz Family (1797-1820)	P-297	3 items
Spielberger Family (1878-1969)	P-609	5 boxes			

C. EPHEMERA MANUSCRIPT COLLECTIONS

NAME	TYPE	CALL #	CITY, STATE	SIZE
Action Central For Soviet Jewry	Soviet Jewry	MS-SOJ.C6	Cleveland, OH	1 box
Adas Israel Congregation	Synagogue	MS-SYN.W2	Washington, DC	3 cartons
Albert Einstein College Of Medicine	Educational	MS-ED.A5	New York, NY	1 carton
Albert Einstein Medical Center	Medical	MS-MD.P3A5	Philadelphia, PA	3 cartons
Alpha Epsilon Phi Fraternity	National	MS-NAT.A13		1 carton
Alpha Epsilon Pi Fraternity	Fraternal	MS-FRA.135		1 box
Alpha Epsilon Pi Fraternity	Fraternal	MS-FRA.A135		2 boxes
Alpha Epsilon Pi Fraternity	National	MS-NAT.A135		2 carton
Alpha Omega Fraternity	Fraternal	MS-FRA.A137		1 box
Alpha Omega Fraternity	National	MS-NAT.A137		1 box
Amalgamated Clothing Workers Of America	Labor	MS-LAB.A14		2 boxes
American Academic Association For Peace In The Middle East	National	MS-NAT .A21		1 box (.5 linear ft)
American Council For Judaism	National	MS-NAT.A2		
American Financial And Development Corporation For Israel	National	MS-NAT.A23	New York, NY	1 box
American Friends of the Hebrew University	National	MS-ED .H50	New York, NY	1 box (.5 linear ft)
American Jewish Alternatives to Zionism, Inc.	National	MS-NAT.A20B1		3 boxes (1.25 linear ft)
American Jewish Committee	National	MS-NAT.A25		23 cartons
American Jewish Joint Distribution Committee	National	MS-NAT.A45		7 cartons
American Medical Center	Medical	MS-MD.D2A5	Denver, CO	1 carton
American Zionist Youth Foundation	National	MS-NAT .A48Y3		2 boxes (.8 linear feet)
American Zionist Youth Foundation	National	MS-NAT.A48Y3		2 boxes
Ampal American Israel Corporation	National	MS-NAT.A47P1		1 box
Anshe Chesed Congregation	Synagogue	MS-SYN.C5	Cleveland, OH	2 cartons
Anshe Emet Congregation	Synagogue	MS-SYN.C3	Chicago, IL	4 cartons
Anshe Emeth Beth Tefilo Congregation	Synagogue	MS-SYN.C6	Cleveland Heights, OH	2 cartons
Anti-Defamation League Of B'nai B'rith	National	MS-NAT.A5		12 cartons
Anti-Semitic Literature	Miscellaneous	MS-MIS.A2		41 cartons
Arlington-Fairfax Jewish Center	Synagogue	MS-SYN.A7	Arlington, VA	1 carton
Assoc. Of Orthodox Jewish Teachers of the New York City Public Schools	Educational	MS-ED .N29	Brooklyn, NY	1 box
Association Of Jewish Center Workers	National	MS-NAT.A75		1 carton
Association Of Jewish Libraries	National	MS-NAT.A77		2 cartons
B'nai B'rith Hillel Foundation	National	MS-NAT.B32		21 cartons
B'nai B'rith Independent Order	National	MS-NAT.B3		11 cartons
B'nai B'rith Independent Order Of Aleph Zadik Aleph	National	MS-NAT.B4		3 cartons
B'nai Jeshurun Congregation	Synagogue	MS-SYN.C62	Cleveland Heights, OH	4 cartons
B'rith Sholom	Fraternal	MS-FRA.B73		1 box
Buffalo Jewish Center	JCC	MS-JCC.B8	Buffalo, NY	2 cartons
Baltimore Hebrew Congregation	Synagogue	MS-SYN.B2	Baltimore, MD	3 cartons
Bay Area Council On Soviet Jewry	Soviet Jewry	MS-SOJ.S3	San Francisco, CA	1 box
Bellefaire	Institutional	MS-INS.C42B2	Cleveland, OH	2 cartons
Berkeley Judah L. Magnes Memorial Museum	National	MS-NAT.B2		1 carton
Beta Sigma Rho Fraternity	Fraternal	MS-FRA.B3		1 folder
Beth El Hospital	Medical	MS-MD.N3B3	New York, NY	1 carton
Beth Israel Hospital	Medical	MS-MD.B5B2	Boston, MA	1 carton
Beth Israel Hospital	Medical	MS-MD.N3B4	New York, NY	1 carton
Beth Israel Hospital	Medical	MS-MD.N4B2	Newark, NJ	2 cartons
Bnai Zion	National	MS-NAT.B5		1 carton
Board Of Jewish Education	Educational	MS-ED.B2	Baltimore, MD	1 carton
Board Of Jewish Education	Educational	MS-ED.B4	Chicago, IL	1 carton
Brandeis Institute	Educational	MS-ED.B8	Brandeis, CA	1 box
Brandeis University	Educational	MS-ED.B7	Waltham, MA	4 boxes
Brith Abraham, Independent Order Of	National	MS-NAT.B7		1 carton
Brith Abraham, Order Of	National	MS-NAT.B72		1 carton
Brith Sholom	National	MS-NAT.B73		1 carton
Brooklyn Jewish Center	Synagogue	MS-SYN.B85	Brooklyn, NY	1 cartons
Bureau Of Jewish Education	Educational	MS-ED.N25	New York, NY	7 boxes
Bureau Of Jewish Employment Problems	Local	MS-LOC.CIE3	Chicago, IL	1 box
Canadian Jewish Congress	National	MS-NAT.C1		15 cartons
Cantors Assembly Of America	National	MS-NAT.C23		1 carton
Center For Jewish Community Studies	Think Tank	MS-ED .C15	Philadelphia, PA	1 box (.5 linear ft)
Central Conference Of American Rabbis	National	MS-NAT.C25		3 cartons
Chicago Action For Soviet Jewry	National	MS-NAT.C33		1 carton
Chicago Action For Soviet Jewry	Soviet Jewry	MS-SOJ.C33	Chicago, IL	1 box
City College	Educational	MS-ED.N23	New York, NY	5 boxes
City Of Hope (formerly Jewish Consumptive Relief Association)	Medical	MS-MD.L5C2	Los Angeles, CA	1 carton
Cleveland Jewish Center	Synagogue	MS-SYN.C67	Cleveland Heights, OH	2 cartons
Columbia University	Educational	MS-ED.C5	New York, NY	1 box

Committee To Free Morton Sobell	National	MS-NAT.C55		2 cartons
Conference of Jewish Material Claims Against Germany, Inc.	Holocaust	MS-HOL.C1	New York, NY	1 box
Conference of Presidents of Major American Jewish Organizations	National	MS-NAT.C57		1 carton
Conference on Alternatives in Jewish Education	National	MS-NAT.C58		1 carton
Congregation B'nai Jeshurun	Synagogue	MS-SYN.N2	New York, NY	3 cartons
Congregation Beth Elohim	Synagogue	MS-SYN.B8	Brooklyn, NY	2 cartons
Congregation Beth Israel	Synagogue	MS-SYN.F5	Flint, MI	1 carton
Congregation Beth Israel	Synagogue	MS-SYN.H3	Hartford, CT	2 cartons
Congregation Emanu-El	Synagogue	MS-SYN.N24	New York, NY	3 cartons
Congregation Emanu-El	Synagogue	MS-SYN.S1	San Francisco, CA	3 cartons
Congregation Mishkan Israel	Synagogue	MS-SYN.H2	Hamden, CT	1 carton
Congregation Ohabei Shalom	Synagogue	MS-SYN.B7	Brookline, MA	2 cartons
Congregation Rodeph Sholom	Synagogue	MS-SYN.N27	New York, NY	3 cartons
Dropsie University	Educational	MS-ED.D7	Philadelphia, PA	2 boxes
Educational Alliance	JCC	MS-JCC.E28	New York, NY	2 cartons
Euclid Avenue Temple	Synagogue	MS-SYN.C52	Cleveland, OH	1 carton
Family Location Service (formerly National Desertion Bureau)	National	MS-NAT.F15		1 carton
Farband - Labor Zionist Order	Labor	MS-LAB.F3	New York, NY	2 boxes
Federation Of Jewish Agencies Of Greater Philadelphia	Federation	MS-FED.P33	Philadelphia, PA	2 boxes
Federation Of Jewish Philanthropies	Federation	MS-FED.N28	New York, NY	5 cartons
Fitchburg Jewish Community Center	JCC	MS-JCC.F3	Fitchburg, MA	1 carton
Free Sons Of Israel	National	MS-NAT.F7		1 carton
Free Sons Of Judah, Independent Order	National	MS-NAT.F72		1 carton
Freemasons, Mount Scopus Lodge	National	MS-NAT.F73	MA	1 carton
Garment Center Congregation	Synagogue	MS-SYN.N2G2	New York, NY	1 carton
Grand Street Boys' Association	JCC	MS-JCC.N28	New York, NY	6 cartons
Gratz College	Educational	MS-ED.G24	Philadelphia, PA	1 box
Greater NY Conference on Soviet Jewry	Soviet Jewry	MS-SOJ.N5	New York, NY	1 box
Habonim	National	MS-NAT.H14		1 carton
Hadassah	National	MS-NAT.H1		6 cartons
Hadassah, Junior Hadassah	National	MS-NAT.H13		3 boxes
Har Zion Temple	Synagogue	MS-SYN.P3	Philadelphia, PA	2 cartons
Harlem Hospital	Medical	MS-MD.N3H2	New York, NY	1 carton
Hebrew College	Educational	MS-ED.B73	Brookline, MA	1 carton
Hebrew Teachers College	Educational	MS-ED.B3	Baltimore, MD	1 carton
Hebrew Theological College	Educational	MS-ED.C23	Chicago, IL	1 box
Hebrew Union College - Jewish Institute Of Religion	Educational	MS-ED.H29	Cincinnati, OH	9 boxes
HIAS	National	MS-NAT.H3		5 cartons
Histadrut	National	MS-NAT.H37		1 carton
Histadruth Ivrith Of America	National	MS-NAT.H51		1 box (.5 linear ft)
Home For Aged And Infirm Hebrews (now known as Jewish Home And Hospital For Aged)	Institutional	MS-INS.N28H5	New York, NY	2 cartons
Home Of The Daughters Of Jacob	Institutional	MS-INS.N28H7	New York, NY	1 box
Hospital For Joint Diseases	Medical	MS-MD.N3H4	New York, NY	1 carton
Icor	National	MS-NAT.I3		1 carton
Independent Order of B'rith Abraham	Fraternal	MS-FRA.B7		2 boxes
Independent Order of the Free Sons of Israel	Fraternal	MS-FRA.F7		1/2 box
Independent Order of the Free Sons of Judah	Fraternal	MS-FRA.F72		1/2 box
Independent Order of the Sons of Benjamin	Fraternal	MS-FRA.S5		1 folder
Industrial Union Department, AFL-CIO	Labor	MS-LAB.I3		1 box
Institute Of Jewish Affairs	National	MS-NAT.I6		2 cartons
International Kosher Foods amd Jewish Life	National	MS-NAT.I85		1 carton
International Ladies Garment Workers Union	Labor	MS-LAB.I9		3 boxes
Jewish Board Of Guardians (formerly Jewish Protectopry and Aid Society, 1907-1921)	Institutional	MS-INS.N28J1	New York, NY	1 box
Jewish Braille Institute Of America	National	MS-NAT.J14		2 cartons
Jewish Chautauqua Society	National	MS-NAT.J185		1 carton
Jewish Colonization Association	National	MS-NAT.J19		3 cartons
Jewish Community Center Of Charleston	JCC	MS-JCC.C2	Charleston, SC	1 carton
Jewish Community Center Of Dallas	JCC	MS-JCC.D1	Dallas, TX	1 box
Jewish Community Centers Association	JCC	MS-JCC.S13	St. Louis, MO	5 cartons
Jewish Community Relations Council of Greater Philadelphia	Local	MS-LOC.P33	Philadelphia, PA	2 cartons
Jewish Consumptive Relief Society	Medical	MS-MD.D2J2	Denver, CO	3 cartons
Jewish Defense League	National	MS-NAT.J20	New York, NY	1 box (.5 linear ft)
Jewish Family Service, (est. 1946 by merger of Jewish Social Service Association and The Jewish Family Welfare Society of Brooklyn)	National	MS-NAT.J29	New York, NY	1 box
Jewish Federation	JCC	MS-JCC.Y4	Yonkers, NY	3 cartons
Jewish Federation Of Metropolitan Chicago	Federation	MS-FED.C35	Chicago, IL	1 carton

Jewish Foster Home & Orphan Asylum	Institutional	MS-INS.P33J1	Philadelphia, PA	1 box
Jewish Hospital	Medical	MS-MD.B7J2	Brooklyn, NY	1 carton
Jewish Hospital Association	Medical	MS-MD.C3J2	Cincinnati, OH	1 carton
Jewish Hospital Of St. Louis	Medical	MS-MD .S5J2	St. Louis, MO	1 box (.5 linear ft)
Jewish Institute Of Religion.	Educational	MS-ED.J25	New York, NY	1 box
(merged into Hebrew Union College-Jewish Institute Of Religion in 1950)				
Jewish Labor Committee	Labor	MS-LAB.J1		3 boxes
Jewish Maternity Association	Medical	MS-MD.P3J3	Philadelphia, PA	1 carton
Jewish Media Service	National	MS-NAT.J21	Wellesley, MA	1 box
Jewish Memorial Hospital	Medical	MS-MD.N3J2	New York, NY	1 carton
Jewish National Home for Asthmatic Children	Medical	MS-MD.D2J4	Denver, CO	1 carton
Jewish Occupational Council	National	MS-NAT.J24		4 cartons
Jewish Pharmaceutical Society of America	National	MS-NAT.J25		1 carton
Jewish Postal Employees Welfare League	Labor	MS-LAB.J3P1	New York, NY	2 boxes
Of Manhattan And Bronx, Inc.				
Jewish Public Library	National	MS-NAT.M55	Montreal, Canada	2 cartons
Jewish Publication Society Of America	National	MS-NAT.J27		1 carton
Jewish Sanitarium For Incurables	Medical	MS-MD.B7J3	Brooklyn, NY	1 carton
Jewish Telegraphic Agency	National	MS-NAT.J34		3 cartons
Jewish Theological Seminary Of America	Educational	MS-ED.J28	Los Angeles, CA	10 boxes
Jewish Theological Seminary, Jewish Museum	National	MS-NAT.J35		2 cartons
Jewish United Fund	Federation	MS-FED.C33	Chicago, IL	2 boxes
Jewish Welfare Fund	Federation	MS-FED.C34	Chicago, IL	2 boxes
Jewish Welfare Fund &	Federation	MS-FED.N15	New Orleans, LA	1 box
Federation Of New Orleans				
Kappa Nu Fraternity	Fraternal	MS-FRA.K1		1 folder
L'alliance Israelite Universelle	National	MS-NAT.A12		8 cartons
Lebanon Hospital	Medical	MS-MD.N3L2	New York, NY	1 carton
Lincoln Square Synagogue	Synagogue	MS-SYN.N2W2	New York, NY	1 carton
Lubavitcher Hasidic Movement	National	MS-NAT.L8		2 cartons
Luing-In Hospital	Medical	MS-MD.N3L9	New York, NY	1 carton
Missionary Literature	Miscellaneous	MS-MIS.A3		8 cartons
Montefiore Hospital	Medical	MS-MD.N3M5	New York, NY	2 cartons
Mosean Fraternity	Fraternal	MS-FRA.M5		1 folder
Mount Sinai Hospital	Medical	MS-MD.M3M4	Minneapolis, MN	1 carton
Mount Sinai Hospital	Medical	MS-MD.P3M5	Philadelphia, PA	1 carton
Mount Zion Hospital	Medical	MS-MD.S2M4	San Francisco, CA	1 carton
Mu Sigma Fraternity	National	MS-NAT.M8		1 carton
Mu Sugma Fraternity	Fraternal	MS-FRA.M8		1/2 box
National Conference Of Christians and Jews	National	MS-NAT.N16		4 cartons
National Conference Of Jewish	National	MS-NAT.N18	New York, NY	2 boxes
Communal Sevice				
National Council Of Jewish Women	National	MS-NAT.N2		8 cartons
National Council On Art In Jewish Life	National	MS-NAT.N22	New York, NY	1 box
National Jewish Hospital	Medical	MS-MD.D2N2	Denver, CO	1 carton
National Jewish Music Council	National	MS-NAT.N23		2 cartons
National Jewish Welfare Board	National	MS-NAT.N25		21 cartons
National Mental Health Center	Medical	MS-MD.D2N3	Denver, CO	1 carton
National Museum Of American Jewish History	National	MS-NAT.N27		1 carton
National Yiddish Book Center	National	MS-NAT.Y2A1	Amherst, MA	1 box
New Haven Jewish Community Center	JCC	MS-JCC.N2	New Haven, CT	2 cartons
New Jewish Agenda	National	MS-NAT.N40	New York, NY	1 carton
New York Board Of Rabbis	National	MS-NAT.N29	New York, NY	2 cartons
Order Of B'nai Zion	Fraternal	MS-FRA.B5		1 box
ORT	National	MS-NAT.O7		5 carton
Palestine Economic Corporation	National	MS-NAT.P9		
Phi Alpha Fraternity	Fraternal	MS-FRA.P32		1/2 box
Phi Alpha Fraternity	National	MS-NAT.P32		1 carton
Phi Delta Epsilon Fraternity	National	MS-NAT.P3		1 carton
Phi Epsilon Pi Fraternity	National	MS-NAT.P2		3 cartons
Phi Lambda Kappa Fraternity	Fraternal	MS-FRA.P23		1/2 box
Phi Lambda Kappa Fraternity	National	MS-NAT.P23		2 carton
Pi Gamma Mu Fraternity	Fraternal	MS-FRA.P24		1 folder
Pi Gamma Mu Fraternity	National	MS-NAT.P24		1 carton
Pi Lambda Fraternity	National	MS-NAT.P25		1 carton
Pi Lambda Phi Fraternity	Fraternal	MS-FRA.P25		1/2 box
Progressive Order Of The West	Fraternal	MS-FRA.P7		1 folder
Progressive Order Of The West	National	MS-NAT.P7		1 carton
Psychoanalytic Institute	Educational	MS-ED.N237	New York, NY	1 box
Rabbinical Assembly Of America	National	MS-NAT.R12		2 cartons
Reconstructionist Rabbinical College	Educational	MS-ED.R2	Wyncote, PA	1 box
Reform Congregation Keneseth Israel	Synagogue	MS-SYN.P37	Philadelphia, PA	4 cartons
Religious Zionists Of America	National	MS-NAT.R35		2 cartons
Rodef Shalom Congregation	Synagogue	MS-SYN.P4	Pittsburgh, PA	1 cartons
School Of Jewish Studies	Educational	MS-ED.N237	New York, NY	1 box

Sephardic Home For The Aged	Institutional	MS-INS.N28S2	New York, NY	3 cartons
Shaare Zion Congregation	Synagogue	MS-SYN.S3	Sioux City, IA	1 carton
Sigma Alpha Mu Fraternity	Fraternal	MS-FRA.S31		1 folder
Sigma Delta Tau Fraternity	Fraternal	MS-FRA.S34		1 folder
Sinai Congregation	Synagogue	MS-SYN.C37	Chicago, IL	2 cartons
Sinai Congregation Of The Bronx	Synagogue	MS-SYN.N2S3	New York, NY	1 carton
Sinai Hospital	Medical	MS-MD.B2S3	Baltimore, MD	1 carton
Sinai Hospital Of Detroit	Medical	MS-MD.D3S3	Detroit, MI	1 carton
Sons Of Benjamin,Independent Order Of	National	MS-NAT.S5		1 carton
Spertus College Of Judaica (formerly College Of Jewish Studies)	Educational	MS-ED.S62	Chicago, IL	2 boxes
Stephen Wise Free Synagogue	Synagogue	MS-SYN.N2S7	New York, NY	4 cartons
Synagogue Council Of Massachusetts	Local	MS-LOC.M1	Boston, MA	1 box
Tau Delta Phi Fraternity	Fraternal	MS-FRA.T1		1 folder
Temple B'rith Kodesh	Synagogue	MS-SYN.R2	Rochester, NY	4 cartons
Temple Beth El	Synagogue	MS-SYN.D3	Detroit, MI	3 cartons
Temple Beth Israel	Synagogue	MS-SYN.C38	Chicago, IL	4 cartons
Temple Beth-El	Synagogue	MS-SYN.P7	Providence, RI	1 carton
Temple Emanu-El	Synagogue	MS-SYN.H5	Honolulu, HI	1 cartons
Temple Emanu-El	Synagogue	MS-SYN.W3	Westmount, Canada	3 cartons
Temple Israel	Synagogue	MS-SYN.B5	Boston, MA	2 cartons
Temple Of Beth Solonom Of The Deaf	Synagogue	MS-SYN.A6	Arleta, CA	1 carton
Temple Of Liberal Judaism	Synagogue	MS-SYN.M5	Monroe, NY	1 carton
Temple Petach Tikvah	Synagogue	MS-SYN.B88	Brooklyn, NY	1 carton
The Jewish Center	Synagogue	MS-SYN.N2J2	New York, NY	1 carton
The Temple	Synagogue	MS-SYN.C57	Cleveland, OH	2 cartons
Torah Umesorah	National	MS-NAT.T5		2 cartons
Touro Synagogue	Synagogue	MS-SYN.N45	Newport, MA	1 carton
Union Of American Hebrew Congregations	National	MS-NAT.U5		16 cartons
Union Of Councils For Soviet Jews	Soviet Jewry	MS-SOJ.U52		4 boxes
United Israel Appeal	National	MS-NAT.U53		2 cartons
United Jewish Appeal	National	MS-NAT.U54		5 cartons
United States Holocaust Memorial Museum	National	MS-NAT.U6	Washington, DC	3 boxes
United Synagogue Of America	National	MS-NAT.U7		9 cartons
United Zionists-Revisionists Of America	National	MS-NAT.U95	New York, NY	1 box (.5 linear ft)
West Side Institutional Synagogue	Synagogue	MS-SYN.N2W2	New York, NY	3 cartons
Workmen's Circle	Labor	MS-LAB.W1		14 boxes
World Conference Of Jewish Organizations, American Committee	National	MSNAT.W05C13		1 box (.5 linear ft)
World Jewish Congress	National	MS-NAT.W4		2 cartons
World Jewish Congress, Latin American Section	National	MS-NAT.W6		6 cartons
World Union For Progressive Judaism	National	MS-NAT.W1	New York, NY	1 box
World Zionist Organization, American Section	National	MS-NAT.W7A1		7-8 boxes
Y.M. And Y.W.H.A.	JCC	MS-JCC.N3	New York, NY	1 carton
Y.M. And Y.W.H.A.	JCC	MS-JCC.S1	St. Louis, MO	2 cartons
Yeshiva U'mesivta Toras Emes Kamenitz	Educational	MS-ED.B75	Brooklyn, NY	2 boxes
Yeshiva University	Educational	MS-ED.Y2	New York, NY	9 cartons
YIVO Institute For Yiddish Research	National	MS-NAT.Y3		3 cartons
Zeta Beta Tau Fraternity	Fraternal	MS-FRA.Z2		1/2 box
Zeta Beta Tau Fraternity	National	MS-NAT.Z2		3 cartons
Zionist Organization Of America	National	MS-NAT.Z3		9 cartons

SOURCES OF INFORMATION

Listed here are the sources of information that were used in the preparation of this book. They serve as footnotes and acknowledgements for each section of this guide.

CENSUS RECORDS:

National Archives and Records Service, *National Archives Microfilm Resources for Research, A Comprehensive Catalog.* (Washington: National Archives and Records Administration, 1990), pages 60-64.

Prologue: Quarterly of the National Archives. XXIII, 2 (Summer 1991), pages 131-147. {1920 Census}.

The Newsletter of the Massachusetts Genealogical Council. XV:1 (Winter-Spring 1996). {1870 Massachusetts Index}.

NATURALIZATIONS:

National Archives and Records Service, *National Archives Microfilm Resources for Research, A Comprehensive Catalog.* (Washington: National Archives and Records Administration, 1990), page 4.

Roger D. Joslyn, "New England Naturalization Records Index", Massachusetts Genealogical Council Publication 3 (1986).

Catherine S. Menand, *A Research Guide to the Massachusetts Courts and their Records.* (Boston: Massachusetts Supreme Judicial Court Archives and Records Preservation, 1987), pages 112, 126, and microfiche supplement.

PASSENGER LISTS:

National Archives Trust Fund Board. NATF Form 81 (Revised 1-91), "Order for Copies of Ship Passenger Arrival Records".

John P. Colletta, *They Came In Ships.* (Salt Lake City, UT: Ancestry, Inc, 1989), pages 29-42.

Michael Tepper, *American Passenger Arrival Records.* (Baltimore: Genealogical Publishing Co., 1993).

National Archives and Records Service. *Pamphlets accompanying M265 and M277: Index to Passenger Lists of Vessels Arriving at Boston 1848-1891; Passenger Lists of Vessels Arriving at Boston 1820-1891.* (1969, 1970).

Thanks to: Walter Hickey.

VITAL RECORDS:

Where to Write for Vital Records: Births, Deaths, Marriages and Divorces. (Washington: U.S. Department of Health and Human Services, March 1993), 30 pp.

News of the Family History Library. Volume II, Number 2. (March/April 1990).

DOROT, The Journal of the Jewish Genealogical Society (New York). XII, 1 (Autumn 1990), page 6; XIII, 1 (Autumn 1991), pages 7-8. {New York vital records}

BOSTON PUBLIC LIBRARY:

George K. Schweitzer, *Massachusetts Genealogical Research.* (Knoxville, TN: the author, 1990), pages 172-174.

Marcia Wiswall Lindberg, ed., *Genealogist's Handbook for New England Research.* 2nd edition. (Boston: New England Historic Genealogical Society, 1985), pages 84-85.

P. William Filby, *Directory of American Libraries with Genealogy or Local History Collections.* (Wilmington, Del.: Scholarly Resources, 1988), page 98.

FAMILY HISTORY CENTERS (LDS):

Family History Library, *Library Services and Resources: Family History Library and Family History Centers.* Series FHL, No. 1, Seventh edition, Jan. 1993; Ninth edition, Jan. 1995.

Estelle M. Guzik, *Genealogical Resources in the New York Metropolitan Area.* (New York: Jewish Genealogical Society, 1989), pages 321-322.

Federation of Genealogy Societies Forum, III, 1 (Spring 1991), page 10.

Daniel M. Schlyter, in *The Encyclopedia of Jewish Genealogy*, Volume I. (New Jersey: Jason Aronson, 1991), pages 128-132.

Thanks to: the Directors of all local Family History Centers.

HEBREW COLLEGE LIBRARY:

Avotaynu, V,4 (Winter 1989), page 16.

MASSACHUSETTS ARCHIVES:

The Massachusetts Archives, *Researching your Family's History at the Massachusetts Archives*. [pamphlet], (March 1989), 9 pages.

The Massachusetts Archives, *Guide to the Records of the Secretary of State in the Massachusetts Archives*. (1987), pages 38, 41, 46, 51-52, 77-78.

Federation of Genealogical Societies Forum, Fall 1990, page 10.

Massachusetts Genealogical Council *Newsletter*. X, 1 (Spring 1991), p2; XI, 1 (Winter 1992), p3.

NATIONAL ARCHIVES - NEW ENGLAND REGION:

The National Archives - New England Region, *Sources for Family History*. [pamphlet], (July 1992), 6 columns.

Estelle M. Guzik, *Genealogical Resources in the New York Metropolitan Area*. (New York: Jewish Genealogical Society, 1989), pages 313-317.

Immigrant and Passenger Arrivals, A Select Catalog of National Archives Microfilm Publications. (Washington: National Archives Trust Fund Board, 1983, 1991).

New England, A Select List of National Archives Microfilm Publications. (Washington: National Archives Trust Fund Board, 1987), pages 6-8, 13.

National Archives Microfilm Resources for Research, A Comprehensive Catalog. (Washington: National Archives and Records Administration, 1990), pages 4, 30, 51-52, 60-64, 70.

Guide to Records in the National Archives - New England Region. (Washington: National Archives and Records Administration, 1989). 25 pp.

Microfilm Publications in the National Archives - New England Region. Special List 46. (Washington: National Archives and Records Administration, 1990). 77 pp.

REGISTRY OF VITAL RECORDS AND STATISTICS:

Massachusetts Genealogical Council, "Civil Records: Massachusetts". Publication 2b. (1988).

Where to Write for Vital Records: Births, Deaths, Marriages and Divorces. (Washington: U.S. Department of Health and Human Services, March 1993), page 12.

YIZKOR BIBLIOGRAPHY:

Estelle M. Guzik, *Genealogical Resources in the New York Metropolitan Area*. (New York: Jewish Genealogical Society, 1989), Appendix A: pages 323-372. Bibliography compiled by Zachary M. Baker.

Bibliography of Eastern European Memorial (Yizkor) Books. Compiled by Zachary M. Baker, Edited by Steven W. Seigel. (New York, Jewish Genealogical Society, July 1992). 51 pages.

DOROT, The Journal of the Jewish Genealogical Society (New York). X, 4 (Summer 1989), page 15; XI, 2 (Winter 1989-90), page 17; XIV, 2 (Winter 1992-93), page 21.

George Sackheim, "Index to *Pinkas HaKehillot*...", *Search: International Quarterly for Researchers of Jewish Genealogy*, VIII, 3 (Fall 1988), pages 17-23; (Summer 1991), pages 22-25.

Catalogs of Yizkor Books from: J. Robinson & Co. (No. 187/C); National Yiddish Book Center.

Thanks to: Zachary Baker; Dr. Maurice Tuchman and Shalva Seigel at the Hebrew College Library; Dr. Charles Cutter at Brandeis University Library.

INDEX

This index contains the names of people, places, and topics mentioned in the text of this book. It does **not** include the names and places in the Appendices, nor the cemetery names in the JCAM chapter (pages 113-117).

Korner, Peter 96
Kranzler, David 74, 103
Kugelmass, Jack 101
Kurzweil, Arthur 2, 74, 102, 103, 162
Lainhart, Ann S. 14, 166
Lamont Library (Harvard) 94
Land Records 232
  Middlesex County 137, 138
  Suffolk County 187
Landsman, Isaac 103
Landsmanschaften 48
Landsmen: Quarterly Publication of the Suwalk-Lomza... 108
Latter-Day Saints
  see Family History Centers (LDS)
Latvia
  Yizkor Book 195
Lawrence
  Voting Lists 183
Lawrence, Amos 6
Lazarus, Emma 34
LDS
  see Family History Centers (LDS)
Lebowich, Joseph 184
Lehmann, Ruth P. 79
Leipzig, Germany 96
Leningrad
  City Directories 95
Leo Baeck Institute 35, 63
Lev, Aryeh 42
Levi, Harry 60
Levine Chapels 112
Levine, Hillel 71, 184
Levy, B. H. 163
Levy, Uriah Phillips 34
Library of Congress
  Genealogies Bibliography 61
  Judaica Section Catalogs 105
Lighthouse Keepers 152
Lindberg, Marcia Wiswall 1
Lithuania
  Jewish Communities 102
  Yizkor Books 196
Local History 51
Lodz 195
Lodz, Poland 97, 98
London Times 63
London, England
  City Directories 64
LOUIS (Brandeis catalog) 81
Lowell
  City Directories 127, 183
  Police Court 127
Lowenstein, Leopold 75
Lucker, Jay K. 132
Lynn
  City Directories 183
  Jewish History 172
Maine
  Maps 65
  Naturalization Records 148
  Vital Records 30, 167
Makovsky, Donald J. 163

Malden
  City Directories 183
  District Court 127
  Jewish History 184
  Voting Lists 183
Maps
  also see Altases, Gazetteers
  Balkans 135
  Central Europe 134
  Eastern Europe 98, 133
  Massachusetts 71, 164, 182
  Poland 133
  Sanborn Fire Insurance Maps 65, 71, 182
  Soviet Union 133
Marburg-Biednkopf, Germany 97
Marcus, Jacob Rader 35, 102, 168
Mariner, Mary Lou Craver 13
Marriage Records
  see Vital Records
Mass-pocha 4, 75, 108, 162
Massachusetts Archives 124
Massachusetts General Hospital 6
Massachusetts Institute of Technology 132
Massachusetts State Archives
  see Massachusetts Archives
Massachusetts State Library
  see State Library of Massachusetts
Mattapan
  Jewish History 56, 184
Mauthausen Concentration Camp
  Death Books 151
Medford
  City Directories 183
Medical Examiner's Reports 128
Medjuck, Sheva 163
Meirtchak, Benjamin 97
Memorial to the Jews Deported from France 96, 106
Mence, Michael 96
Meorei Galacia 104
Metro-Boston Library Network (MBLN) 68
Meyer, Isidore S. 34
Middlesex County
  Divorce Records 141
  Land Records 137, 138
  Naturalizations 20, 127
  Probate Records 67, 128, 141, 166
Middlesex County Registry of Probate 141
Middlesex Registry of Deeds 137, 138
Milhomme, William 124
Military Records 67. 151, 158
Minnesota
  Jewish History 163
Mirsky, Mark 184
Missouri
  Jewish History 163
MIT
  see Massachusetts Institute of Technology
Mokotoff, Gary 2, 3, 61, 80, 102, 164

Monis, Judah 5
Mormon Church
  see Family History Centers (LDS)
Mortality Schedules 14
Morton Allan Directory 22, 66, 165, 238
Moscow
  City Directories 95
Moses, L. 76
Mostov, Stephen G. 173
Muneles, Otto 105
Name Changes
  Massachusetts 166
  New York City 169
Names, Jewish 78, 104, 162
National Archives 143, 154
  Genealogical Research 3, 21, 61, 103
National Jewish Post and Opinion (Indianapolis) 63
National Jewish Welfare Board
  Army-Navy Division 42
  Bureau of War Records 42
National Union Catalogue 135
Naturalization Records 16
  Barnstable County 19
  Berkshire County 19
  Bristol County 19, 126
  Connecticut 147, 150
  Essex County 126
  Franklin County 20, 127
  Hampden County 20, 127
  Hampshire County 20, 127
  Maine 148
  Massachusetts 19, 126, 148, 158
  Middlesex County 20, 127
  New England 17, 146, 158
  New England - Indexes 17, 67, 147
  New Hampshire 149
  New York City 18
  Norfolk County 20, 127
  Plymouth County 20, 127
  Rhode Island 149
  Suffolk County 20, 127
  Vermont 150
  Worcester County 20, 127
Neagles, James C. 16
Neagles, Lila Lee 16
Needleman, Frances R. 132
NEHGS
  see New England Historic Genealogical Society
NEHGS Register 162, 171
Netherlands 163
  Holocaust Survivors 97
  Yizkor Book 195
Neusner, Jacob 184
New Bedford
  Naturalization Records 19
  Passenger Lists 66, 146, 157
  Voting Lists 183
New Brunswick
  Vital Records 167
New England Historic Genealogical Society 161